To Libby, Mom, and Dad

Faustian Bargain

FAUSTIAN BARGAIN

*The Soviet-German Partnership and
the Origins of the Second World War*

Ian Ona Johnson

OXFORD
UNIVERSITY PRESS

OXFORD
UNIVERSITY PRESS

Oxford University Press is a department of the University of Oxford. It furthers
the University's objective of excellence in research, scholarship, and education
by publishing worldwide. Oxford is a registered trade mark of Oxford University
Press in the UK and certain other countries.

Published in the United States of America by Oxford University Press
198 Madison Avenue, New York, NY 10016, United States of America.

© Ian Ona Johnson 2021

First issued as an Oxford University Press paperback, 2024

Library of Congress Cataloging-in-Publication Data
Names: Johnson, Ian Ona, author.
Title: Faustian bargain : The Soviet-German Partnership and the Origins of the
Second World War / Ian Ona Johnson.
Other titles: Soviet-German military cooperation in the interwar period
Description: New York, NY : Oxford University Press, [2021] |
Includes bibliographical references and index.
Identifiers: LCCN 2021008943 (print) | LCCN 2021008944 (ebook) |
ISBN 9780190675141 (hardback) | ISBN 9780197695531 (paperback) |
ISBN 9780190675172 (epub)
Subjects: LCSH: Soviet Union—Military relations—Germany. |
Germany—Military relations—Soviet Union. | Soviet Union—History, Military. |
Germany—History, Military—20th century.
Classification: LCC DK67.5.G3 J64 2021 (print) | LCC DK67.5.G3 (ebook) |
DDC 355/.03109430947—dc23
LC record available at https://lccn.loc.gov/2021008943
LC ebook record available at https://lccn.loc.gov/2021008944

Paperback printed by Sheridan Books, Inc., United States of America

CONTENTS

ACKNOWLEDGMENTS

I have been working on this book, in one form or another, for most of my adult life. Over that time, I've learned that a work of international history like this is as much an odyssey as it is a literary task. This manuscript had traveled tens of thousands of miles before it ever hit shelves. Those many miles from idea to print are impossible to travel without the encouragement of family and friends, and assistance of colleagues, archivists, agents, and editors.

This project began during my first year of graduate school at the Ohio State University. Searching for a dissertation project, I found myself asking how Germany had rearmed so effectively following its defeat in the First World War. That led me to the puzzle of the interwar Soviet-German relationship, the subject of this book. I was fortunate to have a terrific dissertation committee to help steer me through the next six years of graduate work on that project: Colonel Peter Mansoor, who helped me edit the chapters as I wrote them and reminded me along the way not to forget military realities—like doctrine, training, and budgets; David Hoffmann, who provided invaluable advice on the Russian archives; and Alan Beyerchen, who helped throughout the writing process, while also encouraging me to steer this project toward its current emphasis on technology. Most of all, I am grateful for the constant support and guidance of my graduate school adviser, Jennifer Siegel. It was her mentorship that helped me identify the key questions of my dissertation, prepared me for work in the archives, and helped me to structure my dissertation. Further, her advice steered me toward research at key German industrial firms—like Krupp—which ended up revealing the critical role of Soviet-German cooperation in Germany's technological rearmament. I hope to have repaid her very slightly for all her assistance over the years, as I am cautiously optimistic that her annual task of writing dozens and dozens of letters of recommendation on my behalf is finally coming to an end.

From Columbus, the dissertation took me to archives in Essen, Stuttgart, Augsburg, Lipetsk, Kazan, Samara, Berlin, Warsaw, Newport, Palo Alto, and Washington, DC, with longer periods spent in Moscow, Freiburg, and London. The archivists at this myriad of stops—almost without exception—were of great help. In particular, I would like to acknowledge the assistance of the staff at the Russian State Military Archives—where I took up residence for almost a year—and the Bundesarchiv-Militärarchiv in Freiburg. In addition, the staff at the corporate archives in Germany (Krupp, Porsche, Daimler-Benz, and MAN) all uniformly provided enthusiastic assistance. Working in Krupp's Villa Hügel was a particularly rare treat, both from a research perspective and for the beautiful surroundings. In Russia, I am grateful to the archivists at the State Archives of Lipetsk Oblast and the State Archives of Samara Oblast, whose untapped records on the Soviet-German relationship were a great boon.

None of that research would have been possible without generous financial assistance. A Foreign Language Area Studies Fellowship provided the opportunity to hone my Russian language skills in Moscow. The numerous research trips themselves were made possible by grants from the Society for the History of Technology, the Bradley Foundation, the Mershon Center for International Security Studies, and a Fulbright-Hays Fellowship that brought me back to Moscow for a year. I also received generous support from the H. F. Guggenheim and Smith-Richardson Foundations to begin the writing process. But of all the grants that made this dissertation possible, I am most humbled to have received the first research grant from the Lt. Colonel Sean M. Judge Memorial Scholarship. It is named in honor of a friend and fellow graduate student at the Ohio State University who passed away far before his time. I hope he would have enjoyed this book.

From Moscow, the project carried me to New Haven, Connecticut, where I took up a yearlong predoctoral fellowship with International Security Studies (ISS) at Yale University. I cannot say enough to thank Paul Kennedy, both for his company and for his advice, and for the ISS program he built. The latter gave me the chance to finish writing the dissertation among a rich intellectual community of faculty and fellows.

The book was not done moving me across the country yet. After defending my dissertation in 2016, I received a postdoctoral fellowship at the Clements Center for National Security at the University of Texas at Austin. Once again, I was fortunate to find myself in good company, thanks to Clements Center director Will Inboden. I finished the first draft of this book while I was there, while beginning research efforts to expand the scope from the Rapallo Era to the entire Interwar period. The most important event to occur in Austin, though, was that I ran into a lovely young lady while out with friends—my amazing wife, Mariah. This project brought me to her, and that makes it all worth it.

From Austin I (soon to be we!) then headed back to New Haven, where Beverly Gage hired me to serve as the associate director of Yale's Grand Strategy (GS) Program while I finished working on the book. I am grateful to her for the chance to return to Yale for two years, once again enjoying the company of the GS and ISS faculty and fellows. Conversations with faculty, fellows, and my students there helped shape the book in myriad ways. As a result, over my two years as associate director, this manuscript slowly transformed from a dissertation to something beginning to resemble a book.

Mariah and I had one more stop before the marathon would come to an end and I would finally stop tinkering with this manuscript. A year and a half ago, I was offered the P. J. Moran Family Professorship of Military History at the University of Notre Dame. My time here thus far has been an absolute pleasure, bolstered by generous, thoughtful, and welcoming colleagues, great staff members, and terrific students. I am grateful to them all, and to Pat Moran for providing such assistance to the field of military history. In our brief time here, Mariah and I have already come to think the world of the Notre Dame community.

There have been many others along the way who have left their imprint on this work. Mary Habeck was very generous, commenting on my dissertation and sharing her own research extensively. Historian and director of the Deutsches Panzermuseum Munster Ralf Raths was also a great help, commenting on manuscript chapters and enlightening me on German tank design. In addition to the many people already listed, this project has also benefited from the advice, comments, questions, source recommendations, and translation help provided over the last decade by Fritz Bartel, John Bew, Mike Brenes, Bruno Cabanes, James Cameron, Seth Center, Alexander Clarke, Rob Clemm, Susan Colbourn, Alice Conklin, Jonathan Coopersmith, Max Crowder, Michael De Groot, Tony Demchak, Michael Desch, Andrew Ehrhardt, Ryan Evans, Hal Friedman, Zachery Fry, John Gaddis, Frank Gavin, John Hall, Stephen Kotkin, Charlie Laderman, Rebecca Lissner, Alex Martin, John Mearsheimer, Chris Miller, Nuno Monteiro, Eva-Maria Muschik, Paul Niehrzydowski, Geoffrey Parker, Ionut Popescu, James Rogers, Klaus Schmider, Mark Stoler, Matthias Strohn, Ingo Trauschweizer, Will Waddell, Gerhard Weinberg, Corbin Williamson, and Evan Wilson. I am grateful to my agent, Roger Williams, for his encouragement and support in bringing this book to completion. And to my editor, the ever-patient Tim Bent, who was subjected to three completely different versions of this manuscript over the last four years as the book grew in scope and scale. His attention and sage advice helped to turn this book from something that resembled a dissertation into the volume you have in your hands.

Last, but certainly not least, I am grateful to my family for their support throughout the long process of researching, traveling, and writing this book. Beyond moral support, my wife and parents read much of the manuscript and all three—especially my dad, an author himself—provided helpful writing advice. My sister Libby assisted me in organizing the tens of thousands of pages of scans and photocopies I brought back from the archives. And my newborn daughter Madeleine had most of this book read out loud to her as I did the final revisions. It did wonders putting her to sleep; I try not to read too much into that. Finishing this journey—from Columbus to Moscow to South Bend, and everywhere in between—would have been impossible without all of them.

NOTE ON TRANSLITERATION AND TRANSLATION

This work uses the Library of Congress's 2012 Romanization Rules for Russian, with a few exceptions. For the sake of simplicity, I have generally omitted the soft and hard signs. For well-known figures and some first names, I have followed common Anglicizations: Joseph Stalin as opposed to Iosif Stalin, for instance. When German quotations or sources refer to a Russian location or name, I provide the original spelling in the text, unless the variant is likely to be confusing, in which case the phrase is rendered in the Library of Congress system.

LIST OF ABBREVIATIONS

ARCHIVES

AAN	Archiwum Akt Nowych, Warsaw, Poland
BA-L	Federal Archive Berlin–Lichterfelde, Berlin
BA-MA	Federal Archive–Military Archive, Freiburg
DBCA	Daimler-Benz Corporate Archives, Stuttgart
GALO	State Archive of Lipetsk Oblast, Lipetsk
GARF	The State Archive of the Russian Federation, Moscow
HIA	Hoover Institution Archives
JPI-L	Josef Pilsudski Institute, London
JPI-NY	Josef Pilsudski Institute, New York
KA	Thyssen-Krupp Corporate Archives, Essen
MAN	M.A.N. Corporate Archives, Augsburg
NARA	National Archives at College Park, Maryland
NWCA	Naval Historical Collection, Naval War College Archives, Newport, Rhode Island
PA-AA	Foreign Ministry–Political Archives, Berlin
PCA	Porsche Corporate Archives, Stuttgart
RGASPI	The Russian State Archive of Socio-Political History, Moscow
RGAE	The Russian State Archive of the Economy
RGVA	The Russian State Military Archives, Moscow
TNA	The National Archives, Kew
TsGASO	The Central State Archive of Samara Oblast, Samara
Y-RAP	Yale Russian Archive Project, New Haven, Connecticut

GERMAN ABBREVIATIONS

AA	Auswärtiges Amt (German Foreign Ministry)
AG	publicly traded limited corporation
BMW	Bavarian Motor Works
DDP	German People's Party
F.u.G.	Command and Combat of the Combined Arms
GEFU	Society for the Promotion of Commercial Enterprises, cover for German military industrial projects in the USSR

GELA	The Society for Agricultural Products, cover name for German chemical weapons production in the Soviet Union
IAMCC	International Allied Military Control Commission
IvS	Engineering Office for Shipbuilding, secret German naval organization in the Netherlands
IWG	Inspectorate for Weapons and Equipment
KPD	The German Communist Party
M.A.N.	Machine Factory Augsburg-Nürnberg
NSDAP	Nazi Party
Russgetorg	The Russian-German Trading Company
RWM	Reich Ministry of the Economy
SPD	Social Democratic Party
Truppenamt	The Troop Office, the reconstituted German general staff
USPD	Independent Social Democratic Party
Wa. Prüf.	Weapons Testing Division
Waffenamt	Reichswehr Weapons Office
WIKO	Central Business Office, code name for divisions of Moscow Center
WIVUPAL	The Scientific Research and Test Establishment for Aircraft, German code name for Lipetsk
Z.Mo.	Moscow Central, the secret German military headquarters in Moscow

RUSSIAN ABBREVIATIONS

BUZ	The Red Army's Armored Warfare University
CHEKA	Emergency Committee, first Soviet State Security Organization, 1917–1922
GAU	Main Artillery Department
GDD	Long Range Action Group
GKB-OAT	Main Design Bureau of the Arsenal Gun Trust
GPU	State Political Directorate, Soviet State Security Organization, 1922–1923
GRU	Main Intelligence Directorate
NKID	The People's Commissariat for Foreign Affairs
NKPS	The People's Commissariat of Foreign Trade
NKTiP	The People's Commissariat of Trade and Industry
NKVD	The People's Commissariat of Internal Affairs, Soviet State Security Organization, 1934–1946
NKVT	The People's Commissariat of Ways of Communication
OGPU	Joint State Political Directorate, Soviet State Security Organization, 1923–1934
OSOAVIAKhIM	Society for Defense, Aviation, and Construction of Chemical Weapons, Soviet code name for Kama

RKKA	The Workers' and Peasants' Red Army
RKKF	The Workers' and Peasants' Red Fleet
RVS	Revolutionary Military Council
SNK	Council of People's Commissars
SR	Socialist Revolutionary (Political Party)
TEKO	Technical Courses of the Society for Defense, Aviation, and Construction of Chemical Weapons, Soviet code name for Kama
TsGASI	Central Aerodynamics Institute
UMM	Bureau of Motorization and Mechanization
VOKhIMU	The Military-Chemical Defense Committee
VRK	Council of People's Commissars on War and Naval Affairs
VSNKh	The Supreme Soviet of the National Economy
VVS	Air Force of the Red Army

Introduction

A Faustian Bargain

September 1, 1939, dawned over a bloodied Poland. Beginning at 4:30 in the morning, the German air force unleashed terror bombing against 158 towns and cities across the western portion of the country. Several hours later, without a declaration of war, fifty divisions of the reborn German Army crossed the Polish-German border. Despite Polish resistance, within a week, the Wehrmacht's armored spearheads were approaching the suburbs of Warsaw. British and French declarations of war against Germany proved irrelevant to Polish soldiers defending the capital. As the German Army encircled the city, the remnants of the Polish Army retreated toward the Romanian border, intending to maintain control over at least part of the country.

On the night of September 16, the Polish ambassador in Moscow arrived at the Kremlin for a meeting with the deputy commissar for foreign affairs. To his shock, the Soviet diplomat informed him that the "Polish-German war has revealed the internal inadequacy of the Polish state. . . . the Soviet government intends to 'liberate the Polish people from the unfortunate war, where it was cast by its irrational leaders, and give them the opportunity to live a peaceful life.'" A few hours later, half a million Red Army soldiers invaded Poland from the East without a declaration of war. In the face of now-certain defeat, Warsaw surrendered to the Germans on September 27.

The 1939 partition of Poland between Hitler and Stalin has often been described as a moment of opportunism, a temporary alignment of interests between the two dictators. In fact, it was the culmination of nearly twenty years of intermittent cooperation between Germany and the Soviet Union. Following the Treaty of Rapallo in 1922, the Soviet Union hosted hundreds of German soldiers, engineers, and scientists at secret military bases inside Russia. In this first Soviet-German pact, the revolutionary regime in Moscow and aristocratic officer corps in Berlin agreed to work together despite immense ideological differences. Broken off by Hitler in 1933, then renewed again in 1939, the Soviet-German partnership would eventually lead both states into war—first, with their neighbors, and then, with each other.

After the First World War, a Soviet-German alliance seemed highly unlikely, for it was hard to overstate how much the two partners clearly despised each other. Vladimir Lenin had publicly called the German military "savages," "plunderers," and "predators" and had noted that in the First World War "the German robbers broke all records in war atrocities."[1] He thought even less of the German Social Democrats who ran the Weimar Republic after 1918, singling them out as "heroes of philistine stupidity and petty-bourgeois cowardice."[2] After the Social Democrats ordered the German military to suppress the first major attempt at communist revolution outside Russia in January 1919, Lenin wrote that "no words can describe the foul and abominable character of the butchery perpetrated by alleged socialists."[3] For the Bolsheviks, the right-wing military officers who dominated the interwar German Army were archetypes of counterrevolution, and their government even worse.

The German officer corps was hardly more circumspect in articulating its hatred of Bolshevism. Some senior German generals referred to Lenin and Trotsky as "enemies" and the "devil" in their writings.[4] A German veteran and former non-commissioned officer (NCO) would write publicly in 1925 that the Russian leaders— Lenin was dead, so this was mainly Stalin and his abettors—were "the scum of humanity which, favoured by circumstances, overran a great state in a tragic hour, slaughtered and wiped out thousands of her leading intelligentsia in wild blood lust, and now for almost ten years have been carrying on the most cruel and tyrannical regime of all time."[5] This view was more or less common among the German military's officers and NCOs, many of whom were drawn from right-wing veterans' associations that had banded together to put down left-wing insurrections in 1918 and 1919.

Why therefore did two states whose leaders saw the other as the very embodiment of evil make a deal with one another? Much like the old German tale of Faust, whose protagonist bargained away his soul to the devil in exchange for temporal power, the Germans and Soviets would use each other—at great cost—to remedy their own perceived military weaknesses. The Soviet Union, devastated by war and internationally isolated, needed technical expertise, financial capital, and new military technologies, which only the Germans were willing to provide in quantity. For the German military leaders, an alliance with the Soviets held out the best possibility of getting around the terms of the Treaty of Versailles that had ended the First World War. The victorious Allies had all but dismantled the vaunted Imperial German Army, reducing it from over four million to only 100,000 men. The terms of the Treaty of Versailles forbade Germany from producing or purchasing the modern tools of war, such as aircraft and armored vehicles. For German military leaders, a partnership with the Soviet Union meant rearmament and—someday—a war of revenge.

The first tentative connections between the German military and Soviet state would be made almost before the ink had dried on the treaties ending the First World War. In 1919, key figures in Soviet Russia and Weimar Germany began to quietly discuss matters of mutual interest. In April 1922, the two states normalized relations when they signed the Treaty of Rapallo. Secret negotiations conducted later that year would initiate covert military cooperation. This first period of partnership—the Rapallo Era—would come to an end nine months after Hitler's arrival in power in 1933.

During the Rapallo Era the Red Army encouraged German military industry to relocate experts and banned industrial production to the Soviet Union. Several German factories were established on Soviet soil to produce aircraft and other military technologies. The German military also served as an intermediary between the Soviet state and German businesses, drawing in investment to key sectors of Soviet defense industry. As the relationship grew, the Red Army and German army also established a number of joint military ventures on Russian soil. These included a flight school and an armored warfare testing ground, as well as two chemical weapons facilities. In exchange for space to train their own men, German officers helped to educate thousands of Red Army engineers, pilots, mechanics, and scientists. During cooperation's peak between 1928 and 1932, hundreds of German and thousands of Red Army personnel worked together at bases, military academies, laboratories, and factories operated in collaboration.

Hitler's rise to power ended this first period of the relationship. At his orders, the secret facilities closed one by one, the last concluding in September 1933. Although mistrust would pervade Soviet-German relations over the next six years, ties would never be severed completely. Economic exchange continued. Soviet envoys repeatedly probed German diplomats and military officials about renewing their earlier partnership. German diplomats in the Foreign Ministry argued for rapprochement with the Soviet Union. And then, in the first half of 1939, relations rapidly warmed.

That spring, both Stalin and Hitler suddenly proved open to renewing cooperation for a variety of strategic and ideological reasons. On August 23, 1939, the country's two foreign ministers signed the Treaty of Nonaggression between Germany and the Union of Soviet Socialist Republics, better known as the Molotov-Ribbentrop Pact. This new arrangement not only renewed military and economic ties, but also partitioned Eastern Europe between the two states in a secret protocol added to the treaty. Secured against the prospect of a two-front war, Hitler invaded Poland on September 1. Britain and France in turn honored their guarantees to Poland, and declared war on Germany. The Second World War in Europe had begun, sparked by a German-Soviet pact.

Much has been written about the political and administrative aspects of Soviet-German cooperation. That is, historians have provided chronologies of the negotiations, opening, organization, and eventual closure of each of the shared military facilities and the major military-industrial plants in the Soviet Union. With the exception of a handful of works to appear in the 1990s, most books on the subject have treated the collaborative facilities themselves as a sort of "black box"—important because of their very existence, but mysterious in their inner workings.[6] Given that the primary goal of Soviet-German cooperation was to develop new technologies of war, to train new officers and engineers, and to expand military industrial capacities, any attempt to estimate the impact of the secret military relationship between the two states that does not engage directly with the work conducted at the facilities is incomplete. Drawing from twenty-three archives in five countries, this project aims to help elucidate exactly what the Soviets and Germans did together at their secret facilities, and the role that work played in the origins of the Second World War.

As argued here, the technological component of Soviet-German cooperation was in hindsight its most significant element. It was German rearmament that would pose the greatest problem to European stability and lead directly to the events of September 1939. If Hitler had not initiated a European arms race in 1933, a new war would have been unlikely. And it was work conducted in the USSR that laid the foundation for that rearmament program.

This was primarily a product of the Treaty of Versailles. Following Germany's defeat in the First World War, the victorious allies stationed inspectors across Germany to oversee disarmament and the demobilization of Germany's military. But senior German officers in the Reichswehr—the German military—proved unwilling to accept the terms of German defeat. Instead, they immediately embarked on efforts to retain or revive key aspects of German military power, particularly technologies that the Treaty of Versailles forbade: tanks, planes, poison gas, submarines, and heavy artillery. Unable to develop such equipment under the watchful eyes of Allied inspectors, the Reichswehr would turn to the Soviet Union, where Germany would develop and test the next generation of aircraft, tanks, and chemical weapons technology. Work in the Soviet Union also led toward the development of military radios suitable for coordinating formations of fast-moving aircraft and vehicles—a key concept for what would later be called "Blitzkrieg." Nearly every major German industrial firm and most of the significant German aircraft and tank designers of the Second World War participated in this process, many of the latter moving to the USSR to work on new technologies of war. Most of the prototypes they developed and tested at the joint facilities were a generation removed—meaning more primitive—from the combat vehicles of World War Two, but without the former, the latter would not have been possible. The Panzers I, II, III, and IV—the tanks with which Germany would begin the war—all resulted directly or indirectly from work conducted in the USSR.

For the Soviets, the joint facilities enabled partnerships with German firms and opportunities for industrial espionage. Intellectual exchange—and theft—played a key role in the design or modification of many of the Soviet tank designs, including the T-24, T-26, T-28, T-35, and the Bystrokhodnyi Tank (Fast-Moving Tank, or BT) series. These designs represented the bulk of Soviet armored forces when the Second World War began. The German impact on Soviet aircraft design was only slightly less profound. The first generation of Soviet heavy bombers were so derivative of German designs that an impetuous designer working with the German military (to the great embarrassment of his government) sued the Soviet government in international court for patent infringement.

Technological research and development also drove doctrinal changes in both militaries. Only in the Soviet Union could German officers gain hands-on access to banned technologies of war. The work conducted at the joint armored warfare facility led the German military to completely reassess the role and place of tanks, and shift from the production of light to medium tanks—eventually resulting in the Panzer IV, the main German battle tank of the war. The same process unfolded in the German air force. So important was the doctrinal experimentation performed at the

German airfield in the USSR that future Luftwaffe General Wilhelm Speidel would write that "the spiritual foundations of the future Luftwaffe were developed on that aeronautical field."[7] In turn, the intellectual influence of the Reichswehr on the Red Army by 1933 is hard to overstate. The Reichswehr assisted in training thousands of Soviet officers, directly or indirectly. Between 1925 and 1933, 156 senior Soviet officers spent time training or studying in Germany, some for a year at a time. The list of Soviet students in Germany included two Red Army chiefs of staff; two of the Soviet Union's five marshals; the heads of the Soviet Air Force, Directorate of Motorization and Mechanization, and the Soviet Chemical Weapons Program; as well as the country's leading theorists and heads of most of its major military education institutions. Cooperation even led the Red Army to reform along German lines, adopting the German General Staff model as its central organizing principle.[8] And, as they rearmed together, the German and Soviet militaries evolved in similar—though by no means identical—directions.

This book is divided into two parts. The first aims to identify why Germany and the Soviet Union partnered together and what shape that partnership took during the Rapallo Era. The beginning of Part I advances arguments about Imperial German and Imperial Russian defeat in the First World War. It highlights who took power in each state after the war, what their strategic aims were, and how those were products of their respective experiences in the Great War. It then lays out the Treaty of Versailles, the peace treaty drawn up by the victorious Allied Powers. Versailles imposed economic reparations and military limitations upon defeated Germany that would come to define its new government, the Weimar Republic, and shape the Reichswehr.

This work then explores how Soviet and German diplomats, spies, and military officers made contact in 1919 and 1920 during the Polish-Bolshevik War, and how it was that two regimes so intensely hostile to each other in ideological terms would develop a strategic partnership. The key figures in the early relationship between the two states were Leon Trotsky and General Hans von Seeckt. Following chapters then lay out the program of Soviet-German cooperation they created. Initially, the Seeckt-Trotsky partnership centered on military-industrial arrangements between German firms and the Soviet military, negotiated with the assistance of the Reichswehr.

The relationship shifted in significant ways beginning in 1925. Chapters 9 through 14 lay out how the two states increasingly moved toward direct military-to-military cooperation. In particular, the Reichswehr began to relocate training facilities, research laboratories, and prototype development programs to the Soviet Union. This process was interrupted by a political scandal in 1926, then accelerated the following year.

The remainder of Part I explores the height of cooperation between 1928 and 1932. During this period, collaborative work between Germany and the Soviet Union took place on an enormous scale. German firms provided large sums and technological assistance to aid the growth of Soviet military industry under Stalin's First Five Year Plan. Simultaneously, hundreds of German officers trained and tested equipment at secret facilities. They also trained thousands of Soviet officers and engineers as part of the arrangement. Intellectual and technological exchange, particularly rich on questions of aviation and armored warfare, improved the military capabilities of both sides.

The second half of the book, Part II, shifts focus to the consequences of Soviet-German cooperation, highlighting the unraveling of the Soviet-German relationship amid the European arms race that Hitler initiated beginning in 1933. What follows is the story of how years of secret cooperation between Germany and the Soviet Union played a critical role in that arms race.

The final phase of the interwar Soviet-German relationship was marked by the resumption of partnership. In August 1939, Stalin and Hitler resumed military and economic exchange and partitioned Eastern Europe between them. The two states both invaded Poland the following month, marking the beginning of the Second World War in Europe. The book explores the nature of the renewed partnership between Germany and the Soviet Union, while identifying how it shaped the early phases of the Second World War.

In its final pages, this work explains the end of their partnership. Having succeeded beyond his own wildest expectations, Hitler decided to betray Stalin and invaded the USSR on June 22, 1941. In doing so he relied heavily on resources—human, technological, and economic—that had been provided through Soviet assistance. It was the ultimate, tragic conclusion to twenty years of an on-again, off-again partnership.

PART I

Sowing the Wind

CHAPTER 1

The Bolsheviks' Army

In July 1917, as the First World War raged, the Ukrainian city of Tarnopol reverberated with the death knell of the Russian Imperial Army—one site among many. Those present remembered it glowing a hideous red and orange in the twilight as German artillery pounded the strategic rail hub. As the Russian front collapsed in the face of the onslaught, the flow of deserters grew from a trickle to a flood. One eyewitness recalled "unimaginable panic" engulfing the town.[1] Trains overloaded with civilians, bureaucrats, Red Cross workers, and soldiers departed the main rail station headed eastward, illuminated by the light of the burning city. Tens of thousands more took to the roads by foot. Gangs of former draftees roamed the streets, looting and killing. The streets reverberated with the shattering of glass, sporadic gunfire, and the crackling of timber homes ignited either by the bombardment or by those setting fires.

It was a long fall. By the time the Russian Imperial Army had completed its mobilizations in 1914, it was the world's largest military force, mustering almost six million men.[2] However, it was a colossus made of clay, dependent on a weak industrial sector and drawn largely from peasant classes increasingly hostile toward the autocratic Tsarist state. After a series of military disasters in the first twelve months of the conflict, Tsar Nicholas II personally took over management of the war effort, heading to the front in September 1915. He handed over the empire's domestic affairs to his wife and a coterie of hangers-on, including the infamous Rasputin, who wildly mismanaged the home front. At the same time, the Tsar's presence did nothing to end paralysis and incompetence at Stavka (the Army High Command), which failed to adapt to the tactical, technological, and economic demands of modern warfare.[3] In part as a result, the Tsarist army suffered more than any other combatant power in the war—over seven million casualties in three years of intensive fighting against the German, Austro-Hungarian, and Ottoman Empires. In February 1917, soldiers fired into hungry crowds protesting in the Imperial capital, Petrograd. The remainder of the city garrison then mutinied, in some instances killing their officers in the process. Crowds of hundreds of thousands of workers, soldiers, and sailors then occupied the city. As the Russian war effort collapsed amid the ensuing strife, the Tsar's generals abandoned him or begged him to resign. With the Russian rail system paralyzed by strikes, Nicholas II was unable to even return to his capital, abdicating his crown in the provincial town of Pskov in March.

Looking back from that moment, it was clear that the Imperial Russian state had failed to effectively mobilize the country's vast human and natural resources. Russia called to arms the smallest percentage of its population of any of the combatants of the First World War, for two reasons: it did not have enough arms and it did not have enough officers for a larger army. Addressing these two problems—supply and leadership—was decisive to Imperial Russia's performance in the war, and as it turned out, the survival of the state. They would also be the two greatest tests facing the Red Army in the interwar period.

The Russian Empire failed at both. By the fall of 1914, Russia had 5.1 million men on active duty, but 4.5 million rifles. Only with tremendous effort did the state overcome the worst of its industrial and organizational problems by 1916, putting a great strain on the economic, political, and social fabric of the country. The decisive blow was self-inflicted: the state had decided to ban the sale of alcohol as a social measure in August 1914.[4] With budget deficits skyrocketing to 40 percent in 1914, then to 76 percent the following year, the decision to ban alcohol sales was devastating to the economy. Vodka sales (a state monopoly) had contributed 26 percent of the national budget prior to the war.[5] Facing enormous deficits, the Ministry of Finance began printing money at an alarming rate, triggering hyperinflation.[6] As rubles became increasingly worthless, peasant farmers stopped bringing their products to market.[7] Food shortages gripped the major cities, despite rapidly rising industrial output and wages.

Facing the second problem—leadership—the strict class structure of Russian society proved a major handicap. In 1913, less than 1.5 percent of the national population was classified as "noble," yet they constituted half of the Imperial Army's officer corps.[8] In part for social reasons, the army had only 40,000 commissioned officers out of a force of 1.5 million in 1914 (2.6 percent). By comparison, there were 30,739 officers among 761,438 total soldiers (4.0 percent) in the German Army in the same year.[9] This shortage turned into a crisis as the war dragged on. The prewar Russian officer corps disappeared into the maw of combat: more than 100,000 officers would become casualties during the war. Less than 10 percent of prewar officers were still serving in 1917.[10] Increasing the size of the army required a fundamental change in the social demographics of the officer corps. Even when the willingness to do so existed, there simply were not enough educated men to meet the need. Huge shortages of NCOs and officers played a major role in the collapse of discipline in the ranks in late 1916 and early 1917. That would prove disastrously decisive in the summer of 1917, when the Russian Imperial Army at last collapsed.

Stemming that disintegration was beyond the capabilities of the new political authorities. For eight months following the abdication of the Tsar, the Provisional Government, primarily composed of moderate socialists drawn from the Russia's last elected national legislature, tried to steer the vast Russian Empire through the First World War. Throughout its brief reign, its members were challenged by the Petrograd Soviet, a body representing the capital city's workers and soldiers, which claimed popular legitimacy.[11] In late September 1917, the Bolshevik faction of the Russian Social Democratic Labour Party—revolutionary Marxists led by Vladimir Ilych Lenin—took over the Petrograd Soviet. On November 6 (October 24 by the Julian calendar then in use in Russia), Lenin moved to resolve the conflict of power with the Provisional Government by force. Bolsheviks under orders from the party's Military Revolutionary Council seized the major centers of power throughout the Imperial capital. The leadership of the Provisional Government fled to the Winter Palace—the vast palace complex at the heart of Petrograd that had been home to the Tsars for two centuries. Soldiers and sailors under the leadership of Bolshevik Vladimir Antonov-Ovseenko, a senior Bolshevik, besieged the palace.

That evening at 9:40 P.M., the cruiser *Aurora* fired the blank shot to signal the beginnings of the attack against the Palace. It was soon followed by thirty rounds fired at the Winter Palace from ancient artillery pieces in the Peter and Paul Fortress across the river. After some desultory shooting, at two in the morning, orders flew down for the final assault. In his *History of the Russian Revolution*, Leon Trotsky described the scene as one of chaos. Junkers (military cadets) guarded the assembly but were soon overwhelmed. "Workers, sailors, soldiers are pushing up from outside in chains and groups, flinging the junkers from the barricades, bursting through the court, stumbling into the junkers on the staircase, crowding them back, toppling them over, driving them upstairs." Eventually the junkers were disarmed. "The victors burst into the room of the ministers. . . . 'I announce to you, members of the Provisional Government, that you are under arrest!' exclaimed Antonov in the name of the Military Revolutionary Council."[12]

So ended the first military action of the revolution. The image of a maddened mob overrunning the seat of national power was more propaganda than reality. So, too, was the description of intense fighting in the old palace: there had been almost no resistance. The October Revolution was more military coup than popular uprising: the conquest of the Winter Palace had been achieved with a daylong siege in which the Bolsheviks successfully deployed artillery and armored cars, an array of deserting army units, and a naval detachment of five ships from the Baltic fleet. It was the soldiers and sailors of Petrograd and the nearby Kronstadt naval base, more than anything else, who guaranteed the success of the October Revolution.

What were the aims of Russia's new leaders? Lenin sought to build a small, tightly disciplined "vanguard" party capable of imposing revolution upon Russia, rather than waiting for the forces of history to play out. As such, he tolerated little dissent within the ranks of his party, though a degree of interparty democracy—debate by the twenty-one members of the party's Central Committee—existed.[13] Lenin had many goals but the most immediate was to answer the rallying cry that had inspired many to support his party: "Peace, Land, Bread!" Before land and bread could be delivered, Lenin had to deliver peace, and withdraw Russia from the First World War.

To that end, he dispatched Trotsky, the Bolsheviks' new commissar for foreign affairs, to reach a settlement with Germany. Trotsky was already one of the giants of the Bolshevik Party in early 1918, despite the fact that he was a relative newcomer to the organization.[14] When Tsar Nicholas resigned, Trotsky—then living in New York—had immediately booked passage back to Europe. Returning to political chaos, his outstanding oratory and organizational skills helped win many over to the Bolshevik cause, particularly among soldiers of the city garrison.[15] Now Trotsky had to find a way to save the newfound revolution from the German Army. Thanks to the disintegration of discipline at the front, there was little standing between Petrograd and eighty-nine German divisions, numbering over a million men.[16] In a position of strength in the East, but desperate to turn to the Western Front on which the outcome of the war depended, the German Oberste Heeresleitung (Supreme Army Command) requested a ceasefire on December 4, 1917. Two weeks later, German and Soviet delegates arrived at the charred ruins of the German-occupied town of Brest-Litovsk in modern-day Belarus to begin negotiations.

Trotsky aimed to drag out negotiations as long as possible in the hopes that revolution or events on the Western Front would force German capitulation. After two months of deflections and delay, German patience was exhausted. On February 10, 1918, Richard von Kühlmann, the German foreign minister, delivered a speech laden with invective, accusing "the Bolsheviks of inciting the German army to mutiny and to the murder of its Emperor, Generals and officers."[17] Trotsky replied to Kühlmann's claims that he had no "knowledge of such an order. But," he added, in a weighty tone, "the decisive hour has struck. . . . Russia declares, on its side, the state of war with Germany, Austria-Hungary, Turkey and Bulgaria as ended."[18]

The German delegation was stunned. This was entirely unexpected, and without precedent. How could Russia unilaterally leave the war? After a moment, the German commander in the East, General Max Hoffmann, shouted, "Unheard of!"[19] Kühlmann tried to save the conference by calling for a new session, but Trotsky refused, replying that their mission was at an end and they were now returning to Petrograd.[20] With that, Trotsky and the Bolshevik delegation stood and left the conference room. Trotsky had concluded that if Germany resumed its advance eastward, it might destabilize the German home front and lead to the desired communist revolution. Even if the revolution did not happen, should the Germans and their allies resume an advance, they would clearly be the aggressors in the eyes of the world, boosting the Bolsheviks' reputation as the party of peace with Russians at home. In either case, Trotsky concluded, the Imperial German Army would be hesitant to renew the offensive.

The German response shattered these hopes. Nine days after Trotsky's abrupt departure from Brest-Litovsk, General Hoffmann launched Operation Faustschlag ("Fist Strike") with fifty-three divisions.[21] They encountered nearly no resistance as they moved eastward, covering 150 miles in seven days. Hoffmann described the "fighting" in his diaries as "the most comical war I have ever known."[22] At one stop, a single lieutenant and six soldiers received the prompt surrender of 600 Russian cavalrymen.[23]

The reaction in Petrograd was one of despondence. Lenin summoned the Central Committee to deal with the news on February 18. He made it clear that there were only two options: to wage a guerrilla war—which the Bolsheviks might lose—or to surrender and accept German terms. He concluded that it would be best for the revolution to cut its losses, which might require territorial and economic concessions, and accept peace terms with the Germans.[24] Trotsky still refused to admit he had miscalculated. It took three hours of acrimonious debate in the Central Committee before Lenin received a slim majority—7 to 4—in favor of his motion to agree to terms with the Germans.[25] Around midnight that evening, the Bolshevik leadership cabled their acceptance of the terms to the German High Command.[26]

There was a further price to be paid. Hoffmann and his superiors decided to punish the Bolsheviks for their withdrawal from the negotiations: the final terms would be even more onerous than the ones Trotsky had rejected. Trotsky himself refused to attend the signing ceremony in Brest-Litovsk on March 3, 1918.[27] Under the new agreement, Bolshevik Russia renounced control over the Baltic states, Poland, Finland, Ukraine, and Belarus—territories constituting around a third of Imperial Russia's population and 54 percent of its industry.[28] It would also be forced to pay a massive indemnity, even as the workers of Petrograd were starving. The terms were so harsh that Lenin was met with cries of "German Spy!" and "Traitor!" when he first announced the terms at a Communist Party meeting a few days later.[29] Outside of the party, Lenin's surrender triggered the beginnings of violent, organized resistance in Russia to the Bolsheviks, setting off the Russian Civil War.

It was also in this moment of chaos, violence, and revenge that the seeds of the interwar German-Soviet relationship were planted. The Treaty of Brest-Litovsk was the first formal diplomatic interaction between the Bolsheviks and a capitalist state.[30] The Allies refused to recognize the new government in Petrograd. Since relations had been established, however tenuously, with Berlin, the Bolsheviks turned to Germany for industrial goods they desperately needed, especially locomotives and train cars.[31] A Soviet trade delegation would arrive in Berlin almost immediately after the signing of the treaty.[32] In exchange, the German High Command dispatched Count Wilhelm von Mirbach to serve as the German ambassador to Soviet Russia.

In late February 1918, Lenin had decided to move the capital of Soviet Russia from vulnerable Petrograd to the more centrally located Moscow. Now settling in to the ancient Kremlin, the Bolshevik Central Committee was soon fully preoccupied with growing military revolt across the country. The Treaty of Brest-Litovsk had generated enormous anger among Russian nationalists and members of the military, who soon rose in open revolt. To deal with the multiple threats to the revolution, Lenin and the Central Committee appointed Trotsky the first People's Commissar for Military and Naval Affairs on March 13, 1918, two weeks after the signing of the treaty he had fought. Clarifying his objectives in a speech delivered to a session of the Moscow Soviet of Workers', Soldiers', and Peasants' deputies six days later, Trotsky argued that to survive the Soviet Republic needed "a properly and freshly organized army!"[33]

Trotsky found himself in an odd position. He had done everything he could to destroy the Imperial Army, but now that he was in a position of power he needed to reconstitute it. The Raboche-Krestyanskaia Krasnaia Armiia (The Workers' and Peasants' Red Army, hereafter Red Army) began in earnest in March 1918. Trotsky's first task was to find capable military professionals, which meant recruiting officers from the old army. The process proved easier than expected. Petrograd and Moscow received a steady stream of volunteers from a range of political and social backgrounds. Trotsky embraced them, though not without taking precautions—they would be accompanied by a "commissar" system of reliable political officers to monitor their behavior. His decision prevented tens of thousands of officers from joining the political opposition. The Red Army would draw the core of its leadership from former Tsarist soldiers: 314,180 of the 446,729 (70.3 percent) officers who served in the Red Army during the Russian Civil War had also served in the former Imperial Army.[34]

One of the officers who would take advantage of Trotsky's change of policy was Mikhail Tukhachevsky. Born to an impoverished noble family, Tukhachevsky had joined the Imperial officer corps before the war and served with distinction in combat before being wounded and captured by the Germans at the Second Battle of the Masurian Lakes in February 1915.[35] Transferred to a prisoner of war camp in Germany, Tukhachevsky would attempt four escapes between 1915 and 1917, once staying at large for a month and hiking in disguise 300 miles from Prussia all the way to the Dutch border before being recaptured.[36] He eventually escaped from the supposedly impregnable Ingolstadt fortress and made his way back to Russia.[37] A nobleman, an atheist, and a nationalist, Tukhachevsky was reluctant to pick sides in the political chaos that followed the Bolshevik Revolution. It was only the resumed advance of German forces into Russia, and Trotsky's decision to allow former officers full participation in the Bolsheviks' military force, that finally convinced Tukhachevsky he could and should join the Red Army.[38] Like thousands of other officers, defending Russia against foreigners trumped political concerns about the Bolsheviks.

In addition to recruiting experienced officers like Tukhachevsky, Trotsky began to address other major deficits within the Red Army. In particular, he rolled back earlier Bolshevik proclamations eliminating officer ranks and disciplinary measures, such as the beating of soldiers by their commanders.[39] Lenin applauded Trotsky's toughness, writing to him that if it appeared a senior commander seemed to be hesitating in launching an offensive, Trotsky should follow the example of the French Revolution and shoot him.[40]

The reason for the Bolsheviks' reversal was the increasingly dire military situation. In the spring of 1918, a host of enemies had appeared to confront Lenin. The first organized opposition came in May, when the Bolsheviks attempted to disarm a military formation made up of Czech and Slovak prisoners of war, the so-called Czech Legion.[41] The Czechs refused, repelled the Bolsheviks, then seized control of part of Russia's primary artery, the Trans-Siberian Railway. In doing so, they effectively cut off Bolshevik forces in central European Russia from the rest of the country. Their actions emboldened formations of former Tsarist officers who had organized themselves into an anti-Bolshevik resistance. These units soon occupied Siberia, the Urals, and the Lower Volga.[42] Despite a motley array of political beliefs and leaders, these forces would become known collectively as the "Whites."

As the Whites and Czech Legion threatened the Bolshevik hold on power, the Allied powers—Great Britain, France, the United States, Italy, and Japan—decided to intervene. Beginning in July 1918, they landed forces along Russia's Black Sea, Arctic Sea, and Pacific Ocean coasts. Their aim was to prevent either the Germans or the Bolsheviks from seizing huge stockpiles of military equipment that had accumulated in Russian ports. They also began delivering military aid to the Whites.

Perhaps most dangerously, forces within Soviet territory also threatened Lenin's new regime. The Bolsheviks had held a previously scheduled national election in November 1917 but—to Lenin's great surprise—lost badly. When members of the new National Assembly arrived in Petrograd in January 1918, the Bolsheviks arrested most of the elected representatives and then outlawed all but one other political party. The one exception was that of the Left Socialist Revolutionaries (SRs), who had backed Lenin during the October Revolution. On July 6, 1918, the Left SRs rose in revolt against the signing of the Treaty of Brest-Litovsk. They assassinated German ambassador Count Mirbach, arrested head of the Secret Police Feliks Dzerzhinsky, and besieged the Bolshevik leadership, who were occupying the Kremlin. The Left SRs were eventually beaten back in fierce street fighting led by the pro-Bolshevik Latvian Riflemen.[43] Nonetheless, the internal danger remained. One of the Red Army's most experienced military commanders attempted to defect to anti-Bolshevik forces along with several thousand of his men before being shot by his commissar in mid-July 1918.[44]

In the midst of this desperate scene, Lenin tried to rally the forces of the revolution in Moscow. On August 30, 1918, he gave a speech to workers at the Michelson Factory, warning them about the dangers of democracy. "Wherever 'democrats' rule you find plain, straightforward theft. We know the true nature of such democracies!" He concluded by shouting, "We have only one way out: victory or death!"[45] He then waved and began working his way through the crowd to the exit. Caught in the throng of workers leaving the building, one of his bodyguards, Commissar Baturin, fell behind. As he caught up to Lenin, Baturin heard what he thought was a car backfiring. After a moment, he realized the noises were gunshots, fired by an SR assassin. He saw Lenin face down next to his car. "I did not lose my head," Baturin recalled, "but shouted 'Catch the killer of Comrade Lenin!' "[46] Lenin was not dead, however. After being driven back to the Kremlin, he even walked up three flights of stairs to his apartment before collapsing. Doctors summoned to the scene rapidly ascertained that he had been shot twice, in the neck and the shoulder, with the potential for serious complications.

The Bolsheviks faced their most dangerous moment. With Lenin incapacitated, the burden fell on Trotsky to revive the military fortunes of the revolution. He attempted to do that in person at the front. To make the process easier, he centralized military administration under the Revolutsionnyi Voennyi Soviet (Revolutionary Military Council, or RVS), and named himself its chairman.[47] With this reorganization came new commanders. Trotsky replaced most of the Bolsheviks in positions of command with former Imperial Army officers, closely watched by newly appointed communist commissars.[48] His goal was to professionalize the Red Army as best he could.

As a result of Trotsky's leadership, the army that young Tukhachevsky among others joined during the summer of 1918 was largely composed of peasants, commanded by officers and NCOs who had served under the Tsar, and supervised by a relatively small group of Bolsheviks.[49] Indeed, workers never made up more than

18 percent of the Red Army's strength.[50] The wooing of 300,000 Imperial officers and NCOs who formed the core of the Red Army was decisive in sustaining its fighting strength. Arming and maintaining this heterogeneous force, essential to the survival of the new communist state, would require enormous investment. And external help. As the Russian Civil War was beginning in earnest, there was only one state that had established diplomatic relations with Bolshevik Russia, and could provide aid: the former archenemy, Germany.

CHAPTER 2

Revolution and Reaction

A s Trotsky sought to build a new military for the Bolsheviks in 1918, Imperial Germany faced disaster. After the Treaty of Brest-Litovsk, the military rulers of Germany—Commander-in-Chief of the Oberste Heeresleitung Paul von Hindenburg and his domineering deputy, General Erich Ludendorff—had transferred hundreds of thousands of soldiers from the Russian front to France, hoping to win the war in one last great offensive.[1] However, opposed by growing numbers of American soldiers, it petered out 70 miles from Paris. The German Army was forced back on the defensive, short on men and shells. On August 8, the Allies launched an offensive of their own at Amiens, which, with the aid of tanks, tore a 15-mile hole in the front. The Germans began retreating eastward.

Conditions on the Western Front deteriorated fast. On September 30, General Ludendorff informed Kaiser Wilhelm II that the war was lost. The Oberste Heeresleitung—now effectively ruling the country—decided to replace the pro-war chancellor Georg Hertling with a liberal, Prince Maximilian von Baden. Hindenburg and Ludendorff empowered Prince Maximilian to negotiate an armistice, using the United States as the intermediary. When American communiques made it clear that the Kaiser must step down and the German Army withdraw to Germany's prewar borders as a precondition of peace, General Ludendorff himself had no choice but to resign.

Ludendorff's replacement was Wilhelm Groener, a staff officer from Württemberg best known for managing Germany's wartime economy. He was much more inclined to listen to demands for peace and political reform than was his predecessor.[2] His political skills would soon be put to the test: as Groener assumed his new office on October 23, the German Army and the Imperial government were falling apart. On October 28, the Reichstag (the German Parliament) declared that it had the power to dismiss the cabinet and chancellor. This "October Constitution" was reinforced as soldiers', sailors', and workers' committees seized power in major cities, leading to the abdication of all of the country's surviving noble houses, save Kaiser Wilhelm himself. On November 3, the German Hochseeflotte (The High Seas Fleet) in Kiel mutinied. Within twenty-four hours, more than 40,000 soldiers and sailors had taken up arms against their own government. It was clear that Germany could not continue to fight.

Yet, at this critical moment, the German military suddenly deferred to the new civilian government, passing responsibility for seeking an armistice with the Allies to Secretary of State Matthias Erzberger. On November 7, Erzberger drove across the front lines under a flag of truce, rendezvousing with French general Ferdinand Foch in the forest of Compiègne to discuss an armistice. In the words of General Groener, this was done to "keep the armor shining."[3] By abjuring responsibility for defeat and the treaty to come, the military could blame civilian leaders for Germany's downfall and remain the most popular institution in postwar Germany, as Hindenburg and Groener had intended. This would serve as the basis for the "stab-in-the-back" conspiracy theory that would help Hitler rise to power.

Still, even as defeat loomed, Kaiser Wilhelm II dithered about abdicating, wondering about the possibility of retaining his crown, at least in Prussia. Groener finally lost his patience on November 9, declaring to the Kaiser that the army would march home "in peace and order under its leaders and commanding generals," but not under the Kaiser's command, "for it stands no longer behind Your Majesty."[4] When Hindenburg reluctantly seconded Groener's statement, the Kaiser abdicated and went into exile.

Within hours of the announcement of the abdication, the largest party in the Reichstag, the Sozialdemokratische Partei Deutschlands (Social Democratic Party, or SPD), effectively took charge, handed power by the remnants of the Imperial government. Led by Friedrich Ebert, the SPD's leadership mostly hoped to retain the monarchy and extant Imperial German constitution despite the Kaiser's resignation.[5] But the SPD's radical antiwar wing, the Unabhängige Sozialdemokratische Partei Deutschlands (Independent Social Democratic Party, or USPD, which had broken away in 1917), demanded more radical change. Full of uncertainty, a huge crowd of spectators assembled outside the Reichstag building on the afternoon of November 9, demanding that Ebert address them.[6]

Ebert refused, sending word for them to disperse. But his SPD cochair Philip Scheidemann, with whom he was at lunch that afternoon, concluded on his own some public statement was necessary, especially given rumors the USPD might declare a republic later that day. Without telling Ebert, he appeared in front of the Reichstag, shouting to the crowd below: "That old and rotten thing, the monarchy, has collapsed. Long live the new! Long live the German republic!"[7] Ebert was furious with this unilateral declaration, but had few choices. The SPD would back a new republic. Following Scheidemann's announcement, USPD leaders occupied the former Imperial Palace, declaring a rival "free socialist republic" inspired by the Russian Revolution.[8] It seemed that events might follow the course of the February Revolution in Russia, with a workers' soviet and a bourgeois provisional government competing for power. Faced with two rival regimes, the German military intervened. That night, General Groener called the Reichskanzlei, where Ebert had taken up residence. He told Ebert that the army was at the "disposal of his government" and that he expected it to be used to maintain law and order, and to resist Bolshevism. As he recalled, "Ebert accepted my offer of an alliance."[9]

While political drama unfolded in Berlin, the war continued on the Western Front, with German forces in full retreat. On that same dramatic day, Chancellor Ebert finally ordered Secretary of State Erzberger, still in France, to sign the armistice agreement. Erzberger did so in the early morning hours of November 11. The final ceasefire went into effect at eleven in the morning on November 11, 1918. The First World War was over.

The war might have been over, but the German Revolution had just begun. The state was now leaderless. Power was wielded by three forces: the military, led by Hindenburg and Groener; the Reichstag, where the SPD championed a moderate socialist republic; and the mushrooming councils of radicalized soldiers, sailors, and workers, inspired by the Soviet model. United against revolutionary violence, the tenuous alliance between Ebert and the SPD on one hand, and General Groener and the Reichswehr on the other, would define the Republic.

The armistice had major ramifications for the Soviet-German relationship, too. With the declaration of the Armistice, Lenin and Trotsky immediately renounced Brest-Litovsk, eager to cease paying reparations and reestablish control over much of the former Tsarist Empire. Prisoner of war exchanges had been conducted for the previous eight months under the terms of the treaty. However, when the Armistice arrived, more than a million Russian prisoners were still in German hands. Facing a political crisis, famine at home, and without the resources to care for the hundreds of thousands of Russians in captivity, the German government began packing the POWs onto train cars, shipping them east to the truce line between the German and Bolshevik forces in modern-day Belarus, and releasing them. A German diplomat on his way home from Moscow to Berlin recalled that the "pitiful sight" of Russian soldiers shuffling past his train on both sides. "Many of the Russians collapsed from hunger, cold or exhaustion, and remained lying beside the tracks."[10]

As tens of thousands of Russian POWs were left to their fate in wintry Belarus, the Imperial German Army disintegrated. Many soldiers simply started walking home, still in the possession of their weapons. Out of the 10 million rifles and tens of thousands of machine guns in circulation at the end of the war, only 1.3 million rifles and 9,000 machine guns were surrendered to the Allies or to the German government.[11] Armed and organized, common soldiers and sailors helped determine the postwar political landscape. Facing violence from mobs of veterans in Berlin in December 1918, Chancellor Ebert appointed SPD representative Gustav Noske, a former butcher, as minister of national defense and commander-in-chief for Brandenburg, the territory surrounding and including Berlin.[12] Noske had dealt firmly with the naval mutinies in Kiel two months earlier, listening to sailors' grievances but restoring discipline and officers' control, even in the face of armed mutineers. Upon hearing of his appointment, Noske remarked, "someone must be the bloodhound."[13]

Noske understood that the government would not survive without a military force upon which it could depend.[14] Much as Trotsky had concluded earlier that year, Noske decided that the Republic's new military force must be guided by senior German military officers. This entailed serious political risks, as few professional military officers felt anything but disdain for Noske's SPD. To shore up their support, Noske took steps to ensure that the military remained a willing partner by appointing Colonel Walther Reinhardt as Prussian minister of war in early January 1918. The aim was to solidify the tenuous alliance between the military and the SPD by including a member of the military—albeit a junior one—in the ruling circle.[15] Then, with some leadership in place, it was essential to form the rudiments of a new army from the remnants of the old.

The heart of this new force would be drawn from the Freikorps (Free Corps), paramilitary bands that had sprouted up across the country. As early as November 1918, groups of (mostly) right-wing veterans had organized themselves against the forces of revolution, or to protect order and private property in their neighborhoods. The first Freikorps unit drew heavily from Germany's Stoßtruppen (Stormtroopers), elite bands of infantrymen that had been concentrated by the German High Command to break through enemy lines on the Western Front.[16] These men shared attributes. They were uniformly young and physically fit, and they tended to contain a very high percentage of former army officers—as high as one officer per four enlisted.

Freikorps members were volunteers, drawn together by fears about the future. Their typical gathering places were beer gardens and beer halls where they bemoaned the fate of postwar Germany. A typical recruiting poster highlighted their concerns: "Comrades! The . . . [Communist] danger has not yet been removed. The Poles press ever farther onto German soil. Soldiers, Arise! Prevent Germany from becoming the laughing stock of the earth. Enroll NOW in the HUELSEN FREIKORPS."[17] Some enlisted men or NCOs requested their favorite officers organize them into Freikorps. Others were drawn back to service by the calls of their senior officers. Noske and Reinhardt soon began placing loyal officers in charge of existing Freikorps, merging smaller units into larger ones and coordinating their movements.[18]

On December 31, 1918, a variety of radical groups—including the Communist Spartacus League and part of the USPD—united to form the Kommunistische Partei Deutschlands (Communist Party of Germany, or KPD). Four days later, Chancellor Ebert's government dismissed Berlin's chief of police, a radical leftist, for refusing to follow orders. The KPD voted for confrontation with the government to challenge his dismissal. On January 5, 1919, the Spartacist faction—the radical core of the KPD's membership—organized demonstrations that soon swelled beyond their control. Rioters occupied government buildings and newspaper offices and besieged the city center. For eight days, anarchy reigned in the streets of Berlin as nearly 20,000 armed "red guards" and workers organized a Revolutionary Committee and set about dismantling the Republic.[19] Eager to see the German Revolution succeed, several senior Bolsheviks, including Vice-Commissar for Foreign Affairs Karl Radek, attempted to reach Berlin to assist their revolutionary comrades-in-arms. They were denied entry, but Radek—alone—crossed the border secretly, arriving in Berlin.

As these fires of revolution grew, Noske withdrew from Berlin to the suburb of Dahlem, along with a few General Staff officers—the former leadership of the Imperial German Army. There they issued calls to comrades-in-arms and veterans willing to support the SPD government. Volunteer Freikorps units from across Germany began arriving and organizing themselves into a field army. Within three days, there were several thousand well-armed and disciplined troops at Dahlem, answering to the remnants of the General Staff, and to Noske in particular. As these forces swelled in strength, Noske ordered General Freiherr von Lüttwitz, commander of the III Army Corps, to retake Berlin.[20] With the aid of artillery, his soldiers began reconquering the capital on January 8. On January 11, Noske entered the city with 3,000 Freikorps men. At the cost of 13 military and 156 civilian dead—including the nighttime executions of Spartacist leaders Rosa Luxemburg and Karl Liebknecht—Noske and the Freikorps had restored order, at least temporarily.

The turmoil would also entangle the Bolsheviks in German politics. A few weeks after the failure of the January Uprising, government forces caught Karl Radek and locked him up in Moabit Prison in Berlin. Here he would remain for nearly a year, holding a sort of jailhouse salon as an unofficial representative of the Bolshevik regime.[21] He would be visited by senior German politicians, diplomats, and military officers, and allowed to communicate with the outside world.[22] As the SPD and the Reichswehr moved to crush the communists, Radek would serve as a point of contact with the Bolshevik regime in Moscow. Eventually, he would move into the apartments of a German staff officer, an indication of how important the military considered their prisoner.[23] On the political front, the establishment of control in Berlin gave the SPD the time it needed to hold elections to a new National Assembly that would meet beginning on January 20. The radical left refused to participate in the elections. The result was therefore a victory for the moderate parties: the SPD won 37.9 percent of the vote; Zentrum (Center)—a moderate Catholic party—won nearly 20 percent of the vote; and a center-left liberal party, the Deutsche Demokratische Partei (German Democratic Party), received 18.56 percent.[24] All were supportive of the Republican project.[25] Shortly thereafter, these representatives met at Weimar, the birthplace of the German Enlightenment, Goethe's adopted home, and one of the country's great cultural centers. There they drew up the Republic's constitution. Crucially, they created a strong legislature and weak executive, except for one provision: Article 48, which allowed the president—with the countersignature of the chancellor, who was appointed by the president—to rule by decree in the event of a national emergency. This would later turn out to be the Republic's mortal weakness. For the time being, however, the democratic order seemed to be stabilizing, as Chancellor Ebert won the presidency in a landslide on February 11, 1919.

While the constitutional order solidified in Weimar, violence across the country was just beginning to erupt. Noske acted quickly after the legitimation of the elections, dispatching Freikorps units to reconquer city after city from revolutionary councils or anti-government forces. Bremen fell after a daylong battle on February 4. Cuxhaven, Bremerhaven, and Wilhelmshaven were captured with minimal fighting by February 19. Meanwhile, in Berlin, the remaining Spartacists staged another attempted revolution on March 3. Raising 15,000 armed workers, Russian POWs, and red militiamen, the revolutionaries announced a general strike, murdered police officers, and seized control of the eastern half of Berlin. Noske immediately declared Berlin under a "state of siege" and rallied Freikorps units to the government's defense.

The fighting in February and March proved much bloodier than in January. One Freikorps officer told his peers that it was "a lot better to kill a few innocent people than to let one guilty person escape."[26] Violence matched the rhetoric: revolutionaries deployed chemical munitions while Freikorps bombed the capital from the air and rolled their tanks through the streets.[27] Both sides committed atrocities. On March 9, Noske issued an order that read, "Every person who is taken, arms in hand, fighting against government troops, is to be shot immediately."[28] This order was interpreted broadly by the Freikorps officers leading the counterrevolutionary forces. It may have been effective. From March 9 to March 16, the city's working-class neighborhoods were taken, block by block. Between 600 and 1,200 people were killed and thousands more wounded.[29] The final reconquest of Berlin was followed by short but effective campaigns across the country by the increasingly well-organized Freikorps.

The last major bastion of the revolution was in Bavaria, where a brief-lived "People's Republic" had formed. It proved to be one of the strange footnotes of history. Its half-mad commissar of foreign affairs Franz Lipp sent off a series of lewd telegrams to the Pope and Vladimir Lenin regarding the Bavarian Chancellery toilets. Another, sent to the government in Berlin, read, "My dear colleague: I have just declared war on Württemberg and Switzerland because these dogs did not send me 60 locomotives immediately. I am certain of victory."[30] The local SPD government, which had been chased out of Munich, was forced to turn to a Bavarian Freikorps unit led by rabidly right-wing Franz Ritter von Epp. This was awkward, as SPD functionaries had ordered Epp's arrest for treason not long before. Epp, the future Nazi Reichskommissar for Bavaria, began the reconquest of Bavaria on April 29. Hundreds were killed in four days of street fighting. By May, the country was largely pacified and under government control.

The Weimar Republic had surmounted only one of the many hurdles it faced. It now had a large number of men under arms, loyal to the former General Staff but less committed to SPD's program of nationalizations, high taxation, and constitutionalism.[31] In addition, the Ebert government needed to formally end the war with the Allies—the final terms of a peace treaty had yet to be decided. In this context, Noske proposed forming a new national army by concentrating many of the Freikorps.[32] He forced the proposal through a hostile Reichstag, as the SPD allied with the center and right against the other leftwing parties.

The integration of the Freikorps into the Vorläufige Reichswehr (Provisional Reich Defense Force) began on March 6, 1919, with a government decree reorganizing the military.[33] This law established several significant aspects of the Reichswehr. First, the president would be the supreme commander of all German military forces.[34] Second, the Reichswehrminister (minister of defense) within the chancellor's cabinet would manage the incorporation of Freikorps units, oversee discipline, reform regulations, and hear complaints from enlisted and junior officers against commanding officers.[35] For Deputy Chief of the General Staff Wilhelm Groener, the question was how to integrate the Freikorps units into the military structure. The law reinstated the old imperial system of promotion, meaning that regimental and battalion commanders handled the appointment of all junior officers. This in turn meant that the old Imperial officer corps, hostile to the republic, was in the position to reshape the army as it saw fit.[36]

The man who would play the critical role in this process was General Hans von Seeckt. Thin, almost skeletal, his stern, monacled mien suggested the epitome of the Prussian warrior class. Despite his laconic air—for which he had earned the nickname "The Sphinx"—Seeckt was not a typical Prussian officer. Born in 1866, he was the son of a military family of noble status from Pomerania, but took an unusual route to the Prussian Army. He received a civilian primary education, then enrolled in the "Kaiser" Alexander I Guards Regiment, a unit formed in honor of its Russian namesake during the Napoleonic Wars. His intelligence and self-discipline led to a position at the General Staff Course in 1893, then the coveted promotion to the General Staff Corps. He was unique among his cohort for his wide-ranging intellect, his grasp of several languages (including French, English, and Russian), and his love of travel—he had seen most of Europe, as well as Egypt and India.[37] At the same time, however, he could be aloof, arrogant, and thin-skinned. His close subordinates found him difficult to work with, although the officer corps at large would come to revere Seeckt for his strong hand and capable leadership. He had spent the bulk of his wartime service on the Eastern Front, and at the end of the war Hindenburg had assigned him to lead all the German armies in the east, which meant maintaining discipline, withdrawing them in good order, and managing the chaotic occupation of Ukraine and the Baltic states. His interest in Russia was undoubtedly strengthened during this period.

The spring of 1919 found Groener and Seeckt—whom Groener had appointed to manage the structure of the army—deliberating what should be done with the armed bands now spread across Germany. The chaotic months since the armistice provided the evidence for excluding or including particular Freikorps units. They agreed that any unit that had refused to follow their orders during the revolutionary events of the preceding four months should be disbanded. This included a number of pro-Republic formations. In addition, units—including on the extreme right—that had proven undisciplined in their behavior would not find service in the Provisional Reichswehr. While they considered the future shape of the military, they awaited word from the peace conference then ongoing in Paris that was to determine Germany's fate.

As they waited for the terms to be imposed, Germany's officer corps began to evaluate why they had lost the war, conducting an extensive historical study of that question.[38] The consensus was that Germany's basic strategic, operational, and tactical decisions had been entirely correct, particularly in its emphasis on offensive war. Some believed that the Oberste Heeresleitung had failed to carry out the initial invasion of France correctly. Others argued that Germany had lost the technological arms race. Colonel Kurt Thorbeck of the Gewehr-Prüfungskommission (The Rifle Examination Board, responsible for developing new military technologies), for example, argued that "the German General Staff did not properly recognize the material demands of a world war," particularly with regard to economic mobilization and advanced weapons like tanks.[39] The latter proved a popular view among German officers, in part because it relieved them of responsibility for a host of strategic and operational errors during the war.[40]

Even as they debated the causes of defeat, Hans von Seeckt immediately turned to the next conflict. Victory would require alliances and Germany's allies from the war—the Austro-Hungarian and Ottoman Empires—no longer existed, dissolved amid national uprisings that had broken out in late 1918. But one of the former leaders of the Ottoman Empire happened to be in Berlin, at Seeckt's behest. With his help, Seeckt intended to remedy Germany's disastrous strategic position.

After the defeat of the Ottoman Empire, Enver Pasha, the former Turkish minister of defense (and one of the architects of the Armenian mass killings) had fled aboard a German submarine.[41] He was tried in absentia by the new Turkish government and sentenced to death, leaving him in permanent exile. With grandiose plans about returning to Turkey and establishing a pan-Turkic Empire, he met with Karl Radek—then held in a German prison—to seek the help of the Bolsheviks. He also met with Seeckt, whom he had first met in 1916.[42] Radek encouraged Enver to go to Moscow. In April 1919, Seeckt agreed to dispatch Enver as a liaison to Moscow, too.[43] His task was to open communications between Seeckt's Reichswehr and the new Bolshevik government, then in a pitched fight against the Whites. It was a risky assignment. The Allies were at war with the Bolsheviks, and had not yet decided upon the price of peace to be levied against Germany. News that the Germans were negotiating with the Communist enemy very well might cause the war to resume.

Pasha was spotted in April 1919 by German Major Fritz Tschunke, who was then serving as a liaison officer with the Lithuanian army in the then-capital city of Kowno. The Reichswehr had assigned him to assist in dismantling Germany's short-lived empire in Eastern Europe. While sitting in his orderly room, he was shocked to see a pale-looking and disheveled man passed his line of sight, surrounded by armed guards, and being taken to a cell. Tschunke recognized the Pasha because he had been on Seeckt's staff when he had served in Turkey. He also knew that the Pasha was on the Allied Power's list of war criminals, with a bounty on his head. Tschunke concluded that "the Lithuanians did not know the Turk's true identity."[44] He was right. The Pasha, who was carrying forged identity papers, had told his captors he was a Turkish Red Cross volunteer named Mohamed Ali Sami.[45] Suspicious, the Lithuanians decided to hold him until his identity could be confirmed.[46] Had they known whom they had in custody, they would have immediately turned him over to British and French forces stationed elsewhere in Kowno.[47]

Sometime in the next few days Tschunke managed to get a minute alone with the Pasha. He learned from the prisoner that he had been traveling from Berlin to Moscow on a secret mission. His plane had developed mechanical problems and been forced to make an emergency landing near Abeli, Lithuania.[48] Then, to Tschunke's horror, the Pasha informed him that "important maps and documents from the German General Staff were in fact hidden in the airplane."[49] Tschunke realized he had to act fast. If the Allies got hold of these documents the consequences could be catastrophic.[50] The British and French had in fact learned of the mysterious aircraft, and requested the Lithuanians impound it and arrest its passengers until more could be learned about their reason for flying to Moscow.[51]

That night, Tschunke broke into the damaged airplane with the assistance of a German pilot in the employ of the Lithuanian Air Force, and managed to retrieve all of the sensitive materials inside. Now he had to get the Pasha out of the country. Taking advantage of his position as liaison, he convinced the Lithuanian guards to let the prisoner go for "successively longer walks" while the investigation was pending.[52] Tschunke arranged for these walks to go through fields on the edge of an airstrip on the Aleksotas military base not far from the Pasha's holding cell. Next, Tschunke had a German pilot acquaintance and some accomplices prepare an aircraft on the runway. At a designated date and time, they were to have the aircraft, engine on, taxiing on the runway. On one of his walks the Pasha and his guards came within sight of the airstrip. Suddenly, the former minister took off at a dead run across a meadow toward the plane. The guards opened fire as the Pasha managed to hop into the aircraft, which had roared to life, without being hit. The plane accelerated, lifted off, and wheeled in the direction of Germany.

Tschunke would eventually learn why Enver Pasha had landed in a Lithuanian cell. The Pasha had been dispatched to Moscow to facilitate a partnership aimed at rearming Germany.[53] Although it would take two more attempts and another brief spell behind bars before the Pasha was able to open channels between Seeckt and Trotsky, his attempt in 1919 was nevertheless important, particularly given its date. Seeckt had dispatched Enver before the terms of the peace treaty to end the First World War were known—it would not be revealed until the following month. Seeckt made clear his intent to forge a Soviet-German partnership—one predicated on sharing intelligence, economic partnership in areas of military importance, and possibly even an alliance against the new state of Poland—even before the consequences of defeat were known. In other words, it was not an unfair peace that motivated Seeckt and his fellow officers. It was the far more ambitious aim of reversing Germany's defeat in the First World War.

CHAPTER 3

The Treaty of Versailles

Paris in May 1919 still bore the scars of war. It was crowded with refugees. Windowless buildings and piles of rubble remained in some neighborhoods like the Fourth Arrondissement, where the German aerial and artillery bombardment had been worst. Invalids in their military uniforms lined the Champs-Élysées, begging.[1] The famed Louvre art museum remained closed, its collections having been spirited out of the city when the first great German offensive had come within 45 miles of the city in 1914.[2] It was hardly a promising sight for the German delegates who arrived in May to hear the terms to be imposed upon them. There was consensus among the Allied delegates, who had been meeting since January, that Germany must be punished for having begun the war. Its behavior in occupied Belgium, Romania, and throughout Eastern Europe did little to help the German case. American president Woodrow Wilson told his confidantes that the German people "would be shunned and avoided like lepers for generations to come."[3]

On May 7, 1919, German foreign minister Count Ulrich von Brockdorff-Rantzau was handed a 440-article draft text of the Allied terms. There was to be no negotiation. Germany had three weeks to respond to the treaty with "observations," which might result in a few minor changes. When the German delegation saw the full text of the treaty, they were shocked. The treaty stripped the country of all its colonies, assessed preliminary reparations to be paid by Germany at 20 billion gold marks ($241 million), established a committee that would oversee further reparations payments, set up the Allied occupation of western Germany, reduced the military to a shadow of its former strength, and, most painfully, ceded large tracts of eastern Germany to the new state of Poland.[4] The delegation immediately protested that if these terms held they would be unable to defend themselves against Bolshevism.[5] Brockdorff-Rantzau issued a counterproposal, trying to reduce the price of peace. It was rejected by the Allies, who on June 16 told the German minister that he had five days to accept the treaty or their armies would begin marching east.[6]

When German military officers learned of the terms, they were furious about the required reduction of the German army by 97.5 percent, from over 4 million to only 100,000 men.[7] They also were enraged by Article 228—which sought the extradition and trial of German war criminals—and Article 231, the "war-guilt" clause, which placed blame for the entire conflict squarely upon Germany.[8] These portions of the Treaty so inflamed passions within the army that there was serious debate of a coup to overthrow the SPD government, install Gustav Noske as military dictator, and resume the war.[9] On the morning of June 19, senior military leaders secretly gathered in a stable to discuss a plan of action. Groener, who attended as representative of the General Staff, called the conference "a dangerous war council which could have caused the greatest possible political catastrophe for Germany." Reinhardt predicted that acceptance of the terms would cause "a general insurrection in the east," an insurrection that he advocated the government support. General Groener attempted to convince those present such a course was folly, noting that the gentlemen present "spoke as if fighting in the East were completely separate from the potential events in the West."[10] The bellicose faction at the gathering proposed Hans von Seeckt as the new chief of staff if the war was to be renewed. Only when Seeckt advised against resuming the war did Groener win his case.[11]

Meanwhile, Foreign Minister Brockdorff-Rantzau had resigned rather than accept the Allied terms. Philipp Scheidemann, now chancellor, delivered a fiery speech in the Reichstag in which he decried the peace terms as "so unacceptable that I still cannot believe that the whole world could tolerate it."[12] Afterward, he resigned from the government, too. The matter passed to the National Assembly, where members asked Hindenburg, as head of the Oberste Heeresleitung, whether resistance was feasible. He replied in the negative.[13] On June 22, 1919, the National Assembly voted to accept the treaty—with reservations. The following day, the newly appointed cabinet agreed to sign the treaty, claiming that the previous day's vote authorized their decision. On June 28, new Foreign Minister Hermann Müller and Minister for Colonies and for Transport Johannes Bell—who had jointly been in office for seven days— signed the Treaty of Versailles, officially ending the First World War.

The reaction among the German military was one of astonishment. Despite having imposed far more draconian financial and territorial conditions on Russia in the Treaty of Brest-Litovsk, the terms—particularly those regarding demobilization and war guilt—were unbearable to the officer corps. Versailles had significant effects on the relationship between the state and the Provisional Reichswehr, which saw the Weimar coalition government as discredited by signing the treaty. Two cabinet ministers associated with it—Matthias Erzberger and Walther Rathenau—would be assassinated by former Freikorps members in 1921 and 1922, respectively. Noske, who had been popular within the military for his decisive leadership against the communists, suddenly faced calls to resign for his acceptance of the treaty terms.[14] And Groener, who had kept the officer corps together through the revolutionary turmoil, would also be blamed for accepting the treaty. He resigned on September 30, 1919. Groener was the most politically astute senior officer in the Reichswehr in 1919. His retirement and Noske's loss of popularity opened a wide chasm between the military and the Republic.

The military terms of the Versailles Treaty require some examination, given the influential role they played in shaping the Reichswehr and its relationship with the Soviet Union. Section IV of the treaty (specifically Articles 159 to 213) called for the

German military's immediate and rapid demobilization and disarmament, allowing it to retain only a small force, intended by the Allies to guarantee internal order and resist Bolshevism. Article 160 required the reduction of the German army to no "more than seven divisions of infantry and three divisions of cavalry"—numbering no more than those aforementioned 100,000 men. All soldiers in excess of this figure were required to be demobilized by March 31, 1920.[15] The officer corps could consist of no more than 4,000 men in total. Conscription, now eliminated, was to be replaced with twelve-year enlistments. This was to ensure that the German military could not train large numbers of men in brief periods, a trick that the Prussians had used to frustrate similar terms imposed by Napoleon in 1807. Versailles also eliminated the German General Staff and nearly all military schools and academies in the country. The navy was to be shrunk to 15,000 men, manning six old battleships, six light cruisers, twelve destroyers, and twelve torpedo boats.

The German military was also to give up all the modern technologies of war: submarines, aircraft, heavy artillery, poison gas, and tanks were all explicitly banned. Those already in existence were to be turned over to the Allies. To prevent future rearmament, the treaty established the Inter-Allied Commissions of Control (IACC), consisting of boards of officers from the victorious powers whose job it was to police German industry and keep careful watch over its military. Three commissions were tasked with destroying German war material: the Inter-Allied Military (IAMCC), Naval (IANCC), and Aeronautical Control Commissions (IAACC). The first, headed by French General Charles Nollet, was by far the most powerful, tasked in the Treaty of Versailles with closing down all "establishments for the manufacture, preparation, storage or design of arms, munitions or any war material whatever" except for a short list approved by the Allied government.[16] Nollet also was assigned to oversee the other two commissions. Marshal Foch dispatched him to Berlin with an admonition: "The war is not yet over."[17]

There was urgency to the question of German disarmament, as the British and French could not demobilize their own enormous armies safely until Germany had done the same, especially given the precipitous withdrawal of American forces from Europe after the war's end.[18] Even as the disarmament conversations began in Paris, Foch drew up plans for an invasion of Germany should the German government reject the disarmament demands.[19]

The Germans did eventually accept the terms, as noted. But there were barriers to a successful disarmament program. Almost immediately after the IANCC, IAACC, and IAMCC commissions were organized, the Reichswehr set up counter-organizations to monitor and hinder them.[20] In a further sign of trouble, there were disagreements within the inspection teams about their roles and responsibilities. This was a product of broader divergences over the postwar order. Foch and Prime Minister Georges Clemenceau sought French hegemony on the continent, which they viewed as the only guarantee of their long-term security.[21] France's population and economy were smaller than those of Germany, so the only solution was to permanently weaken their larger neighbor. On the other hand, British prime minister David Lloyd George and senior British military officials preferred a balance of power on the continent. A strengthened Germany could serve as a trading partner and resist the spread of communism.[22] One of his cabinet members coined the term "appeasement" in 1919 to suggest gradual concessions to German interests might over time eliminate the most contentious elements of Versailles.[23] The policy would stick, serving—in the words of historian Martin Gilbert—as the "corner-stone of inter-war foreign policy" for Great Britain.[24]

To manage the disarmament of Germany—whatever that might mean—Nollet had at his disposal 1,300 officers, men, and translators, all of whose salaries were to be paid by the defeated Germans.[25] The IAMCC began by ordering the collection of banned war materiel for destruction, as well as administering surveys and conducting surprise inspections of industrial installations across the country.[26] IAMCC inspectors began arriving in Germany in the summer of 1919 and were met with constant hostility as they carried out their work. Workers threw stones at their cars, local policemen arrested them as spies, and, in at least a few instances, IAMCC teams were attacked by mobs.[27] In one instance, a German policeman cut off a French inspector's finger with a sword.[28] Most memorably, during an IAMCC visit to the Krupp Corporation—Germany's largest arms manufacturer—the board of directors hosted a dinner for the visiting officers. One British inspector, complaining about obfuscation at the factory, recalled remarking, "I suppose that the nations will be all fighting each other again in 30 years' time! Whereupon Herr Bauer, one of the senior [Krupp] directors laid down his knife and fork, looked at me and asked, 'Not before that?'"[29]

Nonetheless, the IAMCC was able to achieve some results. Destruction of military equipment commenced in early 1920. By January of the following year, the majority of German industry had been surveyed, their military machinery decommissioned, and the remaining industrial plant certified for non-military production.[30] Two thousand six hundred plants were temporarily closed until they could be certified safe for civilian production.[31] All "Category A" equipment, which could not be used for civilian production, was to be destroyed immediately. German industry and the remnants of the army surrendered nearly 3 million rifles, more than 40,000 artillery and mortar pieces, and 70,300 machine guns.[32]

In his 1920 book *The Economic Consequences of the Peace*, John Maynard Keynes, who would become the most influential economist of the twentieth century, argued that the terms imposed on Germany would provoke a new war.[33] After 1945, it became accepted wisdom that the Allies' harsh treatment of Germany had been largely responsible for the rise of Adolf Hitler. On the whole, the claim does not stand up to close scrutiny.[34] Germany paid relatively little in terms of the reparations demanded of it.[35] And the war, not reparations for it, was the primary cause of economic turmoil during the Weimar period. Versailles' territorial revisions were not particularly harsh. The border changes created problems precisely because of the Allies' failure to define Germany's new borders with clarity. Finally, Versailles' military restrictions did little in the long run to hamper the growth of German military power. The greatest weakness of the Treaty of Versailles was that its authors declined to enforce its military and economic clauses.

Perhaps the greatest evidence of this involves disarmament. While the IACC commissions managed to conduct some of its work successfully, they started from a step behind the Reichswehr, which had begun to move quickly to counter the restrictions of Versailles as soon as they became public. It took almost a year and a half after the armistice for the IAMCC to begin inspections, giving the Reichswehr time to prepare countermeasures. The size of the Allied commissions meant that they could not destroy German equipment, but only supervise German teams assigned with the decommissioning. Reichswehr leadership took advantage of their role in disarmament to bury or hide huge caches of weapons across the country. It also exported large quantities of military equipment for resale or storage in Turkey, Spain, Sweden, and particularly the Netherlands.[36] To avoid the restrictions on numbers, Reichswehr officers coordinated with veterans' organizations to maintain paramilitary forces that might be called up in the event of war. These organizations became known as the "Schwarze Reichswehr" (Black Reichswehr).

German industrial firms played the British and French delegations against each other. At its main facility, for example, Krupp claimed that 95 percent of its machinery had been retasked for civilian production. With the acquiescence of British inspectors, Krupp was even able to save 36 heavy artillery lathes—used to bore gun barrels—on the grounds that they could be repurposed for the production of chemical cylinder tubes or for naval armaments that were still permitted under Versailles.[37] As a result of all of this, the disarmament of Germany was only partial, at best.

More generally, Versailles provided the German military with a number of advantages. First, the postwar Wilsonian vision of self-determination improved Germany's strategic position to the east (see Map 1). Instead of two major powers—the Russian Empire and the Austro-Hungarian Empire—Germany now faced nine

Map 1 Germany after Versailles, 1920

smaller states (Finland, Estonia, Latvia, Lithuania, Poland, Czechoslovakia, Austria, Hungary, and the Kingdom of Yugoslavia), many of which would become economically dependent on Germany in the interwar period.[38] Arguably, only one—Poland—was a real strategic opponent.

Although its leaders would not see it this way, the limitations on German military spending played a role in the economic recovery that fueled growth after the war.[39] Between 1919 and 1930, Germany spent the least, in both absolute and per capita terms, of any of the European powers on its military.[40] Lower taxes—which successive governments refused to raise for a variety of reasons—likely improved German economic performance.[41] More generally, the country enjoyed net capital inflows, averaging 2.1 percent of national income between 1919 and 1931.[42] Even with the inflationary crisis that so famously followed the war, German GDP in 1930 would be 32.9 percent higher than a decade earlier, compared with contractions in Great Britain and Italy, and more modest growth in France.[43]

Versailles also had a number of major unintended consequences on the German military during the interwar period. The ban on conscription and the long terms of service required by the treaty guaranteed that the military would remain highly professional and an exclusive preserve of the former Imperial officer corps. This in turn handicapped Weimar's ability to alter the composition of the military to make it more democratic, one of the major goals of the SPD throughout the 1920s. Instead, given the tiny numbers of officers allowed under the treaty, Generals Groener and Seeckt could hand-select Germany's new officer corps. They determined that there be a disproportionate number of General Staff officers in the new army.[44] As a result, the Reichswehr's new officer corps was even more socially cohesive than it had been under the Kaiser: 48 percent of the officer corps in 1926 were members of "military families" (and thus likely the nobility) versus only 24 percent in 1912.[45]

The officer corps was drawn primarily from the General Staff and the Freikorps— as noted, often overlapping categories. The latter had been formed specifically as the forces of counterrevolution, further shaping its political orientation.[46] The Imperial German military did not simply become the Weimar Republic's Reichswehr; instead it was transformed in an overtly political way. Versailles thus guaranteed that the new German Army would be no friend of the Republican government it claimed to serve and become the home of monarchists, revanchists, and right-wing nationalists, many of whom sought to overturn the Treaty of Versailles by force.

Even before demobilization had been completed, it was clear there was little love for the Weimar Republic within the remnants of the army's officer corps. In July 1919, the new German National Assembly had ratified the Treaty of Versailles into German law, as required by the victors, and began overseeing the Reichswehr's disarmament and demobilization. Members of the radical right within the military—many of whom had played crucial roles during the German Revolution of the previous year— decided to halt their own forthcoming discharges. In the early morning hours of March 12, 1920, news arrived at the Chancellery that Colonel Hermann Ehrhardt, a naval officer commanding a Freikorps scheduled for disbandment, was leading a column of 5,000 men with heavy artillery into Berlin. He had been authorized by

Wolfgang Kapp, a radical right member of the Reichstag, and his commanding officer, General Walther von Lüttwitz, to seize control of the city and establish a military dictatorship.[47]

Minister of Defense Noske immediately summoned a council to which Minister of War for Prussia Reinhardt and his rival, General von Seeckt, soon arrived. Noske and Reinhardt agreed that the officers present should immediately organize defenses in the city with the 12,000 soldiers and policemen available.

To their surprise, Seeckt refused. So did the other generals who were present. Declaring that "Reichswehr does not fire on Reichswehr," he asked Noske whether the minister intended to set "the stage for a battle before the Brandenburg Gate" between soldiers who had previously fought "side by side."[48] Furious at this betrayal, Noske announced that he would go alone in person to rally troops to the capital's defense. Seeckt replied that most of the garrison had already declared for the rebels.[49] At this, the normally stalwart Noske—the former butcher who had put down the naval mutinies in Kiel—lost his nerve, shouting, "Everyone has deserted me; nothing remains but suicide!"[50] He and Reinhardt rushed off to meet with President Ebert. Seeckt meanwhile withdrew to his family estate to await the course of events.

The pro-revolution coup plotters had badly miscalculated. The government fled Berlin, declared a general strike, and rallied the public. Within a few days, the coup's ringleaders were captured and either sent into exile or pensioned off. This event, known as the Kapp Putsch for its political ringleader, would cast shadows over the next several years in Germany. Weimar's survival showed it possessed greater durability than anyone on either the left or right had supposed. It also demonstrated the gulf between the Reichswehr and the state.

The Kapp Putsch's impact on the Reichswehr was considerable, most notably by bringing about a change in leadership and structure. Seeckt replaced Reinhardt as head of the army immediately after the Putsch's failure.[51] In that role, he would oversee a reformation of the Reichswehr's structure, formalized in the Defense Act of March 23, 1921. The Reichswehrminister, a civilian cabinet-level official answering to the Chancellor and the Reichstag, oversaw the German military as a whole. Under him was the Chef der Heeresleitung (Chief of the Army Command)—Seeckt's position—the senior ranking army officer who oversaw the day-to-day functions of the German army. Also answering to the Reichswehrminister was the Chef des Marineleitung, who oversaw the tiny German navy. In a sign of the navy's insignificance, from 1921 onward, the term "Reichswehr" was generally used to identify both the German army and German military as a whole.[52]

Within the army, there were initially five, and later six, departments, among which three were of particular importance. These were the Truppenamt (the Troop Office, in charge of operations, training, and organization), the Waffenamt (the Weapons Office, responsible for weapons research, design, and procurement), and the Inspekteure (Inspectorate), responsible for overseeing the different subbranches of the army—education, infantry, cavalry, artillery, motorized troops, and signals units.

Now head of this reorganized army, Seeckt did not want the Reichswehr to serve as the police force intended by the architects of Versailles or by many of Germany's civilian leaders—a view that had become apparent during the Kapp Putsch. To distance the army from domestic politics, Seeckt now demanded the army be "Überparteilichkeit" (above party politics): he forbade officers and men from membership in political parties or organizations. Instead, Seeckt's aim was to rebuild the German Army into a fighting force. To that end, he sought to develop the core of a future German army, one that would someday be capable of projecting power on the world stage. Seeckt immediately determined that the Reichswehr was incapable of defending Germany's national boundaries given the limitations imposed on it by Versailles. Efforts at border security were largely to be left to the police and others.[53] He focused his attention instead on new tactical and operational doctrine, and training an officer cadres that would serve as the core of a military force that could be expanded in the event of war. Seeckt also further organized the Black Reichswehr, which at this time consisted of Freikorps members organized into "labor battalions" who served as a secret (and under Versailles, illegal) reserve of manpower in the event of war.[54]

Seeckt shared the common Reichswehr view that tactically and operationally, the German Army had done most things right in the First World War. Artillery and infantry could overcome tough defenses by use of storm-troop tactics. In Seeckt's first field regulations, issued in 1921, tanks and aircraft were auxiliary arms of limited importance.[55] Their very presence was significant, though, given that both technologies were banned by Versailles—the fact the Allies had barred Germany from possessing them was a further demonstration of their importance, in Seeckt's view. Seeckt's field regulations went on to deal with the Reichswehr not as it was, but instead as the army "of a modern military great power."[56] The manual concluded that the lesson of the First World War was that a "mass army" was not agile enough to win victories; it could only succeed by "sheer weight."[57] The smaller the army, the easier to arm it with the latest equipment.[58] Seeckt hoped thereby to turn necessity into a virtue. He concluded that the pace of technological change improved the prospects for offensive warfare.[59] As a result, his field manual emphasized the traditional German offensive doctrine of *Bewegungskrieg*, or a "war of movement," but now relying—at least in part—on new technologies of war.[60] Only a mobile army with the latest weapons could guarantee the future defense of Germany against its likely adversaries, the larger armies of France and Poland.[61]

However, Versailles meant Germany would not have access to essential elements of modern warfare. To overcome this obstacle meant getting creative. Although Germany could not build or buy tanks, Seeckt established the Inspekteur der Kraftfahrtruppen (Inspectorate of Motorized Troops), which was headed by officers with experience with armored vehicles during the First World War. Using *Panzerattrapen*—automobiles with wood and sacking added to give the rough appearance of a tank—these officers oversaw armored formations in maneuvers and training.[62] Similar efforts were made to simulate aircraft in any way possible during maneuvers.[63]

Seeckt believed that Germany needed a thoroughly modern army. This required the Reichswehr to master new technologies of war. If changing technology was key to future German security, Seeckt knew he had to look for partners outside of Germany, where Allied inspection teams prevented military research and development. That conclusion reinforced Seeckt's desire to seek a partnership with the one other state equally hostile to the European order: the Soviet Union.

CHAPTER 4
The Polish-Bolshevik War

Seeckt's eagerness for a Soviet partnership was not matched—initially—by most of Germany's military and political leadership. Enormous barriers to any sort of partnership stood in the way. Within the relevant German ministries lay deep division over the question of cooperating with the revolutionaries to their east. The German government had considered, and rejected, rapprochement with the Bolsheviks in May 1919.[1] The first major figure outside of the military to consider the possibility of working with the Soviets was the German minister of economic affairs, Robert Schmidt, who saw restored Soviet-German economic ties as a means out of Germany's dire postwar economic circumstances. Germany had been Russia's top trading partner in 1912–1913, while Russia had been the second-largest importer of German goods before the First World War.[2] There was hope that the logical exchange of German industrial products for Russian raw materials might resume, despite the new Bolshevik government in Moscow.

Schmidt would be joined by a small cohort of diplomats in the German Foreign Ministry, a group that would become known as the *Ostpolitik* (Eastern politics) faction. Chief among this group was Baron Ago von Maltzan, who managed the Foreign Ministry's Russia desk. From that position, he sought to normalize relations with Russia and push for economic collaboration.[3] Arrayed against them was much of the ruling SPD and their *Zentrum* allies in the Reichstag. They were dedicated to policies of *Erfüllungspolitik* (fulfillment politics)—that is, fulfilling Allied peace terms in the hopes of reducing reparations and eventually reintegrating with the Western powers.[4]

In Moscow, a similar debate raged over relations with Germany. On one hand was a large faction that saw any accommodation with Germany's new government as a betrayal.[5] Lenin himself had written that the Revolution was "doomed" were there no comparable event in Germany. Shortly after the founding of the Communist International (Comintern), Lenin approved that body to send 42 million gold marks (equivalent to $505,000 USD at that time) to the KPD, the most funding provided to any foreign party.[6] At the same time, he viewed German economic assistance to Bolshevik Russia as essential, though he also hoped that such assistance would be brought about under the aegis of a communist federation. However, given the defeat of communist uprisings in Germany in January and March 1919, the Bolsheviks had to consider the alternative of initiating cooperation with Germany while simultaneously seeking to undermine its government.[7]

In November 1919, a year after the Armistice, the Allies had returned control of Soviet-German POW exchanges to the German government.[8] Shortly thereafter, the Reichszentralstelle für Kriegs- und Zivilgefangene (Reich Central Office for Military and Civilian Prisoners)—staffed largely by diplomats from the German Foreign Ministry—requested that President Ebert's government give it permission to open direct communication with the Soviets regarding POW exchanges. This was granted. At their invitation, Viktor Kopp, a revolutionary serving in the new Soviet Commissariat of Foreign Affairs, arrived in Germany to negotiate the POW repatriation process.[9] Kopp's own instructions were to open "normal diplomatic relations" between Germany and the Soviet Union, as well as to explore the possibilities of military and economic cooperation.[10] In April 1920, Kopp and the German Foreign Ministry agreed to establish two POW repatriation offices—one in Moscow and one in Berlin. On July 7, Kopp and his German opposite number, a Moscow-born ethnic-German diplomat named Gustav Hilger, were extended diplomatic prerogatives. Thus, by the summer of 1920, the German Foreign Ministry had an envoy—Hilger—in Moscow, and the Russians one of their own—Kopp—in Berlin.

As the two states increasingly developed the means to communicate, events in Eastern Europe began to push them toward cooperation. In the fall of 1919, the Bolsheviks had defeated a series of White offensives, the most dangerous of which had come within 250 miles of Moscow.[11] Now holding the initiative, Trotsky's Red Army began reconquering much of the former Tsarist Empire, including Ukraine. But as the Russian Civil War drew toward a close, the Bolsheviks found themselves threatened from the West. The head of state of newly independent Poland Josef Pilsudski led the Polish Army into what is now Ukraine and Belarus in April and May 1920.[12] Pilsudski's invasion made clear the alignment of German and Soviet strategic interests. In the aftermath of Versailles, more than a million ethnic Germans resided in the new state of Poland. The Polish corridor created by Versailles further cut off East Prussia from the main body of Germany. Both brought intractable conflict between Poland and Germany, accentuated by strong prejudices against Poles in Germany. For the Soviets, the new state of Poland was also a problem. Trotsky wrote in 1920 that "Poland can be a bridge between Germany and us, or a barrier."[13] Soviet leadership believed that the revolutionary Bolshevik regime could survive only with access to the industrialized economies of the West—and Poland stood in the way. Lenin called Poland Versailles' "bastard child,"[14] and, like Seeckt, saw the destruction of Poland as in the Soviet interest.

The Polish Army's advance into Ukraine in the spring of 1920 was poorly timed. Not only were most of the White armies defeated, but the Red Army was increasingly effective as a fighting force. By this juncture in the Russian Civil War, Trotsky had found and promoted talented officers. One of them was the aforementioned Mikhail Tukhachevsky, whom Trotsky placed in a command role, subordinated to commander-in-chief of the Red Army, but functionally the senior military commander on the western front.[15]

The Polish Army took Kiev on May 7. But soon after, the Poles began encountering veteran Red Army units; between January and May, Red Army strength on the Polish front had quintupled.[16] On July 4, Tukhachevsky launched a massive counteroffensive. Outnumbered and far from their logistical bases, the Polish army began a headlong retreat. Red Army forces chased them westward, advancing more than 500 miles in just over a month.

In this precarious moment, leading figures in the German military were torn. A number of radical nationalists such as Ludendorff hoped to ally with Poland against the Bolsheviks.[17] But his adherents had mostly been driven from the army in the aftermath of the Kapp Putsch. Others inclined to work with the Poles and their French allies were discredited by ongoing French efforts to break up what remained of Germany. Most blatant was the French-backed "declaration of independence of the Rhineland," made on June 1, 1920, trying to stir secession across all of Germany west of the Rhine.

Centrist German politicians were also interested in a partnership against the Bolsheviks. At the Spa Conference in July 1920, the victorious Allies invited the German government to discuss disarmament and reparations. There Constantin Fehrenbach, the new German chancellor and Zentrum Party politician, proposed to British and French representatives that Germany be allowed to retain a standing army of 200,000 men rather than 100,000.[18] This, he argued, was necessary to resist a potential communist invasion. The Allies refused. It was now clear that Germany would not be included in an anti-Bolshevik crusade, something German government representatives had repeatedly proposed.[19] At that juncture, the *Ostpolitik* faction decisively gained the upper hand.

Seeckt was the leader of the pro-Russia faction within the military. During the First World War, he had advocated ethnic cleansing in the East, arguing for the expulsion of 20 million Russians and "riffraff of Jews, Poles, Masurians, Lithuanians, Letts, Esthonians, etc." from the former Tsarist Empire. This region, he continued, should then be resettled with ethnic Germans: "Once there are 200 millions of healthy and mostly German people," Germany would be permanently secure in the East.[20] While he still favored the destruction of Poland, his views on Russia itself had changed. Now Seeckt himself wrote that Germany's national strategy should be to "fight a war against the West in partnership with the East."[21] He concluded that only Soviet Russia was equally dedicated to the destruction of Poland as a sovereign state.[22] He further considered Poland the linchpin of the Versailles system. Only with an ally to the east could France maintain its encirclement of Germany. In partnership, Germany and Soviet Russia together could destroy Poland, and then Germany could defeat France.[23] As his adjutant Ernst Köstring recalled, Seeckt believed that "war with Russia should never happen again."[24] The lesson of the two-front war in 1914 had been clear.

Seeckt had little ability to aid the Red Army in June 1920. Instead, he quietly began encouraging connections between German businesses and the Soviet government.[25] Although Allied powers had demanded Germany participate in a total economic blockade of the Bolsheviks, German businesses ignored this provision, with the Reichswehr encouraging its circumvention.[26] During the summer of 1920, the Reichswehr assisted the Soviets in acquiring a total of 27 million marks' worth ($325,000 USD) of equipment from Krupp and other German firms, most notably locomotives and train cars intended to strengthen the Red Army's logistical capabilities.[27] Most of these purchases arrived too late to play a decisive role in the conflict, but they spelled the beginning of bigger things.[28]

While German officers and politicians debated the Red Army's prospects against Poland, victorious Soviet forces began to approach Germany's frontiers. General Tukhachevsky, at Lenin's direction, was to "liberate" Danzig and the Polish corridor, and hand them over to Germany.[29] In the process of fighting the Polish Army along the new borders in July 1920, Red Army units increasingly strayed across the borders of East Prussia. Seeckt obeyed orders relayed from Chancellor Fehrenbach and Minister of Defense Otto Gessler for strict neutrality in the Polish-Bolshevik conflict, but his interpretation of German neutrality clearly favored the Bolsheviks.[30] He issued orders that all Reichswehr officers must "avoid any conflict with Russia or even the outward display of a hostile attitude toward Russia." He also instructed that "any cooperation or assistance toward representatives and troops of the Entente Powers must be avoided."[31] Seeckt went on to note that members of the military or general public openly supporting White Russian or Anti-Bolshevik forces should be taken into "protective custody."[32] As the summer of 1920 progressed, the Polish government consistently complained to the Allies that as German forces left in Eastern Europe after the First World War withdrew in 1919 and 1920, they provided material aid to Bolshevik forces, looted local towns, and even attacked Polish garrisons.[33] The Poles also produced evidence that the Reichswehr was passing intelligence on the Polish Army to the Soviets.[34]

While Seeckt was hoping for Soviet success on the battlefield, Lenin was considering his next steps.[35] Germany seemed ripe for revolution but the threat of a broader war loomed. Allied troops had occupied the Rhineland and were monitoring plebiscites on Germany's eastern boundaries.[36] The Soviet state was meanwhile unable to feed its own people, let alone fight a major war against the victors of World War I.

For much of July 1920, Lenin was busy with the Second World Congress of the Comintern (the Communist International) in Moscow. It became clear to those around him that he was struggling with the question of how aggressively to export the Revolution. Lenin's opening speech to the Congress on July 19, 1920, revealed his priorities, centering on Germany and Western Europe.[37] Shortly thereafter, two French Communists asked Lenin how quickly the Red Army would move forward into Central Europe. Lenin replied, "'if Poland gives itself to Communism, the universal revolution would take a decisive step.'" The Frenchmen recalled that then Lenin stopped, paused, and, as if "thinking out loud," said, "'Yes, Soviets in Warsaw, it would mean Germany shortly falling due . . . it would mean bourgeois Europe cracking apart."' A few days later, they said he ruminated, "Should we stop at the frontiers? Declare 'Peace'? It is vain to imagine this!" He then added that if communist uprisings did not occur in Poland and military situation deteriorated, he remained opposed to "risking a dangerous turn of events."[38] By this, he meant triggering a new general war in Europe.

While maintaining a certain rhetorical ambiguity, Lenin aggressively pursued both diplomatic and military objectives. In mid-July, as Red Army troops advanced on Warsaw, the Bolsheviks opened talks with Great Britain and France through representatives stationed in London. The Soviet delegates offered to halt their offensive in exchange for imposing "Versailles-like" conditions against the Poles: the disbandment of most of the Polish Army, limitations on arms, and potential reparations for soldiers.[39] Yet simultaneously, Lenin personally sent a stream of telegrams to the front (particularly to Joseph Stalin, then a commissar on the front lines) with orders for action. On July 12, Lenin told Stalin to "hasten orders for a furious intensification of the offensive."[40]

By early August, the fate of Poland reached a critical moment. The Red Army moved westward at a rate of over 20 miles a day.[41] Tukhachevsky's primary objective was Warsaw, but as the front dissolved in front of them, senior Red Army commanders began to entertain the possibility of overturning the entire European order. Tukhachevsky—now nicknamed the "Red Napoleon" by the foreign press (his rival Stalin preferred "Little Napoleon")—was enormously ambitious. He issued orders exhorting his soldiers, '"To the West! Over the corpse of White Poland lies the road to worldwide conflagration."'[42] Lenin had already begun organizing the government of a new communist Poland. Things looked so dire in the Polish capital that Chief of State Pilsudski resigned and headed off to the front to lead a desperate gamble to halt the Soviet offensive. While Tukhachevsky was preaching world revolution, Soviet envoy Kopp in Berlin told his German counterparts that he would press for the transfer of the Polish territory to Germany in the planned peace settlement.[43]

The climactic battle at the gates of Warsaw began on August 13. As it commenced, Seeckt made his position vis-à-vis the Soviets very clear for the first time in a memo to a handful of senior officers. He wrote that the Soviet victories against Poland had "aroused moods and hopes within the German military" and that these had muddied the picture of how to proceed. He noted that he knew many German officers hoped to "overthrow" Versailles and with the help of Russian armies fighting in Poland, wage a new war against the Entente.[44]

Seeckt's memo also highlighted the general weakness of the Soviet regime, however. He described the dilapidation of its war industries, noting that its largest factories, like the Putilov Works—the country's top producer of artillery—were producing only a tiny fraction of their pre-1917 output.[45] He added details of the chaos of Russia's transportation network and its agricultural difficulties. The point was that the country would be in no condition to back Germany in a general European war, especially one fought in the face of another long-term blockade, as had occurred in the First World War. Seeckt proposed an alternative, entering into a "friendly economic exchange with Russia to help Russia resume its internal development and undermine the very idea of the Soviet system by making sound alternatives available."[46] Turning Russia into an ally through economic cooperation would not only moderate communism, but make it a potential source for raw materials in a future European war.

Seeckt envisioned that a relationship with Russia might provide the sort of leverage necessary to keep the Bolshevik regime from aiding the KPD, which he viewed as the biggest threat to Germany's survival: "We must face Bolshevism as a unified state and reject international Bolshevism," he wrote in the same 1920 memo. "This requires absolute order domestically and the most rigorous struggle against any revolution."[47] The Soviet state continued to sponsor the KPD, a fact known by the German government.[48] Seeckt hoped to use a relationship with Soviet Russia to force the Bolsheviks to abandon their support for the KPD and revolution in Germany generally.[49]

Seeckt's decision to avoid direct involvement in the Polish-Bolshevik War was the logical one, given Germany's military weaknesses. It was also prescient, given the course the war would take: between August 13 and 17, 1920, a sudden shift in military fortunes changed the strategic landscape dramatically. As Soviet forces moved to encircle Warsaw, the speed of their advance and poor communications caused Tukhachevsky to briefly lose control over the advance. Simultaneously, the interference of Stalin, then, as noted earlier, serving as senior political commissar, delayed the movement of the fearsome First Cavalry Army into its intended position.[50] Already overstretched, this left a huge gap in Soviet lines. Pilsudski took full advantage of the weakness in the Red Army's front. The Polish Army began a major counterattack on August 16 and caught Soviet forces completely off guard. Instead of seizing Warsaw, the Red Army now risked encirclement. Two entire Soviet army groups were driven into the newly delineated borders of East Prussia, where between 65,000 and 90,000 soldiers were interned by the German government.[51]

Even as the Red Army retreated from Poland, Enver Pasha, who had tried and failed to reach Moscow in April 1919, finally succeeded in traveling to the Bolshevik capital.[52] He was accompanied and assisted by Ernst Köstring, one of Seeckt's aides, highlighting the importance with which the Reichswehr viewed a possible Soviet connection.[53] Shortly after the Battle of Warsaw, Enver managed to gain an audience with Trotsky, then had a longer conversation the following day with Trotsky's aide E. M. Skliansky.[54] On August 26, 1920, he wrote to Seeckt, notifying him of the success of his mission, connecting the German military with Bolshevik leadership. In his letter, Enver informed Seeckt that Trotsky represented a faction with "real power" that favored an "understanding" with Germany and was willing to acknowledge Germany's 1914 borders.[55] This would require abnegating the Treaty of Versailles, the destruction of Poland, and the establishment of a new order in Europe. Given the defeat of the Red Army, Germany's weaknesses, and the international situation, such a prospect was not likely to happen immediately. Instead, it would require a long-term, mutual commitment to undermining the European status quo.

Two months after the Battle of Warsaw, the Poles and the Soviets agreed to a ceasefire, followed by a peace agreement the following spring.[56] The survival of Poland convinced the German military that Versailles would remain in force.[57] For the Soviets, the defeat of the Red Army in front of Warsaw in August—called the "Miracle on the Vistula" by their opponents—broke the revolutionary spell cast by the Bolshevik leadership. With the survival of their mutual enemy in the new Polish state, Germany and the Soviet Union now shared at least one strategic aim, one that would endure for the next twenty years.

CHAPTER 5

The Corporate Program

B olshevik Russia in the aftermath of its civil war and the war against Poland was a landscape of devastation. Over the course of the war, Lenin promulgated "War Communism," a program of expediency marked by nationalization, confiscation of property, and runaway inflation.[1] Further, the competing sides in the civil war had seized what provisions they could from local peasants. Over several years, this drastically reduced seed for future planting. When bad weather hit in 1920, crop production suffered further. But Lenin assumed that decreased grain collections that fall were a campaign of passive resistance by middle-class and "rich" farmers, and ordered more aggressive measures to feed the increasingly hungry Soviet cities. This greatly compounded the problem.

As food supplies became exhausted in the "grain belt" of the Volga River valley during the winter of 1920–1921, the specter of starvation began to stalk the land. An English writer invited by the Bolsheviks to report on famine conditions described his impressions of starving refugees in Samara—"everything that is human is lost in this terrible, slow public waiting for death."[2] Accompanying the famine were cholera and typhus, preying on the malnourished. Amid these horrors, a massive peasant rebellion broke out in the central Russian province of Tambov, 300 miles south of Moscow, in the fall of 1920. Conditions in the cities were little better. Shortages of fuel and food emptied most of the factories. Strikes broke out among the working class, supposedly the bedrock of the Revolution.

In response to declining grain supplies, the government cut rations for the country's largest navy and army garrisons by 30 percent over the winter.[3] On February 24, 1921, officers of the Cheka, the Bolshevik secret police, fired into a crowd of protesters in Petrograd. Twelve were killed, and nearly a thousand others arrested. On March 7, a group of Soviet sailors, considered one of the core groups of the Revolution, mutinied. From their base on Kronstadt Island, 20 miles west of Petrograd in the Bay of Finland, they demanded new elections, loosening of market controls, an end to grain confiscation, the right of assembly, free speech, and investigations into the Cheka concentration camps. In a panic, the Bolshevik Party leader in Petrograd, Grigory Zinoviev, wrote to Lenin in Moscow that the workers were joining the soldiers and that they were "going to be overrun."[4] An initial attack against the rebels launched by loyal members of the city garrison was repulsed. Lenin and Trotsky ordered a massive concentration of forces in Petrograd to crush the uprising. Once again, they called upon Mikhail Tukhachevsky to deal with the threat.

At 3 A.M. on March 17, under the cover of darkness and fog, Tukhachevsky ordered the first Red Army units forward across the frozen Gulf of Kronstadt. Part of the assaulting wave made it across the ice unseen. Others were caught in the beams of Kronstadt Island's searchlights. Artillery from the island's forts broke up the ice, drowning hundreds. The rebelling sailors yelled to the Bolshevik troops attacking them, "We are your friends. We are for soviet power. We won't shoot you."[5] Their words were unintelligible to many of those attacking: Trotsky and Tukhachevsky had dispatched many non-Russian speaking units to assault Kronstadt, knowing it would decrease the chances of fraternization. Just in case, any hesitation among the Red Army forces was dealt with mercilessly: when a pair of soldiers abandoned the assault to hide in a barge trapped in the ice, their commander found them, shot both of them without hesitation, then ordered the rest of his forces forward. The assault against the sailors soon prevailed, though at heavy cost of 10,000 Red Army casualties. A few of the surviving rebels fled across the ice to Finland. Hundreds of those unfortunate enough to remain were executed immediately by the Cheka.[6] Several thousand more, and their families, were sent to slave labor camps.

In Moscow, defeat by the Poles had led to an increasingly sober assessment of Soviet foreign policy by Lenin and Trotsky. The Kronstadt rebellion and its aftermath provided further impetus toward a normalization of Soviet international and domestic affairs. Lenin inaugurated the so-called New Economic Policy (NEP), which would allow peasants to be compensated for their grain.[7] It also permitted limited free enterprise, created a new gold-backed currency, and established the possibility of large-scale exchanges with foreign corporations. The goal was to stabilize Soviet Russia's dire economic situation. Germany was a logical partner for economic exchange. To acquire arms and economic assistance, Lenin dispatched Soviet delegates to reach agreements with major German firms.[8]

The timing of these missions was opportune. Financial catastrophe loomed in Germany, as well. In January 1921, the government of Chancellor Constantin Fehrenbach (which had only been in office for six months) announced it would be unable to continue making payments on reparations liabilities under the terms of Versailles, though the final sum to be paid had yet to be determined. The German economy struggled in the aftermath of the war, but the causes of Fehrenbach's announcement were primarily political.

Shortly thereafter, on May 5, 1921, the Allied Reparation Commission finally issued its assessment of Germany's reparations liabilities. The sum they considered recoverable was $12.5 billion.[9] This figure was not, in fact, extraordinary. Later American estimates placed the damage inflicted by the German military on Western Europe at more than $40 billion.[10] While the German economy was in poor shape after the war, the amount was well within the means of the German state to repay, especially given that the Allies were expending large sums to feed Germany's population in the occupied zones.[11] Nonetheless, Germany claimed that the amount was impossibly high, a claim the Commission did not recognize.[12] Shortly thereafter, Aristide Briand, the prime minister of France, declared French military mobilization and a plan to occupy the Ruhr if Germany did not comply. In the face of this crisis, German Chancellor Fehrenbach resigned. His successor, Joseph Wirth, resumed payment, but, rather than attempt the politically toxic maneuver of raising taxes on a weakened economy, his government sought a way out by printing money at an accelerated rate.[13]

As the parallel economic crises unfolded, the channels of communication between the Kremlin and the Reichswehr's headquarters in Berlin grew. In his strategic assessment during the Polish-Bolshevik War, Seeckt had argued that open trade, conducted legally, would both moderate Bolshevism and help Germany. Seeckt had an additional concern, however: the decline of the German armaments industry. He was particularly worried about the drastic circumscription of technological expertise and research. In 1921, while Germany was in the final stages of its Versailles-mandated reductions, the country's armament industries experienced severe losses. To offset those losses, and to find an outlet for the development of banned technologies, Seeckt decided to provide funding to German military manufacturers in critical areas of future development.[14] Some of this work, particularly in areas that had civilian utility, could be conducted through German-owned subsidiaries and shell corporations, many of which would be established in Sweden, Switzerland, the Netherlands, and elsewhere. But for weapons systems like combat aircraft, tanks, and chemical weapons, Seeckt required a partner state willing to host and conceal research, development, and testing. An alliance with Soviet Russia would provide a place for those activities, as well as a market for German goods.

Such efforts required state support in the difficult economic circumstances of 1921. To that end, Seeckt ordered the establishment of a secret bureau, Sondergruppe Russland (Special Group Russia), under which military relations with Russia would be managed.[15] To staff Sondergruppe R—as it was called—he drew heavily from his former associates. By December, five officers under the command of General Wilhelm Heye had been appointed to the group. Most were close colleagues of Seeckt or had been members of his staff when he had been assigned to Turkey during World War One.[16] These included Fritz Tschunke, who, as seen earlier, had served with Seeckt in Turkey and rescued Enver Pasha in Lithuania in 1919; Major Herbert Fischer, Seeckt's personal aide since early 1920; and Major Wilhelm Schubert, the former military attaché to Russia. In a senior supervisory role was General Otto Hasse, who would become Chef des Truppenamts (Chief of the Troop Office) in 1922.[17] Seeckt—concerned about the political consequences were the arrangement to be made public—would serve as the architect of the cooperative measures in Russia, but remained behind the scenes, avoiding meeting with Soviet officials. Hasse would play that role instead.[18]

These officers were joined by Oskar von Niedermayer.[19] An explorer and spy, Niedermayer is sometimes called "the German Lawrence of Arabia."[20] He had spent two years traveling across Asia while on paid leave from the military before World War One. After a brief stint on the Western Front, he was dispatched to Afghanistan in December 1915.[21] His mission was to incite the Afghans into an uprising against the British government. After limited success, he went to Persia and Turkey, where he spent most of the remainder of the war.[22] After the war, he completed a PhD in geography, then joined the extreme right-wing Freikorps of Ritter von Epp in Bavaria.[23] Through the Freikorps, he reentered the military, though this second stint would prove brief; he "resigned" from the Reichswehr in 1921 to supervise the activities of Sondergruppe R in Moscow.[24]

The early work of Sondergruppe R centered on expanding economic cooperation in areas relevant to military industry. Seeckt considered airpower to be critical to the future of warfare. He worried about the declining production capacities and loss of expertise by the German aviation industry. As a result, he expended particular effort in trying to shift combat aircraft production to Russia, enthusiastically supporting the creation of a cartel of German aircraft manufacturers called Aerounion, which would target the Soviet market.[25] However, Aerounion eventually decided against manufacturing aircraft in Russia because the costs would make Russian-built aircraft uncompetitive on the world market.[26] In addition, the risks of working with a government hostile to the very idea of private property appeared to them to be too great.[27] Aerounion did agree to a concessionary agreement that established the Soviet Union's first passenger airline, but declined to move production facilities there.[28]

While Aerounion debated partnering with the Soviet state, Seeckt also turned to Hugo Junkers, an engineer who had manufactured aircraft for the German military during the First World War. His firm, Junkers AG, had declined to participate in Aerounion and was looking to enter in the Soviet market.[29] The firm had already developed several foreign production facilities—in Turkey and elsewhere—to avoid Versailles restrictions that handicapped the sale of civilian aircraft. In early 1921, Niedermayer reached out to Junkers, promising him financial support from the Reichswehr if he would expand his operations in Soviet Russia. From the outset, Junkers expressed worries over the costs and risks of the joint venture. To make the contract possible, Hasse agreed to cover any costs arising from the difficulties of working in Soviet Russia.[30] Mollified, Junkers moved forward with negotiations. In December 1921, Director Gotthard Sachsenberg of AeroLloyd, a Junkers subsidiary and Germany's state airline, traveled to Moscow in the company of Junkers AG's corporate director. Sondergruppe R set up a meeting between Junkers and Leon Trotsky that winter.[31] Although no deal was immediately forthcoming, Soviet interest in a partnership with Junkers was clear.

Lenin was eager to take advantage of German firms' interest in investing in the Soviet Union—whatever their motivations. Even before the Junkers' trip to Moscow in late 1921 and the Krupp agreement in January 1922, he had already moved to create a framework for cooperation with foreign industrial firms, German and otherwise. To encourage investment in both military and civilian sectors of the Soviet economy, Lenin personally formulated a new policy—the *kontsessionnoe soglashenie* (concessionary agreement)—which would come to play a major role in Soviet-German economic relations.[32] The concession was at its core a legal arrangement by which foreign firms leased mines, factories, or land and managed them at their own discretion, but provided the Soviet government with a portion of their profits.[33] The contracted firm also agreed to import the most advanced available technology to maximize production, thus helping to modernize the Soviet Union—as well as provide Soviet intelligence with a chance to steal and copy advanced Western technology. Lenin would later write that "the concession system of state capitalism is a tribute to capitalism itself." For him, however, the real advantage was gaining time, "and to gain time to win means everything."[34] Offering raw materials concessions to German firms in order to acquire machine tools, technology, and industrial equipment was win-win.[35]

The Soviet Council of People's Commissars ratified the first concessionary agreement with a German firm on July 21, 1921.[36] Several others followed. The most important was made with German shipping company Otto Wolff Aktiengesellschaft (Aktiengesellschaft—usually abbreviated AG—meaning a publicly traded company) to establish Russgertorg—"the Russian-German Trading Company," which would oversee Soviet imports from and exports to Germany.[37] Within twelve months of its creation, Russgertorg was handling 20 percent of all Soviet trade.[38]

As the framework for economic investment in the Soviet Union grew clearer, another German firm also proved eager to participate in Seeckt's schemes—steel giant Krupp AG, the leader in German military industry. One of the largest companies in the world prior to 1914, Krupp had been Germany's biggest wartime manufacturer, employing more than 168,000 people at its height.[39] As a result, Krupp was particularly hard hit by the terms of Versailles. Its central plant in Essen in the industrial Ruhr Valley lost more than half of its heavy machinery, which was removed by IAMCC inspectors and given to France as reparations. A series of strikes, hyperinflation, and revolutionary violence in the Ruhr had cost Krupp. Further fueling a desire to work with the Reichswehr were the family's politics. The Krupps had a long history of militant nationalism; future head of the company Alfred Krupp would become a major Nazi Party donor and join the Nazi paramilitary organization Schutzstaffel (Protection Squadron, or SS) in 1931.[40]

In January 1922, Gustav Krupp, then the head of the family, signed a secret "gentlemen's agreement" with the Reichswehr to participate in a vast, long-term program for the rearmament of Germany.[41] The document stated that "in the common interest, Krupp must use its own expertise for the development of up-to-17 cm caliber guns, ammunition and vehicles, as well to make available to the Ministry of Defense the capabilities of Krupp on these subjects."[42] Many of the items detailed in the agreement, such as tanks, heavy artillery, naval guns, and other military equipment, were explicitly banned by Versailles—hence the secrecy. In exchange for Krupp's cooperation and the considerable liability it assumed, the Reichswehr guaranteed Krupp precedence to patents and licenses in areas of future military development, specifically those curtailed by Versailles.[43] Krupp also gained priority when it came to Reichswehr military purchases. Simultaneously, and with help from the Reichswehr, the Krupp Corporation proposed to Soviet emissary Viktor Kopp a vast program of fifty-year leases on industrial properties in the Soviet Union for the "production of agricultural machines and appliances, production of machined instruments, household-merchandise and mass-produced articles for rural economies, the repair of locomotives, construction of locomotives and rail-wagons, construction of merchant-ships." Also included in the deal were agreements on the production of "artillery, shells, gun-barrels, gun mounts, munitions wagons" and even submarines.[44]

There can be no doubt about the objective of these agreements, whose particulars reveal German strategic thinking. For instance, the Waffenamt sent Krupp a memorandum with specifications of a new tank they were to build in contravention of Versailles. Among the technical details was a note that the dimensions "should be such that the vehicle can be loaded onto an open railway car in keeping with the lowest gauge of the French and Belgian" railways.[45] The aim, clearly, was to rebuild a German military capable of offensive action. The entire program of economic partnership with the Soviets intended to create a source of strategic depth—in both economic and physical terms—for a new war of revenge. Specifically, the agreement with Krupp was a central part of Seeckt's master plan for a potential war against both France and Poland. Between Junkers and Krupp, Seeckt was collecting the partners he needed to fulfill his vision.

Numerous foreign firms and businesses—ranging from Italian carmaker Fiat to American financier Averell Harriman—sought entry to the Soviet market, despite the political and economic dangers. Thanks to superior organization, historic ties, and the assistance of its government, German firms would acquire the largest share of concessionary agreements: in 1922, nearly 39 percent of concessionary firms were of German origin.[46] Military concessions were even more heavily tilted toward Germany. During the Rapallo Era between 1922 and 1933, the Red Army negotiated 526 concessionary or "technical aid" agreements.[47] Of those, 255, or 48.5 percent, were with German firms.[48] In all, German business invested tens of millions of rubles worth of capital annually in the Soviet economy.[49] Nor was this traffic all one-way. By 1924, the German Foreign Ministry estimated that 40 percent of Russian exports— primarily raw materials and foodstuffs—went to Germany.[50]

By the spring of 1922, channels of communication between Germany and the Soviet Union, and in particular, from the Reichswehr to Moscow, were fully open.[51] Through the POW offices, as noted, there were already official envoys in each capital. Sondergruppe R had been established to supervise the Reichswehr's program of corporate cooperation. Krupp and Junker had signed preliminary contracts to invest in Soviet military industry. Large-scale trade began to resume under the concessionary agreement system. Powerful figures in both Germany and the Soviet Union concluded that they had mutual interests in opposing the postwar status quo in Europe. This would pave the way for a major, formal declaration of mutual interests, one that would shock Europe.

CHAPTER 6

The Road to Rapallo

In early April 1922, representatives from thirty-four countries began to arrive in Genoa for an economic summit. There were two subjects to be discussed. The first involved shifting the world economy back toward a gold standard, abandoned by most of the Great Powers under the financial pressures of the war. The other was to seek the reintegration of Russia into the global economy. Both Weimar German and Bolshevik Russian delegations were invited to attend the conference, the first time either had been invited as an equal member of the international community to a summit of this sort. The conference's host, Italian prime minister Luigi Facta, declared in the conference's opening speech, "In this place the memories of the hatreds and resentments of the war must be forgotten; here there are no longer friends and enemies, victors and vanquished, but only men and nations striving in common for the attainment of a lofty ideal."[1] There was a feeling of hopefulness in the air that three years after the disaster of the war, the moment to return to economic prosperity and political stability had arrived.

On their way to Genoa, the Soviet delegation stopped in Berlin. They had two crucial tasks there. First, Soviet commissar for foreign affairs Georgy Chicherin pressed for an agreement to settle outstanding disputes of a diplomatic and economic nature between the German and Soviet governments. This included war claims leveled by each state against the other. Article 116 of the Treaty of Versailles had included language suggesting Russia's right to German war reparations, in part as a measure to divide the two states. In 1922 it remained an impediment to reestablishing formal diplomatic ties. During the Berlin visit, the two sides worked to draft an agreement settling all outstanding issues between the two governments. They ran out of time, however, to reach a final agreement.[2]

While in Berlin, members of the Soviet delegation also met with Hugo Junkers.[3] Both the Reichswehr and the Soviet government were eager to formalize some form of military-industrial cooperation. Although still concerned about operating manufacturing facilities in the USSR, Junkers was persuaded by verbal guarantees from the Reichswehr that they would give Junkers priority on aircraft purchasing contracts from the German government.[4] On March 15, 1922, during the Soviet delegation's visit, Junkers and Sondergruppe R, represented by Otto Hasse, had signed an agreement to jointly establish production facilities in Russia.[5] To make the concession possible, Hasse agreed to subsidize Junkers with a grant of 140 million paper marks ($333,659 USD); 100 million was to serve as the capital for Junkers' Russian venture, while an additional 40 million was to cover the costs of any complications arising from the unique logistical difficulties of working in Russia, such as shortages of raw materials, transportation difficulties, and the lack of skilled labor.[6] The details with the Russian side remained to be worked out, but with the financial support of the German military, Hugo Junkers was willing to move forward. With progress on both diplomatic reconciliation and private military cooperation, the German and Soviet delegations proceeded separately to Genoa.

On April 10, the negotiations in Italy began. The British and French delegations immediately pressed the Soviets for the payments of Tsarist-era war debts and remuneration for foreign (mostly French) property seized by the Soviet state. Chicherin countered with offers for partial repayment of foreign property losses in exchange for diplomatic recognition and large loans with which to rebuild the Soviet economy. Chicherin knew that the proposal was unlikely to be accepted.[7] Instead, his primary job at the summit was to propose measures that would divide Western leaders and prevent them from presenting a unified front against Soviet Russia.[8]

The German delegation arrived in Genoa shortly after their Bolshevik acquaintances. It included Chancellor Joseph Wirth, Foreign Minister Walther Rathenau, Colonel Hasse (representing the Reichswehr), and Baron Ago von Maltzan, the head of the Foreign Ministry's Russia Desk. Rathenau, the delegation's dominant personality, hoped for rapprochement with the West. He would quickly be disappointed. The French proved entirely intransigent on the issue of German war debt and reparations. During the first five days of the conference, the German delegation achieved none of its objectives.[9]

The question of returning to the text of a Russo-German Treaty soon arose, if in a curious fashion. After midnight on Sunday, April 16, Soviet diplomat Adolf Joffe telephoned the Germans and suggested that both countries' delegations slip out of the conference and head to Rapallo, a small town on the Italian Riviera near Genoa, to complete the treaty negotiations they had begun in Berlin. At that early hour, dressed in their pajamas, the leadership of the Weimar Republic assembled in Rathenau's hotel bedroom to debate whether or not to meet with the Bolsheviks at Rapallo.[10] Maltzan and Wirth were adamantly in favor and convinced the wavering Rathenau. The next morning, after a half-hearted attempt to inform the British delegation (who would have opposed their plan) the Germans departed for Rapallo. By 5 P.M., Rathenau and Chicherin had affixed their signatures to a final draft of a new treaty.

The Treaty of Rapallo contained six articles and there was nothing particularly remarkable in any of them. Yet collectively, the agreement would rock the postwar European order. The two states agreed to "waive their claims for compensation for expenditure incurred on account of the war" or for lost property, and called the immediate resumption of "diplomatic and consular relations" and the reestablishment of commercial ties on the basis of "most favored nation" status.[11] Germany was therefore the first capitalist state outside the former Tsarist Empire to formally normalize relations with the Soviet Union.[12] Rapallo meant escape from international isolation for both states.

Six days after the conclusion of the treaty, the *London Times*, soon followed by nearly every other major newspaper in Europe, began to publish documents purporting to prove Germany and the Soviet Union had agreed to a secret military alliance against Poland at Rapallo. The document was a forgery, likely inspired by fears of revived German military power and specter of communism. Seeckt himself confirmed this. In a letter to General Hasse in May 1922 he wrote that "no political-military agreements exist; however the possibility of their existence is believed. Is it in our interest to destroy this weak Nimbus [halo]?"[13] While Rapallo was not a formal alliance, Seeckt did aspire to exactly that: a partnership with the USSR against Poland. He wrote that "Poland must and will be wiped off the map, with our help, through internal weakness and Russian action. Poland's fall will be that of one of the key columns supporting the Treaty of Versailles."[14] But Germany remained too weak militarily to risk war, even with Poland alone. Rapallo, to Seeckt and many *Ostpolitikers*, instead represented a future opportunity for territorial revision of Eastern Europe, once rearmament had been accomplished. It marked a spirit of mutual understanding that started Soviet-German relations down a path to a grand bargain to divide Eastern Europe. In April 1939, Stalin would receive word of Hitler's desire that "a new Rapallo stage should be achieved in German-Soviet relations."[15] Five months later, the two armies would complete the partition of Poland, just as Seeckt had proposed in 1922.

The immediate result of Rapallo was a joint military-industrial project in the field of aviation. German aviation had been among the world's leaders in 1914. Versailles required that all existing combat aircraft were to be turned over to the Allies to be destroyed immediately. The Reichswehr duly handed over 15,000 aircraft, 28,000 aircraft engines, and 16 Zeppelins.[16] The Allies further banned all aircraft production and flights over Germany for a period of six months, a deadline repeatedly extended until May 5, 1922.[17] When German firms were allowed to build aircraft again, they faced strict limitations enforced by the Inter-Allied Aeronautical Control Commission. Those included limiting new aircraft to speeds of no more than 100 miles per hour (mph), as well as placing limitations on payload, flight ceiling, and flight range.[18] Collectively, these measures prevented Germany from redeveloping its military aviation industry. As a result of the costs imposed by Versailles, the entire German aviation industry after the war consisted of only seven aviation companies, which owned eight airframe and four aircraft engine factories.[19]

Junkers AG was one of those survivors, buttressed by successful foreign subsidiaries. Soviet interest in Junkers AG was based upon the technological superiority of its aircraft. When negotiations began, the firm's latest and most innovative design was the Junkers F-13. A sleek, aluminum passenger plane with an enclosed cockpit, it was the first mass-produced, all-metal commercial monoplane in the world, representing a revolutionary step forward from the biplane design common during the First World War.[20] A demonstration for Russian state officials in Moscow in the spring of 1922 resulted in the F-13 crash landing. In a wooden aircraft the crew would have been killed and the plane destroyed. But the F-13's crew did not even suffer injuries, and the plane was ready to fly again within a day.[21] Trotsky was convinced that cooperation with these world-leading German manufacturers was worth considerable investment.

However, lack of trust and the economic difficulties in both Germany and the Soviet Union led to long and contentious negotiations before Junkers could actually begin manufacturing aircraft in the USSR. The Soviet government proposed a concessionary agreement with Junkers AG for a thirty-year lease on the "Second Russo-Balt Automobile Factory," located in the Moscow suburb of Fili. To guarantee the project's profitability, the Soviet military agreed to buy a certain proportion of the resultant aircraft. During negotiations in May 1922, a Junkers representative wrote Trotsky that for the Russia venture to be worthwhile to his corporation, "the Junkers Corporation would need to bring into the company an approximate value of DM 1 billion"—an extravagant sum, even in the era of growing inflation.[22] The Russians apparently scoffed at the idea of providing any portion of that figure themselves. Instead, Hugo Junkers wrote to Seeckt's Sondergruppe R, noting that for the company to operate in "the truly vast and uncertain conditions," the Reichswehr would have to procure the required capital "in full."[23] This meant at least 600 million paper marks ($120,000 USD), the stated sum necessary for the manufacture of aircraft frames and engines in the USSR. Junkers added in his letter that "Junkers AG must be secure against any risk created by internal and external political conditions."[24] Such a guarantee was clearly beyond the abilities of the Reichswehr in 1922. Junkers then indicated he could not accept the terms as they stood. The whole project seemed to be falling apart before it began.[25]

While letters flew back and forth between Junkers AG and Sondergruppe R, Seeckt applied pressure in another way. The Reichswehr did not have the financial resources to guarantee Junkers anything substantial beyond what had already been promised. However, over a dinner with Hugo Junkers, Truppenamt chief Otto Hasse and Waffenamt chief Ludwig Wurtzbacher "talked about the common interests of both parties." Over the course of the meal, there was some drinking and the "two gentlemen" made a number of toasts, convincing Junkers that they had agreed to guarantee him against possible financial losses.[26] He took these promissory toasts as a contract, assuming, perhaps naturally, that given the clandestine nature of the work, not all of the negotiations would be drawn up on paper. This would later come back to haunt him.

By the end of the summer of 1922, Junkers considered his company financially protected by these verbal guarantees from Reichswehr representatives. He wrote back to Arkady Rosengoltz, the Soviet representative handling the concession negotiations, expressing renewed interest. Rosengoltz replied that Junkers needed to make a swift decision. Negotiations had already been drawn out for eight months and if he could not come to an agreement, "a large part of the [aircraft] orders could go on to other companies."[27] Finally, on October 23, 1922, Junkers' representatives wrote back to Rosengoltz in Moscow: "We have decided to abandon our previous position and to welcome a concession for the Russo and Russo-Balt Fili and Russo-Balt Petersburg [factories]."[28] Investment at the Russo-Balt Petersburg factory was to follow the Moscow Fili plant if the latter was successful. Junkers AG was now committed.

Several members of Sondergruppe R appeared as signatories on the final treaty text, guaranteeing Junkers' investment in the Fili facility, though exactly what this guarantee entailed were unclear. In addition, the agreement noted that the Soviets expected at least 650 million paper marks to be invested by the company before production would begin.[29] Trotsky was intimately involved in the final negotiations; his name appeared on the document as well, showing the value the Soviets placed in assisting the German firm in establishing industrial facilities on their soil.[30] The Soviets expected Junkers AG to begin manufacture in early 1924 with a goal of producing 100 aircraft a month at peak capacity. They followed this concessionary agreement with a purchase agreement intended to provide a guaranteed market to Junkers AG and the Fili plant. On November 26, 1922, they finalized this contract, which required Junkers AG to manufacture 300 aircraft and 450 aircraft engines on Russian soil by the second year of the agreement.[31]

The Second Russo-Balt Automobile Company factory had been built in 1917, though it had failed to produce any automobiles before being nationalized in the aftermath of the October Revolution. Automobile production began there in 1922, but under the extremely difficult circumstances of post–civil war Russia—lacking raw materials, skilled workers, or even a market for vehicles—only five automobiles rolled off the lines.[32] The facility at Fili would reopen on January 23, 1923, when an engineering team from Junkers AG would arrive to begin updating the factory's equipment. Since it lacked the necessary heavy machinery, the factory could not initially produce finished aircraft engines. Instead, throughout 1923 and into 1924, Junkers AG sent to Fili German engineers and managers, who supervised a largely Russian staff. Their main task involved assembling aircraft from parts shipped from Germany.[33]

Connected to the center of Moscow by a direct rail line, the factory consisted of six buildings during the time of German production. A main factory building, laid out in open floor style to accommodate a Ford-inspired assembly line, sat along the road from Moscow. In 1922, Fili stood at the outskirts of the Soviet capital; even so, it was only 6 miles from the Kremlin, with the political, logistical, and economic advantages that conferred. Behind the main factory building stood the assembly hall, where component parts were put together. Next door, an armory stored munitions and the machine guns to be mounted on each aircraft, a clear sign of the facility's main function. Several hundred yards away from the factory grounds stood three large hangars that housed assembled aircraft. A separate rail line ran directly to the hangars for easy transport of the finished product.[34] While some F-13 passenger planes were also to be produced there, the vast majority of Fili's production would be warplanes.

One of the early debates at Fili involved the question of precisely which aircraft to manufacture. In 1920, Hugo Junkers had hired a twenty-three-year-old engineer named Ernst Zindel for his engineering team at Junkers AG's corporate headquarters in Dessau. Junkers paired the young man with one of his longtime associates, Otto Mader.[35] The Zindel-Mader team would be responsible for all of the new plane designs that were to be produced in Russia—four in all. Versailles' restrictions meant that their prototypes were to be assembled only at Fili. Given that all four were explicitly designed for military use, their construction required secrecy that only Fili could provide.[36]

Versailles had of course severely limited German aircraft design. Across the rest of the world, however, cutting-edge designs appeared that had been commissioned but not finished during the war, pushing the limits of aeronautical engineering. These new designs relied more and more on lightweight metals. In the early 1920s, the top-of-the-line single-seater aircraft was the French Nieuport Delage NiD 29. With a top speed over 130 mph, it repeatedly broke world speed records in 1919 and 1920, until it was superseded by the Nieuport-31 sesquiplane.[37]

In the glamorous, rapidly evolving world of racing and fighter aircraft design, Zindel's designs were not trailblazers. Two of his four designs were rejected for mass production after initial prototypes performed poorly.[38] Instead, the Soviets concentrated their orders on his J-20 and J-21 design. The bulk of the initial order—fifty aircraft—were the latter, whose primary use was reconnaissance.[39] Cutting corners to speed up the design process, Zindel based the J-21 on earlier, First World War designs, though it used a new Bayerische Motoren Werke (BMW) engine. The J-21 was designed to be a two-seater observer aircraft, but could also serve as a fighter. Each was armed with two 7.62 mm machine guns, the standard armament for World War One fighter aircraft.[40] The Junkers plant in Dessau clandestinely began building two J-21s prototypes in 1922, with the aim of shipping them to Fili in early 1923 as models for the production line.

The Soviets were not thrilled with this Junkers design. Even with the engine upgrade, the J-21 remained underpowered.[41] The Soviets wanted to use the J-21 to replace their Tsarist, World War One–era reconnaissance aircraft, but it proved to be only a slight improvement on the old designs.[42] Hugo Junkers had stated in the purchase agreement with the Soviet Air Force in 1922 that the J-21 would have a maximum speed of 116 mph; this was already slower than the best Allied fighters at the end of the war.[43] But when actually delivered, Soviet tests indicated that the plane could barely break 100 mph.[44] Soviet engineers also reported the aircraft was 440 pounds heavier than Junkers himself had claimed, and took twice as long to climb to altitude as he had promised.[45] An instructor at a Soviet Air Force training facility was killed flying a J-21 not long after the first delivery. The Soviet Air Force blamed technical issues, further aggravating tensions over the issue.[46] As 1922 came to an end, the Junkers Plant at Fili was failing to live up to the expectations of either the Reichswehr or the government of the renamed (December 1922) Union of Soviet Socialist Republics. Events further isolating Germany on the international stage would intervene to prevent the unraveling of the nascent Soviet-German relationship.

CHAPTER 7
Poison Gas

In December 1922, economic conditions in Germany and political maneuvering by the government led to a default on reparations payments. This convinced French prime minister Raymond Poincaré that the Germans were intentionally violating Versailles to test the political will of the Allies. To that end, in January 1923, the French and Belgian governments ordered the military occupation of Germany's Ruhr Valley. They were stationed there to enforce reparations, particularly in the form of steel, coal, and timber.

Germans in the heavily urbanized and industrialized Ruhr region met this occupation with a vast campaign of passive resistance. They refused to work, hampered the movement of local troops, and protested constantly. The German government organized and financially supported much of this activity. Sometimes resistance took more active forms. When mine workers learned that one of their own was collaborating with the French, reported one Ruhr-based mine manager, they beat him to death.[1] These sorts of acts were accompanied by constant strikes, refusals to work, and an accelerating program of hyperinflation by the German government. The French responded with force: violent confrontations with protesters throughout the Ruhr left more than 130 German civilians dead.[2]

In the ongoing chaos of German parliamentary politics, new chancellor Wilhelm Cuno—the fifth German chancellor since the since the signing of the Treaty of Versailles—had few good options. He decided he had little choice but to rely on this passive resistance to pressure the French into withdrawing, as acquiescence to occupation would be tantamount to political suicide.[3] Germany did not possess military forces capable of expelling the French. Many in Berlin were convinced that the French and Poles would occupy the entire country if they tried to resist with military force.

In the face of this painful reminder of German impotence, Seeckt organized two secret meetings. The first, on February 13, 1923, brought together senior German military officers, mostly from Sondergruppe R, who were ordered to depart immediately for Moscow. The next day, he arranged a second meeting that brought together industrialists and Reichsbank officials. The aim of the two gatherings was to increase weapons stocks and ammunition procurement for the Black Reichswehr. By the end of March, the Reichswehr earmarked an additional 200 million Reichsmarks for weapons purchases. Complicating all of these activities was the continued presence of the IAMCC. Their network of inspectors—and their spies—was at its most extensive in 1923.[4] As a result, most of these weapons would have to be procured abroad.

The German military's February visit to Moscow produced little in the way of concrete results, other than a general sentiment on both sides that armaments cooperation should precede direct military arrangements.[5] A second visit in April had a more satisfactory conclusion. Led by one of Seeckt's lieutenants in the Truppenamt, the Reichswehr toured major industrial facilities across the Soviet Union that Trotsky hoped to modernize with German assistance.[6] The visit concluded with a Reichswehr agreement to deliver a small preliminary sum of 35 million Reichsmarks for Soviet military industry. Soviet factories would in turn produce munitions for the Reichswehr in the event of war.[7] This was not without controversy even among those privy to the secret talks. German Ambassador in Moscow Count Ulrich von Brockdorff-Rantzau was on poor terms with Seeckt personally and generally ambivalent to military cooperation with the Soviets. The ambassador protested that he had not been informed of the negotiations, and that, as a result, the Reichswehr had failed to receive basic guarantees regarding potential weapons shipments. Seeckt's response was to direct all Reichswehr agents in Moscow to send all correspondence to Berlin using Russian couriers rather than relying upon German diplomatic channels, as he no longer trusted the German Foreign Ministry.[8]

Nevertheless, the government in Berlin would express enthusiasm for the idea of armament manufacturing in the Soviet Union. Chancellor Cuno would expand the credit a few months later to 60 million Reichsmarks as part of a broader policy of luring the USSR into economic and political cooperation against Poland, a project that would eventually come to nothing during his tenure.[9] For the entire German government, the Ruhr crisis had highlighted an immediate need to find new partners, and in particular arms suppliers.

The immediate result of the Moscow visits would be a partnership in a new arena: chemical weaponry. Germany had introduced chemical weapons to the battlefield in the First World War in 1915. The mastermind behind it was the chemist Fritz Haber, who, when the war began had, been the head of the renowned Kaiser Wilhelm Institute for Physical Chemistry and Electrochemistry. He took over as head of the Chemistry Section of the German Ministry of War nearly as soon as the war started and personally supervised the deployment of chlorine—the first fatal gas used—during the Second Battle of Ypres.[10] Chlorine marked the beginning a chemical weapons arms race that would end only with Germany's defeat. Haber supervised the nation's chemical weapons program at great personal cost: his first wife, a chemist and pacifist, would kill herself in protest of his work.

As the war drew to a close, Haber convinced the German Ministry of War to transfer funds to his institute to continue work on military technology.[11] This was part of their broader program to conceal German war materiel and industrial capacity wherever possible. In Haber's case, this money was intended to maintain German expertise in chemical warfare after defeat. These funds supported Haber's surreptitious work until 1920.[12]

The need for concealment proved well-founded. The Treaty of Versailles required the German government to disclose and then destroy their poison gas stockpiles, and further barred the future manufacture, purchase, or storage of chemical warfare agents.[13] The Allies also labeled Haber, who had disappeared, a war criminal and called for his arrest. Only when he unexpectedly received the Nobel Prize in Chemistry in 1919 for his work on nitrogen fixation did the Allies reluctantly abandon their efforts. Haber emerged from hiding in Switzerland, and returned to Germany to resume his work.[14]

In January 1920, the first IAMCC inspectors had arrived to begin its work in dismantling Germany's chemical industry, with a particular eye toward its gas warfare program.[15] Due to delays by industry and by the German Ministry of Defense, the IAMCC did not begin its full inquiry into chemical weapons network until 1922, and its start was not auspicious. British commissioner Sir Harold Hartley approached Haber, now back in Germany, to demand he hand over all materials related to the program. Haber responded that he wished they had come sooner, as there had been a fire and all the documents destroyed.[16] Such lies were difficult to challenge. Haber's efforts were effective at concealing the extent to which the German chemical weapons program had survived intact after the war.

In truth, it was extensive. At the end of 1918, Haber's network of scientists and corporate partners had gone underground and continued much of their work. Some found employment at universities, where they continued their weapons research in other forms. Others plied the chemical weapons trade more openly. Besides Haber, the key figure in this transition was Hugo Stolzenberg, a young army officer who had joined Haber's chemical weapons program after suffering severe wounds at the front in 1916. Stolzenberg's background as a research assistant at the Chemical Institute at the University of Breslau recommended him to Haber; his management skills would lead to rapid promotion.[17] Stolzenberg worked first in Haber's laboratory, then managed a gas shell-filling plant near Berlin, and finally transitioned to managing a vital portion of Germany's mustard gas program at Breloh.[18]

After the war, Stolzenberg left the military and started a private chemical business, the Chemische Fabrik Stolzenberg in Hamburg. As Allied forces and inspection teams were concentrated in the Ruhr and Rhineland—where most of Germany's chemical industry was based—Stolzenberg was able to evade Versailles' restrictions better than his competitors. In 1920, Haber directed a large Reichswehr "decontamination" contract to Stolzenberg's firm. Ironically, the task was to decommission the very mustard gas plant he had helped to build and manage during the war at Breloh, near Hamburg.[19] Under the nose of Allied inspectors, Stolzenberg smuggled crucial chemical warfare agents from Breloh to his own firm's depots, rather than destroying them as he had ostensibly been hired to do.[20]

This secret reserve would soon prove its value. In 1921, the Spanish government quietly approached Haber for assistance in procuring chemical weapons. A rebellion had broken out in their North African colony, Spanish Morocco. Haber relayed the information to Stolzenberg and to the Reichswehr. Stolzenberg traveled to Spain and in January 1922 signed a contract for the provision of chemical war materiel and the construction of a production facility in Spain.[21] Most of the weapons shipped to

Spain in 1922 and 1923 were from Germany's wartime reserves, the ones suppos-edly destroyed by Stolzenberg's firm. As this supply reached exhaustion, Stolzenberg oversaw the construction of La Mariñosa, a mustard gas production facility in Melilla, Spanish North Africa.[22] His influence in Spain reached into the highest levels of government. Stolzenberg would personally brief Spain's military dictator, Primo de Rivera, and Spain's king, Alfonso XIII, on the use of chemical weapons against rebels in the so-called Riffian Republic.[23]

This work proved of interest to the German military. Sondergruppe R approached Haber to discuss whether or not it was realistic to establish similar chemical weapons production facilities in Russia.[24] Haber brought up Stolzenberg's work in Spain and agreed to provide an introduction. Haber also took the additional step of reaching out to the Soviets personally. In early 1923, Haber—in his role as head of the Deutsche Chemische Gesellschaft (German Chemical Society)—invited Vladimir Ipatieff, the Russian scientist then functionally heading the Soviet chemical weapons program, to deliver a lecture in Berlin.[25] In a private conversation, the two men discussed the possibility of building up the chemical weapons industry in Russia.

That industry was in parlous condition in 1923. In the immediate aftermath of the Russian Civil War, only one chemical weapons laboratory remained operational and it barely functioned, with technicians paid only in food (and apparently, not much of that).[26] Ipatieff, the head of the program, did little besides provide weekly lectures in an unheated classroom to scientifically illiterate officers from the Artillery Directorate, the department then overseeing the chemical weapons program.[27] The program had a significant network of facilities at its disposal, including storage grounds, a chemical-artillery firing range at Kuzminki near Moscow, a central laboratory in Petrograd, and an officer training school.[28] None of these was in good condition.

History compelled the new Soviet government to remedy these shortcomings. In the First World War, Russian soldiers had suffered more than those of any other army from poison gas—at least 475,000 soldiers became casualties. Lacking a strong chemical industry, Russia had only deployed small quantities of gas themselves. And the failure to provide even rudimentary countermeasures to its soldiers meant that its death rate from gas exposure was far higher than the other Great Powers: 11.8 per-cent of gassed Russian soldiers died, versus only 4.2 percent of British and French soldiers on the Western Front.[29] The Soviets were keenly aware of Russian tech-nical inferiority in the area of chemical weapons and rectifying this became a top goal of the new regime, as well as a critical marker of industrial progress.[30] When Ipatieff returned to Russia from his visit to meet with Haber, he suggested to his superiors that the Red Army invite Stolzenberg for a visit to discuss the possibility of collaboration.

They did, and Stolzenberg accepted, arriving in April 1923.[31] By the end of his six-week trip, Stolzenberg and Trotsky had arrived at the basic terms of a contract to construct a joint chemical weapons plant in the environs of Samara Oblast, some 600 miles southeast of Moscow, along the Volga River. This preliminary agreement laid out plans for a German-managed, Russian-staffed facility, and marked the begin-ning of an intimate relationship between the German and Soviet chemical weapons programs.[32]

With two major corporate projects—aircraft and chemical weapons—underway by the spring of 1923, the need for an organizational structure became a critical one for the Reichswehr. To cloak their activities in Russia in legality, Seeckt authorized the foundation of a private company to provide cover for the Reichswehr's economic activities in Russia. Colonel Kurt von Schleicher supervised the negotiations founding the dummy company.[33]

The forty-one-year-old Schleicher hardly looked like the Machiavellian mastermind some would accuse him of being. Bald, with a thin mustache and a weak chin, Schleicher appeared more avuncular than implacable. His peers considered him garrulous, but in the words of contemporary British journalist Elizabeth Wiskemann, he was "damned charm[ing]."[34] Schleicher had been born the son of an officer, and followed in his father's footsteps. He rose rapidly through the ranks, gaining a coveted Prussian General Staff position in 1913.[35] During the First World War, he worked primarily on managing the German war economy, with a brief stint on the Eastern Front in 1917. Along the way, he cultivated close relationships with General Hindenburg (through his son), General Groener, and General Seeckt, who trusted Schleicher's political sensibilities and gave him a significant role in developing Sondergruppe R.

The new umbrella organization, entitled Gesellschaft zur Förderung gerwerblicher Unternehmungen (Society for Promotion of Commercial Enterprise, or GEFU), was officially incorporated and capitalized on August 9, 1923.[36] Unofficially, the firm was placed under the direct supervision of Waffenamt chief General Wurtzbacher, the same officer who had made guarantees to Hugo Junkers over drinks the previous summer. GEFU's board included a mix of military officers and businessmen Seeckt considered trustworthy, critical given Seeckt's concerns about the IAMCC. Officially, chairing the new supervisory board was Otto Henrich. Henrich was a respected businessman who had been the CEO of industrial giant Siemens, but was fired after his affair with the wife of the Siemens' family heir became public.[37]

GEFU immediately established offices in Berlin and in Moscow. In the latter, they took up residence at 28 Khlebnyi Pereulok, a leafy part of east-central Moscow, just down the street from the British embassy.[38] Its immediate goal was to convince German industrial firms to invest in Soviet weapons industry and to convince the Soviets to agree to conditions—logistical, political, and financial—essential to their success. It was also given responsibility of secret weapons purchases in Russia as part of Seeckt's effort to stockpile arms.[39] On September 27, the new GEFU headquarters would attempt to finalize a concessionary contract between Stolzenberg and the Soviet government to take over the chemical facility near Samara that he had visited in May.[40]

GEFU also took over responsibility for the unfolding Junkers AG arrangement. Some eight months after Junkers AG had taken over Fili, GEFU's board found nothing had been accomplished toward engine production at the site, and that aircraft orders lagged far behind expectations. Informed of this, Sondergruppe R dispatched two representatives to Moscow in October 1923 to investigate for themselves.[41] One was a uniformed Reichswehr officer, Major Helmuth Wilberg, whom Seeckt had assigned to serve—illegally under Versailles—as head of a concealed German air force general staff within the Reichswehr.

Wilberg's traveling partner was Hermann von der Lieth-Thomsen. By 1923, though his exploits were legendary, Lieth-Thomsen was a portly, balding retiree. Prior to the First World War, he had been one of the architects of German air power. He had—wisely—advocated for aircraft over dirigibles as the basis of German air power, as well as coordinated relations between Germany's nascent air force and its army and navy. His administrative role in the war was seen as so essential that Kaiser Wilhelm had awarded him the Pour le Mérite, Germany's highest military honor, in 1917, despite the fact that Lieth-Thomsen had not personally been involved in combat. For the last two years of the war, Lieth-Thomsen had served as chief of staff of the German Air Force. Allied victory had meant retirement, as Germany was no longer allowed to possess an air force.

Lieth-Thomsen and Wilberg arrived in Moscow late in October and set to work trying to identify what was going wrong at the Fili Aviation Plant. The original concession agreement, signed a year earlier, required Junkers AG to manufacture the engines at Fili. Yet during the intervening year, almost no machinery had been imported from Germany to begin that manufacturing process. As a result, Lieth-Thomsen noted to his superiors, Fili was still not capable of production.[42] He also noted after having toured the facility that the absence of trust between Arkady Rosengoltz (now the head of the Soviet Air Force) and Hugo Junkers was "understandable."[43] Given the state of aircraft production in Russia as a whole, the Fili agreement project was of immense importance to the Soviet Air Force. Junkers AG's Fili plant would soon consume about 10 percent of the entire Soviet Air Force's annual budget.[44] Rosengoltz would repeatedly complain to his Reichswehr counterpart General Hasse about the state of affairs. This meant several return trips to Fili for Lieth-Thomsen and Wilberg over the course of the next twelve months to investigate the continuing difficulties at Fili and to try to mediate between Junkers and the Soviet Air Force.

In the meantime, the Reichswehr also began sketching out alternative ways to reviving German air power. Wilberg and Waffenamt representative Kurt Student—the future father of the German paratroopers—had started drawing up a multistage program of aircraft production. They laid out basic design principles for four types of aircraft: a daytime fighter, a nighttime fighter, a reconnaissance plane, and a long-range bomber.[45] In 1923, they discreetly contacted four firms.[46] One, Berlin-based Albatros, was a well-established aviation company, having manufactured thousands of aircraft in the First World War. Germany's top ace, the famous "Red Baron" Manfred von Richthofen, had flown Albatros aircraft for most of the war. But aside from Albatros, Wilberg decided to invest in new firms, each founded by aircraft designers who left struggling aviation companies following the end of the First World War. Each would play a major role in the Second World War. The most established of the three was Arado, which had been reconstituted from a bankrupt First World War firm and placed under the management of designer Walter Rethel. Arado would produce the Arado Ar 234-Blitz, the first jet-powered bomber, late in the Second World War. Also agreeing to participate was young designer Wilhelm "Willy" Messerschmitt. He would later end up managing the Bayerische Flugzeugwerke, which would eventually bear his name and manufacture the Luftwaffe's most-produced fighter aircraft of the war, the Messerschmitt Bf 109.

The fourth firm—Heinkel Flugzeugwerke, named for founder Ernst Heinkel—would become best known for its bomber aircraft designs in the Second World War. Most notable was its He-111, which would terrorize British cities during the Blitz.[47] There was some risk in contracting prototype development with the new firms, but between the Treaty of Versailles and the end of the First World War, the entire German aviation industry had shrunk to just seven aeronautical engineering firms. In such circumstances, the Waffenamt had little choice but to work with new companies.[48]

The expectation was that each firm would produce a handful of prototypes for testing and redesign. According to their plans, all testing would be conducted by 1928, when the Ordnance Office would issue a new set of specifications based on the results of technical testing. A second generation of aircraft would be designed by 1931 or 1932, and then enter mass production. By 1933 or 1934, German air power would not only be restored but start to surge ahead of their Western competitors.[49] All these ambitious plans would require a safe place to test prototypes, however— ideally, they hoped to do so in the Soviet Union.

As for the progress of the chemical weapons program, it was now clear that Samara Oblast would become the heart of operations. A couple of years earlier, two large *arteli* (unions) of construction workers had begun assembling dormitories, several chemical plants, and a number of auxiliary buildings in settlement of Ivashchenkovo, a town 25 miles from Samara.[50] The "Bertoletovoy Soli" Facility, or Bersol (the Russian term for potassium chlorate), was designed to produce a compound with a broad array of industrial applications, including plastic explosives and percussion caps. The site enjoyed the benefits of good rail access, plentiful water, and workers already on site. On September 18, 1923, Stolzenberg submitted a large budget request to GEFU to update the facility and get it operational.[51]

On September 27, representatives from both sides assembled in Moscow. These included an engineer representing Metachim (the Soviet state agency for metal and chemical production); V. I. Ipatieff, representing the Soviet military; Officers Eckhardt and Tschunke, representing GEFU (and the Reichswehr); and Stolzenberg, joined by a staff member from his Hamburg office. They formalized an agreement to produce a variety of industrial chemicals. To oversee production, GEFU and Metachim created a joint legal framework by established a holding company, also entitled "Bersol." Its board was to be composed of two Soviet and two German representatives. The two sides contributed considerable capital to bankroll the project: over 10 million gold rubles (roughly $2 million USD), with the Soviets paying 57 percent and the Germans 43 percent of the total costs.[52] Those funds were intended to make Bersol one of the most modern and productive chemical weapons plants in the world, with the expectation its poison gas would help to arm both German and Soviet militaries in the event of war.

Bersol's primary goal would be the production of the blister agent mustard gas and the asphyxiating agent phosgene.[53] The contract stipulated that mass production would begin no later than May 15, 1924, or about six months after the agreement had been signed.[54] The planned scale of this enterprise was nothing less than breathtaking: Bersol was to produce half a million gas shells a year.[55] The contract also called for the production of seven chemical agents in large quantities, beginning with initial annual production of around 525 tons.[56] These were relatively small figures when compared to peak German production in 1918, but more than 260 times the sum of all poisonous gases the Russian Army had deployed to the front in the First World War.[57] Together, the two sides aimed to mass-produce poison gas for the next war.

CHAPTER 8

Coups and Countermeasures

As Stolzenberg finalized the contract to produce poison gas in Soviet Russia, the next war looked like it might be approaching faster than anyone had predicted. Chancellor Cuno, who had initiated passive resistance in early 1923, spent the next eight months trying to get the French and Belgians to compromise on the issue of reparation payments. His policy of printing money triggered the rapid devaluation of the German currency, starting a hyperinflationary crisis that wiped out the remaining savings of the working and middle classes. The chaos inspired strikes across the country. After a vote of no-confidence in August 1923, Chancellor Cuno resigned.[1]

Cuno was replaced by a coalition government headed by Gustav Stresemann, who would become the dominant figure in German politics for the next six years. Stresemann, who resembled an aging boxer, was the son of a beer bottler in Berlin. He completed a doctorate, worked as a journalist for a while, and then—after marrying into a wealthy Jewish family—he entered the political arena. By 1907, he was a member of the Reichstag, representing the left wing of the National Liberal Party. After the war, he formed his own party, the center-right German People's Party (DVP), drawing together many middle-class voters and pro-business elites.[2] Stresemann had ardently supported Germany's war effort, but after it was over he spoke frequently of "a concept of Germany as part of European concert of powers."[3] Whether or not he believed in the pan-European vision he espoused publicly, his primary aim was to free Germany from the strictures of Versailles through whatever means necessary.[4] One British journalist skeptical of his sincerity argued that Stresemann had "discovered that the way to get away with being a good German was to pretend to be a good European." The new chancellor might seem "good-hearted and a little muzzy with beer," but was actually "as quick and sharp as a buzz-saw."[5] His subordinates described him as a man of "personal courage and an idealism which was admirable even if it was disappointed," who inspired great devotion in his subordinates despite being "thoroughly unbureaucratic" and "lower-middle class."[6] Stresemann's time in power suggests that both portraits are accurate. He played the pro-European role convincingly, while following his deeply rooted convictions about Germany's place in the world.

Stresemann realized passive resistance to Versailles and the Allies was not succeeding. As hyperinflation grew ever worse, Germany would have to abandon it to get the French and Belgians out of the country. Only then could the German economy finally recover enough to deal with reparations payments and the broader economic crisis. The political costs of such a decision were going to be high—nationalists and the far left were both broadly supportive of the efforts against the French and Belgian occupiers. Nonetheless, in late September 1923, Stresemann declared an end to the passive resistance campaign, simultaneously invoking Article 48 of the Weimar Constitution. This provided President Ebert with the power to rule by decree during the crisis. Ebert in turn gave extraordinary powers to Minister of Defense Gessler to maintain order.[7]

As Stresemann had feared, violence soon erupted across the country. Members of the Black Reichswehr launched an anti-government putsch at Küstrin near the Polish border. The army had to be called in to put down the revolt. Three weeks later, in Hamburg, communists—who had failed to seize power in 1919 and 1920—launched yet another attempt at revolution. They occupied police stations and armed themselves. The Comintern in Moscow moved to provide support, while Trotsky immediately began mobilizing Red Army forces to invade Poland and move to the assistance of the KPD in Germany if the opportunity presented itself.[8] But after a day of fighting, during which more than 100 were killed, the Reichswehr was able to crush the Hamburg rising.

After this third abortive attempt at revolution, senior Soviet leaders—particularly Stalin—were convinced that a German revolution was not likely to succeed, at least immediately. He wrote that fall that "I think that communists do not have a majority among the workers. . . . The majority were for the revolutionary struggle at certain moments, but not for the communists."[9] From the fall of 1923 onward, Bolshevik leaders were increasingly skeptical that the KPD could effectively seize power, and instead emphasized maintaining good relations with the sitting government in Berlin.

While the communist insurrection had failed, another danger to the Republic loomed. In response to the growing national political crisis, the state government of Bavaria, the heartland of the radical right, declared a state of emergency. The local Reichswehr commander, the state commissioner (governor), and the chief of police took control of the government. Fearful lest they be preempted by those even further to the right—like the Black Reichswehr soldiers who had seized Küstrin—the ruling trio banned public meetings other than those they themselves had set up.[10] On November 8, during a rally they had organized in the Bürgerbräukeller, one of Munich's gigantic beer halls, the three leaders of Bavaria were rudely interrupted by a sallow thirty-four-year-old with a narrow moustache. He stood on a table, picked up a beer stein, drank it to the dregs, smashed it to the floor, then drew a pistol and fired into the ceiling. With the attention of a crowd of more than 6,000 upon him, he then shouted, "The National Revolution has begun!"[11] At gunpoint, he seized the ruling triumvirate and led them into a back room. There, he tried to force them to agree to participate in a new government he planned to organize.

This young political agitator was Adolf Hitler, the head of a tiny radical party, the Nationalsozialistische Deutsche Arbeiterpartei (National Socialist German Worker's Party, or Nazi Party). The so-called Beer Hall Putsch was Hitler's first real appearance on the national German political scene. Disorganized and unable to rally popular support, the entire coup collapsed after a brief shootout in the center of Munich on November 9. Hitler fled the scene, only to be apprehended a few days later. After a dramatic trial, one that would gain him a great deal of national attention, Hitler was sentenced to five years in prison. He would serve only nine months, during which time he would dictate his political thoughts to a fellow prisoner, the basis for his book, *Mein Kampf*.[12]

Stresemann's gamble, on the other hand, had succeeded, despite the violence. His reasonableness and acquiescence in the face of enormous domestic pressure had made the French and Belgians appear the villains on the global stage. The military had managed to maintain order and resisted seizing power themselves when presented with the opportunity. Stresemann's reputation with the British and French skyrocketed. Here, they believed, was a man with whom they could work. Stresemann left the chancellorship, but remained foreign minister.[13] In that role, he sought to renegotiate German reparations payments, as well as conclude the activities of the IACC commissions as quickly as possible. In September 1923, Stresemann (over Seeckt's fierce resistance) had agreed to allow the IAMCC to conduct a special national disarmament tour, consisting of over 800 inspections.[14] These two actions led, eventually, to the withdrawal of French and Belgian forces from the Ruhr.[15] The Weimar Republic had survived the great crisis.

Even as the workers' revolt in Hamburg ended in gunfire, Seeckt had dispatched negotiators to establish a new organization to function alongside GEFU. The general had decided that it was time to press ahead with the other aspect of his rearmament plan: training officers in new technologies of war. He envisioned a secret office in Moscow that could supervise German officer training programs, safely hidden from Allied inspectors inside the Soviet Union.

His ideal candidate to oversee the military programs in the Soviet Union was Hermann von der Lieth-Thomsen, the retired aviator whom Seeckt had commissioned to investigate conditions at Fili. His time as chief of staff for the Luftstreitskräfte (the Imperial Flying Corps) meant that he knew all of the Reich's top pilots, and was thus in an ideal position to supervise the rebuilding of German air power in Russia, one of Seeckt's major goals.[16] Better yet—for the purposes of deniability—Lieth-Thomsen was retired. With a contract in place, Seeckt and Hasse dispatched him to Moscow in October 1923.[17] His duties were to work alongside the Soviets, gathering information and directing military-to-military exchanges. In most important respects, Lieth-Thomsen's role was that of a covert military attaché. Germany had been banned from having military attaches under Versailles, so his appointment was handled with the greatest secrecy.

Lieth-Thomsen's visit marked the establishment of Zentrale Moskau (Moscow Central). Initially, this organization served as the Truppenamt's home in Moscow—overseeing German training programs in the USSR—while GEFU and its weapons production programs continued to report to the Waffenamt. Oskar von Niedermayer would serve Moscow Central's deputy director, and one of its two central figures through 1931. Originally, Seeckt had intended Niedermayer to be the first director, but his personal behavior (such as his contacts with arms dealers of ill repute) and tendency to overpromise had led to complaints from Lenin and Chicherin. Nevertheless, Niedermayer's presence—his language skills, his connections, and his passion for clandestine activity—was too valuable, and he would remain a central player in Russia for the next eight years.[18]

Niedermayer moved to Moscow in the fall of 1923.[19] Lieth-Thomsen visited Russia several times, then moved to Moscow permanently the following summer. The two men soon assembled a small staff in a building near the GEFU headquarters at Ulitsa Vorovskogo No. 48.[20] In addition to the two of them, Moscow Central's staff also included a personal assistant and a secretary.[21] They would serve as the core of the Truppenamt's program in Russia. At its height in 1931, about 30 percent of the Reichswehr's training budget would be earmarked to the secret facilities in Russia, paid for through Moscow Central.[22]

While the Weimar Republic struggled to survive the crises of late 1923, the Soviet Union faced its own political emergency. Lenin had suffered a series of strokes in 1923, likely the consequences of the gunshot wounds he had received in 1918. His health continued to deteriorate and factionalism over the question of his successor grew. In May 1923, a document had appeared in Lenin's name, circulated among only a handful of senior Communist Party elites, which purportedly laid out Lenin's thoughts on his likely successors.[23]

Lenin (or his wife, who may have drafted the document, given that Lenin was largely incapacitated) identified the weaknesses of his potential heirs. In the "Testament," as it has become to be known, Lenin listed the six most influential Bolsheviks, dismissing four of them in short order. He identified two as the "most able figures in the present central committee."[24] One was obvious. In addition to being in charge of the military, Trotsky was the party's leading speaker, having churned out treatises on Marxist doctrine while serving in half a dozen administrative roles. His organizational and intellectual abilities were clear to everyone in the party.[25] The other was Stalin, the short, pockmarked Georgian who had quit seminary to take up bank robbing on behalf of the Bolsheviks. Stalin now served as the general secretary of the Communist Party. In that role, he promoted officials loyal to himself, soon coming to dominate the Communist Party apparatus.[26]

Both men were targets of criticism in the Testament. Trotsky, it read, was "the most able man in the present Central Committee—but also by his too far-reaching self-confidence and a disposition to be too much attracted by the purely administrative side of affairs." Stalin was "too rude," and indeed, according to the Testament, Lenin was proposing ways of removing him from the post of general secretary.[27] Lenin (or his ghostwriter) went on to enumerate the dangers of an internal conflict between the two leaders, and the damage that might inflict on the Communist Party of the Soviet Union.[28]

On January 21, 1924, Lenin fell into a coma. He never awoke, dying later that day. The Central Committee immediately renamed Petrograd "Leningrad" in his honor, then organized a series of ceremonies on January 26 and 27, 1924, to allow the public to mourn. Hundreds of thousands attended, eager to view Lenin's body despite the freezing cold.[29] Most of the major figures in the party gave eulogies. But Trotsky was in the Caucasus on vacation; when he cabled Moscow about the funeral arrangements, Stalin gave him the wrong date for the ceremony, and he missed it.[30] Trotsky's absence was a major mistake. After delivering a stirring eulogy, Stalin rapidly began working on expanding his own base of support at Trotsky's expense.

Stalin and Trotsky had been sparring since the Russian Civil War. With Lenin dead, the stakes were now much higher. Stalin calculated after Lenin's death that one of Trotsky's greatest vulnerabilities was his management of the military. The Red Army had been largely neglected following the civil war, as economic aims took priority. This inattention soon became a matter of political factionalism. In 1923, a military commission had been established to investigate the state of the Red Army; its conclusions suggested serious mismanagement and disastrous material conditions. Following its conclusion, Stalin convinced the Central Committee to appoint a new committee to investigate Trotsky's handling of the military, led by a Red Army hero from the civil war, Mikhail Frunze.[31]

Frunze's committee delivered a report highly critical of Trotsky to the Central Committee on February 3, 1924.[32] In his address, he condemned the lack of professionalism, logistical shortages, and the complete absence of modern technologies of war. Stalin reacted with rehearsed horror at the details of the report, commenting in the meeting, "If we should be involved in war, we would be broken to pieces and ground to dust."[33] Frunze's report became a pawn in the chess match between Stalin and Trotsky. Stalin aimed to use Frunze, and the damning report, to strip Trotsky of his most powerful position.[34] Immediately following Frunze's report, the Central Committee sacked a number of Trotsky's subordinates within the Red Army.

The criticisms of the parlous state of the Red Army were not entirely unfair, but hardly Trotsky's fault alone. He and his subordinates had been attempting to remedy its major weaknesses, particularly its deficiencies in training and technology, in part through partnership with the Germans.[35] At that juncture—early 1924—Fili was finally productive, with 1,500 workers employed on site.[36] With enormous efforts from Junkers AG, the Soviet Air Force had received the first seventy-three aircraft on time later that year.[37] However, Arkady Rosengoltz, then heading the Soviet Air Force, had expected larger quantities of aircraft, and there remained concerns about the quality of the aircraft produced.[38] Rosengoltz complained to GEFU about the delay in the remaining aircraft, demanding action to get Junkers AG moving. Given the difficult conditions of manufacture, supply, and transportation in the Soviet Union in 1924, Junkers' completion of most of the first order was actually quite an accomplishment, but the news was not positive enough to help Trotsky's cause.

Concern over the continuing failure of Junkers AG to manufacture critical component parts in Russia led to a special Reichswehr meeting on February 24, 1924.[39] Held in the Waffenamt's office in Berlin, the session included representatives of both Junkers and BMW, whom the Reichswehr had invited. Since Junkers AG had been attempting to manufacture BMW engines under license for their J-20s and J-21s, the Reichswehr had decided that the two firms should merge their Russian operations and together construct an engine production facility on the grounds of

Fili to supplement the assembly work already being done. Sondergruppe R clearly considered this second facility to be of paramount importance. Given escalating Russian complaints about the quality and quantity of German production in Russia, it was necessary to demonstrate the Reichswehr's dedication to military-industrial cooperation. To that end, Lieth-Thomsen returned to Moscow in the company of the general director of BMW himself, Franz Joseph Popp.[40] The Reichswehr invited Junkers AG to attend or send representatives, but according to Reichswehr records, Hugo Junkers refused, perhaps because of the failure of the Reichswehr to place any aircraft orders with his firm.

The meeting between BMW and Rosengoltz was a disaster, according to Reichswehr reports. Rosengoltz demanded the previous contract for aircraft be fulfilled before talk of a new facility could begin.[41] When the Reichswehr again spoke to Hugo Junkers, he responded to Russian charges by claiming Russian intransigence and failure to make payments on time. He went on to request 20 million gold marks ($4.79 million USD) to fund the production of BMW motors at Fili.[42] Instead, Seeckt offered to arrange an 8 million mark ($1.9 million USD) credit line.

Junkers might have been satisfied by this offer, yet soon learned that Seeckt intended to purchase aircraft from the Netherlands-based Fokker firm for a secret flight school he planned to establish in Russia. This meant that a large purchase order Junkers had anticipated for Fili would not be forthcoming. He threatened to file for arbitration against the German military.[43] The correspondence between Seeckt and Junkers turned nasty.[44] Seeckt made it clear that the covert and secret nature of the Fili project meant that no such arbitration would be possible.[45] After Junkers first threatened the Reichswehr with legal action in their last letter exchange of 1924, Seeckt replied, "I have no doubt that every other German aircraft company would have taken the step [to work in Russia] under such conditions."[46] This was factually untrue, as Aerounion had already turned the project down. Seeckt continued by accusing Junkers of being motivated by mere greed, rather than "by our national political interest."[47] When Junkers retorted by recalling the oral agreements made over dinner in the spring of 1922, Seeckt and Otto Hasse denied any such conversations had taken place, stating that the only "truly binding contract was that which was drawn up in writing and dated March 15, 1922."[48]

Only a few years into operation, Seeckt's vision of German factories throughout the Soviet Union seemed to be in trouble. A handful of other contracts were active, but Fili remained the showpiece of his plan to transfer military industry to the Soviet Union. Not only was Seeckt's grand plan in danger of failure, his program's problems were having an impact on the ongoing struggle for power in the Soviet government.

CHAPTER 9

The Frunze Era

It remained unclear how the Soviet government would respond to these difficulties in their relationship with the Reichswehr. It would fall to new leaders within the Red Army to make that decision. In response to reports of shortcomings within the Red Army, Stalin arranged to have Mikhail Frunze named deputy commissar for military and naval affairs, serving as Trotsky's direct subordinate. Beginning in April 1924, Frunze set about reorganizing the Red Army.

His central strategic principle was the idea of Unified Military Doctrine, drawing from a mix of Marxist ideology and his perceptions of the German army.[1] Frunze argued the Imperial German Army had been the most combat-effective force in the First World War. It had possessed clear strategic aims, centralized leadership, and had mobilized society, technology, and its armed forces effectively to achieve its strategic ends.[2] He wanted to replicate those elements in the USSR, but with a communist orientation. He sought the mobilization of society in the name of military preparedness, the technological modernization of all branches of the Red Army, and military reorganization to match the structure of Soviet society.

Germany was his chief model for such reforms. As deputy commissar of war, he established a new general staff along German lines and inspectorates to oversee the development of the army, air force, and navy. He also drew up a broad new program of officer and enlisted education. Perhaps his greatest concern was in the technological realm; he soon proposed to the Central Committee that considerable investment be made to modernize the Red Army's communications, chemical weaponry, and aircraft.[3]

Under the terms of Frunze's reforms, the Red Army's air power was reorganized as the Voenno-Vozdushnye Sili RKKA (Air Force of the Red Army, or VVS). Appointed to head this new organization was Peter Ionovich Baranov, a thirty-two-year-old army veteran.[4] Tall and thin, Baranov looked out of place in the cockpit of an aircraft. Indeed, he had little experience with planes—he'd been conscripted into the Russian Imperial Army in 1915, only to be arrested for political agitation. He was released during the February Revolution, serving in increasingly senior roles with the Bolsheviks. Despite a limited education, Baranov was deeply interested in technology and had served as commander of the Red Army's armored forces.

Baranov—and his superiors Frunze and Trotsky—all had personal and political motivations to build the VVS from next to nothing into a substantial force. The Imperial Russian Air Service had limited claims to success in the First World War. Perhaps its most remarkable feat was the first combat "kill" of the war. In August 1914, pilot Peter Nesterov had rammed an enemy aircraft, marking the first air-to-air "victory" during the war. Unfortunately but unsurprisingly, this had also resulted in Nesterov's death. When the war ended, unlike all the other belligerents, the Russian Imperial Air Service had not yet even begun producing reliable synchronized machine guns—which could fire through the propeller of an aircraft—except on a few prototypes.[5] In Germany these devices were universal in fighter aircraft by the end of 1915. This technical disparity made it nearly impossible for a Russian aviator to bring down a German fighter. While the literature on the Imperial Russian Air Force is thin, one statistic indicates the short life spans and inferior equipment. The top Russian ace of the war, Alexander Kazakov, had only twenty kills, the fewest of any combatant nation in Europe other than Turkey.[6]

In the aftermath of the October Revolution, the Soviets inherited 1,116 aircraft and roughly 600 spare engines, but most of these were obsolete or in poor shape.[7] Trotsky had attempted to make the most of these aircraft, dispatching squadrons to each front. He also organized the country's first aviation research lab, the Tsentralnyi Aerogidrodinamicheskii Institut (Central Aerodynamic Institute, or TsGASI).[8] These changes failed to alter realities on the ground, however. By the end of the first year of the civil war, the Red Army had only 255 operational aircraft, a figure that would dwindle to 77 in 1919 and 43 in 1921.[9]

The challenges the VVS faced were immense. Russia lacked the vital components of an air force: an aviation industry, engine production facilities, large numbers of skilled pilots, training facilities, or even airstrips. From the end of the civil war until 1924, there were only two operational flight schools in the entire Soviet Union.[10] Germany's aviation achievements during the First World War had not escaped the notice of the young VVS commander. Cooperation with Germany offered solutions to both the immense training and technical problems plaguing the VVS. With that end in mind, on June 9, 1924—despite his own personal concerns about working with the Soviet military—Ambassador Brockdorff-Rantzau met with Trotsky in Moscow. Their conversation focused on the possibility of dispatching German aviation "consultants" to help train Soviet pilots and technicians. The Reichswehr would agree to dispatch seven experts to the USSR no later than August, marking the first military-to-military cooperation initiated by the Soviet and German militaries.[11]

Frunze's reforms also reorganized the Soviet chemical weapons program, placing all relevant agencies and facilities under a single agency called the Chemical Defense Directorate, shortly thereafter renamed Voenno-Khimicheskogo Upravleniia (the Military Chemical Directorate, or VOKhIMU).[12] The first head of the new agency, appointed in the midst of the struggle for power between Stalin and Trotsky, was an ally of Stalin's, Yakov Fishman. He was the most significant figure in the interwar Soviet chemical weapons program.[13]

Born to a Jewish family in Odessa in 1887, Fishman was a precocious student. Radicalized in his youth, he was in and out of jail and exile from 1906 to 1911. He moved to Italy in 1911, where he received an advanced degree in chemistry.[14] He affiliated himself with the Left Socialist Revolutionaries—allied to the Bolsheviks— and returned to Russia to serve in the Red Army in 1917. After the civil war, Fishman served as an assistant military attaché in Germany, a position in which he became well acquainted with its world-leading chemical industry.[15] Fishman also had good political connections. His patron and mentor was Josef Unschlikht, the deputy head of the Soviet secret police and then the deputy commissar for military and naval affairs. Unschlikht, in turn, was a close associate of Stalin, who used Unschlikht to keep an eye on the Red Army.[16] As a result, Fishman's star rose while Trotsky's influence within the Red Army declined.

Now in charge of VOKhIMU, Fishman became aware of the dismal state of the Soviet chemical weapons program. He would later write to the Red Army's Chief of Armaments Ieronim Uborevich that he had been handicapped from the start by "a lack of chemical engineering specialists and researchers, a chemical laboratory system in a desperate state [and] the lack whatsoever of engineering organizations specializing in chemical weaponry."[17] In essence, Fishman had inherited a single, semi-functioning laboratory in Petrograd staffed by former Tsarist-army chemists, a dilapidated testing ground near Moscow, and a stockpile of aging and unreliable chemical weapons. A Red Army report described the main storage facility as a "chemical trash heap."[18] And there was almost no civilian Soviet chemical industry from which to draw expertise and resources.[19]

Despite these shortcomings, Fishman believed that reforming VOKhIMU was of central importance to the survival of the Soviet Union. "Explosives," he wrote in 1924, "will in future wars have only secondary importance; they serve only to shatter the shell of the gas bomb and atomize the chemicals, and further to eliminate mechanical obstacles to make way for the gases."[20] Preventing the Soviet Union from taking a lead in the field of chemical weaponry, he believed, was skepticism about their use by a number of the Red Army's military specialists.[21] In particular, he was disappointed by the Red Army's emphasis on defensive technologies—gas masks and poison gas treatments—rather than offensive chemical weaponry.[22] Fishman supported his views in favor of the latter with an outpouring of articles, mostly published in the Red Army military journal *Voina i Tekhnika* (*War and Technology*).[23]

Because of this—and because of his admiration for Germany's chemical weapons program—Fishman soon became one of the staunchest advocates of cooperation with the Reichswehr. He traveled to and from Germany extensively during the interwar period and developed relationships with a number of senior German officers. He also corresponded and consulted with Fritz Haber, who, from his vantage as head of the German Chemical Society, provided advice to the Soviet chemical weapons program.[24]

On July 8, 1924, Fishman met with Colonel Fischer of Sondergruppe R in Moscow to establish a more concrete plan of cooperation in the field of gas warfare.[25] Fishman's eagerness was almost overbearing. After demanding a meeting with General Hasse to discuss the beginning of chemical weapons testing together,

Fischer complained to his superiors about the "very aggressive behavior of Mr. Fischmann [sic]."[26] But, irritating though he could be, Fishman also provided the Germans with intelligence estimates regarding the chemical weapons programs of America, England, and France in the hopes of future cooperative work.[27] He proudly informed Moscow Central that he had been in personal contact with Haber, whose advice he had been soliciting.[28] In exchange, the Reichswehr assisted Fishman in hiring suitable German scientists to staff his chemical weapons training school and fill other technical positions.[29] The Reichswehr's own ambitions, defined by Wilberg and one of Seeckt's aides in a July 24 report, were to develop an effective chemical aerobomb as well as aviation sprayers for chemical weapon dispersal by aircraft.[30] Versailles meant that such technologies could not be developed or tested in Germany. Russia was the logical alternative.

Fishman had his own grand ambitions for partnership with the Germans, and for the Bersol plant. He made clear to the Reichswehr his frustrations with the slow progress of the production facilities. Throughout 1924, the Bersol complex had yet to produce chemical agents in any significant quantities, yet had more than 1,400 employees and two plants undergoing updating near Samara.[31] While there was much activity at the site, Hugo Stolzenberg, who managed it, was running into many of the same problems facing Soviet industry elsewhere: a lack of skilled labor, supply and transportation problems, and a shortage of heavy machinery.[32] The latter, all of which had to be imported from Germany, had delayed the plant's operations by nine months.[33] Stolzenberg claimed that more than 75 percent of the material at the primary Bersol plant required replacement or updating.[34] He also had to import skilled labor. An inability to find trained chemists in the Soviet Union led Stolzenberg to hire thirty to forty skilled German workers as managers, paying them a premium for their discretion and the hazards of working with chemical agents.[35] One noted that when he was engaged by Stolzenberg's firm, he was told that he would receive a good salary if he remained silent, but that if he "sent something home in writing," he would either be tried for treason at home or shot in Russia.[36]

More Germans headed eastward to assist the Red Army that August—this time, in uniform. That month, seven German officers departed for the Soviet Union under the terms of the June arrangement between Trotsky and the Reichswehr.[37] Upon arrival in Moscow, they were given Red Army uniforms and ranks, and dispatched to VVS facilities across Russia.[38] The roles of these "consultants" varied widely. The group's overall leader, Martin Fiebig, was an experienced pilot who had risen to command a bomber wing during the First World War. His task was to provide advice on the management of the Soviet flight schools at Smolensk and Vitebsk, as well as help to establish the Soviet's first night-flying courses.[39] Of the six other officers, one was posted to serve as an adviser in VVS training facilities. The five others served in technical roles within design bureaus, workshops, and factories. After a brief stay in 1924, the German consultants left, with the intention to return for a much longer residency the following year.

The Soviets were pleased enough with the results of their visit that the VVS proposed a joint flight school be developed at the Soviet air base near Lipetsk in south-central Russia.[40] The first German pilots visited Lipetsk in October 1924.[41]

They reported that the site had the advantage of being relatively southerly and enjoying particularly good flying weather for the Soviet Union. There were only rudimentary facilities on site, but good rail links with the rest of the country. Nothing was decided in 1924, but the offer remained for Seeckt's consideration.

New avenues of cooperation seemed to be growing even as the corporate ventures failed to live up to expectations; Seeckt had even agreed to allow Soviet officers to attend Reichswehr maneuvers and training courses. A single Red Army officer had duly been dispatched for three months in 1924—but more were anticipated for the following year.[42] Such measures were a small start for direct military cooperation, but signaled the possibility of much more. In particular, the possibility of combining the ongoing endeavors in aviation and chemical weaponry seemed to promise a revolution in warfare.

CHAPTER 10

Command of the Air

From Berlin the memo came:

> Between 4 o'clock and 5 o'clock this morning, French Aerial forces . . . have thrown
> hundreds of tons of explosive, incendiary, and poison bombs on the cities of Köln,
> Bonn, Koblenz, Bingen, Mainz, Worms, Mannheim, and Speyer. Damage to per-
> sons and buildings are incalculable; thousands of citizens, aged people, women,
> and children have been killed or lie dying. The German government has ordered its
> Independent Air Force to act in reprisal.[1]

This passage appears in a 1925 science fiction novel called *The Command of the Air*,
written by Giulio Douhet. Douhet, an Italian general who was also one of the foremost air power strategists of the interwar period, speculated that future warfare
would be determined entirely in the air through the strategic bombing of civilians.[2]
In Douhet's fictional account of a future war between France and Germany, intense
and brutal air warfare provided a decisive conclusion to the conflict in only forty-
eight hours. He wrote, "Air power makes it possible not only to make high-explosive
bombing raids over any sector of the enemy's territory, but also to ravage his whole
country by chemical and bacteriological warfare." He also argued that the shortness
of the conflict rendered its means—the mass gassing of women and children—moral.

Even as gases deployed during the First World War grew more effective, dispersal
methods lagged. In the early phases of chemical usage, German chemical battalions
had simply waited for a wind of the requisite strength and direction, and opened
valves on large gas canisters. As the war progressed, both sides used gas-filled artillery shells, which came with their own technical issues. Toward the end of the war,
seeking a better deployment method, the Allies filled train cars with chemical agents,
accelerated the train toward the front at top speed, and then opened the chemical
valves as the train decelerated, creating a cloud that would drift across the German
lines.[3] All of these methods were imprecise and risked endangering one's own troops.

Veterans of the chemical battalions in the First World War believed that there
was great potential in deploying chemical agents by air. British scientists at their

Porton Down research facility had tested chemical "aero-bombs" in 1918, but they were not used during the war. And, according to internal reports, the Red Army had used chemical weapons in conjunction with aviation at least once during the Russian Civil War.[4] Soviet intelligence also recorded that the Germans had begun developing a phosgene air bomb in 1918, but it was never deployed in combat.[5] Chemical aviation, as Soviet and German theorists termed it, seemed to be the future of warfare. However, it remained to be seen whether chemical weapons could be effectively used in conjunction with mobile, offensive operations, or strategic bombing. This was an area assigned high priority by General Seeckt, who hoped to learn whether chemical aviation would work in conjunction with a future war of movement, or not.[6]

The theoretical basis for chemical aviation came from a number of sources,[7] including in the United States, where findings were (more or less) public.[8] General Amos Fries, the second head of the US Chemical Warfare Service, had written in a book in 1920 in which he argued that chemical weapons "will be used in the future by the Air Service, and probably on a large scale."[9] The following year, Army Air Force General Billy Mitchell—the United States' best-known and most influential proponent of air power between the wars—had testified before Congress that "the combination of chemical weapons and aircraft could effectively 'kill every inhabitant' of New York City."[10] He followed up this pronouncement with a public display. On September 23, 1923, Mitchell organized a trial attack against the derelict USS *Alabama* using white phosphorus bombs.[11]

In a 1925 article, "Chemical Air Force Experiences," which appeared in the Soviet military journal *Voina i Tekhnika*, Fishman wrote glowingly of "the American bombing experiment on the battleship Alabama."[12] He noted that the Americans had dropped a phosphorus bomb combined with a lachrymatory agent, noting that "its effect was such that the 'experts' could not board the ship for up to 45 minutes after the bombing of the ship without gas masks."[13] He concluded his article with the note that "modern chemical weapons provide tremendous power when fully utilized with effective aviation."[14]

Under the terms of Versailles, the Reichswehr was barred from pursuing chemical weapons research or manufacturing, and allowed only limited facilities for gas mask and respiratory equipment production. Its official chemical weapons program in 1925 was very small, comprising three facilities at Spandau, Kummersdorf, and a Gasschutzschule (poison gas defense school) near Berlin.[15] As a result, the Reichswehr relied upon an underground network of corporate and university partners for banned research and development.[16] At the beginning of 1925, the Waffenamt organized this network through the formation of a "Council of Scientific Workers" on chemical defense.[17] This group included senior faculty from five universities, two government bureaus, and a corporate representative from Auergesellschaft, a firm specializing in the procurement and production of poisonous chemicals and radioactive materials.[18] When not assisting the German military in illegal rearmament activities, the unconventional Auer firm was becoming well known as a purveyor of a radioactive toothpaste called Doramad guaranteed to make customers' teeth sparkle. In 1934, the Reich would force Auer's Jewish owner to sell the firm to chemical conglomerate Degussa, the company that later produced their patented Zyklon B pesticide for the gas chambers of the Holocaust. In this new corporate structure, Auer would use slave labor to procure uranium sheets for Germany's atomic bomb program.[19]

In February 1925, as part of this reorganization of the illegal German chemical weapons program, Seeckt, Stresemann, and Interior Minister Schiele agreed to the foundation of an Institut für Gasanalyse at Germany's elite technical university, the Technische Hochschule zu Berlin.[20] Its first head was Haber's protégé and Council of Scientific Workers member Fritz Wirth, who was also a professor of biology. Ostensibly, Wirth's work was to focus on civilian defense. With government funding, he maintained a laboratory where he focused on "degassing [living] tissue"—treating those who had been exposed to poisonous agents.[21] But other academic teams worked on purely offensive technologies. One university research laboratory was assigned to develop a new variant of mustard gas that would be suitable for "spraying purposes," and thus useful in strategic bombing.[22] A third laboratory, managed by the head of the Pharmacology Department at the University of Würzburg, worked on trying to synthesize new poison gas agents.[23] Despite this network, the Reichswehr still could not perform essential tests at home. It was to remedy that deficit that the Reichswehr sought to relocate its chemical weapons research to the Soviet Union.

The effort already underway to do exactly that—the chemical weapons facility at Bersol—was not going well. By 1925, Bersol was only producing superphosphates (a fertilizing agent) and small quantities of the asphyxiating agent phosgene.[24] The Soviets had anticipated production of half a million shells a year, a figure nowhere near reality. Frustrated by the slow progress at the facility, Soviet representatives dispatched Vladimir Ipatieff, former head of their chemical weapons program, back to Bersol. He reported to Moscow that the plant appeared unsafe and totally unfit for mass production of chemical agents.[25] The Reichswehr began their own investigation, and soon concluded that Stolzenberg had been lying to them about matters at the plant.[26]

The other corporate venture—the aviation plant at Fili—was in even worse shape, having temporarily shut down production. In the early spring of 1925, Junkers claimed Fili would either require additional contracts for its financial solvency or be forced to close.[27] Neither the Reichswehr—which had purchased aircraft from the Fokker Company in the Netherlands—nor the Soviet Air Force was willing to make additional purchases from Fili. As a result, in March, Junkers AG's managing director Gotthard Sachsenberg ordered Fili to shut down production and reduce staff at Fili by 98 percent, keeping only a skeleton crew of thirty on site.[28]

The failure of Fili and struggles of Bersol shifted Soviet-German cooperation in a new direction. For the Germans, there was clearly a sense of urgency as the corporate ventures fell apart—the entire vision of partnership with the Soviet Union seemed to be at risk should the existing enterprises collapse without any substitute form of partnership. As noted, the Soviets had offered the Reichswehr use of an airbase near Lipetsk in 1924. In 1925, Seeckt decided to move forward with this venture.

For Seeckt, the development of a flight school in Russia was part of his multi-directional program to rebuild German air power despite Versailles. At the end of the First World War, the Reichswehr had attempted to retain at least the nucleus of a future air force, despite the Versailles ban on aircraft. Seeckt saw to it that the

Reichswehr retained the services, in one capacity or another, of 200 pilots. Of these, 180 were army aviators and 20 were naval aviators.[29] Quite a few of these officers were assigned to cavalry units, alongside general staff officers hidden throughout the ranks of the Reichswehr. As noted, Helmuth Wilberg was assigned to supervise this network of flyers.

Outside of the Reichswehr, other measures were taken with an eye toward the revival of a future German air force. The Reichswehr patronized aerial sports groups as one means of developing a reserve of pilots.[30] These clubs, flying unpowered gliders, taught the very basics of flight to a new generation of young men. In addition, Wilberg took advantage of airlines and mail services, arranging contracts for former pilots with mail and passenger companies in Europe and South America. In 1925, the Reichswehr's exploitation of these civil aviation opportunities remained rudimentary, however.[31]

In any case, such measures proved insufficient for Seeckt's vision. Almost all the pilots embedded in the Reichswehr were First World War veterans, already in their thirties or forties. Younger pilots were therefore needed for a future conflict that might be a decade away. Efforts to expand the glider and civilian aviation programs in Germany in the 1920s proved too difficult. Future Luftwaffe General Wilhelm Speidel—who would learn to fly at Lipetsk in 1928—recalled that the use of civilian airlines quickly became problematic as the number of officers had made it "increasingly difficult to maintain outward camouflage. While pilot and observer training could be conducted in Germany, Speidel noted, "the training of fighter pilots . . . was not possible in Germany."[32]

The other missing element of the Reichswehr's secret aviation programs at home was the development of new aircraft prototypes. The Fili enterprise had not resulted in cutting-edge designs. Given the limitations imposed by Versailles and the continued presence of IAMCC inspection teams in Germany proper, some other place would have to be found to test new aircraft prototypes that might serve as the basis for a renewal of German air power at a later date. In the minds of senior Reichswehr personnel, it was critical to preserve the hard-won engineering expertise of the First World War, as well as to find a place to test the new prototypes Wilberg and Student had commissioned with Arado, Alabros, Messerschmitt, and Heinkel in 1923. To both the challenges of training new pilots and testing new aircraft, the solution was the Soviet-German partnership.

Seeckt's interest in expanding the direct partnership was met with equal enthusiasm from the Red Army, particularly Mikhail Frunze. In January 1925, Frunze had replaced Trotsky as commissar for military and naval affairs.[33] He added other jobs to his portfolio as Stalin hounded Trotsky out of his management of the Red Army. In May, Frunze became a candidate member of the Politburo, and then, some six months later, replaced Trotsky as chairman of the RVS. Throughout the spring and summer of 1925, he demonstrated keen enthusiasm for working with the Germans, not only seeing them as a model for his reforms but actively seeking to continue the Junkers AG arrangement at Fili despite the difficulties that had become apparent.[34]

Frunze saw an opportunity at Lipetsk to develop the Soviet military's own cadres. One of his central tasks for the Soviet military as a whole was to replace Tsarist-era officers of questionable loyalty with a generation of loyal communists from the working class. Developing that expertise meant creating a whole new generation of pilots, mechanics, and engineers. As noted, one Soviet officer had attended Reichswehr training and maneuvers in 1924.[35] Frunze aimed to expand those sorts of officer exchanges massively in scope—providing opportunities for new, communist officers to improve their professional military education. He hoped to develop similar opportunities within the Soviet Union.

In addition, Frunze wanted to gain direct access to German technology. At this early stage in its development, the Soviet military in general—and the VVS in particular—largely depended on reverse-engineering foreign technology. If German prototypes began arriving at Lipetsk, the Soviets could study them—with or without German consent. The Reichswehr, initially eager for the opportunities Lipetsk might provide, would agree to allow the VVS to inspect all technical equipment sent to the airbase. This provision would become more contentious as Lipetsk would grow into the Reichswehr's primary aviation testing ground.

It was in this context that in mid-March 1925 the Reichswehr held a secret conference in Berlin. A small group of German officers met to draw up a clear program for leasing the Lipetsk Air Base before a final contract was negotiated with the Soviets. For Lieth-Thomsen—heading the project—the critical question was whom to hire to supervise the work at Lipetsk. His criteria were quite specific: "a manager of the old type and a good flier" who could maximize the Reichswehr's limited resources.[36] Simultaneously, however, in order to conceal the illegal nature of the enterprise, Lieth-Thomsen wanted a retired officer to run it, thus giving the illusion of being a private enterprise so as not to contravene Versailles.[37] All of the school's activities and communications would be subordinated to Lieth-Thomsen's office in Moscow, but Lieth-Thomsen intended to leave Lipetsk's commandant with considerable autonomy.[38]

Lieth-Thomsen's ideal candidate was Colonel Walter Stahr, an old friend of his and former commander of the Seventh Army's Air Wing, whom he had invited to the discussion sessions in Berlin. Lieth-Thomsen described Stahr as "an extraordinarily practical person . . . who has often made the most of slim resources."[39] Further, Stahr had the advantage of being (like Lieth-Thomsen) retired, having left the Reichswehr as a major in 1922. But Stahr proved hesitant to commit to Lipetsk, in part because of his young wife and two children. The conditions in Russia in 1925 were still very inhospitable for foreign residents, both politically and economically. That year, one German officer had resigned and another requested to take an extended leave of absence, both citing the poor living conditions. Stahr eventually agreed to take over management of the school at Lipetsk for a hefty salary, paid in US dollars.[40]

Stahr's first month on the job was a busy one; he traveled to Russia to meet with Soviet counterparts, and also began searching for suitable personnel in Germany to staff the new base.[41] In conversations with Stahr, Lieth-Thomsen had described his ideal flight instructor as an combat veteran not currently in the Reichswehr who had flown both the Fokker D-XI and XIII fighter aircraft and could teach "dogfighting, squadron flying, shooting, and theoretical training."[42] In addition, Lipetsk required the services of a master mechanic, who knew the latest engine designs and could teach how to build and test them.[43] This officer would have teams of mechanics training under him while at Lipetsk. This role Stahr and Lieth-Thomsen filled more easily, as Lieth-Thomsen knew an "excellent mechanic" who had also spent five years in a Russian POW camp and therefore spoke fluent Russian.[44]

Lieth-Thomsen also made it clear to Stahr that he wanted as few German staff present as possible, given concerns over cost and the terms of Versailles. He told Stahr that the total staff for the first summer session in 1925 should be only about a dozen "retired" officers, equipped with eighteen total aircraft for use by both the staff and the Russians.[45] While circumstances had improved, it remained uncertain what would happen should the British or French intelligence learn about covert German rearmament plans. After all, the late payments of reparations had led to the occupation of part of Germany. Secrecy and deniability were key.

With these details arranged, the Germans presented their program for a flight school at Lipetsk to Baranov. After some negotiation in Moscow, Lieth-Thomsen and Baranov signed a protocol establishing a flight school at Lipetsk on April 15, 1925.[46] The contract provided for the immediate lease of the base at Lipetsk by Sondergruppe R for the purposes of establishing a flying school and factory for the testing and modification of aircraft. As there were almost no buildings on site, the treaty required the establishment of a "hangar, workshop, administrative office, storage facilities" and barracks to be built on site no later than the end of June 1925, only three months away.[47] According to Speidel, Seeckt himself oversaw the development of a seven-point program for the proposed flight school, centered on training pilots and testing aircraft.[48] The task was to develop the nucleus of a new German air force.

CHAPTER 11

The Wooden Titan

A tremor in the political landscape seemed to make Seeckt's ambitious plans more realistic: the election of a military officer as Germany's head of state just as construction at Lipetsk began. On February 28, 1925, President Friedrich Ebert died. He had been ill for much of his presidency, his poor health exacerbated by the constant attacks and court cases brought against him by his political opponents. Ebert delayed medical treatment to testify at a slander trial where he sought charges against a journalist who had accused him of treason. Shortly thereafter, he collapsed. He was diagnosed with appendicitis, but too late to be saved.[1]

His death opened a chasm in Germany's political scene. The two-stage election for his successor splintered the electorate between radical right, radical left, and the two largest centrist parties, the SPD and Zentrum. After a crowded first round of the election in March, the leading candidate, Karl Jarres of the German National People's Party, stepped aside in favor of Field Marshal Paul von Hindenburg. Hindenburg was well known among the German public as a war hero for his victory over the Russian Army at Tannenberg and his role as functional military dictator of Germany from 1916 to 1918. He had enjoyed wild popularity early in the war, which manifested itself in the construction of gigantic wooden Hindenburg statues as a morale-boosting measure. Such displays led one British observer to nickname him "the wooden titan," appropriate given his stolid temperament.[2]

Hindenburg was an ironic choice for president. A monarchist who had little positive to say about the Republic, he supposedly met with Kaiser Wilhelm II (then in exile in the Netherlands) to get his approval before eventually agreeing to run. Hindenburg would eventually beat Wilhelm Marx, the candidate of the pro-Republic center parties, in a close vote on April 26, 1925.[3] His assumption of the presidency further handicapped the ability of the Republic to respond to political challenges, while increasing the role of the military. He proved surprisingly willing to abide by the German constitution, but was less willing to engage in the inter-party disputes upon which the life of the Republic depended.[4] This meant that the role of the chancellor became all-important. That office would be held by no one of international standing for the next five years, by which time the democratic experiment of the

Weimar Republic was approaching its end. The Reichswehr would take full advantage of Hindenburg's support for the military, as well as the political uncertainty, setting the stage for broader national rearmament.

While Hindenburg was settling into the Reichspräsidentenpalais, Reichswehr Captain Martin Fiebig was busy trying to assist the Soviet Air Force. After his visit in 1924, the Reichswehr had ordered Fiebig to return for a longer stint in May 1925—another means of maintaining the relationship with the VVS. Per the Reichswehr's agreement with the Soviet Air Force, he was to stay for one year to help train and advise in any capacity they might request. Baranov assigned him to the Zhukovsky Air Force Engineering Academy, where his tasks were to give occasional guest lectures and provide advice on reformulating the curriculum.[5]

Fiebig was not alone. He oversaw a team that once again included six other Reichswehr officers, scattered across the Soviet Union. One young lieutenant was assigned to serve as an aviation adviser with the VVS's Scientific and Technical Committee. Three officers were appointed to assist construction and manufacturing projects across the USSR.[6] Another was sent to assist the Soviets with aviation engine development, helping the Soviets to reverse-engineer foreign engines and mass-produce them.[7] A sixth joined the VVS's first bomber training facility in Serpukhov, providing design and training advice.

Given that the VVS had so short a history and also suffered from massive material shortages, it was perhaps not surprising that it was in a very poor state when Fiebig's team began arriving in May. Indeed, Fiebig's initial descriptions of Zhukovsky Academy were withering. Training was very brief, with each officer studying at the academy for only five months. During examinations, instead of forcing students to make decisions on the spot—as was standard in German training—the Soviet instructors assigned tactical problems as homework. Trainees wrote orders or reports that tended to "degenerate into long written pieces, lacking precision of expression or brevity entirely."[8] When assigned basic technical work, he noted, the "lack of education" of the cadets was extremely evident.[9]

Taking to his task with gusto, Fiebig provided a long list of suggestions to Baranov and the VVS. At their core were concerns about the academy's organization and management. The evaluation system was pass-fail, and nearly every attendee graduated, which hardly motivated conscientiousness. Further, VVS instructors enforced almost no discipline at the academy. As Fiebig noted, "missing lessons is hardly even reprimanded. And it is actually rare to experience a lecture that begins punctually or ceases at the correct time."[10] Fiebig saw graduates as ill-prepared for serious responsibilities. Most were posted to senior positions in Soviet Air Force general staff after only three months, a prospect Fiebig found bizarre. He summed up his initial observations by saying that "One cannot help but think that the Academy is a 'quick fix' in the truest sense of the word."[11]

Perhaps unsurprisingly given the pejorative tone of his reports back to Germany, Fiebig's suggestions were ignored by Baranov, at least at first. Baranov proved more willing to listen to German advice on VVS technical facilities, however. While posted at the Zhukovsky Academy, Fiebig, in the company of VVS instructors, visited a laboratory located in Eastern Moscow called Nauchnyi Avtomotornyi Institut (the

Scientific Institute for Engine Research, or NAMI). His group was given a tour of the engine and motor workshops, taking them through three laboratories. In the first, there were three BMW and Junkers aviation engines, as well as a twelve-cylinder Kondor-Engine, all from Germany.[12] In the second, there was a Junkers L-5 engine mounted on a testing block. In the third, a 400-horsepower American Packard Motor Company Liberty Engine was mounted on a testing stand and surrounded by mechanical equipment.[13] Fiebig concluded that the work being done at NAMI mainly consisted of reverse-engineering foreign component parts. He was right. Particularly in its first decade, the Soviet Union borrowed heavily from foreign technical developments in an effort to catch up technologically. They would do so with remarkable success, mass-producing knockoffs of the Liberty Engine during the course of 1925. Several of the German officers on Fiebig's team would assist the Soviets in this work.

While these Germans worked in the USSR, there were also Soviet officers studying in Germany. Following on the previous years' trip, the training program for Soviet officers in Germany expanded markedly. As part of the broader expansion of military-to-military cooperation, Seeckt agreed to allow some Soviet commanders to participate in tactical exercises in the field and maneuvers "on a mutual basis," as well as to attend German military academy courses, including the famed general staff course.[14] In May and June 1925, four instructors from the Soviet Voennouchebnykh Zavedenii (Military Instruction Facilities, or VUZy), which supervised all Soviet military education, had arrived to study the "methodology and program of German military schools."[15] They were joined by two engineers who were tasked with studying how they were organized and run.

While officer exchanges proved promising, Lipetsk neared completion. Working— oddly enough, given secrecy concerns—with the local city government in Lipetsk, Lieth-Thomsen at Moscow Central arranged for the construction of warehouses, hangars, workshops, repair facilities, barracks, and assorted outbuildings between April and June 1925.[16] Initial efforts to have the Russian side construct barracks and hangars from scratch were canceled when it became apparent that because of materiel shortages in Russia it would be far cheaper simply to import prefabricated buildings from Germany.[17] As a result, most of the equipment for construction was imported. The Soviets provided land and labor. The Reichswehr shipped equipment via sea to Leningrad or used aircraft, which Speidel recalled flew "at the greatest heights and without landing in the border states."[18] Despite these difficulties, the base reached readiness in only a few months. By June 1925, as planned, the facilities at Lipetsk were ready for the arrival of personnel.

German pilots began arriving over the summer of 1925, taking to the skies over Russia, their first such flights since the war. Sondergruppe R oversaw the import of a contingent of Fokker D-XIII biplanes and one L-69 racing monoplane from the Albatros Flugzeugwerke (Aircraft Company).[19] With aircraft on site, some of Germany's aces could now reacquaint themselves with flying. Training centered on fourteen-day fighter pilot courses for new pilots and 180 minutes of flight time "retraining" for veterans. Some of the veterans enrolled in fighter pilot instructor training, mastering additional tactical and technical information to teach the next generation. Lieth-Thomsen hoped to supplement the small number of Germans by attracting as many Russian mechanics and staff people as possible, in order to reduce the cost of managing the school—Russians would be cheaper than Germans.[20] A short, but successful, flying season over the summer of 1925 suggested the possibility of Lipetsk's expansion for the following year.

While Lieth-Thomsen and Stahr were quite happy with the results of their first summer of operations, Martin Fiebig—who felt his advice was too often ignored while stationed at the VVS Academy—was convinced he had not accomplished much of anything. He wrote to Lieth-Thomsen at the end of his tour that "Everything here is in vain."[21] However, the Soviets thought otherwise, noting the Fiebig team's valuable assistance in developing technology, training, and management in the country's nascent military-aviation industry.[22] Baranov himself praised their work, taking pains to keep the German consultants on staff after their planned departure and encouraging the Reichswehr to appoint a replacement for Fiebig, who requested reassignment after returning to Germany.[23] Fiebig himself would return to the USSR only with the German invasion, commanding the German Eighth Air Corps outside of Stalingrad in 1942 and barely escaping encirclement. He would be executed for war crimes in Yugoslavia after the war for his role in the terror bombing of Belgrade.[24]

Soviet enthusiasm for working with their German partners proved so great that even as Lipetsk took off and Fiebig's team advised the Soviet Air Force, Frunze and the RVS sought to revive the failed Fili plant. After production shut down in March, the RVS attempted to renegotiate the terms of the contract with Junkers. The whole Soviet government soon became involved. In a broader indication of the need for German technical assistance, Georgii Pyatakov, the deputy chairman of the Supreme Council of the National Economy—a government body separate from the Soviet military—expressed his willingness to do whatever it took to keep the facility afloat in the name of expanding Soviet industry, even offering to fund another purchase order if necessary.[25] Eventually, the RVS offered a contract to Junkers AG for the purchase of 120 aircraft and 150 motors, and a twelve-year extension of its contract with 20 percent profits per year "calculated into" the overall cost per aircraft.[26] Bribery to two Soviet state officials may have helped facilitate this proposal, which, however, soon collapsed amid mutual recriminations.[27]

The Politburo would later censure the senior leadership of the RVS for having offered such generous terms, noting that the Soviet Air Force had been "unconditionally accepting" the Junkers planes, though they were not what had been ordered. The Politburo blamed the RVS's trying to keep the Junkers concession "at all costs."[28] Junkers AG turned down even this generous Soviet offer, instead making a counterproposal that even the RVS considered unreasonable. At that juncture, the People's Commissariat for Military and Naval Affairs—which oversaw the Soviet military—recommended that the contract be terminated. For the next eighteen months, the Fili facility would remain half-shuttered and staffed by a skeleton crew, as both sides argued over its future.

Even though Fili remained a sore point in the relationship, officer exchanges and the growth of Lipetsk seemed to promise new opportunities. The RVS, apparently satisfied with the experiences of the six Soviet officers then studying in Germany, decided to dispatch a much larger contingent at the end of the summer. In August, the first of thirty-five Red Army officers began to arrive for extended stays. The group included engineers, chemists, professors at the Red Army's main training facilities, and a number of division commanders who were to study German tactics and training. They were also joined by Yakov Fishman, the director of the Soviet chemical weapons program, who spent seven weeks in Germany studying new developments in chemical warfare and consulting with his German counterparts.[29]

On August 30, a military celebrity joined the Soviet delegation: Mikhail Tukhachevsky himself, disguised as a Bulgarian military officer. Then serving on the Red Army's General Staff, Tukhachevsky returned to Germany for the first time since his escape from a POW camp there during the First World War. He participated in maneuvers, discussed tactics with German officers during six days of meetings, and met with General Seeckt.[30] With over forty senior Soviet officers and technicians in Germany, and a German air base now operating on Soviet soil, the alliance between the Red Army and the Reichswehr Seeckt had envisioned was finally taking shape.

CHAPTER 12

New Faces

The first nine months of 1925 were a period of remarkable growth in the Soviet-German partnership. Within the space of a year, though, Frunze would be dead, and Seeckt forced into retirement. The durability of the partnership would be put to the test.

Stalin had promoted Frunze to drive Trotsky from the military, but he quickly became almost as much of a problem as his predecessor. Popular, independent-minded, and increasingly close to Stalin's rival Grigory Zinoviev, Frunze posed a genuine threat to Stalin's position in the midst of an intense competition for Soviet leadership in the fall of 1925. In October, Frunze was ordered by the Central Committee, at Stalin's direction, to undergo surgery as a treatment for ulcers—against his will.[1] He died on the operating table of a chloroform overdose in what has often been regarded as an assassination.[2] Frunze's untimely death shifted control over the Soviet-German network to new Commissar for Military and Naval Affairs Kliment Voroshilov. He not only inherited Frunze's mantle in 1925; he also adopted his children and raised them as his own.

In October 1925, Voroshilov was a "jaunty cavalryman better known for his personal bravery than for scintillating intellect," in the words of historian Sheila Fitzpatrick.[3] In the interwar period, he was one of the most popular men in the Soviet Union, his portraits common.[4] Voroshilov was the son of an ethnic Russian railway worker, and his was the sort of upwardly mobile proletarian family that produced many Bolshevik leaders. He joined the Bolshevik party in his twenties, then spent much of the next twelve years in and out of exile in Siberia. He became an early friend of Stalin's, having been roommates with him at a party conference in 1906.[5] With the outbreak of the Revolution, Voroshilov took over control of the Petrograd Revolutionary Military Council, and then helped to organize the Cheka. His experience in the Civil War, much of it spent with Stalin on the Tsaritsyn Front, highlighted his courage, but not his command ability. Voroshilov had proved reasonably successful as a junior commander. However, he was soon promoted beyond his competence.[6] His close association with Stalin and his political background nonetheless guaranteed him a continued voice in military matters. This was the man who would head the Red Army through one its most intensive phases of development. One of his first tasks would be to reassess the Soviet-German military partnership with a critical eye.

He was not alone. At the end of 1925, the Politburo—increasingly bending to Stalin's will—decided to expand cooperation with Germany. In a meeting in January 1926, the Soviet ambassador to Berlin Nikolai Krestinsky told his German counterparts that it would be useful to have representatives of the two militaries sit down and discuss cooperation in military technology.[7] The Politburo designated Deputy Chairman of the Revolutionary Military Council Iosef Unschlikht to serve as its military representative. They dispatched him to Berlin, urging him to reach an agreement to replace the faltering corporate arrangements at Fili and Bersol. Unschlikht arrived in Germany in late March, under conditions of great secrecy.

The German government placed tremendous importance on this trip, as well. At the first event held on March 30, they hosted a breakfast for Unschlikht, whose guest list included the brief-serving Chancellor Hans Luther, Foreign Minister Stresemann, Minister of Defense Gessler, General von Seeckt, and a number of other senior Reichswehr officers.[8] At this first meeting, Unschlikht and Ambassador Krestinsky made expansive proposals on future cooperation, envisioning a broadening of industrial partnerships and direct German state investment in Soviet war industries; the establishment of new joint military bases; training of Soviet officers in Germany; joint participation in maneuvers; and intelligence sharing.[9] Unschlikht noted that Russia did not want to start a war, but wanted to "prepare for war, for it knew that other states planned military action against Russia, as they did against Germany, too." He added that the Soviets were aware that military "training for Germany is only possible in Russia."[10] In their totality, Unschlikht's statements not only called for a broad program of Soviet-German cooperation, it articulated more fully than ever before the reason behind it: reshaping the European status quo.[11]

While the Reichswehr shared many of Unschlikht's aims, Germany's civilian leadership reacted coolly. Chancellor Luther replied to Unschlikht's comments by citing Germany's "great interest" in working with Russia "for the cause of peace."[12] He studiously ignored mention of any of the military exchanges proposed by the Soviet side. Stresemann, the major figure in the cabinet, also avoided any endorsement of the Soviet proposals. On December 1, 1925, in London, he had affixed his signature to the Locarno Treaties, which normalized relations between Germany and France, and guaranteed Germany's existing western borders.[13] Locarno was a step toward securing German entry to the League of Nations and Stresemann did not want a pact with the Soviets to threaten that or his careful diplomatic efforts toward France and Great Britain. He sat sphinx-like throughout the exchanges.

While Seeckt had said nothing during the formal proceedings, he would play host to Unschlikht afterward. Unschlikht reported that he had met privately with Seeckt, with whom "reigned 'complete unanimity.'"[14] Seeckt introduced him to the individual department heads within the Reichswehr, briefing him on the technical particulars of potential cooperation. These discussions bore greater fruit than the earlier meetings, despite German reluctance to fully embrace the "big program" proposed by the Soviet side. By the end of Unschlikht's visit in April, the groundwork had been laid for a new phase in the relationship. Seeckt agreed to an exchange of technical information, including submarine blueprints, as well as the continued production of some military equipment in the Soviet Union.[15] The Reichswehr also committed itself to expand the flight school at Lipetsk. Both sides agreed to mutual participation in the formation of a joint armored-warfare training and testing ground. Further, they cemented in place the exchange of officers in each other's maneuvers and field exercises. While the Soviets were still not fully satisfied, this represented a major expansion of the partnership. Critically, Chancellor Luther's government was not fully informed of Seeckt's decisions.[16]

Although Weimar's civilian leaders had declined the "big program" of military cooperation pitched by Unschlikht, they did agree to improve their diplomatic relationship with the Soviet Union. In April 1926, Stresemann and Soviet ambassador Krestinsky signed the Treaty of Berlin, a renewal and expansion of the Treaty of Rapallo of four years earlier. It reiterated Germany's complete neutrality in the event of a clash between the Soviet Union and other powers—a clause the Soviets intended to target Great Britain, then considered by the Kremlin to be the greatest threat to Soviet security.[17] Commissar for Foreign Affairs Chicherin sought to maintain a lifeline to Germany, the one state in the West with which the Soviet Union had decent relations. At all costs, he concluded, Russia needed to avoid becoming completely isolated, which might happen should Germany reach a modus vivendi with Great Britain and France.[18] Stresemann, for his part, prioritized good relations with the West, but he believed good relations with the Soviets might give him a card to play against France and Great Britain.[19]

Following the Soviet visit and in response to the lack of success of the corporate ventures, Seeckt reorganized the German ventures in Russia. On April 1, the Truppenamt took control of the various agencies in Russia, some of which had previously been managed by the Waffenamt.[20] Lieth-Thomsen in Moscow Central was made responsible for all German ventures in Russia, which were organized into four units: WIKO R, or GEFU, which managed the German corporate ventures; WIKO L, the airbase at Lipetsk; WIKO K, a proposed tank school that would begin construction later that year; and WIKO V, which would be responsible for "all administrative, financial and economic issues," such as handling the frequent negotiations with German firms seeking to enter the Russian market and assisting the Red Army with weapons procurements. In addition, WIKO V served as the mailing and telegram address for the various secret ventures.[21] WIKO R and V were based in Moscow, and so, in the name of secrecy, were instructed to brief Lieth-Thomsen orally on all important matters. To maintain security and control, all communications with Berlin were to go through Lieth-Thomsen and Moscow Central.[22]

With the new structure in place, technological cooperation could expand, particularly in aviation. Already at Lipetsk were German pilots, and aircraft. And work had already begun to coopt major German aircraft manufacturers, as noted, a process that would expand rapidly as Lipetsk grew. After the first season of activity at Lipetsk, four former Luftstreitskräfte pilots met in Berlin to discuss the results of Lipetsk. They were led by Major Wilberg. Also present was Captain Hugo Sperrle, a First World War pilot, who would soon head to Lipetsk to serve as a flight instructor.

He would become better known as the command of the Condor Legion in the Spanish Civil War and eventually, during the Second World War, commander of the Luftwaffe in Western Europe. The pilots' initial assessment of Lipetsk was that it made financial sense to expand the program, particularly its research component.[23] In particular, they noted that testing machine guns or poison gas could not be conducted as conveniently anywhere else.[24]

These basic experiments meant an expansion of the mission of Lipetsk, which had been purely for flight training. Testing military equipment was another matter and required the presence of active-duty military officers. To that end, one of the other pilots present—who had a strong engineering background—agreed to travel to Lipetsk to oversee machine-gun testing. [25]

Prototype devices, including bombs, machine guns, and optical sights, could only be tested in Lipetsk, not produced there. The supervising officers would provide detailed notes on the performance of each item, which would be sent back to Germany for German firms to pore over. From Germany's perspective, this had real advantages. As Wilhelm Speidel later commented, this policy was shown wise in light of the "relentlessly progressive development of tactics and technology" that continued throughout the interwar period.[26] Building a few prototypes and testing them extensively was a cheap way to maintain pace technologically with work being done in rival states, particularly Great Britain and France. A likely adversary, France remained among the world leaders in aviation technology, holding most of the world speed records set between 1919 and 1926.[27]

Wilberg hoped to begin research and development work immediately in the summer of 1926. To that end, he proposed to Seeckt a vast technical testing program, including new bomb prototypes, gun scopes, a new fireproof gas tank, high-altitude oxygen tanks, military camouflage, prototype ski runners for landing aircraft on snow, several types of aviation machine guns, and new ammunition types, all of which were soon to enter development in Germany.[28] German industrial firms had designed some of this equipment through subsidiaries outside of Germany (particularly in Sweden, Switzerland, and the Netherlands), but none of it had been tested in conjunction with combat aircraft. Wilberg was also able to utilize the newly formed Lufthansa—the national airline formed in 1926—to test some equipment that had civilian utility. But for most of the key systems—particularly weapons—there was nowhere else to go aside from Lipetsk.

The most ambitious element of the testing program would involve testing new aircraft prototypes commissioned by the Reichswehr beginning in 1923 with partner firms in Germany's struggling aviation industry. The first of these would begin arriving in the summer of 1926. Ernst Heinkel, head of the Heinkel firm, recalled his introduction to the aircraft testing program at Lipetsk:

> When I returned to Warnemünde from Sweden, I was told that a certain visitor [Kurt Student] wished to see me. When I met him, he didn't introduce himself . . . in spite of his civilian clothes, I felt from the outset that he was a military man. He made it a condition that our talk should be kept in confidence. After our first conversation, it still was not clear whom he really represented. Only some time later I understood

who he was and the real reason for his visit. . . . [At that time, Helmuth] Wilberg headed the Reichswehr Aviation Department. He made a trip to Russia to study the possibility of training pilots there using airplanes built secretly in Germany. At the time, I could not understand why the visitor asked whether I would be able to make a landplane with a speed of 220 km/h [136 mph] and ceiling of 6000 meters [19,685 feet], which could be employed as a short-range reconnaissance aircraft. I asked him what financial resources he had. The man smiled and said that he was ready to buy such an airplane immediately after it was built.

Heinkel eventually agreed to the arrangement, and from then on his company became involved in providing the Reichswehr with arms while "playing cat-and-mouse with the Allied Commission on Aircraft Construction." Heinkel was aware that it was a game he could lose and in the process either lose his business or have it placed "under strict surveillance and constant supervision." But he was never caught, later recalling that "I think fortune was on my side."[29]

After Student's visit, the Reichswehr had issued Heinkel a contract for prototype development of a fast (150 mph) reconnaissance biplane to be tested at Lipetsk. His design, the Heinkel HD-17, would be the first German prototype to arrive at Lipetsk in 1926.[30] That facility would become the home of Heinkel's—and all the other— prototype combat aircraft commissioned by the Reichswehr. Most of the designs would not see mass production, but even those that failed provided essential practice, experience, and ideas to those young engineers who would come to dominate the German aviation industry in the 1930s.

Unlike the industrial cooperation mentioned earlier, the Reichswehr managed and directly supervised all the work conducted at Lipetsk. The stakes were too high, and the importance of the new design work too important. Within the Waffenamt, Prüfwesen 8 (Weapons Testing Department 8, or Wa.Prüf 8)—the "statistics" bureau—was responsible for highly secret aviation development.[31] This group was well represented at Lipetsk, where between 1926 to 1928 there were at least six Wa.Prüf 8 team members, five of whom had engineering backgrounds.[32] This team was headed by Wilhelm Wimmer, a future Luftwaffe general who would oversee the Luftwaffe's building program between 1936 and the outbreak of the war in 1939.

When necessary, the Wa.Prüf 8 supplemented its team at Lipetsk by hiring civilian aviation engineers as consultants and then dispatching them there. Captain Roluf Lücht, for instance, worked as an engineer for the German aviation firm Rohrbach after the First World War. In 1926, he was hired by the Reichswehr as a "technical adviser" and sent to Lipetsk.[33] The research team would eventually grow to include additional Soviet and German engineers, twelve aircraft mechanics, five hangar staff, six armorers, four bomb specialists, three pyrotechnical experts, and a three-man demolition squad.[34] Including German and Russian pilots, engineers, and support staff, the number of men present at Lipetsk would soon be in the hundreds. The core of the new German air force was beginning to form—inside the Soviet Union.

CHAPTER 13

Chemist Gypsies

As Lipetsk's mission grew more expansive, German and Russian representatives began discussing the establishment of a jointly operated chemical weapons laboratory and testing group dedicated to exploring chemical dispersal techniques. Unlike the chemical weapons facility at Bersol, this would center on weapons testing, including the use of poison gas in conjunction with air power. In May, Hermann von der Lieth-Thomsen and Unschlikht met to hammer out the specifics, initially discussing a site called Luga near Leningrad. But by July, Luga was rejected in favor of a military base already under Yakov Fishman's control, just southeast of Moscow.[1]

As the summer of 1926 dragged on, the Reichswehr grew increasingly eager to formalize an agreement before winter conditions in the Soviet Union rendered testing impossible. On August 19, a team, including Lieth-Thomsen, Student, and Fishman, visited the site near Moscow.[2] Two days later, they signed the formal cooperative agreement to take joint management of the site, which was called Podosinki and located on a forested estate formerly owned by Prince Nikolai Dmitrievich Golitsyn, the last Tsarist prime minister of Russia at the time of the February Revolution.[3] The base's technical work would be managed by German scientists and military officers, while its administration would be managed by a Soviet officer. Soviet chemists would participate fully in the work, gaining expertise in the process. The Soviets added a provision to the contract stating that the leading Soviet officer at the facility, or his deputy, must be present for all experiments and weapons testing.[4] Trust was at a premium in the USSR—even when relations were at their best, the Soviets sarcastically called the Germans "friends" (in quotation marks!) in their own internal correspondence.

By 1926, Podosinki was also the home of the Moscow Military District's Gas Battalion, as well as neighboring a VVS airfield; the visiting delegation noted that the main testing ground was pockmarked with craters and reeked of mustard gas.[5] The German team expressed some concern about the airfield and testing field's close proximity to Moscow's suburbs–the base was only 12 miles from Central Moscow. Fishman assured them that he "took full and total responsibility for all the trials" and any possible civilian casualties that might result.[6]

To provide their team with cover from allied intelligence agents, the Reichswehr formed a new corporate entity, entitled the Gesellschaft für landwirtschaftliche Artikel (the Society for Agricultural Products, or GELA). In September, a team of twelve German scientists, engineers, and pilots journeyed to Moscow to begin work at the facility, after being briefed and given a fictitious backstory about working on agricultural pesticides. Most of the team had been affiliated with Germany's chemical weapons program in the First World War, and understood the stakes of their research. Supervising them was Hans Hackmack, who had served as a pilot in the First World War. He spent two years after the war as a private flight instructor in the Soviet Union, not far from Lipetsk. Hackmack, who would go by the alias "Amberg" during his time in the Soviet Union—secrecy was still paramount—was repeatedly lauded by his military superiors for his organizational skills, and for handling the civilians under his management despite being their junior by decades.[7]

The intention of the agreement signed in August was to manufacture small quantities of chemical agents for testing purposes. Two tons of lachrymatory agents—also known as tear gas—were expected during the first four months of operation.[8] These agents would then be used in conjunction with aircraft to test the possibilities of aerial bombardment with chemical weapons. However, when the Germans arrived at Podosinki they were in for a rude surprise. There were almost no facilities present. Materials that had been shipped from Germany before their departure had not yet been delivered, some appearing only weeks later. Almost nothing was available in Moscow for construction. The head of the research team complained that even "every single hammer will have to be obtained from Germany!"[9]

Hackmack's job was also complicated by Soviet policies. In October 1926, the Red Army liaison passed Hackmack a copy of "Rules for Guests," a twenty-nine-point guideline for German behavior at Podosinki penned by one of Fishman's assistants.[10] Germans were forbidden to travel to Moscow without permission, and then only in groups of "two or smaller." They were forbidden from congregating outside their facilities, talking with Russian guards or officers not directly involved in the work, or walking to any other buildings around the military airfield besides the ones in which they were quartered or working. The second-to-last point added emphatically that "ignorance or lack of understanding of the Russian language" was no excuse, as the instruction had been translated into German.[11] In other words, the Germans were treated as some sort of capitalist bacilli that might contaminate all of the Red Army officers with whom they came into contact. Mediating between Soviet policy and his team consumed much of Hackmack's time.

Complicating matters was a changing of the guard in Berlin. Over the course of 1926, instead of building alliances with similar-minded members of the government, the arrogant and thin-skinned Seeckt antagonized President Hindenburg and waged an unnecessary struggle with Foreign Minister Stresemann over control of foreign policy, especially foolish given Stresemann's support for German rearmament.[12] Both were highly inappropriate actions for a man who was not even in the cabinet. Facing an increasingly hostile political environment, Seeckt made one last critical mistake: he allowed the Hohenzollern crown prince—heir to the German throne if the monarchy were to be restored—to attend the Reichswehr's September maneuvers in uniform.[13] This was both a slap in the face of the constitution and a violation of military rules. Seeckt's political adviser Kurt von Schleicher very likely leaked the indiscretion to the public, guaranteeing a political firestorm.[14] Hindenburg did not defend Seeckt, nor did Minister of Defense Gessler.[15] After a brief discussion about "resisting" his departure with senior military officers, Seeckt gave in, and retired on October 5, 1926.[16] Appropriately, his last major act had been to superintend a preliminary agreement to establish a "tank school" in the Soviet Union for testing armored vehicles and training armor officers on October 2.[17]

Hindenburg did give Seeckt a chance to nominate his successor as chief of army command. There were four potential candidates. Seeckt intentionally backed the man he deemed most pliant, Wilhelm Heye, whom he thought he could control even in retirement. Heye was duly selected to become chief of army command. Heye was a genial man, well-liked among the fellow officers, though not regarded as particularly brilliant or tough.[18]

Heye filled important positions with a new cohort of younger military officers. Most significant of these was general staff officer Werner von Blomberg.[19] Blomberg was a scion of a right-wing Prussian military family. During the First World War, he had served as a staff officer, participating in the Battle of the Marne and Verdun, among others. For his service, he would receive the Pour le Mérite, Germany's highest military honor, from the hands of Kaiser Wilhelm himself in 1918.[20] Ardently dedicated to rearmament, Blomberg was more favorably inclined toward political radicalism than most of his peers in the interwar Reichswehr. With Heye's promotion in 1926, Blomberg would first be placed in charge of army training, then the following year, become chief of the Troop Office—the second-most senior rank in the Reichswehr. In that role, he would become a frequent visitor to the Soviet Union.[21]

As Heye assumed his office, the Reichswehr received a stream of complaints from Podosinki outside of Moscow. Despite a good relationship with the enthusiastic Fishman, everything was in short supply. Moscow Central noted that "his goodwill for the common cause certainly cannot be denied," but that Fishman did not have much support in his own ranks. Niedermayer wrote in November 1926 that Fishman "constantly issues orders that are either not complied with, or under the circumstances, cannot be followed."[22]

VOKhIMU's lack of resources rapidly became apparent to the Germans. Given that the facility was so close to Moscow, the German team expected some of the comforts of home.[23] Concerns regarding secrecy and a terrible housing shortage in Moscow derailed that possibility. Instead of apartments in Moscow, the Germans present— four of whom were middle-aged or elderly academics—reported that living at Podosinki meant living like "gypsies" and "under the most primitive of conditions."[24] The group's doctor, Otto Muntsch, reported that they were brought buckets of rainwater for cleaning and drinking. In particular, the team complained about subsisting on nothing but tea and sausage. In a report back to Berlin, Muntsch reported that "in the long term this is unsustainable physically, mentally and spiritually."[25]

Muntsch added, however, "The experimental work itself I find extremely interesting."[26] That work centered on the possibility of fulfilling Giulio Douhet's vision of strategic bombing using chemical weapons. The primary delivery system proposed was the chemical aero-bomb. In the 1920s, these were ordnance containing a timed fuse and explosive designed to detonate above the ground for maximum dispersal of the chemical agent. The other possibility pursued during the interwar period was the use of chemical sprayers, similar to those used in pesticide crop dusting. Low-flying aircraft could saturate large areas evenly with a properly designed sprayer. However, each of these technologies required significant adjustment to the chemical agents themselves in order to maintain dense concentrations capable of wounding or killing enemy combatants. Trying to solve those issues was the key challenge of the testing program.

After two months of improving the camp's facilities, the staff at Podosinki were finally ready to test some of Douhet's and Fishman's propositions about chemical aviation.[27] In November, the German team began conducting forty tests involving spraying "neutral agents" that resembled mustard gas from various heights to test dispersion.[28] Using aircraft from the nearby airfield, the Germans dropped five tons of chemical agents via fourteen different aero-bomb and sprayer configurations, testing concentration and dispersion of the agents.[29] During the remainder of the testing season, they also tested bombing timers, new percussion fuses, the development of an effective aero-bomb, and a poison gas dispersing armored vehicle built by Krupp, as well as the "degassing" of contaminated terrain.[30] It was a substantial achievement in a short space of time given the immense difficulties of operating at Podosinki, including inclement weather.[31] Hackmack's reports to Lieth-Thomsen and Moscow Central grew in confidence as the fall progressed. He wrote in the last report of the year that the results at Podosinki were "valuable in spite of the difficulties."[32]

With weather conditions getting worse (and the cold affecting test results), Hackmack's team decided to hold a major demonstration of their results in first week of December. Lieth-Thomsen, accompanied by Fishman and Unschlikht, arrived at Podosinki for a presentation of their efforts.[33] These involved releasing chemical agents from an aircraft at a number of different heights onto the testing ground. Hackmack wrote that the testing allowed them "to draw precise conclusions on evacuations and organization for emergencies, etc."[34] What he meant by "evacuations and organization" was the preparation of Germany's cities against massive chemical warfare bombardment from the air. In Hackmack's mind, as well that of his team, this was the beginning of a new era in warfare, where the systematic bombing of civilian populations with chemical agents would now be a vital tool in the military arsenals of the Great Powers. Germany needed to be prepared.

Writing some two weeks after the exercise, Lieth-Thomsen described the test as a tremendous success. While he reported that Fishman had had some problems in gaining the "interest of higher agencies" for the experiments, he now had their attention.[35] The observation was an astute one. Two weeks after the tests, Unschlikht would write to Stalin and the Politburo: "The use of mustard gas via aviation for the purposes of contamination and attacking human settlements is technically possible and of great value."[36] With the success of the demonstration at Podosinki, the Soviets agreed to an expansion of the cooperative chemical weapons program. In addition, Fishman gained vital political support: VOKhIMU's research budget increased more than 60 percent the next year.[37] However, despite the triumph of the December tests, Podosinki's brief role in Soviet-German cooperation was nearing an end.

CHAPTER 14

The Junkers Scandal

On December 3, 1926, residents of Manchester, England, awoke to a startling headline in the *Manchester Guardian*: "Cargoes of Munitions from Russia to Germany! Secret Plan between Reichswehr Officers and Soviet[s]. STARTLING DISCLOSURES. Military Intrigues to be stopped by German Government."[1] This was not the first time that Germany had been accused of undermining Versailles through secret rearmament, but the *Manchester Guardian* revelations were exceptional for the amount of evidence they produced to support their claim, including material provided by left-wing members of the Reichstag.[2] The Guardian's foreign correspondent alleged that Junkers AG had built an airplane factory, and that poison gas was being developed, essentially identifying German activities at Fili and Bersol. It singled out Seeckt's role as commander in chief of the Reichswehr, and accused him of being "on the best of terms with the Russians, particularly with officers of high rank in the Soviet army."[3]

Every word was accurate.

Soon after the article, German newspapers themselves called attention to the connection, though not accusingly, and if anything approvingly.[4] Only *Rote Fähne* (Red Banner), the KPD's paper, decried the story: "The Social Democrats throw 'lie grenades' against the Soviet Union."[5] An ineffective denial by their paper seemed to confirm in the minds of many this unlikely partnership between the archconservative German officer corps and the revolutionary leaders of the Soviet Union.

The reaction in the Reichstag was dramatic. On December 15, 1926, Philipp Scheidemann, now the head of the SPD (the leading opposition party at that juncture) delivered a furious speech over the roars of the government benches. "The German people want peace and reconciliation with the Allies," Scheidemann thundered. "But the military activities of the Nationalist elements endanger that peace." Scheidemann called for a detailed accounting from anyone involved with these "sub rosa armaments." "To Russia I say that we want to be friends," he concluded, "but it is a foul friendship so long as the Soviets preach world revolution and help disrupt the German Reichswehr."[6]

The floor erupted in shouts of "Traitor! Blackguard! Treason!" Others gestured toward the American ambassador, who was sitting in the diplomatic box. "'Why reveal these things to our enemies?!'"[7] As members of the right angrily stormed out of the Reichstag, the Social Democrats called for a vote of no-confidence in the sitting government.

This speech, coupled with revelations about Junkers AG, brought down the government of Chancellor Wilhelm Marx, a moderate Catholic from the Zentrum Party. Joined by the far right and far left, the SPD's vote of no confidence succeeded on December 17. However, in the parliamentary struggle that followed, it soon became clear that the next coalition would have to move to the right in order to form a stable government. That meant including a number of nationalist, right-wing parties in the government. Chancellor Marx, supported by Stresemann, stayed on as chancellor. The two men soon cobbled together a coalition of nationalists and centrists; as part of the arrangement, Minister of Defense Gessler would not be replaced, as Scheidemann had demanded. Neither would his subordinates. Ironically, the Junkers affair had brought down one German government and ushered in another further to the right, many of whose members openly approved of the Reichswehr's activities in Russia.

Nevertheless, the international outcry that resulted from the Junkers scandal would result in what historian Sergei Gorlov termed the *politicheskaia pausa*—"the political pause"—in Soviet-German relations.[8] The Soviet government was embarrassed by revelations of its work with the archconservative Reichswehr; there was talk of ending the entire relationship in Moscow.[9] The German government—most of all Stresemann—was concerned primarily about the lack of supervision over Reichswehr activities in the Soviet Union. He too wanted to reassess the relationship.

Amazingly, even as the German military fretted about the Western reaction to the Junkers Scandal, as all this was now being called, the Allies' Interallied Military Control Commission was coming to an end. The British had long grown tired of continental commitments. The French were unwilling to maintain the status quo without British support, and more generally, were exhausted by the costs of enforcing reparations and disarmament. In mid-December—just as the scandal exploded—the British and French governments indicated to Stresemann their general satisfaction that Germany had met the disarmament terms of Versailles. They ordered the withdrawal of the IAMCC from Germany effective January 31, 1927.[10] Its final report, delivered in January 1927, was ominous: "Germany has never disarmed, has never had the intention of disarming, and for seven years had done everything in her power to deceive and 'counter-control' the Commission appointed to control her disarmament."[11] The Conference of Ambassadors, a council of Allied representatives, would continue to monitor disarmament compliance; a small number of military inspectors would remain behind to assist them. But the stringent enforcement of Versailles was at an end. In the face of broad evidence of German rearmament efforts, the British and French governments decided to do nothing. The ongoing British policy of "appeasement" had won the day.

With a tepid Allied response, both Germany and the USSR reassessed the relationship. Work at the chemical weapons grounds at Podosinki was mostly discontinued.

The flight school at Lipetsk continued training small numbers of pilots, but its expansion was put on hold. The scandal had threatened too much to proceed without the greatest caution.[12] Most troubled were Fili and Bersol, neither of which had met expectations. Deputy Chief of the Revolutionary Military Council Unschlikht wrote to Stalin immediately after the scandal had broken, laying out the state of the Soviet-German relationship. He noted that "the main task we put forward at the beginning of our cooperation, i.e., the improvement of the material bulk of the RKKA [Red Army] (in the organization of the military industry), has not yet yielded the expected results." He added that it would be in his view a good idea to keep the German Ministry of Defense out of any mediation with German firms, given that the added bureaucracy "results in nothing."[13]

In the aftermath of the Junkers Scandal, the Politburo met to discuss the future of the corporate ventures, and in particular, to consider the Reichswehr offer to sell their share of Bersol. On January 17, 1927, the Soviet government agreed to end the concession at Bersol, taking total control of the facility.[14] In March, they likewise concluded the Junkers contract, with Junkers handing over the facility to the Soviets for a nominal sum.[15] Many other German firms continued to work with Soviet defense industry, but these two Reichswehr attempts to directly manage the restoration of German military industry in the Soviet Union had failed. The first phase of cooperation had effectively come to an end.

However, both Fili and Bersol had an active afterlife, playing a major role in Soviet military industrialization. Bersol would eventually become productive under the Soviet aegis. Poison gas production figures grew rapidly in the late 1920s; in a sign of its growing importance, in 1931, when relations between the German and Soviet militaries were at their best, the Soviets denied Reichswehr personnel access to the facility.[16] By 1932, factory hands at Bersol were filling tens of thousands of artillery gas shells a month.[17] By 1936, Bersol was producing four tons of mustard gas a day, making it one of the largest centers of poison gas production in the world.[18]

The aviation plant at Fili also took on new life. Historians have generally dismissed the Junkers facility as a total failure, but that conclusion derives entirely from the German experience there. It is true that the plant produced only a small portion of its planned aircraft, and relatively low-quality ones at that. In total, during its two and a half years of operation, the Fili plant had assembled 150 aircraft of J-20 and J-21 design, as well as modifying a handful JuG-1/G24 three-engine bomber prototypes.[19] Still, to put Fili's production figures into perspective, the entire Soviet Air Force consisted of 173 functioning aircraft in 1924.[20] The head of VVS estimated that Fili was the fourth-most productive aviation facility of any kind in the Soviet Union at the end of 1925.[21] Fili was an essential source of aircraft during its years of operation.

The factory eventually became quite successful under Soviet control, with German contractors remaining on site to assist in production. After upgrades and expansion after Junkers' departure, the Fili plant was renamed Moscow Aircraft Factory N22. It began producing high-quality BMW engines under license agreements with that German firm in 1927.[22] As of 1931, the factory was still open to German visitors; at that time, it was the primary center for the production of famed Soviet aviation designer Andrei Tupolev's early reconnaissance and bomber aircraft.[23] Tupolev's designs, too, drew their origins from Fili. The first generation of Tupolev aircraft were reverse-engineered from Junkers' duraluminum monoplane designs, some of which had been stolen from the plant by Soviet employees.[24] The first fruit of Tupolev's work, the TB-1 (the Soviet Union's first monoplane bomber), was mass-produced exclusively at Fili beginning in 1928, as it was the only plant in the entire Soviet Union that could accommodate the complicated production work. So derivative was it of Junkers' designs that Hugo Junkers sued the Soviet Union in international court at The Hague for patent infringement—an embarrassment for both German and Soviets governments.[25] Under Tupolev's management, Fili was the sole source of all of the Soviet Union's heavy bombers for four years, which numbered 218 by 1932.[26] By that date, Fili had provided the intellectual and physical capital necessary for the future expansion of the Soviet Air Force.

While German expectations for Fili and Bersol were disappointed, Soviet aims, after considerable additional investment, were largely met. In this way, Reichswehr assistance played a critical if indirect role in the early development of Soviet military industry in key fields, particularly aviation and chemistry. With the corporate projects concluded, the big question for Reichswehr and RVS officials was what would come next.

CHAPTER 15

Resetting Relations

The new phase of relations began even before the old one ended. As noted, Seeckt's last act in office had been to reach a preliminary agreement for the construction of a joint tank facility in the Soviet Union. On December 2, just as the Junkers scandal was breaking, Commissar of Military and Naval Affairs Voroshilov and Director of Moscow Central Lieth-Thomsen had finalized terms for a three-year lease on a to-be-determined military facility for the purpose of joint tank training and testing.[1] The contract stated that the Germans would have forty-two men and the Soviets thirty men in residence, with the aim of having twenty or so students at a time complete three-month-long armored warfare courses using tanks to be provided by the German side.[2]

There was great eagerness on each side to develop a joint armored-warfare facility. Neither the Soviet nor the German army had had much experience with armored vehicles. Germany had ended the First World War with a decided disadvantage in tank technology. By 1918, the British and French had produced 6,891 tanks, while the Germans completed only 20 of their own heavy tank design, the A7V.[3] As a result, Germany did not have the technical and operational expertise that the Allied powers had.

This presented problems, but also opportunities: the huge stockpiles of tanks left over from the First World War handicapped the evolution of British and French doctrine and slowed their investment in new vehicles, while German officers were freer to think about the future of armored warfare and the types of tanks to develop.[4] As part of this process, after the war, the Reichswehr's Ausbildungsabteilung (Training Department) managed study groups of officers who examined the conduct of the war and the causes of German defeat. These reports repeatedly stressed the role of the tank in Entente victory, as well as their future potential.[5] This further spurred Reichswehr interest in the pursuit of new armored warfare technologies and ideas.

As noted earlier, in 1920, Seeckt had begun requiring the inclusion of *Panzerattrapen* (dummy tanks) in all maneuvers and major war games.[6] He pushed for the mechanization of artillery within the bounds allowed by the treaty.[7] Further, he placed all mechanized vehicles (at the time, only a handful of armored cars qualified) under the control of a reorganized Inspektion der Kraftfahrtruppen (Inspectorate of Motorized Troops), which put tank development in the hands of its strongest proponents.[8]

The work of one these proponents, Ernst Volckheim, paved the way for a refinement of German armored principles. Volckheim had been one of the first armor officers in the German Army, serving in the first tank-on-tank combat at the Battle of Villers-Brettoneux in 1918.[9] Retained after the downsizing of the Reichswehr, he was assigned to the new Inspektion der Kraftfahrtruppen in 1923. He began teaching armored warfare courses in 1925. Between 1923 and 1927, he wrote three books on armored warfare, penned a number of influential articles in the Reichswehr's weekly journal, the *Militär-Wochenblatt* (*Military Weekly*), and served as the leading contributor to an insert published alongside *Militär-Wochenblatt* entitled *Der Kampfwagen* (*The Combat Vehicle*). *Der Kampfwagen*, which appeared in six volumes between October 1924 and March 1925, had only one named author besides Volckheim: Heinz Guderian, famed future tank commander and theorist, who would later claim all of the credit for Germany's high-speed armor doctrine.[10] As a sign of Volckheim's immense importance to the development of German armor doctrine, his work *Der Kampfwagen in der heutigen Kriegsführung* (*The Tank in Today's Warfare*) was assigned as the primary textbook for all would-be German armor officers beginning in 1924.[11]

Volckheim's writings spurred broad interest in tanks among the German officer corps. One of his arguments was that improvements in technology would reverse the relationship between tanks and infantry. In the First World War, tanks' slow speeds and mechanical unreliability had meant they could only be used effectively in support of infantry attacks. At some point in the future, Volckheim believed, infantry would become auxiliary to armored vehicles, which would be the decisive arm.[12] In addition, he argued against the status quo at the time by positing that it was the armor and gun of the tank, rather than its speed, which were its key elements. This meant that instead of endorsing the production of light tanks with high speed and maneuverability, the German Army should focus on producing medium-weight tanks that were fast enough to encircle enemy forces but heavy enough to defeat opposing tanks and artillery if necessary.[13] Not everyone agreed, however. And the debate could not be fully resolved until German officers could actually train with tanks and use armored vehicles in maneuvers.

Soviet armored theory and technical design lagged behind even the Germans. The Russian Imperial Army had never managed to deploy tanks in the First World War, although it had built several prototype designs. The nature of warfare on the Eastern Front made slow-moving armored vehicles of limited use. During the Russian Civil War, the Red Army had organized an armored forces corps made up of armored trains, armored cars, and improvised armored vehicles. These last were usually trucks or cars with metal plates welded on, perhaps mounting a heavy machine gun. During the war, a number of British Mark V and French Renault FT-17 tanks were delivered to the Whites, all of which were captured and put to use by the Red Army. Reverse-engineering the Renaults led to the first Soviet-built tank, called the "Freedom Fighter Comrade Lenin," which was produced by workers in Nizhny

Novgorod in 1920.[14] But given the limited role performed by tanks in both the First World War and the civil war, this was not a priority area in the crafting of doctrine.

In the waning days of the civil war, the Red Army established the Avto-Bronetankovoe Upravlenie (Directorate of Armored Forces) and decided to concentrate their armored vehicles into formations. But in the rush of demobilization after the war, most of the tanks were either left to rust or put to work elsewhere—in 1922, for instance, six of its tanks were dispatched to Ukraine to help with the harvest as tractors.[15] In a further sign of conditions, the armored forces were merged into the Glavnoe Artilleriiskoe Upravlenie (Main Artillery Department, or GAU) in 1923.[16] Given the lack of resources and experience, the Soviets (just like the Germans) kept a close eye on foreign developments. They were particularly familiar with the works of British armored war theorist J. F. C Fuller (Tukhachevsky supervised the translation of his work into Russian) and Captain Basil Liddell-Hart, the military historian and theorist.[17]

As part of the reorganization of Soviet armored forces in 1923, the Red Army established its first tank design bureau, staffed with ten engineers.[18] These began working on home-grown tank designs, but still generally drew most of their inspiration from prototypes in England, the United States, and France. The Soviet Union's first domestically designed tank (the T-16) was more or less a copy of the French FT-17, the most advanced tank captured during the civil war.[19] But it took years before even that small, two-man tank could be replicated in significant numbers. Thanks to neglect, what little armored forces the Red Army possessed deteriorated badly. An inspection of the top tank regiment in the Soviet military revealed that it had only nineteen tanks in its motor pool, six of which had no guns and nine of which were mechanically unfit for active service.[20]

By the time of the political pause in 1927, Soviet and German armored forces were in much the same place. Almost no vehicles had been produced domestically, which in turn handicapped development of doctrines or strategies. Both relied on foreign, particularly British, experience with armored vehicles. In early 1927, new Chief of the Army Command General Heye dispatched a major named Wilhelm Malbrandt to select, in cooperation with Red Army officials, an appropriate location for an armored-warfare training school. They soon settled on an old Tsarist cavalry base near Kazan, a major city situated along the banks of the Volga River.[21] The Red Army officially transferred the former barracks of the Fifth Dragoons Regiment to the Reichswehr on February 1, 1927.[22] Soon after, the RVS selected an open range—a *polygon* in Russian—for tank maneuvers and gunnery drills on a site some 6 miles from Kargopol Barracks.[23] The Soviets selected the codename "KaMa" for the whole facility, combining the words "Kazan" and "Malbrandt." This turned out to be a comically poor choice, as a river near the site also bore the same name.[24] They would eventually re-code the camp "TEKO," short for "Technical Courses of the Society for Defense, Aviation and Construction of Chemical Weapons."[25] The name Kama stuck, though, particularly on the German side.

However, little progress would be made on the facility at Kama for some time because of political circumstances. Soviet ambassador Krestinsky had made it clear to Gustav Stresemann in the aftermath of the Junkers Scandal that the Soviet Union wanted only to resume relations on a "legal basis": that is, all policies regarding joint Soviet-German military cooperation had first to be approved by the German government in Berlin to prevent scandals of the sort that had just occurred.[26] With that conversation fresh in his mind, and a few days after the Red Army's transfer of the site at Kama, Stresemann determined it was time to reassess the Soviet military partnership.[27] On February 4, 1927, he met with the Reichswehr's senior leadership to discuss the existing situation. He laid out some of the basic preconditions for the Reichswehr's continued work in the Soviet Union but, perhaps to their surprise, Stresemann did not dismiss the idea of working with the Russians entirely. Shortly thereafter, Minister of Defense Gessler forwarded a report to Stresemann with a long list of suggestions for bolstering national defense. While Stresemann's office balked at many of the requests (such as plans to begin secret preparations for a large standing field army), it opened a dialogue between the Foreign Ministry and the Ministry of Defense regarding national defense strategy. Critically, as part of the "legalization" of secret rearmament measures, Chancellor Marx's government authorized a Reichswehr proposal for a unified, modern armaments program for the whole state, using funds concealed from the Reichstag.[28] This meant additional resources could be devoted to the programs in Russia.

Prospects for continuing growth in the Soviet-German relationship seemed good. In late February 1927, the Marx government managed to kill a Reichstag investigation into the Junkers Scandal. When forced to testify, Defense Minister Gessler read a prepared statement before the Reichstag's foreign relations committee. The committee members asked a few minor questions about the financing of the projects in Russia, concluded that "under previous cabinets, military agreements had been concluded without the necessary constitutional bases," and ended the inquiry.[29] Enthusiasm for cooperation with Russia was high. Immediately afterward, former chancellor Wirth gave a rousing plea for Ostpolitik on the floor of the Reichstag, aided by loud applause from the KPD.[30] The scandal receded as quickly as it had come.

With the conclusion of this public cover-up, German military-diplomatic rapprochement moved forward. The next step came on May 18, when Generals Blomberg and Heye met with Stresemann again to discuss German activities in the Soviet Union.[31] The two men reached an agreement on a long list of points intended to reassure the Foreign Ministry. Stresemann required an improvement of the relationship between the Reichswehr and Foreign Ministry if Soviet-German cooperation was to continue. First, that meant that his office would need to provide an official (though not publicly announced) declaration of its consent before the armored-warfare training and testing ground at Kazan could open for operations. He also demanded the Reichswehr make certain that there were no uniformed personnel at any of the joint facilities.[32] At the same time, however, Stresemann granted permission, even Foreign Ministry assistance, for mutual exchanges of officers to attend maneuvers. And he endorsed the establishment of language-training courses for Germans headed to the Soviet Union. At the end of the meeting, he made it clear that a full review of all joint military activity should be made at the end of the year, at which time policy toward the Soviet Union could be reassessed.

As the Reichswehr waited on permission from the Foreign Ministry, Major Malbrandt and two assistants moved to Kazan to begin preparations at the site.[33] With the political circumstances somewhat improved, a German engineer and a team of Russian workmen remodeled the staff offices, living facilities, classrooms, the base armory, and the shooting range.[34] They also made the building of a *kasino* (officer's mess) an early priority.[35]

Soviet sources recorded that the Reichswehr allocated between 1.5 and 2 million marks ($356,000-$475,000 USD) on the facility in 1927.[36] This amount paled in comparison to the more than 20 million marks ($4.75 million USD) invested in Podosinki and other joint chemical weapons work, and the nearly 22 million marks ($5.22 million USD) spent on Lipetsk through that year.[37] The minimal investment—a product of the political pause—meant that during these first few months of construction only a handful of individuals were present at Kama. Although significant activity waited on the Foreign Ministry, throughout the summer the Reichswehr did dispatch a number of civil and military engineers that spring, mostly singly or in pairs.[38] Lacking prototypes, they decided they would keep themselves busy by attempting to turn commercial tractors into self-propelled armored guns. The engineers made use of two tractors built by the Hanomag Corporation.[39] The first attempted modification involved the addition of a 37-mm anti-tank gun mounted on a pedestal, which could only traverse 30 degrees. Mounted on the rear of the tractor was a machine gun. The vehicle itself, a 1922 model, had an engine about as powerful as a riding lawnmower today.[40] It was a small start for the development of a German tank service.

While the engineering teams present at Kama were just getting started, things at Podosinki were heating up. On a quiet Thursday evening in March 1927, a Russian cook ran into the room of a German army mechanic at the Podosinki site.[41] He said that he smelled smoke. The mechanic must have had a sinking feeling at those words. The two men rushed into the kitchen, checked the furnace, and could find no source of the smell, which was growing stronger by the minute. The mechanic decided he would check upstairs. Opening the door to a large storage room, he was greeted with a wave of heat and choking smoke. He must have felt tremendous fear at that moment, given Podosinki's role as a secret chemical weapons laboratory.

The mechanic struggled against the heat and smoke. He was not sure what chemicals might be in the cloud of smoke filling the room, but it could be deadly. He knew he had to get to a gas mask. With visibility no greater than an arm's length, he later reported that he struggled to reach the masks because he was "half-fainting in the stifling smoke and had to grope for the exit."[42] Coughing and gasping, he dashed back down the stairs. At that moment, another German soldier ran up, accompanied by a few Russian guards. One had brought a gas mask with him. The German soldier took the mask and made another effort at the upstairs room. Braving the heat and smoke, he managed to return with a pair of heavier German gas masks, then collapsed half-conscious outside the building. The mechanic attempted to use the rescued masks to investigate the fire, but found the "fumes from inside had penetrated into the seams" of the masks, rendering them useless.[43]

Elsewhere in the building vital laboratory equipment was at risk. After the Russian guards tried and failed to extinguish the blaze, the group began rapidly evacuating all material from the building. Throwing water on the floor and closing doors to slow the fire, the Russian guards managed to save all the materiel from the lower floors. Both Germans had to restrain one of the Russian soldiers who tried to brave the fire upstairs by himself—by that time it was too late to contain the blaze. Just as the men managed to drag the building's portable electrical generator outside, "the house went up in flames."[44] It was a little after midnight on a cold spring night as the crew began sifting through the goods they had managed to salvage. Shortly thereafter, a truck from the Moscow fire department arrived on scene, too late to do any good.[45]

Discussions had begun even before the fire about the possibility of moving the Soviet and German research teams to a site in the vicinity of Orenburg, in the Urals. When General Wilhelm Adam (then chief of staff to the Seventh Division) visited the location on May 3, 1927, accompanied by the young pilot Hackmack, Niedermayer from Moscow Central, and Fishman's Deputy at VOKhIMU, the Germans recorded their total dissatisfaction with the location.[46] The site was too close to the city, too distant from European Russia (their clothes would be noticeable, they complained), and lacked water.[47] A German team would visit to observe a Soviet chemical defense maneuver there, but not relocate.[48] In the meantime, they continued testing at Podosinki until July 20, 1927, while Moscow Central sought a new arrangement with VOKhIMU.[49] After learning that decontamination would "require the presence of the entire staff for 8–14 days and involves more dangers than the operation of the facility," the Germans decided to board up the facility and turn it over to the Red Army, in exchange for a proviso that the Germans could rent it the following spring (1928) if they so desired.[50] They would not return. Podosinki would become part of the Red Army's chemical weapons program, serving as the testing ground for gas masks and chemical agents produced in five factories located around Moscow.[51]

Despite the issues at Podosinki, the termination of the Junkers and Fili ventures, and the political pause, the Soviet-German partnership continued to expand in 1927. By the end of the year, Lipetsk was fully operational, and had hosted 144 men, including several dozen older pilots, ten new trainee pilots, and a number of visiting Russian flight instructors.[52] The school also boasted six different types of aircraft.[53] Soviet workers had meanwhile largely finished construction at Kama, which awaited German political approval, armored vehicles, and students.

The training program for Soviet officers in Germany also continued, hosting nineteen senior officers in 1927.[54] In that year, the visitors included Robert Eidemann, head of the Frunze Military Academy; Vladimir Triandafillov, an influential Soviet military theorist; and Ieronim Uborevich, chief of armaments for the Red Army.[55] Six senior German officers reciprocated, attending Soviet maneuvers or studying at Soviet military education facilities.[56] The Junkers Scandal and the delicate political situation had kept the Reichswehr and Red Army from expanding their collaboration, but just as it appeared the political pause might finally be at an end, another military scandal threatened to bring down the new German government.

CHAPTER 16

The Lohmann Scandal

On January 20, 1928, Chancellor Marx stood before the Reichstag to announce the discovery of "inconsistencies" in Ministry of Defense accounting standards. These had been discovered when an investigation into the extravagant spending by a mistress of Reichsmarine [Imperial Navy] Captain Walther Lohmann led to an official investigation.[1] The increasingly bizarre revelations centered on Lohmann's Russian girlfriend, a movie studio, and, oddly enough, pig farming. It was only thirteen months after the Junkers Scandal had brought down the German government.

The son of the former president of Norddeutscher Lloyd shipping company, Lohmann had been a middling logistics officer when the war ended.[2] After playing a major role in the German Navy's decommissioning negotiations at Versailles, he showed considerable skill in purchasing back large numbers of German commercial vessels from British custody. He also adeptly managed to get German naval POWs released from custody and supervised their return.[3] His skills in this regard earned him praise from his senior officers, and in October 1920, he was promoted to head the Naval Transport Section of the Reichsmarine.[4] In that position he was twice sent to Leningrad to negotiate for the release of German vessels interned during the war.[5] He visited first in late 1921, helping to conclude an agreement for the repatriation of German ships that were still seaworthy. Lohmann returned to Leningrad in May 1922 with a German delegation, to conclude an arrangement with the Soviet Admiralty.[6] During his two trips, Lohmann, who was married, became closely acquainted with Else Ektimov, a Russian woman of German descent whom he brought back with him to Germany. She soon became entangled in his professional life, as he secretly tried to support her financially.[7]

While his personal life began to grow complicated, Lohmann's career was on a meteoric rise in the postwar German Navy. His success in the negotiations with Russia led to his further promotion. In fact he was given total control over the Reichsmarine's "black funds." Following Versailles, the German Navy had illicitly amassed more than 25 million dollars' worth of hard currency through the sales of military vessels. The head of the Reichsmarine, Admiral Behnke, gave Lohmann total control over these funds to improve the Navy's capacity for a future war.[8] This meant getting around the restrictions of Versailles. The Navy assigned only an accountant to supervise Lohmann, and Lohmann was even responsible for hiring him. Essentially, he could do whatever he wanted with the small fortune.

Initially, Lohmann used his black fund to discreetly return dozens of merchant vessels impounded during the war, restoring the German merchant marine fleet as cheaply as possible.[9] Using a Berlin-based bank as a cover, he then began to buy shares in German shipyards and naval facilities, where he used the money to retain skilled personnel and construct vessels—ostensibly for civilian purposes but really for future military use. The Reichsmarine, through Lohmann's intervention, also arranged to have banned weapons stockpiled at corporate facilities outside of Germany. As noted earlier, the Netherlands was a favorite destination for large quantities of aircraft, munitions, guns, and optical equipment, which were stored at warehouses at safe industrial sites.[10] Through his growing business connections, Lohmann also purchased an aircraft manufacturing company (Casper) and a small airline (Severa) to expand the Navy's aviation wing and train new pilots. His superiors were very impressed by his early work and his discretion: unlike the Army, the Navy did not have to deal with public scandals.

The scandal-free period was soon to end as Lohmann went too far. Most of his early business ventures had clear naval applications. Sometime in 1926, with his funds depleted, Lohmann decided he would start to buy businesses he thought could turn a profit to replenish the black fund. He invested heavily in some bizarre research projects, including one that was attempting to make gasoline from potatoes, and in a company claiming that it could use ice to float sunken shipwrecks. Then he poured millions of marks into the Berlin Bacon Aktiengesellschaft, a firm that claimed to have invented a new, special bacon-curing process that it was thought would particularly appeal to British tastes, thus threatening the near-monopoly of Danish pork exports to the United Kingdom.[11] When asked later to explain this rather strange investment, Lohmann would argue that he thought the bacon transport ships might find future use as troop transports. As it turned out, Berlin Bacon had not found the secret of catering to British tongues, and his investment evaporated.

While Lohmann's bacon foray had been a mistake, it was a different project that would prove ruinous to him. For reasons that were more ideological than financial, he bought a huge number of shares in a movie studio, Phoebus Films. At the time, it was Germany's third largest film producer.[12] Unlike the case with the Berlin Bacon Company, Lohmann had some not entirely unreasonable arguments for his initial investment. He planned to have the studio produce nationalistic films that portrayed the military, and particularly the Navy, in a good light. Then he planned to establish a network of subsidiary studios throughout the world. By hiring actors and employees who could also serve as German spies, he hoped to create a vast intelligence network.[13] His first international target was the Soviet Union.

It may have been the glitz and glamour of the new film industry that swayed Lohmann the most. He made certain that his investment entailed a job for Else Ektimov, one that involved little work and a good deal of money.[14] With Lohmann's assistance, she also came into ownership of a twelve-bedroom apartment, which he also used from time to time. It was her ostentatious displays of wealth that first brought journalists sniffing around the story.

Perhaps unsurprisingly, Lohmann had failed to do his due diligence before investing in Phoebus Films, which was in financial straits at the time. Even Lohmann's injection of funds could do little to slow the company's decline. By 1927, it was bankrupt, as was Lohmann. Already beginning to attract some media attention, the story broke wide open when a disgruntled former company director told a journalist from the *Berliner Tageblatt* all about the Reichsmarine's role in the company. The Reichsmarine quickly tried to sweep the incident under the rug, forcing Lohmann into an early retirement at a slightly lower pension rate than he might otherwise have enjoyed.[15]

While Lohmann dodged major consequences for his actions, the German government could not. The Phoebus Scandal, as it became known, again rocked the Republic and forced a spate of resignations, including that of Minister of Defense Gessler, who had served in that role since 1920. He would be replaced by retired general Wilhelm Groener. As noted, Groener had arranged the partnership between the Reichswehr and the civilian government to put down the communist uprisings of early 1919. He was also on friendly terms with Stresemann. As a result, Groener was both able and willing to improve the relationship between the Foreign Ministry and Defense Ministry.[16] And unlike his predecessor, he intended to closely supervise the Reichswehr. His assumption of office would dramatically improve relations with the civilian government, and with it, bring fresh resources to bear on rearmament.

Behind Groener's calculations and caution was his understanding of the broader strategic landscape. Much more than Seeckt or Gessler, he saw politics and war as connected, in the vein of Carl von Clausewitz. Once in office, Groener laid out some of these thoughts in a report entitled "The Organization of the Entire People for War." In it, he ignored the specific operational questions that had consumed his predecessors' time. Instead, he focused on industrial mobilization, natural resources, manpower, standardization of tanks and planes for faster production, and nationwide industrial planning, all of which he saw prerequisites for German victory in the next war. This sort of broad thinking led him to seek closer accommodation with German political leaders.[17]

Among Groener's concerns was the unsupervised rearmament work being conducted by the German Army and Navy. As soon as he took over Defense, he promptly demanded an assessment of Navy activities "outside the Treaty of Versailles." Grudgingly, the Navy acquiesced. Groener soon discovered the broad network of illegal activities, both at home and abroad.[18] At home, the Navy—through shell corporations—owned an airline, several shipyards, armament, ammunition, and optical equipment factories.[19] Abroad, Groener discovered the network of naval facilities was even larger, spread across Spain, Turkey, Finland, and the Netherlands.[20] In 1922, in partnership with Germany's three largest shipbuilders—Vulkan AG, Krupp's Germaniawerft, and Weser AG—the Reichsmarine had organized the acquisition of Ingenieurskantoor voor Scheepsbouw (Engineering Office for Shipbuilding, or IvS) in The Hague.[21] Staffed by German naval officers and submarine experts, the Reichsmarine maintained technical expertise and developed new designs at the facility. It also used the IvS to acquire stakes in the Crichton-Vulkan Shipyard in Turku, Finland, and the Echevarrieta Shipyards in Cádiz, Spain.[22] By 1925, the Reichsmarine was building eight submarines in Finland and in Spain, all in violation of Versailles.[23] This network was the main reason the Reichsmarine repeatedly declined offers of partnership from the Soviet Navy: it was able to evade Versailles effectively elsewhere.[24]

The Phoebus Scandal briefly brought to light the breadth of Germany's commitment to rearm. Not only was the Army actively seeking to develop aircraft, armored vehicles, chemical weapons, and artillery, Versailles or no, but the Navy, too, had extensive rearmament programs in operation. The Phoebus revelations further highlighted the unwillingness of the British or French to do anything about Germany's rearmament programs. The scandal was widely publicized. The *New York Times* alone ran eight stories on the subject in seven weeks.[25] The German Navy had spent $7.5 million on a mixture of schemes that all but indicated illegal rearmament, yet the news created little stir in Paris or London.[26] Neither did the news a few weeks later in March 1928 that Germany would begin building new "pocket battleships"— fast, heavily armored 10,000-ton battlecruisers that were permissible (barely) under Versailles.[27]

The lack of consequences encouraged not just hardline military officers, dreaming of a war of revenge. They also seem to have convinced Germany's civilian authorities that rearmament was a safe proposition. Despite the Phoebus Scandal, Stresemann held his promised meeting with senior Reichswehr officials to reassess cooperation with the Soviets. On February 6, 1928, he and Groener approved plans for the broadening of military rearmament work in the Soviet Union.[28]

With the support of the new minister of defense and Stresemann, it was time for Moscow Central to expand the existing network of bases in the Soviet Union (see Map 2). On February 23, 1928, Lieth-Thomsen entered negotiations with Red Army officials for a new joint chemical weapons facility to replace Podosinki.[29] A few weeks later, the Russian and German negotiators visited a test site near Volsk in south-central Russia along the Volga River. It met all of the German requirements: far from big cities, with plentiful water, and large open spaces for testing purposes. With the assent of both sides, construction of a new base began there a few months later. The Soviets called the site Shikhany, but found the Germans could not pronounce the name easily. The Reichswehr instead referred to the site as "Tomka," a reference to one of the train stations near the Podosinki facility where staff had disembarked, Ukhtomskaya.[30] As the name reflected, "Tomka" was to be a new and improved version of the previous site, centered on the same testing program and including many of the same personnel.

In the spring of 1928, those selected to staff the facility met in Berlin. A number of alumni of Podosinki were in their ranks, including the senior scientist and best-known academic, Fritz Wirth. The rest of the team included an accountant, two explosives experts, a medical doctor and his assistant, a university meteorologist, a toxicologist, two chemists, three pilots, seven mechanics, one driver, one aircraft engineer, three laboratory technicians (graduate students in chemistry), and

Map 2 Major Reichswehr Facilities in the Soviet Union

two animal keepers.[31] After a planning session, this menagerie of German technical knowledge slipped out of Berlin and headed for the Soviet Union.

To head this new program, General Blomberg, now head of the Truppenamt, appointed Colonel (later Major General) Wilhelm von Trepper to head the new facility. Trepper, a Prussian artillery officer, had been the functional head of Germany's gas warfare program in his position as the head of the Artillery Inspectorate since 1925.[32] To preserve the secrecy of the program, Trepper "resigned" from the Reichswehr and was appointed commandant of Tomka effective the next day.

The German team members had a number of things in common. First, the officers involved in the work at Tomka were very young. Only two of its team members were over the age of forty. Perhaps not surprisingly, most were veterans of the First World War, a majority (among those whose military records are known) having served in artillery units. In addition, they were drawn from the far right: for instance, the camp chemist and the "Ground Research Expert" (Alexander von Grundherr) had been members of the Freikorps unit which had brutally suppressed the communist uprising in Munich in 1919.[33]

The staff would depart Germany in the spring of 1928. The journey was an arduous one. Divided into groups of no larger than six, these teams journeyed either by train to Riga or by ferry to Leningrad, and from there by train to Moscow. Upon their arrival they were greeted by Niedermayer, the representative of Moscow Central.[34] After some recuperation and sightseeing organized by Moscow Central, the groups boarded trains for distant Saratov. Twenty-four hours later, they boarded a steamer on the banks of the Volga; there were no roads to their final destination. At the small town of Volsk, they switched to trucks and continued overland. One of the Germans later noted that when they reached the last tiny peasant village, Shikhany, one of the villagers helped with directions, despite the fact that the site—located a few miles away—was supposed to be shrouded in secrecy.[35]

Like the other Reichswehr facilities in Russia, much of the base had been built in Germany: prefabricated buildings included barracks for housing and administration, medical and chemical laboratory buildings, a hut for housing test animals, and a protective tent for aircraft.[36] In addition, Russian workers built a cellar for food supplies, as well as special tunnels for the storage of chemical weapons, gas masks, and degassing equipment.[37] The extreme local temperatures—according to German reports, ranging from −49° to 113° Fahrenheit—required special accommodations, such as furnaces in every conceivable space, including the tunnels that ran under the base.[38] Throughout this process, one German observer noted that the Russian workers were "very skilled, willing to work and always cheerful."[39] They were also kept busy. While Tomka was being built, a major Soviet chemical weapons base was under construction 3 miles away.[40] Although no Germans would reside there, they were frequently invited there as guests.[41] By August 1928, there would be twenty-four wooden buildings on site at Tomka.[42] The Germans lived near the primary laboratory facilities, while separate residence barracks were built for the Russian team a few hundred yards away. Besides the work facilities, there was also an officers' club, the ubiquitous *Offizierskasino*, where membership was fifteen rubles to join and one ruble a month for "entertainment and the improvement of *kasino* facilities."[43]

Trepper organized Tomka's staff into three research teams—Aviation, Ground, and Gas Defense—each headed by a German with PhD-level credentials and staffed with several German researchers. Each German team member was in turn shadowed by two to four Soviet scientists or assistants whose educational background matched that of the German with whom he was paired. Head chemist Leopold von Sicherer, for instance, had four Soviet chemists assigned to him, each of whom, in his words, "had completed tertiary education."[44] The Soviet team members all spoke fluent German, and participated extensively in the work; Sicherer noted that "before them [the Russian academics] there were no secrets."[45] In total, there were around forty Soviet scientists and assistants living at Tomka alongside their German counterparts at any one time. In 1928, Sicherer recorded that fraternization between German and Russian staff members was strictly forbidden off-duty. But the close working and living conditions at Tomka, the isolation of the base, as well as the fact that all of the Soviet officers spoke German led to increasingly amicable relations between the two sides. As Sicherer recalled, "twice a year, the Russian commander hosted a summer garden party in a forest glade, and once in the winter a drinking party in the Russian barracks. Consultation with the Russians was consistently good, and over the years, friendly relations developed."[46]

General Blomberg visited the Soviet Union in 1928 to inspect the Soviet-German facilities there, initiating a new tradition of annual visits to the Soviet Union by the chief of the Truppenamt.[47] He toured all three facilities and was impressed, describing the newly built Tomka as "very well organized" and the staff "very effective."[48] It represented a remarkable upgrade on the Podosinki facilities. Blomberg's enthusiasm for their shared work was matched by Kliment Voroshilov, with whom he spent a great deal of time on this trip. Their discussions were marred only by Voroshilov's insistent prodding about the possibility of war with Poland. When he asked whether the Soviet Union could count on Germany in the event of a Polish attack, Blomberg remained silent and redirected the discussion to Kama and Lipetsk.[49]

As Blomberg and Voroshilov jointly toured the Soviet-German bases, Lipetsk was undergoing a major change of course. In 1928, the senior officers managing Lipetsk initiated a new policy.[50] It was becoming apparent that the flight officers of the First World War might be too old for the next war, which might be ten or more years away. By 1926, 80 of the 180 pilots retained by Seeckt had already become ineligible for active flight duty.[51] Most of the German pilots who trained between 1925 and 1928 at Lipetsk were between thirty and forty years old, and almost none were under twenty-five. While First World War veterans filled command positions and the ranks of the training schools, younger pilots would be needed to serve as the leaders in combat itself. To remedy this, Reichswehr planners initiated a new training program for a younger generation of pilots, to be nicknamed the *Jung-Märker*, or "Young Marks."[52] Many of those selected for the program were in fact so young that Sondergruppe R wrote letters to their parents providing instructions on what to pack. One memorandum instructed them to have their sons pack a box of fifty cigars to bring to Lipetsk. A note clarified that the cigars were not for the pilots, whom the command staff assumed would be too young to like cigars. Rather, they were for the senior officers; the base was experiencing a cigar shortage.[53]

To train these very young future officers, the instructors and staff at Lipetsk developed the program that would be adopted by the Luftwaffe after its restoration in 1935. Courses lasted a year. They began with six months of basic flight training at a "commercial flight school" administered by the Reichswehr in Germany. Simultaneously, students were given a series of technical and tactical training lessons taught on the ground by German veterans. Among other skills, candidates had to master the use of a radio.[54] The best graduates of this program then departed to Lipetsk in the spring. Upon arrival, they were put through a strict training schedule. Monday through Saturday, the cadets woke up early for two hours of flight time, led by First World War aces. Among the instructors were aces Carl-August von Schoenebeck and Werner Junck, both of whom would serve as generals in the Luftwaffe during the Second World War. The young pilots then had an hour of class about aircraft maintenance and an hour of technical instruction, followed by a lunch break. Their meal was followed by rotating lectures covering topics including tactics, organization, and metal aircraft, followed by a tea break. Their long day concluded with shooting and tactical lessons, with Russian-language training filling the evenings.[55]

The first order of duty was to master tactical flying. Trainees were instructed to fly at the highest altitude their aircraft could reach that did not require an oxygen tank for the pilot.[56] They were also required to practice "blind flying," in which they were guided by instruments alone, essential practice for flying at night.[57] Because of the declining quality of the aircraft, there were a large number of accidents among the young pilots, particularly during "blind flying" exercises. Weapons testing accompanied these flying lessons. Instructors were told to use "frequent repetition" to get the rookie pilots to produce "a flawless shot pattern."[58] These firing lessons usually took place on the ground against stationary targets to avoid mishaps.

Once their young pilots' individual skills had been honed, instructors then began to teach them to work together. This involved first flying alone, then in a *Kette* (chain) of three aircraft, then in a *Staffelverband*, a flight of nine aircraft flying in formation. In the *Kette* exercises, instructors simulated foreign fighter formations—particularly those developed by the French—to add an element of realism to the air exercises. The culminating lessons of "*Jagdsaison*" (hunting season), as the fighter pilot instructors termed it, involved dogfighting simulations of two *Staffelverbände* engaging each other. After the flights were over, the pilots held discussions about them with combat veterans, who recounted lessons from their own experiences. As the future commandant of Lipetsk Max Mohr recalled, these follow-up seminars "fostered tactical understanding."[59] Tellingly, these tended to center on discussions about French and Polish air power.[60] The aim was to understand the enemy in order to beat them in the next war in the sky.

Those who completed the rigorous Lipetsk course—and survived, as there were many training accidents—returned to Germany to be commissioned into the Reichswehr.[61] The program proved highly successful: thirteen Second World War German aces can be identified with certainty as having been *Jung-Märker* from Lipetsk's fighter pilot training school.[62] But air power alone was not enough to fulfill Seeckt's vision of a modern army.

CHAPTER 17

The Tanks Arrive

While Lipetsk began to prove effective at training pilots and the chemical facility at Tomka approached completion, at Kama, the small Reichswehr engineering team already in place had spent the summer and early fall of 1928 working on their own experiments. They had modified a pair of Hanomag tractors the previous season. This time around, the engineers would work with a higher-powered (50 horsepower) tractor, mounting a 75 mm gun on it that could, in theory, be used against other armored vehicles.[1] That caliber would eventually become the standard for later medium tank designs like the Panzer IV.[2] Their work at Kama was preliminary, though, waiting on the arrival of actual armored vehicles.

In 1926, Captain Hans Pirner, head of the Waffenamt Prüfwesen 6: Panzer- und Motorisierungsabteilung (the Waffenamt's Weapons Testing Bureau Section 6 for Tank and Motor Vehicles—hereafter Wa.Prüf 6), had commissioned two separate tank design projects.[3] One would be a light tank (under 10 tons), the other a "heavy" tank (less than 20 tons). The Waffenamt gave priority to the heavier design, contracting with three of Germany's largest industrial firms—Krupp, Rheinmetall, and Daimler—to build the prototype.[4] The companies were ordered to use the designation of *Grosstraktor* (heavy tractor) in all communications and financial reports. This was to hide their real purpose, which was clearly illegal under Versailles. It was to be faster and more heavily armed than any previous German tank, weighing sixteen tons, reaching a top speed of over 25 miles per hour, and mounting a powerful 75 mm cannon.[5]

Participating in the Krupp project was a young engineer named Erich Woelfert. Prior to the First World War, Woelfert had graduated with an engineer's degree from one of Germany's elite schools, the Technische Hochschule in Charlottenburg, and immediately gotten a job as a car designer.[6] During the war, he had worked on military engineering projects, including a cutting-edge aircraft engine and one of Germany's first tanks. After the war, he had been hired by Krupp AG's design office for motorcar engineering in Essen.[7] He was reassigned to the *Grosstraktor* prototype project along with four other engineers in 1926.

To Woelfert, it must have been clear from the moment he saw the specifications for the new tank that it would violate Germany's treaty obligations. Woelfert's superior swore all five men on the Krupp engineering team to secrecy before they began working on the prototype.[8] One coworker noted that "when we started working on building tanks in 1926, we didn't speak about the Treaty of Versailles."[9] At first, the team worked on preliminary designs in Krupp's car manufacturing facility, before moving their offices and construction work to the largely empty "Verwaltungsgebäude III" (Administrative Building III), where they could work more openly.[10] The Reichswehr had given them two years to attempt to build the world's most advanced tank.

By March 1927, the engineering team working on the *Grosstraktor* had advanced far enough to produce a wooden model, which was inspected and approved by the Waffenamt.[11] Over the summer of 1927, preliminary production began. By August 1928, Krupp workers assembled the chassis and installed a powerful BMW airplane engine in the vehicle.[12] They completed a second prototype shortly thereafter. With the Krupp *Grosstraktor* prototypes mostly complete, engineers could turn their attention to the Reichswehr's other requested design, the light tank.

In the spring of 1928, Pirner drew up specifications for the second set of prototypes he wanted to test at Kama. Codenamed the *Leichttraktor* (light tractor), the model was to weigh between eight and nine tons, mount a 37 mm cannon, and have a rotating turret.[13] Daimler's team, led by a young engineer named Ferdinand Porsche, had encountered considerable difficulties in completing a working *Grosstraktor* model, so only Rheinmetall and Krupp would receive contracts for new prototypes.[14] Pirner traveled to Essen personally to brief the Krupp team on the specifications for the new prototype in May, indicating that the Reichswehr hoped to test the new vehicle at Kama in 1930.[15] The head of the Krupp team must have noted great potential in the young Woelfert to bring him to the meeting, as he soon thereafter promoted Woelfert ahead of several older Krupp engineers to head up the *Leichttraktor* program. From this meeting onward, Woelfert was the heir apparent to Krupp's tank development program.[16]

Woelfert rapidly put together a preliminary wooden model of the *Leichttraktor*, loosely based on a prototype design from the end of the First World War. Pirner reviewed the designs during the summer of 1928, assisting Woelfert in selecting an engine before approving construction. By October 1928, two prototypes had entered production, designed with several new technical elements (including an upgraded tracked suspension and new rubber track, as well as a new and much superior air filter), all based upon early lessons learned at Kama.[17]

The Reichswehr wanted to test the prototypes at Kama. Up until 1928, the major technological components shipped to the various secret Reichswehr–Red Army facilities in the Soviet Union had been relatively small—airplane engines, disassembled component parts, and laboratory equipment for chemical weapons testing. Besides Krupp's two prototypes, Rheinmetall and Daimler had their own models. Transporting six 16-ton tanks over 1,200 miles—secretly, no less—was a new challenge entirely. The Reichswehr decided to double down on their tractor euphemism to camouflage the vehicles. To that end, in September 1928, Krupp was ordered to make external modifications to their *Grosstraktoren* to make them appear like commercial vehicles.[18] Included in the shipment, just in case, were a number of tractor "plows" to lend the cover story credibility.[19] Of course, these "tractors" were being shipped with turrets mounting 75 mm cannons, which might have given everything away. Although preparations were complete for shipment, the modified tractors remained in Germany, waiting for the spring thaw.

Tank prototypes were not the only item missing from Kama. As of yet, there were no students, either. On New Year's Day, Reichswehr Lieutenant Hans Joachim von Köppen[20] was informed via letter that he was being discharged from the Reichswehr with the rank of captain due to lack of "mental capacity."[21] A model officer and future commander of one of the Wehrmacht's armored warfare training bases during the Second World War, Köppen was entirely unfazed by this strange pronouncement. Ten days later, a "civilian" Köppen received new orders. An identification card arrived, accompanied by orders to head to the barracks of the Wachregiment in Berlin.[22] He was to obey his instructions to the letter. Köppen arrived later that day, only to discover a number of businessmen and engineers standing "hat in hand," as he remembered it, in the barracks to which he had been assigned.[23] Several other "dismissed" military officers also joined them, as well as two Russian officers.[24]

This motley group was soon met by a man in civilian clothing who introduced himself as Herr Hacher.[25] As the men would later learn, Hacher was the pseudonym of Reichswehr Major Josef Harpe, the director of a secret Soviet-German armored warfare school and testing grounds located inside the Soviet Union. Harpe, future commander of the Fifth Panzer Army during the Second World War, also managed the preparatory program for all Germans being sent to Kama each winter.[26] For the next four months, the civilians and former officers took courses on their respective technical subjects to prepare them for their time in Russia.[27] In addition, they studied the basics of the Russian language.[28]

Beginning in June, Köppen and the other students left the Wachregiment's Moabit Barracks and made their way to Bahnhof Zoo Station.[29] Each officer received passports from the German Foreign Ministry with false identities. They were instructed to dress as tourists. By the time the tank facility at Kama became operational, the Reichswehr had learned lessons regarding secrecy. German officers destined for Russia had always been easy to spot. Large groups of them, dressed in similar clothes, had arrived at the train station with identical, numbered suitcases. Former officers found it difficult to hide their military bearing; in more than one group photo they all instinctively lined up by height, as they would have on a parade ground.[30] Some lessons were hard to unteach.[31]

To prevent the Allies from growing suspicious, Köppen and his acquaintances were dispatched over the course of several weeks in groups of three or four. Unfortunately, the most direct rail line from East Prussia to Moscow passed through Klaipeda, a strip of German territory that had passed to French administration under the terms of Versailles. Should they have to pass through the customs post there "all of our secrets soon would have been known," as one officer noted.[32] Instead, each group was given directions to go a different route. Some went by boat to Leningrad, while the rest took a variety of train routes through the Baltic states.[33] The most common route was the "Nord Express Paris-Riga" train from Germany to the city of Daugavpils, where specially assigned Soviet customs personnel on the border awaited their arrival. After their meandering journeys, Köppen and the others arrived in Moscow, where they were met by German military representatives.

The fatigued travelers were brought by their compatriots to the German house on Khlebnyi Pereulok, a Tsarist-era stone building in northeastern Moscow. It stood a short distance from the famed Revolutionary Theater, which was run by the Russian-German actor Vsevolod Meyerhold, later executed by the NKVD for being a spy. Some of them might also have noticed that just down the street, at Khlebnyi Pereulok 19, was the British Mission in Moscow.[34] Upon arriving, Lieutenant Colonel Niedermayer and his wife offered their guests hot tea. Niedermayer then briefed each man on their remaining travel arrangements, explaining the currency exchange process and mail service with Germany.[35] He also told them that they would have a few days to explore the city before they left.[36] Niedermayer helped German officers get tickets to the Bolshoi Theater, visit the Kremlin Museums (which had reopened to the public), and take guided tours of the city.[37]

The Soviet secret police (later the NKVD, then referred to as the OGPU) assisted Moscow Central in these efforts; for instance, they organized a regular weekly "express" from Moscow to Lipetsk.[38] That was not Köppen's destination, however. After a few days of playing tourist, he and his peers boarded a sleeper train headed toward Murom, and from there along the Volga River to Kazan.[39] A German-made Benz car was waiting to pick them up from the station, driven by a man who introduced himself as "Comrade Ivan." Through the cobblestone streets of Kazan, the car rumbled southward to the highly restricted Kargopol barracks, about 5 miles south of the train station.[40] In 1929, it remained mostly empty, under construction, and without its raison d'être—the armored vehicle prototypes. Nevertheless, the students and staff began arriving in early 1929, and by March, there were forty-five Germans at Kama, including nine women, mostly the wives of senior German officers. Their presence was greatly appreciated by the Soviets; one Soviet intelligence report complained that Germans were trying to fraternize with Russian women and that partly due to the arrival of the wives, "such communications ceased."[41]

The German team was dwarfed in numbers by their Soviet counterparts. During the first full training course beginning in 1929, the Soviets had a total of 131 staff and 10 students at Kama.[42] A civilian academic mentioned in correspondence and known only as "Nikolai Fedorovich" handled the daily needs of the Russian students. The Soviets also had a party secretary present whose primary responsibility was to prevent too much contact between local Russians and the Germans. With such political preparations complete, the first full complement of 10 German and 10 Russian students commenced armored warfare coursework in March 1929.[43]

The German cadets' first assignment was to return to their Russian-language studies, suspended during the long trip to Kama. To that end, there were two instructors on the German staff.[44] In addition, per a Soviet requirement in the original agreement, a university professor from Kazan gave the Germans a series of talks that centered on the successes of Stalin's Five-Year Plan.[45] After completing these introductory courses the other cadets began their armored warfare studies.

Lessons were divided between theory and practical training. On the theoretical side, students took three courses: tactics, radio technology, and tank mechanics.[46] Given the lack of expertise in all three areas (because of Versailles, of course), most of the instructors would eventually be former students who had already spent a year or two at Kama and, as one officer recalled, "having mastered one area of knowledge or another, were then classified as a teacher."[47] The tank mechanics course, first taught by Captain Hans Pirner, focused on memorizing the varieties of tanks, the models of engines, and ammunition types.[48] Pirner and his successors also lectured on the form and function of tank components.[49] An engineer from Krupp named Johann Hoffmann taught the tank mechanics courses at Kama, dressed in a Soviet officer's uniform.[50] In testimony later presented at the Nuremberg War Crimes Tribunals, Hoffmann remembered how he had to improvise in his teaching. In the "workshop lesson" he used what he had at hand as models, which were car parts and "engines that were cut-open and rear axle gears, which I then explained and discussed with the students."[51] This sort of hands-on experience was brand-new for the German cadets, as was training in the use of radio. The emphasis on radio technology was unusual for 1929, and highlighted German interest in command-and-control technologies, which would play a major role in the orientation of Kama's technical testing program.

Tactics classes were first taught by future general Friedrich Kühn. Kühn would become famous as one of Germany's leading tank commanders during the Second World War, winning medals for valor during the Battle of France, Operation Barbarossa, and the Second Battle of Kharkov. In 1943, he would be promoted to manage the Wehrmacht's tank and motor vehicle programs in Berlin, only to be killed in an Allied bombing raid.[52] At Kama, his lessons centered on lectures and seminars about the tactics of tank platoons and companies. These were supplemented by exercises on sand tables—literally, tables covered in sand that were used for simulations and wargaming. Like many German instructors, Kühn believed in the importance of mentally placing officers in the position of a tank commander through such exercises. Subjects included "infantry-tank coordination," "leading tanks in attack against fortifications," "antitank defenses," and the different roles of infantry support and long-range tank groups.[53] Required reading included leading German tank theorist Ernst Volckheim's work, as well as French and British field manuals and reports.[54]

Like Lipetsk, Kama's courses emphasized initiative, independence, and quick thinking from its students. One of those enrolled was Klaus Müller, future commander of the Sixtieth Panzer Detachment and recipient of Knight's Cross during World War II. In one course, remembered Müller, officers would be handed a card with a tactical situation and directed to a corner of the room. The officer then had five to six minutes to "assess the situation, make a decision and write orders" to address it.[55] There were numerous other simulations, either in the field, on a map, or on a sand table in the tank tactics classes.

For the first three years of operation at Kama, German and Russian students took these classes together. Neither side wore insignias or rank, both to maintain anonymity and also to foster an atmosphere conducive to open dialogue and learning.[56]

Müller described the mood of the courses as remarkably "free from restrictive bureaucracy, which meant the possibility of achieving real success in the most serious work."[57] The groups of students also ate lunch together in a shared mess hall at least once a week, a policy aimed at promoting camaraderie between the two militaries.

At first, the Russian students at Kama were hopelessly unprepared for the German style of training. A Red Army regimental tank commander named Yeroshchenko, who attended the courses at Kama as chief Red Army liaison, wrote to Tukhachevsky that the "weak tactical training of the majority of our students forces us to organize last-minute coaching sessions aimed at improving the most basic tactical skills: writing orders, reports, drawing diagrams, etc."[58] German instructors helped them develop them. Yeroshchenko thought that it distracted from the more important goal of gaining experience related to the tactics of tanks.[59] Nonetheless, he argued this was a necessary process, as Red Army officers were finally developing "solid skills and knowledge of tactical work" thanks to both the classroom environment and intensive self-study.[60]

The Soviets themselves were in the midst of a dramatic revamping of strategic thinking, in part as a result of interaction with the Reichswehr.[61] The major movers in this transformation were Mikhail Tukhachevsky and Vladimir Triandafillov, both of whom had studied in Germany. In many respects, Tukhachevsky and his fellow officers were futurists. Like their contemporaries in art, they rejected drawing too many lessons from the past, and embraced new technologies.[62] In 1929, Tukhachevsky completed a three-year project with several other officers exploring "the character of future war," which would play a major role in reshaping Red Army thinking.[63] Their conclusion was that the next war would feature enormous fleets of tanks and aircraft fighting fast, decisive engagements.[64] Technology was everything.[65] The problem with fighting a mechanized war such as this was that the Red Army lagged far behind its likely adversaries, both in theory and in technology.

In a series of reports to the RVS in 1929, Triandafillov laid out his own concept for a Soviet armored force.[66] He foresaw three primary types of vehicles, each with different missions: light tanks of three to seven tons for reconnaissance and exploiting breakthroughs in the enemy line; a medium tank weighing 16 tons that could destroy fortified positions; and a heavy tank of 60 to 80 tons capable of "breaking through powerfully reinforced lines."[67]

The increasing speed of tanks led Triandafillov to an inevitable conclusion: that they would move faster than ground troops and therefore should be independent of them, forming "separate mechanized formations" to take full advantage of their potential.[68] Triandafillov's conceptualization of the tank would become the basis for Soviet tank doctrine for nearly the next decade.[69] It fit into the broader ideas of mechanized, mobile warfare being developed by Mikhail Tukhachevsky. The "three echelon" approach offered the possibility of striking in depth, taking advantage of the different technical attributes of each class of tank.[70] Yeroshchenko, while stationed at Kama, noted that there was much that was similar on this aspect of German and Soviet doctrine, reporting that "our views on the three-tank echelon system in attack . . . they fully share."[71] Doubtless, conversations at Kama and during maneuvers had contributed to that shared perspective.

In general, however, the Soviets stationed at Kama were surprised by the lack of German armored theory. Yeroshchenko wrote of German instruction that "every lesson came across full of ambiguities, contradictions and reticence."[72] The Germans eschewed doctrine to a degree that surprised their Soviet counterparts, who partially credited this to a lack of experience with armored vehicles. This was most clearly revealed by their reactions to German teaching methods in Kama's classrooms, which reflected the theoretical disparities between the two forces. Reports on British maneuvers employing armored vehicles convinced Seeckt that tank technology was rapidly advancing, especially in terms of vehicle speed and reliability. Based on these changes, he had written shortly before his resignation that advances in tank technology meant armored vehicles should attack independently, with the infantry following them.[73] But beyond that, the Reichswehr waited for experience with the vehicles themselves to solve thorny questions of doctrine. A Soviet representative at Kama noted that the Germans criticized Soviet armor doctrine as "quite modern, but too schematic and . . . prescriptive."[74] Given that the Germans handled the teaching at Kama, the courses generally reflected the German way of thinking, deemphasizing theory and emphasizing initiative. Instead, class time centered on debate, discussion, and simulation. Yeroshchenko commented, again with some surprise in his report to Tukhachevsky, that "the lectures which took place were generally insignificant—only a final analysis."[75] This came at a time when the Red Army had moved in the other direction, emphasizing doctrine and hierarchy more than ever before. By 1929, the seminar format had been entirely eliminated from core courses in favor of lectures at the Frunze Military Academy, the Red Army's most prestigious training institution.[76]

The criticisms both sides drew from these early encounters emphasized fundamental differences between the German and Soviet militaries. Specifically, it reflected disparities in their officer corps. The German officer corps was tiny (4,000 men), made up of long-serving professionals as required by Versailles, and, as a result, extremely well educated. By contrast, the Soviet officer corps was enormous and often drawn from first-generation literates. For the former, instilling confidence and technical know-how were critical goals. Doctrine was less essential; initiative – long a part of German military tradition – was much more important. In a large, less-technically proficient army like the Red Army of the 1920s, however, the situation was very different. The Red Army's leadership considered prescriptive doctrine essential in an army where training was, by necessity, limited. There was a cost to such a route: an inflexibility that would affect millions of Red Army soldiers in the first half of the Second World War.

While theoretical training could take place in the classrooms at Kama, for the Reichswehr, the real purpose of the facility was to provide hands-on experience in tank combat for officers and test new prototypes. After a brief test of the *Grosstraktoren* within one of the Krupp buildings to make sure they would run, Pirner arrived to supervise the transfer of the tanks onto rail cars alongside the tractor plows.[77] He accompanied them to Kama, arriving in May 1929.[78] The Reichswehr also purchased armored car, experimental armored personnel carrier, and scout vehicle prototypes from German firms Daimler-Benz, C. D. Magirus, and Büssing, which soon began to arrive.[79] A single model of German-Swedish consortium Merker's "convertible tank," with both tank treads and road wheels, was also under contract but would not arrive until the following year.[80] This plethora of German designs were joined by a number of Russian vehicles, mostly purchased from abroad. These included a British Carden-Loyd tankette (the size of a car, weighing just 1.5 tons), and two medium (12 ton) British Vickers tanks.[81] Both Germans and Soviets saw the British as world leaders in tank design and doctrine at this juncture; they had organized the first armored brigade employing a variety of cutting-edge prototypes in 1926.[82]

The arrival of these vehicles enabled the first formal tank instruction.[83] Practical lessons centered on driving, shooting, and unit maneuvers. Two instructors offered shooting lessons for machine guns and tank cannons out on the *polygon*. The Russian students proved enthusiastic about adding an element of realism to their training exercises—they dressed up the shooting range dummies in Polish and Czech uniforms.[84] There were mishaps. Müller remembered how "very embarrassing" it was when a first-year Russian cadet tried to load a Soeda machine gun and stepped on the trigger, sending bullets flying and wounding two factory workers in Kazan.[85] The German officers were unsympathetic to the injured locals. One of the radio instructors remarked that "when [the guns] start popping, everyone should get out of the way; they know it's a shooting range."[86]

Most of the cadets' hands-on training focused on learning to operate a tank. As most of the vehicles required five or six men, mastering these machines took weeks of practice. Each student had to learn the various roles in the *Grosstraktor*: driver, commander, radio operator, and gunner.[87] The cadets took turns commanding the vehicles, and then together led small formations of the armored vehicles. Instructors gave the cadets an examination at the end of the summer that included maneuvering a tank at night, overcoming various earthen obstacles, and driving through water barriers.[88]

Technical work also accelerated with the arrival of the vehicles. Daimler had designed its own engine for the tank and generally avoided collaborating with the other two firms. They had placed their prototype design in the hands of Ferdinand Porsche, who was already well known.[89] But Porsche's prototype faced a series of problems in 1929, including mobility. Daimler engineers on site decided that the de-sign flaw in the Daimler *Grosstraktoren* could not be resolved.[90] Ironically, Porsche's initial failure at Kama would lead, eventually, to his great success as the founder of the Porsche Corporation. The poor performance results of his *Grosstraktor* led to his departure from Daimler; not long after, he founded his own consulting firm working on automobile designs.[91]

At the end of the testing season that year, General Kurt von Hammerstein-Equord—about to replace Blomberg as head of the Truppenamt—visited the three shared facilities in the USSR. On September 5, 1929, he sat down with Voroshilov to discuss the state of cooperation. Hammerstein told Voroshilov that his general im-pression of the shared facilities was satisfactory, and that he hoped to increase the scope and scale of training at each of the facilities. Voroshilov took a sharper tone, pressing his German counterpart on the question of technology. Where were all of the cutting-edge German technological prototypes? The Soviets were unimpressed by the German tank and plane prototypes they had seen at the joint facilities. He told General Hammerstein that "the question of new weapons and testing, especially chemical weapons, is of the paramount importance." To hammer home his point, he added, ominously, that "no one knows when the next war could break out."[92] The question of that next war—possibly a new Russian civil war—would be on the minds of many in Moscow as political events took a dramatic turn.

CHAPTER 18

Winter of Crisis

As the tanks reached Kama in the spring of 1929, Stalin was busy cementing his hold on power. He had defeated the five other men mentioned by Lenin in his 1923 Testament. He had stripped fellow old Bolsheviks Georgii Pyatakov, Grigory Zinoviev, and Lev Kamenev of their Party membership. He had expelled Leon Trotsky from the Soviet Union in February. Finally, he removed Nikolai Bukharin from his management roles in April, to be followed shortly thereafter by his dismissal from the Politburo.[1]

Stalin was now firmly in charge. He soon set about a radical program of force-paced industrialization. In April, the Politburo re-ratified the first Five Year Plan, which aimed to increase Soviet GDP by 20 percent per year as part of a vast program of industrialization, mechanization, and modernization.[2] That summer, under Stalin's direction, the Politburo voted through two secret decrees related to the military aspects of the Five-Year Plan. The first stated that all of the USSR's neighbors to the West should be considered "likely enemies." The second called for reorganization of the Soviet Union's industrial capacities, particularly highlighting the danger of "wrecking"—sabotage—by Tsarist-era specialists of dubious political reliability.[3]

Immediately after the Politburo decision, Commissar for Military and Naval Affairs Voroshilov held two days of meetings with the RVS to discuss the reorganization of the Red Army's procurement and technological departments. At that time, most of the personnel in the Army's supply directorate were involved with printing publications and propaganda, not armaments or logistics.[4] The latter two services were woefully understaffed. Addressing the problem, August Kork, head of the Supply Directorate, suggested that his own experience in Germany had convinced him of the value of the Reichswehr's organizational structure. He wrote to Voroshilov that "The German army in the thoughtfulness and expediency of its organization, unarguably, can be considered a model."[5] Within a year, the Red Army would follow the German model, spinning off everything not directly related to technological rearmament into separate parts of the army. The new Armaments Directorate itself would be reorganized to have three subdirectories focusing on communications technology, chemical warfare, and artillery.

Accompanying these organizational changes came a greater urgency to speed up the Red Army's modernization, and related military industry. To that end, even as Soviet intelligence rounded up officers in the Red Army's artillery directorate for allegedly committing sabotage, Soviet representatives reached out to the major German firms to develop fresh expertise.[6] On June 17, the Soviet government agreed to terms with Krupp for the provision of technical assistance and machine tools to some of the Soviet Union's largest factories, including the Barrikad Artillery Works in Stalingrad, Nizhny Novgorod's Krasnoe Sormovo (the first tank factory in the USSR), and the Elektrostal metallurgical complex outside of Moscow.[7] In particular, their assistance was sought to improve steel casting and artillery production. Rheinmetall reached a similar agreement focused on artillery production.[8]

This scaling up of Soviet military industry was heartily endorsed by the cohort of young Soviet futurists, including Mikhail Tukhachevsky. He had written repeatedly that changing technology was the single most important element in the formulation of new military doctrine. He coined a term to describe the vast technological changes from 1914 onwards: *avia-mekhanizatsiya* (airmechanization). The most important changes, he wrote, were those taking place simultaneously in "aviation, tank forces, radio communication and chemical warfare."[9] He argued that most of these drew directly from progress in civilian economic sectors, meaning that increases in economic production would directly translate into military capability. As a result, the country with the largest and most adaptable industries in relevant areas—particularly chemicals, tractors, automobiles, and aviation—would prevail in future conflict.[10]

Tukhachevsky's arguments and those of his protégé Vladimir Triandafillov for large-scale military production and high technology—mere fantasies when the military's budget barely covered the cost of uniforms and rifles—suddenly suited the political climate. Inspired by the deterioration of security in Europe and East Asia, the First Five-Year Plan launched the Red Army on a program of modernization. On July 15, 1929, Stalin and the Central Committee agreed to eliminate supply shortages in the Red Army.[11] They specifically formulated that the army needed to maintain "superiority in two of three key technologies: aircraft, artillery, and tanks."[12] Given that Stalin had identified all of the Soviet Union's European neighbors as potential enemies, this meant enormous military production. The Politburo decisions formulated that by 1933, the Red Army should have a mobilized strength (i.e., active plus reserve) of 3 million men, 3,500 aircraft, up to 5,500 tanks, and more than 12,800 pieces of artillery, making it by far the largest military in the world.[13] To achieve that end, the share of Soviet industrial employment consumed by military production went from 3 to 9 percent between 1928 and 1932.[14] That number would rise even more sharply after 1932.[15]

While Stalin pushed the pace of industrialization in the Soviet Union, the capitalist world faced disaster. On October 24, 1929, the American stock market began to collapse. The German economy was heavily dependent on continuing American loans. It was also an export-driven economy, and thus particularly vulnerable to fluctuations in trade. These two factors made Germany one of the worst-hit by the economic disaster that unfolded in October 1929. With an able statesman at the helm, perhaps the Weimar Republic could have navigated the storm. But three weeks before the American markets began to plummet, the one man of that stature—Gustav Stresemann—died. He was only fifty-one years old. The cause was a stroke brought on by months of overwork.[16]

After the American crash, unemployment in Germany skyrocketed from around 5 percent to more than 15 percent in less than twelve months.[17] Five million people would lose their jobs in the next three years.[18] Middle-class families—still recovering from the war and the inflationary crisis—watched their savings once again disappear in a spate of bank collapses.[19] This economic catastrophe accelerated the radicalization of German politics. One sign of the times was a sudden increase in the number of militarist films and books; nostalgia for the last war grew as people idealized the supposed unity of the nation, the leveling of social difference, and the clear sense of place and purpose that it had entailed.[20] The force of this angry wave soon began to drown out moderate voices in German politics and empower the radical wings of the political spectrum.

The developing crisis impacted the Reichswehr in myriad ways. After the rapprochement between Stresemann and the Reichswehr in 1927, civil-military relations, particularly with the Foreign Ministry, had warmed considerably. The Reichswehr had even started inviting diplomats to participate in active roles in their strategic-level war games.[21] However, as the leadership of the Reichswehr became friendlier to the Republic, the Reichswehr's rank and file grew increasingly political in other ways. Seeckt had banned officers adopting political affiliations as part of what he called an "army above politics." That policy unraveled as soldiers radicalized. In a sign of their growing concern, the Reichswehr's Truppenamt began offering "bounties" to soldiers who turned in other soldiers spreading communist propaganda.[22]

While it was easy to target communists, the real danger was from the right. After his failed coup in 1923, Hitler had pursued primarily legal means to power—the ballot box. As the Great Depression hit, Nazism's hostility to both communism and capitalism made it increasingly popular. This became clear to Reichswehr leadership for the first time in March 1930, when Groener put two lieutenants on trial, accused of membership in the Nazi Party and spreading Nazi propaganda in violation of Seeckt's apolitical rules. It was immediately clear that the vast majority of the army favored the Nazi officers' immediate acquittal—including Seeckt himself, who was beginning a political career in the Reichstag.[23] Hitler himself testified as a witness at the trial, securing their acquittal.[24]

Kurt von Schleicher, Minister of Defense Groener's political adviser, received a series of letters highlighting the dangerous growth of radical sentiments. One veteran wrote to him that "younger officers who had still greater ideals than the mere struggle for existence . . . are not pro-Nazi because of the Nazi programme, but because they believe they discover there a force which fights the decline of the Reich, which does what they perhaps expect from the Reichswehr."[25] Another wrote that the rising generation of junior officers was "a fanatical defender of Nazi sentiments with whom it is hardly possible to argue."[26] A third officer estimated that 90 percent of the officer corps favored the National Socialists.[27] The Reichswehr's leadership was losing the battle for the officer corps.

While internal division grew, Schleicher used his influence to marginalize rivals within the Reichswehr.[28] In early 1929, he had convinced Groener to create a new office—the Ministeramt (Ministerial Office)—which soon became an all-powerful political office within the Ministry of Defense. Not coincidentally, Schleicher became its first head. He and his allies used their growing clout to isolate the Heye, chief of the army command, and then get General Blomberg, head of the Truppenamt, demoted. Schleicher maneuvered to have a friend of his appointed as Blomberg's replacement.[29] Schleicher, who had long favored cooperation with the USSR, also took advantage of the new post to press forward with the Soviets.

While the Soviet Union seemed immune to the economic buffeting that descended on Europe and the United States in the fall of 1929, it faced its own internal crisis. Famine loomed as Soviet agricultural policies triggered grain shortages; peasants refused to sell their produce at artificially low state prices.[30] Stalin needed to export grain for foreign capital to buy machine tools to build the factories envisioned by the First Five-Year Plan. On November 7, Stalin wrote an article in the Communist Party's official newspaper, *Pravda* (Truth). He stated that Soviet peasants were now flocking to the collective farms the Party had established throughout rural areas.[31] These were state-owned farms where land, machinery, and livestock were to be held in common. In fact, they were extraordinarily unpopular among farmers. In his article, Stalin called for all Soviet citizens to press the "determined offensive of socialism against the capitalist elements in town and country."[32] This marked the beginning of one of the most significant and tragic periods in Soviet history.[33]

Stalin ordered Soviet officials to collectivize nearly all of the Soviet countryside under the guise of the "Ural-Siberian" method—essentially confiscation—during the 1929 harvests. Communist authorities set fixed quotas for grain deliveries, to be made in exchange for promised industrial goods. Peasants identified as "middle" and "lower" elements were to be forced onto collective farms. "Kulaks"—supposedly rich peasants who might own an extra cow or hire help during the harvest—were to be arrested, exiled, or killed. At least 1.8 million people were deported from their homes in 1930 and 1931, many of them facing extreme privation or death.[34]

The peasant response was natural. Manifestos and calls to arms soon circulated. One in a Siberian peasant village announced that the "hunted and oppressed people will form a mighty partisan green army which will sweep its oppressors from the face of the earth."[35]

Taking up the cry, revolts broke out across the country as villages resisted the seizure of their grain stocks without payment and the deportation or arrest of their members. Many slaughtered their livestock rather than let them be seized by the state. The Soviets recorded 13,753 "mass disturbances" in 1930, including 1,100 murders related to the enforcement of collectivization.[36] The whole country teetered on the edge of civil war.

In March 1930, Stalin wrote a new article entitled "Dizzy with Success." He claimed that the Politburo's policies had been abused by comrades who had "gone too far."[37] This marked a temporary halt in the collectivization campaign. He could be satisfied with the significant increase in grain collection. The Soviet Union would export 3 million metric tons of grain in 1930, with the profits going to purchase industrial equipment, particularly from Germany and the United States.[38] Unfortunately, that surplus had come at great cost. To meet quotas, farmers in many parts of the Soviet Union (particularly Ukraine) had been forced to give up their seed grain. That meant a much smaller harvest the following year. The result, predictably, would be the same sort of horrific man-made famine that Lenin's policies and the civil war had unleashed in the early 1920s.

The Red Army played a central role throughout the process. The Communist Party had sought to build a reliably communist army since the civil war.[39] Simultaneously, it aimed to use the army as an instrument to educate the general population to support regime policies. During the collectivization crisis, the Red Army was used to quell violence, force collectivization, and collect the harvest. But as it did so, it became an increasingly unreliable instrument; large numbers of conscripts expressed hostility over government policies as their families suffered enormously.[40] Nearly 10,000 soldiers were dismissed in 1929–1930 alone for opposing the collectivization line, or being related to a kulak who did.[41] Stalin's embrace of rearmament was first and foremost aimed at strengthening the country's military weaknesses.[42] But it also reflected a long-standing aim of the Communist Party leadership: professionalizing, modernizing, and generally rendering the military more politically reliable, particularly important as revolts broke out across the country.

As excess grain was sold overseas, Stalin sped up the pace of construction in Soviet military industry. In 1930, the Politburo committed itself to a massive technological rearmament program that would increase the size and mechanization of the Red Army.[43] Once again, Germany became the lead partner in helping the Soviet Union achieve those goals. That year, the Soviet Union signed 124 technological aid contracts with Germany companies.[44] Ten of the Soviet Union's eighteen tank factories would be modernized by German engineers or relied on imported German industrial plant.[45] Four classes of Soviet submarines—the Dekabrist, Pravda, Leninets, and Stalinets—would be equipped with German diesel engines, manufactured in Germany or under concessionary agreement.[46] BMW and Daimler signed license agreements with the Soviet state whereby they would build aircraft engines in Russian factories.[47] An entire generation of Soviet aircraft would be equipped with BMW engines as a result.

In January 1930, RVS representative Innokenty Khalepsky arrived in Berlin to conduct negotiations with major German firms Rheinmetall, Krupp, Mafai, Daimler-Benz, and Linke-Hoffman for technical or license agreements regarding tanks, artillery, armored cars, aircraft, and rifles, as well as the temporary hiring of German engineers and the training of Soviet engineers in German plants.[48] At the same time, with the assistance of the Reichswehr and Moscow Central in Moscow, the RVS concluded contracts with M.A.N., Humboldt, Demag, Krups, Ehrhardt, Zemer, and Bütast for artillery pieces, anti-aircraft equipment, machine guns, tank armaments, and machinery for military industry.[49] Another Soviet agent in Germany reached agreements with Heinkel and BMW in the same year.[50] In total, the Soviet government outlaid more than 100 million rubles on technological assistance from the Germans in 1930. By contrast, the entire Soviet military budget for 1929–1930 was 1.05 billion rubles.[51] The results, coupled with vast capital investment, would become apparent almost immediately: over the next twelve months, Soviet military production would increase 78 percent on the previous year.[52] This dramatic increase in Soviet military industry was just the beginning of the broader militarization of the Soviet economy: from 1929 to 1939, Soviet military spending would grow from 3.4 percent of the national budget to nearly 33 percent.[53] Reichswehr help in acquiring German machine tools and hiring engineers was an essential part of that process.

CHAPTER 19

Machines of the Future

As the Soviet state starved its people to build weapons factories, the newest German tank prototype was on its way to Kama for testing. In February and May 1930, Krupp dispatched its first and second new prototypes—a pair of *Leichttractoren* (Light Tractors)—to Kama. Following not long after was its lead designer, Erich Woelfert.[1] After four years of working on tank designs, Woelfert would finally get a chance to see one of his vehicles in action.

Upon arrival at Kama, Woelfert met with the team of Krupp engineers now in residence. By 1930, Krupp had ten employees living at Kama; the rival Rheinmetall Corporation had seven, and Daimler four.[2] From them, he learned that they had been busy while waiting for Woelfert's new prototypes to arrive. Throughout the course of the 1929 testing season at Kama, the *Grosstraktor* medium tank prototypes had been put through their paces. The flood of technical data that had resulted had led to major revisions in the vehicles, including some work performed on site.

Not long after his arrival, Woelfert watched the *Leichttraktor* perform on the *polygon*. He must have been pleased to hear that of the four prototypes being tested (the other two being from Rheinmetall), one of his own models proved to have the best performance.[3] Woelfert later noted that the *Leichttraktor* project was the Krupp team's most important practice in designing tanks, for through it "we gained essential experience, particularly with the engine's machinery and tracked vehicle component parts."[4]

Over the past year, some competition had developed between the Krupp and Rheinmetall teams. Both groups were heavily invested in the possible outcome— lucrative contracts and professional pride were on the line. One Krupp engineer complained about not being allowed near a Rheinmetall vehicle.[5] To overcome that competitiveness, Pirner's office began to force closer cooperation between the Rheinmetall and Krupp engineers at Kama beginning in 1930. For instance, Rheinmetall were ordered to install one of their own successful turret designs onto Woelfert's superior tank chassis.[6] By the end of testing at Kama, the Krupp engineering team reported that their prototype had a Krupp chassis, a "Daimler-Benz engine . . . an Aphon- manual transmission, gears from a factory in Friedrichshafen and . . . a Rheinmetall turret."[7] The *Leichttraktor* was thus the product of extensive corporate collaboration, supervised by the Reichswehr. Their aim was to develop the best possible prototypes from the pooled knowledge and expertise of all of Germany's major industrial firms—a process that was uniquely suited to the environment at Kama and the Reichswehr's limited resources.

As the *Leichttraktoren* underwent modifications, the *Grosstraktoren*, too, continued to see modifications. Pirner's initial specifications had been well beyond the technical capabilities of engineering at the time they had been issued. None of the six prototype vehicles met the Waffenamt's standards.[8] However, modifications improved each vehicle over time. Senior Krupp designer Georg Hagelloch came for a visit in October 1930, and noted a number of improvements, including "a new chain to drive the wheels and casters; a change of the lever pivot of the drive; improvements to the compressor system; the installation of chilled cast iron sleeves and a new conveyer belt in the gearbox."[9] This represented a considerable overhaul to the vehicle. But more important, all of these changes were carefully noted for future development. The next generation of tank specifications then under consideration would benefit enormously from the experience gained through the trial and error process at Kama.

As Kama advanced the limits of coordinated armored warfare, Lipetsk was just beginning to play its own role in prototype testing. The airbase's role in aircraft testing and design was relatively limited until 1930. As noted, back in 1923, Helmuth Wilberg had drawn up specifications for four types of aircraft and commissioned four firms to develop prototypes. Aside from Heinkel's HD-17, the other aircraft commissioned between 1923 and 1928 failed to meet Reichswehr specifications, and so were not tested at Lipetsk. This was mainly a product of their inferior engine design, solved only in 1929 with the introduction of a new BMW aviation engine, the first mass-produced German engine in the 1,000 horsepower class.[10] As a result, until 1930, the training program at Lipetsk depended on now-obsolete biplanes.[11] At that juncture, Lipetsk had thirty-one Fokker D-XIIIs, four HD-17s, and two very old Fokker D-VIIs in working condition.[12]

Beginning in 1930, these older aircraft would be supplemented by the arrival of a dizzying variety of new prototypes and technical equipment, all of them finally up to Wilberg's standards. The Waffenamt's stated priorities before the 1930 season centered on flight testing of several new aircraft prototypes, as well as work on aviation radios, aviation glasses, targeting scopes, and lightweight cameras.[13] Once the summer began, the list of experiments and design work grew rapidly. Staff at Lipetsk tested monitoring and precision instrumentation to allow for night bombing.[14] They added a new parachute design to be tested in July.[15] A type of heavy machine gun manufactured by Rheinmetall in Switzerland—borrowed from Kama and, as it turned out, too heavy for aircraft—also began modification at Lipetsk. Waffenamt staff further listed work on targeting devices, reflex sites, bombing equipment, cameras, machine gun mounts for attaching guns to fighter aircraft, and three types of bombshells in their weekly reports, with research often done in conjunction with Soviet engineers. A Reichswehr report also noted that a Soviet-German team from Lipetsk traveled to Tomka to conduct chemical aviation tests using 22 and 110 pound chemical bombs.[16] The 1930 research program represented a vast investment of capital and expertise, aimed at advancing aviation technology.[17]

Most important, several new prototype aircraft arrived, including the HD-21 and Heitag Arado SD 1 single-seat fighter, the first illegal fighter design produced in Germany.[18] This was the first wave of new designs to arrive in the summer of 1930—in total, fourteen distinct models of aircraft from six different aircraft manufacturers underwent trials at Lipetsk over the next three summers. The participating firms included Arado, Albatros, Dornier, Heinkel, Junkers, and Rohrbach. If one excludes the firm of Messerschmitt AG, which had gone bankrupt and would be reconstituted only in 1933, these six companies produced 98 percent of Germany's combat aircraft in the Second World War.[19] Designers learned or relearned how to build those combat aircraft by working on prototypes for Lipetsk. Although they did not reside at the facility—as designers did at Kama—each of the corporate engineering teams was kept informed of the testing and results of the developments at Lipetsk. They received data and flight reports, and adjusted their designs in response. When the next round of specifications for combat aircraft prototypes was released by the Waffenamt, they were expected to modify their aircraft designs accordingly.

The importance of this work to the development of the German aviation industry can hardly be overstated. As noted, there were only seven aeronautical engineering firms in Germany after the war, which collectively owned four engine plants and eight airframe factories.[20] The number of designers who would craft the warplanes of the Second World War was small, and nearly all of them were involved in the prototypes tested at Lipetsk. Indeed, those prototypes constituted, in several cases, the first time future lead designers worked on combat aircraft. For instance, Hermann Pohlmann, who would later design the famous shrieking Ju-87 "Stuka" dive-bomber—used to such devastating effect in Germany's early "Blitzkrieg" warfare—had his first design, the JuG-1, built in Russia at Fili.[21] Two of his other designs, the K-47 and W-34, were also tested at Lipetsk. He would retain components (like the tail) of the K-47 that had proved successful at Lipetsk in his dive-bomber.[22] Albatros engineer and test pilot Kurt Tank, who would become an influential designer in the Second World War, would also have his own early designs tested and refined at Lipetsk. He would eventually lead the design team on the Focke-Wulf Fw-190, the Luftwaffe's main fighter aircraft in the opening phases of the war.[23] Germany's leading engineers learned their trade designing aircraft for Lipetsk, and modifying their designs as the Waffenamt provided data from flight testing at the base.

The flying itself was performed in combination by the Waffenamt's aviation research group, as well as a collection of test pilots and civilian contractors who began to appear at Lipetsk in 1930.[24] Among the pilots who came to test fly aircraft at Lipetsk were several of Germany's most famous aces, including Emil Thuy, a Pour le Mérite recipient and ace with thirty-five kills to his name in the First World War.[25] He was joined by at least three others, including fighter ace Carl-August von Schoenebeck – now test pilot for Dornier, Heinkel and Arado – who returned to Lipetsk in 1930 as a private citizen. Soviet intelligence, which carefully monitored all arrivals, described Schoenebeck as "the best pilot, the leader of the fighter pilot group."[26] The test pilots' main duties involved flying the array of prototypes and experimental aircraft that would soon begin to arrive.

The life of a test pilot was always a risky one, especially when the designs in question were prototypes. On June 11, 1930, Thuy took up a new Albatros L-76 biplane fighter for a test flight at Lipetsk. The aircraft experienced mechanical failure and crashed, killing him.[27] He had survived more than three years of combat over the Western Front, only to die in a test flight in Russia in peacetime. Despite this setback, testing continued on the Albatros line, which would evolve into the L-101 trainer.

Their Soviet counterparts were also busy at the airbase. From its inception, the VVS had faced a gargantuan task in developing an aviation industry, training pilots, and devising new aircraft designs almost from scratch. In 1930, a senior Soviet Air Force officer told counterparts at Lipetsk that up to that point they had only "primitive human material" on which to base efforts. "You cannot put primitive people in complicated machines," he told German officers.[28] Building "new men" and new aircraft was the Soviet goal. By 1930, the VVS was beginning to succeed on both marks, thanks to Lipetsk.

Lipetsk remained throughout its period of operation the most "German" facility in the Soviet Union—it had the largest German staff and the greatest independence of action and management. Nonetheless, Lipetsk had numerous Russian personnel, too. To begin with, the Reichswehr's lease required the Germans to train large numbers of VVS personnel. The number of pilots, engineers, mechanics, and support staff who received some training from the German side was considerable. In the 1927 summer program the 140 German pilots and engineers present were joined by 20 Soviet pilots-in-training and 24 test pilots.[29] By 1930, that number had grown to 26 military pilots and 234 other workers, mechanics, and technicians.[30] Their education was an important part of the professionalization of the VVS.

The other Soviet ambition at Lipetsk was to gain access to German technology. In June 1930, a German officer at Lipetsk reported back to Berlin that base personnel had heard growing rumors about an "intensive new rearmament effort of the Soviet Air Force."[31] He also reported that all future Soviet army aircraft would be made of metal; the Soviets were vastly expanding their light and heavy bomber fleets; and the new generation of Soviet fighter aircraft seemed to have specifications better than contemporary German prototypes.[32] The photos included with the intelligence report by its author indicated that the Soviets were acquiring aircraft designs from around the world for their own purposes. Specifically, he observed that a new Soviet fighter design "vividly recalls the American Curtiss fighter."[33] He added that other design components appeared to have been borrowed from Fokker aircraft already in use in the Soviet Union. Their observation was accurate: from 1925 to 1930, nearly every Soviet aircraft design was derivative of foreign designs.

To "catch up" with Western aviation technology, the VVS depended upon legal acquisition of technology through purchases and license agreements.[34] A number of German aviation firms reached these sorts of deals with the Soviet state. Heinkel, for instance, hosted Soviet engineers in 1927, sold production rights to the Soviet Air Force for the HD 37, and then dispatched their own engineers to assist the Soviets in production within the Soviet Union in 1929.[35]

But when such routes proved insufficient, the Soviets used industrial espionage and reverse-engineering of stolen designs to remedy their own shortcomings. The facility at Lipetsk was immensely important for both legal and illegal routes. Beginning in 1930, large Soviet delegations of engineers from TsGASI, now the main aviation research institute in Moscow, arrived in Lipetsk. They were often accompanied by test pilots. Under the terms of the agreement at Lipetsk, they were allowed to "inspect and study the material available" and take any aircraft or equipment present up for a test flight. They began doing this with some frequency when the new German designs began to arrive in numbers in 1930. German pilot Wilhelm Speidel noted that the TsGASI representatives demonstrated "an amazing mastery of individual technical areas." He also noted that they were carefully coached to "avoid revealing surprise, recognition, doubt, rejection, or similar subjective opinions though posture of facial expressions. The mask never fell."[36] This was to avoid, in part, revealing the engineers' familiarity with German technology.

When license agreements and purchase contracts could not fulfill Soviet desires for German technology, espionage often did. The Germans were aware of the frequent borrowing. Some critical pieces of technology never traveled to Lipetsk specifically because of German fears regarding their theft. In negotiations with Moscow Central, Voroshilov or the head of the VVS Baranov often mentioned technologies described in newspaper articles and then demanded an explanation why the Germans were not testing them at Lipetsk. For instance, they requested information repeatedly about a new "wireless image transfer" technology that would allow photographs to be sent instantly from an aircraft to a receiving station. But the Germans insisted repeatedly that the technology was simply not ready.[37] It would never be ready, at least for testing in Russia.

By 1930, the Germans suspected espionage on every component part they brought with them to Lipetsk. These fears proved, for the most part, justified. Most of the parts for the Waffenamt's technical tests were kept "in a small wooden shack" and German engineers often noted that they were sometimes damaged or had been moved around.[38] They suspected that the Russians were sneaking into the storage facility at night to disassemble and map the component parts of each device in order to reverse-engineer them. A number of schematics also disappeared from a German office at Lipetsk during the summer of 1931. The German engineers reported that "The request of the research group at WIVUPAL [Lipetsk] regarding the investigation [of stolen technical plans] has not yet been answered . . . the theft was probably ordered by the Russian Air Force."[39] German suspicions regarding the importance of "spying" to Soviet aviation developments were confirmed in the early 1930s. While team after team of Soviet technical experts arrived at Lipetsk, no completed, modern Soviet designs ever appeared at the facilities. During German tours of Soviet airbases elsewhere, the Soviets generally prevented the Germans from seeing their new aircraft. Speidel complained that every time the Soviets agreed to a demonstration flight of a new aircraft, "at the last minute it was always prevented by unforeseen circumstances." The aircraft they were allowed to see, and fly if desired, were always "museum pieces."[40] The Germans soon realized why: the Soviets were unwilling to reveal how much they had borrowed from German designs.

These thefts undermined the Reichswehr-VVS relationship. Besides German anger at Soviet audacity, they complicated the Reichswehr's relationship with its corporate partners. As noted, many German companies were dispatching equipment for testing at Lipetsk. Those that did not have representatives in Russia required a Reichswehr "commitment . . . over the confidentiality of their transferred equipment."[41] While the Soviets had been allowed to inspect equipment since 1925, the outright theft of German products cut into corporate sales. Pressure at home led Moscow Central to issue a change of policy to the Soviets in 1932, stating that "German firms have patent rights; we must reject the copying or photographing of equipment as well as the disassembly of these devices."[42] But by that juncture, much of the damage had been done. This organized process of technological thievery played a major role in the rapid ascent of the Soviet Air Force in the 1930s.

Espionage aside, there were broader implications to the technological work being conducted at Kama and Lipetsk. As the testing season came to an end in September 1930, Kama received a high-level delegation from Germany. Schleicher's close associate General Otto von Stülpnagel—supervising the Inspectorate of Motorized Troops—and his deputy Colonel Heinz Guderian arrived to observe maneuvers. One of the reasons for their visit was the need to answer key questions about armored warfare. In particular, the Reichswehr needed to decide whether to build small, fast tanks, or slower, more heavily armored vehicles. Should tanks be used independently of infantry, to take advantage of their speed in battles of maneuver? Or in close coordination with infantry, taking advantage of their firepower, but losing the advantage of speed? These central questions would determine the next round of prototypes to be commissioned—and possibly mass-produced for the next war.

Stülpnagel was deeply impressed when he reached the base, describing Kama as the one place where "really positive work" on tanks was taking place, and its "true worth" being considered.[43] His extended visit to Kama led to several important conclusions. First, he was surprised by the technical capacities of the new *Leichttraktoren*. He concluded that they could be ready for emergency production should Germany find itself in a new war in the very near future. At the same time, he disagreed with the assessment of many of his peers within the Reichswehr that small tankettes or light tanks of the kind being mass-produced in France, Italy, and Great Britain were the future of armored warfare. Instead, Stülpnagel recorded his conviction that the larger vehicles then on display at Kama—the *Grosstraktoren*—had greater potential in the future.[44] At this juncture he was in the minority, with most officers believing speed was the most important attribute of armored vehicles, and thus endorsing a light, fast tank. As of 1930, the Reichswehr resolved that no decisions would be made until more senior officers could personally witness the technical capabilities of the prototypes at Kama.[45] Once again, it was clear that technology was shaping the development of doctrine.

Another research project Stülpnagel witnessed during his 1930 visit highlighted this to an even greater degree: the radio. Technicians at Kama demonstrated that radios might enable complex command and control in the near future, including inside a moving armored vehicle.[46] As it turned out, this was—alongside the three-man turret — arguably the most significant technology under development at Kama. It would have momentous implications in the war that followed within the decade.

The issue of command and control of tank units had become apparent toward the end of the First World War. German armored theorist Ernst Volckheim had written, drawing from his personal experience in the war, that "the radio link must be seen as the only and at the same time the perfect solution" to the problem of command and control of armored formations. He added that if radios were not developed to meet the needs of Germany's tank forces, "the successful use of the tank is very much in doubt."[47] Guderian, who had spent much of his early military career in radio communication roles, seems to have agreed.[48] And they were hardly alone. As a result, the Reichswehr devoted considerable resources toward radio development. It was, in many respects, a core part of the offensive-minded, combined arms doctrines developing in both Germany and the Soviet Union; without it, coordinated, mobile warfare using tanks, planes, and infantry was impossible. In short, radio would revolutionize tank warfare.[49]

Versailles had not placed limits upon radio technology, so German radio production during the 1920s kept up with, and in some areas surpassed, developments ongoing in Great Britain and France.[50] However, Versailles handicapped the Reichswehr's ability to test radios in vehicles and aircraft.[51] And the technical problems involved were immense. Radios in the 1910s were made with crystals that required relative stability. Putting a standard commercial radio into a tank would have resulted in these crystals breaking, thus rendering the unit useless.[52] Frequency control also proved extremely difficult. Due to movement and temperature variation, interwar AM radios were more or less impossible to operate while a vehicle was moving.[53] The tremendous noise within a tank also rendered voice transmission or reception very difficult. Finally, the locomotion of the tank itself produced interference, which made radio use very difficult.[54]

When the Reichswehr put in its orders for tank prototypes beginning in 1922, they required that every unit have a radio mount, though the technology for stable transmission from a tank had not yet been developed.[55] This was well before the 1927 British maneuvers often thought to have inspired the German adoption of the radio in tanks. Kama instructor and head of Wa.Prüf 6 Hans Pirner—who had guided many of the Reichswehr's key decisions on tank design—was the inspiration behind this remarkable foresight.[56] This marked a major change from the First World War. Instead of signaling via flare or flag, German prototypes of the interwar period were all intended to have their own transmission and reception capabilities, as well as an on-board radio communications officer. The technical solutions to the question of tank radios had not been remedied by the time of Stülpnagel's visit, but they would remain a priority for the next testing season at Kama.

CHAPTER 20

Yellow Cross

As Stülpnagel observed tanks and radios at Kama, millions of Germans prepared to vote amid a growing political crisis. Facing the crippling economic conditions triggered by the Great Depression, sitting Chancellor Heinrich Brüning had attempted to pass a controversial budget, cutting social benefits and civil service pay.[1] Most of the political spectrum, including the Nazis and Communists, joined forces to vote the budget down. Unable to govern, Brüning had invoked the emergency measures of Article 48, and received President Hindenburg's support to dissolve the Reichstag. With the approval of Hindenburg and General Schleicher, Brüning then issued his budget with minor modifications. Shortly thereafter, on September 14, 1930, a new election was held for the Reichstag. It proved a disaster for Brüning's government and the pro-Republic parties. The center-left SPD lost 10 seats, while their sometime allies the Zentrum Party gained only a few. The Communists added 22 representatives to become the third largest party, while the Nazis grew from 12 to a staggering 107, becoming the second largest faction in the 577-seat Reichstag.[2] Hitler's share of the vote had increased from 810,000 in 1928 to 6.4 million in a little more than two years.[3]

Coalition government was now impossible. The Reichstag was incapable of governing. Brüning remained in office only because no party could cobble together a majority government. From the 1930 election onward, a series of minority governments were able to govern only through the extensive use of Article 48. It was the beginning of the end of parliamentary rule in Germany.

The political chaos in Germany had little impact on the Soviet-German military partnership. As long as Wilhelm Groener stayed on as minister of defense, and General Schleicher continued to dominate civil-military relations, the relationship remained stable. In the early fall, most of the personnel at Lipetsk and Kama winterized camp buildings and began heading home. For the German officers and engineers who returned to Germany instead of braving the Russian winter, the months at home meant time to plan for the next year of testing and training. Only the research team at Tomka stayed, hoping that breaks in the weather might mean another round of chemical testing. By December, they could only report to Berlin that "success in winter proved quite difficult."[4] Resorting to methods more reminiscent of the nineteenth century rather than the twentieth, those still on site were forced to resort to wooden carriages and sleighs just to move around the camp. Fishman, who visited the site, recalled that "only snowshoeing and the occasional celebration, e.g. Christmas and New Year's Eve, kept up the spirits of each individual."[5] Most would depart for home in January.

In February 1931, Niedermayer wrote to Fishman about the chemical weapons test program for the coming year, laying out German priorities. Niedermayer's top agenda item for Tomka was the development of a new variant of mustard gas that might work in conjunction with air power—and thus make Douhet's apocalyptic vision possible. Most of the other items on his list—a ground-based chemical sprayer, as well as new bomb and fuse types for chemical aviation—depended on the success of the mustard gas research. Fishman reviewed the list and made some suggestions, though he agreed that the mustard gas variant should be the priority. The result of their deliberations was a nine-point testing program, centering on aviation and mustard gas experiments.[6]

Mustard gas itself was not new. On July 12, 1917, near Ypres, chemist and future Nobelist Fritz Haber had personally supervised the release his newest project. Hoping to break the war open in a single decisive moment, the Germans had stored huge quantities of their new chemical weapon, codenamed Gelbkreuz (Yellow Cross).[7] A fierce bombardment during the night had proven a rather strange experience for British troops of the Fifteenth and Fifty-fifth Divisions. They had suspected they were getting gassed based on the lack of high explosive shells, but the canisters fired at them instead contained a brownish liquid that pooled on the ground and in the trenches. It caused little pain on initial contact, and the soldiers at the front felt a great sense of relief upon realizing the substance was not the asphyxiating gas phosgene. That would soon change. The following morning they woke up in "intolerable pain" that became so intense that many were given morphine.[8]

This toxic substance seeped through clothing and ate away at the skin, creating huge blisters and painful swelling as layers of skin sloughed off. But the real damage was done to the lungs, as men's windpipes slowly constricted and they suffocated over days. Gelbkreuz had the added attribute of remaining toxic for extremely long periods. It was so powerful that British doctors suffered ill effects from the agent after dissecting a deceased man who had been gassed ten days earlier.[9] This was the agent the Tomka research teams hoped, with modifications, could be deployed by aircraft and thus used against cities.

On May 22, 1931, a German "forward" team of fifteen officers and enlisted men returned to Tomka, meeting Red Army counterparts. They reactivated the telephone lines—which had been shut off for the winter—and began working alongside Russian construction crews in updating the facilities.[10] Three days later, lead chemist Leopold von Sicherer arrived. Although the majority of his research team would not arrive until mid-June, Sicherer wanted to initiate the first tests of the season immediately. And he wanted to begin with the top priority—mustard gas testing. He just needed to wait for the right weather conditions.

In the early morning hours of May 30, officers at the camp noted that it was very warm and that there was "almost no wind—so the best Gaswetter [gas weather]."[11]

Donning their gas masks and suits, the German team, joined by a number of Russian officers and students, detonated two gas bombs. Unfortunately—and perhaps forgetful after the long winter break—several of the officers had not "closed their suits tightly enough because of the intense heat," Sicherer reported.[12] The result was that "participants suffered mustard gas burns to the arms and neck, or even almost their whole bodies."[13]

It might have seemed an inauspicious start to the testing season, but such injuries were par for the course at the facility. Without skipping a beat, Tomka's German commandant Wilhelm Trepper noted in his report that "similar experiments are envisaged for [June] 7th."[14] With only a few short summer months in which to test new equipment and tactics, the teams at Tomka would run experiments almost daily, including on weekends, from May through November.[15] The bulk of testing was conducted on the artillery range with fifteen artillery pieces of four different varieties, firing poison gas and testing dispersion.

For many of the scientists present, the more exciting research work involved experimental poison gas deployment technologies, particularly agricultural sprayers and aircraft.[16] Early on the morning on August 9, Tomka researchers began testing a new prototype: a six-wheeled Krupp armored vehicle mounting an agricultural spraying hose—their first attempt at a chemical tank.[17] The goal was to test concentrations of chemical agents along different types of roadways: dirt, concrete, stone, etc. The aim was to discover if chemical weapons could render roads impassable.[18] If so, chemical tanks might become an important feature of all armored units. The Tomka team decided in this new test not to use the real thing—mustard gas— but instead, a mixture with similar chemical properties. They were nevertheless pleased with the results, recording that the armored cars' drive left "chunks from [the size of] beans to the size of a fist on the ground."[19] By their math, this meant the road would become impassable for at least an hour after spraying. Enthusiastic about the potential implications, the team immediately began working on simplifying the design so that the sprayer "can be mounted on any commercial trucks."[20] That could potentially turn thousands of civilian vehicles into instruments of chemical warfare.

As German and Soviet scientists at Tomka experimented with chemical tanks, research work at Kama continued on the *Grosstraktor*, the *Leichttraktor*, and radio development. Testing at Kama with the six-man *Grosstraktor* led Reichswehr officials to conclude that it was difficult to command the vehicle because there were too many crew members.[21] In addition to being crowded, the design required the commander to load the main gun besides issuing orders.[22] This slowed the process of reloading, and also diminished the ability of the tank commander to issues orders and coordinate with his unit.

After trying out a variety of solutions, two German engineers at Kama—one from Krupp and one from Rheinmetall—came up with a new solution: borrowing the turret design and crew layout of the Soviet T-28 for their next version of a medium tank.[23] This much larger turret, with room for three men, placed the commander in a position to observe and issue commands while a gunner and loader handled the actual work of the main gun.[24]

This three-man turret represented a major and permanent step forward in German tank design. Contemporary enemy tank designs, particularly French, had some technical superiorities to the German prototypes. But their internal configuration meant that the commander was unable to devote himself entirely to leading his vehicle. In equivalent French armored vehicles, the tank's commander had to load and fire his main armament as well as issue orders. The result was a rate of fire around two to three rounds per minute.[25] By comparison, in German tanks equipped with the three-man turret, the commander could focus his attention on coordinating with other vehicles, finding enemy targets, and commanding his crew.[26] Freeing the commander also resulted in a rate of fire three to five times faster. The three-man turret would thus prove a major advantage when French and German tanks met in battle in 1940.[27]

While the revolutionary new turret underwent testing, Kama's engineers also experimented with new radio designs. The Lorenz Corporation had secretly commissioned an engineer named Burkhardt, a radio technician bound for Kama, to bring several of their radio modules with him.[28] There, Burkhardt installed the first 30 watt transmitter and receiver in the *Grosstraktor* prototype.[29] He would be joined by other radio technicians as Kama expanded. They attempted to solve three main problems: improving frequency control, increasing the stability of the radio itself, and finding a means of clearly transmitting and receiving a human voice from within the noisy confines of a tank. The first was partially remedied by improving the suspension of the tank models being tested.[30] They addressed the second by testing newer, more stable versions of Lorenz's audion radio. Here, too, they ran into difficulties with transmission, but improved radio designs could at least endure the rigors of tank movement.

To the third challenge, technicians at Kama attempted to improve the clarity of voice transmission and reception, a difficult task, as noted, within a moving tank. To that end, Burkhardt and other technicians at Kama first tried a "lip reader," which was a modified contact microphone. Unfortunately, after considerable experimentation (and apparently much saliva), they decided the device was disgusting and unsanitary.[31] Other work proceeded with a larynx contact microphone, but that, too, proved unsuccessful. In the end, the engineers invented a new set of headphones that were, as Müller recalled in his memoirs, "embedded in large soft brackets and pressed by a spring clip . . . to the head."[32] With this headset (along with other developments in radio technology), radio operators could at least receive voice commands even in a moving vehicle. This meant that as long as a command tank remained motionless, a squadron commander could send orders to his men. Although in this instance, the Germans remained behind British and American radio technology, work at Kama marked a major step forward for the Reichswehr.[33]

The Germans were not the only ones to notice the importance of the new radio technology under development. Ianis Berzin, the head of Red Army Intelligence (known as GRU) wrote to Marshal Tukhachevsky in September 1931 to discuss radio developments at Kama. He noted that tactical studies had been of immense value in revealing the importance of radios. By that year, the Soviets had begun developing their own tank radios at the Red Army's Institute of Communications based on

German experiments at Kama.[34] Berzin wrote that "the tactics of the tank vehicles depend on communication, and that of the three means of communication: radio, signal flags and tracer shells—radio was the most efficient means of command and control, but that the Red Army had not yet perfected the technology.[35] He ended his notes on the tactical exercises at Kama by recommending that "management and command ought to be given by radio."[36] He added that the technology was still in its infancy. Nevertheless, the conclusion that radios were an essential component of tank command and control—and possible to build—had been firmly established for both the German and Soviet armored forces.[37]

Although Kama did not remedy many of the technical issues with the tank radio, it did advance German expertise considerably. By 1939, most German vehicles at least had receivers, allowing basic command and control. The same could not be said of French or Soviet armies, which employed a mixture of communication systems, most notably flags.[38] When war returned to Europe, armies would learn that popping open the hatch of a tank to wave a flag in the midst of battle was less than ideal. By contrast, when the Battle of France began in 1940, many of the German vehicles that swept across Northern France were equipped with the radio sets that had first been tested and developed at Kama. They enabled the rapid war of maneuver that proved so devastatingly effective in the early years of the war.

CHAPTER 21

Hunger

In 1931, Soviet production of tanks and planes jumped by leaps and bounds: aircraft production rose 87 percent over the previous year, and tank production by 103 percent.[1] That industrial miracle came at a cost. Mass hunger first appeared in the USSR in 1931, growing infinitely worse the following two years. The famine, triggered by Stalin's collectivization and industrialization policies and exacerbated by bad weather, would claim at least 5.7 million lives.[2] In a number of cities, corpses accumulated nightly in the streets; the dead had become commonplace. Those still alive, too weak to properly bury the dead, left the recently deceased in shallow graves. Cannibalism became widespread. The OGPU recorded that "families kill their weakest members, usually children, and use the meat for eating."[3] There was no mercy for the victims. The Soviet state responded by making theft of grain—even tiny amounts from their own farms—punishable by death.[4] The deaths of millions of farmers—and the grain they would have consumed—were the foundation upon which to build the Soviet Union's military might.[5] That was the price to be paid for new tanks and planes.

All three of the joint facilities in 1931 were in the famine zone created by Stalin's collectivization policies. At Lipetsk, the Germans paid the salaries of both their own men and the Soviet employees. This put them in a uniquely uncomfortable position. Lipetsk was in the heart of a region where more than a million Soviet citizens would starve to death during the course of the next twenty-four months. Severe food shortages meant that German wages, paid in rubles to the local staff, were no longer sufficient for survival. Red Army officers and men at the base never suffered from the same food shortages, a sign of the Soviet regime's priorities. The civilian personnel, on the other hand, suffered greatly. As a result, in the fall of 1931 the German commandant agreed to raise the living wages of the Soviet staff at Lipetsk, writing that "the station has an obligation to those who reside on station and the Russian workers and employees . . . to alter their wages given current (that is, general famine) conditions."[6] However, Moscow Central lacked any additional money in their budget, so Lieth-Thomsen was forced to decrease the number of Russian personnel for the winter of 1931 from 309 to 248 in order to pay the remaining Russian staff a living wage.[7] What happened to those terminated from their contracts at Lipetsk is unknown; some must have become casualties of the famine.

The Germans did not have to worry about the food crisis themselves. Pilot Wilhelm Speidel, who was in residence at Lipetsk the following year, recalled being pleasantly surprised that the German side was adequately supplied with food despite the "difficulties and fluctuations in food supplies for the local population."[8] While thousands of Russians were starving just beyond the gates of the airbase, the Germans kept on hand stores of expensive foreign cheese, lemons, pineapples, half a dozen types of German sausages, Japanese seafood, noodles, hams, imported chocolates, and countless other luxuries, as well as huge quantities of staples such as butter, eggs, and flour that were widely unavailable among the civilian population.[9] Some of this food was provided by the Russians. At the height of the famine, the German warehouse staff at Lipetsk apologetically rejected shipments of basic foodstuffs, as the "camp did not have room for any more."[10]

The contrast was stark, as some of the Germans came to understand when they visited town. Before the famine reached its peak, the Soviet liaison requested that the Germans cease "selling and donating goods of German origin."[11] Some of these exchanges were charitable or financial. Others were of a more salacious nature. Soviet border security confiscated pairs of women's stockings and panties from one young German pilot's luggage. When confronted, he claimed that they were gifts for the elderly "base charwoman."[12] Likely they were destined for a mistress in Lipetsk itself. The OGPU recorded that several of the German pilots enjoyed a "large circle of female acquaintances in the city."[13]

Others were not aware of the sharp divide between themselves and the locals. For many of the young German pilots who went through Lipetsk, the whole trip was a grand adventure. There was a certain naiveté in their recollections. Future Luftwaffe ace Wolfgang Falck spent a summer at Lipetsk when he was twenty-two years old. He described the period as a "holiday with flying thrown in." He found his time in town particularly fun. "We all had a great time, and we also got to know the Russian girls there very well." He noted that you had to be careful as "all of these girls would have loved to marry any foreigner just to leave Russia."[14] The OGPU did not view this sort of fun as quite so innocent. In 1929, they had arrested nineteen "friends" of the Germans in Lipetsk. Another eight were arrested in 1937 when the Great Terror swept away hundreds who had known the German visitors, even in passing. When the war began in 1941, thirty-nine more disappeared, mostly former staff members of the facility.[15]

Despite their "friends" and food, most of the Germans enjoyed less-than-luxurious living conditions at Lipetsk. After the expansion of the facility in 1930 with the arrival of twenty-five Reichswehr engineers and close to seventy-five support staff, pilots and researchers were forced to triple up in the bedrooms of the eight German barracks. Only the heads of the experimental group, the leading flight instructor and the camp commandant, received their own rooms that summer.[16] The crowded conditions and complications with keeping families informed led the Reichswehr to request, whenever possible, that the officers and staff be unmarried.[17] The activities of the pilots were kept strictly secret. As Speidel recalled, "nobody, not even next of kin, could be informed of the real reasons for the resignation and the new profession" of their pilot relatives.[18] The legal fiction to spouses regarding their husbands' activities proved a significant strain on families, leading to the suicide of at least one pilot's wife.[19]

Further, the flight training itself was highly dangerous, resulting in frequent fatalities. Between the test pilots and the new trainee pilots, there was some traffic home in corpses. Getting the remains back to Germany proved difficult. As Speidel put it, "coffins with the corpses of downed airmen from Lipetsk were packed in boxes and declared as 'machine parts.' They were then smuggled out of the free port of Stettin using a trusted and known customs officer."[20] The need to write down such a regulation highlights how often bodies needed to be shipped home.

While pilots at Lipetsk risked life and limb learning dogfighting skills, aircraft also circled over the testing grounds at Tomka. Aviation testing remained the most important research work at Tomka in 1931. It was also the most gruesome of the tests to conduct, as it frequently involved large numbers of test animals. Supervised by the camp biologist, dogs and rabbits were left caged at premeasured distances around the chemical testing ground. A Russian (or occasionally German) pilot, flying one of Tomka's four test aircraft, released a bomb payload at a predetermined height. Most of these bombs were small, weighing around eighteen pounds. Each had a glycerin charge, a timed fuse, and a small gas payload. Dropped over the field from a variety of heights, the bombs exploded a distance off the ground, dispersing a chemical agent over an area ranging up to several hundred square feet. After a short wait, the team's scientists would visit the field to measure the damage inflicted on the test animals. Fishman recorded that traditional dispersion tests at Tomka—by gas canisters placed on the ground—were found to kill around 83 percent of all test animals and render the remainder incapacitated.[21] Aerial sprayers and bombs tested at Tomka consistently proved less effective.[22] The chemical agents dispersed too quickly.

For low-altitude tests, real mustard gas was frequently used. But for high-altitude tests, the Tomka researchers used nontoxic chemical compounds with similar properties to test dispersion and concentration; the reason for this was to avoid casualties should the aircraft miss the test field, a lesson learned from experience.

On September 12, 1931, a Russian pilot took up one of these nontoxic test loads. His task was to release 60-pound bombs full of the material on Tomka's *polygon* from heights varying between 65 and 10,000 feet.[23] Both Soviet and German teams looked on. They noted with satisfaction that the low altitude tests coated the *polygon* very effectively.[24] They followed this test up with a high-altitude bombing run, intended to test the possibility of inflicting "the very greatest [damage] in the hinterland."[25]

Fifty enlisted Red Army personnel were tasked with scouring the field after the high-altitude flight. Trepper described a surreal scene: the Soviets had positioned large posters on the field, reading, "Capitalism has rejected our offer for peaceful exchange, so now we have to prepare for defense; you must search this field for [mustard gas] droplets; he is a poor socialist who exempts himself and does not do his full part of the work."[26] A recreation tent set up nearby housed a radio blared a state propaganda program as the soldiers crawled through the grass. The end result of the experiment was disappointing: Trepper recorded that the Soviet soldiers found nothing across the entire *polygon*. This matched months of data collected about poison gas dispersal.[27] The chemical agents dispersed too fast to have any noticeable effect on ground level when dropped from height.

Trepper wrote that this confirmed what the German team had learned over the previous few years: strategic bombing with chemical weapons was deeply problematic. Better fuses, more effective bombs, and different chemical agents would be needed to render bombing from 10,000 feet against targets like cities possible.[28] The alternative would be for bombers to fly close to the ground when dropping chemical munitions, but they would likely suffer huge casualties in the process from anti-aircraft fire. His Soviet co-commandant, Jan Zhigur, seemed disappointed too, but Trepper noted that the Soviets had not yet abandoned the idea.[29] Zhigur added, "wholly in jest but with an inscrutable face," that low-level flights would still be enough to give the Poles "a lesson from which they could recover after a few weeks."[30]

This sort of testing took its toll. Trepper recorded that September that the Russians had "allegedly lost seven people due to the premature opening of a chemical container."[31] The Germans only learned of the incident at their nearby Soviet chemical weapons base (TsVHP) when Tomka's Zhigur urgently appealed to his German equivalent Trepper for medical equipment and decontamination materials for their injured men. The Germans asked whether or not their doctors could be of use; they had the dual motive of hoping to see the men themselves, given that, as Trepper wrote, "this case would have been for our physicians of the highest interest."[32] The Soviets, perhaps suspicious, rejected the offer for direct medical help, limiting their request to medical equipment.

Tests also proceeded throughout the year on chemical defense and medical treatment for chemical injuries. This involved using different bleaches and medical treatments to repair chemical burns inflicted by mustard gas. The best way to test new techniques, naturally enough, was on human volunteers. Lev Fyodorov, a Russian chemist, later recalled this kind of test: "Soldiers would be locked in a bunker with respiratory gear and gassed. Or gassed without wearing any equipment at all. Sometimes soldiers would stand at a certain distance from a release point, while officers measured the effect of their reaction. 'This was standard procedure in the Red Army.'"[33] In other instances, Soviet chemists would douse a uniform in mustard gas, try out a new method of decontamination on the uniform, and then order a Soviet enlisted man to put the uniform on. Sometimes they simply put a mustard gas on a conscript's skin and then test out new decontamination techniques, which were not always effective.[34]

This sort of human testing sometimes took place on a huge scale. In October 1931, Zhigur told Trepper that the Soviet side had decided to run a battalion-size test of a new gas mask and gas-protection system that could filter smaller particles than in the past. This had involved forcing a gas battalion of around 500 men to march through mustard gas, with only the first row of soldiers wearing full protective gear. Trepper replied, in surprise, even shock, that the Soviet side "placed quite extraordinary demands on the gas discipline of their troops." Zhigur answered that "gas discipline is now among the most important of requirements, and that they prefer to suffer some losses than let this opportunity to test many warfare agents pass by."[35] The price of advancing the technology of chemical warfare was high in human terms.

While Trepper reacted with surprise to the Soviet methods, the Germans, for their part, also depended on human testing, though usually on volunteers from their own ranks. When testing decontamination methods or new gas masks at Tomka, the Germans turned to their "experimental unit."[36] In September 1931, for instance, the German team tested a new decontaminant on six volunteers.[37] This involved placing mustard gas on the skin, waiting for the beginnings of a reaction and then applying the decontaminating agent. After noting some of the injuries endured—"severe skin burns, eye conjunctivitis, pharyngeal and laryngeal catarrh"—Trepper praised "the personal courage and devotion of my staff."[38]

Their courage and devotion, and the 1931 test season, seemed to suggest that the dreams of chemical warfare in conjunction with strategic bombing might not be practicable. The vision of cities obliterated by mustard gas was fading, with a war of machines—tanks and planes—rising in its place.

The end of the testing season at Kama brought another high-level delegation from Germany. In this instance, it was Oswald Lutz, newly appointed head of the Inspekteur der Kraftfahrtruppen. Joined by his deputy, Colonel Guderian, Lutz wanted to see what doctrinal lessons could be drawn from the 1931 season of testing and maneuvers at Kama themselves. Most critically, he and Guderian hoped to decide which new vehicle prototypes the Reichswehr should commission that winter.

Lutz and Guderian test-drove the prototypes at Kama. As Müller recalled, after riding in both the *Leichttraktor* and *Grosstraktor*, Lutz and Guderian concluded that the larger machine should be "developed as quickly as possible."[39] Echoing General Stülpnagel's sentiments from his visit the previous summer, they were convinced by the new round of demonstrations at Kama in 1931 that light tanks were at best a "stopgap," as they would struggle against other tanks as well as existing antitank defenses. The increasing performance of the medium tanks further meant that there was not as big a difference in speed and range as had been theorized in the early 1920s. That meant that a medium tank design—like the *Grosstraktor*—might, with improvements, be able to break through enemy defenses and still be fast enough for maneuver warfare. Lutz and Guderian's view on the subject would not be fully accepted for some time, but from 1931 onward, German doctrine shifted toward independent armored elements operating in broad, sweeping maneuvers, coordinated by radio.[40]

The problem was that the *Leichttractor*—developed later—was more technically advanced and closer to mass-production standards than the *Grosstraktor*. And German planners were increasingly eager to shift from prototype development to mass production. With this aim in mind, the officers from the Waffenamt began meeting with key engineers at Krupp and other corporate partners in 1931 to discuss the redesign of the prototypes and the next generation of vehicles. These conferences would become increasingly frequent—between June 1931 and July 1933, Krupp engineers Woelfert and Hagelloch would meet with men from Waffenamt at least sixty-four times, some of the meetings lasting up to a week.[41] At these gatherings, they reviewed reports from the corporate engineers at Kama and made decisions about component changes. This working group would decide on eighteen major component changes for the *Leichttraktor* alone, representing a fundamental redesign of the vehicle.

Despite concerns about the tactical value of light tanks, the data from Kama led the Waffenamt to commission a new prototype for testing at Kama. The specifications listed a vehicle weighing only 6 to 8 tons and capable of speeds of around 25 mph.[42] The Krupp team were to draw on their experiences at Kama, particularly with the *Leichttraktor* and the Red Army's British-made Carden-Loyd tankettes.[43] In 1931, Woelfert was placed in charge of the new project and began work on the vehicle, codenamed "Landwirtschaftlicher Schlepper" (LaS) or "Agricultural Tractor."[44] Woelfert was told to have prototypes ready for testing at Kama in the summer of 1934.

While the end of the summer brought a high-level delegation to Kama, rumors spread of an equally distinguished visitor soon to visit Tomka—Mikhail Tukhachevsky. The reason for the visit was the arrival, at long last, of a new chemical agent ready for testing. For years, Fishman and VOKhIMU had insisted that the Germans must be hiding their research in Germany, as no new chemical agents had been deployed for testing at Tomka.[45] As the Germans noted, "the most important question for the R.A. [Red Army] are new agents."[46] Reichswehr research teams embedded within German universities had concluded, after testing more than 10,000 chemical compounds, that the discovery of new, cheap, and effective poison gas agents was unlikely.[47] But, in part to accommodate the Russians, the Germans announced they were bringing a new chemical agent to Tomka for testing, code-named "Pfiffikus" [crafty one]. Strictly speaking, it was not a new agent, but a mixture of well-known chemical weapons. Nonetheless, great fanfare attended the first of these tests, begun on October 8, 1931.[48]

"Pfiffikus" was a chlorine-arsenic mixture that was intended to combine the effects of Blue Cross (a respiratory agent), Yellow Cross (mustard gas), and Green Cross (a pulmonary agent) into a single superweapon.[49] This agent was meant to trigger both skin blistering and lung poisoning, as well as have the advantages of Blue Cross, which was the least easily detected and filtered chemical agent. Potentially, that meant that gas masks would be useless against it. Tests proceeded throughout October on the *polygon* with artillery shells and aerial bombs.[50] The German scientist who performed autopsies on the test animals reported that "51 percent of the animals died during the cycle time. 42 percent of the animals were affected more or less intensely and 7 percent of animals survived without specific findings."[51] Most of the affected animals died over the following weeks. Despite this "success," Sicherer noted that Pfiffikus had a habit of evaporating or mixing with water vapor and becoming harmless.[52] The results were not awe-inspiring.

Nevertheless, the Germans reported that Tukhachevsky himself might soon arrive to witness testing with Pfiffikus.[53] They regarded him with great respect and were thrilled at the prospect of his visit. Zhigur and one of the German scientists laid out an agenda for their visitor that would involve, according to a report, "a walkthrough of all the laboratories together, with presentations by lecturers" and viewing of a bombing and shooting test.[54] Despite some enthusiasm, Trepper did hasten to complain to his superiors that "our work was thus severely disrupted" by preparations for the visit.[55]

Both Germans and Russians must have been disappointed when instead of Tukhachevsky, his subordinate in the Ordnance Department, General Efimov, arrived on the night of October 11. Efimov, who had studied in Germany and had visited Tomka the year before, was already familiar with the facility and its staff. He spent his first night at Tomka enjoying a large dinner party with fifteen German guests and a number of Russian officers. Trepper's report to Berlin noted that "the party was as great as if it had been an official dinner at a top hotel in Moscow."[56] He added in his official report that "it brought the German and Russian staff a lot closer."[57]

The demonstrations planned for Efimov proved less successful than the dinner. The main event—demonstrating new chemical agents and their use with air power— had to be canceled, as the German head of the chemical aviation bomb unit had a severe attack of angina that left him bedridden. Nevertheless, the laboratory tour and a chemical munition demonstration went off as planned; Efimov apparently was well informed of the work going on at Tomka, leading Trepper to comment gratefully, "I believe Mr. Efimov gained a favorable impression of our work from the reports of Mr. Schigur [Zhigur]."[58] On the night of October 13, Efimov traveled back to Moscow in his own private train car, conveying those impressions to Tukhachevsky.[59] As long nights and deep snowfalls hemmed Tomka in, the German staff began to depart. The testing season had produced mixed results. New agents and deployment methods had been tested, and new defensive treatments employed. It was clear, however, that Pfiffikus was not the miracle agent promised. And chemical aviation testing continued to reveal its limitations.

As German officers returned home for the holidays, Soviet officers were headed the other direction. In 1931, fifty-two senior Soviet officers visited, worked, or studied in Germany.[60] Twenty-three of them stayed for at least a month, to take part in officer training courses. In that year, the delegation included future marshal of the Soviet Union Semyon Timoshenko, as well as the head of military education for the Red Army, the chief of General Staff training, the commander of artillery officer training, and senior lecturers from the Red Army's main military academy specializing in motorization, technical education, cartography, and aviation.[61] These senior visitors aimed to fundamentally reshape Soviet military education and training procedures based upon the German model.

This process of reform was greatly aided by a string of prominent German officers who taught in the major Soviet service academies. Among those who taught military history and tactics at the Frunze Military Academy were future generals Georg-Hans Reinhardt, Kurt Brennecke, field marshals Erich von Manstein, Walter Model, and Friedrich Paulus—famous for his defeat and capture at Stalingrad—and field marshal Wilhelm Keitel, future head of the Oberkommando des Wehrmacht (OKW).[62] By 1931, the RVS recorded that the education plan of the Frunze Academy was "in all areas built on the experience gained from the German Military Academy."[63] One Russian general described the role of German instructors in Soviet education. "It is difficult to say where our staff begins and the German staff ends," he wrote. "Since the civil war we have had a proper military training and have become quite good military specialists. Our military academicians are better educated than was the case before the war."[64] The reshaping of curricula at the major academies and the training of instructors had an inestimable impact on the Red Army, assisting in the development of a new military class. These visits also impacted the shape and structure of the Soviet General Staff, the central "brain of the army," responsible for operational planning and mobilization. It increasingly came to resemble its German counterpart, on which it had initially been modeled back in 1924.[65]

The year 1931 would prove the apogee of Soviet-German military cooperation. Testing at Kama in 1931 had, as noted, reshaped German armor doctrine. Chemical weapons testing began to convince Soviet and German theorists that strategic bombing with poison gas was likely to prove too costly to be effective. And at Lipetsk, the arrival of a fleet of new prototypes marked the early revival of German air power. In addition, more than four dozen senior Soviet officers studied for extended periods in Germany in 1931. Their time in Germany came as the Red Army and VVS developed a bounty of new military technologies, the new designs heavily influenced by German engineering and produced in factories often built with German assistance. But as the snows fell and the bases reduced to skeleton staffs for the winter, the increasingly complicated political situation would soon begin to intrude.

CHAPTER 22

Schleicher

General Kurt von Schleicher was arguably the most significant figure of the later days of the Reichswehr, and the Republic. As described earlier, he entered the story of the German-Soviet partnership at its very beginning, hosting negotiations in 1921, overseeing the formation of GEFU in 1923, and meeting with his Russian counterparts many times over the years. An associate of Generals Seeckt, Groener, and Hindenburg, he had maneuvered all of them to his own advantage. Schleicher considered himself the shrewdest political mind in the Reichswehr. He certainly possessed considerable abilities to convince, cajole, and manipulate. Even with those gifts, however, he overestimated his abilities to control events.[1] As one contemporary observer wrote, Schleicher "does not seem to be constructed upon an heroic scale."[2] The military had become increasingly central to efforts at political coalition-building as government dysfunction peaked. Schleicher attempted to make the most of this, to the benefit of both the army and himself.

Schleicher's central strategy was to "tame" radicals by including them in government, rather than by suppressing them.[3] He had played a role in bringing Stresemann's center-right National Liberal Party into the government in 1920, courted the further-right DNVP in 1924, and sought to do the same with the Nazis between 1930 and 1933.[4] His mentor and superior, Wilhelm Groener, was rightly skeptical of the last project, opposed on many grounds to Hitler and his party. But Schleicher's machinations, divisions within senior leadership of the Reichswehr, and a chance event all intervened to thwart Minister of Defense Groener's efforts to fend off the rise of Hitler. The first disaster was entirely of his own making. Groener, then sixty-three years old, married his mistress, who was thirty-six. A child followed rather too soon after the wedding, and speculation within the Reichswehr abounded.[5] This strained Groener's relationships with his subordinates, and crucially, with the personally conservative Hindenburg. On April 10, 1932, Hindenburg defeated Hitler in the national presidential election. Believing this Nazi setback was his best chance to further weaken the radical right, Groener decided to push for a ban on the Sturmabteilung (Storm Detachment, or SA) and the SS, the two Nazi paramilitary wings. On May 10, 1932, he spoke for forty-five minutes against the Nazis in the

Reichstag, while being shouted and harassed by the large number of Nazi delegates present.[6] It was courageous, but the speech was not well received nationally.

Meanwhile, Schleicher had concluded—without informing Groener—that it was time to draw the Nazis into a governing coalition with the Zentrum Party. Schleicher approached Hindenburg and convinced him that Groener had to resign after his Reichstag "debacle." It was the only hope, Schleicher argued, of persuading the Nazis to join the government. Three days later, Groener, the last real advocate for the Republic in the government, resigned as minister of defense.[7] He remained interior minister for two more weeks, but his removal destroyed the new Heinrich Brüning government, and the whole cabinet was soon recalled.[8]

Brüning's successor as chancellor was Franz von Papen, a man historian Joachim Fest described "almost a caricature of himself . . . nobody took him quite seriously."[9] In the minority government that was formed, Schleicher was rewarded for the betrayal of his mentor by becoming his successor. As minister of defense, he dominated the entire government. From that position, he pushed for Hitler's inclusion in the government, arguing to Hindenburg that it would end two years of minority governments and rule by emergency decree. But as Schleicher sounded Hitler out, he learned that the Nazi leader's price for backing the government was high: he wanted the chancellorship and the crucial cabinet positions.[10] Schleicher was unwilling to concede so much.

While Schleicher continued his political balancing act, Soviet-German cooperation was fraying. The culprit was primarily of Schleicher's own making. In the spring of 1932, the Reichswehr adopted plans to recruit and arm a twenty-one-division army, in violation of Versailles.[11] As it did so, it began to relocate banned weapons testing back to German soil. The results would immediately be felt in the USSR. In May 1932, the Germans informed their Soviet counterparts they would not be resuming testing at Tomka that summer. The new chief of the Truppenamt, General Wilhelm Adam, wrote that "for a year, we will willingly interrupt the experiments at Tomka, and plan to use the resulting break for further improvement and development. It is then possible to save significant funds this year, which can also be used to benefit [us] the next year."[12] The real reason for declining German interest, however, was their growing willingness to violate Versailles at home, as the Reichswehr began opening flight schools and practicing tank maneuvers on German soil beginning that year.

On the Soviet side, Fishman's priority for Tomka was not tactical testing of the kind conducted the previous year. By 1932, the Red Army was conducting similar large-scale field tests themselves at other facilities. Nor did Fishman require military-industrial assistance. Soviet chemical weapons production, with German help, was now taking place on a vast scale. VOKhIMU could report by the beginning of 1931 that it could fill five million artillery shells of twelve different calibers with chemical agents; that its factories were producing 300,000 gas masks a year; and that the organization had five full-strength chemical battalions staffed with well-trained personnel.[13] Instead, Fishman wanted to develop new chemical agents and gain access to German laboratory facilities, neither of which was on offer in May 1932. As a result, he did not protest the facility's temporary closure.

The news about Tomka came as the Red Army underwent a major transformation. In May 1932, Stalin wrote a letter to Tukhachevsky in which he apologized for dismissing the arguments Tukhachevsky had laid out in 1930 arguing for the total militarization of the Soviet state.[14] Tukhachevsky had been briefly exiled to Leningrad for impolitic behavior while serving as chief of staff in 1928; while there, he had written a flurry of theoretical publications, including the letter referenced by Stalin, in which Tukhachevsky had proposed a huge increase in the strength of the Soviet Army. He argued for a field army of 250 divisions (7.5 percent of the Soviet population) and annual production of 122,500 aircraft and 197,000 tanks—sums in excess of all of Europe's armed forces combined.[15] At the time, Stalin had dismissed these figures as absurd—he derisively referred to it as "Red Militarism." But, in the first sign that he had changed his mind, Stalin brought Tukhachevsky back to prominence in 1931. He was made Voroshilov's deputy at the Commissariat of Military and Naval Affairs, while concurrently serving as chief of ordnance for the Red Army.[16] By May 1932, Stalin was willing to concede even more to Tukhachevsky's vision of future warfare. During the course of 1932, Soviet defense spending would grow from 845 million rubles to 2.2 billion.[17] By the end of that year, defense spending constituted roughly 9 percent of the Soviet Union's national income.[18]

The international situation was deteriorating. The economic crisis in the West triggered political instability in their partner, Germany. Poland had moved closer to military dictatorship under anti-Communist marshal Josef Pilsudski. Most worryingly, Japan had become increasingly aggressive, invading Manchuria in 1931. In the first six months of 1932, Stalin shifted priorities. Military production increased by 60 percent.[19] The 1932 arms buildup would witness the Red Army accepting a new generation of military technology into service. And for the first time, Soviet factories began to produce weaponry that was technologically equal to its European rivals.

Much of this technological edge was, of course, a product of years of cooperation with Germany. For instance, in 1932, the Soviet Air Force began deploying the world's first four-engine monoplane bomber, the TB-3 (Heavy Bomber-3). Its designer, Andrei Tupolev, had studied in Germany as part of officer exchanges in 1925, 1928, and 1929. He used the intellectual theft of Junkers' designs freely in his work, leading, as noted, to a copyright infringement lawsuit. His TB-3 bomber was powered by four BMW VI V-12 engines, built under license from the German firm. And it entered mass production at Fili (now N22), where 763 would be built over the next six years.[20]

The production of Soviet armored vehicles also entered a new phase in 1932, with the arrival of large numbers of modern, domestically generated tank designs. Beginning in 1928, the Red Army had purchased dozens of vehicles from Czechoslovakia,[21] Great Britain,[22] and most important, the United States.[23] By 1932, Soviet designs improving upon these foreign purchases began to reach mass production.[24] Most notable was the work of Soviet designers Michael Koshkin and Alexander Morozov, who used an American Christie chassis and transmission as the basis for the fast *bystrokhodnyi tank* (Fast-Moving Tank, or BT) design series. It resulted in the 12-ton BT-5, which entered service in 1932. The BT-5 had a top speed of 45 mph off-road and a stunning 70 mph on roads.[25] And it mounted a 45 mm cannon that could pierce armor. Those two assets made the BT-5 perhaps the best medium tank in the world in 1932.[26] And it was not just a question of quality. Total

Soviet tank production in 1929 had been 26 vehicles; this figure grew to 170 in 1930, then 740 in 1931, rising to 3,121 in 1932.[27]

German designers and interactions at Kama played a significant role in the redesign of these foreign prototypes, as well as the production of new Soviet tank lines. In 1932, the deputy chief of the Directorate of Motorization and Mechanization Ivan Gryaznov wrote to Commissar for Military and Naval Affairs Voroshilov, describing in detail how useful German technology had been in designing the Red Army's new fleet of vehicles, from the suspension to the arrangement of the crew; from the welded housings to periscope sights to machine-gun design; and of course to the use of radios.[28] Gryaznov ended his report by calling urgently for an increase in Soviet students and engineers at Kama, highlighting how significant he thought the German contribution to Soviet mechanization had been.

Mass production of Soviet vehicles also relied on industrial plant and engineers developed in conjunction with Germany. With German assistance, the USSR had begun producing BMW aircraft and tank engines under license: more than 27,500 would be built for the Red Army and VVS.[29] German machine tools or engineering teams assisted in the modernization or construction of ten of the Soviet Union's eighteen major tank production facilities in the interwar period.[30] German engineers and designers also played a significant role in the design process itself. For instance, German tank designer Eduard Grotte worked as one of the leading designers in the bureau that would draw up three of the primary tank designs—the T-26, T-28, and T-35—for the Red Army. Stalin, who paid extraordinarily close attention to tank design, considered Grotte of such value that he instructed, "Do not by any means allow Grotte to go back to Germany. Take all measures up to arrest and compel him to prepare the tank for serial mass production, because he might give away secrets."[31]

These changes in technology and in industrial capacity had a profound impact on Red Army doctrine.[32] Tukhachevsky spearheaded the development of a new operational doctrine that would become known as *glubokaia operatsiia* (usually translated "Deep Battle").[33] In the next war, he argued, states would mobilize the totality of their resources. This would lead to vast mechanized armies dueling over huge distances in massive combined arms confrontations. Tukhachevsky believed that a successful army would need to be able to conduct operations over a front of 275 miles and a depth of 125 miles. It would coordinate the use of airplanes, chemical weapons, and tanks to penetrate deep behind enemy lines, attacking logistical and command and control capabilities. Mainline forces—tanks, infantry, and artillery—would face the enemy's front while fast-moving tank armies swept through the enemy rear.[34] Deep Battle proved a contentious subject in the Red Army, but it provided a rationale and a use for the vast number of vehicles demanded by Stalin. Following the line proposed by theorists in March 1932, Red Army leadership approved the first Soviet armored corps—grouping fast, mechanized units together.[35] By 1932, the Red Army had become the most mechanized military in the world. Germany, by contrast, had ten working tanks in total, all of which were located in the USSR. For Reichswehr officers bristling at the limitations of Versailles and eager to redraw Germany's borders, this was an unacceptable state of affairs.

CHAPTER 23

Rearmament

While the Red Army acquired thousands of new tanks and vehicles, as the summer of 1932 started, the German military began to free itself from the constraints of Versailles. A major disarmament conference ongoing at Geneva seemed to offer an escape from the military restrictions of the treaty. At Schleicher's direction, German representatives demanded that either Germany's neighbors disarm to Germany's level—a process seemingly already begun in France and Great Britain as a product of the economic crisis—or agree to the principle of German military equality. Either would provide Germany an opportunity to rearm itself without consequence, Reichswehr leadership cynically concluded.

In light of these changing circumstances, Inspector of Motorized Troops General Oswald Lutz felt much greater freedom to take risks, even planning maneuvers in Germany itself for that coming autumn that would include "armored vehicles," though these were cars with steel plate attached, rather than the more sophisticated prototypes under testing at Kama.[1] In the meantime, Lutz and Guderian returned to the Soviet Union in July 1932 to see the vehicles at Kama once again.

The school was much more crowded than during their previous visit. For the 1932 training season, the Soviets had dispatched 100 Red Army officers to join the Germans onsite. For the first time, the growth in numbers enabled students to engage in company-sized tank maneuvers. Those who had been dispatched to the base included a mix of academic instructors from the academies, combatant commanders of the early mechanized units of the Red Army, and more junior tankers, gunners, and radio operators. Their tasks, in the words of Gryaznov, were to learn as much as possible about the design of the various German vehicles present; to master armored vehicle driving, marksmanship; and tactics in battle; and to think about the tactical employment of armored vehicles.[2]

Kama's technical testing was in full swing in the summer of 1932 when they arrived. Work continued on the *Leichttraktor*, *Grosstraktor*, and the now thirty Soviet vehicles in the tank park. Five Soviet engineering graduate students had joined the staff at Kama that year to improve their technical knowledge.[3] Training had changed somewhat from the year before, as the increasingly confident Red Army had begun to dispatch its officers to serve as faculty members. These included Andrei Grigorievich Kravchenko, an early tank pioneer and future two-time Hero of the Soviet Union who reached three-star general rank as commander of a tank army in the Second World War.[4]

While Red Army doctrine on the use of armored vehicles was coming into focus, German armor doctrine remained obscured. The problem was that the army had not yet commissioned the successor to the *Grosstraktor*, which meant that mass production of a new medium tank would likely be three to four years away, if not longer. Lutz wanted expanded tank production to begin as soon as possible, to allow for training and maneuvers, which would in turn assist in doctrinal development. After returning from Russia, he immediately commissioned Krupp and Rheinmetall to begin work on a medium tank, code-named the *Neubaufahrzeug* (new-built vehicle). Lutz and Guderian were both aware that it would take years to develop.[5]

In the meantime, the Reichswehr had only one new tank design near readiness: Woelfert's LaS light tankette, in development at Krupp.[6] In July 1932, General Lutz demanded that Krupp accelerate its production schedule, telling its engineering team to push on faster or they would be forced to buy Carden-Loyds from the British government. It was certainly a bluff, given that Germany could not legally buy tanks anywhere. Nevertheless, Krupp engineer Georg Hagelloch wrote to his superiors that "even if it is not exactly true, the statement is enough to force on us the greatest acceleration in the completion [of the tank]."[7] Krupp completed a chassis with a turret made of wood the following month, which they ran through trials for the Reichswehr, to their general satisfaction.[8] By September, the consensus was that the LaS had at least surpassed the Carden-Loyd in terms of maneuverability and reliability.[9] While Lutz would have preferred to have a heavier vehicle at his disposal, it would be the LaS that would be Germany's first mass-produced armored vehicle.[10]

As Lutz and Guderian wrestled with tank prototype design, Lipetsk was witnessing the arrival of numerous new aircraft designs. By the end of 1931, Lipetsk's research division had grown to fifty-seven German engineers, designers, test-pilots and others, plus fifty-eight Russians.[11] This team had received the K-47 monoplane—precursor to the Junkers 87 "Stuka" dive-bomber—the Arado 64 biplane fighter, the Albatros Al-84 biplane fighter, the Heinkel HD-38 biplane fighter, the Messerschmitt M23 monoplane, and the Dornier Merkur monoplane fighter design.[12] In early 1932, an upgraded version of the Arado 64 arrived in Lipetsk (the Ar-65), also powered with a BMW VI engine. It was accompanied by the Heinkel HD-59 biplane torpedo bomber, and a Junkers W-34 monoplane prototype.[13] In addition, Lipetsk's airfleet received the first prototypes of the Dornier XI, the Luftwaffe's first attempt at a *Schnellbomber*, a fast light bomber that could outrun intercepting fighters.[14]

There were two significant things about these new designs. First, they represented the collective work of almost all of Germany's aviation industry. All but one of Germany's airframe companies was now dispatching aircraft to Lipetsk for testing. Second, 1932 marked a generational shift in the aircraft designs themselves. For the first time, a considerable number of Lipetsk's new aircraft were all-metal monoplanes. The K-47, with a top speed of 185 mph, was around 65 mph faster than the fastest German aircraft at the end of the First World War.[15] And the W-34 design would break the flight altitude record, reaching a height of 41,000 feet.[16] While Great Britain, the United States, and Italy all had faster designs, the 1932 prototypes represented significant steps forward for Germany's aviation industry, following ten years of restrictions and financial losses.

While new aircraft underwent testing, the training program at Lipetsk was reaching its zenith. On the morning of July 7, 1932, twenty-one-year old Wolfgang Falck accelerated his Fokker D XIII into the Russian sky. As he circled upward, two other aircraft climbed into formation behind him. His *Kette* (chain of three aircraft) was to engage three other German pilots in a dogfight. He and his wingmen, Ekkehard Hefter and Günther Radusch, circled and climbed to an altitude of 5,000 feet. After ten minutes in the air, their opponents—led by nineteen-year old pilot Günther Lützow—appeared as dots on the horizon, moving directly toward them from the northwest.

Obeying his tactical training, Falck maneuvered his aircraft to a position above the enemy, then began a sharp diving turn to come up behind them. His wingman Hefter followed along behind his squadron leader, dropping several hundred feet in a few seconds as he swooped in behind the leading "enemy" aircraft, piloted by Lützow. Just as Hefter "had Lützow in his scope and decided to 'take him'" there was a collision, and a piece of the wing of Hefter's plane was sheared off.[17] Hefter immediately broke off the maneuver, struggling to keep his plane level. The Fokker D XIII he was piloting was a sesquiplane, a biplane with a lower wing much smaller than the upper. Without half of the upper right wing, Hefter thought it unlikely that he could generate enough lift to keep the plane level and in the air. Constantly eyeing his right wing lest it come off completely, Hefter only just managed to reach the airfield. The landing looked like it would be more of a crash, but Hefter kept his plane level and brought it down smoothly some six minutes after the collision had occurred. Falck recalled that he was "severely chastised for not bailing out, as the plane was in bad shape." He thought he had done the right thing by landing, but was told in no uncertain terms that aircraft were more easily replaced than pilots.[18]

Despite destroying two of the facility's few trainers, their commanding officer wrote of the incident that "the smooth landing by the young pilots . . . proves the self-confidence and good nerves of the pilots."[19]

His praise proved to be well deserved. Their class of graduates from Lipetsk would become known as the "Kameradschaft '31" (for the year they began their training back in Germany), the most elite class to graduate from Lipetsk.[20] Their careers highlight how essential the facilities in Russia proved for German rearmament. The class of 1931–1932 would stay friends, risking execution together fifteen years later when they defied Hitler during the "fighter pilot's revolt." Nearly all of them would have distinguished careers. Falck eventually became commander of Germany's night fighter defense force. Lützow would score 110 kills during the Second World War, only to disappear in action two weeks before the end of the war while flying an ME 262 jet fighter. One of Lützow's wingmen, Hannes Trautloft, would account for fifty-eight planes, eventually being promoted to a series of senior command positions. Günther Radusch would eventually claim sixty-five kills, going down as the Luftwaffe's top night fighter pilot, a skill he had practiced for the first time at Lipetsk. Only

Ekkehard Hefter, who had so barely avoided disaster on this training mission, would fail to become an ace. Instead, he bore the ill-fated title of the first pilot killed in action after the reformation of the German Air Force. His plane crashed on one of the first combat missions of the Condor Legion in Spain.

The course that the Kameradschaft '31 graduated from had evolved considerably since Lipetsk's inception.[21] Frequent meetings, particularly over the winter breaks, resulted in constant changes to the school's manuals and teaching materials, all with an eye to a time when Versailles' strictures would not limit German air power. The list of those teaching or managing the curriculum at Lipetsk included Wilberg, Hugo Sperrle—who served as an instructor and also ran the school in Lieth-Thomsen's occasional absences—Kurt Student, and Hans Jeschonnek, as well as Albert Kesselring and Hans Stumpff.[22] Hans Jeschonnek would become Luftwaffe chief of staff in 1939. Sperrle, Kesselring, and Stumpff would reach the rank of field marshal in the Luftwaffe. In essence, with the exception of Walter Wever, all the major figures of the future Luftwaffe were involved in crafting the training program at Lipetsk. By 1932, their basic objective was clear: develop the cadres, doctrine, and training procedures for a rapid expansion of the German Air Force, with an eye toward war with France and Poland.

Although flight training at Lipetsk had proved a great success in the summer of 1932, there were signs that the relationship might have already peaked. Senior Reichswehr officers had begun to consider the possibility of relocating training back to Germany, as fears of British or French military intervention declined and the costs of training in Russia rose amid the Great Depression. Chief of Staff for Training Hellmuth Felmy would write that "armaments expenditures in Russia are now only carried out for political reasons," adding that it would be best to give up the difficult work abroad as soon as possible."[23]

In July 1932, the Nazis won a dominant electoral victory, nearly doubling their percentage of the national vote to 37.3 percent.[24] The large Nazi and Communist factions continued to block any possible governing coalition. This placed the onus ever more on the eighty-four-year-old Hindenburg and the incompetent Papen. As a result, new Minister of Defense Schleicher became Germany's dominant political figure. Although he had argued that to moderate the Nazis, they should be brought into the government on his terms, their growing electoral clout forced him to consider alternatives. Schleicher instead decided to co-opt parts of the Nazi program. He increased military spending and began plans for a national public works program on August 10.[25]

Schleicher also remained concerned with maintaining the friendly military-to-military relationship with the Soviet Union. At the end of the summer, he personally invited Tukhachevsky, now of course Voroshilov's deputy, chief of ordnance, and most impressively, "the commander-designate of the Red Army in the event of full-scale war in Europe," to visit Germany.[26] Tukhachevsky arrived to a warm reception from the German Army Command in Berlin, where he received the distinct honor of being greeted by President Hindenburg in person. For the next three weeks, he was wined and dined, visited important factories and military installations, received assistance in concluding deals with German armaments firms, and above all, spent a great deal of time with Schleicher.[27] In the aftermath of Tukhachevsky's visit, even Tomka appeared likely to resume operation: a Reichswehr team was dispatched to check on the state of the facility on October 5, 1932, and prepare for the following testing season.[28]

As the fall progressed, the German political environment continued to deteriorate. A new election on November 6, 1932, did little to improve the situation: the Nazi share of the vote declined slightly, with the Communists and the far-right DNVP picking up most of the difference.[29] The outcome made clear the continued inability of any party to form a coalition, so Chancellor von Papen openly tried to convince Hindenburg to dissolve the Reichstag and declare martial law to avoid a potential civil war. To forestall that possibility, and undermine Papen, Schleicher ordered a Reichswehr war game run to practice for a potential outbreak of violence between the Nazis and Communists. In a result that may have been dictated by Schleicher, the Reichswehr failed to prevent or stop a civil war.[30] Hindenburg took the point to heart, and demanded Papen's resignation.[31] It was duly offered on November 17.

After Papen's resignation, there was a two-week interregnum with no chancellor. Hindenburg then appointed Schleicher himself to the chancellorship. It was a role the general would have preferred to hand off to others, as he disliked the limelight. And Schleicher realized only too late that his position was entirely untenable. He tried to cobble together a workable parliamentary majority, either by wooing the Nazis, or by building an alliance of "moderate Nazis on the Right to the Moderate Social Democrats on the Left," an improbable coalition.[32]

The major accomplishment of Schleicher's autumn was to expand the illegal rearmament of the Reichswehr.[33] In early November (still as minister of defense) he approved the Umbau Plan, the first rearmament plan that openly violated Versailles. It called for a twenty-one-division army with 147,000 frontline soldiers, while planning for even greater long-term armament.[34] He had also succeeded—in his brief time in the chancellorship—in creating a 600 million Reichsmark ($183 million USD) public works fund, a sum 50 percent larger than the entire German military budget in 1932.[35] It also provided funding for military-industrial mobilization. Finally, Schleicher achieved a key concession from the Western powers at the ongoing Geneva disarmament talks. In November and December, the French and British conceded in principle the right of Germany to an equality of status with regards to arms, a vague formula that Schleicher planned to argue meant acceptance of partial German rearmament.[36]

However, despite the general success of his foreign policy, Schleicher's domestic position proved increasingly untenable in the absence of parliamentary support and growing street violence. By New Year's Day 1933, he believed he had one last hope of retaining power: declare martial law and crack down on the National Socialists by force. It was something he was reluctant to do, though he told Hindenburg it might succeed. Hindenburg forbade it, based upon the results of the failed war game Schleicher had run the previous November.[37] Nevertheless, on the evening of January 28, 1933, Schleicher sounded out the senior officers of the Reichswehr about the possibilities of military action against both radical right and left. By that juncture, the political reliability of the Reichswehr, particularly its junior officers, was less than certain. Schleicher decided to delay any decisive action.[38]

Then a final disaster struck. Papen, spiteful toward Schleicher after his own removal, convinced Hindenburg privately to agree to Hitler's demands on the broader inclusion of the National Socialists in the government. This meant removing Schleicher and putting that "Bohemian corporal," as Hindenburg contemptuously referred to Hitler, in the chancellorship.[39] When Hindenburg reluctantly agreed, there remained one last hurdle to be cleared in the Nazi quest for power: the possibility that the senior officers of the Reichswehr would oppose the National Socialists, with or without General Schleicher. Had the senior generals of the army stood firmly together, perhaps the crisis could have been managed. It was not to be. The army had lost faith in Schleicher.[40]

Hitler had already found a military partner. General Werner von Blomberg, commander of the Reichswehr's First Division, despised Schleicher for organizing his demotion in 1928. And, after his trips to the Soviet Union, Blomberg was enamored with the idea that a dictatorial regime represented the best means of rearming the state and preparing for war. He told a fellow officer that "I have seen in Russia what can be got out of the masses. I was not far short of coming home a complete Bolshevist. Anyhow, that trip [in 1928] turned me into a National Socialist."[41] He was convinced that Hitler represented the Reichswehr's interests better than the alternatives.[42] On January 28, 1933, Blomberg agreed in principle to take over as minister of defense in a Nazi cabinet. In that role, he would shepherd the army into the era of Nazi dictatorship. Two days later, Hitler accepted the chancellorship.[43] A new era had begun.

PART II
Reaping the Whirlwind

CHAPTER 24

The End of an Era

After dusk on January 30, 1933, Berlin resounded with cheers and noisy celebrations. Brown-shirted SA paramilitaries thronged in the streets, joined by thousands of men, women, and children from all walks of life. A reporter for the *New York Times* noted that "singing and chanting civilians" waving swastika banners "swung through the Brandenburg Gate down Unter den Linden, which was jammed with jubilant crowds of Nazi sympathizers."[1] The celebrations lasted late into the night. In some cases, the cheering revelers were joined by uniformed soldiers. In one instance, a gallant-looking cavalry officer in uniform—Count Claus von Stauffenberg, who would in 1944 try to assassinate Hitler—placed himself at the head of one of these "victory parades."[2]

Hitler had triumphed. After months of political deadlock, several indecisive elections, and rapidly rising violence between radical right and left, the elderly and infirm President Paul von Hindenburg reluctantly appointed Hitler chancellor, responsible for forming a new government. Within hours, communist newspapers had been banned. Gunfire resounded in working-class neighborhoods across Germany as Nazi brownshirts and communists clashed.

While the National Socialist German Workers' Party seemed uncouth and unruly to many bourgeois citizens, growing political and economic instability seemed to threaten even worse. Over the previous week, wild rumors had swirled throughout the country. On one hand, there were whispers of a general strike by the left to pre-empt the Nazis. On the other, there were stories of a military coup on the night of January 29, before Hindenburg's final decision in favor of Hitler. Departing Chancellor Schleicher had indeed summoned the German High Command to discuss "resistance" to Hitler that day, which might have resulted in a military dictatorship.[3] But neither event came to pass.

On February 27, 1933, a fire broke out at the Reichstag. The communists were blamed; most likely, the SA had started the conflagration.[4] Less than a week later, with the country in a frenzy amid widespread fears of a communist uprising, Chancellor Hitler called another national election. SS and SA men guarded the polling places in Prussia to ensure the "right" outcome. Regardless, it was clear that enthusiasm for the Nazis and for Hitler was high. They would receive nearly 44 percent of the vote; their allies, the German National People's Party, received an additional 8 percent, providing Hitler with a foolproof majority.[5] Immediately after the election, he banned the Communists. Not long afterward, all other political parties were banned. On March 1, 1933, the Army was officially subordinated to the Nazi Party. General Blomberg supervised a purge of the office corps, removing those officers who supported Schleicher or could pose a threat. The twelve-year Nazi monopoly on power had begun.[6]

Having at long last attained power, Hitler's grand strategic plan was not entirely clear, even to himself. Perhaps the clearest statement of his immediate intentions in 1933 he confided in a letter to a diplomat in the German Foreign Ministry. His objectives, he declared, were fivefold: to eliminate Marxism; to regenerate Germany; to increase the technical armament of the military; to exploit "all the energy" of Germany's population for a defensive buildup; and finally, to gain legal recognition for the renewal of German power on the world stage.[7] Central to all of these aims was the resurrection of German military strength. Less than six weeks into his chancellorship, Hitler told General Blomberg, "The future of Germany depends exclusively and only on the reconstruction of the Wehrmacht. All other tasks must cede precedence to the task of rearmament."[8] His central goal, from his first days in power, was to rearm in preparation for a war to restore Germany to great power status.

Hitler was not the only one who saw rearmament as the top priority of the state. The Reichswehr and preceding governments had already begun laying the foundations for a large-scale rearmament program. Three elements were necessary to restore German power: a massive increase in the size of the military through the mobilization of manpower; the development of new technologies of war; and the mobilization of the national economy for the mass production of weapons. Germany had prepared for all three tasks before Hitler came to power. Thanks to Minister of Defense Wilhelm Groener, the German state had developed the first mass-mobilization plans for the national economy.[9] By the end of 1932, the German military industry had already begun to "tool up" for mass production, thanks to this financial assistance.[10] And in the USSR, Germany had already developed some of the technological and human resources that would make Hitler's rearmament plan possible.

Thanks to its work at Lipetsk, by 1933, the Reichswehr had more than 300 trained pilots and observers, as well as cadres of skilled engineers and mechanics. These men would serve in key command and training positions as Germany rebuilt its air forces. Some indication of this can be seen from their later service records: twenty-two officers who would later achieve the rank of General der Flieger (General of the Flyers, the equivalent of a three-star general) in the Luftwaffe had either studied, taught, or had a command position at Lipetsk. And by 1933, the Reichswehr had tested nearly two dozen aircraft prototypes at Lipetsk, simultaneously developing skilled engineering talent at nearly all of Germany's aircraft manufacturing firms.

Kama played an equally profound role in preparing the ground for the expansion of the German armored forces. German training manuals already emphasized the importance of independent armored formations as part of mobile, combined arms operations, despite the absence of tanks in Germany.[11] Of the thirty German students

Leon Trotsky rallies Red Army soldiers during the Polish Bolshevik War, 1920. As head of the Red Army, he played a major role in beginning cooperation with the Reichswehr. (Bain News Service photograph collection, Library of Congress Prints and Photographs Division, Washington, DC)

German and Soviet statesmen negotiating the Treaty of Rapallo in 1922. From left to right: Adolf Joffe, Georgy Chicherin, Leonid Krasin, and Joseph Wirth. (Bundesarchiv, Bild 183-R14433 / CC-BY-SA 3.0, 1922)

Chef des Heeresleitung General Hans von Seeckt and Minister of
Defense Otto Gessler attend maneuvers. (Bundesarchiv, Bild 102-
10883, Foto: Georg Pahl, August 1926)

Unable to develop modern technologies of war at home, the Reichswehr used approximations of aircraft and tanks in maneuvers. (Bundesarchiv, Bild 102-14330, Foto: Georg Pahl, 1933)

Lipetsk Air Base, pictured in 1926, was the first joint military facility to begin operation. Visible here are the living quarters and storage facilities; in the foreground, construction is about to begin on a new barracks for the next class of pilots. (Bundesarchiv. RH 2 Bild-02215-056, Spring 1926)

Four Russian guards at Lipetsk Air Base pose for a photograph in the winter of 1926/1927. One Soviet guard would be killed during a break-in—likely an attempt to steal German technical material—in 1933. (Bundesarchiv, RH 2 Bild-02292-233, 1926/1927)

A group of young German pilots arriving at Lipetsk pose for a photograph. Ordered to disguise themselves as tourists to avoid attracting attention on their journey, these young men have had trouble forgetting their military training, lining up by height as if on a parade ground. (Bundesarchiv, RH 2 Bild-02292-134, 1926/1927)

Flying at Lipetsk—either as a test pilot or as a pilot in training—could be a dangerous proposition. Here, a Fokker D-XIII crashed near the airfield. (Bundesarchiv, RH 2 Bild-02292-189, 1926/1927)

Flying at Lipetsk claimed the lives of many German and Soviet pilots during its time of operation, requiring the drafting of rules on the transport of German bodies back to Berlin. Memorial services were held at Lipetsk before the bodies' departure. In this instance, a crash claimed the life of a German pilot named Daurer. (Bundesarchiv, RH 2 Bild-02292-169, 1926/1927)

New equipment being tested at Lipetsk—in this instance, ski runners for a Fokker D-XIII. (Bundesarchiv, RH 2 Bild-02292-072, 1926/1927)

A *Staffelverband* of nine pilots flying in three *Ketten* of three aircraft each during aerial maneuvers. At least thirteen Second World War aces learned to fly at Lipetsk. (Bundesarchiv, RH 2 Bild-02292-141, 1926/1927)

Lipetsk was the only one of the joint facilities where senior officers were allowed to bring their families. Here a party includes many of the base's personnel at the Officer's *Kasino* (Club) in the winter of 1926/1927. The megaphone has printed on the side: "They are so stupid!" (Bundesarchiv, RH 2 Bild-02292-217, 1926/1927)

An aerial shot of the Tomka chemical weapons base, laboratories, and testing grounds. Tomka replaced Podosinki as the home of German chemical weapons research in 1928. There, German and Soviet scientists worked very closely together. This photograph was almost certainly taken by Leopold von Sicherer, one of the base's senior chemists. (Bundesarchiv, MSg 2 Bild-00782-24, December 1928)

The main aims of research at Tomka were to test new ordnance and chemical weapons technology. Here, a German and Soviet team fires poison gas shells from a 105 mm field howitzer. (Bundesarchiv, MSg 2 Bild-00782-30, 1928/1933)

The main focus of testing at Tomka centered on dropping poison gas from planes onto the test range to see if chemical warfare could be conducted alongside strategic bombing. Here animal cages are prepared for dispersal around the testing ground. Rabbits and dogs were usually used as test subjects—note the dogs in the background to the left. (Bundesarchiv, MSg 2 Bild-00782-34, 1928/1931)

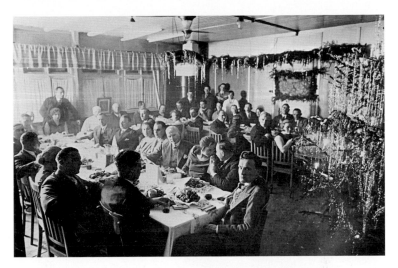

The Christmas party at Tomka in the officer's *Kasino*, possibly in 1928. Those present include German and Soviet scientists and officers, as well as local Soviet women invited as guests. The original caption, likely Sicherer's, reads: "Christmas was the great solemn event of an experimental period. The decorated Christmas tree, the cake plates with delicious pastries at every place on the lovingly laid banquet table, all the Tomkinesen [*sic*] 'into the [punch] bowl' and of course the invited Russian girls with their best possible civilian presentation, all this made for a delightful picture. . . . After the feast, Saint Nicholas and Servant Ruprecht rumbled into the dining room with a large sack. . . . Finally the steaming red wine punch was served, and our hearts grew warm. Who of us back then would not like to think back to it today." (Bundesarchiv, MSg 2 Bild-00782-65, December 1928/1931)

The Red Army's first five marshals. First row, right to left: Alexander Yegorov, Kliment Voroshilov, and Mikhail Tukhachevsky. Second row: Vasily Blyukher and Semyon Budyenny. The brilliant Tukhachevsky was the first to be shot in the purges. Blyukher and Yegorov would soon follow. (Public Domain, 1936)

Derived from the experimental engineering work conducted at Kama, Germany's first Panzer I tanks roll past Hitler during the Party rally at Nuremberg in September 1935. (Bundesarchiv, Bild 146-1995-066-10A, September 1935)

A formation of Junkers Ju-87 "Stuka" dive-bombers in the skies over Poland in September 1939. The Stuka was developed from the K-47, one of the last planes tested at the Lipetsk flight school. Its designer Hermann Pohlmann had his first aircraft designs tested in Russia. Of his several prototypes the Reichswehr dispatched to Lipetsk, the K-47 was the most successful. (Bundesarchiv, Bild 183-1987-1210-502 Foto: Heinrich Hoffmann, September 1939)

Soviet and German officers in Brest-Litovsk during the joint victory parade enjoying a moment of socializing beneath a portrait of Stalin. (Bundesarchiv, Bild 101I-121-0011-20, Foto: Böttcher, 22 September 1939)

A scene during the joint Soviet-German parade through Brest-Litovsk on September 22, 1939. Here a Soviet T-26 Panzer from Semyon Krivoshein's Twenty-ninth Light Tank Brigade passes German motorcycle troops from Heinz Guderian's XIX Panzer Corps. Both commanders were alumni of Kama. (Bundesarchiv, Bild 101I-121-0012-30, Gutjahr, 22 September 1939)

A photo taken in the early hours of August 23, 1939, just after the signing of the Molotov-Ribbentrop Pact; Stalin shakes Ribbentrop's hand before the celebratory drinking begins. (Bundesarchiv, Bild 183-H27337 / CC-BY-SA 3.0, 23 August 1939).

The renewal of the Molotov-Ribbentrop Pact on September 28, 1939. Front row, left to right: Soviet Ambassador in Berlin Alexei Shkvarzev, Vyacheslav Molotov. Back row: Richard Schulze-Kossens (Ribbentrop's aide), Boris Shaposhnikov (chief of staff of the Red Army and alumnus of general staff courses in Germany), Joachim von Ribbentrop, Joseph Stalin, Vladimir Pavlov (translator). (Public Domain, 28 September 1939)

A photo from Molotov's first meeting with Ribbentrop in Berlin in November 1940. As the relationship frayed, Ribbentrop and Hitler pitched an expansion of the state's partnership and a joint war on the British Empire. After the failure of the meeting, Hitler would decide upon the invasion of the Soviet Union. (Bundesearchiv, Bild 183-1991-0207-505, 12 November 1940)

Three alumni of cooperation with the USSR play cards as they wait to be called as witnesses at the Nuremberg War Crimes Tribunals after the war. From left to right: Luftwaffe Field Marshal Hugo Sperrle, Wehrmacht Chief of the General Staff Heinz Guderian, Luftwaffe General Hans-Jürgen Stumpff, and Luftwaffe Field Marshal Erhard Milch. Sperrle had been acting commandant at Lipetsk, Guderian had spent extended time at Kama driving armored vehicles, and Stumpff had learned to fly at Lipetsk. Milch was involved in German rearmament within Germany. (Public Domain, 1945)

who completed the full curriculum there, seventeen would eventually reach the rank of Generalmajor—a divisional commander in the Wehrmacht—or above.[12] Veterans of cooperation with the Red Army included Walter Nehring, future commander of the Afrika Korps, and Georg-Hans Reinhardt, commander of Army Group Center in the latter years of the Second World War.[13] The country's top theorists—Volckheim, Oswald Lutz, and Heinz Guderian—had all either lived at Kama or visited it. Kama had thus helped to train the theorists and future cadres of the reconstituted German armored forces. And, as at Lipetsk, cooperation played a crucial role in the development of engineering expertise: starting in 1933, engineers like Erich Woelfert, Johann Hoffmann, and Georg Hagelloch—all of whom had worked at Kama—would begin designing the next generation of German tanks.

Tomka's role was different, but also important. By 1933, the research performed there redirected German doctrine and resources away from the sort of chemical weapons program Germany had possessed during the First World War. Its research teams had demonstrated the incompatibility of chemical weapons with maneuver warfare, and the high costs of using poison gas in conjunction with strategic bombing. The vision of German military theorists—"the restoration of the primacy of both the maneuver and the offensive in battle"—required a degree of precision that chemical weapons could not provide. It was thus a threat, rather than an aid, to the type of war German officers planned to fight.[14] This conclusion would direct German training and doctrine through the outbreak of the war.

Drawing in part on the resources developed in Russia, Hitler began accelerating German rearmament, though initially with caution. On January 30, 1933, Hitler had authorised the creation of the Reichluftfahrtministerium (the Reich Air Ministry, or RLM). In charge as the new secretary of state for aviation was Erhardt Milch, who had been involved with Lipetsk tangentially throughout the previous half-decade. Milch was half-Jewish, but a dedicated Nazi; he would operate under the supervision of famed pilot and senior Nazi leader Hermann Göring. In February 1933, Hitler ordered the addition of 14,000 new personnel to the Army, in violation of Versailles. The Nazi state announced the formation of a Reich Defense Council in April.[15] But in reality, none of these decisions deviated significantly from Schleicher's rearmament program of the previous fall.[16] Hitler, more than General Blomberg, realized the diplomatic repercussions of rearming.[17]

Hitler's actions against the limitations of Versailles were largely consistent with the arc of Reichswehr planning beginning at the end of the First World War. His program was only possible because German statesmen like Stresemann, Groener, and Schleicher had envisioned and planned for the very same event. Stresemann and Groener saw a revived German military as a tool for renegotiating the status quo in Europe. Their means for achieving that goal were the same as Hitler's: a rejuvenated army, navy, and air force. Hitler's ambitions went much further, of course, but in 1933, he represented continuity, rather than a break on the key question of rearmament.[18] That meant broad support from the Reichswehr.

Hitler's coming to power naturally triggered some alarm in Moscow. His book, *Mein Kampf*, explicitly called for the destruction of the Soviet Union, among other things.

Nevertheless, Stalin consistently saw Germany's Social Democrats—rivals for the hearts of the working class—as a greater threat than the Nazis, even after Hitler's seizure of power. Stalin also hoped that Nazism would bring about a renewal of the military partnership.[19]

It was not immediately clear after he came to power that Hitler would terminate military cooperation with the Soviet Union. Before becoming chancellor, of course, he had inveighed against Bolshevism and the Soviet Union at great length. And he was aware that some sort of military work was being conducted with the Soviets: in his unpublished second book, written in 1928, he devoted an entire chapter to the subject of military cooperation with the Soviet Union. He concluded that "the belief in a German-Russian understanding is fanciful as long as a government that is preoccupied with the sole effort to transmit the Bolshevist poison to Germany rules in Russia. . . . The hope of a German-Russian alliance—a hope that is haunting the minds of many nationalist German politicians—is very doubtful."[20] His basis for this was largely his racial calculus. He claimed that because the Soviet Union was led by Jewish revolutionaries, it revealed the "fundamentally international-capitalistic character of Bolshevism."[21] This, he believed, meant that the Bolsheviks were likely to ally with the Western democracies against Germany regardless of German policy.

Within weeks of coming to power, however, Hitler struck a very different pose toward the Soviet Union. Repudiating one aspect of Versailles, the ban on formal military attachés, he told the Soviets that Germany would like to appoint Colonel Otto Hartmann to that position. Stalin, via Voroshilov, passed along his approval.[22] Publicly, too, Hitler seemed to indicate greater tolerance for international communism. In one of his first addresses to the Reichstag as chancellor on March 23, 1933, he made it clear that his attitude toward the Soviet Union would be amicable, and that his government was "determined to cultivate friendly relations which are productive for both parties." "The fight against Communism in Germany is an internal affair," he announced, "in which we will never tolerate outside interference. The national political relations to other powers to which we are related by mutual interests will not be affected by this."[23] Hitler told his new ambassador to the Soviet Union in late 1933 to take this speech as "the guideline for Soviet-German relations."[24] He also agreed to a renewal of the 1926 Treaty of Berlin.

Despite some signals that Hitler was willing to maintain elements of the relationship, the circumstances that had thrust the Red Army and Reichswehr together had begun to change. Even before Hitler came to power, General Schleicher mentioned the possibility of closing one of the schools—Lipetsk, the most expensive—to Tukhachevsky during his visit the previous fall. With Hitler's formation of a new "civilian" air ministry (subordinated to the Ministry of Defense) and the beginning of flight training in Germany, Lipetsk was redundant.[25] Its training and testing functions would gradually be transferred back to Germany, despite the risk of an Allied response. German interest in cooperation waned as the new Nazi regime proved eager to restart rearmament work at home.[26]

Further, events in Germany highlighted Nazism's attitude toward communism. Brown-shirted SA thugs openly attacked Soviet citizens in the streets of German cities without repercussions. German police officers arrested Soviet government representatives, roughed them up, and then released them without explanation. Soviet diplomat Nikolai Krestinsky recorded in his diary that "All these lawless actions, arbitrary rule, outrage and violence create a very tense atmosphere." Krestinsky noted, "The contradictions between the official statements of the chancellor and other members of the government about the unchanged character of Soviet-German Relations and these daily acts of hostility."[27]

That spring, General Mikhail Tukhachevsky invited the Reichswehr's chief of armaments, General Alfred von Bockelberg, to visit the Soviet Union's top armaments factories. This was intended as a return invitation for Tukhachevsky's own visit the previous fall. Bockelberg arrived in late April and spent nearly a month in the Soviet Union. He repeatedly and generously complimented his Russian hosts, encouraging the maintenance of the tenuous relationship. His personal behavior raised a few eyebrows though: the Red Army Foreign Liaison paired with Hartmann wrote that "[Military Attaché] Hartmann complained to me about Bockelberg's behavior as unworthy of a Prussian officer: he got drunk at the reception, and after we had left, he behaved indecently, finally falling under the table."[28]

Despite this "friendliness," it became clear during Bockelberg's visit that the Soviets were concerned about political circumstances in Berlin. And although Bockelberg himself evinced great enthusiasm for continued cooperation, it became apparent that the new government in Berlin was skeptical.[29] On May 15, Bockelberg and Hartmann met with Yakov Fishman. Tukhachevsky had agreed to a preliminary testing program for Tomka in March 1933, an offer Fishman reiterated on May 10.[30] He told Hartmann that the Soviets planned to continue research alongside the Germans there in 1933 despite disappointments about the proposed research program and the lack of new chemical agents.[31] The two sides even discussed, albeit in vague terms, the possibility of a 1934 program for Tomka.[32] On May 16, Bockelberg reported that he and Fishman had reached a tentative agreement for a ten-week testing season and an exchange of chemical warfare officers.[33]

However, neither side offered any specific objectives for the 1933 testing program, unlike as in years past. While Hartmann reported that "there is among the highest-placed Russians a serious and sincere willingness to deepen our military cooperation," the changed political circumstances were driving the two sides apart.[34] A German report on Bockelberg's trip recorded that "it was immediately clear what was going on: the interests of [the two sides] conflicted with each other."[35] Eventually convinced nothing could be achieved in the 1933 testing year, Bockelberg finally proposed that a team of six men go to Tomka to collect and return equipment there to Germany.

The Soviets had profited enormously from their partnership with Germany, but still had hopes of even greater gains. Soviet aviation and tank production relied upon technical knowledge acquired in part through the Reichswehr, built in factories that had been equipped with German machine tools, and managed by engineers trained in conjunction with the Germans. By 1933, the Red Army estimated that it had a yearly production capacity of up to 40,400 tanks and armored vehicles and 13,100 aircraft, far greater than any other country in the world.[36] Those figures would not have been possible without the concessionary agreements, the training arrangements, and the capital investment that were arranged with Reichswehr assistance—all of which were still ongoing.

The continued role of German officers in training and modernizing the Red Army was still of the utmost importance. Between the visit of Fiebig's group in 1925 and the rise of Hitler in 1933, thousands of Soviet officers had been trained alongside the Reichswehr. Over 150 senior officers trained or studied in Germany, some for a year at a time. They included two Red Army chiefs of staff; two of the Soviet Union's five marshals; the heads of the Soviet Air Force, Directorate of Motorization and Mechanization, Ordnance Department, and the Soviet Chemical Weapons program; as well as the country's leading theorists and heads of most of its major military education institutions. Cooperation led the Red Army to reorganize along German lines, adopting the General Staff model as its central organizing principle.[37] Partnership meant continued professionalization and modernization.

As a result, the Soviet reaction to Bockelberg's suggestion and growing evidence that Hitler intended to terminate the relationship was intense, with Soviet rhetoric and behavior turning sharply negative. During Bockelberg's visit, senior Bolshevik Karl Radek began penning a series of openly anti-Nazi editorials in the Soviet newspaper *Izvestia* [News], arguing for enforcement of the Treaty of Versailles—likely intended as a warning shot to the Germans about the costs of abandoning the partnership.[38] On May 30, the Soviet military attaché told the Reichswehr that the Red Army was officially canceling the 1933 testing schedule for Tomka, regardless of German intentions.[39] In early June—while the flying courses were ongoing—the Red Army abruptly halted all traffic to and from Lipetsk, cutting off the Germans from the rest of the world.[40] In mid-June, the Soviets suspended their activities at Kama. On June 26, the Red Army formally informed the Germans that they considered themselves "released . . . from its previous obligations."[41] That same day, Chief of the Army Command Kurt von Hammerstein-Equord submitted a letter to Voroshilov informing the Russians that Lipetsk would now be closed permanently.[42]

Complicating the dissolution of the decade-long partnership were the mixed messages emanating from the German Foreign Office and Ministry of Defense, where many *Ostpolitik* advocates hoped to maintain the Rapallo relationship. On July 8, General Hammerstein hosted a farewell breakfast for the Soviet officers who were then studying in Germany. Some had been in country for more than six months. Hammerstein was joined by Blomberg, Otto von Stülpnagel, and fluent Russian speaker General Hans Krebs. All four men had spent time in the Soviet Union. On the Soviet side, Ambassador Lev Khinchuk was joined by General Mikhail Levandovsky and six other officers of general rank.[43] Hammerstein began the event with a speech to the "traditional friendship of the two armies."[44] He was answered by Levandovsky who, rather more pointedly, stated his great regret in leaving, and blamed the German Army for the declining relationship.

A similar tone dominated a larger dinner that evening, attended by most of the Reichswehr's senior officers, Minister of Defense Blomberg, Ambassador Khinchuk, and a number of senior Red Army officers. Both sides made speeches emphasizing the need for continued good relations. Blomberg went so far as to say there was "every precondition" for the establishment of trust between the Red Army and the

Reichswehr. "Common efforts of the diplomats and military of such a large country as the Soviet Union and of new Germany will manage to maintain equilibrium in Europe."[45] But not long afterward, the Reichswehr would inform the Soviet Foreign Ministry they no longer intended to participate in joint maneuvers or observe Soviet ones; the Soviets would reciprocate by canceling the dispatch of their annual class to military education courses in Germany.[46]

The "liquidation process" for Kama and Lipetsk began two weeks later, when the Soviet side started packing up German equipment at Kama. The same procedure began at Lipetsk, though the continued presence of German pilots undergoing training delayed the process. Tensions ran high there as late that summer, an unknown assailant shot one of the guard officers on duty. The Germans suspected yet another case of technological theft, this time gone awry.[47]

On July 26, a German team of six men arrived to dismantle the station at Tomka. Soviet military intelligence reported that their orders were "putting everything in order and repairing all the property left" before the handover to the Soviets.[48] The trip was not a pleasant one for the Germans. The Soviets had replaced the popular officer Yan Zhigur with General N. S. Gubanov, who proved much less friendly. The Germans complained that he even denied them permission to leave the camp enclosure to bathe in the river when the temperature reached 104° Fahrenheit. Gubanov also intentionally impeded their work, trying to prevent the removal of any equipment when he could, particularly German-manufactured testing equipment and the camp's vehicles.[49] While the team succeeded in getting the majority of their vehicles out, they were forced to leave valuable laboratory equipment at the Tomka grounds.[50] According to Soviet military intelligence, the abandoned equipment included nine cars, a tractor, one of Krupp's experimental chemical tanks, a complete laboratory with equipment, a newly equipped electrical power station, and a great deal of technical material.[51]

Besides documenting what they were leaving and packing what they could, the German team had another mission: intelligence gathering. They were ordered to record everything they saw at the base, as well as the general state of affairs in the region. They noted that the Soviets were already actively expanding their chemical warfare facilities at Tomka. By the time of their visit that July, in fact, the Red Army had their own aircraft, new testing vehicles, a new rail line direct to the station, and other new facilities.[52] The German officers also noted with horror that the region was still gripped by famine—though they were mostly concerned with the fate of the local Volga Germans, rather than ethnic Russians. Their report estimated that sixty to seventy people were dying each day from starvation, particularly children and the elderly.[53] Underneath that observation, the German author dutifully recorded the prices of food at their hotel, well out of the reach of even skilled laborers. After making these final observations, the German team departed Tomka, officially turning over the facility to VOKhIMU on August 16.[54]

In mid-September, the last German officers departed Lipetsk and Kama, too.[55] As at Tomka, the Soviets assisted German teams in loading railcars with some—but not all—of their technical equipment. The Reichswehr's priority list for material to be shipped home were, first, the newest aircraft; then came all parachutes, experimental weapons, camera and optical equipment, their radios, the base's archive, and all winter clothes, as well as the mess silverware.[56] Much else could not be returned to Germany, ranging from Lipetsk's prefabricated hangars to its engine-testing equipment. As a result, the Soviet Air Force inherited a bounty of technical material when the Germans left on September 14.[57] The following day, the last Germans left Kama, similarly abandoning much equipment. The Soviets would send ten tanks back to Germany via rail car and ship, while retaining more than 220,000 rubles' worth of equipment for themselves.[58] The Red Army immediately began to convert Kama into their own armored warfare training ground.[59]

The final element of the Soviet-German military network remaining was Moscow Central, the headquarters of German military operations in the USSR. The oldest element of the Soviet-German partnership, it was now headed by pilot Lothar Schüttel. Now that Germany was able to openly maintain a military attaché in Moscow, and the joint facilities had all come to an end, his office was no longer necessary.[60] At the end of September, Schüttel was to hand the keys to Moscow Central to German military attaché Hartmann, who would turn it into his official residence.[61]

On September 23, Soviet Foreign Liaison officer Vasily Smagin hosted a goodbye dinner for the departing members of Moscow Central.[62] The guest list included the heads of each Soviet department who had worked alongside the Germans: each sent his excuses. Smagin informed the Germans that their presence was needed at ongoing maneuvers. It was a sign of how the times had changed. At the dinner itself, Hartmann and Smagin had a frank, private exchange where the latter made it clear that the main reason the Soviets had moved to terminate joint military activities with the Reichswehr—in reality, a process driven as much by Berlin as Moscow—was the increasing hostility of the entire German state to the Soviet Union. One Red Army officer had actually been attacked in public earlier in the summer. But Smagin also reassured Hartmann that there were major voices in the military who retained "the desire to resume the military contacts."[63]

Shortly after Schüttel's departure, Minister of Defense Blomberg sent a letter to Commissar for Defense Voroshilov. Blomberg wrote that with the "liquidation" of the three experimental stations, a "long period of close and friendly collaboration has drawn to a close." He added that he hoped it would "remain of continuing benefit to the armies of both countries."[64]

Blomberg wrote another draft of the letter, recommending the resumption of direct military cooperation in the near future. That sentence was cut from the version that Voroshilov would read.[65] The first Soviet-German partnership was at an end.

CHAPTER 25

Enemies Again

Even if he was responsible for it, Hitler worried that the closure of the last of the Soviet-German facilities might damage his long-term rearmament plans. On September 2, 1933, General Blomberg learned that France was pushing the Soviet Union to provide details of German military activity in the Soviet Union.[1] Should the truth come to light, France might then have grounds to impose sanctions through the League of Nations, or even react militarily to enforce Versailles.[2]

The French already had some intelligence about the nature of German rearmament prior to Hitler. On September 25, they approached their British colleagues about taking action against Germany based on a dossier they had prepared. However, the British government, led by Prime Minister Ramsay MacDonald, was unwilling to play along.[3] A socialist, a pacifist, and inclined to be sympathetic to Germany, MacDonald later commented he was thankful that the "blot on the peace of the world, the Treaty of Versailles," was "vanishing." "France has again had a severe lesson," he added, "and I hope it will take this time."[4] Despite reports of rearmament and Hitler's erratic behavior from the British ambassador in Berlin, the MacDonald government refused to commit to coordinated action with the French.[5]

European disarmament talks, which had begun in 1932, were scheduled to resume on October 16, 1933.[6] Hitler had retained as foreign minister professional diplomat Konstantin von Neurath, who had been appointed by his predecessor. During preparatory meetings in Paris, Neurath demanded French disarmament as a prerequisite to any concessions. The French, for their part, insisted upon a halt to covert German rearmament prior to any further reductions to their own already paltry forces. Hitler sought an excuse to withdraw from the negotiations, though only when he could pin the blame on his adversaries. When it became clear that the Americans, British, and French would oppose the German position, he withdrew the German delegation and simultaneously announced his country's withdrawal from the League of Nations.[7]

It was a bold move. The Germans justified their withdrawal on the grounds of the vague British formula given to Kurt von Schleicher before Hitler came to power, guaranteeing Germany "equality of status of arms." Hitler's sudden withdrawal split British and French decision-makers. While British prime minister MacDonald was sympathetic toward Germany, the French lacked clear leadership altogether.[8] Between 1930 and 1940, a carousel of unstable parliamentary coalitions resulted in French cabinets lasting an average of just five months in office.[9] Nevertheless, then-head of government Edouard Daladier considered military action, provided the British would participate. Once again, however, the British would not go along. As Robert Vansittart, the anti-appeasement head of the British Foreign Office recalled, "we paddled in a puree of words."[10] Hitler's professions of peace did not reassure Vansittart, "but, having disarmed ourselves more than the Germans," his government had few options.[11] Without the British, Prime Minister Daladier could not move against Germany, instead stepping down from office on October 26.

Hitler sought to mollify international opinion after his abrupt withdrawal from the League by declaring his pacific intent in a series of addresses that fall.[12] As he privately told General Blomberg, he needed to buy time. Germany could even accept arms limitations, provided they did not impede the general German rearmament plan through 1935. At that point, Hitler argued, any restrictive rearmaments clauses could be safely ignored—presumably because he would possess the strength to deter likely adversaries.[13]

Hitler moved to isolate the French further later that same month. At his direction, Foreign Minister Neurath offered a nonaggression pact to Poland.[14] Jozef Pilsudski, then minister of military affairs and still the most prominent figure in government, proved willing, uncertain about the reliability of the Polish alliance with France. After several months of negotiation, the two countries signed an agreement on January 26, 1934. Notably, it did not recognize the existing border between them, but did succeed in distancing Poland from its French partner. This convinced appeasers in London that Hitler had no intention to revise Europe's borders by force.[15] The agreement with Poland had other consequences, including the continued decline of the Soviet-German relationship, which had long been predicated on shared hostility to Poland. As the Soviets correctly perceived, Hitler hoped to draw the Poles into a coalition against the USSR.[16]

There were figures in the German military and Foreign Ministry who disliked Hitler's pivot toward Poland and away from the USSR—including Minister of Defense Blomberg. Among the diplomats, one of the chief dissenters was the German ambassador in Moscow, Herbert von Dirksen. Since his appointment as ambassador by Gustav Stresemann five years earlier, Dirksen had become an ardent advocate for the Soviet-German military partnership.[17] His insistent stream of messages from Moscow urging the maintenance of cooperation with the Soviet Union led Hitler to order his recall and reassignment to Tokyo.[18] On November 3, 1933, Dirksen wrote to Kliment Voroshilov that the "memories of the years I spent in the Soviet Union will forever be linked in my mind with my feelings of profound respect that I have always had for you."[19] The two men traded personal mementos of their time together. Dirksen's wife had assembled a photo album from their time in Russia, which was delivered to Voroshilov. In turn, Voroshilov would report to Stalin, he had sent Dirksen a Palekh inkstand that he had always admired. Dirksen was indeed pleased, writing in reply that he would "keep it as a good memory of our work together in improving and consolidating the German-Soviet relationship."[20] In fact, Voroshilov had a later gift to bestow: a framed photo of the two men together would save Dirksen from being shot by Red Army soldiers when they occupied his estate in 1945.[21]

Dirksen's departure and Hitler's overtures to Poland encouraged Stalin to consider a new tack in foreign policy, intended to steer Soviet strategy as the German partnership deteriorated.[22] Stalin never abandoned the thought of a renewed Rapallo agreement, repeatedly returning to the possibility, but in the absence of any interest from Berlin he needed an alternative. That new policy would become known as "collective security"—a collection of bilateral partnerships aimed at maintaining the status quo in Europe. The author of collective security was Maxim Litvinov, who had become foreign minister in 1930.

Pudgy, bespectacled, humorless, and dour, Litvinov had been born Meir Wallach to a wealthy Jewish banking family in the Polish portion of the Russian Empire. He had spent much of his life in revolutionary exile, in the process developing outstanding language skills and marrying a British novelist, Ivy Low.[23] Those connections, and his presence in London, led to his appointment as the first Soviet ambassador to London in 1917—where he was rapidly arrested, and then exchanged for British spymaster Robert Bruce Lockhart. Litvinov's return to Russia launched him into the newly formed Soviet Foreign Ministry. By 1930, he had hounded his boss and predecessor Georgy Chicherin out of office as the latter's health declined, becoming commissar for foreign affairs in his stead. In that role, Litvinov would become a major advocate of partnership with the British and French governments, in opposition to Chicherin's preference for a partnership with Germany.

Stalin largely sidelined Litvinov as commissar for foreign affairs until 1933. Only with the decline of the German relationship did Stalin give him greater authority to pursue his proposed collective security strategy. Beginning in that year, Litvinov arranged a series of bilateral arrangements with Eastern European states, as well as a realignment toward France. While often portrayed after the war as a Soviet attempt to block Nazi aggression, this was only half the story.

Continued, quiet efforts at reconciliation made it clear that Germany was still a potential partner in Stalin's eyes. Even as military cooperation collapsed, the Soviet Union remained dependent on German imports, particularly machine tools necessary for further industrialization: in 1932, 72 percent of Soviet machinery imports had been from Germany.[24] There were also strategic reasons for Stalin to continue conversations with Germany: to prevent the great Soviet fear, a united anti-Soviet bloc including both Great Britain and Germany.[25]

As part of this balancing act, surreptitious diplomacy aimed at renewing the spirit of Rapallo would be conducted even as Litvinov signed alliances aimed at containing Germany. In January 1934, while Litvinov finalized a mutual defense pact with France, Alexander Egorov, the chief of the Red Army General Staff, met with Fritz von Twardowski, a German diplomat in Moscow. Egorov informed him of "the Red Army's desire to reestablish its old ties with the Reichswehr."[26] Egorov then approached Hartmann, the German military attaché, to invite General Werner von Fritsch, the new head of the Reichswehr, to visit the Soviet Union and discuss the renewal of direct military ties. Neither effort led to any concrete results.

The events of the winter of 1933–1934, marked by French caution, British acceptance, and Soviet efforts at rapprochement, convinced Hitler that he could gamble more aggressively. He ordered an acceleration in the pace of rearmament, beginning with the reestablishment of German air power. Five days after Germany's withdrawal from the League of Nations, Göring "announced the Führer's intention to re-establish Germany as an air power within the next twelve months" to a group of aircraft manufacturers.[27] The Reichsluftfahrtministerium (the Air Ministry, or RLM) soon began acquiring majority stakes in aircraft producers, beginning with Junkers.[28] The influx of state funds led to a surge of hiring by the aircraft industry, now directed by the state. From January 1933 to January 1935, the number of workers employed in aircraft manufacturing rocketed from 4,000 to 54,000.[29]

In late 1933, at Hitler's prompting, the Defense Ministry drew up the "December Plan." This envisioned the expansion of the Reichswehr to a peacetime strength of 300,000 men. This army, of twenty-one divisions, would be at full strength by March 1938. Terms of service would be reduced to one year in order to enable the rapid training of the largest possible number of men. The aim was clear: the beginnings of a national mobilization of German manpower.[30]

The December Plan was accompanied by proposals for far more ambitious technological rearmament. Lufthansa director Robert Knauss proposed the idea of a *Risiko-Luftwaffe* ("Risk Air Force") to his former boss Erhard Milch, now heading the RLM under Göring's supervision.[31] His concept centered on the early and rapid construction of a significantly sized air force—one with strategic bombing capabilities—that would deter French and British intervention while Germany rearmed its other branches.[32]

Given that Germany had not legally developed any military aircraft since 1918, this process was heavily dependent on the human resources and prototypes that had been developed in the Soviet Union. This was particularly true in terms of personnel, technology, and doctrine. To address the first, the nascent German RLM—still technically a civilian organization—received an influx of 550 officers from General Blomberg to spur its development.[33] These included numerous Lipetsk alumni, faculty, or organizers, including Wilhelm Speidel, Kurt Student, Hugo Sperrle, Helmuth Felmy, Hans Jeschonnek, Albert Kesselring, and Hans Stumpff, all of whom came to dominate the early RLM.[34]

In December 1933, the aircraft ideal to fit this new Risk Air Force did not yet exist, or were in early stages of development. There were two choices: wait for more modern aircraft to be ready for mass-production, or begin producing large numbers of aircraft that were either based upon civilian designs or had been tested at Lipetsk. Milch attempted to do both. On January 1, 1934, he introduced the first effort at nationally coordinated aviation procurement, the Rhineland Program. With it, the RLM began to place large orders for a number of the prototype designs tested at Lipetsk: 104 Arado Ar-64 and 65 single-seater fighters, 150 Dornier Do 11 bombers, and 200 of its successor, the Dornier Do 13.[35] In total, 42.6 percent of Germany's bomber production and 42.4 percent of its fighter production ordered in early 1934 came in the form of aircraft that had been tested and developed at Lipetsk.

The remainder of Milch's orders consisted almost entirely of civilian designs that had been produced for the German airlines. Given the tiny number of aeronautical engineers and aviation firms in operation in Germany, these designs, too, drew heavily from the legacy of Soviet-German cooperation. For instance, Milch sought to use civilian Junkers 52 (Ju-52) and Heinkel 51 (He-51) aircraft as the bombers at the core of the Risk Air Force. The Ju-52 was a lumbering but reliable airliner first produced in 1931. The RLM intended to convert it into its main bomber until more modern prototypes could enter production. Its leading designer, Ernst Zindel, had been one of the first figures in Soviet-German aviation cooperation, learning his trade designing all four aircraft models that would be assembled at Fili between 1920 and 1926.[36] Heinkel, whose firm had tested three prototypes at Lipetsk in its last years of operation, likewise drew from the experience in Russia in the development of the He-51.[37] In other words, without Lipetsk, Germany's aviation rearmament plans in 1934 would have been impossible.

As the Risk Air Force began construction, the RLM's technical office, headed by Wilhelm Wimmer—the former head of research at Lipetsk—also started to issue specifications for the next generation of aircraft. In total, he would commission forty-two total specifications in 1934, including day and night fighters, light bombers, dive-bombers, and bomber-fighter and reconnaissance aircraft. Wimmer disbursed funding via developmental contracts, left firms to their own devices, then had the resultant prototypes compete for production contracts.

Naturally, Wimmer drew heavily from technical data gained at Lipetsk, as well as his own experiences there. For instance, the Soviet emphasis on close air support for ground forces impressed some of those who studied at Lipetsk.[38] With the Soviet experience in mind, the Reichswehr had tested an early dive-bomber design at Lipetsk, the Junkers K-47.[39] Wimmer now issued specifications for the next generation of dive-bomber, which Hermann Pohlmann, the K-47's chief designer, would build. Pohlmann retained a number of the K-47's parts in his new prototype, which would first fly in 1935.[40] The end result was the Ju-87 "Stuka" Dive-Bomber, which would prove devastatingly effective in close air support early in the Second World War.[41]

In Krupp's Bureau of Motor Vehicle Construction in Essen, engineer Erich Woelfert was also very busy. The Reichswehr wanted new tanks, and fast. As noted in Part I, after his visit to Kama in 1932, Oswald Lutz had demanded the acceleration of tank design and production on the LaS, a light tank. The Reichswehr wanted to begin issuing specifications for that next wave of armored vehicles while simultaneously mass-producing vehicles to allow for training, testing, and improving the mass-production capabilities of German military industry.[42]

Hitler was an enthusiastic supporter of tank development, particularly after attending maneuvers organized by Guderian at Kummersdorf Testing Grounds in July 1933.[43] Nevertheless, to avoid an international incident, the first LaS production run, starting in January 1934, consisted of only fifteen turretless hulls. The Reichswehr issued contracts to five different firms in order to help develop armored vehicle expertise broadly.[44] Over the course of 1934, as the Reichswehr grew bolder, they would order first 150, then an additional 450, LaS of the Krupp design, with turrets and armament.[45] The vehicle line would soon be renamed the Panzerkampfwagen (Armored Combat Vehicle, or Panzer) I.

To Lutz and Guderian, the main problem with the Panzer I was that it lacked a main armament to engage other tanks. The medium-tank prototype commissioned in 1933 from Rheinmetall—code-named the Neubaufahrzeug—was far behind schedule, so, in the words of Guderian, "General Lutz decided on a second stop-gap" tank.[46] As a complement for the Panzer I, the Waffenamt drew up another set of specifications in January 1934 for the Maschinenfabrik Augsburg-Nürnberg AG (MAN) version of the LaS, now codenamed the LaS 100. It was based upon an already-completed chassis design for the LaS, which meant it would be ready for production almost immediately. The LaS 100 was heavier than the Panzer Is,[47] and intended to carry a small 2 cm cannon with armor-piercing round capability.[48] Soon renamed the Panzer II, MAN A.G. and Daimler would produce 2,030 from 1934 onward.[49]

While the Panzer II was intended as a stopgap, other designs commissioned in early 1934 were more ambitious. Based on their experiences at Kama, Lutz and Guderian recommended two new sets of specifications. One design would be lighter and faster, engineered for speed. This was intended to be Germany's primary battle tank, armed for tank-to-tank fighting with a smaller caliber but longer-barreled main gun for firing armor-piercing rounds.[50] The other vehicle would specifically be designed to battle enemy infantry and field fortifications, and as such would have heavier armor, slower speeds, and a main gun designed to fire high-explosive rounds.[51] The two concepts would evolve into the 15-ton Panzer III and 25-ton Panzer IV, respectively. The Waffenamt issued specifications for both vehicles on January 11, 1934, drawing extensively, yet again, on the lessons learned at Kama.[52] Most important were the inclusion of the three-man turret concept developed in Russia for both vehicles, and the requirement that both designs have radio mounts.[53] Kama participants Krupp and Rheinmetall won initial contracts to develop prototypes.[54] Thanks to his experience, Krupp's Erich Woelfert, who had lived and worked at Kama, was placed in charge of Krupp's Panzer IV project.[55]

The mass production of the Panzers I and II, as well as the initiation of the Panzer III and IV projects, required massive expansion of the labor force at Germany's major military industrial plants. Krupp, for instance, tripled the workforce in its Bureau of Motor Vehicle Construction from 153 to 473 in 1934.[56] To incorporate the huge numbers of new workers, major industrial firms ran apprenticeship programs, relying on their cadres of more experienced workers—developed during the early years of rearmament.[57] The head of the Krupp Corporation would later boast—at Nuremberg, during the postwar International Military Tribunals—that "through years of secret work, scientific and basic groundwork was laid in order to be ready again to work for the German Armed Forces at the appointed hour without loss of time or experience."[58] Just as in the Army, the engineering cadres had been developed, at least in part, during the partnership with the Soviet Union.

Of course, producing prototypes and expanding industrial capacity were only two of many critical facets of rearmament. As the German military grew, so too did its manpower. Göring's RLM received infusions of officers and men from the Reichswehr, and established training facilities across the country. The RLM initially contained only 900 flying officers.[59] Given that Lipetsk had trained several hundred pilots and observers—almost all of whom joined the new body—they constituted a large part of the RLM's flying strength at its inception, playing a key role in training in the next generation of pilots. "Without Lipetsk," General Speidel would later write, "no military aviation training would have been possible."[60]

The same process unfolded within the Reichswehr. In late 1933, Blomberg established the first armored warfare training facility on German soil at Zossen-Wünsdorf, just south of Berlin. Heading the new facility were two of the former commandants of Kama, Ludwig von Radlmeier and Josef Harpe.[61] A few months later, the Wehrmacht founded its first Tank Gunnery School. Its first three commanders were all former Kama students.[62] And unsurprisingly, the first heavy tank company established at Zossen for training was made up of the four surviving *Grosstraktoren* and three of the *Leichttraktoren* from Kama.[63]

European statesmen were not unaware of German rearmament measures. As a Soviet intelligence report noted in January 1934, "The growth of the military budget shows the high levels of military training by the German Fascists and their swift effort to achieve the military readiness of other imperialist countries. . . . The rearmament of Nazi Germany is acquiring international significance."[64] Between 1933 and 1935, German defense spending would increase from 1 to 10 percent of national income. If Great Britain, France, and the Soviet Union did not react quickly, they would risk falling behind in a new arms race.[65]

Initially, that arms race left Germany in a very vulnerable position. In the spring of 1934, the German military possessed only a few hundred aircraft—most of which were trainers—the eight functioning tanks left from Kama, and fifteen turretless tanks without guns. It would take a minimum of two years for the German rearmament program, in theory, to reach a place where only a determined coalition might stop it. In the words of a German diplomat in March 1934, the coming two years marked the greatest danger for Nazi strategy: "our only security lies in a skillful foreign policy and in avoiding all provocations."[66]

Of course, Hitler was not good at avoiding provocations, even as he preached peace publicly. On June 6, 1934, he accelerated plans to expand the Reichswehr to 300,000 men. The pace Hitler proposed startled General Ludwig Beck, now head of the Truppenamt, who worried the plan would trigger a French military response, or dilute the quality of the small officer corps the Reichswehr had so carefully trained over the past decade. Hitler brushed aside both objections. He also made it clear that it would soon be time to revisit the question of conscription, a measure far more threatening internationally than a limited increase in the Reichswehr's active strength.[67]

All of these decisions unsettled the Reichswehr's leadership. While they were pleased with Hitler's dedication to rearmament, the frantic pace and the seeming unruliness of the Nazi Party membership were matters of grave concern. Nazi SA paramilitaries were increasingly running amok. Their chief, Ernst Röhm, grew ever louder in his demands that his organization, with 2.5 million members, absorb the much smaller Reichswehr.[68] This was Minister of Defense Blomberg's greatest fear. On June 21, 1934, President Hindenburg and General Blomberg warned Hitler that they would declare martial law and put an "end to the Hitler experiment" if he did not bring the "revolutionary trouble-makers . . . to reason."[69] Hitler faced a seemingly stark choice between his rearmament plans or his own party.[70]

CHAPTER 26
Long Knives

On the morning of June 30, 1934, wrote a journalist for the *New York Times*, "Herr Hitler with his guards strode into Captain Röhm's bedroom and himself declared that his Storm Troop chief of staff was under arrest. Captain Röhm made no protest and attempted no resistance."[1] Handed over to SS officers, Röhm was dragged to Stadelheim Prison in Munich to await his fate. The head of the Stürmabteilung had no notion that he would be eliminated by his own party leader. With Röhm's arrest, a wave of bloodletting began, spearheaded by the SS.

Six hours after Röhm's arrest, two young men broke into General Schleicher's house. They found him reading in his armchair, and promptly shot him dead. When Schleicher's wife ran into the room to her husband's side, the assassins killed her, too. Röhm, who remained behind bars while his associates were being killed, refused the option of suicide offered by his jailor. He was shot the day after his arrest. Within seventy-two hours, at least eighty-three prominent Germans, many of them National Socialists, were dead.[2]

This was the infamous Night of the Long Knives, an internal purge designed to solidify the Führer's hold on power. The official Nazi press would claim that those killed had been plotting a coup. The story in the *New York Times* added, "There is mention of a 'foreign power' as being involved. The discerning interpret this reference as being to Russia and the ultimate aim of the rebels as a new national bolshevism."[3] There was no hint of reality in the accusations; Hitler ordered the SS, under the firm control of Heinrich Himmler, to fabricate evidence for senior Reichswehr officers that the SA had been planning a coup.

The Army was pleased with the demise of their paramilitary rivals. Blomberg, who had threatened Hitler's hold on power only a week earlier, thanked the Führer for "the resolute and courageous action by which he had saved the German people from civil war."[4] Hitler's choice of the Army over his own party also confirmed to most of the recalcitrant members of the Reichswehr that Hitler prioritized rearmament over all other ideological goals.[5] Over the next month, Hitler extended the military's prerogatives even further. On July 13, 1934, he declared that Reichswehr members alone would be allowed to carry weapons. He made it clear that his vision for reborn

German military power centered exclusively on traditional military institutions. He required loyalty in exchange, making the entire military take an oath of personal allegiance to him in August 1934.[6] Obsessed above all with their domestic prerogatives and rearmament for a war of revenge, officers like Blomberg were willing to concede most other points to Hitler, and take the oath.

Hitler's power, solidified after the purge, became nearly absolute by the end of the summer. On August 1, 1934, he learned that elderly President Paul von Hindenburg was near death. He ordered a new "law" from his cabinet that would merge the presidency and chancellorship into the new office of Führer (leader). Hindenburg's death the following day eliminated one of the few remaining checks on Nazi power.

Stalin paid close attention to these developments in Germany. He asked his ambassador in Berlin for a detailed report for himself on Hitler's purge of his own party.[7] Upon reading it, he exclaimed to members of his inner circle, "What a guy!" Here, clearly was a leader who "knows how to act!"[8] Stalin saw the Night of the Long Knives as a model of centralizing power. Immediately following the event, and obviously inspired by it, he finalized the reorganization of his secret police agencies, with the Narodnyy Komissariat Vnutrennikh Del (People's Commissariat of Internal Affairs, or NKVD) replacing the OGPU.[9] This was supposed to mark a turn toward "socialist legality."

On December 1, 1934, a disgruntled and unstable young man named Leonid Nikolayev entered the headquarters of the Leningrad Communist Party. There, he found First Secretary Sergei Kirov unguarded and shot him in the neck, killing him. There has been a long-running debate over the culpability of Stalin in Kirov's death. The evidence suggests that he was not involved.[10] Regardless of his role, Stalin took advantage of the death to produce the same sort of terror Hitler had used in Germany some six months before. It was done on a vastly grander scale, however. In the NKVD, Stalin had at his disposal a far larger and more efficient apparatus of terror than Hitler had in the SS. The NKVD's techniques had been honed in the battles over collectivization that had led to the deaths of at least 5.7 million people.[11]

Stalin deployed the NKVD to full effect in the aftermath of the Kirov assassination. Within a few months, 40,000 political oppositionists, including many of the leading Old Bolsheviks who had sided against Stalin on collectivization or NEP, had been arrested.[12] The Kirov assassination also accelerated the Soviet repression of the Volga Germans. In mid-November, the NKVD had begun detaining ethnic German leaders accused of "fascist agitation" on behalf of the German government. By December 25, hundreds had been arrested and charged with treason.[13] Simultaneously, the Red Army began expelling ethnic Germans from its ranks. The accusations of German espionage echoed Hitler's claims that his opponents were in league with the Soviets.

Even as he accused the Germans of coups and conspiracies, Stalin showed little concern with Hitler's rearmament program. By 1934, the Red Army possessed 10,000 armored vehicles, nearly 5,000 aircraft, and had nearly a million active duty soldiers in total.[14] It was—in numerical terms—the most powerful army in Europe. Years of work with the Germans, the crash-course industrialization program, and Stalin's decision to ratchet up military spending dramatically had given the Soviet

Union a degree of security. Cooperation with Germany had given Red Army leaders a fair sense of the distance to be covered by the Germans in rearming, deeming the danger it posed in triggering increased British and French military spending a greater threat than German militarism itself.[15] As a result, following the horrific famine of 1932–1933, Stalin halted bread rationing, increased incentives for individual workers, and slowed the growth rate of military industrial production in favor of consumer goods.[16]

Instead, Stalin responded to the shifting power balance in Europe diplomatically rather than militarily. Commissar for Foreign Affairs Litvinov was given leeway to press ahead with his collective security project. He had led the Soviet Union into the League of Nations in September 1934, and pursued improved relations with the United States, Great Britain, and France. Together, these states might enforce a peaceful status quo, giving the Soviet Union time to continue its industrialization program. But in March, Litvinov's project for maintaining peace was dealt a new, unexpected blow.

On March 16, 1935, millions of Germans—many using the new mass-produced Nazi radio, the Volksempfänger 301—tuned in for a major speech.[17] The Führer, expected to unveil a new defense policy, greeted his audience first with a description of the end of the First World War. He argued that the German people had trusted in President Wilson's program of Fourteen Points, believing "they had rendered a service not only to tormented humanity but also to a great idea per se." That idea, he claimed, was the concept of complete and total disarmament. Hitler continued his historical fiction by claiming that Germany's statesmen had only agreed to Versailles because they believed that "the beginning of international general disarmament would be marked and guaranteed." He singled out the Soviet Union as the greatest disruptor of this proposed international order, stating that the German government sees "in the creation of a Soviet Russian Army of 101 divisions . . . an element that at the time of the conclusion of the Versailles treaty could not have been divined."[18] A pacific Germany, armed with only the best intentions for mankind, had been betrayed since the peace conference. The country had surrendered only because the Allies had promised to disarm themselves, too. After reciting a long list of the war materiel given up by Germany in the aftermath of the war, he drew toward his grand conclusion. Germany would rearm not to in order to attack but, rather, "exclusively for defense and thereby for the maintenance of peace."[19] He announced a new law, dated March 16, that would introduce universal military conscription and expand Germany's peacetime army from ten to thirty-six divisions.[20] Thus, in the name of peace and the good of mankind, Hitler announced his preparations for war.

Surrounding this announcement were a great number of name changes and reformed institutions. In February 1935, the Air Ministry was reorganized into the Luftwaffe (Air Force), and any pretensions of its civilian nature were cast aside. Hitler reestablished the Kriegsakademie (War Academy) and the famed General Staff, now to be called the Oberkommando des Heeres (the Army High Command, or OKH).[21] Tellingly, he also renamed the Reichswehrministerium (the Ministry of Defense) to the more belligerent Reichskriegsministerium (the Ministry of War).

The Reichswehr (Defense Force) following suit, becoming the Wehrmacht, while the Reichsmarine (Imperial Navy) became the Kriegsmarine (War Navy).

Hitler followed these organizational changes with a number of new appointments in senior military positions. Minister of War Blomberg would also serve as commander-in-chief of the armed forces. To head the new Wehrmacht, at Blomberg's request, Hitler appointed Werner von Fritsch. Fritsch was a popular but personally ascetic staff officer. Guderian described the monacled, mustachioed general as "extremely reserved and even shy at large gatherings."[22] Truppenamt head Beck was promoted to serve as OKH chief of staff.[23] These were popular choices, demonstrating Hitler's respect for the officer corps.

With his announcement of conscription, Hitler had switched tactics. Until March 1935, he had understated the military capacities of the Reichswehr. Now he would overstate his military capabilities, aiming to deter foreign intervention, rather than dissuade it by peaceful rhetoric. As new tanks rolled off assembly lines, the Luftwaffe grew, and German manpower was mobilized on a scale not seen since the First World War, one question remained. Would anyone stop Hitler?

CHAPTER 27

The End of Versailles

The French center-right government headed by Pierre-Etienne Flandin had only been in office for four months when Hitler announced German rearmament. "France hates war," Flandin declared. "All measures necessary to maintain peace will be taken." That included issuing a note of protest, asking for action in the League of Nations and hosting a conference to discuss German behavior.[1] It all meant nothing. Without the British, France would not oppose Hitler.

The British reaction was once again muted. Elder British statesman David Lloyd George counseled, "Let us keep our heads. The co-signatories with Germany to the Versailles Treaty are in no position morally to enforce those parts of the treaty which they themselves have flagrantly and defiantly broken."[2] Labour Party Prime Minister Ramsay MacDonald's health had grown so bad that, as Robert Vansittart noted, he "was no longer equal to public tests."[3] He began to experience memory loss and struggled to dress himself. Most embarrassingly, he delivered one short address at an international conference that was so rambling and incoherent that his French interpreter stood silent, then asked one of MacDonald's aides what he should say. The interpreter was quietly told to "make the speech which will best combine caution and encouragement."[4] MacDonald was hardly the man to take forceful action in the spring of 1935.

At the end of March, MacDonald's cabinet did dispatch Foreign Secretary Sir John Simon to Berlin to meet with Hitler, with the aim of limiting German rearmament. Over two days of intensive meetings, Hitler argued that his limited military build-up was aimed only at the Soviet Union. Sir Simon reported that in Hitler's view, Russia "was of all states the one which could most easily start a war, and which would itself be least threatened by the war."[5] He pointed out to Hitler that thirty-six divisions would "result in a German superiority which the other Western Powers could not accept as a basis for discussion."[6] Hitler replied that Germany only sought parity with Great Britain, and "again emphasized the danger threatening from Russia."[7] Simon's visit produced no results.

Not all leaders were willing to ignore Hitler's plans for rearmament. There were voices in London that sought to build a coalition capable of limiting the expansion of

German arms. In London, they included Robert Vansittart at the Foreign Office and the Under-Secretary for Foreign Affairs Anthony Eden.[8] They found an unlikely ally in Italy, where Fascist dictator Benito Mussolini remained wary of Hitler. In particular, Mussolini sought to block Germany's ambitions with regard to Austria, which had become economically dependent on Italy after the First World War. Mussolini and his Foreign Minister Count Ciano further feared that the fall of Austria might stir the ethnic German population of Italy's South Tyrol region.

Diplomatic efforts to contain Hitler and German rearmament commenced quickly after the March 16 speech. In April 1935, British, French, and Italian diplomats gathered in Stresa, Italy, to draw up a unified response. They reiterated their willingness to enforce Versailles, and made a general commitment against certain unnamed states that might seek to upset standing international treaties. This was, in theory, aimed at Hitler. Their loose alliance took the forceful-sounding name of the Stresa Front.

The French were the most dedicated to halting German rearmament, following up on the Stresa agreement by seeking an arrangement with the Soviet Union to contain German ambitions in Eastern Europe. The previous year, the French Foreign Ministry had initiated negotiations with Soviet Foreign Minister Litvinov. However, the talks had been derailed by the accidental assassination of French Foreign Minister Louis Barthou. The killer was a Bulgarian nationalist whose real target, the king of Yugoslavia, happened to be riding in the same car as Barthou. Both men died, as did the assassin, who was promptly beaten to death by an enraged crowd.

Barthou's successor in the Foreign Ministry, Pierre Laval, resumed talks with Litvinov immediately after Germany's announcement of rearmament, hurriedly reaching an agreement, the Franco-Soviet Treaty of Mutual Assistance, on May 2, 1935. The two states agreed to aid each other in the event of aggression, though only after proceeding through the League of Nations arbitration process. It was a feeble effort at containment, but suggested the beginnings of an anti-Hitler alliance. For Stalin, its purpose was clear: Stalin told Laval, who in the intervening period had been elevated to prime minister, that the treaty was "absolutely directed against one particular country—Germany" and that he foresaw that if things did not change, the path of German policy was to either seize Poland or, with some foresight, "share her with another power."[9]

There was little military muscle to back up these diplomatic measures, however. By April 1935, between regular and irregular forces, Hitler possessed an army of 336,000 men and 450 tanks, and a growing air force of 2,500 aircraft.[10] Budget deficits, unstable governments, and antiwar activists had slowly stripped France of its ability to wage war.[11] From 1921 to 1924, French military strength dropped from fifty-two to thirty-two divisions, with spending declining even more rapidly.[12] Conscription remained, but by 1928 the terms of service declined from three years to twelve months. Those few soldiers conscripted had very little training.[13] All these activities were justified in terms of ongoing disarmament talks, but those in fact were just a rationalization for disarmament measures taken out fiscal and political necessity. They were to get worse in the context of the Great Depression; French military funding dropped an additional 17 percent from 1930 to 1934.[14] What money there was went largely to fortification of the Maginot Line, a politically popular but strategically useless investment.[15] The French military was armed primarily with obsolete tanks and planes and had only 195,000 front-line first-division troops in France itself.[16] The French minister of war concluded by April 1935 that Germany was already "the strongest military power in Europe," and that the postwar status quo had already been shattered.[17] That Hitler was able to deter French and British intervention just two short years after becoming chancellor was a testament to the success of German rearmament measures taken before 1933—particularly efforts in the Soviet Union to develop German aviation and armored warfare capabilities.

In Berlin, even without full knowledge of French military weakness, there was little fear of the Stresa Front. As the French and Soviets finalized their treaty, the German ambassador to France informed Berlin that he considered a stable Franco-Soviet relationship unlikely, for political and military reasons.[18] French requirements that any pact remain within the terms of the League of Nations further handicapped any real military commitment between the two states. Similarly cautious optimism was expressed by German diplomats in Italy. Foreign Minister von Neurath met with the Italian ambassador in Berlin in early May and emerged convinced that even after the Stresa Front agreement, Mussolini was "striving to improve the atmosphere with Germany somewhat" mainly to "free his rear in Europe for his adventures in Abyssinia [Ethiopia]."[19]

German fears about Great Britain were dispersed with equal rapidity. Just weeks after the Stresa Front agreement, the MacDonald government proposed naval "conversations" between the German and British navies. Hitler seized upon the possibility of a deal with the British with alacrity, agreeing to naval talks in London in late May.[20] Hitler was thus aware that there was no serious coalition developing against him, despite what it might appear.

In response to Hitler's declaration of rearmament and the formation of the Stresa Front, Stalin, characteristically, moved in two directions at once. In April 1935, Soviet trade representative in Berlin David Kandelaki—who may have been empowered directly by Stalin to improve both economic and political relations—reached a new, long-term credit and trade deal with the German government worth 200 million marks ($80.6 million USD).[21] Even as the political relationship soured, Germany would supply between one third and two thirds of the Soviet Union's machine tool imports between 1933 and 1938.[22] Kandelaki's credit deal was followed by another round of diplomatic maneuvers aimed at improving Soviet-German relations: Soviet ambassador Yakov Surits and diplomat Sergei Bessonov in Berlin and Litvinov and Tukhachevsky in Moscow all approached their German counterparts with various soundings about possibilities of improving relations. Tukhachevsky went so far as to tell the German military attaché in Moscow that "if only . . . both countries enjoyed their friendship and political relations as in the past, they could dictate peace to the world."[23] All these hints were ignored.[24]

At the same time, Stalin hedged his bets. After the announcement of German conscription, Tukhachevsky penned a scathing piece in *Izvestia* on Hitler's war plans that got distributed internationally. Tukhachevsky estimated "in a year or two Germany can put an army into the field equal in size to the German army at the end of the World War."[25] Given its content and distribution, it seems clear that Stalin—who had personally edited the piece—intended the article as a signal to the West.[26] Diplomacy followed this public warning, as Stalin directed Commissar for Foreign Affairs Maxim Litvinov to continue to develop allies against Germany. Two weeks after the signing of the Franco-Soviet Treaty of Mutual Assistance, the Soviets reached a similar agreement with Czechoslovakia.[27]

While Stalin cultivated his options, Hitler was not idle diplomatically. Following the British offer of naval conversations, on June 4, 1935, Hitler dispatched Joachim von Ribbentrop as "ambassador extraordinary and plenipotentiary" to London. Ribbentrop, a former wine salesman, was widely reviled even within Nazi circles. Nazi propaganda minister Joseph Goebbels said of Ribbentrop that he "bought his name, he married his money, and he swindled his way into office."[28] The flamboyant, scheming Ribbentrop arrived in London in pomp. Within minutes of their first meeting, Ribbentrop informed the British delegation, led by Sir John Simon, that Hitler would offer Britain a guarantee limiting German rearmament to 35 percent of British naval strength, but that a formal agreement codifying that ratio was a precondition for future talks.[29] Simon, shocked, excused himself to go meet with Prime Minister MacDonald. Two days later, to the surprise of Germany's traditional foreign policy elite and Britain's allies in France, the British government agreed to the German proposal.[30]

On paper, it was an attractive agreement for the British. Germany was clearly rearming under Hitler. This pact might limit that rearmament program to levels that did not threaten British interests. The entire arrangement suggested to them that Hitler was dedicated to a modest program of territorial revision and legal equality. There were military reasons for the British to find the terms of the proposal acceptable, too. British naval negotiators at the talks were deeply concerned about qualitative advancements by the German Navy, particularly its 10,000-ton "pocket battleships" (legal under the terms of Versailles) that were technologically cutting-edge, and thus threatened the 1921 Washington Naval Treaty then maintaining British naval preeminence. It was feared that these fast, heavily armed vessels, of which eight were planned, might race through the North Sea and inflict far more damage than the submarine war had done to British shipping in the First World War.[31] British naval planners felt that allowing Germany modest rearmament would lead them back to more traditional capital ships, and thus prevent a new technological arms race that might draw in France, Italy, and the Soviet Union, and render much of the British Navy obsolete.[32] On these grounds, some sort of agreement with Germany made sense.

However, in the broader international landscape, the agreement was disastrous to the effort to contain Hitler. For the first time, one of the signatories and enforcers of the Versailles agreement had formally abandoned its provisions by agreeing to allow German rearmament. The French, who had not been consulted, were shocked. Laval felt betrayed, having cobbled together a coalition of Eastern European states and offered concessions to Mussolini to keep him as a partner in the Stresa Front.[33] Hitler was gleeful. The German Navy privately recorded that "any substantially larger figure than that permitted by the agreement could hardly be reached in the next decade" anyways.[34] In other words, in exchange for an empty promise to limit his naval buildup, Hitler had split the Stresa coalition within six weeks of its formation. The last nail in the coffin of containment came only a few months later. Laval, in his effort to bring the Italians into an arrangement against Hitler, had given Mussolini a blank check to proceed as he wanted in East Africa.[35] With dreams of empire and a desire for war, Mussolini had grand plans for the conquest of Ethiopia, one of the two remaining independent states in Africa. Laval regarded it as a necessary, if unfortunate, concession in the face of German revanchism. On October 3, 1935, Italian forces invaded Ethiopia from the Italian colony of Eritrea, not bothering to declare war. The British public was outraged. A Franco-British attempt to broker a ceasefire (which would have given Italy part of Ethiopia without Ethiopia's consent) ended when the details became public, leading to the resignation of the British foreign minister.

The Italian invasion of Ethiopia demolished what remained of the Stresa Front. Idealists like Anthony Eden responded in horror, demanding sanctions and in turn angering Mussolini. Realists like Vansittart and Laval thought Hitler was the greater menace, and were willing to concede all of Ethiopia to Mussolini in exchange for help containing German aggression.[36] The resulting muddled, contradictory noise emerging from London and Paris completely halted any efforts at British-French-Italian reconciliation.[37]

In the face of that confusion, Hitler continued to accelerate his rearmament program: German military expenditures grew from 0.3 percent of GDP in 1932 to 2.9 percent in 1934 and then 5.5 percent by the end of 1935.[38] By the end of the year, the new Luftwaffe had received 5,568 aircraft from German industry.[39] More than 500 Panzer I's had already been issued to Wehrmacht units. In October 1935, the heavier Panzer II had already entered into mass production.[40] The window to halt German rearmament without a world war was shrinking rapidly.

The weakness of the response to accelerating German rearmament further emboldened Hitler as the New Year came and went. The one meaningful clause of Versailles that remained in effect domestically involved the Rhineland. This heavily populated industrial region of Germany located on the border of France had been demilitarized under the terms of the treaty, with French troops stationed there as a guarantee until 1930. In January 1936, a report reached Foreign Minister Neurath suggesting that the French military considered itself unready to do anything militarily should Germany try to remilitarize the Rhineland.[41] It remains unclear whether or not Neurath—a conservative member of the traditional foreign policy establishment—shared this information with Hitler, but he did inform the Führer he did not think the French would respond militarily to any move to violate Versailles.[42]

In February 1936, at a meeting with Göring, Blomberg, Fritsch, Neurath, and Ribbentrop, Hitler informed them that he was considering using the Franco-Soviet Treaty of 1935 as an excuse to move troops into the Rhineland.[43] He told them that he had not planned to violate this last tenet of Versailles until 1937, as bringing German troops to the very borders of France might stir even the politically divided French into action. However, while "militarily Germany was not yet ready," a German diplomat recorded Hitler saying, "the right psychological moment for addressing the

Rhineland issue may have arrived. Russia was only intent on having peace in the West. England was in a bad state militarily, and much hampered by other problems; France was distracted by internal politics."[44]

While they were weak and divided now, in Hitler's estimation, the strength of Germany's potential opponents—particularly the Soviet Union—was growing. He meant to strike before military victory might be impossible. Blomberg and Göring were horrified, considering the German military to be in the early stages of rearmament and entirely unprepared for war.[45] Despite their concerns, on the morning of March 5, 1936, Hitler decided finally and firmly to move into the Rhineland.[46] Two days later, nineteen German army battalions marched into the demilitarized zone. The 25,000 German soldiers dispatched into the Rhineland were greeted rapturously by the local population, read the coverage in the New York Times: "When, with banners flying and bands blaring, the troops staged their formal entry into their new home towns, they did so amid thunderous cheers which re-echoed through the narrow ancient streets."[47] According to a reporter on the scene, 15,000 Nazi stormtroopers marched behind the army formations, signing a song whose refrain ran "For today we own Germany and tomorrow the entire world."

As news of the event circulated via radio and newspaper, the German public held its collective breath, waiting for the international response. The French began mobilizing forces along the border. War seemed like a real prospect. General Blomberg panicked at the news, begging Hitler to withdraw German forces. Neurath, with his secret intelligence report, urged Hitler to continue, repeatedly reiterating that France would not strike.[48]

Neurath's intelligence had been correct. In Paris, there was despondency. When the French government, now led by Albert-Pierre Sarraut, met to deliberate on its response, the chief of the French General Staff informed the cabinet that the French military would be ready to respond, with proper investment and mobilization— but not for twelve months.[49] He concluded that, should the French move into the Rhineland to stop Hitler, they would likely start a general war, which would devolve into trench warfare. In the long run, Germany would win thanks to its larger population and military industry.[50] Therefore, he argued, no military action could or should be taken.

Hitler was triumphant. He ordered a referendum two weeks later to add a veneer of legality to his rearmament of the Rhineland. It was approved nearly unanimously. It was clear that the measure was of enormous popularity. Propaganda Minister Joseph Goebbels wrote in his diary: "Everything worked out wonderfully . . . the leader is beaming. England remains passive. France refuses to act alone. Italy is disappointed, and America is uninterested."[51] Hitler had brought Europe to the brink of war and walked away with yet another major victory, his greatest to date. It would only embolden him, improving his domestic position in the face of economic turmoil, and increasing confidence in his leadership among skeptical members of the military.

CHAPTER 28

Terror

In 1936, an opportunity for the German military to test some of the new prototypes under development presented itself. On July 18, the Spanish military, led by Generals José Sanjurjo, Emilio Mola, and Francisco Franco, staged a coup d'état, attempting to overthrow the leftist government of President Manuel Azaña. Poor coordination, the early arrest of several coup leaders, and the prompt arming of the workers' unions by the government prevented the coup leaders from seizing much of the country.[1] Even worse for the plotters, mutinies among pro-Republic sailors in the navy led to the deaths of most of the pro-coup naval officers, which prevented the large Spanish North African Army from moving to the mainland.

At this juncture, General Franco, the dominant figure among the coup leaders, communicated with Hitler, requesting aid in the form of air support.[2] Hitler chose to intervene. He immediately ordered two German naval vessels into the Straits of Gibraltar to prevent the Spanish Navy from firing on convoys of Franco's soldiers. More significant, German pilots conducted a critical airlift of Franco's forces from North Africa into southern Spain. German pilots flying Junkers 52 transport planes would bring more than 1,500 soldiers, and Franco himself, across the Republican-controlled waters.[3] This made possible Franco's seizure of much of the south and west of the country, though his forces remained too weak to take Spain's major cities in the center and northeast of the country. The coup's half-success created a stalemate, marking the beginning of a bloody, three-year-long civil war.

In August, British prime minister Stanley Baldwin (who had replaced Ramsay MacDonald in June 1935) and his French counterpart—now Leon Blum—organized a Non-Intervention Agreement to prevent the world's major powers from getting involved in the unfolding war. Hitler, Mussolini, and Stalin all agreed to its terms, then proceeded to make a mockery of its fundamental principles. All three would dispatch advisers and technology to Spain—the Italians and Germans backing General Franco's Nationalists, and the USSR backing the Republican government.

At first, both German and Soviet commitments in the Spanish Civil War were limited. They sent small numbers of aircraft and armored vehicles, with the first

Germans arriving on August 1 and the Soviets two months later.[4] In the early days of the civil war, stubby Soviet I-16 fighter planes easily bested German Arado Ar-68 and He-51 biplanes, which were slower and less heavily armed. Despite early successes, Stalin remained wary of a large commitment. There would never be more than 800 Soviet pilots or advisers in Spain at any one time.[5]

By contrast, Hitler expanded the German role in Spain in the fall of 1936 once it became apparent that Great Britain and France would not assist the Spanish Republican government in any meaningful way.[6] Luftwaffe head Hermann Göring advised the Führer that Germany should test out new technologies, tactics, and the new generation of pilots on the battlefields of Spain: "With the permission of the Führer I sent a large part of my transport fleet and a number of experimental fighter units, bombers, and antiaircraft guns; and in that way I had an opportunity to ascertain, under combat conditions, whether the material was equal to the task."[7] Here was the first opportunity to reveal the capabilities that had been developed over fifteen years.

The officers sent to staff the Condor Legion—the German formation deployed to Spain—unsurprisingly included a large number of the pilots trained at Lipetsk. The First World War generation was too old for active combat, while the thousands of new pilots being inducted into the Luftwaffe lacked experience. Students who had begun training between 1927 and 1933 at Lipetsk were now in their prime, with, in some instances, ten years of flying under their belts. As a result, they dominated the Condor Legion. In September 1936, an alumnus of Lipetsk, Ekkehard Hefter, crashed and died on a combat mission, the first German pilot killed in combat since the First World War. Other alumni gaining their first combat experiences in Spain included future aces Hannes Trautloft and Günther Lützow.[8]

Heading the Legion was another Lipetsk alumnus, Hugo Sperrle, the scowling, monacled former flier so villainous in appearance that Hitler invited him to state meetings when he wanted to intimidate foreign guests.[9] By November 1936, under Sperrle's watch, the Condor Legion grew to 4,500 men, with three bomber and three fighter squadrons. It also began receiving state-of-the-art aircraft.[10] After fifteen years of flying civilian aircraft or biplanes, some of the new designs elicited wonder from the pilots; Hannes Trautloft described his first flight in the new Bf 109 fighter by saying that "as soon as I am in the air I feel at home in the new bird. Its flight characteristics are fantastic."[11] The technological tables now turned and German pilots faced slower, less maneuverable Soviet aircraft. Lützow, who would claim 105 aerial victories in the Second World War, shot down his first five aircraft in Spain. He would also help to rewrite Luftwaffe fighter tactics, developing with Werner Mölders the "finger-four" formation that would become standard Luftwaffe doctrine in the Second World War.[12]

The weight of the German air power commitment made itself felt in the larger war. By April 1937, the Nationalists began to achieve air superiority. Most infamous of the signs of that increasing dominance was a Condor Legion bombing raid on April 26. As Franco organized an offensive to capture the resisting Basque region of northern Spain, he ordered the Condor Legion to support their efforts against the ancient city of Guernica. Their orders were to destroy the town's central bridge and block the roads, in order to hamper efforts of Republican forces to move through the town.[13]

The day was Monday, the market day in Basque country. As a result, the town was brimming with refugees, farmers, and shoppers. Beginning in the late afternoon, German Ju-52s swept over the hills around the town, accompanied by fighter escorts. They targeted the bridge in the center of town, dropping around 75,000 pounds of bombs. The result was mayhem: one eyewitness recalled that "it is impossible to describe the horror of that moment. Wounded, dead, prayers, cries and weeping. For an hour, two hours, three hours there fell steel and flames which burned and destroyed."[14] Fire spread, engulfing much of the city and destroying nearly 70 percent of its buildings. Foreign press reported a death toll of nearly 1,700—though the real number was likely around 300. Such horrors and the exaggerated press coverage in Great Britain and France seemed to confirm the premise of the "Risk Air Force": that Germany now possessed the capacity to inflict grievous damage on France or Great Britain should they attempt to halt rearmament.[15]

While Guernica was subject to terror at the hands of German pilots, Stalin unleashed his own terror within the Soviet Union. Following the Kirov assassination, the scope of state repression grew; in August 1936, sixteen senior Communist Party leaders had been tried and sentenced to death in a public "show trial." As the international environment grew worse, Stalin and the Politburo also demonstrated concern about political control of the Soviet military. Only about 11 percent of the Red Army were Communist Party members, a steep decline driven in part by the army's expansion.[16] To guarantee party control, the Politburo reintroduced the party commissars into military units in May 1937.

Stalin took more dramatic steps later that month. On May 10, 1937, Tukhachevsky was suddenly relieved of his senior posts and reassigned. Stalin met with him in his offices at the Kremlin on May 13, assuring his marshal that the Politburo's security concern had to do with one of his mistresses, and would soon be resolved.[17] Tukhachevsky duly left for his new post in Kuibyshev on May 16. He was arrested a week later, brought back to Moscow, and tortured for four days, at which point he began to sign confessions that implicated fellow officers in a plot to overthrow the government.[18]

On June 2, 1937, in front of those members of the Revolutionary Military Council who remained outside of prison, Stalin made an appearance to announce the shocking news of Tukhachevsky's "treason." There he warned, "Comrades, I hope no one doubts now that a military-political plot against Soviet power existed." After a meandering and contradictory speech, he eventually reached the climax, which was to accuse Tukhachevsky of passing along operational plans—"our operational plans, the holy of holies"—to the German army.[19] Tukhachevsky and nine fellow officers were accused of being part of a Trotskyite Anti-Soviet spy ring working with the Germans.[20]

Nine days after Stalin's speech, the trial of the senior leadership of the Red Army was publicly announced. A few of Tukhachevsky's close associates—Yakov Alksnis and Vasily Blyukher—were among those forced to serve as military judges during a trial on June 11. Eight of the accused were found guilty. On June 12, in a dank cellar in Lubyanka Prison, Tukhachevsky was shot.

Tukhachevsky was dead but the purges had yet to spread much beyond his immediate circle. They soon would. General Alexander Vasilievich Gorbatov had risen through the ranks of the Red Army by merit. A peasant by birth, he had become a cavalryman in 1912 in the Tsarist Army. After the Bolshevik Revolution, he journeyed home to see his family, eventually joining the Red Army as a private. In 1937, Gorbatov had risen to command the Second Red Army Cavalry Division in Ukraine. This emblem of Soviet social mobility and a man who owed everything to communism woke to a surprise one June morning when he read the paper and learned of Tukhachevsky's conspiracy.[21]

At a Military District Party Conference a few days later, Gorbatov's popular commanding officer Iona Yakir was "morose and tense." Within a week, Yakir had been pulled off a train on his way to Moscow and arrested. Gorbatov said nothing to his peers, but continued to hope it was all a misunderstanding.[22] Soon, senior officers were disappearing from the district in droves. The NKVD seized Gorbatov's corps commander in August. During a public meeting about his arrest, Gorbatov made the mistake of speaking up on his superior's behalf. Not long after, he was stripped of his position and expelled from the Communist Party for "contacts with 'enemies of the people.'" But he was not arrested.

After weeks of uneasy waiting, Gorbatov was given a new post. Shortly after his arrival, he went to collect his winter uniform. But the corps storekeeper sheepishly told him that the political commissar had telegrammed him, instructing him not to issue Gorbatov his winter uniform: he had been expelled from the army. Deeply distraught about what might come next, Gorbatov journeyed to Moscow. There, he managed to meet with the head of the Chief Directorate for Personnel, who told him, reassuringly, "We'll try to find out what your position is." Then he asked where in the city Gorbatov was staying.

At two the next morning, there was a gentle knock on the door. When asked who was there, a woman's voice told him that it was a telegram. Gorbatov was sure that the telegram was from his wife, then with her family. When he opened the door, "Three uniformed men came into the room and one of them told me point-blank that I was under arrest. . . . Thereupon one began to tear the medals off my tunic, and another to cut the badges of rank from my uniform, while the third watched me dress."[23] He was whisked off to Lubyanka, where he was thrust into a pitch-dark cell sometime before dawn.

Gorbatov would endure months of torture. He recalled his interrogation sessions ending with his torturer's "evil voice hissing, 'You'll sign, you'll sign' as I was carried out, weak and covered in blood."[24] According to his own account, he did not sign any confessions or indict any of his fellow officers. This was unusual; ten fellow officers had testified against him. For his recalcitrance, he was sentenced to fifteen years' hard labor in the Kolyma gold mines. Within a short time of his arrival, starvation rations and "killing labor" caused his teeth to begin to fall out. His legs swelled up and he lost the ability to walk. Only by being transferred to a less strenuous assignment by a merciful camp commander was he saved from certain death.[25]

Gorbatov was part of the lost generation of Soviet military leadership. The purges had begun sometime before with the arrests of thousands of Party members. The sudden turn against the military marked a major change. In the first round of arrests, the NKVD seized the entire circle of officers around Tukhachevsky: Iona Yakir, Ieronim Uborevich, Roberts Eideman, August Kork, B. M. Feldman, Vitaly Primakov, Yan Gamarnik, and former military attaché in Germany Vitovt Putna.[26] Yakov Fishman would soon follow.[27] Their writings and ideas went with them, too. The 1936 Red Army Field Manual disappeared along with its authors, leaving the Red Army without an effective operational doctrine until the early disasters of the Second World War forced it to revive some of Tukhachevsky's ideas about "Deep Battle."

The circle of victims would soon grow. In the ten days after Tukhachevsky's execution, nearly a thousand senior commanders were arrested, and many were tortured and shot.[28] In total, the purge claimed 3 of 5 Marshals, all 13 deputy commissars for defense, 75 of the 80 members of the RVS (which was abolished), 13 of 15 army commanders, 8 of 9 fleet commanders and admirals of first grade, 50 out of 57 corps commanders, and 154 of 186 divisional commanders.[29] The arrests would also decimate military intelligence, logistics, research, and support services. Between June and December 1937, nearly 8 percent of the officer corps lost their posts. A year later, an additional 3.7 percent were removed.[30] In total, three to four times as many general officers would be shot by Stalin in the purges as died in the Second World War.[31]

The logic of the Great Terror, as the growing maelstrom of repression became known, remains debated, with scholars variously arguing that Stalin sought to consolidate control over the military, that he was concerned about the political reliability of the many Tsarist-era officers in positions of power, or that he actually believed a coup was imminent. German intelligence did leak false documents through Czechoslovakia implicating Tukhachevsky and other members of the Soviet High Command in a conspiracy against the Soviet government. It remains unclear whether Stalin took that evidence seriously.[32]

The German role in educating so many Soviet officers between 1922 and 1933 has been neglected among the explanations for Stalin's decision to initiate the purges. This is surprising, as it was the ostensible reason Tukhachevsky was shot. At his show trial, prosecutors claimed Tukhachevsky had been acting under the "direct supervision" of the German General Staff since 1925.[33] In the event of war, "the front would be opened to the Germans" with the expectation they would in turn help Tukhachevsky launch a military coup in Moscow to seize power.[34] Prosecutors brought up Tukhachevsky's past work with Seeckt and the Reichswehr as evidence.[35] The great preponderance of historical analysis suggests the entire plot was invented by the Kremlin, but some elites running the Soviet state may have actually believed Tukhachevsky or parts of the Red Army would collaborate with the Germans in the event of war.[36] Future commissar for foreign affairs Vyacheslav Molotov, for instance, maintained until his dying day that Tukhachevsky had such plans in mind, saying that "if trouble started, which side would he have been on?"[37] Stalin himself thought in terms of a parallel with the French revolution. His nickname for Tukhachevsky was telling: Napoleonchik, the little Napoleon, referencing the French general who had overthrown a revolution and established a military dictatorship.[38] That historical analogy was also explicitly mentioned at the show trials.[39]

Whether he believed Tukhachevsky was capable of playing Napoleon, Stalin was clearly concerned that the Red Army might not be a reliable instrument in the event of war with Germany. Officers who had worked with the Germans dominated the senior ranks of the Red Army. Paranoid as he already was, Stalin must have noted how many of his commanders had lived, studied, or trained in Germany, his most likely military adversary. In this light, some of Stalin's private comments make greater sense. In late 1937, for instance, Stalin explained to senior NKVD officers tasked with making arrests that the purges were a preemptive strike to prepare frontier areas for war by eliminating hostile elements that might be loyal to potential adversaries.[40]

This logic can be seen in the selection of victims. Stalin's Politburo requested lists of all senior officers who had lived in Germany.[41] In 1937, the list of alumni included two of the Soviet Union's five marshals, the commander of the Soviet Air Forces, the head of the Soviet military education, the head of Soviet Civil Defense, the head of the Frunze Military Academy, the director of naval construction for the Soviet Navy, the commanders of the Northern Caucasus and Belorussian Military Districts, and the first deputy commissar for defense, as well as numerous corps and division commanders.[42] Almost none survived to 1941. The obliteration of those who had worked with the Germans went far lower in the ranks, too: According to the memoirs of a Red Army officer stationed at Kama after the purges, everyone he knew who had been there had been purged by 1938.[43] This included plumbers, janitors, and even waitresses at the camp mess hall.[44] The accusations made at the show trials, the internal justifications for the purges, and the selection of victims all suggest the history of cooperation between the Reichswehr and Red Army were among the reasons Stalin decapitated the Soviet military.

Whatever Stalin's motivations, the purges had cataclysmic effect on Soviet diplomacy. In the summer of 1937, the NKVD also began to ravage the Foreign Ministry, exacerbating existing confusion in Soviet foreign policy by the eliminating the Soviet Union's diplomatic capabilities just as they were needed most. Stalin replaced his ambassador in Berlin, Yakov Surits, who happened to be Jewish, in July 1937 with an ethnic Russian, Konstantin Yurenev. Hitler interpreted this favorably, and invited Yurenev to meet near his personal retreat at Berchtesgaden and greeted him with relative warmth, causing a mild stir in Moscow.[45] In an abrupt about-face, Stalin then recalled Yurenev to Moscow two months later and had him shot. Soviet trade official David Kandelaki, who had done much to pitch rapprochement in Berlin, was first proposed as his replacement, but then summoned home and arrested in mid-1937.[46] Stalin continued to send hints that he was willing to negotiate with Germany, but the furor of the NKVD roundups clouded the picture.[47]

That picture globally was just as bleak. Soon, the Soviets would have no ambassadors in nine crucial foreign capitals, including Washington, Tokyo, and Warsaw.[48] So many typists had been purged from the London embassy that Ambassador Ivan Maisky was unable to report any news to Moscow for several months.[49] Foreign Minister Maxim Litvinov reported to Stalin that seven out of eight Foreign Ministry departments were headed by temporary appointees or empty, and that "nine counsellors, 22 secretaries, 30 consuls and vice-consuls and 46 other official posts" were empty.[50] The purge would inflict similar damage on the Soviet intelligence services overseas.

Stalin's mutilation of his diplomatic, military, and intelligence apparatuses in the midst of a deteriorating international environment still defies easy understanding. It had immediate negative repercussions on Soviet security. The Wehrmacht's internal journal noted that "in shooting these well-known military leaders of the Soviet Union, they self-consciously sacrificed fighting ability and leadership of the Red Army to politics." The journal noted that getting rid of Tukhachevsky, "the most outstanding of all the Red Army commanders" created an irreparable loss.[51] Hitler would see the murders as an opportunity.

Other countries watched the immolation of the Soviet state with alarm. New British prime minister Neville Chamberlain commented that the purges had made "Russia an unreliable friend with very little capacity for assistance but with an enormous irritative effect on others."[52] At the same time, American ambassador in Moscow Joseph Davies reported that the French had no confidence in the USSR.[53] The purges had wrecked Litvinov's collective security policy. Nevertheless, he would continue to work on forging alliances even as his experienced diplomats disappeared into the maw of the NKVD's prisons and mass graves.[54] It was an impossible task, given the environment: at the end of the summer of 1937, the Soviet Union had a semi-functioning foreign ministry, a decimated intelligence service, a demoralized and leaderless army, and a great number of tanks and planes that were rapidly becoming obsolete. And the country was now completely isolated, beginning to move back toward its status as international pariah from which it had seemingly just emerged.

CHAPTER 29

The Technological Window

A s Stalin murdered his generals, Hitler gathered his together to plan the next war. On November 5, 1937, he brought together the heads of each of the military services—Werner von Fritsch for the Army, Erich Raeder for the Navy, Hermann Göring for the Luftwaffe, and Werner von Blomberg as minister of war—at the Reich Chancellery in Berlin. They were joined by Neurath, representing the Foreign Ministry, and Hitler's military adjutant, Colonel Friedrich Hossbach. He began the four-hour meeting, which became known as the Hossbach Conference, by telling them that he was going to share matters of such importance that he had excluded even the Reich cabinet from participating. He went on to say, somewhat melodramatically, that "his exposition be regarded, in the event of his death, as his last will and testament."[1]

As Hitler made clear to his five military leaders, his entire policy centered on the necessity of achieving autarky—complete independence. Germany as it currently stood was dependent on other states for critical raw materials, including food, which could not be grown in the "tightly packed racial core" of Germany itself. The solution was conquest. Germany's greatest opportunities lay in the East, as he had argued for the last twenty years. He then highlighted the immediate gains that were to be made with the conquest of Czechoslovakia and the annexation of Austria. The war to redraw Germany's borders must take place prior to 1943. He based this upon several facts. First, Germany had a head start in the global arms race that he had started and its equipment and armament were the most advanced. Delaying war meant "the danger of their obsolescence."[2] Further, although Hitler had ordered armaments production to be given top priority in his Four Year economic plan of August 1936 (inspired by the Soviet five-year plans), bottlenecks had begun to appear and armaments production was plateauing.[3] By 1943, the rest of the world would have increased their own military readiness to an unacceptable degree; Germany might even face a "food crisis."[4] War must come, and come swiftly.[5]

The military officers immediately protested. Generals Blomberg and Fritsch both made clear that they thought Germany was incapable of defeating Britain and France, should they intervene. Foreign Minister Neurath echoed the point, suggesting that the opportune circumstances Hitler had envisioned—a civil war in France or a Franco-Italian conflict—were not likely to materialize. The head of the German Navy, Admiral Raeder, sat silently. Only Göring voiced his approval.[6]

Hitler had outlined his immediate plans and clarified his strategic vision. What drove his proposed timing was his perception of a "technological window," when Germany would enjoy significant advantages in armament versus its likely opponents. The reasons for this were myriad, but depended upon on three facts. First, the rearmament work that had been conducted prior to 1933 had laid the ground for a rapid expansion of German military power and the rapid commissioning of new technologies of war. Second, Hitler had made rearmament his top priority from the moment he took office; the slowness with which the democracies had responded meant he had a head start that would diminish over time. And third—oddly—was the fact that the Treaty of Versailles had eliminated the normal process of research and development in Germany, resulting in the simultaneous appearance of large numbers of new aircraft and armored vehicle designs.

During the interwar period it took an average of four years to develop an armored vehicle or aircraft frame from specifications to mass production. It usually took another two years to reach maximum production efficiency and fix glaring technical problems. A new engine system took around six years to design from scratch. These developments could rarely be accelerated, even by major infusions of money. For instance, Luftwaffe General Wolfram Freiherr von Richthofen pressured engineers to accelerate the speed of innovation in aviation engines in the mid-1930s. But despite pouring funding into the program, it still took five to six years for results—not the two he had hoped for.[7] The design, development, and testing process could rarely be sped up.

By the time of the Hossbach Conference, the Luftwaffe had 162 different aircraft designs in production or under development. Many of these had been commissioned for the Air Ministry in 1933 or 1934, hence they were in the middle of their design timeline in the summer of 1936. For instance, the RLM had drawn up specifications for a single-seat fighter in 1933, then issued developmental contracts the following year. Willy Messerschmitt produced the first BF-109 prototypes for testing in the summer of 1935. Test flights indicated engine and structural defects, and the aircraft went through a total redesign in the summer of 1936. One model would be flown over the Olympic Games hosted in Berlin in August 1936, highlighting the rebirth of the Luftwaffe for international audiences.[8] But additional teething problems meant that the aircraft would not begin mass production until the following year. Refinements in design would lead the BF-109 F to be the most-produced airframe of the war, but not until 1940.[9]

Armored vehicles followed a similar timeframe. Oswald Lutz, as we've seen, had laid out the Panzer IV's specifications in January 1934. In 1936, Woelfert and the Krupp team began testing their first Panzer IV prototypes. In October 1937, the first models would enter mass production, with the Wehrmacht receiving its first Panzer IV models in January 1938. A final, major redesign resulted in the most mass-produced variant of the Panzer IV, but not until November 1941, when Operation Barbarossa was fully underway.

The Treaty of Versailles completely altered the normally staggered process of military-technological commissioning. It bears repeating: all of the research conducted in the 1920s meant that German military engineering did not lag significantly behind ongoing work in France, Great Britain, and the Soviet Union in aircraft and armored vehicle design. Then the bonds of Versailles were very suddenly shed between 1933 and 1935, leading to the initiation of a vast number of design contracts in a relatively narrow period. Given the relatively similar timelines of research and development, this in turn meant the Wehrmacht had a large number of technological systems reaching maturity and mass production *simultaneously* between 1939 and 1941. None of the other major powers was in that position. Rather than constraining Germany, the ban on military technologies under Versailles guaranteed that it would have a greater percentage of its new military technology reaching combat effectiveness than any other of the great powers.

By contrast, Great Britain and France remained reluctant to embrace full-scale rearmament in late 1937. Over the preceding decade, Britain had fallen behind Germany technologically thanks to the "ten-year rule"—that armed forces budgets should be prepared with the assumption that war would not happen in the next decade. This led to the decline of military-industrial expertise and the closure of many of the country's First World War arms manufacturers. By 1930, the only major, privately owned military-industrial complex left in the country was Vickers-Armstrong.[10] Great Britain had raised defense spending very slightly under Stanley Baldwin in 1935, but his successor Neville Chamberlain entered office in 1937 as a fiscal hawk: his first act was to halve the war office budget recommended by the Defence Requirements Committee, impeding efforts at preparing British industry for large-scale military production.[11] As a result, Britain lacked prototypes under development in many areas—Chamberlain's budget cuts halted all tank development, for instance.[12]

The one branch that had received ample financial support over the previous ten years was the Royal Air Force. As a result, the British had several outstanding aircraft prototypes entering mass production as the European crisis deepened. The Hawker Hurricane fighter was well along in development, and would enter service in small numbers at the end of 1937.[13] The famed Spitfire single-seater fighter was not far behind, with the first models planned to arrive at Fighter Command in June 1938.[14] The RAF remained several years away from having a heavy bomber, but had several excellent prototypes in early phases of development.[15]

Ironically, given their lead in armored warfare technology in the 1920s, British tank design lagged behind Germany's. Armored vehicles had been neglected as the Army focused on imperial policing; the vehicles produced were primarily light tanks and tankettes. In 1936, British specialists attended Soviet tank maneuvers run by Tukhachevsky. These emphasized fast, medium-sized tanks such as the BT series. The Soviets had borrowed from the British, and now the British would return the favor, though it would take some time for usable medium (or "cruiser," in the British lexicon) tanks to enter their arsenals in large numbers. The first prototypes of a medium British tank that could conceivably match the Panzer IV—the Crusader—remained several years away from mass production in 1938, especially following budget cuts.[16]

All of this lay behind the eventual British conclusion that more time was needed to bring its military readiness up to par with Germany.[17]

Even slower to embrace rearmament, the French government greeted news of Hitler's arrival in power by cutting nearly 30,000 soldiers from its standing army in metropole France—nearly 10 percent of the total.[18] Battles over whether or not military industry should be allowed to profit from government contracts caused the stagnation of research and development. In the early 1930s Renault, France's leading military-industrial giant, debated halting all design work on military projects until its intellectual property rights were guaranteed in some way by the military and the state.[19]

The first significant efforts to rearm France, begun under the Popular Front (Radical-Socialist-Communist) coalition government, proved disastrous. Prime Minister Leon Blum sought to resolve the Gordian knot of French rearmament by slicing through the problem, attempting to nationalize all of France's war industries in July 1936. The resultant dislocations, carried out unevenly, hampered mass production and raised costs. By 1942 or 1943, perhaps, these problems might have been rectified. Over the short term, it meant a haphazard mess, hampering efforts to catch the Germans in technological and industrial terms.[20] Follow-on efforts, such as a new national rearmament bill in September 1936, proved unsustainable as the Blum government was unable to secure long-term financing.[21]

Even with additional resources, French technology lagged behind German designs.[22] Little had been invested in the Air Force over the previous two decades, meaning there was a shortage of pilots, engineers, and skilled workers.[23] These factors all hindered the development of modern aircraft. The French Air Force had issued specifications for a fast, single-seater fighter in 1934, but by 1938 few designs were near readiness. Those aircraft in mass production were inferior to the German aircraft they were likely to face: the main French fighter was 50 mph slower than its German equivalent.[24] A better fighter aircraft—the Dewoitine D520—remained in the development stage.[25]

In tank production, the picture was only slightly less gloomy. The French Army possessed some excellent anti-tank weapons, but most of its armored vehicles were either old, mechanically problematic, or not yet ready for mass production.[26] The French armored forces consisted primarily of light tanks and tankettes. Its medium and heavy tanks—the Char B1, B1 bis, and Somua medium tank—had some significant advantages over their German opponents, including heavier armor and main armament. But the Char designs were old (first produced in 1924), slow, and mechanically outdated, while the Somua had significant mechanical and design problems.[27] Tactically, extremely conservative French armor doctrine and plans to remain on the defensive consigned the tank to a secondary role.[28]

The nature of French rearmament was only part of the strategic problem. The internecine French culture wars have received a great deal of attention as a cause of later French defeat. Pacifism, the disastrous state of labor relations, the low birth rate, and other such factors certainly played a role in perceptions of national weakness. But there were the hard realities: Germany had 20 million more people than France in 1936. Germany's industrial capacity was more than twice that of France.

France also imported key resources essential for its war industries, including nearly all of its petroleum, rubber, lead, copper, tin, manganese, sulfur, and pyrites.[29] French dependence on Great Britain was the essential conclusion drawn from these facts. France could not hope to defeat Germany by itself.

Of the other states on the continent, only the Soviet Union possessed both economic and demographic resources to pose a strategic threat to Germany's rearmament plans. But the Soviets lacked both a common border with Germany and the partners necessary to reach Germany—they faced decidedly hostile regimes all around their periphery. And German military intelligence assessed the Red Army as functionally useless in the immediate aftermath of the purges.[30] As a result, Hitler felt safe to ignore Soviet military capabilities by the time of Hossbach Conference.

The essence of the problem was that it took time to reorient a modern economy to war production, and even longer to develop the engineering and industrial capacity to produce large quantities of effective military materiel. In November 1937, German factories were already producing the new generation of aircraft and tanks commissioned in 1933 and 1934, and based upon the preceding years of secret rearmament work. Twenty-three medium Panzer IIIs would be produced by the end of 1937. The first tanks of the Panzer IV design—the project headed by Erich Woelfert at Krupp—rolled off of assembly lines by the end of 1937.[31] The Messerschmitt Bf 109 first entered mass production in February 1937. The new, fast Do-17 light bombers had begun arriving at Luftwaffe squadrons in the same month, with the new He-111 E series of medium bombers following not long after.

Thanks to the combination of secret rearmament measures—particularly those conducted in the Soviet Union—and his all-out embrace of rearmament, Hitler believed he was winning the European arms race, temporarily. That lead had enabled him to overturn Versailles at shockingly little cost. He also concluded that his aggressive rearmament program had provided the tools necessary for a quick victory in a future war, provided it was fought before the British and French had caught up militarily.[32] Convinced that his military forces were strong enough to deter the French and British for a few years, he sought to isolate and quickly conquer other states in Eastern and Central Europe. First and second on his list were neighbors Austria and Czechoslovakia. A month after the Hossbach Conference, the Wehrmacht amended its war plans to give precedence to an invasion of Czechoslovakia.[33] Hitler wanted war. Now he was prepared to start one.

CHAPTER 30
Purges and Panic

In late 1937, Blomberg, now a field marshal, approached Göring to discuss a personal matter. The fifty-nine-year-old widower had fallen hard for one of the secretaries in the War Ministry. Pursuing the relationship would fall somewhat outside of the social expectations for the most powerful military man in the Reich. He therefore asked Göring as a friend and an officer whether he thought the potential marriage would be acceptable.[1] Göring replied that he had no objections—in fact, the marriage seemed to him politically advantageous, highlighting the new, classless social order. Göring proceeded to assist the field marshal "in the disposal of a rival admirer, whom the Minister-President [Göring] obligingly shipped off to South America."[2] No doubt anxious about the precedent of his predecessor Wilhelm Gröner, Blomberg went so far as to ask Hitler for his personal blessing. The Führer endorsed the marriage and promised to attend himself. A small ceremony was duly held in Berlin on January 12, 1938, with Hitler and Göring standing in as witnesses.

There was only one problem. According to police records, Blomberg's bride, Erna Gruhn, had been a prostitute and posed for pornographic magazines. The incriminating documents turned up by chance on the desk of Count Wolf-Heinrich von Helldorf, who was then serving as the police-president of Berlin. A former army officer, he decided to discreetly deliver the documents to General Wilhelm Keitel, Blomberg's son-in-law, in the hopes of avoiding a scandal. Keitel, not wanting to confront his father-in-law, instead allowed them to be turned over to Göring, who "felt in duty bound to pass them to Hitler."[3] It may not have been so happenstance. Some have argued that Göring had masterminded the conspiracy, though Hitler was in all likelihood not involved.[4]

Field Marshal Blomberg had no choice but to resign. The entire officer corps felt shamed; his close subordinate Ludwig Beck told Blomberg to his face that "he was not even fit to command a regiment."[5] So incensed was one former adjutant of Blomberg's that he followed the retired marshal and his new wife on their honeymoon to Italy. In Rome, he confronted Blomberg with a pistol, demanding Blomberg either kill himself or file for divorce to redeem the honor of the military. Blomberg declined, writing that the young officer "had quite different views and standards of life from my own."[6]

Hitler had been genuinely surprised by the Blomberg revelations—one subordinate said he was so shocked he had a "nervous breakdown."[7] Regardless, the political opportunities created by the scandal were already becoming clear in his mind. Fritsch, then commanding the Wehrmacht, was Blomberg's logical successor. Unlike Blomberg, he lacked any personal rapport with the top Nazi brass. Göring wanted the job of minister of war himself. The head of the SS, Heinrich Himmler, wanted a different Nazi in the position.[8] A cabal against Fritsch soon formed, predicated on another scandal. In this case, it was the false claim that the elderly, monastic Fritsch—who was unmarried—was a closeted homosexual.[9] Himmler and Heydrich produced a witness who would testify against the general. Fritsch demanded a court-martial to clear his name.[10] Hitler refused him the opportunity.

While the Army High Command had lost respect for Blomberg, they rallied around General Fritsch. General Beck, now one of the most ardent anti-Nazis among the senior officers (he would be shot for trying to kill Hitler in 1944), proposed that Fritsch use the opportunity to remove Hitler from power and "to cleanse once again not only the Government of the Reich but also the honor of the Army."[11] Groener or Schleicher might have considered the attempt. But Fritsch proved to lack the necessary willpower. He resigned his commission and retired in disgrace.

Hitler took full advantage of the crisis. Rather than replace Fritsch and Blomberg, he reorganized the military entirely, assuming the role of commander in chief himself.[12] He eliminated the Ministry of War altogether and replaced it with the Oberkommando der Wehrmacht (the High Command of the Armed Forces, or OKW) to oversee all three branches—Army, Navy, and Air Force. Hitler then placed the OKH under the OKW. Hitler rewarded General Keitel for his betrayal of his father-in-law Blomberg by appointing him chief of staff of the OKW. The Army was now firmly subordinated to Hitler and the Nazi Party, and its few leaders capable of resistance stripped of real power. A minor purge of potentially disloyal officers followed. Though nowhere on the scale or violence of Stalin's purges, the intention was similar, as was stated in the list of indictments at the Nuremberg trials after the war: "to get rid of the men who might stand in the way of aggressive warfare."[13] In a final blow to the Wehrmacht's prestige, in August 1938, Hitler authorized the SS to use their forces in combat. Within eighteen months, the SS would develop a military wing with more than 100,000 men and support personnel.[14] The Army had lost its monopoly on force.

Like Stalin, Hitler also "cleaned house" at the Foreign Ministry. Foreign Minister Konstantin von Neurath—one of the few senior Weimar-era holdovers—was pushed out of office, and the entire Foreign Ministry brought directly under Nazi Party control.[15] The three men who had spoken up against Hitler's plan for war at the November 1937 meeting—Neurath, Blomberg, and Fritsch—had all been removed from office by February 1938. Hitler now completely dominated the security and foreign policy apparatus of the state. Now in firmer control of the military, Hitler would begin moving quickly. Within a week, Hitler began demanding German self-determination in Czechoslovakia.[16] He also moved against Austria. These were the two states he had marked for annexation in the Hossbach Conference.

In Austria, the right-wing authoritarian government of Kurt von Schuschnigg faced great danger. Hitler met with Schuschnigg on February 12, 1938, and demanded greater Austrian Nazi participation in the government, including its total control over the country's police forces. Schnuschnigg agreed, hoping to stave off invasion. As riots grew and in the face of increasing German demands, Schuschnigg declared that a national plebiscite would be held on the question of Austrian independence on March 8. Hitler hoped to absorb Austria on the grounds of self-determination but a major victory for Austrian independence at the ballot box might spell disaster for his plan, rendering annexation of Austria much more difficult. On March 11, he gathered the new military leadership of the Reich and told them to prepare for an invasion of Austria by noon of the following day. Schuschnigg became aware of the danger and tried to cancel the plebiscite. But German forces invaded on March 12, resulting in the long-promised Anschluss (union) of Austria with the German Reich.

Even as German troops prepared to cross the border, Hitler solicited Mussolini's approval for the invasion, which, to his great satisfaction, was forthcoming. Mussolini's Ethiopian and Spanish adventures had permanently severed his ties with the Western powers.[17] There was little succor for Austria from London or Paris, either. In Great Britain, Chamberlain continued to preach appeasement. In France, there was near-complete political chaos: there would be three different national governments in power between February and April, with a new one, led by Leon Blum, forming only on March 13, in the midst of the crisis. While there was alarm across Europe, no concrete measures were taken to deter Hitler. Nothing emerged from Paris other a pledge of support to Czechoslovakia on March 14, followed by a similar one from Moscow.[18]

Hitler was fortunate in that the occupation of Austria had not actually required any military force. In part because of lack of experience and in part because of limited preparation time, the entire "invasion" had been haphazard and badly organized. The Wehrmacht had only been able to move across Austria by fueling up at local gas stations.[19] Hitler nonetheless immediately turned his attention from Austria to Czechoslovakia, where Sudeten German demands for annexation had grown ever louder. On May 28, in a meeting with military leaders, Hitler told them that a war with Czechoslovakia was necessary in the event of conflict with the Western powers—now his main preoccupation—but that it would have to wait until German defenses in the West had been built up further, and until the Wehrmacht possessed greater "striking power" for overcoming Czech fortifications (see map 3).[20] That being said, he believed that no one would come to Czechoslovakia's aid should he strike: the British were not yet rearmed, and the French and Soviets were incapable of offensive action.[21] On May 30, he ordered the military to begin making preparations for the invasion of Czechoslovakia, to take place no later than October 1, 1938.[22]

Five thousand miles to the East, the possibility of a very different war was starting to grow, and under bizarre circumstances. Early in the morning of June 13, 1938, two Chinese policemen working for the Japanese occupation authorities in Manchuria

Map 3 Central Europe, 1938

stumbled upon a strange sight. Wandering through the undergrowth in the morning fog was a short, overweight, and bedraggled Russian man with a Hitler-like mustache.[23] When the policemen challenged him, the man threw two pistols on the ground and raised his hands high. When they approached, they discovered that he wore the uniform of a Soviet general. As they went through his things, they found a card that identified him as Genrikh Lyushkov, the senior NKVD official for all of Siberia and the Far East. And he wanted to defect.[24]

Lyushkov carried with him immense knowledge about the Soviet state, having spent time with Stalin as well as the senior leadership of the Red Army.[25] A close affiliate of NKVD boss Nikolai Yezhov, the Kirov assassination and subsequent roundups and purges had meant promotion for Lyushkov. He fit right in; a junior officer who later defected to the West described him as "arrogant, arbitrary and [a] sadistic bully." Among his particular accolades, he had received a medal from Moscow for supervising the ethnic cleansing of Koreans and Chinese from the Soviet Far East.[26]

It was perhaps Lyushkov's enthusiasm for executing his fellow NKVD officers that most earned him Stalin's approbation. In July 1937, Stalin had met with him privately, ordering him to root out traitors in the government, party, and military in the Far East, near the tense Japanese border. Stalin gave Lyushkov a clear rationale: "War with Japan is inevitable; the Far East is undoubtedly a theater of war. It is necessary to clean up the army and its rear in the most determined manner from hostile spy and pro-Japanese elements."[27] Among those to be watched was Marshal Vasily Blyukher, the independent-minded and capable commander in the Far East. After Blyukher had served on the tribunal that sentenced Tukhachevsky and other friends of his to death, he had developed a serious drinking problem. In his cups, he had become somewhat indiscreet, sharing his thoughts on Voroshilov and the purges.[28]

When he was invited to Moscow in June 1938—the usual precursor to arrest for senior officers—Lyushkov decided his odds were better in militarist Japan than in the murderous Soviet Union. He shared with his captors his stories about the decimation of the Red Army, as well as the much larger than expected strength of Soviet forces in Siberia. Not long after, Japanese intelligence in Manchuria learned that the Soviets were moving forces into a disputed territory near their border. Stalin was responding to Lyushkov's defection with a show of force, increasing security in the Far East and moving additional border guards to the disputed area between the Soviet Union and Japanese-occupied Manchuria. This, naturally, heightened tensions. Stalin refused Japanese demands to withdraw his forces in mid-July. Local Japanese commanders in Manchuria, now well informed about the magnitude of the purges and dispositions of Soviet forces, decided to risk escalation without the consent of their senior officers in Tokyo.[29]

On the night of July 30–31, the Japanese struck, launching attacks on fortified positions in territory that the Soviets had occupied earlier that month. Although the Soviets possessed a sizeable advantage in vehicles, aircraft, artillery and infantry, the deadly work of the purges had drastically reduced morale and removed many effective officers. As a result, Soviet forces blundered into Japanese defenses, suffering enormous casualties. Gradually, though, the Japanese were pushed back. On August 10, Japanese diplomats reached out for a return to the status quo ante, which the Soviets accepted the following day.[30]

The border "skirmish," in which the Soviets had suffered more than 4,000 casualties, confirmed the danger of a war in the East, though it left the border unresolved. While the Japanese had technically conceded the seized ground, the attack highlighted weaknesses in the Red Army that convinced some Japanese Army planners that defeating the Soviets and seizing the Far East was possible. Stalin's reaction indicated his thoughts on the matter. He had Marshal Blyukher tortured to death not long after the battle's conclusion.[31]

With Stalin distracted by the threat of war in the East, Hitler continued his game of brinksmanship in Europe, convinced of the unwillingness of Great Britain and France to confront his increasingly powerful Wehrmacht and Luftwaffe. Planning had already begun for the invasion of Czechoslovakia. Hitler told General Keitel that he wanted a war either after an incident provided justification, or "action after a period of diplomatic discussions which gradually lead to a crisis and to war." He ruled out a surprise attack, which, because of world opinion, must be saved for the "last enemy on the continent."[32] Whether he chose to strike west or east, eliminating Czechoslovakia would weaken France's hand, and provide the Wehrmacht with critical resources.[33] And in Czechoslovakia, the case of the 3 million Sudeten Germans allowed him to use the language of self-determination to justify his seizure of territory. Who in Great Britain would go to war to stop a national minority from expressing its own political preferences?[34] The conflict would split the British and French. And while the Soviets had a military agreement with Czechoslovakia, it seemed unlikely that they would intervene, especially given Stalin's ongoing purges and the crisis in the Far East. Here, it seemed, Hitler had the war he wanted.

His own military leadership disagreed, however. As his planned date at the end of September drew nearer, the senior ranks of the Wehrmacht resisted his plans. In particular, OKH head General Beck told Hitler repeatedly that German rearmament was not far enough advanced to defeat France and Great Britain should they intervene. On August 10, Hitler tried to bypass Beck by meeting with his subordinates, endeavoring to convince them that a rapid attack on Czechoslovakia could lead to victory in four or five days, obviating the political risks of a war in the West.[35] They, too, were skeptical. A circle of conspirators began to plot to remove Hitler in the event of war. Beck—who was one of them—resigned on August 18 in protest of Hitler's determination to go to war.[36] His successor, General Franz Halder, was even more resistant to Hitler's plans, but lacked the political capital and will of his predecessor.

In Prague, Czech president Eduard Beneš was theoretically willing to go to war, should the British and French commitment prove trustworthy.[37] Beneš refused to meet with Hitler directly, placing Czechoslovakia's fate in the hands of its allies, who would negotiate on its behalf. They were unprepared to do so effectively. The French, led from March 1938 by Prime Minister Édouard Daladier—now in his third stint as prime minister—were largely focused on social reforms at home. In August, following a Nazi-orchestrated visit to a Luftwaffe base, Chief of the French Air Force Staff General Joseph Vuillemin told Daladier, "If war breaks out at the end of September as you think it will, there won't be a single French aircraft left after 14 days."[38] Daladier used this excuse of supposed German air supremacy to argue France could do little, ceding initiative to British prime minister Neville Chamberlain.[39] Chamberlain, too, felt unready to take on Germany, in part due to Germany's perceived armaments advantage.[40] The British Foreign Office and the British Chiefs of Staff were convinced that Germany could not be stopped by military means in the short term, and that to attempt to do so would bring Italy and Japan into a conflict that would be prolonged and global in scope.[41]

Nevertheless, war threatened. On September 23, the Czechoslovak Army mobilized. On September 24, the French government ordered their own partial mobilization. Desperate to avoid war, Chamberlain initiated shuttle diplomacy, aimed at reaching an "acceptable" compromise short of war.[42] This led to the infamous summit in Munich on September 29 and 30, hosted by Hitler and attended by Daladier, Chamberlain, and Mussolini. There, Hitler reiterated demands for the ethnically German regions of Czechoslovakia. Mussolini presented a "compromise plan"—one that was in fact drawn up by the German Foreign Ministry.[43] When asked for a delay to ascertain Czech willingness to accept some of the terms (given that they had refused to negotiate directly with Hitler), the Führer flew into a fury.[44] The final product was the Munich Agreement, where Hitler received all of his territorial demands without the need to go to war. Germany's armaments lead had produced another bloodless victory: American ambassador in Paris William Bullitt reported home that it was the perceived strength of German air power that had convinced the French and their British partners to surrender yet again to German demands.[45]

Hitler was far from happy in the aftermath of his latest bloodless victory. He had wanted a war on the right terms and he had not gotten it. And his military officers had proven truculent. Almost immediately after Munich, he abandoned the pacific rhetoric in which he had cloaked his aggression and rearmament to date. Now, he declared Germany's need to break "the spirit of Versailles" in a more systemic way.[46] Hitler had achieved the two swift victories he had planned at the Hossbach Conference. Now the question was where he would turn next.

CHAPTER 31

Stormclouds

While Hitler was disappointed he had not gotten his short, victorious war, Stalin was irate. As noted, three years earlier, Litvinov had negotiated the 1935 Soviet-Czechoslovak Treaty of Mutual Assistance. Under its terms, the USSR would assist in the defense of Czechoslovakia if that state were threatened, but only if the French rendered assistance first.[1] During the crisis in 1938, Stalin offered to commit military forces to assist Prague, even ordering a partial mobilization of the Red Army. It remains unclear whether this offer was genuine, especially given possible Soviet interest in directing Hitler's aggression westward.[2] The most recent evidence from the Russian archives suggests that had the French acted, the Soviet Union would have fulfilled its obligations under the terms of the 1935 treaty, but that the Kremlin was fairly confident the French would not act.[3] At the time, neither France nor Britain seriously considered Soviet assistance, refusing to even invite a Soviet delegation to attend the Munich Conference where Czechoslovakia's fate was decided.[4] In practice, this meant that Soviet collective security policy had failed once again.

Stalin had kept his options open throughout the 1930s. He had maintained channels to Germany and continued to offer openings for political rapprochement from 1933 to 1938, even while Litvinov pursued collective security. Following the Munich Conference, the German option became much more attractive.[5] The series of negotiations that would eventually lead to a renewal of the Soviet-German partnership began over trade relations shortly following the Munich Conference. As noted, German-Soviet economic exchange did not cease in 1933, though it did decline from its peak in 1930.[6] Much of the continuing trade was conducted under credit agreements, whereby the German government provided credits to the Soviet government to purchase industrial and finished goods from German firms. Every year between 1933 and 1938, Germany remained one of the top three exporters to the USSR. And Germany continued to import key raw materials from the USSR as its rearmament measures rapidly used up existing stocks of resources in Germany. This led German officials—including Hermann Göring, then managing German war production—to seek expanded trade agreements with their Soviet counterparts five times in 1937 and 1938.[7] However, these attempts failed, in part because the Soviets demanded political talks as part of any economic agreement.[8]

Circumstances changed after Munich. By December 1938, German raw material needs had become desperate, with former Reichsminister of Economics Hjalmar Schacht informing Hitler that without further resource imports in critical areas like oil, rubber, iron, manganese, phosphates, tungsten, and chrome, "armaments production had reached the limit of peacetime expansion possibilities."[9] With few other options, the Germans stepped up their negotiating efforts with the USSR. On December 1, 1938, the head of the Eastern European Economic Section of the German Foreign Ministry, forty-one-year-old Karl Schnurre, decided to renew the German approaches. A member of the *Ostpolitik* faction, he devised a generous credit proposal designed to bring the Soviets back to the negotiating table. The Germans would offer credits to cover Soviet purchases worth 500 million Reichsmarks in Germany in exchange for 300 million Reichsmarks' worth of Soviet raw materials.[10] The Soviets responded with a proposal for trade talks in Moscow on January 11, 1939.

Behind the scenes, there was enthusiasm on the Soviet side. Kliment Voroshilov sent Anastas Mikoyan, then managing foreign trade, a list of requested purchases to be made from Germany's military industry as part of the deal.[11] The final proposal stretched to seventeen pages. The Soviet Air Force alone planned to request from German industry four complete fighter and bomber prototypes, seven engine designs, thirteen different machine gun and bomb designs, nine types of laboratory equipment, and ten kinds of optical and electrical equipment. The total list included 112 items. The fact that the Red Army would consider presenting German trade representatives such a list during a period of supposed hostility shows how essential German designs and expertise remained for the Red Army.[12] It also indicated that the Soviets had in mind broader rapprochement, as the Germans would never agree to sell such a list of weaponry without a political understanding.

The Soviets soon found themselves disappointed, however. Hitler, steered by Ribbentrop, remained committed to his approaches to Poland. With his assent, Ribbentrop canceled Schnurre's proposed trip to Moscow on January 28.[13] Instead, Ribbentrop ordered Ambassador Schulenberg to enter into trade negotiations, but without the power to conclude an agreement. Negotiations seemed to be making progress, but Soviet demands for large quantities of military materiel proved unpalatable to Hitler, who still believed Ribbentrop's promises about the construction of an anti-Soviet coalition. On March 11, the German Foreign Ministry ordered Schulenberg to bring negotiations to a "standstill in a suitable way," while leaving room for their future resumption.[14]

A change in circumstance would ultimately present new opportunities. With German connivance, Czechoslovakia had begun to disintegrate following the Sudeten crisis of the previous year. Its remaining national minorities—particularly the Slovaks—were encouraged to clamor for independence, or at least greater autonomy. Hitler took advantage of the disorder that followed, ordering the Wehrmacht to prepare to occupy the remainder of the Czech state.[15] On March 14, 1939, he ordered the president of Czechoslovakia, Emil Hacha, to Berlin. At one in the morning, Hitler—who had kept Hacha waiting for hours while he watched a movie—summoned the elderly lawyer into his presence. He announced that as he spoke, the German Army was invading Czechoslovakia. He told Hacha he could either order the Czech military to lay down arms and prevent bloodshed, or force would be used, including the terror bombing of Prague. Hacha's reaction to this was a heart attack. While under medical treatment, he signed Hitler's demands, and ordered the surrender of the Czech military to the occupying Germans.[16]

There was little legal pretext for the invasion; one German representative in Prague recorded that the Germans "deplored the perfectly correct, even accommodating, attitude of the Czechs everywhere."[17] It was an act of naked aggression. Hitler's reward was the powerful Czech military arsenal, carefully built up throughout the interwar period: more than 1,000 modern aircraft, 2,000 artillery pieces, and 800 modern tanks.[18]

The German invasion stunned Neville Chamberlain. He delivered a quiet and cautious address to Parliament shortly after the news came in on March 15.[19] Two days later, he addressed a crowd in Birmingham, saying, "Public opinion in the world has received a sharper shock than has ever yet been administered to it, even by the present regime in Germany." He went on to insist defensively, "Really I have no need to defend my visits to Germany last autumn, for what was the alternative?" But there was a hint of resolve in the speech that was new. He concluded by saying that "No greater mistake could be made than to suppose that, because it believes war to be a senseless and cruel thing, this nation has so lost its fibre that it will not take part to the utmost of its power in resisting aggression."[20]

Hitler had more shocks in store. Seven days after taking Czechoslovakia, he seized the city of Memel from Lithuania. The following day, he forced Romania into a pro-German trade treaty, providing the Wehrmacht with a guaranteed supply of oil.[21] Hitler also began exerting heavier pressure to bring Poland into the German orbit.[22]

Chamberlain finally acted. During a cabinet meeting on March 18, he made clear that it was time to take a stronger line, even to the point of risking war.[23] After brief deliberation, his government publicly announced a security guarantee to Poland, promising to protect Polish sovereignty should Hitler invade.[24] The aim was to deter further aggression. But Chamberlain's decision was made hastily, without consulting the Foreign Office. His speech announcing the policy indicated that he had chosen Poland over the Soviet Union as a partner in the East.[25] The problem was that Britain could offer little military support to Poland directly, and Poland was too weak to defeat Germany without considerable assistance.

Realistically, cooperation between Poland and the Soviet Union was the only means of deterring German aggression toward the East. Unfortunately, by emphasizing commitments to Poland without serious overtures to Stalin, Chamberlain had simultaneously alienated the Soviet Union and made his foreign policy dependent upon it. He had some reasons for ignoring Moscow: the broad consensus among British and French intelligence continued to be that the Red Army had become useless after the purges. In the spring of 1939, for instance, the French General Staff described the Red Army as "virtually worthless," while the head of the British Secret Intelligence Service reported that it "could do nothing of real value."[26] Combined with general distrust of Soviet ideology and lingering horror from collectivization and the purges, the Soviets seemed a hopeless ally.

For his part, Hitler was furious about the guarantee to Poland. It ended any possibility he could cajole Poland into supporting a crusade against the Soviet Union.[27] Upon receipt of the news of the British statement, Hitler shouted, "I'll cook them a stew that they'll choke on!"[28] On April 3, 1939, he ordered plans drawn up for the invasion of Poland, to begin no later than October 1 of that year.[29] By way of explanation, he told German military leadership that "We have nothing to lose; we have everything to gain . . . the power of initiative cannot be allowed to pass to others."[30]

The Wehrmacht's own rearmament programs were leveling off, approaching maximum production possible given resource, manpower, and finance constraints.[31] Technologically, prototypes commissioned between 1933 and 1935 now made up the bulk of German production, providing—as noted—a temporary lead in armaments that would gradually fade. The British and French were now committed to serious rearmament, and across the Atlantic, the United States had also begun to gear up for national mobilization.[32] Hitler's window for war was closing. After four years, nothing had come of Ribbentrop's efforts to persuade Polish foreign minister Józef Beck to ally with Germany – Beck understood the stakes too well.

The idea of a new Soviet partnership would first emerge from veterans of the old. There were constituencies within both the German military and Foreign Ministry— primarily veterans of the Rapallo Era—that favored a renewal of ties with the Soviet Union. [33] To sway the Führer, members of the German Foreign Ministry fed information to key members of Hitler's entourage indicating that Stalin was interested in rapprochement in March—some of which was at best misleading.[34] In this context, Göring—likely seeking to undermine rival Ribbentrop's influence with Hitler— suggested to Hitler the abandonment of overtures to Poland and a reorientation toward the Soviet Union. To further sway Hitler, he even traveled to Rome in mid-April to discuss with Mussolini the Italian reaction should Germany pursue an anti-Polish agreement with Moscow.

The guarantee to Poland had triggered a reaction in Moscow, too.[35] Immediately, the Soviets renewed their approaches to Germany. On April 17, 1939, Soviet ambassador Alexei Merekalov in Berlin met with State Secretary Ernest von Weizsäcker to discuss whether the now German-occupied Škoda Works in Czechoslovakia would fulfill military orders that had been placed there by the Soviet government.[36] Merekalov concluded his remarks by noting that the German reaction would demonstrate whether Germany wanted to "cultivate and expand economic relations with Russia," or not.[37] Stalin also ordered the recall of his ambassadors in London, Paris, and Berlin for consultations.

On April 21, Stalin summoned his foreign policy team to the Kremlin, including Ambassador in London Ivan Maisky, Merekalov, Vyacheslav Molotov, Voroshilov, Mikoyan, and Litvinov. The air was tense, particularly between Commissar of Foreign Affairs Litvinov and his rival Molotov. Stalin made clear that he was "manifestly dissatisfied with England," and that he was concerned "there might be a plot in London or Paris to involve Moscow in a war and then leave her in the lurch."[38] Molotov suggested opening negotiations with Germany. Merekalov made clear that Berlin would be open to an agreement.[39] Given the hostile attitude toward his collective security project, Litvinov then dramatically offered his resignation. Stalin rejected it, then turned to Maisky, asking his assessment of the situation in London. Sensing the mood in the room, Maisky suggested that a new British act of appeasement toward Germany was indeed possible, possibly with the purpose of encouraging Hitler to attack the Soviet Union.[40]

On May 3, Stalin removed Maxim Litvinov, who was Jewish, from office. Stalin replaced Litvinov with his closest associate Molotov, who was ethnically Russian and supportive of renewed cooperation with Germany. Molotov, known as "stonearse" by his associates for his dull personality and long working hours, would later describe his understanding of the role of foreign minister as "expand[ing] the borders of our fatherland."[41] Stalin's first order to him, in Molotov's own recollection, was to "purge the ministry of Jews."[42] This was intended as a signal to Hitler.[43] Other signals were immediately forthcoming, too. On May 4 and 5, Soviet diplomat Georgii Astakhov sought out German diplomats in Berlin to discuss the Škoda contract issue.[44] During those meetings, one of them recalled, Astakhov "spoke about the removal of Litvinov and tried to ask indirectly whether this event would bring us to a changed attitude of the Soviet Union." [45] Astakhov wrote back to Moscow that "the Germans are trying to create the impression of an impending or even immediate improvement in the German-Soviet relations," and that their motives for doing so were so obvious—the Polish guarantee—that such signals should be taken seriously.[46]

That assessment was accurate. Hitler ordered a halt to media attacks against the USSR, then recalled Ambassador Schulenberg, diplomat Gustav Hilger, and military attaché Ernst Köstring from Moscow to Berlin for his own round of consultations. On May 10, he met with Hilger—the most experienced Russia expert in the Foreign Ministry, resident in Moscow for twenty years—and trade negotiator Karl Schnurre. Unusually for Hitler, he listened attentively, asking thoughtful questions on the nature of Soviet foreign policy.[47] He met with Köstring shortly thereafter, behaving similarly.[48] These men, veterans of the Rapallo Era and advocates of rapprochement with the USSR, described a Stalin willing to collaborate and with much to offer economically.[49]

On May 17, Astakhov approached Karl Schnurre to discuss renewing the stalled trade talks. He also noted that "there were no foreign policy disagreements between Germany and the Soviet Union, and that, as a result, there was no basis for hostility between the two states."[50] Astakhov then explicitly cited the precedent of the Treaty of Rapallo, a subject laden with military and political meaning.[51] Three days later in Moscow, new Commissar for Foreign Affairs Molotov visited Ambassador Schulenberg for an hour-long conversation. Molotov suggested that economic talks could resume once the necessary "political bases" for them had been constructed. He proposed both governments think about "the way in which better political bases could be built."[52] He would not say more when pressed, leaving Schulenberg—to Molotov's amusement—temporarily bewildered.[53] Schulenberg conveyed to Berlin his belief that Molotov had "almost invited political discussions" and that "our proposal of conducting only economic negotiations had appeared insufficient to him."[54]

In light of these signals and ongoing talks between the Soviets and Great Britain, Hitler decided to reopen negotiations in Moscow. On May 30, the German Foreign Ministry informed Schulenberg, "Contrary to the policy previously planned, we have now decided to undertake definite negotiations with the Soviet Union."[55] But after years of mistrust, neither side was certain whether talks were entirely tactical— aimed at isolating the other from other potential partners. Astakhov, Merekalov, and Weizsäcker in Berlin and Schulenberg and Molotov in Moscow spent much of June cautiously sounding each other out. For instance, Astakhov visited the Bulgarian ambassador in Berlin—whom he hardly knew—and spent two hours explaining Soviet attitudes toward Germany to him apparently on the assumption he would relay the information. Most notably, the Bulgarian ambassador told his hosts, Astakhov had stated that of options available to the USSR, "a rapprochement with Germany . . . was closest to the desires of the Soviet Union."[56]

On June 17, the German Foreign Ministry informed Mikoyan of their interest in sending Schnurre back to Moscow to reopen trade negotiations. He rejected this offer as being too risky, given that there were British and French emissaries in Moscow. Mikoyan eventually offered to send a delegation to Berlin instead.[57] Stalin seems to have been playing for time. Hitler, growing frustrated, briefly canceled further talks, though only four days later, Schulenberg and Molotov discussed the political basis upon which a trade deal could be negotiated.[58] Between July 7 and July 12, the Germans dropped one of their major reservations in the economic negotiations: they would sell armaments to the Soviets.[59] This marked a change in the German negotiating position, which had essentially blocked weapons sales to the USSR since 1935.

On July 21, Schnurre formally opened new economic talks with Soviet envoys in Berlin. Hitler told the German Foreign Ministry that "we will here act in a markedly forthcoming manner, since a conclusion, and this at the earliest possible date, is desired for general reasons."[60] Specifically, Hitler now planned to launch a war against Poland in late August. An economic partnership with the USSR would provide critical raw materials to maintain the German war machine in the face of a possible British blockade. Given that German military planners calculated Germany had only three to six months of oil in the event of war—and even greater shortages of other raw materials— Wehrmacht officers concluded that "making our greater economic sphere blockade-proof can only be achieved through close economic cooperation with Russia."[61] In essence, this was the idea that had motivated Seeckt back in 1920: that the USSR might serve as strategic and economic depth in the event of a new war between Germany and the Western powers. Even better, in the German view, an agreement with Stalin might deter the British from honoring their guarantees to Poland at all, thus handing Hitler yet another easy victory. Ribbentrop, who spent nearly every moment by Hitler's side in the critical months of 1939, told the Führer this would in fact be the case.[62]

Stalin, whose intelligence agencies allowed him to read much of the German diplomatic traffic, was well aware of the German position.[63] He resolved to extract the highest possible terms from Hitler before reaching an accommodation. The Germans began negotiations by proposing a large credit arrangement at high interest, centering on raw material deliveries to be made over a short period of time in exchange for finished goods.[64] The Soviets countered every one of the German terms, and won each at the negotiating table as Hitler pressed the German Foreign Ministry to reach an arrangement. By August 4, the two sides had reached the basic contours of a credit deal.[65] But the Soviets refused to finalize the arrangement, waiting to see if they could improve their bargaining position before political talks began.

Hitler was impatient for Stalin's agreement. On August 11, Hitler informed Mussolini that he was considering temporary rapprochement with Stalin to deter any British or French action over Poland.[66] The same day, he declared to an amazed foreign visitor, "Everything I am doing is directed against Russia; if the West is too stupid and too blind to grasp this, I shall be forced to come to an understanding with the Russians, strike West, and then after its defeat turn against the Soviet Union with my assembled forces."[67]

As Hitler waited for Stalin, London and Paris sent representatives to Moscow to negotiate a military alliance with the Soviets against Germany. Inexplicably, they were sent via slow-boat, were not authorized to sign any documents, and, in the British case, had not even been credentialed by their own government.[68] Their primary goal may have been to keep the Germans and Soviets from concluding a deal. On August 11, they finally arrived, greeted with a huge feast hosted by Commissar for Defense Kliment Voroshilov. Despite the warm reception, Stalin was not impressed. The envoys had low ranks, lacked credentials, and could not communicate in Russian—the large delegation had only one Russian-speaker as an interpreter. At a meeting of a Politburo that day, Stalin formally decided to begin political negotiations with Germany.[69]

The Germans had far more to offer than the British and French. Sympathetic Stalin observer and *New York Times* journalist Walter Duranty would later write, "I do not doubt that the Soviet [*sic*] would always have preferred to retain its friendship with Germany rather than rapprochement, however close, with Britain, France, and Poland."[70] That view was broadly shared in the embassies of the other great powers in Moscow in August 1939.[71] Hitler could give his assent to Soviet occupation of the Baltic states, eastern Poland, and Bessarabia, whereas London and Paris would not. Hitler could supply huge quantities of machine tools and military technology to the USSR, while the British and French could not, especially as they tried desperately to catch up with the German lead in armaments.

There were also ideological reasons behind Stalin's preference for a German partnership. Stalin perceived of the capitalist world as a hostile bloc, divided between "rich" and "poor" states.[72] Great Britain stood at the head of the "rich" states; Germany was a revisionist "poor" state. Stalin's goal remained to avoid any unity between these two groups, which might result in a capitalist crusade against the Soviet Union. Instead, however, if the two fought an extended war, the Soviet Union might profit enormously, staying on the sidelines until its weight could be added decisively to the scales.[73] As Molotov would explain to a party member in 1940, a long war between Germany and the British and French would trigger revolutions and civil wars in which the Soviets would intervene militarily. A decisive victory "somewhere near the Rhine" would permanently establish communist rule across Europe.[74]

The final steps had not been taken, yet. On August 12, the Soviets informed the German Foreign Ministry that they were willing to begin talks of a political nature, provided they could be held in Moscow.[75] Hitler was amenable, driven above all by the desire to reach an agreement before he invaded Poland. On August 13, the Polish government ordered a partial mobilization of its army, further increasing Hitler's sense of urgency.[76] On August 14, Ribbentrop communicated to the Soviets his request for a personal meeting with Stalin to discuss "the restoration of German-Soviet friendship, and where appropriate, to resolve territorial issues in Eastern Europe together."[77] Molotov indicated his approval during a meeting with Schulenberg the following day, presenting a few key items that should be included in negotiations.[78]

On August 19, Molotov provided the Germans with a Soviet draft of a nonaggression pact.[79] It included five brief articles, roughly based upon the 1926 Treaty of Berlin, which in turn had been an extension of the 1922 Treaty of Rapallo. There were two unusual terms. First, the draft treaty did not include a section that rendered the treaty null and void in the event Germany or Soviet Union committed aggression against a third country—language that had been included in all other Soviet nonaggression treaties to that point.[80] Second, it stated that the pact would be valid only if it included a special secret protocol covering key points in foreign policy between the two states.[81] The Germans interpreted these terms to indicate Soviet interest in the partition of Poland, and other possible territorial agreements besides. Before they could turn to the Soviet draft treaty, however, Molotov insisted that a credit deal be finalized first.[82] Urged on by the German Foreign Ministry, Schnurre and a Soviet envoy signed the delayed trade agreement in Berlin after midnight that day. The final agreement included a low-interest credit worth 200 million Reichsmarks ($80 million USD) to be used by the USSR for the purchase of German machine tools and weapons.[83] In exchange, the USSR would export 180 million Reichsmarks' worth of Soviet raw materials over two years, with shipments to begin immediately.[84] Given the interest rates, the German concession to sell weapons, and uneven value of the deal, it was clear Stalin had won the negotiations.[85] The raw material exports listed, while substantial, were hardly at the level of German expectations needed to maintain an extended war against Great Britain.[86]

On the afternoon of August 20, dismayed by breaking news of the Soviet-German economic agreement, the French delegation in Moscow agreed to a major Soviet demand: that the Red Army be allowed to cross Polish and Romanian territory in the event of a German invasion.[87] They did so without the consent of their Polish and Romanian allies, both of whom were concerned that such an agreement would result in permanent Soviet occupation. Although the Soviets claimed this was key to any military arrangement, Stalin had already made his decision: he had agreed to political discussions with the Germans nine days earlier and already provided the Germans with the draft text of a treaty that strongly hinted at the partition of Poland. Given the course of events, it seems probable that Stalin had inclined toward a German pact since May, and had only allowed the British and French delegations to visit Moscow in order to get better terms from the Germans. In any case, on August 21, Stalin temporarily suspended negotiations with Great Britain and France. Immediately afterward he sent his lead negotiator in those talks, Kliment Voroshilov, on a duck-hunting expedition to halt any attempts to recommence the process.[88] The same day, Stalin ordered the Soviet Foreign Ministry to give Ambassador Schulenberg an official memorandum on the subject of further negotiations.

Now just days from his planned invasion, Hitler sent a personal cable to Stalin, writing that he considered it "urgently necessary to clarify questions connected with it [the political talks] as soon as possible," and urging Stalin to accept a visit from German foreign minister Ribbentrop, who would be delegated full powers to sign an agreement.[89] At 8:30 P.M. on the evening of August 21, Hitler learned that Stalin had authorized Ribbentrop to arrive on August 23. He declared, "Now I have the world in my pocket!" and immediately ordered champagne to be broken out.[90] The next morning, Hitler spoke to his senior military leadership, outlining his plans for war against Poland. He told Germany's military leaders that "because we have sources of supply in Eastern Europe" there was now limited danger from the Western powers.[91] Bolstered by an out-of-touch Ribbentrop, he was confident that agreements already made with Italy, Japan, and now the Soviet Union would deter any British or French military interventions—he would finally have his short victorious war. Amateur "peace feelers" from London behind the scenes also strongly suggested to him that the British and French lacked the will to go to war.[92] A final measure of reassurance arrived when a British diplomat delivered a fresh offer from Chamberlain to negotiate over Poland—hinting that the British guarantee to Poland was not in fact ironclad.[93] But with the renewal of Rapallo imminent, Hitler was ready to start his war, and would not allow any peace talks or concessions to divert him from that aim. On the evening of August 22, Ribbentrop boarded Hitler's personal Condor aircraft and departed for Moscow.

CHAPTER 32
Fulfillment

German foreign minister Joachim von Ribbentrop's plane touched down in Moscow in the early afternoon of August 23. His flight had not been uneventful: Soviet border guards, unaware of the visit of the German delegation, opened fire on his aircraft as it crossed the border.[1] Ribbentrop received a warmer welcome once he landed. Waiting for him on the runway were the Soviet Union's deputy foreign minister Vladimir Potemkin, Stalin's personal bodyguard Nikolai Vlasik, and a bulletproof limousine flying a Nazi flag.[2]

Ribbentrop headed directly for the German embassy, where he was met by several longtime veterans of diplomacy in Russia. Ribbentrop's translator for the trip was the Russian-born diplomat Gustav Hilger, who, as noted, had been the first German representative to arrive in Moscow in 1920. He had been there ever since. Hilger was joined by the military attaché Ernst Köstring, Seeckt's former adjutant who had worked at Moscow Central from 1931 to 1933.[3] Köstring was initially unimpressed by Hitler's diplomatic troubleshooter, who appeared "nervous and agitated."[4] Much rested upon this former wine merchant's visit to Moscow.

After a brief rest, Ambassador Friedrich von der Schulenberg and Hilger accompanied Ribbentrop to the Kremlin. To their surprise, Stalin met them in person.[5] In five years in Moscow, Schulenberg had never met the reclusive Soviet leader. Ribbentrop presented a short letter from Hitler indicating he had the full powers to conclude an agreement between the two states. Given that both sides had presented the other with drafts, negotiations proceeded rapidly. Stalin immediately moved the conversation to the division of spheres of influence (see Map 4). The two sides quickly agreed to a partition of Eastern Europe between them, with Finland and Estonia falling in the Soviet sphere, and Lithuania in the German. Poland would be partitioned along the line of the Narew, Vistula, and San rivers. Germany declared its disinterest in Romanian Bessarabia.[6] Aware of Hitler's urgent need for a final agreement, Stalin raised Soviet demands: all of Latvia—previously to be divided along the line of the Dvina River—was now to be included in the Soviet zone. Ribbentrop dashed to the German embassy and cabled Hitler with the new demands. Hitler, who had nervously stayed up late watching films, replied almost immediately with his assent.[7] Ribbentrop returned to the Kremlin, where he informed Soviet leadership of Hitler's agreement.

The major issues resolved, Stalin and Ribbentrop turned to global affairs. Ribbentrop expressed confidence Germany could handle the Western democracies and Poland; Stalin expressed some doubts, but added that "the Soviet Union is interested in preserving a strong Germany, and in the event of military conflict between Germany and the Western democracies, the interests of the Soviet Union and Germany coincide completely. The Soviet Union shall never tolerate letting Germany fall into difficult straits."[8] While they talked, staffers finished drafting the text of the nonaggression pact. There remained only some brief final haggling over the preamble. The German draft contained florid prose about "natural friendship" between the two states, to which Stalin objected: "Don't you think that we have to pay a little more attention to public opinion?" he asked the Nazi foreign minister. "For many years now, we have been pouring buckets of shit on each others' heads. . . . And now, all of a sudden, are we to make our peoples believe that all is forgotten and forgiven? Things don't work that fast."[9] Ribbentrop conceded. After a brief review, Molotov and Ribbentrop signed the text of the seven-paragraph treaty at 2 A.M. Moscow time on August 24. It went into immediate effect. Ribbentrop called Hitler from the Kremlin—with Stalin present, though not speaking to the Führer himself—to share the news.[10] The celebratory drinking then began: champagne was served, with Stalin offering an unexpected toast: "Let's drink to the new anti-Cominternist—Stalin!" In Molotov's recollection, Stalin immediately followed the toast with a private wink.[11] Stalin, Molotov, Ambassador Schulenberg, and Ribbentrop then toasted each other in turn.[12] Bleary-eyed photographers documented the moment.

The Molotov-Ribbentrop Pact shocked the world. Contemporary American journalist Walter Lippmann summed up the feelings of many when he wrote, "In all history it would be hard to find another conspiracy so terrible in its consequences, or to match its perfidy."[13] Communists and Fascists both regarded the agreement as a betrayal. French, British, and American communists were horrified at Stalin's deal; a trickle, then a flood, began to depart the Party.[14] Ardent Nazis felt much the same way. Propaganda minister Joseph Goebbels wrote of his own distaste at the news in his diary: "We are in a tight spot, and like the devil, have to eat flies." He confidently added that, in any case, "at some point we will come into conflict" with the Soviet Union.[15]

There were other reactions, though. Many German officers felt that a partnership with the Soviet Union was the best possible strategic decision. Old veterans of the Rapallo days like Oskar von Niedermayer wrote, "The time of Versailles and the interventions has come to an end. . . . Careful thinking and action has superseded a military miracle. . . . The destinies of Germany and Soviet Russia are now closely connected; war against Germany also means war against Soviet Russia."[16] General Max Ludwig—former head of the Waffenamt during the Rapallo Era—celebrated the "'Führer's ingenious decision to alleviate the tensions and return to our long-established friendship.'"[17] That long-established friendship had first emerged from shared hostility to Poland, the state that would soon suffer greatly from the renewal of the Soviet-German partnership.

Map 4 Territorial Changes, 1939–1941

On the night of August 31, SS forces staged an attack against a radio tower on the German side of the border, dumping concentration camp victims in Polish uniforms as supposed proof of Polish aggression. The following morning at 4:40 A.M., without a declaration of war, the German attack began. The aging battleship *Schleswig-Holstein*, supposedly on a goodwill visit to Danzig, opened fire point blank on Polish defenses. The Luftwaffe followed, striking hundreds of targets across the western Poland. Then the Wehrmacht—which numbered 1.5 million men in the east and now possessed five Panzer divisions—began crossing the border. The Polish government had ordered a national mobilization on August 29, but anxious British and French governments had demanded they cancel it lest they "provoke" a German response.

As a result, only about half of frontline Polish units were in their assigned defensive positions when the German attack began.[18]

Hitler, who announced the attack to the Reichstag that morning, was certain the Western Allies would do nothing. Ribbentrop had convinced him his partnerships with Italy, Japan, and the USSR would deter their intervention. He was genuinely surprised when—with great reluctance—they fulfilled their promises to Poland, and on September 3 declared war on Germany. When the news arrived, Hitler stood silently, then looked at Ribbentrop and said, "What now?"[19] Stalin, for his part, could be satisfied that the new war looked like it would be fought primarily in the West, with the Soviet Union as a neutral observer.

Despite determined Polish resistance, the coordinated use of aircraft, armored vehicles, and infantry rapidly overwhelmed Polish defenders. On September 9, the Luftwaffe began terror-bombing the Polish capital. Guderian, commanding the XIX Panzer Corps, led his tank formations in a rapid encirclement of a large Polish force near the town of Andrzeievo—northeast of Warsaw—which surrendered two days later. He later described the campaign as "a baptism of fire for my armoured formations. I was convinced that they had fully proved their value and that the work that had gone into building them up had been well spent."[20] With German forces south, north, and east of Warsaw, armored columns succeeded in cutting off the Polish capital on September 13. The Luftwaffe continued bombing Warsaw long after it ceased to be militarily expedient; more than a thousand German aircraft attacked the city on September 24, after most of the Polish army had been defeated. The Polish capital would suffer 40,000 civilian deaths in a month of combat.[21]

As the Germans rapidly overran their "sphere of influence" in Poland, the Soviets provided navigational aids to the Luftwaffe via radio, but otherwise remained quiescent.[22] During the first week of the German invasion, the Politburo initiated plans for significant increases in the size of the Red Army. Voroshilov ordered the mobilization of Red Army reservists in seven border districts and canceled scheduled discharges from the ranks. And the NKVD began organizing "operational groups" for the occupation of Eastern Poland.[23] But despite these preparations, when the German government asked whether or not Russian forces would immediately invade eastern Poland, Molotov informed Schulenberg, "We agree with you that at a suitable time it will be absolutely necessary for us to start concrete action. We are of the view, however, that this time has not yet come."[24] The aim, he implied, was to avoid being drawn into war with the British and French. He told Schulenberg a few days later that the Red Army was mobilizing and planned to launch military action following the fall of Warsaw, which would enable his government to claim the USSR was coming "to the aid of the Ukrainians and the White Russians 'threatened' by Germany," which would make intervention "plausible to the masses" and "avoid giving the Soviet Union the appearance of an aggressor."[25] This was true, but not the whole truth: the USSR had been taken by surprise by the speed of the German advance and had not yet completed diplomatic and military preparations to seize their portion of Poland.[26]

On September 15, in a seemingly unrelated piece of news, the Soviet Union announced that an agreement with the government of Japan had finally concluded a months-long border conflict in Manchuria following a Soviet military victory at Khalkin Gol.[27] Late the following evening, the Polish ambassador was summoned to the Kremlin, where he was informed by Potemkin that the "Polish-German war has revealed the internal inadequacy of the Polish state" and that therefore the Soviet government intended to "liberate the Polish people from the unfortunate war, where it was cast by its irrational leaders, and give them the opportunity to live a peaceful life."[28] A few hours later—the morning of September 17—nearly 500,000 Red Army soldiers, equipped with nearly 10,000 tanks and armored vehicles, as well as 2,000 aircraft, crossed the Polish frontier.[29]

Soviet and German forces began to encounter each other east of their demarcation line because of the speed of the German advance. Guderian's men first met a Russian reconnaissance unit on September 18 outside of Brest-Litovsk, which they had just taken following heavy fighting. Twenty years earlier, that city had played host to the negotiations between Trotsky and the German government that would end Russia's involvement in the First World War. Now, the two sides would share a brief joint occupation until German soldiers could withdraw to the demarcation line agreed to in the Molotov-Ribbentrop Pact. Red Army soldiers were discouraged from fraternizing with the Germans, but both sides shared cigarettes, exchanged mementos, and inspected each other's equipment.[30] Local Poles, who at first thought the Red Army was coming to protect them, were horrified.

Guderian's orders were to hand over the city to the Soviets and withdraw. The two sides arranged to do so on the morning of September 22, following a brief conference. Guderian then met with his Soviet counterpart, Twenty-ninth Light Brigade Commander Semyon Krivoshein. Krivoshein had been among the Soviet students enrolled at Kama; it is possible he and Guderian already knew each other. In any case, they shared a common language—French—and agreed after brief discussion to review German forces, accompanied by a Soviet band and a few Soviet regiments, prior to German departure from the city.[31]

At 4 P.M. on that cool autumn afternoon, Guderian and Krivoshein met on a hastily constructed wooden platform to watch the joint procession through town.[32] Guderian and Krivoshein, both tank pioneers, chatted pleasantly as their soldiers began to pass the reviewing stand. The crowd lining the parade route consisted of German and Soviet soldiers, as well as many non-Polish locals, temporarily enthusiastic about their Soviet "liberators." The German formations impressed the crowd with their smart *feldgrau* (field gray) uniforms, their modern motorcycles, trucks, half-tracks and tanks, and their disciplined ranks. The Soviet Twenty-ninth Light Brigade, by contrast, included obsolete tanks like the T-26—one of which slid off the road into a ditch near the reviewing stand.[33] Red Army soldiers wore shoddy olive-colored uniforms, and instead of trucks, relied on horses. The men themselves had "dirty boots, dusty greatcoats and stubble on their faces."[34] It would have been hard for the audience to imagine that the slovenly Soviet soldiers had marched only 150 miles without encountering much resistance, while Guderian's men had fought their way across more than 325 miles of Polish terrain, inflicting more than 25,000 casualties on the Poles in the process. The purges and rapid expansion of the Red Army had clearly taken a toll on Soviet military discipline.

Five days after the victory parade, Warsaw surrendered to the Germans. On October 6, the last Polish military resistance ceased. Both occupiers immediately began mass arrests, deportations, and murders of the local Polish population, intending to keep them submissive. General of the Armia Krajowa (the Home Army, the primary Polish resistance organization) Tadeusz Bór-Komorowski recalled that in some ways the Soviets were worse than the Germans, at first. The Germans behaved as brutes: they beat people to death in the streets and left piles of corpses. In September alone, they murdered more than 12,000 Polish citizens, mostly in public.[35] By contrast, Bór-Komorowski wrote, "Soviet methods of police procedure were more refined and efficient."[36] In their zone, people disappeared at night. Their effective network of spies created prisons of the mind, leaving "mutual distrust of which the greatest use was made."[37] Following the arrival of the Red Army, the NKVD deported 100,000 Polish citizens to Siberia, where nearly half were starved to death or executed.[38] In the Katyn Forest outside Smolensk, they also shot 21,892 Polish officers taken prisoner during the war.[39] The Germans, by contrast, were just learning how to industrialize death. That process would begin the same month as the invasion of Poland with the Aktion T-4 program, which euthanized hundreds of thousands of handicapped people in Germany.[40] It would culminate in the Holocaust. Nearly 6 million Polish citizens—half of them Jewish—would be killed by the Nazis over the next six years.

CHAPTER 33

Uneasy Allies

Victory over Poland came with a cost for both Germany and the Soviet Union. Germany was now cut off from most international trade and desperate for raw materials as the unplanned war against Great Britain and France began. The USSR, though not formally a belligerent, soon found itself facing some of the same concerns. The United States, the Soviet Union's largest source of machine tools and industrial equipment in 1939, soon barred the USSR from making armaments or re-lated purchases in America.[1] The result was that Germany and the Soviet Union had to reorient their economies toward greater collaboration.[2]

To that end, Ribbentrop and Schnurre returned to Moscow on September 28 to negotiate a much more substantial political and economic settlement, intended to place Soviet-German cooperation on a more permanent basis.[3] At five in the morning on September 29, the two sides signed a new arrangement, the Boundary and Friendship Treaty. To adjust for territories in Poland still held by the Wehrmacht around Lublin and Warsaw, Germany ceded all of Lithuania to the Soviet sphere of influence, with the understanding that the Soviets would soon invade and annex Lithuania and then turn over a border strip around Memel to German custody.[4] The two sides made general promises about economic collaboration, while the Soviets guaranteed transshipment of key raw materials to Germany across their terri-tory.[5] The Germans were frustrated, however, that Molotov refused to agree to the terms of a new, much broader economic deal to solve Germany's desperate resource shortages, particularly in oil and rubber. So severe were German shortages by the fall of 1939 that some military planners were uncertain whether the Wehrmacht would be capable of launching an offensive against France.[6]

In October, Schnurre returned to Moscow for new negotiations, seeking imme-diate raw material deliveries.[7] Later that month, as part of the negotiating process, forty-five Soviet officials—divided into eight working groups—arrived in Berlin.[8] Their task was to draw up lists of goods to be acquired in exchange for Soviet raw materials. Highlighting Stalin's aims, three teams were to visit machine tool and high-technology firms, while the other five visited armaments plants.[9] Most facilities were open to these delegates, as Hitler ordered German industrial firms to make all equipment that was already in use in the Wehrmacht available to the Soviet visitors. He believed that such a display of German technological superiority might frighten the Soviets into concessions.[10]

On November 30, the Soviet envoys provided a forty-eight-page list of their requested purchases, with an estimated value of 1.5 billion Reichsmarks—a sum roughly equivalent to 10 percent of Germany's national budget from the previous year.[11] In the face of gargantuan German demands for Soviet raw materials, the Soviets had replied in kind. General Keitel called the Foreign Ministry to complain about "voluminous and unreasonable" Russian demands.[12] Half the value of Soviet requests were naval in nature, including a complete cruiser and destroyer, the blueprints for the massive German battleship *Bismarck*, naval guns, precision equipment, mines, torpedoes, and enormous amounts of construction equipment for further shipbuilding.[13]

These orders came directly from Stalin. In 1934, at the XVIIth Party Congress, Voroshilov had announced that Stalin "would now manage the build-up of the Navy himself."[14] Over the course of the next year, more and more work was done on acquiring capital ship designs and armament overseas, particularly from Italy.[15] On May 27, 1936, the Soviet government had approved a naval construction program including a staggering 24 battleships, 20 cruisers, 182 destroyers, and 344 submarines, plus numerous auxiliary ships.[16] Stalin's personal involvement and increasing obsession with massive warships made these plans even more elaborate over the next few years. He even sent feelers out to British firms regarding technical assistance for the construction of a 59,150-ton battleship, a vessel 30 percent greater in displacement than the *Bismarck*, then under construction.[17] Even without the construction of such a monstrosity, by 1940, it was estimated that the Soviet battleship program likely absorbed a third of the Soviet defense budget.[18]

The reasons behind this largesse were opaque to the Soviet Navy: Admiral Nikolai Kuznetsov, commander in chief of the Soviet Navy, recalled that the navy was not consulted on these expenditures. As to Stalin's demands for naval equipment from Germany, he believed that perhaps Stalin hoped to slow down German naval rearmament by demanding so much naval equipment, thus drawing out the war in the West between Germany and Great Britain.[19] Another possibility is that Stalin saw an opportunity to conduct the kind of technological borrowing and espionage of German naval equipment that had been so successfully carried out in armored vehicle and aircraft design during the Rapallo Era, in which the German Navy had declined to participate.

The disparity between the two sides' demands, and Stalin's willingness to once again play for time, meant that no agreement was reached that fall, despite German needs. Nonetheless, military cooperation resumed in other forms. On September 6, 1939, within a week of the signing of the Nonaggression Pact, the German ship *Bremen* had steamed into Murmansk harbor in northern Russia. Over the next month, seven other German-flagged merchantmen arrived in Murmansk, where they were welcomed.[20] The Soviets even briefly considered assisting the Germans in arming some of these former merchant ships to operate as commerce raiders against British shipping out of Murmansk harbor.[21] Realizing this might embroil them in war with Great Britain, the Soviets would soon alter this offer, with Molotov telling Ambassador Schulenberg that "Murmansk was not sufficiently isolated for this purpose [for harboring German warships]."[22] Instead, Molotov suggested the possibility of using an empty bay east of Murmansk, Zapadnaia Litsa (Western Face), for whatever purposes the Germans desired.

Admiral Erich Raeder (head of the Kriegsmarine) was thrilled by this possibility. In words of German naval planners, the offer "opened up entirely new operational possibilities for the German Naval High Command."[23] During a meeting on October 12, Raeder and his staff drew up a list of requests to be made to the Soviet Navy based upon their offer of a Soviet harbor. The list more or less required Soviet entry into the war on the German side. It included "the use of suitable harbors, say Murmansk and Vladivostok" as bases for German warships; assistance in supplying German commerce raiders in both the Atlantic and Pacific; repair and maintenance assistance on German vessels in both oceans; the use of Soviet flags to cloak German naval convoys as "neutrals" in the Atlantic and Baltic; and the cancellation of "all direct or indirect Russian exports to the enemy countries."[24] Although the Soviets would reject some of these terms, on October 22, the German naval attaché relayed the news to Berlin that the Soviets had agreed to put Zapadnaia Litsa at their disposal, noting that "Germany may do whatever she wishes [there]; she may carry out whatever projects she should consider necessary." Any type of vessel would be permitted to call there, including heavy cruisers, submarines, and supply ships.[25]

The offer was immediately accepted. Admiral Raeder ordered the German naval attaché to travel to Murmansk and select two ships for conversion as a floating submarine support base in Zapadnaia Litsa, now called "Basis Nord" [North Base] in German communiqués. A German naval officer arrived in Murmansk on November 28, 1939, to supervise the transfer of goods and military stores to the selected vessels, the *Phoenicia* and *Cordillera*. The arrival of the two vessels established a German military presence at Basis Nord just two days before a new front in the war opened less than 80 miles away.[26]

On the morning of November 30, 1939, without a declaration of war, the Soviet Union attacked Finland. A few hours later, the Soviet Air Force launched a bombing attack on Helsinki. The Finnish border was only 20 miles from the outskirts of Leningrad.[27] To protect the city, Stalin requested that a Finnish delegation come to Moscow to discuss a rearrangement of the border in October 1939.[28] These demands came on the heels of Soviet negotiations with Latvia, Lithuania, and Estonia, which had resulted in Soviet military bases in all three countries. This seemed to Finnish leaders—correctly—to be a prelude to Soviet occupation. The Finnish government was split, eventually deciding against surrendering territory, believing that any concession would mean the loss of sovereignty. Marshal Carl Gustaf Emil Mannerheim, a hero of the Finnish Civil War, was appointed commander in chief in mid-October. He began a quiet mobilization of Finnish troops and a review of the country's defenses.

After the successful invasion of Poland and the victory at Khalkin Gol in the Far East, Stalin was confident in the strength of his Red Army, despite the damage inflicted by the purges. He was dismissive of tiny democratic Finland; there were more soldiers in the Red Army than men in their entire country. Further, Finland was diplomatically isolated. Its traditional ally Germany was now unlikely to intervene, Finland's Scandinavian allies were unwilling to assist, and the Western democracies were already embroiled in a war with Germany. In addition, the Red Army had good intelligence, including clear maps of the Finnish defensive systems along the border, possibly provided by German military intelligence as part of the Pact.[29]

Despite enormous material and manpower advantages, Soviet forces were badly led and poorly prepared for what became known as the Winter War. Some Red Army units reported ammunition shortages within a few hours of the war's beginning—following a full month of preparation.[30] The initial Soviet attack on Finland's half-fortified border defenses did not get off to an auspicious start, either. Red Army officers ordered their men to assault in close order—as if on parade—which led to the decimation of entire companies. (According to contemporary rumors, the Red Army may have herded recently captured Polish POWs in front to reduce the damage to their own men.[31]) One Soviet officer described the anguish of his unit after it had been cut off by Finnish ski troops in bitter winter conditions: "The battalion had been badly punished when the men had lit fires to warm themselves and heat food. From the treetops the Finns had machine-gunned every fire, easily picking out the dark silhouettes of the men against the snow."[32] Most of his battalion eventually surrendered to the outnumbered Finns.

While the Red Army's struggles were not yet apparent internationally, Stalin moved quickly to sound out his new German ally. Within hours of the initial attack, the Soviet Navy requested direct military assistance from the Kriegsmarine in two forms. First, they asked for German support in conducting anti-submarine operations off the Finnish coast. Second, they requested that German vessels supply Russian submarines maintaining a blockade of Finnish ports.[33] The Kriegsmarine, despite deep sympathy for Germany's traditional ally in Finland, immediately and even eagerly responded to the requests. The possibility of reciprocal aid of a similar kind—namely the resupplying of German submarines in both the Atlantic and Pacific by neutral Soviet vessels—was immediately grasped by the Kriegsmarine.

A month after the submarine requests, the Soviet Navy and the Kriegsmarine reached an accord for German passage through the Northern Sea Route through the Arctic Ocean.[34] This was a potentially momentous occasion. With Soviet assistance, it would be possible to dispatch an entire fleet to the Pacific to harass and interdict British merchant vessels. Soviet icebreaker technology, far ahead of anyone else's in the world, had made such a passage possible by specially modified ships. Initially, the Kriegsmarine proposed to send an armada of twenty-six ships to the Pacific to wreak havoc on British supply lines.[35] The difficulties of the naval war in the Atlantic and the Kriegsmarine's strained resources, however, diminished this number to six vessels, then to four, and finally, to two: the *Esso* and the *Komet*.

The voyage started poorly: the *Esso* ran aground off the coast of Norway. The *Komet*, commanded by Konter-Admiral Robert Eyssen, arrived off the coast of Murmansk. However, confusion and bureaucratic issues in Moscow meant that *Komet* had to wait nearly a month for its Soviet icebreakers, the *Lenin* and the *Stalin*.[36] Finally, the *Komet* departed for its long journey, with the *Lenin* leading the way. After perils and more than a few mishaps in the icepack, the *Komet* reached the open sea northwest of the Barents Straits. The passage had taken twenty-three days, the fastest traverse of the Northern Route in history to date.[37] In September, after a brief stop in a Soviet harbor, the *Komet*, disguised as a Japanese merchant ship, made its way to the South Pacific. During its voyage, the *Komet* would sink nine ships displacing nearly 43,000 tons and capture a tenth, which was crewed and sailed back to Germany.[38] The *Komet* would successfully dodge British vessels and reach the safe harbor of Hamburg on November 30, 1941, having successfully circumnavigated the globe. Had twenty-six German vessels reached the Pacific, it might have spelled disaster for the British.

While the two sides expanded their work together at sea, a new economic agreement had not yet been reached. Some trade continued under the August credit agreement, but not at the quantities hoped for in either Berlin or Moscow. The August treaty required the USSR to sell 86,800 tons of oil products in total to the Germans over the next twenty-four months. But German military planners expected 60,000 tons of Russian oil per month just to maintain stocks at existing levels.[39] As the British had initiated a blockade, it appeared Germany might even face serious food shortages if grain could not be purchased from the USSR.

Negotiations in December and January 1940 had brought the two sides closer, but no final treaty had resulted. In growing desperation, Ribbentrop sent a personal letter to Stalin on February 3, pleading the German case. It called the partition of Poland a "not inconsiderable advance payment by Germany."[40] Stalin agreed to convene another summit in Moscow to discuss economic conditions. On February 8, Schnurre returned to Moscow, and spent three days in hard negotiations led by Anastas Mikoyan. The result was the German-Soviet Commercial Agreement of February 11, 1940.[41]

This arrangement promised far more than the August agreement. Including the earlier August arrangement, the USSR was expected to deliver 800 million Reichsmarks' worth of raw materials, a list that now included a million tons of grain, 900,000 tons of oil, 800,000 tons of iron, 500,000 tons of phosphates, 100,000 tons of chrome, and smaller quantities of copper, nickel, tin, molybdenum, wolfram, and cobalt.[42] In exchange, the Germans would provide industrial goods and military equipment, including modern aircraft models. Hitler was so certain that the arrangement would mean the defeat of the British blockade that he assigned Soviet orders higher priority even than the German military. For his part, it seems Stalin hoped to be able to control the flow of raw materials—particularly oil—and thus control the pace of the war in the West. If Germany was winning, he could cite delays and reduce the flow; if France or Great Britain, he could offer more raw materials.[43]

Exports did not suddenly start flowing to Germany, however. Particularly in key areas like grain and oil, Soviet deliveries dropped in March, rather than increasing. Ambassador Schulenberg wrote from Moscow, "The Soviet Government is determined to cling to neutrality in the present war and to avoid as much as possible anything that might involve it in a conflict with the Western powers."[44] Although the Soviets had finally broken through Finnish defensive works, British and French intervention seemed possible.[45] Even more worryingly for Moscow, in March 1940, the British Royal Air Force began conducting reconnaissance flights over Soviet oilfields in the Caucasus.[46] This was a possible precursor for a strategic bombing raid to cut off

Soviet oil production, which the British and French believed was fueling the German war effort.[47]

Until the threat of Western intervention diminished, Stalin avoided fulfilling his agreements with his German partner. To that end, the Soviet Union rapidly concluded a peace treaty with Finland on generous terms for the latter, leaving its sovereignty intact and only adjusting its borders to protect Leningrad and Murmansk. On April 9, Hitler launched Operation Weserubung (the Weser River Exercise), rapidly overrunning Denmark and beginning the invasion of Norway. This opened direct combat operations between German and Allied troops in Norway, removing the likelihood of an attack against the USSR in the north. Molotov publicly declared, "We wish Germany complete success in her defensive measures," while privately telling the Germans that any delays in shipments had been a result of the "'excessive zeal of subordinate agencies' which would be immediately remedied."[48] The USSR then began to open the spigots. Although still short of German expectations, between January and May 1940, the USSR would export 155,000 tons of oil, 128,000 tons of grain, and 8,600 tons of manganese, with most of those quantities arriving in April and May.[49] Stalin had made clear that he held the initiative throughout eight months of contentious Soviet-German economic talks: the Germans needed Soviet raw materials more than the USSR needed German military equipment, especially as Germany faced the combined might of Britain and France in the west. That equation would change suddenly.

CHAPTER 34

Blitzkrieg

At dawn on May 10, the Luftwaffe began bombing airfields in the Low Countries and France. The poorly equipped French Air Force could do little to respond. At first, it seemed that the heaviest German concentrations were being launched against the Netherlands and Belgium. But per Erich von Manstein's operational plan—Fall Gelb IV (Plan Yellow Four)—the main thrust in fact came from the Wehrmacht's Army Group A, racing through the heavily wooded, hilly Ardennes of Belgium and Luxembourg. General Heinz Guderian's XIX Panzer Corps spearheaded this force, containing three of Germany's Panzer divisions. Their aim was to reach the English Channel, resulting in the encirclement of the British and French armies that were already moving into the Low Countries to block the perceived German advance there.[1]

On May 13, 1940, Colonel Friedrich Kühn, formerly an instructor at Kama, took part in the largest armored battle up to that point in history.[2] His Third Panzer Brigade had crossed into southeastern Belgium as part of Army Group B less than seventy-two hours earlier. Lead elements of two of his regiments encountered a French armored detachment of thirty or so machines. Kühn's Panzers, mostly light Panzer Is and IIs, were less well armored and armed than their slower, heavier French opponents. They possessed one critical advantage, however: radios.

The French, who coordinated between their vehicles with signal flags, soon found themselves at a distinct disadvantage. As soon as the two sides opened fire, French commander Le Bel battened down the hatch of his vehicle and immediately lost the ability to coordinate with the rest of his unit. Kühn's tanks experienced losses, but soon outflanked Le Bel's squadron. Suffering casualties from the air and from those heavier German tanks that soon joined the fight, Le Bel had no choice but to retreat. The German XVIth Corps diary, of which the Third Panzer Brigade was a part, noted for the day that "the Germany Panzer arm feels itself superior to the enemy."[3]

That superiority depended on years of preparatory work involving not just the tanks themselves, but aircraft designs, radios, the training of personnel, and the doctrine to use them in conjunction. Many of those elements depended on the work conducted in the Soviet Union. Although still relatively few in number—about one third of the German armored force in 1940—the German Panzer III and IVs were, in the words of one armor officer, "superior to all French tanks" encountered during the Battle of France.[4] This was as much a product of doctrine and training as of technology, but those German tanks were generally faster and more reliable in the field. And most importantly, thanks to the three-man turret devised at Kama, German commanders were freed to concentrate on the battlefield, rather than loading and firing the main gun. [5] Also critical for German success was the frequent use of close air support, provided primarily in 1940 by Hermann Pohlmann's Ju-87 Stuka dive-bomber—a plane developed directly from prototypes tested at Lipetsk. And radios, drawing from experimentation conducted at Kama, allowed the close coordination that enabled German tactical and operational doctrine to succeed. Foreign journalists would call this new German style of warfare "Blitzkrieg"—lightning war.

The thrust of Army Group A succeeded beyond the wildest expectations of planners at the OKW. Guderian, whose XIX Panzer Corps began to reach the Channel coast on May 20, felt the plan's success was "almost a miracle."[6] Over the next two weeks, British and French forces in Belgium beat a hasty retreat in the face of constricting encirclement. Many—particularly British soldiers—were saved by the skillful naval evacuation of Operation Dynamo at Dunkirk. Nonetheless, on June 22, the French government surrendered. Stalin's hopes of a long, bloody war in the West had ended in six short weeks. His reaction to the news was despondency: "Hitler was sure to beat our brains in," he told Nikita Khrushchev.[7]

Hitler had not expected the war to come to so rapid a close, either. Initial planning for the campaign had only aimed to seize enough territory in northeastern France to defend the Ruhr and to mount aerial attacks against Great Britain, not entirely defeat France.[8] The triumphant Hitler toured Paris on June 23, returned to a jubilant Berlin, then began discussing next steps for German strategy. Following the defeat of France, Hitler expected the Soviets to make greater concessions to German interests and speed up raw material deliveries, even though German weapons exports to the USSR were well behind schedule. The Soviets did not show the slightest inclination to do so, however, and significant delays continued in raw material deliveries.[9] In fact, so tardy were Soviet deliveries that the Nazis began to relabel imports from Slovakia with "Made in the USSR" to convince the German public that something was being gained from partnership with the Communists.[10]

Other events following the Fall of France further tested the Soviet-German partnership. Soviet leadership decided that the combat in the west provided an opportunity to seize territories that had fallen into the Soviet sphere of influence in the Molotov-Ribbentrop Pact. On June 15 and 16, Molotov issued ultimata to all three Baltic states. The Red Army then invaded each the following week. On June 23, Stalin moved troops to the borders to Romanian Bessarabia, which had previously been protected by a guarantee from Britain and France. While the Germans had acknowledged their "disinterestedness" in Bessarabia in the Molotov-Ribbentrop Pact, they found Stalin's threat to seize the territory alarming, not least as it threatened the delivery of oil supplies from Romania.[11] Given the failure of the USSR to supply the hoped-for quantities of oil, Romania was Germany's most important source; the Soviet move thus proved a strategic threat.[12] It raised further German suspicions when Molotov informed them the Soviets planned to claim Bukovina, a Romanian territory that had not been included in the Molotov-Ribbentrop Pact.[13] When Schulenberg met with Molotov on June 26 to discuss Soviet plans, Molotov agreed to slightly modify Soviet claims, but stated firmly that "the Soviet Government expected German support of this Soviet demand."[14] Two days later, the Soviets invaded Bessarabia, too.

The Soviet occupation of northern Romania triggered a land grab as Romania's neighbors Hungary and Bulgaria sought territories at Romania's expense. They both began making demands against the Romanian government, and in Hungary's case, preparing for an invasion to secure large portions of Transylvania.[15] Hitler, eager to avoid the partition of Romania—or even worse, a war that would disrupt Romanian oil exports—organized a summit with Mussolini in Vienna on August 30. The result was the Second Vienna Award, whereby Bulgaria and Hungary received most of their territorial demands, and Germany and Italy guaranteed the remainder of Romania.

Hitler did not consult the Soviet Union before this redistribution of much of the Balkans. On August 31, Molotov protested to Schulenberg in Moscow that the Soviet government had only learned of the award via a radio news broadcast. He added that the Soviet government considered the German government to have violated the Molotov-Ribbentrop Pact's terms regarding consultation on matters of mutual significance.[16] Learning of this in Berlin, Ribbentrop ordered Schulenberg to present Molotov with a harshly worded report in reply indicating the Germans viewed the Soviets as having violated the Molotov-Ribbentrop Pact's terms in their invasions of the Baltic states and Bessarabia.[17] The Germans also notified the Soviets they were abandoning the naval base offered them at Zapadnaia Litsa, as it was no longer necessary to the German war effort.[18] In addition, the Germans announced they were moving troops through Finland to Norway, though in fact they would remain in Finland assisting that government. Finally, Italy, Japan, and Germany signed the Tripartite Pact at the end of September 1940, forming a defensive alliance that Moscow saw as potentially dangerous.

As relations frayed, the German war effort faced at a crucial moment. On August 7, 1940, Göring's Luftwaffe had launched Adlertag (Eagle Day), a thousand-bomber raid targeting Royal Air Force bases across Southern England. It was the beginning of the Battle of Britain, where the British would contest the skies in an effort to stave off a possible German invasion of the United Kingdom. In early September, German tactics changed. Now, the Luftwaffe began targeting the city of London, inaugurating the Blitz, which would kill over 43,000 British citizens and leave more than 1.5 million homeless. During three critical months of aerial combat between August and October, the Soviets threatened to suspend all raw material deliveries, citing German delays in delivering military equipment and machine tools.[19] Stalin was tightening the flow of supplies in the face of German victories, as British defeat or withdrawal from the war might turn Hitler eastward, an eventuality to be avoided at all costs. Stalin also kept communications open with the new Churchill government that fall.[20]

Hitler learned of the Soviet-British communications, adding to a growing list of issues with his Soviet partner on trade, the Balkans, and the status of Lithuania's border, which remained unresolved.[21] In September, a former diplomat now in military service informed Ambassador Schulenberg that Hitler was considering an attack against Russia. Desperate to avoid this outcome, *Ostpolitiker* Schulenberg persuaded the Foreign Ministry and, eventually, Hitler to a meeting with Molotov to settle outstanding issues with Moscow.[22] To that end, Ribbentrop sent a letter directly to Stalin inviting Molotov to discussions in Berlin on October 13.[23] It concluded with the bold pronouncement that "I should like to state that, in the opinion of the Führer . . . it seems to be the historical mission of the Four Powers—the Soviet Union, Italy, Japan and Germany—to adopt a long-range policy and to direct the future development of their peoples into the right channels by delimitation of their interests of a worldwide scale."[24] It seemed the Führer wanted to discuss a partition of the globe with Molotov in person.

Vyacheslav Molotov did not like to fly, and had never traveled abroad before. He accordingly decided he would make the journey to Berlin via train. Ambassador Schulenberg and Hilger planned to accompany him, along with a contingent of more than sixty Soviet aides and security personnel. Seeing Molotov off at the station were all five marshals of the Soviet Union, tipsy after a reception at the Japanese embassy—their presence gave some hint of the importance of the mission.[25] Molotov's instructions, besides confronting the Germans over Soviet concerns in Finland, Romania, and over the Tripartite Pact, were to "determine the further intentions of Hitler, and as much as possible delay a German aggression."[26] His journey to Berlin did not go without incident, marred by a dispute at the border. Germany and the USSR had different rail gauges, each of which had been extended into conquered Poland; that meant passengers usually had to change trains at the border. To that end, the Germans had a luxurious German train waiting at the Eydtkuhnen border crossing. But the Soviets refused to board it, instead demanding that their own train be converted onto the other gauge. The Soviet reason was simple, as one of the Soviet delegates recorded: "Undoubtedly their carriages were not only equipped with a fine bar, but with a fine lot of bugging apparatus, too."[27] The delegation refused to even eat in the restaurant car on board the train until they received permission from Moscow.[28] A compromise was eventually reached, with a German locomotive pulling the Soviet carriages onward from the border.

Molotov disembarked at Anhalter station in Berlin on the rainy morning of November 12. Alongside German plenipotentiaries—Ribbentrop, Keitel, Henrich Himmler, Franz von Papen—a military band began to play a rapid version of the socialist Internationale to greet him. Ribbentrop worried that locals might sing along in German should they hear it, and so asked the band to speed through it as quickly as possible.[29] Molotov and his entourage were then herded into German Mercedes, and driven down empty streets to their hotel—a sign of disfavor when the Japanese foreign minister would be received by throngs of Berliners organized by the Nazis not long thereafter.[30]

The Soviet delegation was to spend their visit in the luxurious neoclassical Bellevue Palace, former home of Prussian princes and today the official residence of Germany's presidents. After a hearty lunch served by liveried staff, Molotov was transported to Ribbentrop's ostentatious office in the German Foreign Ministry. There, Ribbentrop subjected the Soviet foreign minister to a long, rambling monologue that lasted nearly an hour.[31] The central theme was that the British and

French empires were doomed. In light of that fact, Ribbentrop inquired "whether Soviet Russia could not derive corresponding advantages from the new order of things" alongside the Germans, Italians, and Japanese.[32] Ribbentrop said the Führer believed that the Soviet Union should seek its "Lebensraum" to the south along the sea. A stolid Molotov asked which sea Ribbentrop had in mind, to which Ribbentrop replied with another long rant before indicating that he meant the Persian Gulf. When Ribbentrop had concluded, Molotov indicated briefly that before they divided the world, Germany and the USSR needed to address the existing "spheres of influence between Germany and Russia. The establishment of these spheres of influence in the past year was only a partial solution, which had been rendered obsolete and meaningless by recent circumstances and events."[33] With that cold water tossed on his grandiose schemes, Ribbentrop adjourned the meeting to allow Molotov another meal before his audience with Hitler.

Hitler had issued a directive to the OKW that morning, ordering German forces to concentrate on the war against Great Britain, possibly through the seizure of Gibraltar and other attacks in the Mediterranean.[34] But near the bottom of his memorandum, a sentence noted that "political discussions aimed at establishing Russian intentions in the near future have been initiated. Regardless of the results of these meetings, all oral orders to continue preparations in the east are to be followed."[35] Those orders included Luftwaffe reconnaissance flights over the Soviet border to photograph Soviet defenses, which Hitler had commanded a few days earlier. And even as Molotov arrived, Wehrmacht officers were running secret war games with the Soviet Union as the adversary. Clearly, Hitler was contemplating an invasion of the USSR. At the same time, he expressed his hope to subordinates that he could convince Stalin—through Molotov—to join his war against Great Britain as an ally.[36]

Hitler arranged to meet Molotov in his offices at the New Reichskanzlei building. This gargantuan, neoclassical complex had been finished just the year before. Hitler had informed his favorite architect, Albert Speer, "I shall be holding extremely important conferences in the near future. For those, I need grand halls and salons which will make an impression on people, especially on the smaller dignitaries."[37] To reach Hitler's office in this Nazi monument, Molotov and his entourage were driven through giant gates to a "court of honor." They passed through a series of anterooms to a grand marble-floored gallery, almost 500 feet long and sporting a giant domed ceiling—twice the length of the Hall of Mirrors at Versailles, as Hitler liked to tell guests. Then, at last, the Soviet delegation reached Hitler's reception hall and his office, a cavernous room with fifty-foot ceilings, dark stone walls, and a massive fireplace. Behind an ornate baroque desk sat the Führer, who rose and moved silently to the center of the room to greet the Soviet foreign minister before directing the party to sit in armchairs in front of the fireplace.[38]

Molotov's afternoon session in Hitler's office followed much the same trajectory as had his interview with Ribbentrop. The German leader was as expansive and heavy-handed as the room in which they sat. He began by saying that "in the life of peoples it was indeed difficult to lay down a course for development over a long period in the future." He went on to note that "in the case of Russia and Germany, moreover, two very great nations were involved which need not by nature have any conflict of interests, if each nation understood that the other required certain vital necessities without the guarantee of which its existence was impossible."[39] Again, his aim was the division of the world, with Germany claiming—in addition to its European territories—colonial possessions in Central Africa. Hitler surveyed German relations with Italy, Japan, and Vichy France before returning to the opportunities presented to the USSR by partnership with Germany.

Molotov gave a brief reply to Hitler's long-winded remarks, noting only that the Führer's words had been of a "general nature," and that "in general he could agree with their reasoning."[40] He then stated that he was now to relay the view of Stalin, as "Stalin had given him exact instructions." What followed was a list of Soviet grievances: Was Germany honoring the pact with regard to Finland? What was the nature of the Tripartite Pact between Italy, Japan, and Germany? How, in the German view, did Japan define its sphere of influence in the Far East? What about the status of Bulgaria, Romania, and Turkey? Only after some vague replies from Hitler did Molotov mellow his tone, agreeing that "the participation of Russia in the Tripartite Pact appeared to him entirely acceptable in principle, provided that Russia was to cooperate as a partner and not be merely an object."[41] A possible air raid caused the meeting to end abruptly, with talks to resume the following day.

The discussions the next day did not break the deadlock, however. The tone remained the same: Hitler theatrical, Molotov impassive, the former seeking to discuss global spheres of influence while the latter demanded the removal of German troops in Finland and Romania, information about the Tripartite Pact, and much more besides.[42] Molotov later described Hitler's offering up fresh conquests as "not a serious conversation."[43] It was clear in his mind that Hitler's goal was to get the USSR in the war against Great Britain.[44] Molotov followed directions from Stalin to "stand up" to Hitler, which he did; the meeting concluded without even an agreement for a reciprocal visit by Ribbentrop to Moscow. Hitler, for his part, seems to have been frustrated by Molotov's intransigence.[45]

During Molotov's final night in Berlin, Soviet ambassador Vladimir Dekanozov hosted a large banquet for German and Soviet guests at the Soviet embassy. Molotov once again met with Ribbentrop amid plentiful caviar and vodka.[46] British bombers crashed the party at 9:45 P.M., driving the guests into a bunker under the embassy.[47] For over two hours, the two foreign ministers continued their conversations underground. Ribbentrop became more explicit as the night wore on, revealing a draft text of Soviet membership in the Tripartite Pact—a full military alliance. He made clear that the "decisive question" was whether or not the USSR would "cooperate with us in the great liquidation of the British Empire."[48] Molotov retorted that "the Germans were acting as if the war against Great Britain had already been won." Ribbentrop asserted it had been, but amid the air raid sirens and anti-aircraft fire, Molotov retorted, "why are we in this shelter, and whose are those bombs that fall?"[49] The "party" finally concluded around midnight, without result.

Molotov returned to Moscow—in the words of one diplomat—"swollen-headed and puffed up," confident his mission had been a success.[50] Eleven days later, Molotov presented Schulenberg with the Soviet government's reply to the German proposal that they join the Tripartite Pact. Included was a long list of Soviet demands: the withdrawal of German troops from the Soviet periphery in Finland and elsewhere; a Soviet protectorate over Bulgaria; Soviet bases along the Dardanelles in Turkey; recognition of the "area south of Batum and Baku in the Persian Gulf" (much of the Middle East) as a Soviet sphere of influence; and Japanese renunciation of territorial claims over North Sakhalin.[51] Molotov noted this would require German assistance in negotiating five different protocols with Soviet neighbors to redress Soviet claims and concerns. This was the price of a formal military alliance with the USSR. It was too much for Hitler. Despite repeated inquiries from Moscow, there was no German reply.[52]

CHAPTER 35

Whirlwind

On December 18, 1940, Hitler issued OKW Directive No. 21. It began: "The German Armed Forces must be prepared to crush Soviet Russia in a quick campaign (Operation Barbarossa) even before the conclusion of the war against England."[1] He ordered preparations to start immediately, with the campaign to commence by May 15, 1941. The previous summer he had asked the OKH to consider the question of attacking the USSR, but their efforts were "desultory and halfhearted."[2] By December, growing tensions in the Balkans, frustrations over trade, and the continued resistance of Great Britain brought about a change of course.[3] Molotov's visit further convinced Hitler of the unwillingness of the USSR to join a crusade against the British Empire on German terms—as a German vassal. Now Hitler was in earnest. He had decided upon war with the Soviet Union.

In mid-January, the Wehrmacht began arranging logistics to prepare for the invasion of the Soviet Union.[4] Chief of the OKH Franz Halder crafted the initial plan for Barbarossa, which centered on a limited program of conquest with decisive battles to be fought close to the borders. The accompanying political program, where it appeared, would entail forming independent states in Ukraine and the Baltics to be dominated by Germany. But Hitler rejected this "soft war" approach. He would lecture that while the region would be "dissolved into separate states with their own governments," the real reason for war was eliminating "the Jewish-Bolshevik intelligentsia, the previous 'oppressor' of the people." "The former bourgeois-aristocratic intelligentsia, which continues to exist," he added, "particularly among emigrants, must also be discarded."[5] Germany would acquire its Lebensraum in the east.

In Moscow, it was not immediately apparent German intentions had changed. Schnurre spent much of December and early January with Mikoyan and Molotov, now familiar with each other as negotiators. The results were positive for the Soviets. The Germans agreed to sell Benz 601 aviation engines, Messerschmitt fighters (108, 109, 110s), and Heinkel and Junkers bombers to the Soviet Air Force. This was not quite Germany's most modern equipment, but represented better aircraft than most Soviet designs then in mass-production. The Reichsmarine agreed to dispatch engineers and officers to helping Soviet shipbuilders finish the cruiser Lützow, sold to the USSR as part of the Molotov-Ribbentrop Pact.[6] Machine tools and other weapons, like anti-aircraft cannons, also joined the list of German exports headed east. In exchange, the USSR agreed to increase grain shipments and other key raw materials. In general, Schnurre recorded, the trade talks were "considerably exceeding our expectations."[7] A final series of economic agreements, signed on January 10, solved ongoing issues in the Baltics and Bessarabia, while laying out a pattern that would normalize long-term trade.[8] But even as these developments signaled a normalization in Soviet-German relations, there were warning signs of the course change in Berlin.

On January 17, Ambassador Dekanozov stopped by the German Foreign Ministry to state Soviet concern about the movement of large numbers of German troops in the Balkans, only to be brushed off by his German counterpart.[9] But six weeks later, the German Foreign Ministry informed the Soviet government that Bulgaria would be joining the Tripartite Pact, and that German troops would be entering that country in large numbers, as British actions had forced German preparations against neighboring Greece. Molotov received this news from Schulenberg with "obvious concern."[10] Two weeks later, the Wehrmacht began hustling a Soviet commission "repatriating" political refugees from Lithuania out of German territory. Officially, the Germans claimed the Soviets had stayed beyond an appointed deadline, but in actuality German intelligence feared the Soviets would observe the growing concentration of German troops along the border.[11]

Stalin was concerned by these warning signs, but also convinced that Hitler would not betray the terms of the treaty, not with his ongoing war against the British Empire. His response was to somewhat increase deliveries of raw materials to Germany.[12] If the Germans were satiated until June or July, it would be too late in the season to launch an invasion of the USSR, he concluded, thus buying another year for defensive preparations to be made.[13]

At the same time, Stalin moved to block the Germans elsewhere. Following Yugoslav acceptance of membership in the tripartite pact, there was a coup in Belgrade. It brought to power a pro-British, anti-German government that promptly resumed negotiations on a military pact with Moscow. To deter potential German intervention, the Soviets immediately finalized a nonaggression pact with the new regime on April 5. Molotov informed Schulenberg that "the Soviet government had been actuated solely by the desire to preserve peace," and pointedly urged that Germany needed to do its part to preserve peace in the Balkans.[14] The Germans, who had already massed troops on the border, responded by launching an invasion of Yugoslavia the next day. Stalin's signal of Soviet interests in the Balkans had been ignored.[15]

Stalin also attempted to block a possible Japanese-German alignment against him. In March, Japanese foreign minister Yosuke Matsuoka began a trip to Europe that included a visit to Berlin, and another to Moscow. In Berlin, Ribbentrop did not tell Matsuoka of the ongoing preparations for the invasion of the Soviet Union, but encouraged him to avoid any commitments with Stalin, saying that "Russia had made conditions that were unacceptable" for joining the Tripartite Pact, and that relations were "not very friendly."[16] During his return through Moscow on April 9,

Matsuoka met with Stalin and Molotov to discuss a possible nonaggression pact.[17] Given ongoing Japanese preparations for an expansion of the war in East Asia, Matsuoka sought Soviet neutrality, at the very least. Ignoring the German request, he concluded the Soviet-Japanese Neutrality Pact on April 13, 1941.[18]

After the conclusion of this pact, there was a great deal of drinking. Stalin took the unusual measure of escorting a barely vertical Matsuoka to his train that evening. On the platform, they encountered Ambassador Schulenberg and acting Military Attaché Hans Krebs. Stalin approached, tapped Krebs on the chest, and said "German?"[19] Krebs replied yes. Stalin slapped his back, shook his hands, then said, "We have been friends with you and we shall remain friends with you." Krebs replied, taken aback, "I am sure of that." He had already been recalled to Berlin at that juncture to discuss invasion plans for the Soviet Union. A tipsy Molotov kept yelling the Soviet pioneers' motto ("I am a pioneer, I am ready!") in the background.[20]

The warning signs continued to multiply. That same month, the British ambassador in Moscow and Prime Minister Churchill both relayed intelligence about a potential German invasion. Stalin interpreted these messages to mean that the British Empire hoped to entangle Germany and the Soviet Union in war to save itself.[21] On May 5, Ambassador Schulenberg, desperate to avoid war, took the unusual step of privately hinting to Soviet diplomats his own government's intentions for war.[22] Stalin may have believed this message was part of a German bluff to drive a better economic deal. Two weeks later, Rudolf Hess, the second-ranking member of the Nazi Party, flew to Scotland on his own initiative to negotiate a peace deal. Stalin again interpreted the information conspiratorially, as an indication of a possible British-German peace arrangement that might be directed against the Soviet Union.[23] Messages from Richard Sorge in Tokyo—relaying highly specific information on German military plans—were also read as part of a plan to force the USSR into accepting economic concessions.[24] In sum, Stalin interpreted the growing mountain of intelligence as either a provocation or a trap.

Stalin had prioritized the expansion of the Red Army above all else over the preceding two years. Between 1939 and June 1941, the Red Army more than tripled in size, but this expansion was "rapid and incoherent."[25] Oversight was so poor that Voroshilov had to report to Stalin in 1940 that the reorganized Soviet Ministry of Defense could not even say definitively how many soldiers were in the Red Army.[26] To fill out the huge numbers of empty positions created by expansion and the simultaneous purges, officers were created post-haste through direct commissioning of enlisted personnel and rushed reservist training programs.[27] The consequences were predictable: in 1941, one in six officer positions were unfilled (one in three in the Soviet Air Force), 85 percent of Red Army officers were under the age of thirty-five, and only half had completed any formal military education program.[28] In the words of historian Roger Reese, when the war began, the Soviet officer corps were "mostly amateurs in skill and civilians in attitude."[29] The Soviet rearmament program and trade with Germany had done much to remedy the country's military-industrial weaknesses, but weapons production had not kept up with the gigantic increase in the size of the army, meaning that many units were poorly armed or had not received much of their equipment by the start of the summer—for instance, front-line tank units on average had received only 35 percent of their armored equipment.[30] Nevertheless, on paper, the Red Army was the largest military in the world by mid-June, mustering some 5.37 million men, 25,000 tanks, and 18,000 aircraft, roughly half of which stood directly along the Soviet Union's western border.[31]

As these dispositions suggested, Stalin was not blind to the mounting evidence of Hitler's intentions. But he remained confident Hitler would not fight a war on two fronts, telling his inner circle that "as long as Germany does not settle her account with Britain . . . Germany would not fight on two fronts and would keep to the letter of the obligations undertaken in the non-aggression pact."[32] And he was certain that an ultimatum would immediately precede an attack—a demand for the territory or the raw materials Hitler coveted. Stalin angrily rejected calls for a national mobilization, telling Commissar of Defense Timoshenko that mobilization along the frontier would provoke Hitler into war.[33]

Nevertheless, Stalin began to feel that "danger was imminent," in the words of Khrushchev.[34] He grudgingly granted Marshal Timoshenko permission to begin additional preparations as the growth of German military forces along the border became apparent. On June 1, Stalin issued partial secret mobilization orders.[35] On June 2, an order to increase preparedness was dispatched to frontline forces.[36] On June 14, the Soviet press publicly signaled its awareness of a German military build-up in Eastern Europe, perhaps hoping to change German behavior.[37] On June 18 and 19, the Red Army was put on alert. Additional forces began moving toward the border. On the night of June 21, 1941, Stalin paced endlessly, working into the late hours. At 10:20 P.M., following reports of broad border violations and interrogation reports of a German defector suggesting an imminent attack, Stalin allowed his General Staff to issue orders for a national mobilization—just in case. He then went to bed, still unconvinced that Hitler would violate their agreement so soon.[38]

As Stalin slept, the storm broke. By the early hours of June 22, Germany had concentrated along the border 3 million soldiers, as well as 690,000 soldiers from the allied armies of Hungary, Slovakia, Romania, and Italy, 600,000 trucks, 3,350 tanks, 7,146 artillery pieces, and 2,770 aircraft.[39] Operation Barbarossa began at 3 A.M. local time as 1,280 German aircraft crossed the frontier on their way to bomb cities and airfields throughout Ukraine, Belarus, and the Baltic states.[40] Parked in neat rows, more than 1,200 Soviet aircraft would be destroyed on the first day of the war.[41] On the ground, three massive Heeresgruppen (Army Groups) of around a million men each began their offensives with orders to drive on Leningrad, Moscow, and Ukraine respectively.

Heinz Guderian, promoted to command of Panzer Group 2, was once again tasked with taking Brest-Litovsk, now on the Soviet side of the frontier. He recalled that "on the fateful day of June 22nd, 1941, I went at 02.10 hours to my group command post . . . it was still dark when I arrived there." He watched as German artillery began pounding Soviet positions at 3:15 A.M. Half an hour later, the sound of airplane engines became clear, followed by the shriek and explosion of Ju-87 Stuka dive-bombers launching their attacks. Half an hour after that, German tanks began to rumble across the Bug River, encircling the massive fortress of Brest-Litovsk.

When Guderian followed his men across the river and into Soviet territory a few hours later, he "found nobody except some Russian pickets." The shocked Russian guards took off running at the sight of German armored vehicles.

Leonid Rosenberg, a Red Army lieutenant in an artillery battalion, recalled the Soviet experience years later. He woke up to the sound of hundreds of planes flying overhead. "Everyone at first thought it was some huge thunderstorm, and then realized it was war. It was sheer horror when the Germans started shelling us. Huge artillery explosions next to us, horses screaming, people screaming for help."[42] Among the officers responding to the attack was the recently pardoned General Gorbatov, still recovering from his time in the Gulag at Kolyma. Upon news of the German attack, he immediately headed for the front. As his forces drew closer to the sounds of battle, he saw huge masses of Red Army soldiers on the roads heading east, away from the German onslaught.[43] Inexperienced, poorly led, and often—in the case of reservists—not even familiar with their weapons, they were running away. Gorbatov hardly knew where to start. He went to stop the rout of one regiment, screaming "Halt! Halt! Halt!" then ordering them to "about-face" and lay down with their weapons toward the enemy. As he shouted orders, one confused soldier told the general, "We saw everyone else retreating and so we began to retreat as well."[44] When he had a moment to pause, Gorbatov later recalled, "My earlier fears still made my hair stand on end: how were we going to be able to fight when we had lost so many experienced commanders even before the war had started?"[45] The result was chaos and carnage: during the first eighteen days of the invasion, the Soviets averaged 44,000 casualties a day.[46]

Rarely in the annals of history have two opponents spent so much time preparing each other for war. Invading German forces marched on rubber boots made with materiel shipped over the Trans-Siberian railroad. [47] Their rations included Soviet grain, which had continued to arrive up to the very day of the invasion. Their ammunition contained chrome, nickel, steel, and manganese from the USSR. German vehicles and aircraft drew heavily from the legacy of engineering work conducted in Russia, and were fueled by oil that had been pumped in the Caucasus. Many senior German commanders had trained in the USSR—quite a few even spoke good Russian from their time there. And when they issued orders, they drew at least in part from lessons learned alongside the Red Army between 1922 and 1933.

Across the lines, the story was much the same. Although few living Soviet officers had trained alongside the Germans, most had been trained in facilities reorganized along German lines, and in some instances staffed by German officers. Their operations were managed by a Soviet General Staff modeled on its German counterpart and reporting to Marshal Timoshenko, who had studied in Germany in 1931. The tanks, aircraft, and artillery the Red Army used to resist the German invasion drew heavily from German designs—in some instances, copies of German designs produced under license or equipment acquired as part of the various Soviet-German economic agreements. Many of their vehicles were powered by German-designed engines. And much of their equipment had been built in factories constructed with German help, equipped with German machine tools, and powered by coal mined in the Ruhr and Saar.[48]

As the news of German attacks began to filter in from the west, Stalin reacted with disbelief; surely Hitler would not just attack "like some brigand."[49] He told Foreign Minister Molotov to find German ambassador Schulenberg. As dawn broke over Moscow, Schulenberg arrived at Molotov's office, accompanied by the long-serving German diplomat Gustav Hilger.[50] As Molotov sat quietly, Schulenberg began reading a memorandum accusing the Soviet Union of breaking the German-Soviet Pact.[51] Schulenberg concluded his remarks, and a pregnant silence hung in the air. Molotov asked, "Is this supposed to be a declaration of war?" Schulenberg merely shrugged. Molotov replied heatedly that it could be nothing else, as "German troops have already crossed the Soviet border, and Soviet cities, like Odessa, Kiev and Minsk, have been bombed by German aircraft for an hour and a half."[52] Schulenberg said nothing. At the end of the interview, "all Molotov could stutter was, 'What have we done to deserve this?' "[53]

Conclusion

A Faustian Price

In Goethe's retelling of Faust, it was the title character's ambition that nearly cost him his soul. So it was with German military leadership, who in 1919 sought rearmament and the destruction of Poland as part of a program to overturn the results of the First World War. Bolshevik leaders in Moscow were even bolder, dreaming of worldwide revolution. Their shared antagonisms produced the partnership at Rapallo that started Europe down the road to renewed war. As has been argued here, many of the key milestones along that path—the Reichswehr's acceptance of Hitler, the speed of German rearmament, British and French appeasement, the Soviet purges, the inability of the European powers to contain Hitler, and finally, the Molotov-Ribbentrop Pact—can only be fully understood in light of the Rapallo relationship.

The Reichswehr – and Seeckt himself – embraced Hitler in 1933, albeit with some reservations. Their shared views on rearmament and the revision of Germany's borders played a major role in that process. So too did the general instability of the late Weimar Republic, to which Reichswehr rearmament efforts had contributed. The secret budgets and semi-autonomous foreign policy conducted by the Reichswehr between 1919 and 1933 strengthened the hand of the military and weakened the state. It was no coincidence the two most significant political figures in Weimar immediately before Hitler came to power—Hindenburg and Schleicher—were both military men. It was they who would hand Hitler the chancellorship of a country already possessing the essential elements needed for a revival of its military power.

While Hitler's arrival in power spelled trouble for the European order, it was German rearmament that was the essential precondition for a new war. Seeckt had written in 1923 that "the Frenchman has occupied the Ruhr area. The Lithuanians have occupied the Memel area. Instinctively, the hand goes where the sword used to be. It only grabs air: we are unarmed. Today, one cannot conduct a war with flails and hayforks."[1] Replacing those flails and hayforks with tanks and planes was only possible for Germany in the USSR. Lipetsk, Kama, and Tomka provided the foundation for the rapid expansion and technological rearmament of the German military, a process Hitler accelerated when he took power. Without the Rapallo Era, rearmament, at least on Hitler's timeline, would have been impossible.

Thanks to preparatory work conducted in the Soviet Union, the speed of German rearmament between 1933 and 1939 caught European leaders by surprise. In 1933, Germany had 100,000 men in arms and possessed fewer than a dozen tanks and a few dozen combat aircraft, all hidden in the USSR. On the eve of the invasion of Poland, Hitler had at his disposal over 3 million men, 4,000 aircraft and nearly 3,500 tanks. The training, arming, and equipping of that vast German force in six brief years was only possible because of the work that had already been done before Hitler came to power.

The speed and timing of German rearmament under Hitler was of the utmost significance. Reluctant to commit to their own rearmament programs, London and Paris fell behind in a new arms race. That meant the perceived strength of German military forces deterred British and French intervention at key moments between 1935 and 1938, resulting in the most infamous acts of appeasement. Those acts further convinced Hitler that he had a lead in the arms race, and a "technological window"—a brief moment of superiority in arms—in which to launch a war to reclaim German territory in the east, and more besides. That window of opportunity, which he believed would close after 1942 or 1943, drove him to decide upon an invasion of Poland in 1939, before his likely adversaries could catch up militarily.

The failure of the Western democracies to contain Hitler was not only a product of their own apparent military weaknesses, but also a result of the difficulty of building a coalition with either Mussolini or Stalin. Mussolini was a faithless partner, bent on his own conquests, but British and French reluctance to partner with Moscow derived, in part, from Stalin's Great Terror. It had been initiated, at least in part, because of the Red Army's past relationship with Germany. London and Paris became convinced that Stalin had little to offer in efforts to contain Hitler, eliminating whatever enthusiasm there might have been for a military accommodation. The result was Munich, the Polish guarantee, and the half-hearted, failed diplomacy of 1939.

While France and Great Britain were wary of a Soviet partnership, Hitler was not, at least from March 1939 onward. The Molotov-Ribbentrop Pact marked a resumption of the Rapallo Era partnership. The logic behind it was much the same. For Stalin, Germany had far more to offer than its rivals. Germany could supply the machine tools and military technology upon which the Red Army had become dependent in the course of the 1920s and early 1930s. And Hitler might also agree to the expansion of Soviet territory in Eastern Europe. By contrast, the British and French could only offer possible military conflict with Germany in the name of defending the hostile state of Poland. For Hitler, the Soviet Union offered strategic depth, economic resources, and the chance to destroy Poland, that "pillar of Versailles"—the same factors that had driven Seeckt toward Russia in 1919. Perhaps prophetically, shortly before his death in 1936, Seeckt had told the Führer that "we were one in our aim; only our paths were different."[2] Seeckt had identified that path in 1922 when he wrote that "Poland must and will be wiped off the map, with our help, through internal weakness and Russian action," but that such action would need to wait for

German rearmament.[3] In 1939, Germany was rearmed, and the partition of Poland Seeckt (and Soviet leaders) had imagined finally came to pass.

The Soviet-German partnership formed at Rapallo not only helps to explain the outbreak of the Second World War in Europe; it also offers some insights into the course, conduct, and eventual conclusion of that conflict. The Rapallo pact cast long shadows on the war itself, offering some explanation for initial German successes, the horrors of the fighting on the Eastern front, and ultimate Soviet victory.

The German army enjoyed unmitigated success over the first six weeks of Operation Barbarossa. During that span, the Soviets would suffer a quarter of a million casualties and the destruction of one sixth of their equipment—tanks and planes—*per week.* There are various factors contributing to these early victories, but from the German perspective, advantages in leadership, doctrine, and materiel were key.

Those German advantages were due, in part, to the high standard of the German officer corps, which succeeded in expanding as war approached with far fewer difficulties than their Soviet counterparts. The Soviet-German partnership played a key role in providing the experienced officers who would make that possible. Between 1922 and 1933, hundreds of German officers or future officers taught, visited, or trained at the facilities in Russia—at a time when the entire German officer corps only numbered 4,000. More than sixty of them would reach the general officer rank, the cadre at the core of the reborn Luftwaffe and the Wehrmacht's Panzer divisions. When flight schools and armored warfare training grounds began appearing in Germany after 1933, they were usually commanded by alumni of Lipetsk or Kama, the only places where such training had been conducted since 1918.

The Wehrmacht and Luftwaffe also possessed key advantages in materiel born from the Rapallo partnership. As argued here, it laid the foundation for the technological rearmament of the German military, providing the basis for the generation of tanks and planes with which Germany would begin the Second World War. Thanks to this work, and to the Treaty of Versailles, almost all the German equipment used in Operation Barbarossa had been manufactured after 1935. By contrast, their Soviet adversaries possessed some outstanding equipment—the T-34 in particular—but most Red Army units were equipped with tanks and planes that had been built in the early to mid-1930s, and designed even earlier. Only 11 percent of Soviet armored vehicles on the western frontier were new models in 1941.[4] Of the remainder, 73 percent required repair.[5] In the Soviet Air Force, less than two thirds of aircraft were fit for flying in 1941, and of those deployed to the Western Front, only 20 percent were modern designs.[6] As a result, the average German vehicle or plane could best the average Soviet one on the battlefield, especially given German advantages in communications and control, doctrine, logistics, and leadership.

If German military successes in 1941 were, in part, products of its partnership with the Soviet Union, so too was the execrable conduct of the German Army and the trailing Einsatzgruppen death squads against Soviet civilians. The experience of living in Stalinist Russia had affected many German officers, if in contradictory ways. While some senior officers—like Blomberg—returned from Russia enthusiastic about the Soviet model, many more German officers studying in the Soviet

Union became rabid anti-communists after seeing Stalinism up close. The Soviet secret police carefully monitored the political affiliations of the German officers at Kama, Lipetsk, and Tomka, and noticed that many—particularly junior officers—became more likely to support Nazism as their time in Russia progressed. This was particularly true at Lipetsk and Kama during the worst of the famines triggered by Soviet collectivization.[7] Erich von Manstein, for instance, visited Kama in 1931 as part of a Reichswehr delegation. He returned for a longer visit in 1932 to attend Red Army maneuvers.[8] He wrote that "the shadow of Asian despotism hung over the country, its people and its events."[9] One of his biographers has argued that his visits to the USSR resulted in his enthusiastic support for the Nazi program of extermination in the Soviet Union. Manstein would be convicted of war crimes after the war.[10] In like fashion, General Wilhelm Keitel, who had lived in the USSR and taught at the Frunze Military Academy, was responsible for issuing the infamous Barbarossa Decree authorizing Wehrmacht officers to shoot Soviet civilians as they saw fit in May 1941. He would be executed following conviction at the Nuremberg War Crimes Tribunal. In sum, the experience of seeing the worst of Stalinism reinforced existing racial prejudices and anti-communism among the officer corps, encouraging support of—or nonresistance to—Nazi brutality during the invasion of the Soviet Union.

Ironically, the German experiences at the Rapallo sites may also help to explain another historical mystery: the disastrous state of German military intelligence on the Soviet Union on the eve of Barbarossa.[11] The Wehrmacht's handbook on the USSR in January 1941 indicated no knowledge of the size or organization of the Red Army, but confidently concluded that it lacked modern equipment, and was "unsuited for modern warfare and incapable of decisive resistance against a well-commanded, well-equipped force."[12] Prewar Wehrmacht estimates of the number of Soviet divisions were off by more than a hundred, while the Luftwaffe similarly underestimated the Soviet Air Force by a factor of two.[13] This seems shocking on its face, given the number of officers who spoke Russian and were familiar with the Red Army. In fact, that experience may have been the reason such assessments were accepted uncritically by senior officers like Keitel, Manstein, and Guderian: low estimations of the Red Army matched their impressions from much earlier. Guderian, for instance, told Hitler and his superiors that based on his experience in Russia in the early 1930s (and again in 1939 at Brest-Litovsk), he felt that Soviet armored forces were unlikely to be prepared for war or effective in combat.[14] On August 11, 1941—six weeks into the German invasion—General Halder would write in his diary, "It is becoming ever clearer that we underestimated the strength of the Russian colossus, not only in the economic and transportation sphere but above all in the military."[15] Experiences during the Rapallo Era, coupled with German hubris following the Fall of France and deep-seated prejudices against Soviet Russia, help to explain why the Wehrmacht disastrously underestimated the strength and equipment of the Red Army prior to the invasion of the Soviet Union.

That Russian colossus of Halder's description had come into being only with German assistance over the preceding two decades. At the beginning of the Rapallo Era, the Red Army had been in a promethean state. Emerging from the Russian Civil War, its form and function remained undefined. Some senior Bolsheviks envisioned a national militia, while Tukhachevsky argued for a mechanized, technically sophisticated professional army. Stalin eventually chose the latter, though the early Soviet state lacked all the essential prerequisites for building such a military—a professionalized officer corps, strong industry in relevant fields, and coherent operational doctrine.

Technology, in particular, came to be seen as a panacea for a range of the challenges facing the Red Army, which at first lacked the ability to produce aircraft, tanks, or chemical weapons. With few options, Trotsky, and then Stalin, came to depend upon foreign expertise to remedy those weaknesses. Throughout the interwar period, the Red Army bought (or stole) numerous foreign designs and reverse-engineered them. Up to 1940, 97 percent of Soviet tank production was of foreign designs or their derivatives.[16] Aviation followed a similar pattern: as late as 1933, a report from the chief of staff of the Soviet Air Force called for the extensive "borrowing" of technical developments from Arado, Heinkel, and Junkers models at Lipetsk.[17] The Red Army modernized through the acquisition of technology abroad, with Germany as its top partner. However, while these efforts resulted in a Red Army equipped with vast arsenals of new weapons, the Soviet military neglected much else, suffering from constant shortages of trained personnel, spare parts, logistical support, and maintenance officers. This was a product of the uneven process by which the Red Army had mechanized and modernized—a process described by one visiting German officer as a "quick fix."[18] In one early engagement of the war, for instance, a unit of Soviet KV tanks—which had higher-caliber guns and thicker armor than their German opponents—were ordered to ram enemy vehicles because there was no ammunition and their guns had not been bore-sighted, which meant they could not fire with any accuracy. In the event, ramming proved out of the question, as the unit had no fuel, either.[19]

A related development was the role that Germany played in expanding Soviet military industry over the same period. Germany was the Soviet Union's largest trading partner in the interwar period as a whole, particularly as a source of machine tools and technology. It played an essential role in Stalin's first two Five Year Plans, the crash-course industrializations he had initiated in 1928, which would see Soviet military spending grow from 3.4 percent of the national budget to nearly 33 percent.[20] By 1941, around half of the Soviet Union's tank production, a majority of its chemical weapons production, and much of its aviation production depended in some way upon German assistance provided during the interwar period. This productive capacity, much of it moved from the western Soviet Union to the Urals during the "Great Evacuation" of Soviet industry in 1941, would prove enormously important. From 1941 to 1945—despite German occupation of the most populous parts of Soviet Union—the USSR would produce nearly 30,000 more aircraft and 50,000 more tanks than Nazi Germany.[21]

The other essential aspiration of the Red Army in partnering with the Reichswehr had been to professionalize its personnel. German assistance aimed to help address this problem. During the period of cooperation, 156 senior Soviet officers visited or studied in Germany. This led to the fundamental redesign of the structure of the Red Army—in the form of the General Staff—and the reshaping of Soviet military education. The Reichswehr trained thousands of junior Soviet officers, too—directly and indirectly. For instance, the 187 Soviet students who passed through Kama, were, in the words of Red Army planners, primarily "combat commanders or teachers of the tactical and technical courses at the Armored Warfare University (BUZ)," while "a smaller percentage were engineering staff."[22] They formed a central part of the Soviet armored forces, teaching new armor officers and designing the next generation of tanks.

The ultimate value of cooperation in terms of this cadre development in the Soviet Union was limited by the purges. Whereas the German alumni of the cooperative facilities played central roles in the Second World War, most of the officers who served alongside the Germans disappeared in the Great Terror between 1936 and 1938.[23] There were some survivors: all three generals who would be promoted to marshal in 1940—Grigory Kulik, Semyon Timoshenko, and Boris Shaposhnikov—had studied in Germany for extended periods.[24] At least five graduates of Kama also survived to reach general rank.[25] But they were exceptions, rather than the rule. In total, at least 24,026 officers, disproportionately from the upper ranks of the army and air force, were arrested or dismissed.[26] By 1938, not a single graduate of the Red Army's main training institution, the Frunze Military Academy, was serving as a regimental commander.[27] In the midst of the simultaneous expansion of the Red Army, the purges were particularly catastrophic: by December 1938, the Red Army was short 93,000 officers, or 34.1 percent of its strength, a shortage that would not be remedied by 1941. This reality undoubtedly contributed to the disastrous Soviet performance early in the war.[28]

Despite the uneven modernization of the Red Army and shortcomings of the Soviet officer corps in 1941, the Red Army survived Operation Barbarossa and emerged victorious after four horrific years of war. While the USSR had produced almost no combat vehicles prior to 1928 and only a few aircraft, by 1941, it had over 20,000 armored vehicles and the world's largest air force. It would outproduce Germany in tanks, planes, artillery, and rifles during the war. Although purges and rapid expansion had significantly diluted the quality of the Red Army officer corps, Red Army military education facilities had produced 170,000 commissioned officers by 1940—four times the number of commissioned officers in the entire Tsarist Army in 1914.[29] While its modernization and professionalization remained uneven, the Red Army had made clear progress—with German help—in addressing both challenges that had led to the defeat of Tsarist Russia in 1917. The result was a Red Army that proved more resilient and robust than the Germans—or any other European power—had anticipated.

The bargain that the Soviets and Germans made to rearm would pay its final dividend in blood. Their partnership, based upon military cooperation and economic exchange, could justifiably be described as an "alliance" at times: a formal political arrangement for mutual benefit. But the Soviet-German relationship in the interwar period hinted at something larger. From Trotsky and Seeckt to Hitler and Stalin, leaders in each country saw the future of the two states as intertwined. German ambassador Brockdorff-Rantzau called the Soviet-German relationship a *Schicksalgemeinschaft*, a "community of fate."[30] The term implied that the destinies of the two states were bound up, for good or for ill. German officers and statesmen hoped that the Soviet Union would serve as a partner against the Western democracies, a role that the Soviets did in fact fulfill from 1939 to 1941. In turn, Soviet leaders Lenin, Trotsky, and Stalin all saw in Germany a future partner in revolution. It was a part that would be forced upon East Germany for over four decades. The futures of both countries and their hundreds of millions of residents were inextricably linked. By June 22, 1941, thanks to years of work in collaboration, Germany and the Soviet Union shared a border, a capacity for making war, and exterminationist ideologies. More than 30 million people would die in the struggle that then unfolded between Berlin and Moscow, the final price of the Faustian Bargain.

NOTES

INTRODUCTION

1. Vladimir Ilyich Lenin, *Collected Works: Volume 28, July 1918–March 1919*, trans. and ed. Jim Riordan (Moscow: Progress Publishers, 1965), 42, 52, 54, 64.
2. Ibid., 434.
3. Ibid.
4. Wilhelm Groener, *Lebenserinnerungen: Jugend, Generalstab, Weltkrieg* [Memoirs: Youth, General Staff, World War], ed. Friedrich Frhr. Hiller von Gaertringen (Göttingen: Vandenhoeck und Ruprecht, 1957), 469–472. Also see Friedrich von Rabenau, *Hans von Seeckt: Aus seinem Leben (1918–1936)* [Hans von Seeckt: From His Life] (Hass und Koehler, Leipzig, 1940). Gustav Hilger, Alfred G. Meyer, *The Incompatible Allies: A Memoir-History of German-Soviet Relations, 1918–1941* (New York: Hafner, 1971), 191–192.
5. Adolf Hitler, *Mein Kampf* [My Struggle] (New York: Reynal and Hitchcock, 1925/1941), 479. This view was more or less representative of the Freikorps members from whom much of the army was drawn between 1919 and 1921. Hitler was discharged from the Reichswehr during one of its last draw-downs at the end of March 1920.
6. The three most important works to date are German historian Manfred Zeidler's *Reichswehr und Rote Armee* [The Reichswehr and the Red Army] (1994), which was based on his dissertation. He was the first to argue that secret Soviet-German cooperation in fact played a substantial role in the rearmament of Germany. The best book to utilize newly released Russian-language archival material is the work of Russian Foreign Ministry researcher and diplomatic historian Sergei Gorlov in *Sovershenno sekretno: Alianz Moskva-Berlin, 1920–1933* [Top Secret: Alliance Moscow-Berlin, 1920–1933] (2001). The third is Mary Habeck's *Storm of Steel* (2003), which explores in great detail Soviet-German cooperation in armored warfare using both German and Russian sources.
7. Wilhelm Speidel (writing under the name Helm Speidel), "Reichswehr und Rote Armee," in *Vierteljahrshefte für Zeitgeschichte, Quarterly Journal for Contemporary History*, 1:1 (1953): 28.
8. Philip A. Bayer, *The Evolution of the Soviet General Staff, 1917–1941* (New York: Garland, 1987), 226–228.

CHAPTER 1

1. "Report of July 22, Narrative of M. Lembitch, Chief Russian Observer at the Front," in *Source Records of the Great War; A Comprehensive and Readable Source Record of the World's Greatest War*, ed. Charles F. Horne (Indianapolis: American Legion Press, 1923), 259–260.
2. David Stone, *A Military History of Russia: From Ivan the Terrible to the War in Chechnya* (Westport, CT: Praeger Security International, 2006), 158.
3. Norman Stone, *The Eastern Front, 1914–1917* (London: Hodder and Stoughton, 1975), 85–91.
4. David Stone, *A Military History of Russia*, 167.

5. Jennifer Siegel, *For Peace and Money: French and British Finance in the Service of Tsars and Commissars* (Oxford, UK: Oxford University Press, 2014), 128; Stephen Broadberry and Mark Harrison, *The Economics of World War One* (Cambridge, UK: Cambridge University Press, 2005), 247.

6. The state first abandoned the gold standard, then began accelerated printing. Hyperinflation would reach 702 percent of 1914 values by mid-1917. Steven G. Marks, "War Finance (Russian Empire)," in *1914–1918: International Encyclopedia of the First World War*, ed. Ute Daniel, Peter Gatrell, Oliver Janz, Heather Jones, Jennifer Keene, Alan Kramer, and Bill Nasson (Berlin: Freie Universität Berlin Digital Press, 2014), 10. http://dx.doi.org/10.15463/ie1418.10159, citing Figures on Inflation, *The Russian State Archive of the Economy* (hereafter RGAE), f. 7733, o. 1, d. 166, l. 11.

7. Norman Stone, *The Eastern Front, 1914–1917*, 287.

8. Peter H. Lindert and Steven Nafziger, "Russian Inequality on the Eve of Revolution," *The Journal of Economic History*, 74:3 (Sept. 2014), 767–798, Table 2; Bryan D. Taylor, *Politics and the Russian Army: Civil-Military Relations, 1689–2000* (Cambridge, UK: Cambridge University, 2003), 58.

9. David Stone, *A Military History of Russia*, 166–167.

10. Ibid., 167.

11. For an eyewitness account of the brief-lived Republic that the Bolsheviks overthrew, see *Boris Sokoloff, The White Nights: Pages from a Russian Doctor's Notebook*, ed. Ian Ona Johnson (Tyler, TX: Bowen Books, 2018).

12. Leon Trotsky, *The History of the Russian Revolution*, trans. Max Eastman (London: Haymarket Books, 2008), 814–815.

13. Victor Sebestyen, *Lenin: The Man, the Dictator, and the Master of Terror* (New York: Pantheon, 2017), 341–343.

14. Dmitri Volkogonov, *Trotsky: The Eternal Revolutionary*, trans. and ed. Harold Shukman (New York: Free Press, 1996), 9.

15. Ibid., 70.

16. David T. Zabecki, ed., *Germany at War: 400 Years of Military History* (Santa Barbara, CA: ABC-CLIO, 2014), 410.

17. John W. Wheeler-Bennett, *Brest-Litovsk: The Forgotten Peace, March 1918* (London: Macmillan, 1938), 226–227; *Proceedings of the Brest-Litovsk Peace Conference: The Peace Negotiations between Russia and the Central Powers, 21 November, 1917–3 March, 1918* (Washington, DC: Government Printing Office, 1918).

18. Wheeler-Bennett, *Brest-Litovsk*, 226–227.

19. Ibid., 227–228.

20. Volkogonov, *Trotsky*, 111.

21. Ibid.

22. Evan Mawdsley, *The Russian Civil War* (New York: Pegasus, 2005), 34–35.

23. Wheeler-Bennett, *Brest-Litovsk*, 244.

24. Ibid., 249.

25. Sebestyen, *Lenin*, 378.

26. Ibid.

27. Paul von Hindenburg, *Out of My Life*, trans. F. A. Holt (1920; reprint, London: Forgotten Books, 2013), 334–335. See Wheeler-Bennett, *Brest-Litovsk*, 477.

28. Sebestyen, *Lenin*, 378–379.

29. Ibid.

30. Robert M. Slusser and Jan F. Triska, *A Calendar of Soviet Treaties, 1917–1957* (Stanford, CA: Stanford University Press, 1957), 1–3.

31. Anthony Heywood, *Modernizing Lenin's Russia: Economic Reconstruction, Foreign Trade and the Railways* (Cambridge, UK: Cambridge University Press, 1999), 76.

32. R. H. Haigh, D. S. Morris, and A. R. Peters, *German-Soviet Relations in the Weimar Era: Friendship from Necessity* (Totowa, NJ: Barnes and Noble, 1985), 28.

33. Leon Trotsky, "We Need an Army," 19 March 1918, in *The Military Writings and Speeches of Leon Trotsky, Volume I: 1918* (London: New Park Publications, 1979), 23.

34. John Erickson, *The Soviet High Command: A Military-Political History, 1918–1941* (London: Frank Cass, 2001), 34.
35. Neil Harvey Croll, "Mikhail Tukhachevsky in the Russian Civil War" (unpubl. diss., University of Glasgow, 2002), 37.
36. Iuliya Kantor, *Voina i Mir Mikhaila Tukhachevsogo* [Mikhail Tukhachevsky's War and Peace] (Moscow: Ogonyok, 2005), 53, 64.
37. Ibid., 86–88.
38. Ibid., 92–102, 106.
39. Orlando Figes, "The Red Army and Mass Mobilization during the Russian Civil War 1918–1920," *Past & Present*, 129 (Nov. 1990), 196.
40. Mawdsley, *The Russian Civil War*, 67–68.
41. The Czechoslovak Legion is usually referred to as the Czech Legion, as less than 10 percent of its membership was Slovak. They had been armed by the Tsar to fight against the Austro-Hungarian government that controlled their homelands.
42. None of the commanders of the White Russian forces demonstrated much political acumen, nor did they come up with coherent political programs. One of the most able of them, Anton Denikin, infamously allowed his soldiers to kill thousands of Jewish residents of Ukraine in a series of bloody pogroms, which brought international condemnation and also handicapped recruiting efforts. Worse, it made it politically difficult for the British, Denikin's chief ally, to support broader aid, something Churchill pointedly told Denikin in a letter. And Denikin's difficulties with the Cossacks, who were essential to his military efforts, also highlight a lack of diplomatic ability. Cossack forces were reluctant to move beyond the borders of their home territories and were often politically divided. During one exchange with the head of the Don Cossack Army, Denikin said that "the Don Host is a prostitute, selling herself to whomever will pay." In response, the general of the Cossack Army replied that "if the Don Host is a prostitute, then the Volunteer Army [Denikin's force] is a pimp living off her earnings." The unified military leadership of the Bolshevik Party proved much more effective in strategic planning. Mawdsley, *The Russian Civil War*, 165.
43. Earl Ziemke, *The Red Army, 1918–1941: From Vanguard of World Revolution to America's Ally* (New York: Routledge, 2001), 95.
44. See Trotsky, "The Socialist Fatherland in Danger," 29 July 1918, in *The Military Writings and Speeches of Leon Trotsky, Volume I: 1918*, 286–302.
45. Dmitri Volkogonov, *Lenin: A New Biography* (New York: Free Press, 1994), 220.
46. Ibid.
47. Erickson, *The Soviet High Command*, 56.
48. Jonathan D. Smele, "Aleksandr Alekseevich Baltiiskii," "Tikhon Serafimovich Khvesin," "Mikhail Mikhailovich Lashevich," and "Mikhail Nikolaevich Tukhachevsky," in *Historical Dictionary of the Russian Civil Wars, 1916–1926* (New York: Rowman and Littlefield, 2015), 172, 575, 656, 1187.
49. Figes, "The Red Army and Mass Mobilization," 168.
50. Erickson, *The Soviet High Command*, 76.

CHAPTER 2

1. F. L. Carsten, *The Reichswehr and Politics, The Reichswehr and Politics, 1918–1933* (Berkeley: University of California Press, 1966), 4.
2. See Groener, *Lebenserinnerungen*, 466.
3. Carsten, *The Reichswehr and Politics*, 6.
4. Groener, *Lebenserinnerungen*, 466, quoted in Carsten, *The Reichswehr and Politics*, 6.
5. Alexander Watson, *Ring of Steel: Germany and Austria-Hungary in World War One* (New York: Basic Books, 2014), 66, 554–556.
6. Anthony McElligott, *Weimar Germany* (Oxford, UK: Oxford University Press, 2009), 27.
7. Ibid.

8. Mark Jones, *Founding Weimar: Violence and the German Revolution of 1918–1919* (Cambridge, UK: Cambridge University Press, 2016), 13, 81–82.

9. Groener, *Lebenserinnerungen*, 467, quoted in Carsten, *The Reichswehr and Politics*, 11.

10. Hilger and Meyer, *The Incompatible Allies*, 22.

11. Barton Whaley, *Covert German Rearmament, 1919–1939: Deception and Misperception* (Frederick, MD: University Publications of America), 7–8; Hans von Seeckt, "General Von Seeckt's Statement on German Disarmament at the Spa Conference," 7 July 1920, The British National Archives (Hereafter BNA), CAB 24/108, 94, 1–6.

12. Harold J. Gordon, *The Reichswehr and the German Republic, 1919–1926* (Princeton, NJ: Princeton University Press, 1957), 15.

13. William Shirer, *The Rise and Fall of the Third Reich* (New York: Simon & Schuster, 1960), 55.

14. Gordon, *The Reichswehr and the German Republic*, 14.

15. Ibid., 15.

16. Robert G. L. Waite, *Vanguard of Nazism: The Free Corps Movement in Postwar Germany 1918–1923* (New York: W. W. Norton, 1952), 26–27.

17. Ibid., 39.

18. Ibid., 157.

19. Gordon, *The Reichswehr and the German Republic*, 28–29.

20. Ibid., 26.

21. Hilger and Meyer, *The Incompatible Allies*, 73.

22. Edward Hallett Carr, *German-Soviet Relations between the Two World Wars, 1919–1939* (Baltimore: The Johns Hopkins Press, 1951), 17–20.

23. Vasilis Vourkoutiotis, *Making Common Cause: German-Soviet Secret Relations, 1919–1922* (New York: Palgrave Macmillan, 2007), 50, 60.

24. Ralf Lindner and Rainer-Olaf Schultze, "Germany," in *Elections in Europe: A Data Handbook*, eds. Dieter Nohlen and Philip Stöver (Baden-Baden: Nomos Verlagsgesellschaft, 2010), 776.

25. John Wheeler-Bennett, *The Nemesis of Power* (London: Macmillan, 1967), 37.

26. Waite, *Vanguard of Nazism*, 89.

27. Ibid., 71.

28. Gordon, *The Reichswehr and the German Republic*, 31.

29. Jones, *Founding Weimar*, 287

30. Waite, *Vanguard of Nazism*, 83; Gordon, *The Reichswehr and the German Republic*, 48.

31. Helmut Heiber, *The Weimar Republic*, trans. W. E. Yuill (Munich: Deutscher Taschenbuch Verlag, 1966), 24.

32. Waite, *Vanguard of Nazism*, 78.

33. "Gesetz über die Bildung einer vorläufigen Reichswehr" [Act on the Formation of the Provisional Reichswehr], *Der historischen Dokumenten*, 6 March 1919, Weimar Republic Document Collection, accessed 1 May 2011, http://www.documentarchiv.de/wr/vorl-reichswehr_ges.html.

34. Ibid.

35. Gordon, *The Reichswehr and the German Republic*, 55.

36. Ibid., 69–70, 431–438. Seeckt's military experiences in World War One shaped his strategic and operational thinking. Carsten, *The Reichswehr and Politics*, 107; Matthias Strohn, "Hans von Seeckt and His Vision of a 'Modern Army,'" *War in History*, 12:3 (2005), 320. James S. Corum, *The Roots of Blitzkrieg: Hans von Seeckt and German Military Reform* (Lawrence: University Press of Kansas, 1992), 25–27.

37. Corum, *The Roots of Blitzkrieg*, 25–26.

38. For more on the subject of German conclusions about the First World War, see Corum, *The Roots of Blitzkrieg*, 24 and Robert Citino, *The Path to Blitzkrieg: Doctrine and Training in the German Army, 1920–1939* (Boulder, CO: Lynne Rienner Publishing, 1999), 7–42. As James Corum argues, the initial impulse of the German officer corps was to argue that General Moltke had failed to carry out the Schlieffen plan satisfactorily.

39. Corum, *The Roots of Blitzkrieg*, 23.

40. For the realities of German tank production during the war, see Ralf Raths, "German Tank Production and Armoured Warfare, 1916–18," *War and Society*, 30:1 (2011), 24-47.

41. Azade-Ayse Rorlich, "Fellow Travellers: Enver Pasha and the Bolshevik Government 1918–1920," *Asian Affairs*, 13:3 (1982), 288.

42. Rorlich, "Fellow Travellers," 289.

43. There is some dispute in the historiography over the date of this first trip. Vasilis Vourkoutiotis's analysis of the primary sources—he saw the original versions of documents—strongly suggests that the date was April 1919, not October 1919.

44. Vourkoutiotis, *Making Common Cause*, 44. This story is confirmed by Seeckt's correspondence. See Rabenau, *Hans von Seeckt*, 306.

45. Rorlich, "Fellow Travellers," 291.

46. Vourkoutiotis, *Making Common Cause*, 42.

47. There were four passengers on board the aircraft, including an engineer with the Junkers firm. The latter had a letter on his person that was seized by the Lithuanians and given to the British, indicating he had orders to "1) start trade relations with the Soviet government, 2) to take from German a person, who was of great importance to the Bolshevik government." Despite this note, the British did little to investigate, leaving the matter in the hands of the Lithuanians. Rorlich, "Fellow Travellers," 291, citing "Notes of a Meeting of the Heads of Delegations of the Five Great Powers Held in M. Pichon's Room at the Quai d'Orsay, Paris on Wednesday, October 22, 1919 at 10:30 am," in *Documents in British Foreign Policy, 1919–1939* (hereafter DBFP), Series I, Volume 2, eds. E. L. Woodward and Rohan Butler (London: His Majesty's Stationery Office, 1948), 43–47.

48. Rorlich, "Fellow Travellers," 291.

49. Vourkoutiotis, *Making Common Cause*, 42.

50. Being a conscientious officer, Tschunke first called his superior officer in Germany, Hans von Seeckt, to inform him of the situation.

51. No. 4, DBFP, Series I, Volume 2, 45–47.

52. Vourkoutiotis, *Making Common Cause*, 42.

53. Rorlich, "Fellow Travellers," 291, citing Ernst Köstring, *General Ernst Köstring: Der militärische Mittler zwischen dem Deutschen Reich und der Sowjetunion 1921–1941* [General Ernst Köstring: The Military Intermediary between the German Reich and the Soviet Union, 1921–1941], ed. Herman Teske (Frankfurt: Mittler, 1965), 42.

CHAPTER 3

1. Margaret MacMillan, *Paris 1919: Six Months That Changed the World* (New York: Random House, 2001), 26–27.

2. Claire Maingon and David Campserveux, "A Museum at War: The Louvre 1914–1921," *L'Esprit Créateur*, 54:2 (Summer 2014), 127–128.

3. MacMillan, *Paris 1919*, 161.

4. All German exchange rates use contemporary dollar amounts, and are drawn from Lawrence H. Officer, "Bilateral Exchange Rates: 1913–1999" [Consistent currency units], in *Historical Statistics of the United States, Earliest Times to the Present: Millennial Edition*, eds. Susan B. Carter, Scott Sigmund Gartner, Michael R. Haines, Alan L. Olmstead, Richard Sutch, and Gavin Wright (New York: Cambridge University Press, 2006), Series Ee662–678, https://hsus.cambridge.org/HSUSWeb/search/simpleSearch.do?id=SIMPLE&searcField=lawrence%20officer; and Lawrence H. Officer, "Exchange Rates between the United States Dollar and Forty-one Currencies," MeasuringWorth, 2018, http://www.measuringworth.com/exchangeglobal/.

5. MacMillan, *Paris 1919*, 159.

6. Heiber, *The Weimar Republic*, 36.

7. David J. A. Stone, *The Kaiser's Army: The German Army in World War One* (London: Bloomsbury, 2015), 133.

8. Groener recorded that "the 100,000 man army was for me completely out of the question, because it would not even be capable of ensuring peace at home." Groener, *Lebenserinnerungen*, 492.
9. Carsten, *The Reichswehr and Politics*, 39-41.
10. Groener, *Lebenserinnerungen*, 503.
11. Carsten, *The Reichswehr and Politics*, 42.
12. Ben Fowkes, ed., *The German Left and the Weimar Republic: A Selection of Documents* (Leiden: Brill, 2014), 204.
13. Heiber, *The Weimar Republic*, 40.
14. Ibid., 40–41.
15. Ibid.
16. Article 168, *The Treaty of Versailles*.
17. David G. Williamson, *The British in Interwar Germany: The Reluctant Occupiers, 1918–1930* (London: Bloomsbury, 2017), 55.
18. Ibid., 37.
19. Ibid., 50.
20. Ibid., 57.
21. See, for instance, Ferdinand Foch's proposal on the terms of a peace treaty in Foch, "To British Empire Delegation, Note by Marshal Foch: Preliminaries of Peace with Germany," February 18, 1919, BNA, WO 158/109, 1–5.
22. Williamson, *The British in Interwar Germany*, 66.
23. Martin Gilbert, *The Roots of Appeasement* (London: Wiedenfeld and Nicolson, 1966), 52.
24. Ibid., 55.
25. General Nollet, "Administrative Statute: The Interallied Commissions of Control," March 27, 1920, FO 893/7, BNA, 1-6; 66; Richard J. Shuster, *German Disarmament after World War I: The Diplomacy of International Arms Inspection, 1920–1931* (London: Routledge, 2006), 27.
26. Williamson, *The British in Interwar Germany*, 57.
27. Ibid., 125
28. Shuster, *German Disarmament after World War I*, 122.
29. Ibid.
30. Williamson, *The British in Interwar Germany*, 118.
31. Shuster, *German Disarmament after World War I*, 68.
32. Ibid., 49.
33. See John Maynard Keynes, *The Economic Consequences of the Peace* (New York: Harcourt, Brace and Howe, 1920).
34. There is a very rich historiography on the subject. Most the recent publications on the subject argue that the treaty terms were not uniquely harsh, not the primary impetus behind Weimar Germany's political or economic problems, and not the main driver of Hitler's rise to power. Even Keynes himself later regretted writing his work after the rise of Hitler. For an excellent review of the literature on this subject, see Sally Marks, "Mistakes and Myths: The Allies, Germany, and the Versailles Treaty, 1918–1921," *The Journal of Modern History*, 85:3 (September 2013). See also Manfred Boemeke, Gerald Feldman, and Elisabeth Glaser, eds., *The Treaty of Versailles: A Reassessment after 75 Years* (Cambridge, UK: Cambridge University Press, 1998), especially William Keylor, "Versailles and International Diplomacy," 469–505.
35. Thanks to currency manipulation and heavy borrowing that was never repaid (particularly from the United States), Germany actually posted a net gain of 17.75 billion RM in capital inflows between 1919 and 1931. Stephen A. Schuker, "American 'Reparations' to Germany, 1919–33: Implications for the Third-World Debt Crisis" (Princeton, NJ: Princeton Studies in International Finance, No. 61, 1988), 118.
36. Shuster, *German Disarmament after World War I*, 57, 115, 119, 120.
37. "IAMCC Memorandum to Marshal Foch," December 30, 1924, BNA, WO 155/14, 1–3; Williamson, 119.

38. Heiber, *The Weimar Republic*, 42.
39. For the best evidence of this, see Max Hantke and Mark Spoerer, "The Imposed Gift of Versailles: The Fiscal Effects of Restricting the Size of Germany's Armed Forces, 1924–1929," *The Economic History Review*, 63:4 (November 2010), 849–864. They conclude that the limitations on Germany's military likely saved up to 650 million Reichsmarks per annum, even factoring in reparations payments.
40. Richard M. Boeckel, "Military and Naval Expenditures," *Editorial Research Reports, 1930, Volume III* (Washington, DC: CQ Press, 1930), digitized at http://library.cqpress.com/cqresearcher/cqresrre1930072500. For the years 1928–1929, for instance, official German military expenditures constituted only 1.28 percent of national income, versus 4.6 percent in France. Even taking into account Germany's black funds, of the major powers, only the United States spent less on defense as a percentage of national income during this period.
41. For a discussion of German tax rates, see Harold James, *The German Slump: Politics and Economics, 1924–1936* (Oxford, UK: Clarendon Press, 1986), 39–64.
42. Schuker, "American 'Reparations' to Germany," 10–11.
43. Angus Maddison, J. Bolt, and J. L. van Zanden, "Global Economic Statistics Database," Angus Maddison Project, Accessed 2014, http://www.ggdc.net/maddison/maddison-project/home.htm.
44. Gordon, *The Reichswehr and the German Republic*, 69.
45. Dirk Richhardt, "Auswahl und Ausbildung junger Offiziere 1930–1945: Zur sozialen Genese des deutschen Offizierkorps" [The Selection and Training of Young Officers, 1930–1945: The Social Genesis of the German Officer Corps] (unpubl. diss., Philipps-Universität Marburg, 2002), 23.
46. Gordon, *The Reichswehr and the German Republic*, 59, 78–79
47. Robert B. Kane, *Disobedience and Conspiracy in the German Army, 1918–1945* (Jefferson, NC: McFarland and Company, 2002), 46–49.
48. Rabenau, *Aus seinem Leben*, 221, also quoted in Gordon, *The Reichswehr and the German Republic*, 114.
49. Rabenau, *Aus seinem Leben*, 221–222.
50. Gordon, *The Reichswehr and the German Republic*, 115.
51. Strohn, "Hans von Seeckt and His Vision of a 'Modern Army,'" 330–332.
52. There is some confusion about the terminology of the Reichswehr versus the Reichsheer in the literature. Reichswehr was the name of the German army from 1919 to 1921 under a law passed by the Reichstag on March 6, 1919. The Defense Act of March 23, 1921, changed the terms for army and military, with Reichswehr applying to the German military (army and navy) as a whole, and the term Reichsheer [Imperial Army] introduced. However, the lexical confusion that resulted meant that most contemporaries and all English language literature since has used Reichswehr to refer to the German army throughout the Weimar period. I've followed that convention, not introducing Reichsheer to avoid confusion.
53. Otto Gessler, "Schutz der Ostgrenzen" [Protection of the Eastern Border], 2 August 1920, BNA, GFM 33/3591, 1–3.
54. For more on the Schwarze Reichswehr, see James M. Diehl, *Paramilitary Politics in Weimar Germany* (Bloomington: Indiana University Press, 1977).
55. James S. Corum and Richard R. Muller, ed. and trans., *Heeresdienstvorschrift 487, Führung und Gefecht der Verbundenen Waffen, Teil I (1921), Teil II (1923)* [Army Regulations 487: Leadership and Battle with Combined Arms, Part I (1921) and Part II (1923)] (Baltimore: The Nautical and Aviation Publishing Company of America, 1998). Seeckt was responsible for the overall production of F.u.G., writing the introduction and editing the final product; it was his creation.
56. Citino, *The Path to Blitzkrieg*, 11, 12, 23.
57. Quoted in Strohn, "Hans von Seeckt and His Vision of a 'Modern Army,'" 322.
58. Hans von Seeckt, "Moderne Heere," in Hans von Seeckt, *Gedanken eines Soldaten* (Leipzig: K. F. Koehler, 1935), 61.

59. Matthias Strohn, *The German Army and the Defence of the Reich: Military Doctrine and the Conduct of the Defensive Battle 1918–1939* (Cambridge, UK: Cambridge University Press, 2011), 98–99.
60. Citino, *The Path to Blitzkrieg*, 18; Corum, *The Roots of Blitzkrieg*, 31.
61. For more on the perceived threat from Poland, see Paul Niebrzydowski, "Das deutsche Polenbild: Historicizing German Depictions of Poles, 1919–1934" (unpubl. master's thesis, The Ohio State University, 2012).
62. David J. A. Stone, *Hitler's Army: The Men, Machines, and Organization: 1939–1945* (Minneapolis: MBI Publishing Company, 2009), 28.
63. Aircraft, for instance, were simulated by motorcyclists who were allowed drive around the maneuver grounds unhindered but not to converse with anyone. In this way, they would imitate observation aircraft. Citino, *The Path to Blitzkrieg*, 13.

CHAPTER 4

1. Richard K. Debo, *Survival and Consolidation: The Foreign Policy of Soviet Russia, 1918–1921* (Montreal: McGill-Queen's University Press, 1992), 66
2. John P. McKay, *Pioneers for Profit: Foreign Entrepreneurship and Russian Industrialization, 1885–1913* (Chicago: University of Chicago Press, 1970), 33; B. R. Mitchell, *International Historical Statistics: Europe, 1750–2000* (New York: Palgrave Macmillan, 2003), 645.
3. Debo, *Survival and Consolidation*, 292–293.
4. Hilger and Meyer, *The Incompatible Allies*, 68.
5. Debo, *Survival and Consolidation*, 65.
6. Sebestyen, *Lenin*, 463.
7. David R. Stone, "The Prospect of War?: Lev Trotskii, the Soviet Army, and the German Revolution in 1923," *The International History Review*, 25:4 (Dec., 2003), 816. They would maintain, briefly, a German communist government "in-exile" in Moscow: in the summer of 1918, the Soviets had encouraged a group of German POWs to establish the Central Revolutionary German Workers' and Soldiers' Committee. In November 1918, this group took over what had been the German embassy, giving them a sort of de facto recognition as an alternate government to that of the SPD. Hilger and Meyer, *The Incompatible Allies*, 34.
8. Moritz Schlesinger Papers, "Reports of the *Reichszentralstelle für Kriegs- und Zivilgefangene*," November 1919, Manuscripts and Archives, Yale University (Hereafter MA-YU), Collection 1590, Box 5, Folder 128.
9. Technically, he returned to Germany. Kopp had been there before as a trade delegate. Robert C. Williams, "Russian War Prisoners and Soviet-German Relations, 1918 to 1921," *Canadian Slavonic Papers*, 9:2 (Autumn 1967), 270–271.
10. Viktor Kopp, "Tov. V. I. Leninu" [To Comrade Lenin], 14 August 1920, The Russian State Archive of Socio-Political History (hereafter RGASPI), f. 5, op. 1, d. 2136, l. 4, 1–3.
11. Mawdsley, *The Russian Civil War*, 144, 146, 133.
12. Ibid., 250.
13. Xenia Joukoff Eudin and Harold Henry Fisher, *Soviet Russia and the West, 1920–1927: A Documentary Survey* (Stanford, CA: Stanford University Press, 1957), 181–182.
14. Norman Davies, *God's Playground: A History of Poland, Volume II: 1795 to Present* (Oxford, UK: Oxford University Press, 2005), 291. Future foreign minister Vyacheslav Molotov preferred the term "monstrous bastard of Versailles." Stephen Kotkin, *Stalin, Volume I: Paradoxes of Power, 1878–1928* (New York: Penguin, 2014), 358.
15. Davies, *White Eagle, Red Star* (London: Macdonald, 1972), 132.
16. Ibid., 2. M. Tukhachevsky, "The March beyond the Vistula," in Jozef Pilsudski, *Year 1920 and Its Climax Battle of Warsaw during the Polish-Soviet War, 1919–1920* (New York: Pilsudski Institute of America, 1972), 87.
17. Vourkoutiotis, *Making Common Cause*, 3–4.

18. Sergey Alexeyvich Gorlov, *Sovershenno sekretno: Alianz Moskva-Berlin, 1920–1933* [Top Secret: Alliance Moscow-Berlin, 1920–1933] (Moscow: Olma Press, 2001), 34. Unless otherwise noted, "Gorlov" in the footnotes refers to *Sovershenno sekretno*.

19. "Memo Regarding German Use of Reichswehr," 3 August 1920, BNA, WO 32/5784, 1.

20. Hilger, Meyer, *The Incompatible Allies*, 191–192. Much the same could be said of the German political establishment. When then-chancellor Brüning met Hitler for the first time in 1930, Hitler made it clear his goal was to defeat France and destroy the Soviet Union; Brüning's main concern was not the objective, but attacking "before one was sufficiently armed on the home front." Wolfram Wette, "Ideology, Propaganda, and Internal Politics as Preconditions of the War Policy of the Third Reich," in *Germany and the Second World War, Volume I: The Buildup of German Aggression*, ed. the Militärgeschichtliches Forschungsamt [Research Institute for Military History], trans. P. S. Fall, Dean S. McMurry, and Ewald Osers (Oxford, UK: Clarendon Press, 1990), 50.

21. Hans Meier-Welcker, *Seeckt* (Frankfurt am Main: Bernard und Graefe, 1967), 210.

22. Haigh, Morris, and Peters, *German-Soviet Relations*, 72.

23. The Soviets did indeed offer, through the approaches of Kopp and an unknown Red Army officer, to help restore Germany's former frontier to the East. But the Soviets may have reneged on that offer; Kopp told Maltzan when victory seemed assured in early August 1920 that "if a Soviet regime was instituted in Poland, [Russia] would determine Poland's frontier with Germany based on ethnographic factors." Robert Himmer, "Soviet Policy toward Germany during the Russo-Polish War, 1920," *Slavic Review*, 35:4 (December 1976), 678.

24. General Ernst Köstring, *Profile bedeutener Soldaten, Band 1, General Ernst Köstring* [Profile of Important Soldiers: Volume 1, Ernst Köstring], ed. Herman Teske (Frankfurt: E. S. Mittler und Sohn, 1966), 46.

25. Vourkoutiotis, *Making Common Cause*, 52; Manfred Zeidler, *Reichswehr und Rote Armee, 1920–1933: Wege und Stationen einer ungewöhnlichen Zusammenarbeit* [The Reichswehr and the Red Army, 1920–1933: Paths and Facilities of an Unusual Collaboration] (Munich: Oldenbourg Verlag, 1994), 59. Unless otherwise noted, "Zeidler" in the footnotes refers to *Reichswehr und Rote Armee*.

26. "Geschäftliche Beziehungen der Firma Krupp mit der Sowjet-Regierung in Russland in den Nachkriegsjahren" [Krupp's Business Relations with the Soviet Government in Russia in the Postwar Years], Kruppisches Archiv, Essen (hereafter KA-E), WA/40 B 1350, 1. See also Norbert H. Gaworek, "From Blockade to Trade: Allied Economic Warfare against Soviet Russia, June 1919 to January 1920," *Jahrbücher für Geschichte Osteuropas, Neue Folge*, 23:1 (1975).

27. "Top Secret: To Comrade Lejava," 20 August 1920, Russian State Military Archive (hereafter RGVA), f. 33987, op. 3, d. 52, l 430, reprinted in *The Red Army and the Wehrmacht: How the Soviets Militarized Germany and Paved the Way for Fascism, from the Secret Archives of the Former Soviet Union*, eds. and trans Yuri Dyakov and Tatyana Bushuyeva (Amherst, NY: Prometheus Books, 1995), 32.

28. "Protokol No. 36, Zasedaniya Politicheskogo Biuro TSK ot 13 Avgusta 1920 g." [Minutes of a Meeting of the Politburo of the Central Committee on 13 August 1920], 13 August 1920, RGASPI, f. 17, op. 3, d. 102, 1, 2.

29. Kotkin, *Stalin: Paradoxes of Power*, 364.

30. This was not true of the entire German government. Members of the German Foreign Ministry and some of the civilian leaders of East Prussia hoped for a Polish victory in the Polish-Bolshevik war. "Memo on Poland," 6 Aug 1920, BNA, GFM 33/3591, 1.

31. Hans von Seeckt, "Fernschreiben vom Offizier an Offizier" [Telegram from Officer to Officer], 23 July 1920, GFM 33/3591, BNA, 1.

32. Ibid.

33. Colonel H. H. Wade, "Cipher Telegram to Mr. Balfour," 18 January 1919, BNA, FO 608/266, 196, 1. Colonel Wade detailed the fighting between German and Polish forces in his reports back to London.

34. "Report, Polish Military Mission to the Supreme Allied Command," 7 July 1920, Instytut Józefa Piłsudskiego w Ameryce in New York (IJP-NYC), Box 3, Folder 2, 10–18, 1–8.

35. Some material excerpted with permission from Ian Johnson, "The Fire of Revolution: A Counterfactual Analysis of the Polish-Bolshevik War, 1919 to 1920," *The Journal of Slavic Military Studies*, 28:1 (March 2015), 156–185. https://www.tandfonline.com/.

36. Silesia and Danzig were two of the most important Entente occupation zones in the aftermath of World War I, each hosting thousands of allied soldiers. For more, see Nicolas Beaupré, "Occuper l'Allemagne après 1918" [The Occupation of Germany after 1918], *Revue historique des armées*, 254 (2009), 9–19; and T. Hunt Tooley, *National Identity and Weimar Germany: Upper-Silesia and the Eastern Border 1918–1922* (Lincoln: University of Nebraska Press, 1997).

37. V. I. Lenin, "First Session Speech," *Second Congress of the Communist International. Minutes of the Proceedings* (Moscow: Publishing House of the Communist International, 1921), 1.

38. Thomas Fiddick, *Russia's Retreat from Poland: From Permanent Revolution to Peaceful Coexistence* (London: Macmillan, 1990), 122–124.

39. "Peace Negotiations between Poland and Russia," July 1920, BNA, FO 688/6, 7, 1.

40. Ziemke, *The Red Army, 1918–1941*, 124.

41. Michael S. Neiberg and David Jordan, *The Eastern Front 1914–1920: From Tannenberg to the Russo-Polish War* (London: Amber Books, 2008), 218.

42. Conan Fischer, *Europe between Democracy and Dictatorship: 1900–1945* (Hoboken, NJ: John Wiley and Sons, 2011), 124.

43. "Besprechung mit Herr Kopp" [Meeting with Mr. Kopp], 19 July 1920, Politisches Archiv des Auswärtigen Amtes, Berlin (hereafter PA-AA), KO 095872, 2. The Polish government was so concerned that Germany might invade in the spring of 1920 that it had drawn up plans for a defense and then counterattack into eastern Germany, assigned troops to form a defensive front, and requested General Charriou, a French military adviser, be sent to reconnoiter the likely German invasion routes. "Instruction au sujet des reconnaissances a effectuer sur la frontière occidentale" [Instruction Regarding Reconnaissance to Be Carried Out on the Western Frontier], 28 February 1920, Josef Pilsudski Institute–NYC (hereafter JPI-NYC), 2/9/367, 1–5.

44. Hans von Seeckt, "Memorandum," 31 July/8 August 1920, Bundesarchiv-Militärarchiv, Freiburg im Breisgau (hereafter BA-MA), RH2-29/1, 1–2.

45. Seeckt, "Memorandum," 31 July/8 August 1920, 1–2. For more on the importance of the Putilov Works, see Jonathan A. Grant, *Big Business in Russia: The Putilov Company in Late Imperial Russia, 1868–1917* (Pittsburgh: University of Pittsburgh Press, 1999).

46. Seeckt, "Memorandum," 31 July/8 August 1920, 1–2.

47. Ibid.

48. "Unterbringung deutscher Kommunisten in russischen Betrieben" [Accommodating German Communists in Russian Enterprises], 25 November 1925, Bundesarchiv Lichterfelde (hereafter BA-L), R/1501/20330.

49. But the Bolsheviks would do so only after the failure of a last uprising in 1923. "Die Welt erobern" [Conquering the World], *Der Spiegel*, 30 October 1995, http://www.spiegel.de/spiegel/print/d-9224698.html; "Memorandum," 19 December 1932, PA-AA, R31497/E496919, 1.

50. Kotkin, *Stalin: Paradoxes of Power*, 362.

51. Annemarie H. Sammartino, *The Impossible Border: Germany and the East 1914–1922* (Ithaca, NY: Cornell University Press, 2010), 147.

52. Felix Dzerzhinsky, "Telegrammi F. E. Dzerzhinskogo v Moskvu V. I. Leninu i v Minsk v RVS zapadnogo fronta I. T. Smigle o pribyvshem iz Germanii Enver Pashe" [Telegrams from F. E. Dzerzhinsky to Moscow and V. I. Lenin and to the Revolutionary Military Council on the Western Front and to I. T. Smigla about the arrival from Germany of Enver Pasha], 11 August 1920, RGASPI, f. 76, op. 3, d. 106, l. 1–2.

53. Rorlich, "Fellow Travellers," 292.
54. Ibid.
55. Rabenau, 307, quoting a letter between the Pasha and Seeckt.
56. For more on the foreign policy decisions surrounding the Battle of Warsaw, see Johnson, "The Fire of Revolution."
57. Jeffrey Korbel, *Poland between East and West: Soviet and German Diplomacy toward Poland, 1919–1933* (Princeton, NJ: Princeton University Press, 2015), 65.

CHAPTER 5

1. R. W. Davies, *Soviet Economic Development from Lenin to Khrushchev* (Cambridge, UK: Cambridge University Press, 1988), 19.
2. Carl Eric Bechhofer-Robert, *Through Starving Russia, Being a Record of a Journey to Moscow and the Volga Provinces, in August and September 1921* (London: Methuen, 1921), 41–46.
3. Stephane Courtois, Nicolas Werth, Jean-Louis Panne, Andrzej Paczkowski, Karel Bartosek, and Jean-Louis Margolin, *The Black Book of Communism: Crimes, Terror, Repression*, trans. Jonathan Murphy and Mark Kramer (Cambridge, MA: Harvard University Press, 1999), 119.
4. Ibid., 112.
5. Paul Avrich, *Kronstadt 1921* (New York: W. W. Norton, 1970), 205.
6. Ibid., 207, 211, 215.
7. For more on the context and consequences of NEP see R. W. Davies, Mark Harrison, and S. G. Wheatcroft, *The Economic Transformation of the Soviet Union, 1913–1945* (Cambridge, UK: Cambridge University Press, 1994).
8. These included Viktor Kopp, who first arrived in Berlin in July 1919, and Leonid Krasin, who arrived in April 1920. "Geschäftliche Beziehungen der Firma Krupp mit der Sowjet-Regierung in Russland in den Nachkriegsjahren" [Business Relationships between Krupp and the Soviet Government in Russia in the Postwar Years], KA-E, WA4/1361, 0197, 1–43, 1.
9. This sum was disguised in a total reparations claim of $27.9 billion for reasons related to the Allied Reparation Commission's domestic audiences, who sought maximum reparations payments from defeated Germany. Marks, 642; Jürgen Tampke, *A Perfidious Distortion of History: The Versailles Peace Treaty and the Success of the Nazis* (Melbourne, Australia: Scribe, 2017), 169.
10. Marks, 643.
11. Tampke, 164–165.
12. Haigh, Morris, and Peters, *German-Soviet Relations*, 92–93.
13. Tampke, 171–172.
14. "Geheim-Abkommen, Vereinbarungen über Zusammenarbeiten von Reichswehr-ministerium und der Firma Fried. Krupp Aktiengesellschaft, Essen" [Secret-Accord, Agreement on Cooperation between the Ministry of Defense and the Fried. Krupp Firm], 25 January 1922, KA-E, WA/40 B 1350, 1.
15. Zeidler, 54.
16.
17. Ibid., 49, 54.
18. Köstring, *General Ernst Köstring*, 46–47.
19. "Ritter Oskar von Niedermayer," in Gerd R. Ueberschär, *Hitlers militärische Elite: 68 Lebensläufe* (Zürich: Primus Verlag, 2011), 78–84. The only major work on Niedermayer's career to date, besides Niedermayer's own writings, is Hans-Ulrich Seidt, *Berlin, Kabul, Moskau: Oskar Ritter von Niedermayer und Deutschlands Geopolitik* [Berlin, Kabul, Moscow: Oskar von Niedermayer and German Geopolitics] (Munich: Universitas Press, 2002).
20. Hilger and Meyer, *The Incompatible Allies*, 195. Hans-Ulrich Seidt, "From Palestine to the Caucasus—Oskar Niedermayer and Germany's Middle Eastern Strategy in 1918," *German Studies Review*, 24:1 (Feb., 2001), 1–18, at 1.

21. For the best treatment in English of this mission, see Peter Hopkirk, *Like Hidden Fire: The Plot to Bring Down the British Empire* (Tokyo: Kodansha International, 1994).
22. Seidt, *Berlin, Kabul, Moskau*, 97–119.
23. Ibid., 125.
24. Ueberschär, *Hitlers militärische Elite*, 78–84.
25. "Expose: Aerounion," 19 November 1921, Daimler-Benz Corporate Archive (hereafter DBCA), DB 167, 1–3; "Aufnahme einer Flugzeug- und Motoren, Fabrikation im Russland" [Report on Aircraft and Engine Manufacturing in Russia], 20 March 1922, DBCA, DB 167, 1–2.
26. "Zweiter Schriftsatz des Reichsministeriums zur Klärung seiner Beziehungen zu Prof. Dr. Junkers," 15 February 1926, BA-MA, RH/2, 1130, 4, 6.
27. Ibid., 6.
28. Wolfgang Wagner, *Hugo Junkers Pionier der Luftfahrt—seine Flugzeuge* [Hugo Junkers, Pioneer of Aviation: His Aircraft] (Bonn: Bernard und Graefe, 1996), 201.
29. The Soviets had already granted Junkers AG a monopoly upon air travel on the Sweden-Persia air route via the Soviet Union and would pay it to conduct a number of aerial surveys of Soviet territory. "Vereinbarung zwischen der russischen Regierung und den Junkerswerken" [Agreement between the Russian Government and the Junkers Works], 6 February 1922, BA-MA, RH/2, 1130, 1–5.
30. These included the problems of transport, shortages of skilled labor, inconsistent deliveries of raw materials, food shortages, and the still unstable political regime. "Zweiter Schriftsatz des Reichsministeriums zur Klärung seiner Beziehungen zu Prof. Dr. Junkers," 7.
31. Vourkoutiotis, *Making Common Cause*, 122–123; Zeidler, 54. Niedermayer and Wilhelm Schubert organized the meeting.
32. "Thezisi Prezidiuma VSNKh o kontsessiakh," 25 March, 1920, RGASPI 5/1/2694, 2–3, reprinted in S. S. Khromov, *Innostrannie kontsessii v SSSR: Istoricheskii ocherk. Dokumenti, Chast I* [Foreign Concessions in the USSR: Historical Essay, Documents, Part I] (Moscow: Rossiiskaia Akademiya Nauk Institut Rossiiskoi Istorii, 2006), 117–121.
33. A. Köves, "Chapters from the History of East-West Economic Relations," *Acta Oeconomica*, 17:2 (1976), 159–176; 159–160.
34. Khromov, *Innostrannie kontsessii v SSSR*, 11.
35. M. V. Klinova, *Gosudarstvo i chastnyy kapital v poiskakh pragmatichnogo vzaimodeistviya* [The State and Private Capital Searching for Pragmatic Cooperation] (Moscow: IMEMO RAN, 2009), 41–42.
36. Khromov, *Innostrannie kontsessii v SSSR*, 236.
37. Antony C. Sutton, *Western Technology and Soviet Economic Development, 1917–1930* (Stanford, CA: Hoover Institution on War, Revolution and Peace Press, 1968), 272–273. Sutton's work has been regarded, rightly so, as controversial. While this early monograph is generally considered reliable, I have here relied on his work only when it clearly cites German Foreign Ministry archival records or published Soviet document collections.
38. Sutton, *Western Technology and Soviet Economic Development*, 273; Haigh, Morris, and Peters, *German-Soviet Relations*, 172–173. Russgertorg's financial success helped encourage a wave of capital investment in Soviet industry and resource exploitation. In fact, it was so successful that by 1925, the Soviet state viewed it as a threat to the economic independence of the Soviet Union and began shifting its responsibilities to state organs.
39. Harold James, *Krupp: A History of the Legendary German Firm* (Princeton, NJ: Princeton University Press, 2012), 141.
40. Ibid., 208–209.
41. "Geheim-Abkommen, Krupp" [Secret-Accord, Krupp], 25 January 1922, 1.
42. Ibid.
43. Ibid.

44. Vourkoutiotis, *Making Common Cause*, 122–123.
45. "Vorgang: Bb. Nr. 3566 vom 11 November 1927," 16 November 1927, KA-E, WA 40/ 252, 255, 140–143, 2.
46. Khromov, *Innostrannie kontsessii v SSSR*, 17.
47. Not all of these were finalized: RGVA contains lists of 526 contracts filed between 1921 and 1933, but not all of them were signed by both sides.
48. "Archivist's Note," 1933, RGVA, f. 31863, op. 1.
49. Concessionary investment in 1925 totaled 32.6 million gold rubles; in 1926, that figure was 48.8. (E. Kantinik-Ulina, "Kharakteristika raboti sushchestvyushchikh kontsessii," 26 November 1926, 8350/1/512, 312–317, State Archive of the Russian Federation (Hereafter GARF), reprinted in Khromov, *Innostrannie kontsessii v SSSR*, 284–288. Much of the capital generated by the concessionary agreements was plowed back into purchases from German firms. For instance, the "Association of German Locomotive Building Companies" would arrange the sale of 700 German locomotives and (along with an English company) the sale of 1,000 oil tanker cars in 1922 alone; those two contracts were worth more than 100 million gold rubles, or 37 percent of *all* Russian imports in 1922. Heywood, *Modernizing Lenin's Russia*, 216–217.
50. "Niederschrift über die informatorische Besprechung über die gegenwärtige Lage der deutsch-russischen Beziehungen im Auswärtigen Amt" [Minutes of an Informational Meeting in the Foreign Ministry about the Current State of German-Russian Relations], 25 June 1924, PA-AA, R 31492K/KO96760, 1.
51. Foreign governments were not unaware of German activities. Polish intelligence in particular remained cognizant of German investment and intentions in the USSR. Polish embassy staff in Moscow drafted a report on the growth of German concessionary activity in the USSR in 1922. The Polish Foreign Ministry ordered the report dispatched to their London and Paris embassies, indicating that such information was likely shared with the British and French governments in 1922—and then ignored. Adam Zielesninski, "Do pana Ministra Spraw Zagranicznych: Stosunki sowiecko-niemieckie" [To the Minister of Foreign Affairs: Soviet-German Relations], 22 October 1922, Archiwum Akt Nowych (hereafter AAN), 510/22, 1–11.

CHAPTER 6

1. Carol Fink, *The Genoa Conference: European Diplomacy, 1921–1922* (Chapel Hill: University of North Carolina Press, 1993), 152.
2. Carr, *German-Soviet Relations*, 63. The primary difficulty was German foreign minister Walther Rathenau's reluctance to make a deal with the Soviets, hoping instead for a better arrangement—particularly regarding reparations—with France and Great Britain at the upcoming Genoa Conference.
3. Richard Byers, *Flying Man: Hugo Junkers and the Dream of Aviation* (College Station: Texas A&M Press, 2016), 52.
4. "Junkers–Von Seeckt Correspondence," 1922–1924, BA-MA, RH 8, 3681.
5. Byers, *Flying Man*, 53.
6. "Zweiter Schriftsatz des Reichsministeriums zur Klärung seiner Beziehungen zu Prof. Dr. Junkers," 15 February 1926, 7. This agreement would be formalized a month later, when Junkers AG would sign a preliminary agreement with Ivan Peterskii, the head of the Soviet Civilian Aviation Office; Wagner, *Hugo Junkers*, 195.
7. Fink, *The Genoa Conference*, 161–162.
8. Vourkoutiotis, *Making Common Cause*, 125.
9. Fink, *The Genoa Conference*, 162–163. For Rathenau's assessment of the lack of consideration for German interests by the Entente powers, see Walter Rathenau, "Telegramm," 18 April 1922, PA-AA, R 83435, 113–114, 1–2.
10. Carr, *German-Soviet Relations*, 64.
11. "[Rapallovertrag zwischen] Die deutsche Regierung, vertreten durch Reichsminister Dr. Walter Rathenau und die Regierung der russischen sozialistischen föderativen Sowjet-Republik, vertreten durch Volkskommissar Tschitscherine" [Rapallo

Agreement between the German Government, represented by Reich Minister Dr. Walter Rathenau and the Government of the Russian Socialist Federative Soviet Republic, represented by People's Commissar Tschitscherin], 16 April 1922, PA-AA, R 83435/102–104, 1.

12. Herbert von Dirksen, *Moscow, Tokyo, London. Twenty Years of German Foreign Policy* (Norman: University of Oklahoma Press, 1952), 49, 167, 169; Vourkoutiotis, *Making Common Cause*, 159.

13. Vourkoutiotis, *Making Common Cause*, 151.

14. Gottfried Schramm, "Basic Features of German Ostpolitik, 1918–1939," in *From Peace to War: Germany, Soviet Russia, and the World, 1939–1941*, ed. Bernd Wegner (Providence, RI: Berghahn Books, 1997), 23.

15. Ivan Maisky, *The Maisky Diaries: Red Ambassador to the Court of St. James, 1932–1932*, ed. Gabriel Gorodetsky, trans. Tatiana Sorokina and Oliver Ready (New Haven, CT: Yale University Press, 2015), 203.

16. Georg Cordts, *Junge Adler: Vom Luftsport zum Flugdienst, 1920–1945* [Young Eagles: From Air Sports to Flight Duty, 1920–1945] (Munich: Bechtle Verlag Esslingen, 1988), 9.

17. Edward L. Homze, *Arming the Luftwaffe: The Reich Air Ministry and the German Aircraft Industry, 1919–1939* (Lincoln: University of Nebraska Press, 1976), 2–3.

18. Homze, *Arming the Luftwaffe*, 3.

19. Ibid., 26.

20. Wagner, *Hugo Junkers*, 142.

21. Alexander Baikov, "Voenno-promyshlennoye sotrudnichestvo SSSR i Germanii—kto koval sovetskii mech" [Military-Industrial Cooperation between the USSR and Germany—Who Forged the Soviet Sword?], 218–302 in *Nepravda Viktora Suvorova* [The Untruth of Victor Suvorov] (Moscow: Yauza, 2008), 247.

22. "Vereinbarung zwischen der russischen Regierung und den Junkerswerken" [Agreement between the Russian Government and the Junkers Works], 6 February 1922, 1–5.

23. Hugo Junkers, "Letter to Hans von Seeckt," 19 May 1922, BA-MA, RH/2, 1130, 1.

24. Ibid.

25. In a letter sent to the Reichswehrministerium on July 7, Junkers apparently made it clear he could not accept the terms currently being offered for the Fili facility. He received a mollifying reply from Sondergruppe R, which argued that Junkers had a misconception of the whole idea of Fili and had imposed upon it "unfavorable assumptions and unsustainable business terms." The letter continued by assuring him that a workable arrangement could be made between himself and Arkady Rosengoltz, the Russian then in charge of managing foreign concessions: "The Russians desire to come to an agreement and will eventually accept reasonable conditions." "Letter to Herr Professor Junkers," 12 July 1922, BA-MA, RH/2, 1130.

26. Ibid., 1.

27. Rosengoltz, "Letter to Junkers AG," 30 August 1922, BA-MA, RH/2 2305, 1.

28. "Letter to Herrn Rosengoltz," 23 October 1922, BA-MA, RH/2 2305.

29. "Vereinbarung zwischen der russischen Regierung und den Junkerswerken," 6 February 1922, BA-MA, 1–5; "Liefervertrag" [Contract of Delivery], 4 December 1922, BA-MA, RH/2/2293/586-189, 1–4.

30. Ibid.

31. "Junkers, Fili (Russland) bis zum Herbst '25," 13 January 1926, 1–2.

32. "History," Khrunichev State Research and Production Space Center, Accessed 17 October 2013, http://www.khrunichev.ru/main.php?id=36.

33. "Mitglied das Obersten Konzession, Moskau," 23 October 1922, BA-MA, RH/2, 230, 1.

34. "Bericht den Besuch des Flugzeugwerkes in Fili," 17 February 1931, BA-MA, RH/12/ 1, 56, 1.

35. Antony Kay, *Junkers Aircraft & Engines 1913–1945* (London: Putnam Aeronautical Books, 2004), 42.

36. Ibid., 45–46.
37. A sesquiplane has one large and one small wing. In the aftermath of the war, designs increasingly shifted from biplanes toward sesquiplanes or parasol-winged monoplanes, with just an upper wing. Enzo Angelucci, *The Rand McNally Encyclopedia of Military Aircraft, 1914–1980* (New York: Military Press, 1980), 116, 127.
38. Some of his aircraft did not get much further than prototype production. The first two, J-22 I and IIs, were single-seat, parasol-winged monoplane fighters armed with a 7.62 mm machine gun, the standard aircraft weapon of the First World War. To hurry the aircraft into production, Zindel based his design on an earlier model called the T-2. The results were mixed. The positioning of the wings on J-22 prototypes was somewhat awkward, restricting the pilot's vision to a narrow slit ahead and to the sides of the aircraft—a serious disadvantage in a fighter aircraft. Only two prototypes were ever successfully produced before the design was determined unfit for mass production. Kay, *Junkers Aircraft*, 44–45.
39. "Das Junkers-Unternehmen in Fili (Russland) in seiner Entwicklung und seinem Verhältnis zum Reichswehrministerium bis zum Herbst '25" [The Junkers Operation at Fili (Russia) in Its Development and Its Relationship with the Ministry of War through the Fall of 1925], 13 January 1926, BA-MA, RH/2, 1130, 1.
40. Kay, *Junkers Aircraft*, 45–46.
41. Peter Baranov, "RVS–Junkers Doklad" [Revolutionary Military Council–Junkers Report], 11 June 1925, RGVA, f. 4, op. 2, d. 14, l. 1–5. It appears that Junkers used an engine that exceeded the horsepower limitations of the IAACC in their Fili models, but just barely.
42. "J-21," Ugolok Neba, Aviation Encyclopedia (Russian), http://www.airwar.ru/enc/other1/ju21.html.
43. "Junkers, Fili (Russland) bis zum Herbst '25," 13 January 1926, 11.
44. Ibid.
45. Ibid.
46. Peter Baranov, "RVS–Junkers Doklad," 11 June 1925, 3. Baranov very much wanted the Fili project to succeed, and blamed the crash on the pilot involved in his report to the RVS.

CHAPTER 7

1. Cyril Brown, "Angry Resistance Down in Ruhr Mine to French Control: Men in the Shafts Declare That Any Invader Who Enters Invites Death," *New York Times*, 23 February 1923, 1–2.
2. See Conan Fischer, *The Ruhr Crisis, 1923–1924*.
3. Ibid.
4. Zeidler, 68.
5. Ibid., 72.
6. Ibid., 74.
7. Carsten, *The Reichswehr and Politics*, 144.
8. Ibid., 233.
9. Zeidler, 76.
10. Dietrich Stolzenberg, *Fritz Haber: Chemist, Nobel Laureate, German, Jew* (Philadelphia: Chemical Heritage Press, 2004), 109, 129.
11. Stolzenberg, *Fritz Haber*, 148–149.
12. Ibid., 149.
13. Treaty of Versailles, Article 171–172.
14. Stolzenberg, *Fritz Haber*, 150.
15. Shuster, *German Disarmament after World War I*, 66–67.
16. Harold Hartley, "Speech at the Royal Society Club Dinner," 14 November 1968, *Notes and Records of the Royal Society of London*, 24:1 (June 1969), quoted in Stolzenberg, *Fritz Haber*, 162.
17. Stolzenberg, *Fritz Haber*, 145.

18. Ibid., 145.
19. Ibid., 163.
20. Ibid., 163.
21. Ibid., 164.
22. For more on Stolzenberg's work in Morocco, see Rudibert Kunz and Rolf-Dieter Müller, *Giftgas gegen Abd El Krim: Deutschland, Spanien und der Gaskrieg in Spanisch-marokko, 1922–1927* [Poison Gas against Abd El Krim: Germany, Spain, and the Gas War in Spanish Morocco, 1922–1927] (Mannheim: Rombach, 1990).
23. Gorlov, 164.
24. Stolzenberg, *Fritz Haber*, 166. Hasse was then heading the Reichswehr's Ordnance Office (TA-1). Hasse ran the ordnance office until April 1922, when he was promoted to head the Truppenamt. His successor was Joachim von Stülpnagel. Rüdiger Schönrade, *General Joachim von Stülpnagel und die Politik: Eine biographische Skizze zum Verhältnis von militärischer und politischer Führung in der Weimarer Republik* [General Joachim von Stülpnagel and Politics: A Biographical Sketch on the Relationship between Military and Political Leadership in the Weimar Republic] (Berlin: Carola Hartmann Miles, 2007), 59.
25. The name of the German Chemical Society changed slightly in 1949, hence the different word order. Stolzenberg, *Fritz Haber*, 166.
26. Lewis Schmerling, *Vladimir Nikolaevich Ipatieff, 1867–1952, a Biographical Memoir* (Washington, DC: National Academy of Sciences, 1975), 93.
27. Ibid., 92.
28. Marina Katys, "Voenno-khimicheskie poligon v Moskve" [The Military Chemical Testing Grounds in Moscow], *Radio Liberty*, 20 December 2000, http://www.svoboda.org/content/transcript/24197763.html. The intention of this last facility was to train "chemical officers," who would be responsible for teaching basic methods of defense and managing defensive materiel for each regiment in the event of a gas attack. It would be reestablished in 1932 as the Timoshenko Military Academy of Chemical Defense. "Betrieb: Gaskrieg. Sowjetrussland" [Gas Warfare, Soviet Union], 14 November 1924, BA-MA, RH/12/4/46, 2.
29. Györgyi Vásárhelyi and László Földi, "History of Russia's Chemical Weapons," *The Journal of Academic and Applied Research in Military Science*, 6:1 (2007), 135–146.
30. See Ian Ona Johnson, "Prophet of Poison Gas: Yakov Fishman and the Soviet Chemical Weapons Program, 1924–1937," *Vulcan: The International Journal of the Social History of Military Technology*, 6:1 (August 2018), 16–36.
31. Stolzenberg, *Fritz Haber*, 166.
32. They officially signed the agreement on May 15, 1923. The Red Army and the Reichswehr would have equal access to the military materiel to be produced at the plant. "V Samarkskii GubKomGosOr" [To the Head Government Organ Committee of Samara] 16 June 1921, The Central State Archive of Samara Oblast (TsGASO), P24/5/331, 1, 1.a.
33. Erickson, *The Soviet High Command*, 151.
34. Elisabeth Wiskemann, "Europe's Two New Premiers," February 1933, *The Living Age*, 343, 4397, 1.
35. Wolfram Pyta, "Kurt von Schleicher," in *Neue deutsche Biographie* [New German Biography], ed. Otto Stolberg-Wernigerode, Vol. 23 (Berlin: Duncker und Humblot, 2006), 51.
36. Zeidler, 79.
37. "Otto Henrich," *Siemens Personalities*, accessed 2016, https://www.siemens.com/history/en/personalities/chairmen_of_the_managing_board_parent_companies.htm#toc-6. He was joined by Theodor Eckhardt, a businessman based in Berlin whom the German Foreign Ministry had recommended to the Reichswehr. Captain Fritz Tschunke, the man who had rescued Enver Pasha and who had earned Seeckt's continued trust during his successful trips to Russia in 1923, joined as representative of the Truppenamt. Lieutenant-Colonel Mentzel, whose second trip to Russia in

April had led to the founding of GEFU, joined as a representative of the *Waffenamt*. Zeidler, 79.

38. Ibid., 79.
39. Ibid., 101.
40. Ibid., 80–82.
41. "Junkers, Fili (Russland) bis zum Herbst '25," 13 January 1926, 1–2.
42. Ibid., 12.
43. Ibid., 1.
44. "K spravke po assignovaniam 24–25 goda i namechennim potrebnim assignovaniam na 25–26 god krasnomu vozdushnomu flotu SSSR" [Inquiry into Appropriations for the 1924–1925 year and projected appropriations requirements for the 1925–1926 year for the Red Air Force of the Soviet Union], 7 July 1925, RGVA, f. 4, op. 2, d. 14(2), l. 1.
45. Homze, *Arming the Luftwaffe*, 25.
46. Ibid.
47. For details on these aircraft, see Smith and Kay, *German Aircraft of the Second World War*.
48. Homze, *Arming the Luftwaffe*, 26.
49. Ibid., 25.
50. "Poisku k zavodu Bersol" [Finding for the Bersol Plant], 25 March 1926, TsGASO, 357/43/112, 1–2.
51. Zeidler, 8.
52. Gorlov, 104.
53. Ibid., 104.
54. Ibid., 104.
55. Ibid., 105.
56. Five of these chemicals had industrial or agricultural use; the other two—mustard gas and phosgene—had use only as weapons. The nonmilitary agents were produced primarily to disguise the military function of the site. Gorlov, 105.
57. Alexei Kojevnikov, "The Great War, the Russian Civil War, and the Invention of Big Science," *Science in Context*, 15:2 (2002), 246.

CHAPTER 8

1. Hermann J. Rupieper, *The Cuno Government and Reparations 1922–1923: Politics and Economics* (The Hague: Martinus Nijhoff Publishers, 1979), 195–199.
2. There is a rich literature on Stresemann and his foreign policy, much of it recent. For more, see Jonathan Wright, *Gustav Stresemann: Weimar's Greatest Statesman* (Oxford, UK: Oxford University Press, 2002), John P. Birkelund, *Gustav Stresemann: Patriot und Staatsmann*; *Eine Biographie* (Hamburg: Europa, 2003); and Eberhard Kolb, *Gustav Stresemann* (Munich: C. H. Beck, 2003). Two older, classic works are Hans W. Gatzke, *Stresemann and the Rearmament of Germany* (Baltimore: Johns Hopkins Press, 1954); and Henry Ashby Turner's *Stresemann and the Politics of the Weimar Republic* (Princeton, NJ: Princeton University Press, 1963).
3. Adam Tooze, *The Wages of Destruction: The Making and Breaking of the Nazi Economy* (New York: Viking Penguin, 2007), 3–9. Tooze has argued that Stresemann's internationalism was fired by a vision of European economic power in competition with the United States.
4. Wright, *Gustav Stresemann*, 385–386.
5. Claud Cockburn, *In Time of Trouble. An Autobiography* (London: Rupert Hart-Davis, 1957), 97, cited by Jonathan Wright, "Stresemann and Locarno," *Contemporary European History*, 4:2 (Jul., 1995), 110.
6. Dirksen, *Moscow, Tokyo, London*, 45–46.
7. Hans Mommsen, *The Rise and Fall of Weimar Democracy*, trans. Elborg Forster and Larry Eugene Jones (Chapel Hill: University of North Carolina Press, 1996), 137.
8. For the best assessment of Soviet activity during the September–October 1923 crisis, see David R. Stone, "The Prospect of War?"

9. Stalin, "Pismo, Tov. Arvid" [Letter to Comrade Arvid], November 11, 1923, RGASPI, f. 326, op. 2, d. 21, l. 139–145, 1–3. He added that "This majority must also be won over. . . . If Ilyich were in Germany, he would say, I think, that the main enemy of the revolution are the Social Democrats, especially from the left, that is the very left part of it which has not yet lost the confidence of the workers, and which contributes to doubts, hesitations, and the uncertainty of a united struggle."

10. Joachim C. Fest, *Hitler* (Orlando: Harcourt, Inc., 1974), 178–181.

11. Fest, *Hitler*, 182–183.

12. Ibid., 199–201.

13. Gatzke, *Stresemann*, 26–27.

14. Ibid., 27.

15. For more on the Dawes plan, see Stephen Schuker, *The End of French Predominance in Europe: The Financial Crisis of 1924 and the Adoption of the Dawes Plan* (Chapel Hill: University of North Carolina Press, 1976).

16. Dennis Showalter, *Instrument of War: The German Army, 1914–1918* (New York: Bloomsbury Press, 2016), 170–172; Thomas Menzel, "Lipezk. Die geheime Fliegerschule und Erprobungsstätte der Reichswehr in der Sowjetunion" [Lipetsk: The Secret Reichswehr Flight School and Testing Facility in the Soviet Union], 2013, Bundesarchiv.de, https://www.bundesarchiv.de/DE/Content/ Virtuelle-Ausstellungen/Lipezk-Die-Geheime-Fliegerschule-Und-Erprobungsstatte-Der-Reichswehr-In-Der-Sowjetunion/lipezk-die-geheime-fliegerschule-und-erprobungsstatte-der-reichswehr-in-der-sowjetunion.html.

17. Zeidler, 108.

18. Gorlov, 89; Vourkoutiotis, *Making Common Cause*, 100.

19. Gorlov, 88–89.

20. Zeidler, 108.

21. Thomsen, "Organisation und Dienstgliederung des Wiko/Moskau" [Organization and Operating Structure of Wiko/Moscow], 1–2. The assistant's name was Rath, and the secretary was Frau von Griseheim.

22. Speidel, "Reichswehr und Rote Armee," 23–24; "Fl. Bericht 312" [Flight Report 312], 2 February 1931, BA-MA, RH/12/I/57, 209–213, 1.

23. Kotkin, *Stalin: Paradoxes of Power*, 498–501.

24. Vladimir Lenin and Leon Trotsky, *The Suppressed Testament of Lenin, with "On Lenin's Testament" by Leon Trotsky* (New York: Pioneer Publishers, 1946), 6.

25. Sebestyen, *Lenin*, 493–497.

26. For the best description of Stalin's rise to power, see Kotkin, *Stalin, Volume I: Paradoxes of Power, 1878–1928* (New York: Penguin, 2014).

27. *The Suppressed Testament of Lenin*, 7.

28. The testament itself would be revealed to the Central Committee not long afterward, when it was read aloud by Central Committee member Lev Kamenev. Kotkin, *Stalin: Paradoxes of Power*, 546.

29. Sebestyen, *Lenin*, 500–501.

30. Kotkin, *Stalin: Paradoxes of Power*, 538–539.

31. Erickson, *The Soviet High Command*, 164.

32. Ibid., 169–170.

33. Erickson, *The Soviet High Command*, 170.

34. N. Varfolomeyev, "Strategy in an Academic Formulation," in *The Evolution of Soviet Operational Art 192–1991: The Documentary Basis, Vol. 1*, trans. Harold S. Orenstein (London: Frank Cass, 1995), 40; Erickson, *The Soviet High Command*, 167.

35. See, for instance, Leon Trotsky, "Prospects and Tasks in Building the Army," May 18, 1923, *Trotsky's Speeches and Military Materials and Documents on the History of the Red Army, The Military Writings and Speeches of Leon Trotsky How the Revolution Armed, Volume IV: The Years 1921–23*, ed. Brian Pearce (London: New Park Publications, 2003), 142–152.

36. Zeidler, 94.

37. "Das Junkers-Unternehmen in Fili (Russland) in seiner Entwicklung und seinem Verhältnis zum Reichswehrministerium bis zum Herbst '25," 13 January 1926.
38. For a technical assessment of Soviet complaints, see Wagner, *Hugo Junkers*, 217–229.
39. "Das Junkers-Unternehmen in Fili (Russland) in seiner Entwicklung und seinem Verhältnis zum Reichswehrministerium bis zum Herbst '25," 13 January 1926, 19.
40. Ibid., 19.
41. Ibid., 20.
42. Ibid., 21.
43. Ibid., 25.
44. "Junkers–Von Seeckt Correspondence," 25 March 1924, BA-MA, RH 8, 3681, 1.
45. "Junkers–Von Seeckt Correspondence," 1926, BA-MA, RH 8, 3681 (1924–1926), 1–4.
46. Ibid.
47. "Junkers–Von Seeckt Correspondence," 26 November 1924, BA-MA, RH 8, 3681, 1.
48. "Zweiter Schriftsatz des Reichsministeriums zur Klärung seiner Beziehungen zu Prof. Dr. Junkers," 2 February 1926, 1.

CHAPTER 9

1. Richard W. Harrison, *The Russian Way of War: Operational Art, 1904–1940* (Lawrence: University Press of Kansas, 2001), 129.
2. Mikhail Frunze, "Unified Military Doctrine and the Red Army," trans. David R. Stone, originally published in *Armiia i Revoliutsiia*, No. 1 (July 1921), http://www-personal.k-state.edu/~stone/FrunzeDoctrine.
3. Thomas Lafleur, "Mikhail Frunze and the Unified Military Doctrine" (unpubl. MMAS thesis, Fort Leavenworth, KS: US Army Command and General Staff College, 2004), 91.
4. Erickson, *The Soviet High Command*, 836.
5. See Alan Durkata, Tom Darcey, and Viktor Kulikov, *The Imperial Russian Air Service: Famous Pilots and Aircraft of World War One* (Mountain View, CA: Flying Machines Press, 1996).
6. At least one of Kazakov's kills also involved ramming. By contrast, the top ace for Germany had 80 kills; France's best had 75; Canada's 72; Britain's 61; Australia's 47; Belgium's 37; Austria-Hungary's 35; Italy's 34; America's 26 (in only six months of combat); New Zealand's 25; and Serbia's 22. Turkey's aviation wing was almost nonexistent during the war and commanded by German officers, which explains its lack of combat aces.
7. Robert Jackson, *The Red Falcons: The Soviet Air Force in Action, 1919–1969* (Brighton, UK: Clifton Books, 1970), 12.
8. " Voenno-Vozdushnye Sili " [Air Force], in *Sovetskaia voennaia entsiklopedia* [The Soviet Military Encyclopedia], ed. Andrei Antonovich Grechko (Moscow: Voenizdat, 1980), 245.
9. "Spravka o Vosdushnogo Flota Rossii" [Information about the Russian Air Fleet], 26 July 1925, RGVA, f. 4, op. 2, d. 14, 1. 1.
10. Ibid.
11. "Archivist's Note," BA-MA, RH2/2920-2942/81, 1, 1.
12. The agency would be reorganized again the following year, On August 15, 1925, the RVS, then headed by Mikhail Frunze, again reorganized its chemical weapons program into VOKhIMU (the Military-Chemical Defense Committee). Fishman, who had served for a year as head of the Red Army's Chemical Defense Directorate, was promoted to head this larger and more independent organization. See Johnson, "Prophet of Poison Gas: Yakov Fishman and the Soviet Chemical Weapons Program, 1924–1937," 6.
13. Benjamin C. Garrett and John Hart, "Fishman, Yakov Moiseevich (1887–1962)," in *Historical Dictionary of Nuclear, Biological and Chemical Warfare* (Lanham, MD: Scarecrow Press, 2007), 76–77.
14. Yaroslav Leontiev, "V mir—Bakh" [Into the World—to Bang, The Fate of Yakov Fishman], *Russkaia zhizn* [Russian Life], 10 September 2008, http://rulife.ru/mode/article/899/.

15. Garrett and Hart, "Fishman," 77.
16. Kotkin, *Stalin: Paradoxes of Power*, 461.
17. Yakov Fishman, "V osnovnom soglasen, Uborevichu" [A Summary of the Agreement, to Uborevich], 30 December 1930, RGVA, f. 33988, op. 3, d. 162, l. 141-165, 45, 1–25/2. This report summarizes Fishman's first five years running VOKhIMU.
18. Ibid., 2.
19. "Die chemische Kriegsindustrie in der S.S.S.R." [The Chemical Military Industry in the Soviet Union], 9 November 1925, BA-MA, RH/12/4/46, 1.
20. Zeidler, 124.
21. Fishman, "V osnovnom soglasen, Uborevichu," 2.
22. In 1925, the Revolutionary Military Council assigned VOKhIMU to focus on defensive weaponry as was appropriate for an organization "formed under the Geneva Protocols [on chemical weapons]." Fishman, "V osnovnom soglasen, Uborevichu," 2.
23. Yakov Fishman, "Betrieb: Erscheinungsformen der chemischen Luftwaffe" [Subject: Forms of the Chemical Air Force], 1925, BA-MA, RH/12/4/47, 26; V. N. Levichev, ed., *Voina i voennoe delo: Posobie po voennomu delu dlya partiinogo, sovetskogo i profsouznogo aktiva* [War and Military Affairs: A Handbook on Military Affairs for Party, State, and Trade Union Activists] (Moscow: Government Military Publishing House, 1933), 339, 378; *Tekhnicheskaya entsiklopedia* [Technical Encyclopedia], Vol. IV, ed. L. K. Martens (Moscow: Joint Society for the Soviet Encyclopedia, 1928), 98; Zeidler, 124.
24. Garret, Hart, "Fishman," 77.
25. This was Colonel Herbert Fischer. "F.L. Nachrichten #2" [Fl. Report #2], 11 July 1924, BA-MA, RH2/2216/329-330, 1–2.
26. Zeidler, 126.
27. "F.L. Nachrichten #2" [Fl. Report #2], 11 July 1924, 1–2.
28. Ibid.
29. "Prepodavatel' boevikh gazov—Khimik" [Teacher of Military Gas—Chemist], 9 January 1931, 33988/3/192-191, 113, 1–2.
30. Even before the two militaries laid out their technical aims, Hugo Stolzenberg's firm had reached an agreement to begin testing aero-chemical devices with Junkers AG in Russia. "Fl. Nachricht Nr. 3" [Fl. Report Nr. 3], 24 July 1924, RH2/2216/542-544, 1–5.
31. Gorlov, 104.
32. "Firma Stolzenberg, Pismo, Inspektoru Truda" [Stolzenberg Firm, letter to the Inspector of Labor], 4 May 1925, TsGASO, 818/3/96, 101, 1.
33. Gorlov, 106.
34. Ibid., 104–105. "Die Giftgasfabrik in Trotsk" [The Chemical Weapons Factory in Trotsk], *Vorwärts*, 11 January 1927, PA-AA, R 31493K, K 097076, 1. This interview is drawn from the Social Democratic Newspaper in Germany, *Vorwärts*, but was in the German Foreign Ministry Archives with notes suggesting that the interview was of concern to the German government because of its factual accuracy. The interviewee notes that he is only revealing information because he had not been paid and the company that had hired him—GEFU—no longer existed.
35. "Die Giftgasfabrik in Trotsk" [The Chemical Weapons Factory in Trotsk], 1. By 1925, there were approximately fifty workers working just on superphosphates, so the total of Russian and German workers was significantly higher than forty. "Zavkom Khimikov" [The Factory Committee of Chemists], 17 March 1925, TsGASO, 818/3/96, 69, 1.
36. "Die Giftgasfabrik in Trotsk" [The Chemical Weapons Factory in Trotsk], 1.
37. "Archivist's Note," BA-MA, RH2/2920-2942/81, 1, 1.
38. Zeidler, 109; "F.L. Nachrichten #2" [Fl. Report #2], 11 July 1924, 1–2.
39. Zeidler, 110.
40. Speidel, "Reichswehr und Rote Armee," 18. Their visit had sparked a proposal from the Soviet Air Force to host German pilots on a long-term basis; not long after, the VVS had extended a proposal to the Reichsmarine (the German Navy) for a joint training

base at Odessa on the Black Sea. But the Reichsmarine—already developing its own aviation programs outside of Germany—declined. Instead, the VVS extended the offer regarding Lipetsk.

41. "Fl. Bericht Nr. 6" [Flight Report Number 6], 23 October 1924, BA-MA, RH/2/2216, 299, 4.

42. That officer, Goretsky, visited Berlin for three months. "Spisok komandno-nachal'stvuiushchego sostava RKKA, byvshikh v komandirovke v Germanii s 1924 po 1936 gg." [List of Commanders of the Red Army Who Were Assigned to Visit Germany between 1924 to 1936], June 1938, RGVA, f. 33987, op. 2, d. 218, l. 37–60 (available through the Yale-Russian Archives Project, no. 260), 45. The Yale-Russian Archives Project, copies of documents not currently available in the Russian State Military Archives in Moscow, is hereafter cited as Y-RAP.

CHAPTER 10

1. Giulio Douhet, "The War of 19—," 292–405, in *The Command of The Air*, trans. Dino Ferrari (Washington, DC: Air Force History and Museums Program, 1998), 372.

2. Giulio Douhet, *The Command of the Air*, trans. Dino Ferrari (Washington, DC: Air Force History and Museums Programs, 1998), 6–7.

3. Robert Harris and Jeremy Paxman, *A Higher Form of Killing: The Secret History of Chemical and Biological Warfare* (New York: Random House, 2002), 32.

4. Fishman, "Betrieb: Erscheinungsformen der chemischen Luftwaffe" [Subject: Forms of the Chemical Air Force], 1925, 1.

5. "Doklad itogakh raboti gostei za 1930 g." [Report on the results of work by the guests for 1930, 15 January 1931, RGVA, f. 33988, op. 3, d. 162, l. 10, 6–7. Whether this is true or not seems uncertain; Sonderkommando Z noted in a report dated 1924 that "Chemical aviation: since we have no prior experience in this field, I am unable to nominate a candidate. But I will get in touch with Stolzenberg." "Fl.N.Nr. 4" [Flight Report Number 4], 8 August 1924, BA-MA, RH2/2216/311–312, 1–2.

6. Corum, *The Roots of Blitzkrieg*, 106.

7. Col. Phillip S. Meilinger, "Giulio Douhet and the Origins of Airpower Theory," in *The Paths of Heaven: The Evolution of Airpower Theory*, ed. Col. Phillip S. Meilinger (Maxwell Air Force Base, AL: Air University Press, 1997), 17.

8. American experiments are mentioned repeatedly by authors in both the German *Militär-Wochenblatt* and the Soviet *Voina i Tekhnika* in the early 1920s.

9. Amos A. Fries and Clarence J. West, "The Future of Chemical Warfare," in *Chemical Warfare* (New York: McGraw-Hill, 1921), 436.

10. Christopher A. Warren, "GAS, GAS, GAS! The Debate over Chemical Warfare between the World Wars," *Federal History*, 4 (Jan. 2012), 43–60; 55.

11. Fishman, "Betrieb: Erscheinungsformen der chemischen Luftwaffe" [Subject: Forms of the Chemical Air Force], 1925; Thomas Iain Faith, "Under a Green Sea: The US Chemical Warfare Services, 1917–1929" (unpubl. diss., George Washington University, 2008), 119.

12. Fishman, "Betrieb: Erscheinungsformen der chemischen Luftwaffe," 2.

13. Ibid.

14. Ibid.

15. Yakov Fishman, "Predsedateliu, Revolutionnogo Voennogo Soveta" [To the Head of the Revolutionary Military Council], February 1929, RGVA, f. 33987, op. 3, d. 285, l. 13, (Y-RAP 152), 2.

16. Ibid., 1.

17. Stolzenberg, *Fritz Haber*, 168.

18. Stolzenberg, *Fritz Haber*, 168–169. The committee was headed by Reichswehr General Max Ludwig.

19. Peter Hayes, *From Cooperation to Complicity: Degussa in the Third Reich* (Cambridge, UK: Cambridge University Press, 2009), 132–133, 214–215.

20. Zeidler, 124.

21. Fishman, "Predsedateliu, Revolutionnogo Voennogo Soveta," 2.
22. Ibid.
23. Zeidler, 202. Many of these researchers were reintegrated into the German military after Hitler came to power. Professor Neumann of the University of Würzburg joined the SA in 1934 and the Wehrmacht in 1937. A number of his students would be commissioned into the Wehrmacht during the Second World War, too. See Stefanie Kalb, "Wilhelm Neumann (1898–1965)—Leben und Werk unter besonderer Berücksichtigung seiner Rolle in der Kampfstoff-Forschung" [Wilhelm Neumann (1898–1965)—Life and Work with a Special Emphasis on His Role in Poison Gas Research] (unpubl. diss., University of Würzburg, 2005).
24. "Politburo—Iz Protokola No. 78" [From Politburo Protocol Number 78], 13 January 1927, RGASPI, f. 17, op. 162, d. 4, l. 45, 1.
25. V. N. Ipatieff, "Original Manuscript of 'My Life as a Chemist,'" 1946, Ipatieff Collection, Boxes 1 and 2, Hoover Institution Archives at Stanford University (Hereafter HIA), 608–639.
26. Zeidler, 98.
27. "Das Junkers-Unternehmen in Fili (Russland) in seiner Entwicklung und seinem Verhältnis zum Reichswehrministerium bis zum Herbst '25," 13 January 1926, 25.
28. Zeidler, 94; Gotthard Sachsenberg, "Brief Zampred RVS SSSR Tov. Frunze" [Letter to the Chairman of the RVS of the USSR, Comrade Frunze], 13 July 1925, RGVA, f. 4, op. 2, d. 90, l. 148, 1–4, 3–4.
29. "Reichswehrministerium, Nr. 722/20 Stab vom 10.2.1920," 10 February 1920, RH/2/2280, 175, 1–2.
30. Carsten, The Reichswehr and Politics, 221–222.
31. Citino, The Path to Blitzkrieg, 12–13.
32. Speidel, "Reichswehr und Rote Armee," 21.
33. Kotkin, Stalin: Paradoxes of Power, 557.
34. Gorlov, 101.
35. That officer, Goretsky, visited Berlin for three months. "Spisok komandno-nachal'stvuiushchego sostava RKKA," June 1938, 45.
36. "Fl. Bericht 27; Schule Lipetsk" [Flight Report Number 27; School Lipetsk], 12 March 1925, BA-MA, RH/2/2216, 2.
37. Ibid.; "Fl. Bericht Nr. 28" [Flight Report Number 28], 19 March 1925, BA-MA, RH/2/2216, 1.
38. "Fl. Bericht Nr. 28" [Flight Report Number 28], 19 March 1925, 3.
39. "Fl. Bericht 27; Schule Lipetsk" [Flight Report Number 27; School Lipetsk], 12 March 1925, 5–7.
40. "Vertrag zwischen Herrn v. d. Lieth und Herrn Stahr" [Contract Agreement between Herr von der Lieth Thomsen and Herr Stahr], 12 March 1925, BA-MA, RH/2/2216, 1.
41. "Fl. Bericht Nr. 28" [Flight Report Number 28], 19 March 1925, 1.
42. Ibid., 2.
43. Ibid.
44. Ibid., 2–3.
45. Ibid., 4.
46. "Protokoll über die Vereinbarungen zwischen der Russischen Luftflotte und dem Vertreter der Sondergruppe in Moskau über Einrichtung einer Fliegerschule und eines Gerätelager in Lipezk" [Details of the Agreement between the Russian Air Force and the representatives of the Special Group in Moscow regarding a flying school and an equipment warehouse in Lipetsk], 15 April 1925, BA-MA, RH2/2214, 2, 1–4. Speidel believed that the VVS and Reichswehr agreed to a contract for Lipetsk in 1924, but the contract in the German national archives is dated the following spring. He might have believed an arrangement had been reached earlier because of the dispatch of a group of German pilots to Lipetsk the previous summer.
47. "Protokoll, Lipezk" [Agreement, Lipetsk], 15 April 1925, 1.
48. Speidel, "Reichswehr und Rote Armee," 25.

CHAPTER 11

1. Hans Mommsen, *The Rise and Fall of Weimar Democracy*, trans. Elborg Forster and Larry Eugene Jones (Chapel Hill: University of North Carolina Press, 1996), 234–235.
2. This was diplomat and historian John Wheeler-Bennett, who lived in Germany for much of Hindenburg's presidency. See his biography of the Field Marshal: *Hindenburg: The Wooden Titan* (London: Macmillan, 1936/1967).
3. Mommsen, *Rise and Fall of Weimar Democracy*, 237.
4. Andreas Dorpalen, *Hindenburg and the Weimar Republic* (Princeton: Princeton University Press, 1964), 94.
5. "Betr. Strategische Aufgabe Nr. 1 und ihre Durchführung bei der Kommandeur-Fakultät der Luftakademie" [Report on Strategic Problem No. 1 and Their Implementation at the Commander-Faculty of the Air Academy], 15 February 1926, BA-MA, RH/2/2217, 4–6.
6. Zeidler, 110–111.
7. "Fl. Bericht Nr. 56" [Flight Report Number 56], 25 September 1925, 1.
8. "Betr. Strategische Aufgabe Nr. 1 und ihre Durchführung bei der Kommandeur-Fakultät der Luftakademie" [Report on Strategic Problem Nr. 1 and Their Implementation at the Commander-Faculty of the Air Academy], 15 February 1926, 4–6.
9. Ibid., 4–5.
10. Ibid.
11. Ibid., 4–6.
12. "Betrieb: Wissenschaftliches Institut für Motorforschung—NAMI" [Subject: Scientific Institute for Engine Research], 18 February 1926, BA-MA, RH/2/2296, 1.
13. Ibid., 1–2.
14. Ianis Berzin, "Doklad nachal'nika 4-go Upravlenie Shtaba RKKA Ya. K. Berzina K. E. Voroshilovu o sotrudnichestve RKKA i Reikhsvera" [Report of the Chief of the Red Army Staff's 4th Directorate Ia. Berzin to K. E. Voroshilov on Cooperation between the Red Army and the Reichswehr], 24 December 1928, RGVA, f. 33987, op. 8 d. 295, l. 71–79, (Y-RAP 146), 1–8.
15. Roger Reese, *Stalin's Reluctant Soldiers: A Social History of the Red Army, 1925–1941* (Lawrence: University Press of Kansas, 1996), 102; "Spisok komandno-nachal'stvuiushchego sostava RKKA," June 1938, 45.
16. "15 sego iunia ya predstavitelya nemskoi gruppi Lip." [On the 15th of June I took a Group of German Representatives to Lipetsk], 17 June 1925, RGVA, f. 4, op. 2, d. 14 (1), l. 1.
17. "Fl. Bericht Nr. 28" [Flight Report Number 28], 19 March 1925, 3.
18. Speidel, "Reichswehr und Rote Armee," 32.
19. "15 sego iunia ya predstavitelya nemskoi gruppi Lip." [On the 15th of June I took a Group of Russian Representatives to Lipetsk], 17 June 1925, 1; "Fl. Bericht Nr. 56" [Flight Report Number 56], 25 September 1925, 1–3; "Fl. Bericht Nr. 57" [Flight Report Number 57], 2 October 1925, BA-MA, RH2\2216, 58, 1–4, 3.
20. Ibid., 3.
21. "Letter from Fiebig to Lieth-Thomsen," 31 March 1926, BA-MA, RH 2/2296, 54, 1–8; Hermann von der Lieth-Thomsen, "Fl. Bericht Nr. 90 vom 3.IV.26" [Flight Report Number 90 on June 3, 1926], 10 June 1926, BA-MA, RH/2/2297, 298, 1–8.
22. "15 sego iunia ya predstavitelya nemskoi gruppi Lip." [On the 15th of June I Took a Group of Russian Representatives to Lipetsk], 17 June 1925, 2–3.
23. Hermann von der Lieth-Thomsen, "Fl. Bericht Nr. 90 vom 3.IV.26" [Flight Report Number 90 on June 3, 1926], 1–8.
24. Samuel W. Mitcham Jr., *Eagles of the Third Reich: Men of the Luftwaffe in World War II* (Mechanicsburg, PA: Stackpole Books, 1997), 138.
25. Zeidler, 94.
26. Voroshilov, "Predmet: Iunkers" [Subject: Junkers], 12 April 1925, RGVA, f. 4, op. 2, d. 90, l. 1–2.
27. Zeidler, 95.

28. "Postanovlenie Sekretariata TSK po delu o kontsessii 'IUNKERSA'" [Resolution of the Secretariat of the TSK on the Matter of the Junkers Concession], 4 March 1926, RGASPI, f. 17, op. 3, d. 550, l. 19, 1–7.
29. "Spisok komandno-nachal'stvuiushchego sostava RKKA," June 1938, 45–46.
30. Gorlov, 145–147. Tukhachevsky wrote to Moscow that because of the "extremely difficult position of the German army due to Versailles"—the Reichswehr's lack of funding, men, and materiel—"only in discipline, fidelity, their offensive spirit, and their precision do they undoubtedly have superiority over the Red Army and likely others, too." Iuliya Kantor, *Zaklyataya druzhba: Sekretnoe sotrudnichestvo SSSR i Germanii 20–30kh godov* [Vow of Friendship: Secret Cooperation between the USSR and Germany in the 1920s and 1930s] (Moscow: Rosspen, 2014), 71.

CHAPTER 12
1. Harrison, *The Russian Way of War*, 120.
2. Erickson, *The Soviet High Command*, 199.
3. Sheila Fitzpatrick, *On Stalin's Team: The Years of Living Dangerously in Soviet Politics* (Princeton, NJ: Princeton University Press, 2015), 26.
4. Ibid., 11.
5. Ibid., 26.
6. Mawdsley, *The Russian Civil War*, 89–91.
7. Gorlov, 168.
8. No. 102, Serie B, Band II, 1 (Dezember 1925 bis Juni 1926), *Akten zur Deutschen Auswärtigen Politik, 1918–1945* [Documents on German Foreign Policy, hereafter ADAP] (Göttingen: Vondenhoeck und Ruprecht, 1950–1995), 259–264.
9. Zeidler, 137–139; No. 102, *ADAP*, B:2, 260–264.
10. No. 102, *ADAP*, B:2, 260–264.
11. Erickson, *The Soviet High Command*, 249.
12. No. 102, *ADAP*, B:2, 263.
13. Locarno was part of a broader British strategy to improve Germany's strategic position in Europe, with the aim of promoting stability within Germany and a balance of power on the continent. Zara Steiner, *The Lights That Failed: European International History, 1919–1933* (Oxford, UK: Oxford University Press, 2005), 396–398, 611.
14. Gorlov, 172.
15. Ibid.
16. No. 43 *ADAP*, B:II,1 (Dezember 1925 bis Juni 1926), 129–133.
17. Harvey L. Dyck, "German-Soviet Relations and the Anglo-Soviet Break, 1927," *Slavic Review*, 25:1 (Mar., 1966), 67–83, 75.
18. Dyck, 69–70.
19. Ibid., 70–71.
20. Zeidler, 103.
21. Hermann von der Lieth-Thomsen, "An WIKO Z/Moskau: Organisation und Dienstgliederung des WIKO/Moskau" [To WIKO Z/Moscow: Organization and Service Structure of the Business Offices in Moscow], 4 June 1926, BA-MA,RH/2/2297/311–312, 1–2.
22. Ibid., 2.
23. "Ergebnis der Besprechung über das Programm der Schule Lip 1925–1926" [Results of the Meeting Regarding the Program of the School at Lipetsk, 1925–1926], 14 November 1926, BA-MA, RH/2/2293, 1.
24. Ibid., 2.
25. This was Adolf Bäumker, who would play a major role in research and development in the Luftwaffe.
26. Speidel, "Reichswehr und Rote Armee," 30.
27. "Records, 1919–1926," Fédération Aéronautique Internationale, accessed September 2020, https://www.fai.org/records?order=field_date_single_custom&sort=asc&f%5B0%5D=field_country%3AFR&page=3. For a more detailed description of

the decline of French air power in the 1920s, see Robin Higham, *Two Roads to War: The French and British Air Arms from Versailles to Dunkirk* (Annapolis, MD: Naval Institute Press, 2012), in particular 84–96.

28. "Ergebnis der Besprechung über das Programm der Schule Lip 1925–1926" [Results of the Meeting Regarding the Program of the School at Lipetsk, 1925–1926], 14 November 1926, 3–4.

29. Ernst Heinkel, *Stormy Life: Memoirs of a Pioneer of the Air Age*, ed. and trans. Jürgen Thorwald (Boston: Dutton Press, 1956), 72–73. Cited in D. A. Sobelev and D. B. Khazanov, *Nemetskii sled v istorii otechestvennoi aviatsii* [The German Imprint on the History of Domestic Aviation] (Moscow: Rusavia, 2000).

30. "Betr: Ausbildung Lehrgang L 1927" [Subject: Training Course at Lipetsk for 1927], 20 November 1926, BA-MA, RH/2/2299, 62, 1–6. Heinkel was likely ahead of his rivals because he had begun producing combat aircraft that violated the restrictions of Versailles in Japan, where he was supported by the Japanese government.

31. Zeidler, 337.

32. "Bericht T-3 V[ersuchsgruppe]" [Report from Section T-3 Research Group], 22 May 1931, BA-MA, RH12/I/57, 298, 1.

33. "Besprechungsprotokoll vom 20.12.1932" [Meeting Transcript from December 20, 1932], 20 December 1932, BA-MA, RH/12/I/60, 141–149, 1.

34. "Stellungnahme zu den Ru. Vorschlägen" [Opinion on the Russian Proposals], 18 January 1932, BA-MA, RH12/I/60, 23–35, 3.

CHAPTER 13

1. "Bericht über die Besichtigung des Flugplatzes und des Versuchsfeldes in der Nähe der Stadt Moskau" [Report on the Survey of Airfields and Experimental Testing Grounds Near the City of Moscow], 19 August 1926, BA-MA, RH/2/2213/407–417, 1–14.

2. Zeidler, 140.

3. Gorlov, 134–135.

4. Ibid., 135.

5. Zeidler, 140; "Bericht über die Besichtigung des Flugplatzes," 19 August 1926, 1–14.

6. Colonel Hermann von der Lieth-Thomsen, "Erfahrungen und Eindrücke bei den Arbeiten der Gruppe Amberg" [Experiences and Impressions on the Work of the Group Amberg], 17 December 1926, BA-MA, RH/2/2297/610–612, 1–4.

7. Lieth-Thomsen, "Erfahrungen und Eindrücke bei den Arbeiten der Gruppe Amberg," 17 December 1926, 2. Hackmack, who continued to work as a test-pilot for the Reichswehr, died after bailing out of a test aircraft in 1928.

8. Otto Muntsch, "Fl. Bericht Nr. 106 von 24 Sept." [Fl. Report Nr. 106 from September 24], 29 September 1926, BA-MA, RH2/2216/117, 1.

9. Muntsch, "Fl. Bericht Nr. 106 von 24 Sept.," 29 September 1926, 2.

10. "Instruktion für die Gaeste" [Instruction for the Guests], 28 October 1926, BA-MA, RH/2/2304/28–31, 1–3.

11. Ibid.

12. In the words of Hans Gatzke, Stresemann's "frequent quarrels with Seeckt did not arise because of any basic divergence of views on the necessity of German rearmament. On several occasions Stresemann actually regretted the lack of a strong army as 'the main factor in a successful foreign policy.' What he objected to was the well-nigh unassailable position which Seeckt and his Reichswehr had cut out for themselves within the Weimar Republic." Gatzke, *Stresemann*, 25.

13. "German Army Chief Resigns: Von Seeckt Withdraws Following Scandal of Wilhelm, Crown Prince's Son," October 8, 1926, *Cornell Daily Sun/Chicago Daily News Company*, 5.

14. Wheeler-Bennett, *The Nemesis of Power*, 151–152.

15. For the reasons they abandoned Seeckt, see Gaines Post Jr., *The Civil-Military Fabric of Weimar Foreign Policy* (Princeton, NJ: Princeton University Press, 1973), 139.

16. Köstring, *General Ernst Köstring*, 50.

17. "The Main Treaty between VIKO [sic] MOSKVA and KA-MOSKVA about Tank School Organization," 2 October 1926, RGVA, f. 33987, op. 3, d. 295, l. 58–64, reprinted in Dyakov and Bushuyeva, 164–170.
18. Carsten, *The Reichswehr and Politics*, 298.
19. See Kirsten Schäfer, *Werner von Blomberg: Hitlers erster Feldmarschall, eine Biographie* [Werner von Blomberg, Hitler's First Field Marshal, a Biography] (Munich: Paderborn, 2006).
20. Ibid., 29.
21. Ibid., 59–64.
22. Zeidler, 141.
23. Muntsch, "Fl. Bericht Nr. 106 von 24 Sept.," 29 September 1926, 4.
24. Ibid. This report (among others) frequently revealed hints of German racial attitudes: they often subtly or overtly referenced racial notions of German superiority and Slavic backwardness. Doubtless their preconceived notions were exacerbated by the poverty of Russia in the aftermath of the Russian Civil War.
25. Muntsch, "Fl. Bericht Nr. 106 von 24 Sept.," 29 September 1926, 4.
26. Ibid., 5.
27. Hans Hackmack, "Schlussbericht 1926" [Final Report 1926], 21 December 1926, BA-MA, RH/2/2304/32–40, 1.
28. Gorlov, 136–137.
29. Hackmack, "Schlussbericht 1926," 21 December 1926, 3.
30. Gorlov, 223.
31. Lieth-Thomsen, "Erfahrungen und Eindrücke bei den Arbeiten der Gruppe Amberg," 17 December 1926, BA-MA, 2.
32. Hackmack, "Schlussbericht 1926," 21 December 1926, 3.
33. Gorlov, 136–137.
34. Hackmack, "Schlussbericht 1926," 21 December 1926, 4.
35. Lieth-Thomsen, "Erfahrungen und Eindrücke bei den Arbeiten der Gruppe Amberg," 17 December 1926, 3.
36. Gorlov, 127.
37. Yakov Fishman, "Kratkii doklad o rabote Khimicheskogo Komiteta VOKhIMU za 1926–1927 god i o plane rabote na 1927–1928 gg." [Short Report on the Work of the Chemical Committee VOKhIMU for 1926–1927 and the Plan of Work for the 1927–1928 year], May 1928, RGVA, f. 33988, op. 3c, d. 98, l. 201. In 1926–1927, VOKhIMU's research budget was 536,359 rubles. In 1927–1928, it was 858,000.

CHAPTER 14

1. "Cargoes of Munitions from Russia to Germany, Manchester Guardian," 3 December 1926, PA-AA, R 31493 K096972, 1.
2. The Reichstag had been made aware of the allegations before the news story broke. Indeed, the *Guardian*'s German correspondent based his report upon on a document provided to every member of the Reichstag and passed to him by a socialist elected official. One of its coauthors seems to have been the disgruntled German industrialist Hugo Junkers, whose business had been ruined in Russia. Byers, *Flying Man*, 90–91; Haigh, Morris, and Peters, *German-Soviet Relations*, 171.
3. "Cargoes of Munitions from Russia to Germany," 3 December 1926, 1.
4. "Russland und Reichswehr, *Vorwärts*," 7 December 1926, PA-AA, R31493K-K096979, 1; "Sowietgranaten für Reichswehrgeschütz, *Vorwärts*," 5 December 1926, PA-AA, R31493K-K096979, 1–2.
5. "Sozialdemokratische Lügengranaten gegen Sowjetrussland," 7 December 1926, PA-AA, *Rote Fähne* R 31493 K-K096987, 1.
6. "Berlin," *New York Times*, 16 December 1926, 6.
7. Ibid.
8. Gorlov, 224.

9. Josef Unschlikht, "Unschlikht to Stalin: 'Both We and They Were Interested in Strict Secrecy,'" 31 December 1926, RGVA, f. 33987, op. 3, d. 151, l. 18–23, reprinted in Dyakov and Bushuyeva, 57–62.

10. Shuster, *German Disarmament after World War I*, 162–164.

11. Whaley, *Covert German Rearmament*, 33.

12. Byers, *Flying Man*, 92.

13. Unschlikht, "Unschlikht to Stalin: 'Both We and They Were Interested in Strict Secrecy,'" 31 December 1926, 58.

14. Gorlov, 114.

15. Ibid., 3; Alexander Nekrich, *Pariahs, Partners, Predators: German Soviet Relations, 1922–1941*, ed. and trans. Gregory Freeze (New York: Columbia University Press, 1997), 30.

16. "Protokoll über die Sitzung am 16.10.32 über das To.-Programm" [Minutes of the meeting on October 16, 1932, on the Tomka Program], 16 October 1932, BA-MA, RH 12/4/54, l, 5.

17. "Direktoru Zavoda No. 15, OB khimsnariadov" [To the Director of Factory Number 15, Chemical Shells], 31 January 1932, TsGASO, 2700/10/28, 3, 1.

18. Milton Leitenberg and Raymond Zilinskas, *The Soviet Biological Weapons Program: A History* (Cambridge, MA: Harvard University Press, 2014), 740. Bersol also became a locus of experimentation and production of "prussic blue" (hydrogen cyanide), which was marketed as "Zyklon B" in Germany. It remained a central part of the Soviet chemical weapons program through the end of the Cold War. The legacy of the Bersol plant can be seen today: Ivashchenkovo (known as Chapayevsk since its renaming in 1929), is known as the "Town of Death." The extensive chemical works built during the period of cooperation with the Germans (and expanded after that period ended) have poisoned the groundwater and led to one of the world's highest rates of birth defects. Fridman and Baleev, "Otchet o rabote ispitanie poglotitel'noy sposobnosti protivogazovoy korobki po otnoshenii k sinil'noy kislote" [Report on the Testing of Absorbency of Anti-Gas Shells with Regard to Hydrocyanic Acid], 18 April 1933, TsGASO, 2305/3/9, 9, 12–13; B. Revich, E. Aksel, T. Ushakova, I. Ivanova, N. Zhuchenko, N. Klyuev, B. Brodsky, and Y. Sotskov, "Dioxin Exposure and Public Health in Chapaevsk, Russia," *Chemosphere*, 43 (2001), 951–966.

19. "From Baranov, Chief of VVS RKKA to Voroshilov," RGVA, f. 33987, op. 3, d. 151, l. 36–37, reprinted in Dyakov and Bushuyeva, 140–143; Bill Gunston, *The Osprey Encyclopedia of Russian Aircraft 1875–1995* (London: Osprey, 1995); Wagner, *Hugo Junkers*, 225.

20. "Spravka o Vosdushnogo Flota Rossii," 26 July 1925, 1.

21. "Programma zavodov Aviatresta na 1927–1928," 5 March 1925, RGVA, f. 4, op. 2, d. 457–461, l. 1, 1.

22. "Bericht den Besuch des Flugzeugwerkes in Fili," 17 February 1931, BA-MA, RH/12/1, 56; "Daimler und Benz Erzeugnisse in Russland" [Daimler and Benz Products in Russia], Archivist's Note (1971) citing material from 1926, DBCA, 1–4, 2.

23. "Bericht den Besuch des Flugzeugwerkes in Fili" [Report on a Visit to the Aircraft Factory at Fili], 17 February 1931, RH/12/1, 56, BA-MA. After the Second World War, the facility switched production to astronautic technologies; it is now known as the Khrunichev State Research and Production Space Center.

24. Paul Duffy and Andrei Kandalov, *Tupolev: The Man and His Aircraft* (Hong Kong: SAE Printing, 1996), 12.

25. Ibid., 12. Junkers lost, as Tupolev could claim a different production method and a slight increase in strength of his monoplane wing. Interestingly, Tupolev had gone on a study tour of German aviation plants during the time he was working on his design for the TB-1.

26. Ibid., 37–43, 4. Another 763 TB-3 heavy bombers, 385 R-6s, and 61 ANT-6 would be built at Fili between 1930 and 1938.

CHAPTER 15

1. Zeidler, 189.
2. "The Main Treaty between VIKO [sic] MOSKVA and KA-MOSKVA about tank school organization," 2 October 1926, 167.
3. Mary Habeck, *Storm of Steel: The Development of Armor Doctrine in Germany and the Soviet Union, 1919–1939* (Ithaca, NY: Cornell University Press, 2003), 3.
4. Robert Doughty, *The Seeds of Disaster: The Development of French Army Doctrine, 1919-1939* (Mechanicsburg, PA: Stackpole Books, 1985), 137; Corum, *The Roots of Blitzkrieg*, 99.
5. Murray, "Armored Warfare," 37–41.
6. Corum, *The Roots of Blitzkrieg*, 133; Stone, *Hitler's Army*, 28. Also, "Betrieb: Kampfwagenausbildung im Heere" [Operation: Armored Warfare Training in the Army], 24–25 March 1924, RH12/2/51, 2673, Bundesarchiv-Militärarchiv, Freiburg im Breisgau (BA-MA), 13.
7. R. L. DiNardo, *Germany's Panzer Arm* (Westport, CT: Greenwood Press, 1997), 75–77.
8. Corum, *The Roots of Blitzkrieg*, 133.
9. "Personal-Nachweis, Ernst Volckheim" [Personnel File of Ernst Volckheim], 1945, National Archives at College Park, Maryland (Hereafter NARA), R242, A 3356, 879.
10. "Der Kampfwagen 1–6," October 1924–March 1925, ed. Ernst Volckheim, ZAN 2511/109, New York Public Library Archives (hereafter NYPL); Russell A. Hart, *Guderian: Panzer Pioneer or Myth Maker?* (Washington, DC: Potomac Books, 2006), 23.
11. "Betrieb: Kampfwagenausbildung im Heere" [Operation: Armored Warfare Training in the Army], 24–25 March 1924, 13.
12. Habeck, *Storm of Steel*, 51.
13. Ibid., 49.
14. Mikhail Svirin, *Bronya krepka: Istoria Sovetskogo tanka 1919–1937* [The Armor Is Strong: The History of the Soviet Tank 1919 to 1937] (Moscow: Iauza i Eksmo, 2006), 40–41.
15. Habeck, *Storm of Steel*, 30.
16. Svirin, *Bronya krepka*, 56; Habeck, *Storm of Steel*, 35. This would have a major impact on the development of tank doctrine: from 1923 to 1929, ideas on the deployment of tanks rested on the assumption that tanks were more or less motorized artillery pieces. The language of Soviet doctrine made this exceedingly clear: tanks were organized into *batteries*, and later *field* and *headquarters* units, just as artillery were. Habeck, *Storm of Steel*, 34–35; 107.
17. Mikhail Tukhachevsky, "Preface to J. F. C. Fuller's 'The Reformation of War,'" in Richard Simpkin, *Deep Battle: The Brainchild of Marshal Tukhachevskii* (London: Brassey's Defence Publishers, 1987), 135–153.
18. Larisa Vasilieva, Igor Zheltov, and Galina Chikova, *Pravda o Tanke T-34: Fakti, dokumenti, vospominania i raznie tochki zrenia ob odnom iz chudes XX veka* [The Truth about the T-34: Facts, Documents, Reminiscences, and Different Points of View about One of the Wonders of the 20th Century] (Moscow: Atlantida–XXI Veka Press, 2005), 13.
19. Steven J. Zaloga and James Grandsen, *Soviet Tanks and Combat Vehicles of World War Two* (London: Arms and Armour Press, 1988), 36.
20. Habeck, *Storm of Steel*, 89.
21. Gorlov, 75–89.
22. "The Main Treaty between VIKO [sic] MOSKVA and KA-MOSKVA about Tank School Organization," 2 October 1926, 165.
23. "Spetsialnaia svodka o sostoanyi 'Tekhnicheskikh kursov OSOAVIAKhIM'" [Special Report on the Technical Courses of OSOAVIAKhIM], 15 August 1930, 109–115, 1–8, Archive of the FSB of the Russian Federation in the Republic of Tatarstan, digitized by Bulat Sultanbekov and Sirena Khafizova, reprinted in "Kama na Volge" [Kama on the Volga], *Nauchno-dokumentalnyi zhurnal "Gazirlar avazi"* [Scientific-Documentary Journal *Gasirlar avazi*], 2 (2005).
24. Habeck, *Storm of Steel*, 81.

25. "Spetsialnaia svodka," 15 August 1930, 1–8.
26. Gorlov, 206.
27. Wright, *Gustav Stresemann*, 386–387.
28. Wilhelm Deist, "The Rearmament of the Wehrmacht," in *Germany and the Second World War, Volume I: The Build-Up of German Aggression*, ed. Militaergeschichtliches Forschungsamt (Oxford, UK: Clarendon Press, 1990), 382.
29. Zeidler, 149.
30. Ibid.
31. Ibid.
32. He did, however, make clear that Reichswehr could use sleight of hand to satisfy this requirement.
33. "Donesenie nachal'niku osobogo otdela PP OGPU TR vremennogo nachal'nika otdeleniya osobogo otdela Akhmetova" [Chief of Special Branch, OGPU Report to Department Head, Special Branch Akhmetov], 3 April 1933, f. 109–115, 1, 18, Archive of the FSB of the Russian Federation in the Republic of Tatarstan, digitized by Bulat Sultanbekov and Sirena Khafizova, reprinted in "Kama na Volge" [Kama on the Volga], *Nauchno-dokumentalnyi zhurnal "Gazirlar avazi"* [Scientific-Documentary Journal *Gasirlar avazi*], 2 (2005).
34. This was Conrad Baumann. Klaus Müller, *So lebten und arbeiteten wir 1929 bis 1933 in Kama* [So We Lived and Worked at Kama, 1929–1933] (unpubl., 1972), 11. I am very grateful to Mary Habeck for providing me a copy of this unpublished memoir by a key German participant in the armored facility at Kama, one of the few extant accounts of the life of officers stationed in Russia.
35. "Spetsialnaia svodka," 15 August 1930, 1–8.
36. Ianis Berzin, "Berzin Report: On Cooperation of WPRA and the Reichswehr," 24 December 1928, in *The Red Army and the Wehrmacht: How the Soviets Militarized Germany, 1922–1933, and Paved the Way for Fascism, from the Secret Archives of the Former Soviet Union*, 68–75; "Spravka o Kame" [Information about Kama], 1928, RGVA, f. 33987, op. 3C, d. 329, l. 150, l. 1.
37. "Vereinbarung zwischen der russischen Regierung und den Junkerswerken" [Agreement between the Russian Government and the Junkers Works], 6 February 1922, BA-MA, RH/2, 1130, 1–5; Ianis Berzin, "Berzin Report: On Cooperation of WPRA and the Reichswehr," 24 December 1928, 68–75.
38. "Donesenie nachal'niku osobogo otdela PP OGPU TR," 3 April 1933, 18.
39. Peter Chamberlain and Hilary L. Doyle, *Encyclopedia of German Tanks of World War Two: A Complete Illustrated Directory of German Battle Tanks, Armoured Cars, Self-Propelled Guns and Semi-Tracked Vehicles, 1933–1945* (New York: Arco, 1978), 146.
40. Ibid., 146–147.
41. Thoms, "Bericht über die Feuersbrunst im Wohnhaus Po. der Gruppe Amberg" [Report on the Fire in the House Po. the Group Amberg], 31 March 1927, BA-MA, RH/2/2304/56–58, 1.
42. Ibid., 1–2.
43. Ibid., 2.
44. Ibid.
45. Ibid., 3.
46. "Bericht über die Erkundung des Geländes Or. als Versuchsfeld für die gesamten Veredelungsarbeiten" [Report on the Exploration of the Terrain Near Or[enburg] as a Testing Ground for the Entire Processing Work], 3 May 1927, BA-MA, RH2/2304/139, 1–8. Fishman's deputy was Vladimir Rockinson.
47. Ibid.
48. Gorlov, 207.
49. "Zum dortigen Bericht vom 8.7, Ziffer 4. Betrifft: Veredelung" [For Local Report of 8.7, Paragraph 4. Subject: Refining/Improvement], 7 July 1927, BA-MA, RH/2/2304/222, 1–4.
50. Ibid., 1-4.

51. Gorlov, 224.
52. "Stärke und Ausrüstungsnachweisung Schule Stahr für das Rechnungsjahr 1927/ 1928" [Strength and Equipment Instructions for School Stahr in the Fiscal Year 1927/ 1928], 1927, BA-MA, RH/2/2218/42–57, 44, 57.
53. "Bericht über die Tätigkeit der Schule Stahr in der Zeit vom 1–17 X 1926" [Report on the Activities of School Stahr in the Period October 1–17 1926], 21 October 1926, BA-MA, RH/2/2297/83–86, 1; "Bericht über die Tätigkeit der Schule im August 27," 27 August 1927, BA-MA, RH/2/2302/153–158, 1. (That list included a Heinkel HD-21, a Junkers A-20, an Fokker D-VII, an Albatros L69, 3 Heinkel HD-17s, and 16 Fokker XIIIs.)
54. "Spisok komandno-nachal'stvuiushchego sostava RKKA," June 1938, 40.
55. Ibid.; Habeck, *Storm of Steel*, 83.
56. Habeck, *Storm of Steel*, 83.

CHAPTER 16

1. "Reich Funds Loaned to Finance Movies: Marx Admits to Reichstag Move in 1926 Against Our Films—Irregularities Found," 21 January 1928, *New York Times*, 26.
2. Captain Schuessler, "The Fight of the Navy against Versailles," 1937, NARA, RG 238, R3–6, 24.
3. Ibid.
4. "The Lohmann Affair," CIA Historical Review Program, accessed 1 November 2014, https://www.cia.gov/static/57c8b16fd41a83887a104f85c27b1e32/The-Lohmann-Affair.pdf.
5. Zeidler, 61.
6. Gorlov, 137.
7. "Russo-German Naval Relations, 1926–1941: A Report Based on Captured Files of the German General Staff," 1947, Office of Naval Intelligence, Naval Historical Collection, Naval War College (NWC), Newport, Rhode Island, 7. This report is a compilation of primary sources taken out of Germany at the end of the Second World War by US Naval Intelligence. "The Lohmann Affair." "Russo-German Naval Relations, 1926–1941," 13. German naval documents claimed that their relationship was purely platonic, as Lohmann was married; given the details of their relationship, this seems unlikely.
8. "The Lohmann Affair."
9. Schuessler, "The Fight of the Navy against Versailles," 1937, 25.
10. Ibid., 10–13.
11. Ibid., 35.
12. Ibid., 30–31.
13. Schuessler, "The Fight of the Navy against Versailles," 1937, 30–31.
14. "The Lohmann Affair," CIA.
15. He would die of a heart attack in 1930.
16. Post, *The Civil-Military Fabric of Weimar Foreign Policy*, 141.
17. Wilhelm Groener, "Die Organisation des gesamten Volkes für den Krieg" [The Organization of the Entire People for War], Undated Memorandum from Office of the Minister of Defense, NARA, M137, R25, 1–3.
18. "Russo-German Naval Relations, 1926–1941," 17–18; "Postanovlenie P.B." [Decision of the Politburo], 1928, RGVA, f. 33987, op. 3C, d. 329, l. 146–147, 1–2. Based on the newly established facilities at Tomka and Kama, Admiral Romuald Muklevich, heading the Soviet Navy, suggested the construction of a similar facility dedicated to submarine construction and training somewhere along the Black Sea coast. Two weeks later, Niedermayer sent another memo to Zenker, requesting some sort of reply for his Soviet counterparts. None was forthcoming. Another attempt was made in early 1928: the Soviet Politburo, perhaps at the suggestion of Voroshilov—who talked to Niedermayer on the subject prior to the meeting—agreed to an exchange of naval officers. While a Soviet delegation would visit Kiel and a German delegation Sevastopol in 1930, no concrete arrangements would result. No agreements would be

reached between the two navies prior to 1933. "Russo-German Naval Relations, 1926–1941," 26; Tobias Philbin, *The Lure of Neptune: German-Soviet Naval Collaboration and Ambitions, 1919–1941* (Columbia: University of South Carolina Press, 1994), 20.

19. Carsten, *The Reichswehr and Politics*, 287.
20. Schuessler, "The Fight of the Navy against Versailles," 1937, 39.
21. Ibid., 39.
22. Ibid., 39.
23. Ibid., 38–40.
24. Some limited exchange did happen in 1926: German officers visited the Soviet Union, while Soviet naval personnel visited the German naval construction bureau in the Netherlands, as well as touring Germany's newest vessel in 1926, the cruiser *Emden*. Philbin, *The Lure of Neptune*, 14.
25. The *New York Times* ran its first story about the scandal on January 21. With growing information, eight more stories appeared, on February 6, 24, and 28, and March 8, 13, 14, 25, and 28.
26. "Reich Acts to Veil Film Fund Scandal: Committee Is Named to Investigate and Expunge Phoebus Investments of $7,500,000 Losses to Be Kept Secret; Groener Denounces High Navy Officials and Resignation of Admiral Zenker Is Rumored," *New York Times*, 14 March 1928, 5.
27. Gerhard Koop and Klaus-Peter Schmolke, *Pocket Battleships of the Deutschland Class: Warships of the Kriegsmarine* (Barnsley, UK: Seaforth, 2014), 9–10.
28. Zeidler, 153.
29. Zeidler, 199.
30. Leopold von Sicherer, "Tomka: Ein deutsches Geheim-Unternehmen hinter dem Eisernen Vorhang in den Steppe des Wolga-Gebietes bei Wolsk in den Jahren 1928 mit 1931, Abbau 1933" [Tomka: A German Secret Operation behind the Iron Curtain in the Steppe of the Volga Region near Volsk in the Years 1928 to 1933], 1933, BA-MA, N 625/209, 3.
31. Sicherer, "Tomka," 1933, 3.
32. Zeidler, 199.
33. Henning Sietz, "'Es riecht nach Senf!': Auf Einladung der Sowjets erprobten deutsche Militärs zwischen 1926 und 1933 an der Wolga chemische Kampfstoffe" ["It smells like mustard!": At the invitation of the Soviets German Military between 1926 and 1933 Tested Chemical Warfare Agents on the Volga], *Die Zeit Online*, 22 June 2006, 1–4. http://www.zeit.de/2006/26/A-Tomka.
34. Ibid., 4.
35. Ibid., 5.
36. Ibid.
37. Sicherer, "Tomka," 5.
38. Müller, *So lebten und arbeiteten wir*, 5.
39. Sicherer, "Tomka," 5.
40. Yakov Fishman, "V osnovnom soglasen Uborevichu" [A Summary of the Agreement, to Uborevich], 30 December 1930, RGVA, f. 33988, op. 3, d. 162, l. 141-165, 45, 1–25.
41. Gorlov, 225.
42. Zeidler, 199.
43. Kasino-Ordnung" [Casino Rules], 3 April 1931, BA-MA, RH/12/I/63, 42, 1.
44. Sicherer, "Tomka," 6.
45. Ibid., 7.
46. Ibid., 1–12.
47. Erickson, *The Soviet High Command*, 263.
48. Carsten, *The Reichswehr and Politics*, 220, quoted in Zeidler, 198.
49. Erickson, *The Soviet High Command*, 265.
50. Speidel, "Reichswehr und Rote Armee," 26, 28.
51. Homze, *Arming the Luftwaffe*, 20.
52. Ibid., 20–21; Zeidler, 175.

53. "Austrüstung für die Reise nach Lip." [Equipment for the Journey to Lipetsk], 2 May 1928, BA-MA, RH/8/V/3623, 11, 1.
54. Speidel, "Reichswehr und Rote Armee," 29.
55. "Entwurf für die Aubildung 1927" [Draft Plan for Training 1927], 11 June 1927, BA-MA, RH/2/2302/1–3, 3.
56. "Bericht über die Ausbildungstätigkeit der Station im Sommer 1931" [Report over the Training Program for the Station in the Summer of 1931], 8 November 1931, BA-MA, RH12/I/60, 2–17, 3.
57. Ibid., 5.
58. Ibid.
59. Ibid., 4.
60. "Ergebnis der Besprechung über das Programm der Schule Lip 1925–1926" [Results of the Meeting Regarding the Program of the School at Lipetsk, 1925–1926], 14 November 1926, 6.
61. Homze, *Arming the Luftwaffe*, 20.
62. "Fl. Bericht No. 324," [Flight Report Number 324], 28 April 1931, BA-MA, RH12/I/57, 278, 1; "Vergütungssätze der z. Zt. vorhandenen" [Current Salary Roster], 1 April 1932, BA-MA, RH12/1/60, 44–49, 45. The actual number is likely higher.

CHAPTER 17
1. Gorlov, 203–265.
2. Corum, *The Roots of Blitzkrieg*, 110–113. For more detail, see Herbert Jäger, *German Artillery of World War One* (Ramsbury, Marlborough, Wiltshire: Crowood Press, 2001).
3. Willi Esser, *Dokumentation über die Entwicklung und Erprobung der ersten Panzerkampfwagen der Reichswehr* [Documentation about the Development and Testing of the First Reichswehr Tanks] (München: Krauss Maffei AG, 1979), 7. I am indebted to Mary Habeck for providing me with a copy of this excellent technical monograph.
4. "Bericht über die Entwicklung von Panzerfahrzeugen bei der Fried. Krupp AG" [Report on the Development of Tanks by Friedrich Krupp], 7 August 1945, KA-E, WA 40 B.1354, 2319.
5. Esser, *Dokumentation*, 7.
6. Erich Woelfert, "Fragebogen, Erich Woelfert, Allied War Crimes Tribunal" [Questionnaire], 23 May 1947, KA-E, WA40B/1350, 897. The Technische Hochschule is now known as the Technical University of Berlin. Its illustrious alumni and former faculty include Wernher von Braun and Gustav Hertz.
7. His superior, Georg Hagelloch, had deep ties to the Reichswehr. Not only had Hagelloch served in the military before and during World War I, but he had also been the assistant head of Krupp's tank development program during World War I.
8. Esser, *Dokumentation*, 6.
9. Ibid., 2.
10. "Verhandlungsprotokoll," Johann Hoffmann, Allied War Crimes Tribunal [Transcript of Proceedings], Johann Hoffmann, 7.
11. "Reichswehrministerium Vorgang: Gr. 2" [Reichswehr Ministry, Development of the Grosstraktor 2], 14 May 1935, KA-E, WA 40/252, 88–91.
12. Ibid.
13. Esser, *Dokumentation*, 38.
14. "Betrifft: L.Tr." [Subject: the Leicht Traktor], 27 May 1935, KA-E, WA 40/252, 92–97.
15. "Die Besprechung mit Wa. Prw. 6 am 26.5.28 in Essen" [Conversation with Wa. Prw. 6 in Essen], 26 May 1928, KA-E, WA 40/255, 172.
16. Erich Woelfert, "Fragebogen, Erich Woelfert, Allied War Crimes Tribunal" [Questionnaire], 23 May 1947, KA-E, 897.
17. "Betrifft: L.Tr.," 27 May 1935, 1–5.
18. Nekrich, *Pariahs, Partners, Predators*, 60.

19. Ianis Berzin, "Dokladivaiu 'Druz'yami' predstavleni po Kazanskoi i Lipetskoi Stantsyam opisi" [Reporting: Kazan and Lipetsk Station Inventories Presented by "Friends"], 29 July 1933, Y-183 (Y-RAP 246), 1–18.
20. Müller, *So lebten und arbeiteten wir*, 11.
21. Ibid., 11.
22. Ibid., 11–12.
23. Ibid., 11.
24. Ibid., 11, 26.
25. Ibid., 11.
26. Ibid.
27. Ibid.
28. Ibid.
29. Müller, *So lebten und arbeiteten wir*, 11; Samuel W. Mitcham Jr., *The Panzer Legions: A Guide to the German Army Tank Divisions of World War II and Their Commanders* (Westport, CT: Greenwood Publishing Group, 2001), 8.
30. "Lipetsk Air Base, Image Collection," 1930–1931, Government Archive of Lipetsk Oblast (hereafter GALO), f. 2176, op. 1, d. 1, 10.
31. Müller, *So lebten und arbeiteten wir*, 33.
32. Ibid, 30.
33. Ibid., 11.
34. The main office of Moscow Central was near to the British embassy, less than six blocks from the Kremlin. It seems the Germans reveled operating so nearly under the noses of their British opponents. Müller noted that the locations of the German offices may have imperiled the secrecy of the mission, however. Ernst Köstring claims in his memoirs that the British and Polish military attachés were well aware of their presence. Köstring, *General Ernst Köstring*, 49.
35. Müller, *So lebten und arbeiteten wir*, 11.
36. Number 7 was equipped with a number of guest rooms, apparently, as Müller and Köppen both noted sleeping there.
37. Müller, *So lebten und arbeiteten wir*, 7.
38. "15 sego iunia ya predstavitelya nemskoi gruppi Lip." [On the 15th of June I took a Group of Russian Representatives to Lipetsk], 17 June 1925, 1. The secret police were called the OGPU at the time of this memorandum; the title was changed to NKVD in 1940.
39. Müller, *So lebten und arbeiteten wir*, 11.
40. Müller identified the barracks as formerly called the Astrakhanski Artillery Barracks, but Soviet records refer to the facility as Kargopol Cavalry Barracks.
41. "Spetsialnaia svodka," 15 August 1930, 1–8.
42. Müller, *So lebten und arbeiteten wir*, 11-13.
43. Ibid.
44. "Spetsialnaia svodka," 15 August 1930, 1–8.
45. Müller, *So lebten und arbeiteten wir*, 13.
46. Willi Esser, *Dokumentation über die Entwicklung und Erprobung der ersten Panzerkampfwagen der Reichswehr* [Documentation about the Development and Testing of the First Reichswehr Tanks] (München: Krauss Maffei AG, 1979), 8–9.
47. Müller, *So lebten und arbeiteten wir*, 11.
48. Gorlov, 203–265.
49. "Verhandlungsprotokoll, Johann Hoffmann, Allied War Crimes Tribunal" [Transcript of Proceedings], 15 December 1947, KA-E, WA 40/6, 452, 4. He was stationed there in 1932 and 1933.
50. Müller, *So lebten und arbeiteten wir*, 6.
51. "Verhandlungsprotokoll, Johann Hoffmann, Allied War Crimes Tribunal" [Transcript of Proceedings], December 1947, 6.
52. *Armored Bears, Volume I: The German 3rd Division in World War II* (Mechanicsburg, PA: Stackpole, 2012), 1 (fn 9).

53. Ianis Berzin, "Tov. Tukhachevskomy, predstavlaiu uchebnii otchet no. 2 nach-ka tankovikh kursov v Kazani ob itogakh sovmestnoi c 'druzyami' uchebi za letnii period" [To Comrade Tukhachevsky, Presenting Training Report Number 2 by the Head of the Tank Study Courses at Kazan over the Summer Period with "Friends"], 13 September 1931, RGVA, f. 3988, op. 3, d. 205, l. 237 (Y-RAP 213), 8.

54. Müller, *So lebten und arbeiteten wir*, 34.

55. Ibid., 5.

56. "Rücksprache mit Herrn Ingenieur Franz Böminghaus" [Conversation with Engineer Franz Böminghaus], 25 October 1945, KA-E, WA 40 B/1350, 0904.

57. Müller, *So lebten und arbeiteten wir*, 10.

58. He wrote this in 1931, when he attended the course. Berzin, "Tov. Tukhachevskomy," 13 September 1931, 2; for Yeroshchenko's background, Erickson, *The Soviet High Command*, 268.

59. Berzin, "Tov. Tukhachevskomy," 13 September 1931, 3.

60. Ibid., 1–2.

61. Zaloga and Grandsen, *Soviet Tanks and Combat Vehicles*, 43.

62. Their ideas were inspired in part by contemporary science fiction and simultaneous artistic movements. For more on Tukhachevsky's strategic thought—and the idea of Tukhachevsky's cohort as "military futurists," see Ian Ona Johnson, "Technology's Cutting Edge: Futurism and Research in the Red Army, 1917–1937," *Technology and Culture*, 59:3 (July 2018), 689–718.

63. Tukhachevsky, "New Questions of War," 136. In that context, Tukhachevsky would write that "future forms of battle need not necessarily bear the stamp of past forms, even if they are logical derivatives of these." He believed the French, whose military thinking was "simply held together by the past, for the most part just carrying an intensively crystallized accumulation of experience to a logical conclusion," would be caught completely unprepared by future forms of warfare. Tukhachevsky, "Preface to J. F. C. Fuller's *The Reformation of War*," 133. Tukhachevsky served as the general editor for this volume, the first of Fuller's works to be translated into Russian, which appeared in 1931. This view of future conflict echoed J. F. C. Fuller, who had written in the volume Tukhachevsky had edited, "Today's and tomorrow's wars will never be like yesterday's."

64. Ziemke, *The Red Army, 1918–1941*, 160.

65. Ibid., 161.

66. Vladimir Triandafillov, "Postanovlenie Revolutsionnogo Voennogo Soveta Souza SSR" [Decree of the Revolutionary Military Council of the USSR], 18 July 1929, RGVA, f. 4, op. 2, d. 504, l. 3, 1. He actually listed four categories, but the first two were overlapping in function. The Red Army schema that would emerge would be called the "three-echelon system" as a result.

67. Ibid., 1–2. He suggested a weight of 3 tons for the tankette, 7 tons for the light tank, 16 tons for the medium tank, and 60–80 tons for the heavy tank.

68. Triandafillov, "Postanovlenie Revolutsionnogo Voennogo Soveta Souza SSR" [Decree of the Revolutionary Military Council of the USSR], 18 July 1929, 15–16.

69. Zeidler, 197.

70. Vladimir Triandafillov, "Predmet: Postanovleniye Revolyutsionoogo Voennogo Soveta Soyuza SSR" [Subject: Resolution of the RVS USSR], 18 June 1929, 1–3; Zeidler, 197; Habeck, *Storm of Steel*, 155. Specifically, Triandafillov's proposed "three-echelon system" grouped fast tanks of reasonably heavy armor together as *Dal'nii poderzhok pechoti* [Distant Infantry Support, DPP]; they would lead the assault on enemy positions, seeking to eliminate enemy tanks and machine gun positions. The next wave, which would enter combat alongside infantry, were designated *Neposredstvennii poderzhok pechoti* [Direct Infantry Support, NPP]; heavier, slower tanks, they would lead infantry into combat against fortified positions. The most important and tactically controversial group were the fast, light tank squadrons, referred to as *Gruppa dal'nego deistvia* [Long Range Action Group, GDD or DD]. These

would break through enemy lines with artillery support before the general infantry assault, attacking headquarters, communications hubs, and artillery positions before encircling enemy units.

71. Berzin, "Tov. Tukhachevskomy," 13 September 1931, 11.
72. Ibid., 2.
73. Habeck, *Storm of Steel*, 51.
74. Berzin, "Tov. Tukhachevskomy," 13 September 1931, 5.
75. Ibid., 6.
76. Varfolomeyev, "Strategy in an Academic Formulation," 39.
77. Müller, *So lebten und arbeiteten wir*, 13.
78. "Verhandlungsprotokoll, Johann Hoffmann, Allied War Crimes Tribunal" [Transcript of Proceedings], December 1947, 7; "Bericht über die Entwicklung von Panzerfahrzeugen bei der Fried. Krupp AG" [Report on the Development of Tanks by Friedrich Krupp], 7 August 1945, 1; Esser, *Dokumentation*, 8–9.
79. The armored personnel carriers were designed by the Daimler-Benz, C. D. Magirus, and Büssing corporations. Each had eight to ten wheels, and was intended to carry a large, domed armored platform to protect the troops inside. German instructors and mechanics tested these extensively at Kama between 1929 and 1930, but funding shortages meant that German officers directed their efforts toward tank development rather than armored cars. The Reichswehr decided to drop the designs, though the SdKfz 231, a six-wheeled personnel carrier that Germany mass-produced during the war, was based on these three experimental designs.
80. This was the Rader-Raupen Kampfwagen M-28, built by the German-Swedish consortium Landsverk. German engineer Otto Merker drew up its initial designs at Reichswehr request for a treaded tank whose treads could be removed for fast road travel. Landsverk produced six prototypes by 1930, one of which the Reichswehr shipped to Kama for testing. The Germans did not like the model, and ended up not pursuing the multi-use chassis Merker had developed. Merker would modify the design for international sale a few years later (before returning to Germany to work in German armament production), leading to the L-60. This light tank would end up being used by Hungary on the Eastern Front, with surviving units sold globally. The last to be used in combat would actually be deployed against US Marines during the Dominican Civil War in 1965. B. T. White, *German Tanks and ArmoAured Vehicles, 1914–1945* (London: Ian Allan, 1971), 30–32; for the Dominican saga, see Sebastien Roblin, "In 1965, US and Dominican Tanks Fought Brief, Violent Skirmishes," *War Is Boring*, https://tinyurl.com/y467obtn.
81. "Verhandlungsprotokoll, Johann Hoffmann, Allied War Crimes Tribunal" [Transcript of Proceedings], December 1947, 15 December 1947, KA-E, WA 40/6, 452, 4.
82. Williamson Murray, "Armored Warfare: The British, French and German Experiences," in *Military Innovation in the Interwar Period*, ed. Williamson Murray and Alan Millet (Cambridge, UK: Cambridge University Press, 1996), 23–26.
83. See Bulat Sultanbekov, "Kama na Volge" [Kama on the Volga], *Nauchno-dokumentalnyi zhurnal "Gazirlar avazi"* [Scientific-Documentary Journal *Gasirlar avazi*], Issue 2, 2005, 3 January 2012.
84. Müller, *So lebten und arbeiteten wir*, 29.
85. Ibid. The Söda machine gun, later known as the MG S2-100. Nicknamed for the design bureau where it was conceived—Rheinmetall's Sömmerda facility—the Söda machine gun was one of the first post–First World War machine gun designs drawn up by German military industry. As production within Germany was forbidden under the Treaty of Versailles, it was mass-produced in the town of Solothurn across the Swiss border. For more, see Peter Chamberlain and Terry Gander, *Weapons of the Third Reich: An Encyclopedic Survey of All Small Arms, Artillery and Special Weapons of the German Land Forces 1939–1945* (New York: Doubleday, 1979).
86. Müller, *So lebten und arbeiteten wir*, 29.
87. Gorlov, 220.

88. Sultanbekov, "'Kama' na Volge" [Kama on the Volga], 3 January 2012; "Personnel File of Josef Harpe," 1945, NARA, R242, A 3356, 276.

89. Esser, *Dokumentation*, 58.

90. Müller, *So lebten und arbeiteten wir*, 18.

91. He made the trip in 1932. Ferry Porsche, *We at Porsche: The Autobiography of Dr.Ing. H. C. Ferry Porsche* (New York: Doubleday, 1976), 41–61. One of his first contracts would involve traveling to Moscow to assist the Soviet government.

92. "Zapis priema T. Voroshilovim Generala Gammersteina i Polkovnika Kolental" [Record of a Reception Hosted by Comrade Voroshilov for General Hammerstein and Colonel Kolental], 5 September 1929, RGVA, f. 33987, op. 3c, d. 375, l. 1, 1.

CHAPTER 18

1. Fitzpatrick, *On Stalin's Team*, 318–331.

2. Kotkin, *Stalin: Waiting for Hitler*, 17.

3. Ibid., 21.

4. David R. Stone, *Hammer and Rifle: The Militarization of the Soviet Union, 1926–1933* (Lawrence: University Press of Kansas, 2000), 128.

5. Stone, *Hammer and Rifle*, 129

6. Stephen Kotkin, *Stalin, Volume II: Waiting for Hitler, 1929–1941* (New York: Penguin, 2017), 23.

7. This was arranged through the Main Concession Bureau described earlier. Nekrich, *Pariahs, Partners, Predators*, 24.

8. Ibid.

9. Tukhachevsky, "New Questions of War," 136. Not surprisingly, these areas (plus artillery) were the major areas of military research, development, and acquisition from 1929 onward.

10. Tukhachevsky, "New Questions of War," 137–139. He believed of the three, aviation was probably the most vital, writing that "the strongest country in a future war will be the one that has the most potent civil aviation and aircraft industries."

11. Ziemke, *The Red Army, 1918–1941*, 166.

12. Stone, *Hammer and Rifle*, 125.

13. Ibid., 124.

14. Ibid., 212.

15. Interestingly, the Soviets, in published documents, underestimated their real military budget by a factor of three, presumably to hide the tremendous costs of militarization. Stone, *Hammer and Rifle*, 217.

16. Wright, *Gustav Stresemann*, 440–442, 490–491.

17. Tooze, *Wages of Destruction*, 21, 33, 48.

18. Ibid., 48.

19. Ibid., 18-22.

20. Karl Prümm, *Die Literatur des soldatischen Nationalismus der 20er Jahre (1918–1933): Gruppenideologie und Epochenproblematik* (Kronberg, Taunus: Scriptor Verlag, 1974), 70, quoted in Wette, "Ideology, Propaganda, and Internal Politics as preconditions of the War Policy of the Third Reich," 81.

21. Citino, *The Path to Blitzkrieg*, 157.

22. Carsten, *The Reichswehr and Politics*, 309.

23. Ibid., 317; Wheeler-Bennett, *The Nemesis of Power*, 212–215.

24. Wheeler-Bennett, *The Nemesis of Power*, 219.

25. Carsten, *The Reichswehr and Politics*, 312

26. Ibid., 312–313.

27. Ibid., 320.

28. Ibid., 301.

29. Ibid., 302–303.

30. Kotkin, *Stalin: Waiting for Hitler*, 15–16.

31. See Lynne Viola, *Peasant Rebels under Stalin: Collectivization and the Culture of Peasant Resistance* (Oxford, UK: Oxford University Press, 1999); *The War Against the Peasantry*, ed. Lynne Viola, V. P. Danilov, N. A. Ivnitskii, and Denis Kozlov (New Haven, NJ: Yale University Press, 2005); Sheila Fitzpatrick, *Stalin's Peasants: Resistance and Survival in the Russian Village after Collectivization* (Oxford, UK: Oxford University Press, 1994); and *Anne Applebaum, Red Famine: Stalin's War on Ukraine* (New York: Penguin, 2017) for the best—and very disparate—treatments of the reaction to Stalin's pronouncement.

32. Joseph Stalin, "A Year of Great Change: On the Occasion of the Twelfth Anniversary of the October Revolution," in *Works, Volume 12, April 1929–June 1930* (Moscow: Foreign Languages Publishing House, 1954), 1.

33. David L. Hoffmann, *Peasant Metropolis: Social Identities in Moscow, 1929–1941* (Ithaca, NY: Cornell University Press, 1994), 33.

34. Ibid., 29.

35. Viola, *Peasant Rebels under Stalin*, 118.

36. Ibid., 183, 238.

37. Ronald Grigor Sun, *The Soviet Experiment: Russia, the USSR, and the Successor States* (Oxford, UK: Oxford University Press, 1998), 224.

38. Ibid., 226.

39. For the best treatment of this subject, see Reese, *Stalin's Reluctant Soldiers*, and Stone, *Hammer and Rifle*.

40. Reese, *Stalin's Reluctant Soldiers*, 86–88.

41. Ibid., 91.

42. Stone, *Hammer and Rifle*, 213.

43. Ibid., 166.

44. Ibid., 163.

45. Zaloga and Grandsen, *Soviet Tanks and Combat Vehicles*, 42–44.

46. "Archivists Note: Geschaftsbeziehungen der M.A.N. zu Russland" [Business of M.A.N. in Russia], 15 February 1979, Maschinenfabrik Augsburg-Nürnberg Archives (hereafter MAN), M. 1, 1; Zusammenstellung über erhaltene Aufträge aus Russland seit 1918" [Compilation of Orders Received from Russia since 1918], 23 February 1931, MAN, M. 3, 1. See also Norman Polmar and Jurrien Noot, *Submarines of the Russian and Soviet Navies, 1718–1990* (Annapolis, MD: Naval Institute Press, 1991).

47. "Beziehungen der Daimler-Benz AG zu der UdSSR, 1917–1941" [Relations between Daimler-Benz AG and the USSR, 1917-1941], compiled June 3, 1970, DBCA, Box 79–82, 1–2.

48. I. Khalepsky, "Pismo, Tov. Voroshilovy" [Letter to Comrade Voroshilov], 8 January 1930, RGVA, f. 33987, op. 3c, d. 350, l. 17, 103; "An die Staatliche Vereinigung für Geschützbau, Waffen und Maschinengewehre" [On the State Association for Artillery Production, Weapons, and Machine Guns], 1930, RH8/V/3531, 2–28.

49. "Postanovlenie No. 1148: Presidium VSNKh SSSR ot 3 iulya, 1930 g." [Resolution of the Supreme Economic Council of the Soviet Union from July 3, 1930], 3 July 1930, GARF, 374/8/3384, 10, 1.

50. "Zatrati na tekhpomoshch' v 1930–1931 g." [The Costs of Technical Assistance in 1930–1931], 9 September 1930, RGVA, f. 4, op. 1, d. 1462, 1.

51. "Importnii plan NKVMora na 1930/1931" [Importation Plan of the Commissariat of Defense], 9 September 1930, RGVA, f. 4, op. 1, d. 1462, l. 1–3.

52. R. W. Davies, "Soviet Military Expenditure and the Armaments Industry, 1929–33: A Reconsideration," *Europe-Asia Studies*, 45:4 (1993), 584.

53. Mark Harrison, *Soviet Planning in Peace and War, 1938–1945* (Cambridge, UK: Cambridge University Press, 2002), 149.

CHAPTER 19

1. "Verhandlungsprotokoll, Johann Hoffmann, Allied War Crimes Tribunal" [Transcript of Proceedings], December 1947, 8.

2. Ibid., 4–5; Zeidler, Anlage 12, 353. See also Nehring, *Die Geschichte der Deutschen Panzerwaffe, 1916-1945*, Appendix I, 9-13.
3. Müller, *So lebten und arbeiteten wir*, 22.
4. Ibid.
5. "Verhandlungsprotokoll, Johann Hoffmann, Allied War Crimes Tribunal" [Transcript of Proceedings], December 1947, 4–5.
6. "Aktenvermerk über die Besprechung bei der Fa. Krupp, Mai 22, 1931" [File Memo on the Meeting at Krupp], 2 June 1931 RH8/I/2674 (BA-MA), 134.
7. "Bericht über die Entwicklung von Panzerfahrzeugen bei der Fried. Krupp" [Report on the Development of Tanks by Friedrich Krupp AG], 7 August 1945, 1.
8. "Reichswehrministerium Vorgang: Gr. 2" [Reichswehr Ministry, Development of the Grosstraktor 2], 14 May 1935, 88–91.
9. Ibid.
10. Homze, *Arming the Luftwaffe*, 27.
11. These figures are for the start of the 1931 season, so the aircraft that were still functioning for training purposes at the end of the 1930 year.
12. "Bericht über die Ausbildungstätigkeit der Station im Sommer 1931" [Report over the Training Program for the Station in the Summer of 1931], 8 November 1931, 2.
13. "Anlagen 1–4, Fl. Bericht Nr. 269 [Annex 1–4 for Flight Report 269], 10 April 1930, BA-MA, RH 12/I/57, 23, 1.
14. "Besprechungspunkte mit General v. Mittelberger" [Conversation with General von Mittelberger], 18 November 1930, BA-MA, RH12/1/57, 157, 1.
15. "Fl. Bericht Nr. 285" [Flight Report Number 285], 31 July 1930, BA-MA, RH 12/I/57, 77, 2.
16. "Stellungnahme zu den Ru. Vorschlägen," 18 January 1932, 3.
17. "Protokoll der Besprechung zwischen Herrn Alksnis und Herrn Molt am 26.3.1932 in Mo." [Minutes of a Meeting between Herr Alksnis and Herr Molt on March 26, 1932 in Moscow], 26 March 1932, BA-MA, RH12/I/60, 63-71, 7; Alan Beyerchen, "From Radio to Radar: Interwar Military Adaptation to Technological Change in Germany, the United Kingdom and the United States," in *Military Innovation in the Interwar Period*, eds. Williamson Murray and Allan Millett (Cambridge, UK: Cambridge University Press, 1996), 276.
18. "Besprechung zwischen F. und M in L." [Conversation between F[elmy] and M[olt] in L[ipetsk]], 17 November 1930, BA-MA, RH12/I/57, 113, 1; "Fl. Bericht Nr. 281" [Flight Report Number 281], 3 July 1930, BA-MA, RH12/I/57, 59, 1. The SD 1 was something of a disaster, as it turned out—slow and not very aerodynamic—and it was canceled. It did not serve as the basis for the next line of aircraft.
19. The only other manufacturer then in existence that did not participate in testing at Lipetsk was Henschel. Henschel's aircraft production during the Second World War was mostly other corporations' designs, produced under license agreement. J. R. Smith and Antony L. Kay, *German Aircraft of the Second World War* (London: Putnam, 1972), 11–12.
20. Homze, *Arming the Luftwaffe*, 26.
21. Wagner, *Hugo Junkers*, 252. Technically, the aircraft was manufactured elsewhere, and then assembled, modified, and had its weapons systems added at Fili, much like the previous German designs.
22. Mike Guardia, *Junkers Ju 87 STUKA* (Oxford, UK: Osprey, 2014), 7.
23. Smith and Kay, *German Aircraft*, 155.
24. The Soviets recorded only two business representatives at Lipetsk in 1930. They were businessman and future Luftwaffe General Gottfried Reidenbach and pilot-engineer Ernst Bormann. Both were former Imperial German Air Service officers and future Luftwaffe generals. Both men served in technical capacities in the Luftwaffe during the war. "O buivshem 4-m Nemetskom Aviaotriade, Lipetskoi Gorodskii Otdel MGB Voronezhskoi Oblasti" [Report on the Former 4th German Squadron, Lipetsk City

Department of the MGB in the Voronezh Region], compiled on 18 January 1950, P-2176, 1, 1, GALO, 7.

25. Biographical information from Norman Franks and Greg Van Wyngarden, *Fokker D VII Aces of World War 1, Part 2* (Oxford, UK: Osprey, 2004), 34.

26. "O buivshem 4-m Nemetskom Aviaotriade," 18 January 1950, 14. The author also added the Schoenebeck was a fascist and "very hostile to Soviet power." He would rise to the rank of major general in the Luftwaffe.

27. Sobelev and Khazanov, *Nemetskii sled*, 116.

28. Speidel, "Reichswehr und Rote Armee," 38.

29. Ianis Berzin, "Kept in Secrecy: Information about Lipetsk," January 1929, RGVA, f. 33987, op. 3, d. 295, l. 81, 1, reprinted in Dyakov and Bushuyeva, 157.

30. Sobelev and Khazanov, *Nemetskii Sled*, 118.

31. "Neue Kriegsflugzeuge in der SSSR" [New Warplanes in the SSSR], 16 June 1930, RH12/I/56, 331, 1.

32. Ibid., 1.

33. Ibid., 3.

34. The first example of a major aviation purchase dates to 1923, when the Soviet Air Force bought 25 of Junkers advanced F-13 monoplanes. Lutz Budrass, *Flugzeugindustrie und Luftrüstung in Deutschland 1918–1945* [Aircraft Industry and Air Armaments in Germany, 1918–1945] (Düsseldorf: Droste, 1996), 182.

35. Sobelev and Khazanov, *Nemetskii sled*, 90–93.

36. Speidel, "Reichswehr und Rote Armee," 38.

37. "Notizen aus dem Protokoll der Besprechung vom 22.11.31 zwischen Alksnis, Feodorof, Hoffmeister und Niedermayer" [Notes from the Transcript of the Conversation on November 22, 1931, between Alksnis, Feodorof, Hoffmeister, and Niedermayer], 22 November 1931, BA-MA, RH12/I/61, 2, 2.

38. "Aktenvermerk" [Memo], 9 January 1932, RH 12/I/60, 18, BA-MA, 19.

39. Ibid., 18.

40. Speidel, "Reichswehr und Rote Armee," 39.

41. "Aktenvermerk" [Memo], 9 January 1932, 19.

42. "Stellungnahme zu den Ru. Vorschlägen," 18 January 1932, 1.

43. Otto von Stülpnagel, "Bericht über meine Reise nach Russland von 16.IX. bis 13.X.1930," 12 November 1930, BA-MA, RH 1/V, 14, 5, quoted in Habeck, *Storm of Steel*, 136.

44. Interestingly, the Soviets agreed about the larger versus smaller vehicles; Innokenty Khalepsky, then heading the Directorate of Motorization and Mechanization, suggested the Germans and Soviets jointly develop a next-generation heavy tank. No agreement was forthcoming on that subject, however. Had they agreed, the Germans might have gained an inkling of the Soviet commitment to larger vehicles—like the T-34 and KV-2—that would prove superior on the battlefields of the Eastern Front.

45. Habeck, *Storm of Steel*, 144.

46. Ibid., 136.

47. Ernst Volckheim, "Nachrichtenmittel bei der Kampfwagentruppe" [Communications Media in the Tank Force], *Der Kampfwagen*, no. 6 (November 1924): 11-13.

48. Guderian, *Panzer Leader*, 27, 31, and Appendix I, 477. From 1912 to 1917, Guderian was assigned to signals roles. In this capacity, he worked with telegraph and radio technology.

49. Beyerchen, "From Radio to Radar," 268.

50. Kenneth Macksey, *The Tank Pioneers* (London: Jane's, 1981), 119.

51. To solve the problem in the air, the Reichswehr used Lufthansa aggressively in the interwar period to test military radios and train new pilots.

52. On the development of the radio, see Hugh G. J. Aitken, "De Forest and the Audion," in *The Continuous Wave: Technology and American Radio, 1900–1932* (Princeton, NJ: Princeton University Press, 1985), 162–249.

53. Richard J. Thompson, *Crystal Clear: The Struggle for Reliable Communications Technology in World War Two* (New York: Wiley: 2011), 10.
54. Ibid., 24. The experience of the First World War made clear this challenge. Until 1917, most World War One aircraft equipped with transmission capability needed to trail a radio aerial on a wire 400 feet behind the aircraft in order to effectively communicate with ground radio stations. Russell W. Burns, *Communications: An International History of the Formative Years* (London: Institution of Engineering and Technology, 2004), 406–417.
55. Müller, *So lebten und arbeiteten wir*, 8.
56. Ibid.; Guderian, *Panzer Leader*, 27.

CHAPTER 20

1. Steiner, *The Lights That Failed*, 642.
2. Heiber, *The Weimar Republic*, 177–178.
3. Steiner, *The Lights That Failed*, 642.
4. "Pri sem prilagaetsya doklad o rezultakh raboti Tomka, priedannii nemtsami soglasno prosbi T. Uborevicha" [Attached Herewith a Progress Report on Tomka, Affiliated Germans as Requested T. Uborevicha]), 15 March 1931, RGVA, f. 33888, op. 3, d. 205, l. 375 (Y-RAP 194), 1. Fishman, "V osnovnom soglasen, Uborevichu" [A Summary of the Agreement, to Uborevich], 30 December 1930, 13–14.
5. Fishman, "V osnovnom soglasen," 14.
6. Oskar von Niedermayer, "Perevod pisem g. Nidermayer" [Translation of a letter from Mr. Niedermayer], 7 February 1931, RGVA, f. 33988, op. 3, d. 162, l. 34.
7. In France and Russia, it was Yperite, for the place it had first been used. In Great Britain, it went by mustard gas.
8. Harris and Paxman, *A Higher Form of Killing*, 24.
9. Ibid., 26.
10. Voelcker, "Tätigkeitsbericht über die Zeit vom 18.5.–25.5.1931" [Activity Report on the Period from May 18 to May 25, 1931], 25 May 1931, BA-MA, RH/12/4/55, 251, 1. In the year to come, their work would include building a new barracks for test animals, a new electrical generator building, expanding the food cellar, and retrofitting of the fire-fighting water pump.
11. "9. Tätigkeitsbericht über die Zeit von 29.6 bis 5.7.31" [9. Activity Report on the Period from June 29 to July 5, 1931], 6 July 1931, BA-MA, RH12/4/55, 196, 1–5.
12. Ibid.
13. Ibid.
14. Ibid.
15. "24. Tätigkeitsbericht über die Zeit von 10.–16.10.31" [24th Activity Report of the Period from October 10 to 16, 1931], 17 October 1931, BA-MA, RH12/4/55, 178, 1–6.
16. "Nachrichten über r. Anschauungen, Versuche in chemischer Kriegsführung und Zusammenarbeiten mit uns" [News about Ideas, Research in Chemical Warfare, and Cooperation with Us], 5 September 1931, 5 September 1931, RH12/4/55, 210, BA-MA, 1–4.
17. Ibid., 3.
18. Grundherr, "Bericht Erdreferat To. 1931" [Report: Soil Unit To[msk] 1931], 17 August 1931, BA-MA, RH/12/4/55/221–223, 1–13, 10.
19. Ibid.
20. Müller, *So lebten und arbeiteten wir*, 6.
21. Walter J. Spielberger, *Die Motorisierung der deutschen Reichswehr 1920–1935* [The Motorization of the German Reichswehr] (Stuttgart: Motorbuch, 1995), 282. This was in general reference to tanks with crews of six or more.
22. Ibid., 318.
23. Ibid., 282; Esser, *Dokumentation*, 24.
24. While innovative, it was not entirely new: it had first appeared on the Char 2C, a heavy French tank first produced in 1921. In 1924, German officers got to see this vehicle,

as a short write-up on its design appeared in Ernst Volckheim's *Der Kampfwagen* in its January 1925 issue "Der neue französische Kampfwagen 'Type 2 c'," in *Der Kampfwagen*, Nr. 4 (January 1925), 31. The French failed to follow up on the design, however, only building a handful of prototypes.

25. Steven J. Zaloga, *Panzer IV vs. Char B1 bis: France 1940* (Oxford, UK: Osprey, 2011), 24.
26. Ibid.
27. Interestingly, Soviet designs retained the two-man turret where a commander had to load as well as lead. This remained the case even on the famed T-34. Vasilieva, Zheltov, Chikova, *Pravda o Tanke T-34*, 114–133.
28. Müller, *So lebten und arbeiteten wir*, 16.
29. Ibid., 16.
30. Ibid., 24.
31. Esser, *Dokumentation*, 3.
32. Müller, *So lebten und arbeiteten wir*, 24.
33. See Aitken, "De Forest and the Audion."
34. Gryaznov, "O rabote kursov TEKO v 1932 godu" [About the Course of Work at TEKO in 1932], 14 March 1932, RGVA, f. 33987, op. 3, d. 375, l. 113 (Y-RAP 230), 2.
35. Berzin, "Predstavliau uchebnyi otchet," 29 July 1933, 1–18.
36. Ibid.
37. Ibid. Highlighting how much effort the Germans invested in radio research at Kama, when the facility closed several years later, the list of items left by the Germans included more than 120 radio receivers and transmitters, small mobile "satchel" receivers, and five experimental Lorenz transmitters and receivers.
38. Jeffrey A. Gunsburg, "The Battle of the Belgian Plain, 12–14 May 1940: The First Great Tank Battle," *Journal of Military History*, 56:2 (Apr., 1992), 207–244; Robert Forczyk, *Tank Warfare on the Eastern Front: Schwerpunkt* (Barnsley: Pen and Sword, 2013), 36–37; Chamberlain and Doyle, *Encyclopedia of German Tanks*, 254.

CHAPTER 21

1. Davies, "Soviet Military Expenditure and the Armaments Industry, 1929–33," 596, Table 6.
2. For recent estimates of the death toll, see R. W. Davies and Stephen G. Wheatcroft, *The Years of Hunger: Soviet Agriculture, 1931–1933* (New York: Palgrave Macmillan, 2009), 415.
3. Quoted in Timothy Snyder, *Bloodlands: Europe between Hitler and Stalin* (New York: Basic Books, 2010), 50.
4. Kotkin, *Stalin: Waiting for Hitler*, 102.
5. Lynne Viola, V. P. Danilov, N. A. Ivnitskii, and Denis Kozlov, eds., *The War against the Peasantry*, trans. Steven Shabad (New Haven, CT: Yale University Press, 2005), 124.
6. "Kollektiv-Vertrag 1932–1933" [Collective Agreement, 1932–1933], 31 May 1932, BA-MA, RH 12/I/59, 30–38, 1.
7. Ibid., 1–8.
8. Speidel, "Reichswehr und Rote Armee," 39.
9. "Bericht Nr. 316," [Report Number 316], 9 March 1931, BA-MA, RH12/I/57, 228, 1.
10. Ibid. "Austrüstung für die Reise nach Lip." [Equipment for the Journey to Lipetsk], 2 May 1928, BA-MA, RH/8/V/3623, 11, 1.
11. "Abschrift, Tagesanordnung #3," [Transcript: Daily Arrangement Number 3], 1 January 1930, BA-MA, RH 12/I/64, 34, 1.
12. "Abschrift: Herr Koch, Zollkontrolle Bigossowo" [Transcript, Customs Control, Herr Koch], 1 January 1930, BA-MA, RH12/I/64, 37, 1.
13. "O buivshem 4-m nemetskom aviaotriade," 18 January 1950, 14.
14. Heaton, Lewis, *The German Aces Speak: World War II through the Eyes of Four of the Luftwaffe's Most Important Commanders* (Minneapolis: Zenith Press, 2011), 175–176.
15. "O buivshem 4-m nemetskom aviaotriade," 18 January 1950, 7–8. In 1950, when the MGB reviewed these cases, four of the last thirty-nine arrested (three women) were

found innocent: "the study of archival investigation files revealed that these agents were not in fact unmasked as agents of the German intelligence." After nine years in the GULAGs, they were allowed to return home to Lipetsk.

16. "Bericht: Unterbringung 1930" [Report: Lodging in 1930], 22 April 1930, BA-MA, RH 12/I/57, 25, 1.
17. "Stelle eines Mitarbeiters in Kassenangelegeneheiten Freigeworden" [Employee Position Available in the Accounting Office], 22 March 1932, BA-MA, RH 12/I, 59, 1.
18. Speidel, "Reichswehr und Rote Armee," 33.
19. Kurt von Schleicher, "Letter to General Franz Ritter von Epp," 2 January 1931, NARA, T-84/9, 9304, 1.
20. Speidel, "Reichswehr und Rote Armee," 33.
21. Yakov Fishman, "Ispitanii 8-mm kg. khim. aerobombi" [Testing of the 8 Kilogram Chemical Aerobomb], 27 July 1928, RGVA, f. 33988, op. 3c, d. 98 (22), l. 152, 1–8.
22. "20. Tätigkeitsbericht über die Zeit von 12.9–18.9.31" [20th Activity Report], 19 September 1931, BA-MA, RH12/4/55, 196, 1.
23. Ibid.
24. Ibid.
25. "Nachrichten über r. Anschauungen," 5 September 1931, 3.
26. "20. Tätigkeitsbericht," 19 September 1931, 1.
27. Ibid.
28. Ibid.
29. Jan Matiseevich Zhigur was a Latvian peasant by birth. He joined the Communist Party in 1912 when he was seventeen. During the First World War, he was drafted and served in the Tsarist Army, where a sterling combat record earned him a battlefield commission to lieutenant. In 1918, he joined the Red Army. After successful service in the Russian Civil War, Zhigur transferred to the GRU (the RKKA's military intelligence directorate) and saw a series of postings in China from 1925 to 1928 as a military adviser, before returning to the Red Army and VOKhIMU. In 1927, he would complete a course of study in Germany. He spoke fluent German, and was generally very highly regarded by his German counterparts, and by Fishman. He would be shot during the purges in 1938. Nikolai Semyonovich Cherushev, *Rasstrelyannaya elita RKKA: Kombrigi i im ravnie, 1937–1941* [The Elite of the Red Army Who Were Shot, 1937–1941] (Moscow: Kukovo Pole Publishing, 2014), 90–91.
30. Ibid., 2.
31. "Nachrichten über r. Anschauungen," 5 September 1931, 2–3.
32. Ibid., 2.
33. In this interview, he was talking specifically about the work done at Podosinki. But similar work was conducted at Tomka as well. Katys, "The Military Chemical Testing Grounds."
34. Katys, "The Military Chemical Testing Grounds."
35. "Nachrichten über r. Anschauungen," 5 September 1931, 2.
36. Ibid., 11.
37. "Rezultakh raboti Tomka," 15 March 1931, 11.
38. "Nachrichten über r. Anschauungen," 5 September 1931, 11.
39. Müller, *So lebten und arbeiteten wir*, 27.
40. Habeck, *Storm of Steel*, 162.
41. "Betrifft: L.Tr.," 27 May 1935, 1–5.
42. Müller, *So lebten und arbeiteten wir*, 36.
43. Ibid.
44. "Verhandlungsprotokoll, Johann Hoffmann, Allied War Crimes Tribunal" [Transcript of Proceedings], December 1947, 5.
45. "Zapis priema T. Voroshilovim," 5 September 1929, 1.
46. "Sitzung über To.-Programm am 17.10.32" [Meeting on the To.Programm on October 17, 1932], 17 October 1932, BA-MA, RH12-1/54/36-38, 1–3, 2
47. Zeidler, 202.

48. "Rezultakh raboti Tomka," 15 March 1931, 11.
49. Zeidler, 202.
50. Wirth, "Perstoff-Schiessen vom 14.X.1931" [Perstoff Shooting from October 14, 1931], 10 October 1931, BA-MA, RH12/4/55, 128, 9.
51. Ibid. This was Dr. Wirth.
52. Leopold von Sicherer, "Bericht über das 6 Artl. Schiessen am 13 u 14.10 31—Perstoff-Schiessen" [Report on the 6 Artl. Shootout at 13 and 14.10 31—Perstoff-Shootout], 5 November 1931, BA-MA, RH12/4/55, 124, 1–3.
53. "Bericht Erdreferat To. 1931," 17 August 1931, 6.
54. "15. Tätigkeitsbericht über die Zeit von 10–16.8.31" [15th Activity Report for the Period from August 10 to 16, 1931], 17 August 1931, BA-MA, RH12/4/55, 196, 1.
55. Ibid.
56. He also added a note of disdain regarding the Soviets serving at Tomka: "The conduct of the Russian cadres with Mr Efimov off duty, e.g. at the social evening was extremely proper; also with Mr Schigur they were constantly observing good mil[itary] proprieties. [They] tend to be so sloppy off-duty in attitude and dress [that] the visit is an opportunity to see great discipline and sharp drill." "15. Tätigkeitsbericht," 17 August 1931, 2–3.
57. Ibid., 2–3.
58. Ibid., 1.
59. Ibid.
60. "Spisok komandno-nachal'stvuiushchego sostava RKKA," June 1938, 41–43.
61. Ibid.; Zeidler, 357–359.
62. Gorlov, 247.
63. Ibid.
64. "Artikel der 'Morning Post' über Verhältnisse in der russischen Armee, insbesondere auch den deutschen Einfluss daselbst" [Article in the "Morning Post" about Conditions in the Russian Army, Especially Discussing German Influence], 1930, PA-AA, R31496 K/K098008, 1.
65. Bayer, The Evolution of the Soviet General Staff, 122–128.

CHAPTER 22

1. Theodor Eschenburg, "The Role of the Personality in the Crisis of the Weimar Republic: Hindenburg, Brüning, Groener, Schleicher," in Republic to Reich: The Making of the Nazi Revolution, ed. Hajo Holborn (New York: Random House, 1972), 19.
2. Wiskemann, "Europe's Two New Premiers," 3.
3. Peter Hayes, "'A Question Mark with Epaulettes'?: Kurt von Schleicher and Weimar Politics," Journal of Modern History, 52:1 (Mar., 1980), 37, 39.
4. Ibid., 40–44. Schleicher briefly reversed course in 1931, hoping to use the Nazis outside of government to pressure the West on a variety of fronts.
5. Carsten, The Reichswehr and Politics, 328.
6. Ibid., 346.
7. Deist, The Wehrmacht and German Rearmament (Toronto: University of Toronto Press, 1981), 17.
8. Carsten, The Reichswehr and Politics, 347.
9. Fest, Hitler, 337.
10. Carsten, The Reichswehr and Politics, 371.
11. Deist, "The Rearmament of the Wehrmacht," 395–399.
12. "Ergebnis der Besprechung bei Chef T.A. am 25.4.32 als Beitrag zum Schreiben an Z.M." [Outcome of the meeting with the Chief T. A. on 4/25/32 as a Contribution to Write to Z.M], 25 May 1932, BA-MA, RH/12/4/54/15, 1–3
13. "Rezultakh Raboti Tomka, 15 March 1931, 1. Fishman, "V osnovnom soglasen, Uborevichu" [A Summary of the Agreement, to Uborevich], 30 December 1930, 13–14.
14. Joe Maiolo, Cry Havoc, The Arms Race and the Second World War, 1931–1941 (London: John Murray, 2011), 7.

15. Ibid., 8.
16. Lennart Samuelson, "Mikhail Tukhachevsky and War-Economic Planning: Reconsiderations on the Prewar Soviet Military Buildup," *Journal of Slavic Military Studies*, 9:4 (1996), 834.
17. Kotkin, *Stalin: Waiting for Hitler*, 91–92.
18. Davies, "Soviet Military Expenditure and the Armaments Industry, 1929–33: A Reconsideration," 602, Table 9.
19. Maiolo, *Cry Havoc*, 20.
20. Duffy and Kandalov, *Tupolev*, 42–43.
21. In 1928, the Red Army purchased light tanks from Fiat and KH-50 models from Czechoslovakia, the latter having been designed by German designer Josef Vollmer, designer of Germany's A7V in the First World War. In late 1929, Innokenty Khalepsky, the head of the Directorate for Motorization and Mechanization, departed on a massive worldwide shopping spree to purchase foreign tank designs. His largest agreement was reached with the Vickers-Armstrong Corporation on March 11, 1930, in which the Red Army purchased twenty Carden-Loyd Mark IV light tanks, fifteen 6-ton tanks, and fifteen 12-ton tanks for £205,000. These purchases were arranged through Arcos Limited, a Soviet corporate front established to make military and industrial purchases in the United Kingdom. Its offices had been raided in 1927 for its role in labor unrest in the UK. Correspondence in the same file as the one cited above includes back and forth from Voroshilov to Arcos, confirming the degree of control from Moscow. As one might imagine, this large-scale purchase of armored vehicles required the approval of the British government, which granted it before the end of the month. Facing national recession, the British government concluded that Russian gold meant jobs. "Buying Order Number 549570, Arcos Limited with Vickers Armstrong, LTD," 15 March 1930, RGVA, f. 33987, op. 3c, d. 350, l. 1, 1–4.
22. John Milsom, *Russian Tanks, 1900–1970: The Complete Illustrated History of Soviet Armoured Theory and Design* (New York: Galahad, 1975), 96.
23. Habeck, *Storm of Steel*, 129. Of the eighteen tank production facilities active in the Soviet Union in 1941, two were modernized by German engineers, while two—the Stalingrad Tractor Factory and the Gorki Automobile Factory—were built by American firms with American and German machine tools. Three more were modernized under contract with American firms with German and American machine tools. Three others were built by Soviet construction crews, but equipped with German and American machine tools and factory components.
24. Milsom, *Russian Tanks, 1900–1970*, 98–99; Bean and Fowler, *Red Army Tanks of World War Two*, 65.
25. Tim Bean and Will Fowler, *Red Army Tanks of World War Two: A Guide to Soviet Armored Fighting Vehicles* (London: Amber Books, 2002), 73.
26. Further reverse-engineering—drawn in part from the *Grosstraktoren* at Kama—also led to the 31-ton T-28, the first Soviet heavy tank. Milsom, *Russian Tanks, 1900–1970*, 98, 103–104.
27. Zaloga and Grandsen, *Soviet Tanks and Combat Vehicles*, 108.
28. Gryaznov, "O rabote kursov TEKO," 14 March 1932, 1–2.
29. "Bericht den Besuch des Flugzeugwerkes in Fili," 17 February 1931, RH/12/1, 56, BA-MA; Gunston, *The Osprey Encyclopedia of Russian Aircraft*.
30. Zaloga and Grandsen, *Soviet Tanks and Combat Vehicles*, 43–44.
31. Kotkin, *Stalin: Waiting for Hitler*, 930, ff. 173.
32. See Bayer, *The Evolution of the Soviet General Staff*, 108–109.
33. For more on Deep Battle, see David Glantz, *Soviet Military Operational Art: In Pursuit of Deep Battle* (New York: Frank Cass, 2005); Richard Simpkin and John Erickson, *Deep Battle, the Brainchild of Marshal Tukhachevsky* (London: Brassey's Defence Publishers, 1987); Richard W. Harrison, *Architect of Soviet Victory in World War Two: The Life and Theories of G. S. Isserson* (Jefferson, NC: McFarland, 2010); and G. S. Isserson, *G. S.*

Isserson and the War of the Future: Key Writings of a Soviet Military Theorist, ed. and trans. Richard W. Harrison (Jefferson, NC: McFarland, 2016).

34. Tukhachevsky was only one of many theorists who developed Deep Battle, though he was the most prominent by dint of his successful record in the Russian Civil War and role as chief of the Soviet General Staff. He was also the first to use the term "Deep Battle" in writing in 1931. Habeck, *Storm of Steel*, 151. The other key figures around him were Triandafillov, Kalinovsky, Khalepskii, Sediakin, and Isserson. Triandafillov and Kalinovsky, key authors, were both killed in a plane crash in 1931. Sediakin was Tukhachevsky's deputy chief of staff from 1933 to 1936, in which role he had significant influence on trying to actualize Deep Battle. Kalinovsky was the first chief of the UMM, and shaped armored warfare and procurement. Isserson would go on to write the major "Deep Battle" manual of the 1930s, PU-1936, and would be the lone survivor of the "Deep Battle" theorists to live through the purges.

35. Habeck, *Storm of Steel*, 168.

CHAPTER 23

1. Heinz Guderian, *Panzer Leader*, 28.
2. Gorlov, 219, 222.
3. Ibid., 224.
4. Gorlov, 224; David Glantz, *Companion to Colossus Reborn: Key Documents and Statistics* (Lawrence: University Press of Kansas, 2005), 66.
5. Guderian, *Panzer Leader*, 28; Thomas L. Jentz, ed., *Panzertruppen: The Complete Guide to the Creation and Combat Employment of Germany's Tank Force, 1933–1942* (Atglen, PA: Schiffer Military History), 9–10.
6. "Kl.Tr. Beschreibung" [Light Tractor Description], 8 August 1930, BA-MA, RH/8/I, 2673, 1, 1.
7. Georg Hagelloch, "Aktennotiz über Unterredung mit Herrn General Karlewski am 25.6.1932 in Essen" [Memorandum on a Conversation with General Karlewski on 25.6.1932 in Essen," 25 June 1932, BA-MA, RH/8/I 2675, 345, 1.
8. "Friedrich Krupp A.G., Reichswehrminister," 12 October 1932, BA-MA, RH/8/I, 2676, 1, 1.
9. Habeck, *Storm of Steel*, 161; "Friedrich Krupp A.G., Reichswehrminister," 12 October 1932, 1.
10. See Guderian, *Panzer Leader*, 28.
11. "Bericht über die Sommerversuche der Wa.Prw. 8 1931" [Report on the Summer Research of Waffenamt 8, 1931], 1 December 1931, BA-MA, RH 12/4/52, 25–54, 1–30.
12. "Bericht über die Ausbildungstätigkeit der Station im Sommer 1931" [Report over the Training Program for the Station in the Summer of 1931], 8 November 1931, 1; "Fl. Bericht No. 327" [Flight Report Number 327], 18 May 1931, BA-MA, RH 12/1/ 57, 293.
13. The Junkers W-34 monoplane would also be briefly tested by Germany's state airline Lufthansa through its Brazilian affiliate "Stellungnahme zu den ru. Vorschlägen," 18 January 1932, 2.
14. "Protokoll der Besprechung," 26 March 1932, 1–2; "Stellungnahme zu den ru. Vorschlägen," 18 January 1932, 2.
15. Wagner, *Hugo Junkers*, 315.
16. Ibid., 281.
17. "Bruchbericht, Fokker D XIII Masch. Nr. 37" [Accident Report, Fokker D XIII Number 37], 7 July 1932, BA-MA, RH 12/I/60, 75, 1.
18. Heaton and Lewis, *The German Aces Speak*, 176.
19. "Bruchbericht, Fokker D XIII Masch. Nr. 37," 7 July 1932, 1.
20. They all attended Lipetsk in 1932, but began the twelve-month course that culminated at Lipetsk the previous summer.
21. "Bericht über die Ausbildungstätigkeit der Station im Sommer 1931" [Report over the Training Program for the Station in the Summer of 1931], 8 November 1931, 2;

"Fl. Bericht, Nr. 286" [Flight Report Number 286], 8 August 1930, BA-MA, RH 12/I/57, 80, 1.

22. Whaley, *Covert German Rearmament*, 81.
23. Zeidler, 304.
24. Lindner and Schultze, "Germany," in *Elections in Europe*, 778.
25. Hayes, "'A Question Mark with Epaulettes,'" 53–55.
26. Erickson, *The Soviet High Command*, 341.
27. Ibid., 341.
28. "Bericht über das To.Kdo. vom 5/10–9/11.1932" [Report on the To.Kdo. from October 5 to November 9, 1932], 11 November 1932, BA-MA, RH12/1/54, 129–134, 1. "Stellungnahme zu den ru. Forderungen To." [Opinion on the Russian demands for To.], 1933, BA-MA, RH12/1/54, 39–41, 1–3.
29. Steiner, *The Lights That Failed*, 790.
30. Edward W. Bennett, *German Rearmament and the West, 1932–1933* (Princeton, NJ: Princeton University Press, 1979), 277.
31. Carsten, *The Reichswehr and Politics*, 388; Ian Kershaw, *Hitler* (London: Longman, 1991), 391–415; Irene Strenge, *Kurt von Schleicher: Politik im Reichswehrministerium am Ende der Weimarer Republik* (Berlin: Duncker und Humblot, 2006), 168–170.
32. For the former argument, see Henry Ashby Turner Jr., "The Myth of Chancellor von Schleicher's Querfront Strategy," *Central European History*, 41:4 (Dec., 2008), 673–681. For the latter, see Wheeler-Bennett, *The Nemesis of Power*, 267–268.
33. In December 1932, in an article for foreign audiences, now-Chancellor Schleicher wrote "It is one of the most momentous contradictions in the structure of the German state since 1919 that it is ready to guarantee the maximum of freedom at home, while it lacks the means of defending this freedom from foreign aggression." Here he argued that Versailles made Germany, and Europe, less free and less secure, and only by its abrogation could collective security be achieved in Europe. Kurt von Schleicher, "The Conception of Defense in Present Day Germany," *World Affairs*, 95:3 (Dec. 1932), 160–161.
34. Tooze, *Wages of Destruction*, 26.
35. See Albrecht Ritschl, "Deficit Spending in the Nazi Recovery, 1933–1938: A Critical Reassessment," *Journal of the Japanese and International Economy*, 16 (2002), 582, table 5.
36. Maiolo, *Cry Havoc*, 73, 92; Manfred Messerschmidt, "Foreign Policy and Preparation for War," in *Germany and the Second World War*, 581.
37. Strenge, *Kurt von Schleicher*, 218.
38. Ibid., 219.
39. Henry Ashby Turner Jr., *Hitler's Thirty Days to Power: January 1933* (New York: Basic Books: 1996), 194.
40. Carsten, *The Reichswehr and Politics*, 322.
41. Hermann Rauschning, *Makers of Destruction* (Bloomington: Indiana University Press, 1942), 25, cited by Zeidler, 268.
42. Schäfer, *Werner von Blomberg*, 170.
43. Interestingly, Göring would claim in 1935 that Schleicher had suggested to Hitler when Hitler became chancellor that Hitler should seek a grand bargain with the Soviet Union and partition of Poland between the two states. Whether it was true or not, the thought was clearly in Hitler's mind. Wheeler-Bennett, *The Nemesis of Power*, 327.

CHAPTER 24

1. "Berlin Reds Urge Strike; Two Killed in Riots during Nazi Celebrations in Germany," *New York Times*, 31 January 1933, 3.
2. Carsten, *The Reichswehr and Politics*, 296.
3. Ibid., 392–393.
4. For a long time, Hans Mommsen's conclusion that the fire had indeed been set by a lone communist was the standard in the historical community. But new evidence, most

recently provided by Benjamin Carter Hett, *Burning the Reichstag: An Investigation into the Third Reich's Enduring Mystery* (Oxford, UK: Oxford University Press, 2014), strongly indicates that the Nazis organized the attack on the Reichstag.

5. Lindner and Schultze, "Germany," in *Elections in Europe*, 778.
6. Wheeler-Bennett, *The Nemesis of Power*, 323–329.
7. E. M. Robertson, *Hitler's Pre-war Policy and Military Plans, 1933–1939* (London: Longmans, Green and Co., 1963), 6.
8. Tooze, *Wages of Destruction*, 38.
9. Groener's understanding of the next war as a "total war" led him to commission surveys of national industrial capacity. This in turn led to a new national armaments plan in the form of the Second Armaments Program, which anticipated the mobilization of national industry. Deist, "The Rearmament of the Wehrmacht," 392–397; Maiolo, *Cry Havoc*, 93–94.
10. While the Great Depression had threatened some aspects of covert rearmament, it had benefited some of the Reichswehr's corporate partners. Fearing the collapse of already anemic German military industrial firms, Groener had overseen an influx of cash from the state aimed at keeping the most important firms afloat. Deist, *Wehrmacht and German Rearmament*, 11.
11. Murray, "Armored Warfare," 41. The main Reichswehr manual in 1933 read: "When closely tied to the infantry, the tanks are deprived of their inherent speed," encouraging their independent use.
12. Personnel Records, NARA; Gerd R. Ueberschär, *Hitlers militärische Elite*; and Franz Kurowski, *Panzer Aces: German Tank Commanders of World War Two* (Mechanicsburg, PA: Stackpole Books, 1992).
13. Corum, *The Roots of Blitzkrieg*, 195, citing Walter Nehring, *Die Geschichte Der Deutschen Panzerwaffe 1916 bis 1945* (Berlin: Propyläen Verlag, 1969), 110, 114. See also Nehring, *Die Geschichte Der Deutschen Panzerwaffe*, Appendix I, 9-13.
14. Joachim Krause and Charles K. Mallory, *Chemical Weapons in Soviet Military Doctrine: Military and Historical Experience, 1915–1991* (Boulder, CO: Westview Press, 1992), 74, 76.
15. Deist, "The Rearmament of the Wehrmacht," 411.
16. Ibid., 410.
17. Ibid., 404.
18. Deist, *The Wehrmacht and German Rearmament*, 106.
19. Kotkin, *Stalin: Waiting for Hitler*, 119.
20. Adolf Hitler, *Hitler's Second Book: The Unpublished Sequel to Mein Kampf*, ed. Gerhardt Weinberg, trans. Krista Smith (New York: Enigma Books, 2003), 144–147.
21. Ibid.
22. Dyakov and Bushuyeva, *The Red Army and Wehrmacht*, 314.
23. Adolf Hitler, "Official Speech on the Enabling Act to the Reichstag," 23 March 1933, World Future Fund Historical Documents Collection, http://www.worldfuturefund.org/Reports2013/hitlerenablingact.htm.
24. Nekrich, *Pariahs, Predators, Partners*, 78.
25. Mitcham, *Eagles of the Third Reich*, 9.
26. Despite these signals, the Soviets made clear that if German attitudes toward the Soviet Union improved, cooperation could continue. It seems that the continued possibility of industrial espionage was a particularly strong lure for Stalin. Habeck, *Storm of Steel*, 184.
27. "From Krestinsky's Journal: Reception of von Dirksen and Hartmann," 3 April 1933, RGVA, f. 33987, op. 3, d. 497, l. 81–84, reprinted in Dyakov and Bushuyeva, 293.
28. "On General Bokkleberg's Trip to Tula, Kharkov, Dnieproges, and Sevastopol from May 17 to 24, 1933," 25 May 1933, 33987/3/497, 143–148, reprinted in Dyakov and Bushuyeva, 298.
29. Hartmann, No. 142/33, "The Military Attaché in the Soviet Union to the Head of the Troop Office in the Reichswehr," 16 May 1933, in *Documents on German Foreign*

Policy, 1918–1945 (hereafter DGFP), Series C, *The Third Reich: The First Phase, Volume I, January 30–October 14, 1933* (Washington DC: United States Government Printing Office, 1957), 464.

30. Ibid., 465.
31. Ibid.
32. Erickson, *The Soviet High Command*, 344–345.
33. Bockelberg, No. 143/33, "Minutes of the Conference with the Chief of the Chemical Troops, M. Fischmann," DGFP, Series C, Volume I, 469.
34. Erickson, *The Soviet High Command*, 346.
35. "Gesamtbild der Abwicklung der Station To. 1933" [Overall Picture of the Termination of the Station To. 1933], 22 August 1933, BA-MA, RH/12/4/55/55, 16.
36. Lennart Samuelson, *Soviet Defence Industry Planning: Tukhachevskii and Military-Industrial Mobilization, 1926–1937* (Stockholm: Stockholm Institute of East European Economies, 1996), 208–209.
37. Bayer, *The Evolution of the Soviet General Staff*, 226–228.
38. "From Colonel Hartmann's Reports to the Reichswehr Ministry," 8 October 1933, RGVA, f. 33987, op. 3, d. 505, l. 139–146, reprinted in Dyakov and Bushuyeva, 309.
39. Jodl, "Bericht, Geheime Kommandosache!" 9 June 1933, BA-MA, 18a. RH/12/4, 54, 7, 1.
40. Zeidler, 45.
41. Erickson, *The Soviet High Command*, 346.
42. Ibid., 347.
43. The dinner list also included Vasily Levichev, Vitaly Primakov, Semyon Uritsky, Alexei Vinogradov, Arkady Borisov, and Alexander Girshfeld. All were senior Soviet officers, ranging from brigade to corps commanders. Only one would live past 1940, with most executed in the purges, and another shot in 1940 for poor performance in the Winter War with Finland.
44. "From the Diary of Khinchuk, Plenipotentiary of the USSR in Germany," 8 July 1933, RGVA, f. 33987, op. 3, d. 505, l. 148–156, reprinted in Dyakov, Bushuyeva, 303–304.
45. Ibid.
46. Gorlov, 305–307; Erickson, *The Soviet High Command*, 346.
47. Speidel, "Reichswehr und Rote Armee," 40.
48. Berzin, "Voroshilovu, o khode likvidatsii predpriatii druzei v Tomke Lipetske, Kazani" [To Voroshilov on the Progress of the Liquidation of the "Friends'" Enterprises at Tomka, Lipetsk and Kazan], 14 October 1933, RGVA, f. 33987, op. 3, d. 504, l. 161–165 (Y-RAP 254), 2.
49. "Gesamtbild der Abwicklung der Station To. 1933," 22 August 1933, 16.
50. Ibid, 7.
51. Berzin, "Voroshilovu, o khode likvidatsii," 14 October 1933, 2–3.
52. Ibid., 8.
53. "Gesamtbild der Abwicklung der Station To. 1933" [Overall Picture of the Termination of the Station To. 1933], 22 August 1933, 3.
54. Berzin, "Voroshilovu, o khode likvidatsii," 14 October 1933, 2–3.
55. Ibid., 3–4.
56. Ibid., 4.
57. Gorlov, 305.
58. Ibid.; Berzin, "Voroshilovu, o khode likvidatsii," 14 October 1933, 5–6.
59. Werner von Blomberg, "Perevod, pis'mo, Minister Reikhsvera" [Translation, Letter of the Reichswehr Minister], 29 September 1933, RGVA, f. 33987, op. 3c, d. 505, l. 171, 1; Habeck, *Storm of Steel*, 186.
60. No. 460, DGFP, C:1, 862.
61. Zeidler, 291.
62. No. 460, DGFP, C:1, 856–862.
63. Erickson, *The Soviet High Command*, 348.

64. Blomberg to Voroshilov, "Perevod, pis'mo, Minister Reikhsvera" [Translation, Letter or the Reichswehr Minister], 29 September 1933, RGVA, f. 33987, op. 3s, d. 505, l. 171. 1.
65. Erickson, *The Soviet High Command*, 348.

CHAPTER 25

1. Robertson, *Hitler's Pre-war Policy and Military Plans*, 22; No. 459, 460, DGFP, C:I, 856, 860–862.
2. Robertson, *Hitler's Pre-war Policy and Military Plans*, 22.
3. Stephen A. Schuker, "France and the Remilitarization of the Rhineland, 1936," *French Historical Studies*, 14 (1986), 314.
4. Ibid.
5. See Documents on British Foreign Policy 1919–1939, Ser. 2, Vol. 5, No. 489 (Oct. 24, 1933), 711–713.
6. For an interesting contemporary assessment of the Geneva Disarmament talks, see Allen W. Dulles, "Germany and the Crisis," in *Disarmament, Foreign Affairs*, 12:2 (Jan., 1934), 260–270.
7. Nos. 479, 499, DGFP, C:I, 887, 922. For more analysis of the decision, see Gerhard Weinberg, *Hitler's Foreign Policy, 1933–1939: The Road to World War Two* (New York: Enigma Books, 2010), 131, and Messerschmidt, "Foreign Policy and Preparation for War," 589.
8. For more on the right-wing protests (sometimes claimed to be a coup attempt) in February 1934, see Brian Jenkins, "The Six Fevrier 1934 and the 'Survival' of the French Republic," *French History*, 20:3 (4 August 2006), 333–335.
9. Anthony Adamthwaite, *Grandeur and Misery: France's Bid for Power in Europe, 1914–1940* (London: Bloomsbury, 1995), xviii–xix, 7.
10. Robert Vansittart, *The Mist Procession: The Autobiography of Lord Vansittart* (London: Hutchinson, 1958), 487.
11. Ibid.
12. Robertson, *Hitler's Pre-war Policy and Military Plans*, 26.
13. DGFP, C:I, 882, cited by Robertson, 23.
14. Weinberg, *Hitler's Foreign Policy 1933–1939*, 59-61; Robertson, *Hitler's Pre-war Policy and Military Plans*, 26.
15. No. 83, DBFP, 2:6, 128–133.
16. Anna Cienciala, "The Foreign Policy of Jozef Pilsudski and Jozef Beck, 1926–1939: Misconceptions and Interpretations," *The Polish Review* 56:1/2 (2011), 147. As Beck understood the German offer, the best Poland could hope for in a German-dominated Europe was survival as a weakened satellite, and perhaps much worse. In 1939, he wrote that an alliance with Germany against the USSR would have meant "we would have defeated Russia, and afterwards we would be taking Hitler's cows out to pasture in the Urals." See also Wojchiech Materski and Aleksandr V. Revyakin, "The Interwar Period: Poland and the Soviet Union in the late 1920s and Early 1930s," in *White Spots–Black Spots: Difficult Matters in Polish-Russian Relations*, eds. Adam Daniel Rotfeld and Anatoly V. Torkunov (Pittsburgh: University Press of Pittsburgh, 2015), 72.
17. Dirksen, *Moscow, Tokyo, London*, 110–112.
18. For the correspondence leading up to his recall, see No. 137, *ADAP*, C:1, 243.
19. Dirksen, "Pismo, Voroshilovu" [Letter to Voroshilov], 3 November 1933, RGVA, f. 33987, op. 3S, d. 505, l. 180, 1.
20. Voroshilov, "Politburo, TsVKP, Tov. Stalinu" [To the Politburo TsVKP, to Comrade Stalin], 14 November 1933, RGVA, f. 33987, op. 3S, d. 505, l. 179, 1.
21. Voroshilov's absence meant that Dirksen would receive it from the hands of a staff member. Ambassador Dirksen handed over his letters of recall in exchange. Dirksen, *Moscow, Tokyo, London*, 252–253.

22. Teddy Uldricks, "Soviet Security Policy in the 1930s," in *Soviet Foreign Policy, 1917–1991: A Retrospective*, ed. Gabriel Gorodetsky (London: Frank Cass Publishers, 1994), 67.

23. Hugh D. Phillips, *Between the Revolution and the West: A Political Biography of Maxim M. Litvinov* (Boulder, CO: Westview Press, 1992), 1.

24. Roger Moorhouse, *The Devils' Alliance: Hitler's Pact with Stalin, 1939–1941* (New York: Basic Books, 2014), 164.

25. Kotkin, *Stalin: Waiting for Hitler*, 24–25, 274–275, 298–299; Nekrich, *Pariahs, Partners, Predators*, 64, 80.

26. Nekrich, *Pariahs, Partners, Predators*, 80.

27. Tooze, *The Wages of Destruction*, 126; Homze, *Arming the Luftwaffe*, 67.

28. Homze, *Arming the Luftwaffe*, 67

29. Tooze, *Wages of Destruction*, 127.

30. Deist, "The Rearmament of the Wehrmacht," 415.

31. See Williamson Murray, *Strategy for Defeat: The Luftwaffe, 1933–1945* (Maxwell, AL: Air University Press, 1983) for more.

32. Homze, *Arming the Luftwaffe*, 74.

33. Richhardt, *Auswahl und Ausbildung*, 218.

34. Mitcham, *Eagles of the Third Reich*, 9–10.

35. Homze, *Arming the Luftwaffe*, 80.

36. See Chapter 6.

37. The He-51 project also included engineers who had cut their teeth working on Heinkel's prototype aircraft tested at Lipetsk, including the HD-17, the HD-38, and the HD-59. The German Navy also commissioned a small number of aircraft—149 in total—under the Rhineland plan. Most of those were Heinkel models that had either been developed at Lipetsk or were direct descendants of those models which had been developed there. See Homze, *Arming the Luftwaffe*, 80, for a list of aircraft commissioned.

38. It was partially responsible for the Luftwaffe's later emphasis on fighter-bombers and assault aircraft. Homze, *Arming the Luftwaffe*, 21.

39. This was one of two designs by Pohlmann that were tested at Lipetsk, the other being the W-34.

40. Guardia, *Junkers Ju 87 STUKA*, 7.

41. Homze, *Arming the Luftwaffe*, 81. Another example is the origin of the Bf-109 single-seater fighter, Germany's primary fighter aircraft for much of the war. There was also particularly fierce competition to build the RLM's next-generation single-seater fighter aircraft. In March 1934, German engineer and entrepreneur Willy Messerschmitt's Bf 108 aircraft took off for its maiden testing flight. Messerschmitt's design team included Walter Rethel, who had dispatched three different aircraft to Lipetsk. The resultant design would become the basis for the Bf-109 design, the second-most produced aircraft of all time. See Smith and Kay, *German Aircraft*, 17.

42. "Verhandlungsprotokoll, Johann Hoffmann, Allied War Crimes Tribunal" [Transcript of Proceedings], December 1947, 5.

43. Guderian, *Panzer Leader*, 31–32.

44. Those five firms were Henschel, MAN, Daimler-Benz, Rheinmetall-Borsig, and Krupp. The latter four had all been heavily involved in military activity on Soviet soil during the preceding decade. Chamberlain and Doyle, *Encyclopedia of German Tanks*, 18.

45. Ibid., 19.

46. Guderian, *Panzer Leader*, 28.

47. "Verhandlungsprotokoll, Johann Hoffmann, Allied War Crimes Tribunal" [Transcript of Proceedings], December 1947, 28–41.

48. Ibid.

49. Ibid. The Daimler engineers, some of whom had lived at Kama, also took the lead with the Panzer III, of which 6,404 were manufactured between 1935 and 1945. The Panzer IIIs initially used a coil suspension that had been rejected by Krupp for its own Panzer

I based on testing at Kama. In 1940, Daimler's Panzer IIIa's were all withdrawn due to unsatisfactory performance of their suspensions.

50. Walter Spielberger, *Panzer III and Its Variants* (Atglen, PA: Schiffer Publishing, 1993), 8.
51. Habeck, *Storm of Steel*, 226. Evidence as to the original intent of the Panzer IV includes the fact that it was initially called a *Begleitwagen*, or support vehicle. It would eventually evolve into Germany's main battle tank, as its success against enemy armor proved more important than its slower speeds.
52. Spielberger, *Panzer IV and Its Variants*, 10; Spielberger, *Panzer III and Its Variants*, 8.
53. Spielberger, *Die Motorisierung der Deutschen Reichswehr 1920–1935*, 334.
54. Spielberger, *Panzer IV and Its Variants*, 10–12.
55. Ian Ona Johnson, "The Soviet-German Armored Warfare Facility at Kama, 1926–1933," *Global War Studies*, 14:1 (2017), 40.
56. "Konstruktive Tätigkeit und Weiterentwicklung" [Construction Activity and Development], undated, KA-E, WA 40 B/1350, 973.
57. Homze, *Arming the Luftwaffe*, 86.
58. "Answer of the United States Prosecution to the Motion on Behalf of Defendant Gustav Krupp von Bohlen," *Nuremberg Trial Proceedings, Vol. 1*, 12 November 1945, available digitally through the Avalon Project–Yale Law School, http://avalon.law.yale.edu/imt/v1-11.asp.
59. It reached that figure at the beginning of 1935. Williamson Murray, *Strategy for Defeat: The Luftwaffe, 1933–1945* (Maxwell, AL: Air University Press, 1983), 56.
60. Zeidler, 304.
61. James S. Corum, "Devil's Bargain: Germany and Russia Before World War Two," *World War Two Magazine*, March 8, 2018, http://www.historynet.com/devils-bargain-germany-and-russia-before-wwii.htm.
62. Corum, *The Roots of Blitzkrieg*, 195.
63. Doyle, Chamberlain, and Jentz, *Panzertruppen*, 16.
64. "Svodka po dovoorudeniu Germanii na 1.5.1934" [Summary of Rearmament of Germany on 05.01.1934], 5 January 1934, RGVA, f. 33987, op. 3c, d. 585, l. 3.
65. Maiolo, *Cry Havoc*, 44.
66. Bernhard von Bülow, "Secretary of State Bülow to Foreign Minister Neurath," August 16, 1934, DGFP, C, III, No. 162, 327, quoted in Maiolo, *Cry Havoc*, 50.
67. Robertson, *Hitler's Pre-war Policy and Military Plans*, 33–34.
68. Kershaw, *Hitler*, 72.
69. Tooze, *Wages of Destruction*, 67.
70. It has been argued by William Shirer that a deal had already been reached between the military in the spring of 1934 to allow Hitler to merge the presidency and chancellorship in the event of Hindenburg's death. Newer sources suggest a more complicated picture.

CHAPTER 26

1. Frederick T. Birchall, "Storm Troop Chiefs Die: Killed or Take Own Lives as Chancellor and Göring Strike; Reactionaries Also Hit," *New York Times*, 1 July 1934, 1.
2. Elizabeth Wiskemann, "The Night of the Long Knives," *History Today*, 14:6 (Jun 1, 1964), 371–380, 378.
3. Birchall, "Storm Troop Chiefs Die," 1.
4. Robertson, *Hitler's Pre-war Policy and Military Plans*, 340.
5. Wiskemann, 372.
6. Deist, "The Rearmament of the Wehrmacht," 508–526.
7. Nekrich, *Pariahs, Partners, Predators*, 73–74.
8. Kotkin, *Stalin: Waiting for Hitler*, 175.
9. Ibid., 176.
10. See Matt Lenoe, "Did Stalin Kill Kirov and Does It Matter?," *The Journal of Modern History*, 74:2 (June 2002), 352–380. Lenoe's evidence, provided in his book *The Kirov Murder and Soviet History*, offers convincing evidence that Stalin did not order Kirov's

death. Stephen Kotkin, in his magisterial biographies of Stalin, concurs. See Kotkin, *Stalin: Waiting for Hitler*, 197–213. That hardly exonerates Stalin from the enormity of the crimes to follow, however.

11. Nicolas Werth, "A State against Its People: Violence, Repression, and Terror in the Soviet Union," in *Black Book of Communism*, 167; see also Norman Naimark, *Stalin's Genocides* (Princeton, NJ: Princeton University Press, 2010), 60, 70–71.

12. Robert Conquest, *The Great Terror: Stalin's Purge of the Thirties* (New York: Macmillan, 1973/2008), 45.

13. Nekrich, *Pariahs, Partners, Predators*, 85.

14. Kotkin, 188; Samuelson, *Soviet Defence Industry Planning*, 175.

15. Maiolo, *Cry Havoc*, 173.

16. Ibid., 174.

17. Wolfgang König, *Volkswagen, Volksempfänger, Volksgemeinschaft: "Volksprodukte" im Dritten Reich, vom Scheitern einer nationalsozialistischen Konsumgesellschaft* (Paderborn: Schöningh, 2004), 37–38, 65.

18. Adolf Hitler, "Hitler's Statement: Text of Hitler's Statement on the Reich Army," *New York Times*, March 17, 1935, 1.

19. Ibid.

20. Deist, "The Rearmament of the Wehrmacht," 423.

21. His announcement of universal service and thirty-six divisions went beyond the expectations of the Army Command, who were as surprised as the public at the final figure. Deist, "The Rearmament of the Wehrmacht," 505–509.

22. Guderian, *Panzer Leader*, 32.

23. Ibid. Guderian blamed Beck for blocking the development of Germany's armored forces earlier on, though the evidence now suggests Beck was far from an opponent of tank warfare. See Habeck, *Storm of Steel*, 221–223.

CHAPTER 27

1. "1,950,000 Germans Ready for War, France Declares; Flandin Refutes Hitler's Charges," *The Globe*, 21 Mar 1935, 1.

2. "Germany defended by Lloyd George," *Pittsburgh Post-Gazette*, 18 Mar 1935, 2. For more on David Lloyd George's role in British appeasement, see Stella Rudman, *Lloyd George and the Appeasement of Germany, 1919–1945* (Newcastle, UK: Cambridge Scholars Publishing, 2011).

3. Vansittart, *The Mist Procession*, 519.

4. Ibid.

5. No. 555, DGFP, C:III, 1043–1080, 1050.

6. Ibid., 1068.

7. Ibid., 1073.

8. Vansittart's delightful (and sadly unfinished) memoir has some choice words to describe the Soviet-German partnership from the vantage of the postwar period: "[Seeckt] desired a strong Russia and passed for genius . . . the outstanding German soldier was supported by the prizeman of the German Foreign Office, Maltzan. Mischief-makers were always sure of rising in the Wilhelmstrasse. The first Fellow-traveller pined for contiguity with a giantess who would emasculate him. The German Government balked at Soviet bait for an alliance against the West, but Seeckt nibbled and Maltzan bit. Lenin measured their school: 'Germany wants revenge, we want revolution.' Trotsky had the same idea sooner: 'European war means European revolution.' Natural allies got together under cover of a bogus company, for which the Germans found 75,000,000 Reichsmarks while asking us for more moratorium. They bargained for production in Russia of aircraft and poison gas, for tanks and flying schools. In turn German officers would keep their hand in by training the Red Army. . . . Thenceforth dissatisfied Slavs let dissatisfied Teutons prepare to attack them twenty years on." Vansittart, *The Mist Procession*, 287.

9. *The Maisky Diaries*, 52.

10. Homze, *Arming the Luftwaffe*, 93; Doyle, Chamberlain, and Jentz, *Panzertruppen*, 18–19; Deist, "The Rearmament of the Wehrmacht," 424.
11. Schuker, "France and the Remilitarization of the Rhineland, 1936," 316.
12. Andrew Webster, "From Versailles to Geneva: The Many Forms of Interwar Disarmament," *Journal of Strategic Studies*, 29:2 (2006), 229–230.
13. Ibid., 231.
14. Schuker, "France and the Remilitarization of the Rhineland, 1936," 319.
15. Ibid., 318.
16. Ibid., 319–321.
17. Ibid., 322.
18. No. 44, DGFP, C:IV, 75–77.
19. No. 63, DGFP, C:IV, 113–114.
20. No. 131, DGFP, C:IV, 253.
21. No. 19, No. 546, DGFP, C:III, 28–29, 1028–1030.
22. Manfred Zeidler, "German-Soviet Economic Relations during the Hitler-Stalin Pact," in *From Peace to War: Germany, Soviet Russia, and the World, 1939–1941*, ed. Bernd Wegner, 97. There was some German enthusiasm for these measures, too. The Soviet ambassador in Berlin reported during the negotiations that there was "powerful pressure from influential Reichswehr circles . . . insisting on reconciliation and agreement with us." Geoffrey Roberts, "A Soviet Bid for Coexistence with Nazi Germany, 1935–1937: The Kandelaki Affair," *International History Review*, 16:3 (Aug., 1994), 466–490, 473.
23. Erickson, *The Soviet High Command*, 395.
24. Nekrich, *Pariahs, Partners, Predators*, 91.
25. "Red Army Warns of Reich Military: Defense Vice Commissar Says German Force Will Be 40 Percent Larger than French Soon; Plan for Fast Blow Seen," *New York Times*, 1 April 1935, 6.
26. Dyakov and Bushuyeva, 333. Stalin made sure that the piece highlighted Hitler's interest in attacking the Western Allies, rather than the threat Hitler posed to the Soviet Union; he was concerned that the Western Allies might be encouraging conflict between the Soviet Union and Nazi Germany.
27. Nekrich, *Pariahs, Partners, Predators*, 82.
28. *Encyclopedia of the Third Reich*, ed. Louis Snyder (New York: Marlowe and Company, 1976), 295.
29. No. 131, DGFP, C:IV, 254–255.
30. No. 141, DGFP, C:IV, 277.
31. Joe Maiolo, *The Royal Navy and Nazi Germany, 1933–1939: A Study in Appeasement and the Origins of the Second World War* (London: Macmillan, 1998), 21.
32. Ibid., 16–21.
33. Anthony Adamthwaite, *France and the Coming of the Second World War, 1936–1939* (London: Frank Cass, 1977), 33.
34. No. 275, DGFP, C:IV, 587–591.
35. Vansittart, *The Mist Procession*, 515–516. In Vansittart's opinion, Laval "swore that he only gave the Duce a free hand economically . . . all fair enough, but a wink is as good as a nod, and Laval had a drooping lid. Alexis, who accompanied him, felt convinced that both [military and economic free hand] had been given."
36. No. 465, DGFP, C:IV, 924. Contrary to Vansittart's memoirs, the German ambassador in London wrote to Berlin that "the Foreign Office, in the person of Sir Robert Vansittart, have long since had enough of the sanctions policy and are striving for a solution which will permit a return to normal relations with Italy and the resumption of serious negotiations with Germany."
37. Aaron L. Goldman, "Sir Robert Vansittart's Search for Italian Cooperation against Hitler, 1933–36," *Journal of Contemporary History*, 9:3 (Jul., 1974), 120–126.
38. Tooze, *Wages of Destruction*, 67.
39. Homze, *Arming the Luftwaffe*, 159.

40. Schuker, "France and the Remilitarization of the Rhineland, 1936," 299–338.
41. Zach Shore, "Hitler, Intelligence and the Decision to Remilitarize the Rhine," *Journal of Contemporary History*, 34:1 (Jan., 1999), 5–18.
42. Ibid.
43. No. 564, DGFP, C:IV, 1142.
44. Ibid.
45. Shore, "Hitler, Intelligence and the Decision to Remilitarize the Rhine," 9. Göring's reaction is surprising given his political position and support for equally risky moves in 1937 and 1938. But in the words of Jozef Lipski, the Polish ambassador who spent a great deal of time with Göring, "Göring was visibly terrified by the Chancellor's decision to remilitarize the Rhineland . . . he openly gave me to understand that Hitler had taken this extremely risky step by his own decision, in contradiction to the position taken by the generals." Shore, citing Jozef Lipski, *Diplomat in Berlin, 1933–1939: Papers and Memoirs of Jozef Lipski*, ed. Wachlav Jedrzejewicz (New York: Columbia University Press, 1968), 252.
46. Shore, 18.
47. Otto D. Tolischus, "Army Marches In as Hitler Speaks: In Full War Equipment It Goes to Rhineland, Ending Its Advance Near Frontier," *New York Times*, March 8, 1936, 1.
48. See Stephen A. Schuker, "France and the Remilitarization of the Rhineland, 1936."
49. Ibid., 322.
50. Ibid., 330.
51. Joseph Goebbels, "Diary Entry of March 8, 1936," in *Die Tagebücher von Joseph Goebbels* [The Diaries of Joseph Goebbels]. Referenced Digitally at Die Tagebücher von Joseph Goebbels Online Database, DeGruyter.

CHAPTER 28

1. For the best treatment in English—particularly of the international dimensions of the conflict—see Anthony Beevor, *The Battle for Spain: The Spanish Civil War* (London: Weidenfeld and Nicolson, 2006).
2. Homze, *Arming the Luftwaffe*, 170.
3. Paul Preston, *The Spanish Civil War: Reaction, Revolution and Revenge* (London: Harper Perennial, 2006), 153.
4. Daniel Kowalsky, *Stalin and the Spanish Civil War* (New York: Columbia University Press, 2004), 14/iii, http://www.gutenberg-e.org/kod01/index.html.
5. As the purges in the Soviet Union accelerated, those officers in Spain were frequently replaced as they were recalled for execution. Among the pilots, this proved disastrous for combat effectiveness, as those sent to Spain often had very little flying experience. Kowalsky, 14/v.
6. Messerschmidt, "Foreign Policy and Preparation for War," 621. Italy and a number of smaller states would begin acceding to the Anti-Comintern Pact the following year.
7. "Testimony of Hermann Göring," *Nuremberg Trial Proceedings Vol. 9*, 14 March 1946, http://avalon.law.yale.edu/imt/03-14-46.asp#Göring2.
8. One senior figure in Spain who had almost attended Lipetsk was Adolf Galland. He went through the first six months of Lipetsk coursework in Germany and was selected to go to Lipetsk as one of the Jung-Märker of late summer 1933, but his class was instead diverted to a training camp in Italy after the facility at Lipetsk closed.
9. Weinberg, *The Foreign Policy of Hitler's Germany: Starting World War II, 1937–1939* (Chicago: The University of Chicago Press, 1980), 292; Richard R. Muller, "Hitler, Airpower, and Statecraft," in *The Influence of Airpower upon History: Statesmanship, Diplomacy, and Foreign Policy since 1903*, eds. Robin Higham and Mark Parillo (Lexington: University Press of Kentucky, 2013), 97.
10. Homze, *Arming the Luftwaffe*, 170.
11. Jan Forsgren, *Messerschmitt Bf 109: The Design and Operational History* (London: Fonthill Media, 2017), 93.

12. Christopher C. Locksley, "Condor over Spain: The Civil War, Combat Experience and the Development of Luftwaffe Airpower Doctrine," *Civil Wars*, 2:1 (1999), 79.

13. The bombing of Guernica was not in fact a test of strategic bombing, as is sometimes argued; instead, it was part of consistent prewar Luftwaffe doctrine to prioritize the support of ground operations within 60 miles of the front. The aim of the attack had been to impede the movement of Republican forces retreating from the front by causing panic and destroying bridges. Because of the rapid success of the Nationalist ground offensive following the bombing of Guernica, Wolfram von Richtofen would proclaim Guernica as "the greatest success" in confirming Luftwaffe doctrine. See Locksley, "Condor over Spain," 83.

14. James M. Minifie, "Basques Charge Germans with Guernica Raid: Eyewitnesses Describe Destruction of 'Holy City' in Three-Hour Bombing," *New York Herald Tribune*, 6 May 1937, 12.

15. Ironically, perhaps, the idea of the Risk Air Force itself had been largely abandoned by that juncture in the face of difficulties producing medium and heavy bombers. The Luftwaffe had never shown as much enthusiasm for strategic bombing as Italy or Great Britain in any case. Nevertheless, the explosive growth of the Luftwaffe did discourage British and French action, so in a sense, it succeeded in its ultimate objective. See Murray, *Strategy for Defeat*, 14.

16. Kotkin, *Stalin: Waiting for Hitler*, 411.

17. Ibid., 411.

18. Ibid., 425

19. Ibid., 418–419.

20. Ibid., 422.

21. A. V. Gorbatov, *Years Off My Life: The Memoir of General of the Soviet Army A. V. Gorbatov*, trans. Gordon Clough and Anthony Cash (New York: W. W. Norton, 1965), 103.

22. Ibid., 104.

23. Ibid., 108–109.

24. Ibid., 113.

25. Gorbatov was fortunate. After thirty months of the work camp, Gorbatov was recalled to Moscow, interrogated again, declared innocent, and suddenly released in March 1941. The next day, he was surreally given a face-to-face meeting with Marsal S. K. Timoshenko, the people's commissar for defense, who reinstated him in the army and warned him that there was a major war coming, and that "there's work for you." Gorbatov would rise to become a four-star general in the Red Army. Ibid., 129–130; 152–153.

26. Zeidler, 299.

27. Conquest, *The Great Terror*, 277–278.

28. J. Arch Getty and Oleg V. Naumov, *The Road to Terror: Stalin and the Self-Destruction of the Bolsheviks*, trans. Benjamin Sher (New Haven, CT: Yale University Press, 1999), 446.

29. Erickson, *The Soviet High Command*, 478, 505–506.

30. Getty, Naumov, *The Road to Terror*, 446.

31. Bernd Bonwetsch, "The Purge of the Military and the Red Army's Operational Capability during the 'Great Patriotic War,'" in *From Peace to War*, ed. Bernd Wegner, 396.

32. See Igor Lukes, *Czechoslovakia between Stalin and Hitler: The Diplomacy of Edvard Beneš in the 1930s* (Oxford, UK: Oxford University Press, 1996), 91–112. Iuliya Kantor says that the relevant documents arrived on Stalin's desk in mid-May 1937, too late to suggest they had any influence on the decision to arrest Tukhachevsky. Kantor, *Zaklyataya druzhba*, 150.

33. Kantor, *Voina i mir Mikhaila Tukhachevsogo*, 408–409, 416.

34. Erickson, *The Soviet High Command*, 483–485.

35. Ibid., 485.

36. Getty and Naumov, *The Road to Terror*, 446. See Kantor, *Voina i mir Mikhaila Tukhachevsogo*, for much evidence about the trial. Her ultimate assessment is that "the

question of whether Tukhachevsky was in fact a conspirator does not hold up under scrutiny." Kantor, 501.

37. It is odd that the only one of Tukhachevsky's inner circle not arrested was Georgy Samoilovich Isserson, a native German speaker from the Baltic, who had some of the closest personal connections to Reichswehr officers, having studied in Germany in the 1920s as part of an exchange. Harrison, *Architect of Soviet Victory in World War Two*, 10.

38. Simon Sebag Montefiore, *Stalin: Court of the Red Tsar* (New York: Vintage, 2003), 221–222.

39. Erickson, *The Soviet High Command*, 483–485.

40. Alvin D. Coox, "The Lesser of Two Hells: NKVD General G. S. Lyushkov's Defection to Japan, 1938–1945, part I," *Journal of Slavic Military Studies*, 11:3 (1998), 151.

41. "Spisok komandno-nachal'stvuiushchego sostava RKKA," June 1938, 37–60.

42. Ibid.

43. "Spetsialnaia svodka," 15 August 1930, 1–8. This is the recollection of Ivan Dubitsky. Dubinsky himself served at the Kazan Armored School after the departure of the Germans. He, too, was arrested and tried as a saboteur during the Great Terror. He survived in the camps until Stalin's death and was released. Late in his life, he penned an extensive memoir of his time during the Russian Civil War, the interwar Red Army, and the Gulags.

44. "Spetsialnaia svodka," 15 August 1930, 1–8.

45. Jonathan Haslam, *The Soviet Union and the Struggle for Collective Security in Europe, 1933–1939* (New York: St. Martin's Press, 1984), 145; Kotkin, *Stalin: Waiting for Hitler*, 402.

46. Haslam, *The Soviet Union and the Struggle for Collective Security*, 145.

47. Conquest, *The Great Terror*, 423.

48. Haslam, *The Soviet Union and the Struggle for Collective Security*, 145.

49. This was in early 1939. Albert Resis, "The Fall of Litvinov: Harbinger of the German-Soviet Non-Aggression Pact," *Europe-Asia Studies*, 52:1 (Jan., 2000), 33–56, 34.

50. Ibid., 34.

51. Kotkin, *Stalin: Waiting for Hitler*, 431.

52. Donald Cameron Watt, *How War Came: The Immediate Origins of the Second World War, 1938–1939* (New York: Pantheon, 1989), 235.

53. Erickson, *The Soviet High Command*, 489.

54. See, for instance, No. 627, *ADAP*, D:I, 922.

CHAPTER 29

1. No. 19, DGFP, D:I, 29.

2. Ibid., 34.

3. Tooze, *Wages of Destruction*, 203, 230–241.

4. No. 19, DGFP, D:I, 34.

5. Ibid., 38.

6. Ibid., 39.

7. Deist, "The Rearmament of the Wehrmacht," 493.

8. Forsgren, *Messerschmitt Bf 109*, 32.

9. Ibid., 127.

10. Brian Bond and Williamson Murray, "The British Armed Forces, 1918–1939," in *Military Effectiveness, Volume II: The Interwar Period*, eds. Allan R. Millett and Williamson Murray (Boston: Unwin Hyman, 1988), 98–130, 102.

11. Bond, Murray, "The British Armed Forces, 1918–1939," 103; John Paul Harris, "The War Office and Rearmament 1935–1939" (unpubl. diss., King's College London, 1983), 148.

12. Murray, "Armored Warfare," 11.

13. Angelucci, *Encyclopedia of Military Aircraft*, 217.

14. Ibid., 218.

15. For the process of British heavy bomber development, see Colin S. Sinnott, *The RAF and Aircraft Design: Air Staff Operational Requirements, 1923–1939* (London: Routledge, 2001), 157–216.

16. John Paul Harris, "The War Office and Rearmament 1935–1939," 268; see also Benjamin Coombs, *British Tank Production and the War Economy, 19341945* (London: Bloomsbury, 2013).

17. Harris, "The War Office and Rearmament 1935–1939," 241. British officer Colonel Giffard Martel attended the Soviet maneuvers with General Wavell in 1936. He noted after witnessing more than a thousand Soviet vehicles performing in the maneuvers that "Unless we can improve the A9 [medium tank] to a considerable extent I cannot help feeling dismay at the idea of our building any large number of these tanks which will be inferior to existing Russian tanks." So impressed was he that Martell immediately sought to find Christie, the designer whose suspension and chassis had proven to be the foundation of the success of the BT line. The Soviets refused to supply a vehicle, so Martel tracked down Christie himself. Christie had not fared well, was nearly bankrupt, and had only one prototype left, which he had mortgaged. Martel bought the vehicle, paid off the mortgage, and—to avoid American government attempts to block the export of the vehicle—had it shipped in crates labeled "grapefruit and tractor." This would mark the beginning of the development of Britain's Cruiser tank concept. Harris, "The War Office and Rearmament 1935–1939," 241–242.

18. Robert J. Young, *In Command of France: French Foreign Policy and Military Planning, 1933–1940* (Cambridge, MA: Harvard University Press, 1978), 36.

19. Jeffrey J. Clarke, "The Nationalization of War Industries in France, 1936–1937: A Case Study," *Journal of Modern History*, 49:3 (Sep., 1977), 411–430.

20. Ibid., 420.

21. Martin Thomas, "French Economic Affairs and Rearmament: The First Crucial Months, June–September 1936," *Journal of Contemporary History*, 27:4 (Oct., 1992), 660.

22. Maiolo, *Cry Havoc*, 236; Robert Doughty, "The French Armed Forces, 1918–1940," in *Military Innovation in the Interwar Period*, eds. Williamson Murray and Allan Millett (Cambridge, UK: Cambridge University Press, 1996), 51.

23. Doughty, "The French Armed Forces, 1918–1940," 45–46.

24. Ibid., 51.

25. Julian Jackson, *The Fall of France: The Nazi Invasion of 1940* (Oxford, UK: Oxford University Press, 2003), 20.

26. Doughty, "The French Armed Forces, 1918–1940," 45.

27. See Stephen J. Zaloga, *Panzer III vs. Somua S35: Belgium 1940* (London: Bloomsbury, 2014); Steven Zaloga, *Panzer VI versus Char B1 Bis: France 1940* (Oxford, UK: Osprey, 2011), 8–9.

28. See Doughty, *The Seeds of Disaster*, 1–5, 161–162. French doctrine stated that "Tanks are only supplementary means of action placed temporarily at the disposition of the infantry." Doughty, *The Seeds of Disaster*, 147.

29. Young, *In Command of France*, 17, 19.

30. Andreas Hillgruber, "The German Military Leaders' View of Russia Prior to the Attack on the Soviet Union," in *From Peace to War*, 178–179.

31. Doyle, Chamberlain, and Jentz, *Panzertruppen*, 58–60, 88–90.

32. As John Mearsheimer has argued, examining the origins of the Second World War in Europe, conventional deterrence breaks down when policymakers in one state think that changes in the material balance of power offer them the prospect of a quick and decisive victory. John Mearsheimer, *Conventional Deterrence* (Ithaca, NY: Cornell University Press, 1983), 109.

33. Robertson, *Hitler's Pre-war Policy and Military Plans*, 109.

CHAPTER 30

1. *Nuremberg Trial Proceedings Volume 12*, 195–197.

2. Wheeler-Bennett, *The Nemesis of Power*, 365.

3. Ibid.

4. Harold Deutsch, *Hitler and His Generals: The Hidden Crisis, January–June 1938* (Minneapolis: University of Minnesota Press, 1974), 105–111.

5. Wheeler-Bennett, *The Nemesis of Power*, 366.

6. Ibid.

7. *Nuremberg Trial Proceedings, Volume 12*, 197–198.

8. Wheeler-Bennett, *The Nemesis of Power*, 366.

9. *Nuremberg Trial Proceedings Volume 12*, 198–199. According to witnesses at the Nuremberg War Crimes Tribunal, there was a Gestapo record of a captain named "Frisch" who had indeed hired male prostitutes. It was a relatively easy matter to doctor the records.

10. *Nuremberg Trial Proceedings, Volume 12*, 198–199.

11. Wheeler-Bennett, *The Nemesis of Power*, 369.

12. Gerhard Weinberg, *Starting World War Two, 1937–1939*, 43; Deist, "The Rearmament of the Wehrmacht," 517.

13. *Nuremberg Trial Proceedings, Volume 12*, 197. Several alumni of Soviet cooperation were on the list, including General Oswald Lutz, one of Germany's Panzer pioneers.

14. *Nuremberg Trial Proceedings, Volume 12*, 197.

15. Richard Overy and Andrew Wheatcroft, *The Road to War* (London: Macmillan, 1989), 46.

16. Weinberg, *Starting World War Two, 1937–1939*, 378–464.

17. Robertson, *Hitler's Pre-war Policy and Military Plans*, 114–116.

18. No. 78, DGFP, D:II, 161; No. 87, DGFP, D:II, 170–171.

19. Guderian, *Panzer Leader*, 51.

20. Robertson, *Hitler's Pre-war Policy and Military Plans*, 33–34, 125. See DGFP (D), Vol. II.

21. Robertson, *Hitler's Pre-war Policy and Military Plans*, 126.

22. No. 221, DGFP, D:II, 357–362.

23. In Coox's telling, Lyushkov had gotten lost in a storm, trying to sneak away from his own staff while he "scouted the border."

24. Coox, "The Lesser of Two Hells," 145.

25. Ibid., 148. He was also, incidentally, connected to Germany, once his area of responsibility. Lyushkov had served with Soviet intelligence in Germany, where his task had been to infiltrate Junkers to investigate its aircraft production.

26. Coox, "The Lesser of Two Hells," 150.

27. Ibid., 151.

28. Ibid., 158.

29. See Alvin Coox, *The Anatomy of a Small War: The Soviet-Japanese Struggle for Changkufeng/Khasan, 1938* (Westport, CT: Greenwood Press, 1977).

30. Kotkin, *Stalin: Waiting for Hitler*, 538.

31. Erickson, *The Soviet High Command*, 499.

32. "Major Schmundt: Summary of Hitler-Keitel Conversation of 21 April 1938," No. 133, DGFP, D:II, 2, cited in Messerschmidt, "Foreign Policy and Preparation for War," 655.

33. Messerschmidt, "Foreign Policy and Preparation for War," 654.

34. No. 15, DGFP, D:II.

35. Messerschmidt, "Foreign Policy and Preparation for War," 660.

36. Watt, *How War Came*, 105.

37. On Beneš's orders, the Czech military began a partial mobilization in May 1938 on rumors of a potential German attack. The source of the information about a potential German attack very well might have been Soviet intelligence, aiming either to embroil Germany in war with the Western Allies or to deter Hitler's aggression. See Igor Lukes, "The Czechoslovak Partial Mobilization in May 1938: A Mystery (Almost) Solved," *Journal of Contemporary History*, 31:4 (Oct., 1996), 699–720.

38. Muller, "Hitler, Airpower, and Statecraft," 101.

39. William Keylor, "France and the Illusion of American Support," in *French Defeat, 1940: Reassessments*, ed. Joel Blatt (New York: Berghahn Books, 1998), 233–234.

40. Milan Hauner, "The Sudeten Crisis of 1938: Beneš and Munich," in *The Origins of the Second World War: An International Perspective*, ed. Frank McDonough (London: Continuum, 2011), 364–365.

41. Ibid., 362.

42. No. 487, DGFP, D:II, 786–798. Chamberlain's second visit to meet with Hitler ended with Chamberlain's rather pathetic plea to Hitler that he [Chamberlain] "had risked his whole career" for a deal over Czechoslovakia, and now, rather than a success, "was being accused in certain circles in Great Britain of having sold and betrayed Czechoslovakia, of having yielded to the dictators and so on, and on leaving England that morning he had actually been booed. All this would show the Führer the difficulties he had had to make in order to obtain agreement in principle to the cession of [Czechoslovak] territory. He therefore could not quite understand why his proposals could not be accepted." No. 562, DGFP, D:II, 875.

43. No. 669, DGFP, D:II, 1005.

44. No. 1227, DBFP, 3:2, 630–635.

45. Watt, *How War Came*, 129.

46. Messerschmidt, "Foreign Policy and Preparation for War," 672–673. Shortly thereafter, he also unleashed Kristallnacht, a savage anti-Jewish pogrom that resulted in the deaths of at least ninety German Jews and the incarceration of tens of thousands more.

CHAPTER 31

1. "Treaty of Mutual Assistance between the Czechoslovak Republic and the Union of Soviet Socialist Republics," May 16, 1935, *League of Nations Treaty Series Volume 159* (1935), 1–3. Available digitally at https://heinonline.org/HOL/Page?handle=hein.unl/lnts0159&div=1&id=&page=&collection=unl; see also Anna M. Cienciala, "The Nazi-Soviet Pact of August 23, 1939: When Did Stalin Decide to Align with Hitler, and Was Poland the Culprit?," in *Ideology, Politics, and Diplomacy in East Central Europe*, ed. M. B. B. Biskupski (Rochester, NY: University of Rochester Press, 2003), 175.

2. See, for instance, Lukes, *Czechoslovakia between Stalin and Hitler*; Hugh Ragsdale, "Soviet Military Preparations and Policy in the Munich Crisis: New Evidence," *Jahrbücher für Geschichte Osteuropas*, 47:2 (1999), 210–226; Jiri Hochman, *The Soviet Union and the Failure of Collective Security, 1934–1938* (Ithaca, NY: Cornell University Press, 1984); Zara Steiner, "The Soviet Commissariat of Foreign Affairs and the Czechoslovakian Crisis in 1938: New Material from the Soviet Archives," *The Historical Journal*, 42:3 (Sep., 1999), 751–779.

3. Ragsdale, "Soviet Military Preparations and Policy in the Munich Crisis: New Evidence," 226; David Stone, *A Military History of Russia*, 189–190; Erickson, *The Soviet High Command*, 503.

4. Steiner, "The Soviet Commissariat of Foreign Affairs and the Czechoslovakian Crisis in 1938," 752.

5. There has long been an intense debate over which state took the initiative and when Stalin decided upon an arrangement with Hitler. Roberts long defended a late date, suggesting Stalin's decision was made only in desperation in August and arguing that "Soviet-German contacts in May–June 1939 are of limited significance." He further suggests that Astakhov and other Soviet figures may have been acting independently when they approached their German counterparts in the spring of 1939. Roberts, *The Unholy Alliance*, 144. Of course, initiative of that sort seems unlikely in a Soviet system that was still in the process of murdering hundreds of its diplomats. Fleischhauer suggests that the decision made in mid-August to partner with Hitler was a "logical way out of a hopelessly narrow set of possible Soviet foreign policy options," a conundrum created by French and British intransigence in the August negotiations. Ingeborg Fleischhauer, "Soviet Foreign Policy and the Origins of the Hitler-Stalin Pact," in *From Peace to War*, ed. Bernd Wegner, 45. True, but that French and British "intransigence" vis-à-vis a Soviet Union—in part a reaction to the bloody purges—had become clear well before August 1939, as had alternative Soviet approaches. Watt sees

Soviet demarches in May 1939 as in earnest, opening "the long road to the Nazi-Soviet pact." Watt, *How War Came*, 254. Weinberg agrees, thinking that a Soviet decision was largely made between March and May, with tentative steps initiated by Moscow: "If the earliest hints . . . all came from the Soviet side, this may have been due to the fact that the Russian government was better informed about German intentions than the other way around." Weinberg, *Starting World War II, 1937–1939*, 568. Historian of Russia Jonathan Haslam argues that Stalin actively pursued relations with both Western powers and Germany from 1933 onward, likely deciding on partnership with the latter following the Polish Guarantee. Jonathan Haslam, "Soviet-German Relations and the Origins of the Second World War: The Jury Is Still Out," *Journal of Modern History*, 69:4 (December 1997), 785–797, 791. Anna Cienciala goes even farther, suggesting that "Stalin always preferred a pact with Germany." Cienciala, "The Nazi Soviet Pact of August 23, 1939," 153. The evidence presented here suggests that Stalin repeatedly tried to restore good relations with Germany in the 1930s, in part as a product of Soviet economic and military dependence on Germany; that he feared the formation of an anti-Soviet coalition; and that he believed by the spring of 1939 that he could get far more from a partnership with Germany than he could with France or Great Britain. The latter depended in part on the past history of collaboration, and part on the prospect of a war in Western Europe that would weaken all the states involved and give the USSR a chance to continue to improve its military.

6. Edward E. Ericson III, *Feeding the German Eagle: Soviet Economic Aid to Nazi Germany, 1933–1941* (Westport, CT: Praeger, 1999), 187 (Table 1.1).

7. Ericson, *Feeding the German Eagle*, 30

8. No. 619, DGFP, D:I, 912.

9. Ericson, *Feeding the German Eagle*, 28.

10. Ibid., 30.

11. "Zamestitelyu predsedatelya soveta narodnykh komissarov SSSR, Tov. Mikoyanu" [To Deputy Chairman of the Council of People's Commissars, Comrade Mikoyan], 28 January 1939, RGVA, f. 33987, op. 3s, d. 1237 (1), l. 43.

12. For more details of the trade negotiations, see Nos. 481–485, 488–495, 613, 620–631, *ADAP*, D:4.

13. Ericson, *Feeding the German Eagle*, 34.

14. Ibid., 36. By contrast, Ribbentrop claimed in his memoirs—written rapidly shortly before his execution in 1946—that the entire idea of collaboration with the Soviets had been his idea, and that the idea had come to him following Stalin's speech of March 10, which stated that "Russia did not intend to 'pull the chestnuts out of the fire' to please certain capitalist Powers." Given that the German Foreign Ministry broke off trade talks the following day, this was obviously untrue. Joachim von Ribbentrop, *The Ribbentrop Memoirs*, trans. Oliver Watson (London: Weidenfeld and Nicolson, 1954), 108.

15. Weinberg, *The Road to War*, 534.

16. Fest, *Hitler*, 570–571; Richard J. Evans, *The Third Reich in Power: 1933–1939* (New York: Penguin, 2005), 682.

17. Weinberg, *Starting World War Two, 1937–1939*, 539.

18. Evans, *The Third Reich in Power*, 683.

19. Weinberg, *Starting World War Two, 1937–1939*, 539.

20. Neville Chamberlain, "Speech by the Prime Minister at Birmingham on March 17, 1939," 17 March 1939, *The British War Bluebook*. Digitized at http://avalon.law.yale.edu/wwii/blbk09.asp.

21. Robertson, *Hitler's Pre-war Policy and Military Plans*, 167.

22. Weinberg, *Starting World War Two, 1937-1939*, 537–538.

23. Ibid., 542.

24. G. Bruce Strang, "Once More unto the Breach: Britain's Guarantee to Poland, March 1939," *Journal of Contemporary History*, 31:4 (Oct., 1996), 721–752.

25. Kotkin, *Stalin: Waiting for Hitler*, 616.

26. Strang, "Britain's Guarantee to Poland," 738.
27. Rolf-Dieter Müller, *Enemy in the East*, 148.
28. Fest, *Hitler*, 578.
29. Robertson, *Hitler's Pre-war Policy and Military Plans*, 165.
30. No. 192, No. 193, DGFP, D:VIII, 207–212, cited by Maiolo, *Cry Havoc*, 273.
31. Tooze, *Wages of Destruction*, 316. Behind closed doors, Hitler expressed great frustrations with the slowdown in rearmament and the drive for autarky: "The Four Year Plan has failed and we are finished if we do not achieve victory in the coming war."
32. Maiolo, *Cry Havoc*, 268.
33. Watt, *How War Came*, 239.
34. Ingeborg Fleischhauer, *Der Pakt: Hitler, Stalin und die Initiative der deutschen Diplomatie, 1938–1939* [The Pact: Hitler, Stalin and the German Diplomatic Initiative, 1938–1939] (Frankfurt am Main: Ullstein, 1990), 118.
35. Robertson, *Hitler's Pre-war Policy and Military Plans*, 167; Kotkin, *Stalin: Waiting for Hitler*, 617.
36. Cienciala, "The Nazi-Soviet Pact of August 23, 1939," 171; "Memorandum by the State Secretary in the German Foreign Office (Weizsäcker)," in *Nazi-Soviet Relations 1939–1941: Nazi-Soviet Relations, 1939–1941: Documents from the Archives of the German Foreign Office* (hereafter NSR), eds. Raymond James Sontag and James Stuart Beddie (Washington DC: US Department of State, 1948), 1. For the Soviet side of this approach, see "Telegramma polnomochnogo prestavitelia SSSR v Germanii A. F. Merekalova v narodnyi komissariat inostrannykh del SSSR" [Telegram from the Ambassador Representative of the USSR in Germany A. F. Merekalov to the Soviet People's Commissariat of Foreign Affairs], 18 April 1939, in *God krizisa: 1938–1939, Tom II, Dokumenty i materiali* [Year of Crisis 1938–1939, Volume II, Documents and Materials] (Moscow: Ministry of Foreign Affairs USSR, 1990), 389.
37. Kotkin, *Stalin: Waiting for Hitler*, 622.
38. *The Maisky Diaries*, 179.
39. Kotkin, *Stalin: Waiting for Hitler*, 623.
40. *The Maisky Diaries*, 179.
41. *Molotov Remembers: Inside Kremlin Politics, Conversations with Felix Chuev*, ed. Albert Resis (Chicago: Ivan R. Dee, 1993), 8.
42. Resis, "The Fall of Litvinov," 35.
43. Cienciala, "The Nazi-Soviet Pact of August 23, 1939," 173, citing Andrei Gromyko.
44. No. 1, in *Die Beziehungen zwischen Deutschland und der Sowjetunion, 1939–1941: Dokumente des Auswärtigen Amtes* (hereafter BZDS) [Relations between Germany and the Soviet Union, 1939–1941: Documents from the German Foreign Office], ed. Alfred Seidel (Tübingen: H. Laupp'sche Buchhandlung, 1949), 1–2.
45. Cienciala, "The Nazi-Soviet Pact of August 23, 1939," 174; BZDS, No. 2, No. 3, 2–3. See also Resis, "The Fall of Litvinov," 35.
46. Astakhov, "Pismo vremmenogo poverennogo v delakh SSSR v Germanii G. A. Astakhova zamestiteliu narodnogo komissara inostrannykh del SSSR V. P. Potemkinu" [Letter from the Chargé-d'Affaires of the USSR in Germany G. A. Astakhov to the Deputy People's Commissar of Foreign Affairs of the USSR V. P. Potemkin], *God krizisa, Tom I*, 457–458.
47. Anthony Read and David Fisher, *The Deadly Embrace: Hitler, Stalin and the Nazi-Soviet Pact, 1939–1941* (New York: W. W. Norton, 1988), 75.
48. Köstring, *General Ernst Köstring*, 32 quoted in Ericson, *Feeding the German Eagle*, 45.
49. Fleischhauer, *Der Pakt*, 176-183. Fleischhauer argues that much of the impetus for the Molotov-Ribbentrop Pact and the behind-the-scenes maneuvering that resulted in the prospect being brought to Hitler's attention came from senior diplomats in the German Foreign Ministry like Ambassador Schulenberg, Karl Schnurre, and Gustav Hilger—the *Ostpolitik* faction who believed German security was best guaranteed by a partnership in the East.
50. No. 5, BZDS, 5; No. 332, DGFP, D:VI, 429.

51. No. 5, BZDS, 5–6.
52. "Memorandum by the German Ambassador in the Soviet Union (Schulenburg)," 20 May 1939, NSR, 5.
53. "Zapis' besedy narodnogo komissara inostrannykh del SSSR B. M. Molotova s poslom Germanii v SSSR F. Shulenburgom" [Record of a Conversation between the People's Commissar of Foreign Affairs V. M. Molotov and the Ambassador of Germany F. Schulenberg], 20 May 1939, *God krizisa, Tom I*, 482–483.
54. "The German Ambassador in the Soviet Union (Schulenburg) to the State Secretary in the German Foreign Office (Weizsäcker)," 5 June 1939, NSR, 18.
55. Ericson, *Feeding the German Eagle*, 46.
56. "Foreign Office Memorandum (Woermann)," 15 June 1939, NSR, 20.
57. Ericson, *Feeding the German Eagle*, 46–47
58. "The German Ambassador in the Soviet Union (Schulenburg) to the German Foreign Office," 3 July 1939, NSR, 28.
59. Ericson, *Feeding the German Eagle*, 49.
60. Ibid., 49.
61. Ibid., 54.
62. Watt, *How War Came*, 426–428, 480.
63. Ibid., 231.
64. "The German Ambassador in the Soviet Union (Schulenberg) to the German Foreign Office," 4 August 1939, NSR, 39, quoted in Ericson, *Feeding the German Eagle*, 54.
65. Ericson, *Feeding the German Eagle*, 57.
66. Robertson, *Hitler's Pre-war Policy and Military Plans*, 177.
67. Fest, *Hitler*, 585.
68. Moorhouse, *The Devils' Alliance*, 20–21.
69. Kotkin, *Stalin: Waiting for Hitler*, 657.
70. Walter Duranty, "The Enigma of Germany and Russia: The pact made by Hitler and Stalin explained in terms of their personalities by a close observer of the Russian experiment and the European scene," *New York Times*, 3 September 1939, 1.
71. German diplomat Johnnie von Herwarth wrote that there was "near unanimity amongst the Western embassies in Moscow that summer that Stalin had a higher regard for the Germans than for the other Western powers, and that he certainly trusted them more." Moorhouse, *The Devils' Alliance*, 23.
72. Stalin made this clear in a conversation with Georgi Dimitrov in September 1939: "A war is on between two groups of capitalist countries (poor and rich as regards colonies, raw materials, and so forth) for the redivision of the world, for the domination of the world. We see nothing wrong in their having a good hard fight and weakening each other. It would be fine if at the hands of Germany the position of the richest capitalist countries (especially England) were shaken. Hitler, without understanding it or desiring it, is shaking and undermining the capitalist system. . . . We preferred agreements with the so-called democratic countries and therefore conducted negotiations. But the English and French wanted us for farmhands [*v bastrakakh*] and at no cost! We, of course, would not go for being farmhands, still less for getting nothing in return." Georgi Dimitrov, *The Diary of Georgi Dimitrov, 1933–1949*, ed. Ivo Banac (New Haven, CT: Yale University Press, 2003), 115–116.
73. Kotkin, *Stalin: Waiting for Hitler*, 673.
74. Moorhouse, *The Devils' Alliance*, 15.
75. Kotkin, *Stalin: Waiting for Hitler*, 659.
76. "Zapis' besedy narodnogo komissara inostrannykh del SSSR V. M. Molotova s poslom Germanii v SSSR F. Shulenburgom" [Record of the Conversation between the People's Commissar for Foreign Affairs of the USSR V. M. Molotov and the Ambassador of Germany in the USSR F. Schulenberg," 17 August 1939, in *Dokumenty vneshnei politiki, 1939 god* (hereafter DVP) [Foreign Policy Documents, 1939] (Moscow: Ministry of Foreign Affairs of the Russian Federation, 1992), available digitally through *Militera: Voennaia literatura*, 609.

77. BZDS, No. 33, 56–58, 57.
78. Memorandum by the German Ambassador in the Soviet Union (Schulenburg), 16 August 1939, NSR, 53; "Pamiatnaia zapiska vruchennaia V. M. Molotovu F. Schulenbergom 15 avgusta 1939 g." [Aide-Memoire Given to Vyacheslav Molotov by F. Schulenberg on August 15, 1939], 15 August 1939, in *God krizisa, Tom II*, 232–233.
79. "Zapis' besedy narodnogo komissara inostrannykh del SSSR B. M. Molotova s poslom Germanii v SSSR F Shulenburgom" [Record of a Conversation between the People's Commissar of Foreign Affairs V. M. Molotov and the Ambassador of Germany F. Schulenberg], 19 August 1939, in *God krizisa, Tom II*, 274–278.
80. Cienciala, "The Nazi-Soviet Pact of August 23, 1939," 207.
81. "The German Ambassador in the Soviet Union (Schulenburg) to the German Foreign Office," 19 August 1939, NSR, 63–65.
82. Kotkin, *Stalin: Waiting for Hitler*, 659.
83. "Foreign Office Memorandum: The German-Soviet Trade Agreement," 29 August 1939, NSR, 83–85.
84. This was in addition to 420 million Reichsmarks of ongoing trade and outstanding credit payments owed by the USSR.
85. Ericson, *Feeding the German Eagle*, 61.
86. Geoffrey Roberts, *The Unholy Alliance: Stalin's Pact with Hitler* (London: I. B. Tauris, 1989), 176.
87. Cienciala, "The Nazi-Soviet Pact of August 23, 1939," 209.
88. Moorhouse, *The Devils' Alliance*, 24; Kotkin, *Stalin: Waiting for Hitler*, 661.
89. Kotkin, *Stalin: Waiting for Hitler*, 660.
90. Hilger and Meyer, *The Incompatible Allies*, 300; Kotkin, *Stalin: Waiting for Hitler*, 662.
91. Ericson, *Feeding the German Eagle*, 58.
92. Watt, *How War Came*, 406–407.
93. Kotkin, *Stalin: Waiting for Hitler*, 662; Watt, *How War Came*, 542.

CHAPTER 32

1. *Molotov Remembers*, 12.
2. Kotkin, *Stalin: Waiting for Hitler*, 663
3. Samuel W. Mitcham Jr., *The Men of Barbarossa: Commanders of the German Army* (Havertown, PA: Casemate, 2009), 28–29.
4. Kotkin, *Stalin: Waiting for Hitler*, 663.
5. Ribbentrop, *Memoirs*, 111.
6. "Treaty of Nonaggression between Germany and the Union of Soviet Socialist Republics," 23 August 1939, NSR, 78.
7. Kotkin, *Stalin: Waiting for Hitler*, 664; Joseph Goebbels, "Diary Entry of August 24, 1939."
8. Moorhouse, *The Devils' Alliance*, 27.
9. Read, Fisher, *The Deadly Embrace*, 252.
10. Kotkin, *Stalin: Waiting for Hitler*, 666–667.
11. *Molotov Remembers*, 12.
12. "Memorandum of a Conversation Held on the Night of August 23d to 24th, between the Reich Foreign Minister, on the One Hand, and Herr Stalin and the Chairman of the Council of People's Commissars Molotov, on the Other Hand," 24 August 1939, NSR, 72–76.
13. Walter Lippmann, "Today and Tomorrow: Hitler-Stalin Pact More Extensive Than Disclosed," September 21, 1939, *Washington Post*, 11.
14. Fraser M. Ottanelli, *The Communist Party of the United States: From the Depression to World War Two* (New Brunswick, NJ: Rutgers University Press, 1991), 197–198.
15. Goebbels, "Diary Entry of August 24, 1939."
16. Oskar von Niedermayer, "Sowjetrussland: Ein wehrpolitisches Bild," *Militärwissenschaftliche Rundschau* (1939, Issue 5/6), Russisch-deutsches Projekt zur Digitalisierung deutscher Dokumente in den Archiven der Russischen Föderation

[Russian-German Project for the Digitalization of German Documents in the Archives of the Russian Federation], http://wwii.germandocsinrussia.org/de/nodes/1337-akte-537-artikel-von-oberst-prof-dr-ritter-oskar-von-niedermayer-sowjetrussland-ein-wehrpo#page/29/mode/inspect/zoom/4. Article referenced in Rolf-Dieter Müller, *Enemy in the East: Hitler's Secret Plans to Invade the Soviet Union*, trans. Alexander Starritt (London: I. B. Tauris, 2015), 170.

17. Ibid.
18. Snyder, *Bloodlands*, 119; Steven Zaloga and Victor Madej, *The Polish Campaign* (New York: Hippocrene Books, 1985), 157; Roger Moorhouse, *Poland 1939: The Outbreak of World War II* (New York: Basic Books, 2020), 1–8, 70, 76.
19. Rolf-Dieter Müller, *Enemy in the East*, 155.
20. Guderian, *Panzer Leader*, 82.
21. Zaloga and Madej, 106.
22. Jan T. Gross, "Sovietization of Poland's Eastern Territories," in *From Peace to War*, ed. Bernd Wegner, 63.
23. Albin Głowacki, "The Red Army Invasion and the Fourth Partition of Poland," in *White Spots—Black Spots*, eds. Adam Daniel Rotfeld and Anatoly V. Torkunov, 163.
24. "The German Ambassador in the Soviet Union (Schulenberg) to the German Foreign Office," 5 September 1939, NSR, 87.
25. "The German Ambassador in the Soviet Union (Schulenberg) to the German Foreign Office," 10 September 1939, NSR, 91.
26. Albin Głowacki, "The Red Army Invasion and the Fourth Partition of Poland," 163; Natalia S. Lebedeva, "The Red Army Invasion and the Fourth Partition of Poland," in *White Spots—Black Spots*, ed. Adam Daniel Rotfeld and Anatoly V. Torkunov, 182–208.
27. For more on this engagement—whose timing played a role in the signing of the Molotov-Ribbentrop Pact in August and the subsequent Soviet invasion—see Alvin Coox, *Nomonhan: Japan against Russia, 1939* (Stanford, CA: Stanford University Press, 1985); and Stuart Goldman, *Nomonhan, 1939: The Red Army's Victory That Shaped World War Two* (Annapolis, MD: Naval Institute Press, 2012).
28. Mikhail Semiryaga, *Taini stalinskoi diplomatii* [The Secrets of Stalin's Diplomacy] (Moscow: Visshaia Shkola, 1992), 81–82. He was told this after midnight on September 16—so technically that conversation took place on the 17th.
29. Semiryaga, *Taini stalinskoi diplomatii*, 88; Moorhouse, *Poland 1939*, 195.
30. Moorhouse, *The Devils' Alliance*, xxix.
31. Guderian, *Panzer Leader*, 83.
32. Moorhouse, *The Devils' Alliance*, xxxi.
33. Ibid., xxxi.
34. Ibid., xxxi.
35. Ibid., 35.
36. Tadeusz Bór-Komorowski, *The Secret Army* (London: Victor Gollancz Ltd., 1951), 20.
37. Ibid.
38. Moorhouse, *The Devils' Alliance*, 46; Snyder, *Bloodlands*, 415.
39. Snyder, *Bloodlands*, 415.
40. Richard J. Evans, *The Third Reich at War* (New York: Penguin, 2009), 100–101.

CHAPTER 33
1. Zeidler, "German Soviet Economic Relations during the Hitler-Stalin Pact," 102–103.
2. Interestingly, Stalin also sought to conduct trade negotiations with Great Britain in late September through Ambassador Maisky in London, who assured the British of Soviet neutrality and seemingly sought recognition for Soviet seizures of territory. Stalin presumably looked forward to a long war in the west, and wanted to make sure whoever won would recognize the gains he had made. This also may suggest that he would have seized eastern Poland had a deal been reached with the British and French and transit rights had indeed been granted there. "Telegramma polnomochnogo predstavitelya SSSR v Velikobritanii I. M. Mayskogo v narodnyy komissariat inostrannykh del SSSR"

[Telegram of the Ambassador Representative of the USSR in Great Britain I. M. Maisky to the People's Commissariat of Foreign Affairs of the USSR], 27 September 1939, DVP, 131.

3. "Germano-sovetskii dogovor o druzhbe i granitse mezhdu SSSR i Germaniyey" [German-Soviet Treaty of Friendship and Border Agreement between the USSR and Germany], 28 September 1939, DVP, 134.

4. The secret supplementary text to the September 28 read: "As soon as the Government of the U.S.S.R. shall take special measures on Lithuanian territory to protect its interests, the present German-Lithuanian border, for the purpose of a natural and simple boundary delineation, shall be rectified in such a way that the Lithuanian territory situated to the southwest of the line marked on the attached map should fall to Germany." Ambassador Schulenberg made clear how this was to be interpreted, writing: "I would ask you to consider whether it might not be advisable for us, by a separate secret German-Soviet protocol, to forego the cession of the Lithuanian strip of territory until the Soviet Union actually incorporates Lithuania, an idea on which, I believe, the arrangement concerning Lithuania was originally based." "The German Ambassador in the Soviet Union (Schulenberg) to the German Foreign Office," 3 October 1939, NSR, 112.

5. "The Reich Foreign Minister to the Chairman of the Council of People's Commissars of the Soviet Union (Molotov)," 28 September 1939, NSR, 108.

6. "Pis'mo predsedatelya soveta narodnykh komissarov SSSR, narodnogo komissara inostrannykh del SSSR V. M. Molotova Ministru Inostrannykh Del Germanii I. Fon Ribbentropu" [Letter from the Chairman of the Council of People's Commissars of the USSR, People's Commissar for Foreign Affairs for the USSR V. M. Molotov to the Minister of Foreign Affairs of Germany J. von Ribbentrop], 28 September 1939, DVP, 137.

7. "Foreign Office Memorandum (Schnurre)," October 1939, NSR, 119.

8. Zeidler, "German-Soviet Economic Relations during the Hitler-Stalin Pact," 104.

9. Ericson, Feeding the German Eagle, 86.

10. Ibid., 88; "Memorandum by the State Secretary in the German Foreign Office (Weizsäcker)," 1 November 1939, NSR, 127.

11. Ericson, Feeding the German Eagle, 90; Ritschl, "Deficit Spending in the Nazi Recovery," Table 5.

12. "Memorandum by the State Secretary in the German Foreign Office (Weizsäcker)," 5 December 1939, NSR, 126.

13. Philbin, The Lure of Neptune, 47–48.

14. Jürgen Rohwer and Mikhail S. Monakov, Stalin's Ocean-Going Fleet: Soviet Naval Strategy and Shipbuilding Programmes, 1935–1953 (London: Frank Cass Publishers, 2001), 42–43.

15. See Tony Demchak, Reform, Foreign Technology, and Leadership in the Russian Imperial and Soviet Navies, 1881–1941 (unpubl. diss., Kansas State University: 2016).

16. Rohwer and Monakov, Stalin's Ocean-Going Fleet, 63–64. This was the ten-year building list; these ships would have been scheduled for commissioning by 1947.

17. Donald Mitchell, A History of Russian and Soviet Sea Power (New York: Macmillan, 1974), 373–374. This proposal was for the Sovietskii Soyuz Class Battleship. Philbin, The Lure of Neptune, 34.

18. Philbin, The Lure of Neptune, 23.

19. Ericson, Feeding the German Eagle, 86.

20. "Russo-German Naval Relations, 1926–1941," 38.

21. Ibid., 39.

22. Ibid.

23. Ibid.

24. Ibid., 40.

25. Philbin, The Lure of Neptune, 83.

26. Ibid., 99.

27. Ibid., 76–77.
28. Robert Edwards, *The Winter War: Russia's Invasion of Finland, 1939–1940* (New York: Pegasus, 2008), 76–77.
29. Edwards, *The Winter War*, 112–113.
30. Ibid., 118.
31. Ibid., 118–119.
32. Ibid., 165.
33. Philbin, *The Lure of Neptune*, 43.
34. Ibid.,132–133.
35. "Russo-German Naval Relations, 1926–1941," 136.
36. Ibid., 139.
37. Ibid., 141.
38. Ibid., 108.
39. Ericson, *Feeding the German Eagle*, 101, 211 (Table 5.1).
40. Ibid., 103.
41. "Foreign Office Memorandum—Memorandum on the German-Soviet Commercial Agreement Signed on February 11, 1940 (Schnurre)," 26 February 1940, NSR, 131.
42. Ibid.
43. Ericson, *Feeding the German Eagle*, 113.
44. "The German Ambassador in the Soviet Union (Schulenberg) to the German Foreign Office," 30 March 1940, NSR, 134.
45. See "Memorandum by the German Ambassador in the Soviet Union (Schulenburg)," 11 April 1940, NSR, 138.
46. Watt, *How War Came*, 143–144.
47. See Patrick R. Osborn, *Operation Pike: Britain versus the Soviet Union, 1939–1941* (Westport, CT: Greenwood, 2000), 137–138.
48. "The German Ambassador in the Soviet Union (Schulenburg) to the German Foreign Office," 9 April 1940, NSR, 138; "Memorandum by the German Ambassador in the Soviet Union (Schulenburg)," 11 April 1940, NSR, 138.
49. Ericson, *Feeding the German Eagle*, 116.

CHAPTER 34

1. Jackson, *The Fall of France*, 37.
2. Gunsburg, "The Battle of the Belgian Plain," 232.
3. Ibid.
4. Doyle, Chamberlain, and Jentz, *Panzertruppen*, 123, quoting the commander of Panzer-Regiment 35, Colonel Eberbach.
5. Zaloga, *Panzer IV vs. Char B1 bis: France 1940*, 24.
6. Guderian, *Panzer Leader*, 113.
7. Gabriel Gorodetsky, "Stalin and Hitler's Attack on the Soviet Union," in *From Peace to War*, ed. Bernd Wegner, 347.
8. Murray, *Strategy for Defeat*, 33.
9. Zeidler, "German-Soviet Economic Relations during the Hitler-Stalin Pact," 108.
10. Moorhouse, *The Devils' Alliance*, 173.
11. "The German Ambassador in the Soviet Union (Schulenberg) to the German Foreign Office," 23 June 1940, NSR, 155.
12. It was likely intended by Stalin to remove a potential invasion route should Germany attack, while also weakening Germany's hand in the Balkans. The Soviets also attempted to monopolize trade on the Danube through the blocking of the only navigable arm of the river into the Black Sea. Gabriel Gorodetsky, *Grand Delusion: Stalin and the German Invasion of Russia* (New Haven: Yale University Press, 1999), 31–33, 47.
13. "The Reich Foreign Minister (Ribbentrop) to the German Ambassador in the Soviet Union (Schulenberg)," 25 June 1940, NSR, 158–159.
14. "The German Ambassador in the Soviet Union (Schulenberg) to the German Foreign Office," 26 June 1940, NSR, 161–162.

15. Ignác Romsics, "Hungarian Revisionism in Thought and Action, 1920–1941: Plans, Expectations, Reality," in *Territorial Revisionism and the Allies of Germany in the Second World War: Goals, Expectations, Practices*, eds. Marina Cattaruzza, Stefan Dyroff, and Dieter Langewiesche (New York: Berghahn Books, 2012), 92–101, 98.
16. "The German Ambassador in the Soviet Union (Schulenberg) to the German Foreign Office," 1 September 1940, NSR, 180–181.
17. "The Reich Foreign Minister to the German Ambassador in the Soviet Union (Schulenberg)," 3 September 1940, NSR, 181–183.
18. "The German Foreign Office to the German Ambassador in the Soviet Union (Schulenberg)," 5 September 1940, NSR, 185.
19. "Foreign Office Memorandum (Schnurre)," 26 September 1940, NSR, 196; "Foreign Office Memorandum (Schnurre)," 28 September 1940, NSR, 199–201.
20. Gorodetsky, *Grand Delusion*, 90–91.
21. Read and Fisher, *The Deadly Embrace*, 493–497.
22. Gorodetsky, *Grand Delusion*, 67–69.
23. "Letter from the Reich Foreign Minister (Ribbentrop) to Stalin," 13 October 1940, NSR, 207–213.
24. Ibid., 213.
25. Read and Fisher, *The Deadly Embrace*, 510–511.
26. Kotkin, *Stalin: Waiting for Hitler*, 806.
27. Read and Fisher, *The Deadly Embrace*, 511.
28. Ibid., 512.
29. Ibid., 513.
30. Moorhouse, *The Devils' Alliance*, 197.
31. "Memorandum of the Conversation between the Reich Foreign Minister and the Chairman of the Council of People's Commissars of the U.S.S.R. and People's Commissar for Foreign Affairs, V. M. Molotov," 12 November 1940, NSR, 217–225.
32. Ibid., 222.
33. Ibid., 225.
34. "Weisung Nr. 18 für die Kriegführung," 12 November 1940, *Hitlers Weisungen für die Kriegführung, 1939–1945: Dokumente des Oberkommandos der Wehrmacht*, ed. Walther Hubatsch (Bonn: Bernard und Graefe Verlag für Wehrwesen, 1962), 68–72.
35. Moorhouse, *The Devils' Alliance*, 196
36. Franz Halder, *Halder War Diary, Volume V* (Office of Chief of Counsel for War Crimes, 1947), 3, quoted in Kotkin, *Stalin: Waiting for Hitler*, 814. Chief of the OKH Franz Halder recorded in his diary earlier that month that "the Führer hopes he can bring Russia into the anti-British front."
37. Albert Speer, *Inside the Third Reich* (New York: Macmillan, 1970), 102.
38. Ibid., 103–104.
39. "Memorandum of the Conversation between the Führer and the Chairman of the Council of People's Commissars and the People's Commissar for Foreign Affairs, Molotov, in the Presence of the Reich Foreign Minister, the Deputy People's Commissar, Dekanosov as Well as the Counselor of Embassy Hilger and Herr Pavlov, Who Acted as Interpreters," 12 November 1940, NSR, 226
40. Ibid., 232.
41. Ibid., 233.
42. "Memorandum of the Conversation between the Führer and the Chairman of the Council of People's Commissars and the People's Commissar for Foreign Affairs, Molotov, in the Presence of the Reich Foreign Minister, the Deputy People's Commissar, Dekanosov as Well as the Counselor of Embassy Hilger and Herr Pavlov, Who Acted as Interpreters," 13 November 1940, NSR, 234.
43. *Molotov Remembers*, 15.
44. Ibid.
45. Gorodetsky, *Grand Delusion*, 74–75. Gorodetsky argues that Hitler's aim was to force the USSR to concede the Balkans as an entirely German sphere of influence, and that

it was ongoing clashes over Bulgaria, Romania, Yugoslavia, Danube transit rights, and the Montreux Convention on the Dardanelles that really underlay the inability of the two sides to reach any sort of compromise in November.

46. Kotkin, *Stalin: Waiting for Hitler*, 808.
47. "Memorandum of the Final Conversation between Reich Foreign Minister von Ribbentrop and the Chairman of the Council of People's Commissars of the U.S.S.R. and People's Commissar of Foreign Affairs, Herr Molotov, on 13 November 1940," NSR, 247.
48. Ibid., 248–249.
49. Moorhouse, *The Devils' Alliance*, 209.
50. Kotkin, *Stalin: Waiting for Hitler*, 810.
51. "The German Ambassador in the Soviet Union (Schulenberg) to the German Foreign Office," 26 November 1940, NSR, 258–259.
52. "The German Ambassador in the Soviet Union (Schulenberg) to the German Foreign Office," 17 January 1941, NSR, 270.

CHAPTER 35

1. Adolf Hitler, "Directive No. 21," 18 December 1940, NSR, 260–264.
2. Moorhouse, *The Devils' Alliance*, 211, citing Warlimont Diary. OKH head General Franz Halder's War Diary also contains no mention of serious planning for invasion of the Soviet Union until January 1941. Clearly, no final decision had yet been made. See Halder, *Halder War Diary*, IV.
3. See Gorodetsky, *Grand Delusion* for the Balkan case; Ericson, *Feeding the German Eagle* and Rolf-Dieter Müller, *Enemy in the East*, 233–238 for the economic case; and Andreas Hillgruber's *Hitlers Strategie. Politik und Kriegführung, 1940–1941* (Munich: Bernard und Graefe, 1965/1982) for first articulating the primacy of ideology in Hitler's war plans.
4. Halder, *War Diary*, V, 90–94.
5. Rolf-Dieter Müller, *Enemy in the East*, 240.
6. Philbin, *The Lure of Neptune*, 127.
7. Ericson, *Feeding the German Eagle*, 149.
8. Ibid., 152.
9. "The State Secretary in the German Foreign Office (Weizsacker) to the Reich Foreign Minister," 17 January 1941, NSR, 268.
10. "The German Ambassador in the Soviet Union (Schulenberg) to the German Foreign Office," 1 March 1941, NSR, 278.
11. "Foreign Office Memorandum (Ritter)," 13 March 1941, NSR, 279.
12. "Memorandum on the Present Status of Soviet Deliveries of Raw Materials to Germany," 5 April 1941, NSR, 318.
13. Ericson, *Feeding the German Eagle*, 164, 169–171.
14. "The German Ambassador in the Soviet Union (Schulenberg) to the German Foreign Office," 4 April 1941, NSR, 316–318.
15. "The German Ambassador in the Soviet Union (Schulenberg) to the German Foreign Office," 6 April 1941, NSR, 320.
16. "Memorandum of the Conversation between the Reich Foreign Minister and Japanese Foreign Minister Matsuoka in the Presence of Ambassadors Ott and Oshima at Berlin on March 27, 1941," 27 March 1941, NSR, 284.
17. "The German Ambassador in the Soviet Union (Schulenberg) to the German Foreign Office," 10 April 1941, NSR, 321–322.
18. "The German Ambassador in the Soviet Union (Schulenberg) to the German Foreign Office," 13 April 1941, NSR, 322–323.
19. Gorodetsky, *Grand Delusion*, 198.
20. Ibid., 198; Kotkin, *Stalin: Waiting for Hitler*, 852.
21. Gorodetsky, "Stalin and Hitler's Attack on the Soviet Union," 348.
22. Ingeborg Fleischhauer, *Diplomatischer Widerstand gegen "Unternehmen Barbarossa": Die Friedensbemühungen der Deutschen Botschaft Moskau 1939–1941* [Diplomatic Resistance

against "Operation Barbarossa: The Peace Efforts of the German Embassy in Moscow, 1939–1941] (Berlin: Ullstein, 1991), 318–320.

23. Gorodetsky, "Stalin and Hitler's Attack on the Soviet Union," 351.
24. Ibid., 350–351.
25. Roger Reese, *Stalin's Reluctant Soldiers*, 202.
26. David Glantz, *Stumbling Colossus: The Red Army on the Eve of World War* (Lawrence: University Press of Kansas, 1998), 54.
27. Reese, *Stalin's Reluctant Soldiers*, 130–131.
28. Kotkin, *Stalin: Waiting for Hitler*, 893; Yuri Y. Kirshin, "The Soviet Armed Forces on the Eve of the Great Patriotic War," in *From Peace to War*, ed. Bernd Wegner, 382.
29. Reese, *Stalin's Reluctant Soldiers*.
30. Kirshin, "The Soviet Armed Forces on the Eve of the Great Patriotic War," 385. For similar figures on the lack of preparation in Soviet air units, see Glantz, *Stumbling Colossus*, 202.
31. Kotkin, *Stalin: Waiting for Hitler*, 892; Glantz, *Stumbling Colossus*, 204.
32. Gorodetsky, "Stalin and Hitler's Attack on the Soviet Union," 347.
33. Ibid., 356.
34. Kotkin, *Stalin: Waiting for Hitler*, 892–894.
35. Glantz, *Stumbling Colossus*, 104.
36. David M. Glantz and Jonathan M. House, *When Titans Clashed: How the Red Army Stopped Hitler* (Lawrence: University Press of Kansas, 2015), 50; Glantz, *Stumbling Colossus*, 10, 206.
37. Gorodetsky, "Stalin and Hitler's Attack on the Soviet Union," 352.
38. Kotkin, *Stalin: Waiting for Hitler*, 898–899.
39. Glantz and House, *When Titans Clashed*, 34. Italian forces did not actually reach the front until July.
40. Read and Fisher, *The Deadly Embrace*, 635–636; Glantz and House, *When Titans Clashed*, 57.
41. Glantz and House, *When Titans Clashed*, 57.
42. "Interview with Leonid Rosenberg, Witness: Operation Barbarossa," Witness History Podcast Series, BBC News, 2011, accessed 2015, http://www.bbc.co.uk/programmes/p00h9rx0.
43. Gorbatov, *Years Off My Life*, 157.
44. Ibid., 160.
45. Ibid., 157.
46. Craig W. H. Luther, *The First Day on the Eastern Front* (Guilford, CT: Stackpole Books, 2019), 339.
47. Ericson, *Feeding the German Eagle*, 179.
48. Ibid.
49. Read and Fisher, *The Deadly Embrace*, 637.
50. The latter, some twenty years earlier, had been responsible for the early POW exchanges as the unofficial representative of Weimar Germany in Russia.
51. "The German Ambassador in the Soviet Union (Schulenburg) to the German Foreign Office," 22 June 1941, NSR, 355.
52. Read and Fisher, *The Deadly Embrace*, 640.
53. Richard Overy, *Russia's War* (London: Penguin Books, 1997), 74.

CONCLUSION

1. Strohn, "Hans von Seeckt and His Vision of a 'Modern Army," 330–331.
2. Wheeler-Bennett, *The Nemesis of Power*, fn. 118.
3. Gottfried Schramm, "Basic Features of German Ostpolitik, 1918–1939," in *From Peace to War: Germany, Soviet Russia, and the World, 1939–1941*, ed. Bernd Wegner (Providence, RI: Berghahn Books, 1997), 23.
4. Glantz, *Stumbling Colossus*, 156.
5. Ibid., 117–118.

6. Ibid., 204.

7. Soviet agents tended to identify "Hindenburg followers" as "Fascists," but not "Strong Fascists," which was something of a generalization. The distinction between conservative nationalists and racial nationalists was somewhat stronger than they understood. "O buivshem 4-m nemetskom aviaotriade," 18 January 1950, 3.

8. Benoit Lemay, *Erich von Manstein, Hitler's Master Strategist* (Havertown, PA: Casemate Publishers, 2010), 26; Rauschning, *Makers of Destruction*, 25, cited by Zeidler, 268.

9. Lemay, *Manstein*, 26.

10. Ibid.

11. David Thomas, "Foreign Armies East and German Military Intelligence in Russia 1941–45," *Journal of Contemporary History*, 22:2 (Apr., 1987), 276; Glantz, *Stumbling Colossus*, 107. In 1938, the OKH reorganized its intelligence agencies and placed Abteilung Fremde Heer Ost (Department of Foreign Armies—East) in the hands of Lieutenant Colonel Eberhard Kinzel. He spoke no Russian, had never visited the Soviet Union, and was simultaneously placed in charge of all military intelligence for China, Japan, the United States and the Western Hemisphere, despite having only a tiny staff at his disposal. Hillgruber, "The German Military Leaders' View of Russia," 179.

12. Hillgruber, "The German Military Leaders' View of Russia," 179–180.

13. Halder, *Halder War Diary, VI*, 190; Halder, *Halder War Diary, VII*, 36.

14. Hillgruber, "The German Military Leaders' View of Russia," 181. David Glantz, *Barbarossa Derailed: The Battle for Smolensk, 10 July–10 September 1941, Volume I* (West Midlands, UK: Helion, 2010), 66. Guderian then expressed shock upon his first encounter with a T-34 on July 3, 1941, despite evidence even in the early 1930s that the Soviets were building some larger and more heavily armored vehicles than their German counterparts. Guderian, *Panzer Leader*, 162.

15. Halder, *Halder War Diary, VII*, 36; translation from Charles Burton Burdick, Hans Adolf Jacobsen edition of the *Halder War Diary*.

16. Zaloga and Grandsen, *Soviet Tanks and Combat Vehicles*, 48. The authors also add that "It is curious that the designs which the Soviets so wisely chose, for their excellent capabilities and ease of manufacture, were in most cases not procured in any numbers by the armies of the countries in which they originated."

17. Sobelev and Khazanov, *Nemetskii sled*, 125–126. These adaptions included wing and flap design, engine and turbocharging systems, and navigational equipment that would be incorporated into new Soviet aircraft.

18. "Betr. Strategische Aufgabe Nr. 1" [Report on Strategic Problem Nr. 1], 15 February 1926, 1.

19. Glantz, *Stumbling Colossus*, 145.

20. Harrison, *Soviet Planning in Peace and War*, 149.

21. Glantz and House, *When Titans Clashed*, 306; Chamberlain and Doyle, *Encyclopedia of German Tanks*, 261–262.

22. Gryaznov, "O rabote kursov TEKO," 14 March 1932, 1; Zeidler, 352–354.

23. For two very different assessments of the purges, see Conquest, *The Great Terror*; and Getty and Naumov, *The Road to Terror*.

24. All three had traveled to Germany for maneuvers or training at some point in the interwar period: Kulik in 1928, Shaposhnikov in 1929, and Timoshenko in 1931. The difference in their cases seems to have been personal. Kulik survived because of his slavish loyalty to Stalin. Stalin valued Shaposhnikov's nonpolitical background (he was not a Party member), his military writing, and his administrative competence. The reasons for Timoshenko's survival are less clear, though it may have also been a product of his personal relationship with Stalin.

25. Zeidler, 306.

26. Erickson, *The Soviet High Command*, 505; Conquest, *The Great Terror*, 450; Reese, *Stalin's Reluctant Soldiers*, 134. Erickson and Reese agree on a figure of around 25,000 total purged officers.

27. Conquest, *The Great Terror*, 450. In retrospect, of the Soviet Union's major theorists, it seems that only Igor Svechin had correctly identified the logical course of Soviet strategy: attritional warfare would be the inevitable result of modern warfare between the Soviet Union and a more technologically advanced neighbor to the west. This would rapidly become apparent in early 1941, even to Stalin. He would tell his commanders early in the war to eschew complicated maneuvers in favor of attritional battles, which relied upon the Soviet Union's superior reserves of manpower. Deep Battle as described in the 1936 manual was too fine an instrument for the Soviet Union as it existed in 1941, particularly in the aftermath the purges. Perhaps, in a Red Army headed by Tukhachevsky, it might have been more effective. It would take more than a year of combat for the Red Army to become capable of complex maneuver warfare like Deep Battle, on clear display by the time of *Operatsiya Uran* in November 1942. See Earl Ziemke, "The Soviet Theory of Deep Operations," *Parameters, Journal of the US Army War College*, 13:2 (1983), 23–33.
28. Roger Reese estimated that one third of this shortfall was a direct product of the purge and the rest from the expansion of the Red Army. Reese, *Stalin's Reluctant Soldiers*, 147.
29. Glantz, *Stumbling Colossus*, 39.
30. Hilger and Meyer, *The Incompatible Allies*, 131.

BIBLIOGRAPHY

ARCHIVES CONSULTED
United States
HIA	Hoover Institution Archives, Stanford, California
HRC	Harry Ransom Center, Austin, Texas
JPI-NY	Josef Pilsudski Institute, New York
MA-YU	Manuscripts and Archives, Yale University, New Haven, Connecticut
NARA	National Archives at College Park, Maryland
NWC	Naval Historical Collection, Naval War College, Newport, Rhode Island
NYPL	New York Public Library Archives, New YorkY-RAPRussian Archives

Project, Yale University, New Haven, Connecticut

Germany
BA-L	Federal Archive Berlin—Lichterfelde, Berlin
BA-MA	Federal Archive—Military Archive, Freiburg
DBCA	Daimler-Benz Corporate Archives, Stuttgart
KA-E	Thyssen-Krupp Corporate Archives, Essen
MAN	M.A.N. Corporate Archives, Augsburg
PA-AA	Foreign Ministry—Political Archives, Berlin
PCA	Porsche Corporate Archives, Stuttgart

Poland
AAN	Archiwum Akt Nowych, Warsaw

Russia
GALO	State Archive of Lipetsk Oblast, Lipetsk
GARF	The State Archive of the Russian Federation, Moscow
RGAE	The Russian State Archive of the Economy
RGASPI	The Russian State Archive of Socio-Political History, Moscow
RGVA	The Russian State Military Archives, Moscow
TsGASO	The Central State Archive of Samara Oblast, Samara

United Kingdom
BNA	The National Archives, Kew
JPI-L	Josef Pilsudski Institute, London

PUBLISHED DOCUMENT COLLECTIONS

Akten zur deutschen auswärtigen Politik, 1918–1945 [Documents on German Foreign Policy]. Serie A und B. Göttingen: Vondenhoeck und Ruprecht, 1950–1995. Cited as ADAP.

Documents in British Foreign Policy, 1919–1939. Series I, II, III. London: His Majesty's Stationery Office, 1948. Cited as DBFP.

Documents on German Foreign Policy, 1918–1945. Series C, Volumes I–IV, and Series D,
    Volumes I–VI. Washington DC: US Government Printing Office, 1949–1964. Cited
    as DGFP.
Dyakov, Yuri, and Tatyana Bushuyeva, eds. and trans. The Red Army and the
    Wehrmacht: How the Soviets Militarized Germany and Paved the Way for Fascism,
    from the Secret Archives of the Former Soviet Union. Amherst, NY: Prometheus
    Books, 1995.
Eudin, Xenia Joukoff, and Harold Henry Fisher. Soviet Russia and the West, 1920–1927: A
    Documentary Survey. Stanford, CA: Stanford University Press, 1957.
Getty, J. Arch, and Oleg V. Naumov, eds. The Road to Terror: Stalin and the Self-Destruction
    of the Bolsheviks. Translated by Benjamin Sher. New Haven, CT: Yale University
    Press, 1999.
Nuremberg Trial Proceedings. Vols. 1, 9, 12, 20. 1945–1946. The Avalon Project. https://
    avalon.law.yale.edu/subject_menus/imt.asp.
Orenstein, Harold S., trans. The Evolution of Soviet Operational Art 1927–1991: The
    Documentary Basis, Vol. 1. London: Frank Cass, 1995.
Proceedings of the Brest-Litovsk Peace Conference: The Peace Negotiations between
    Russia and the Central Powers, 21 November, 1917–3 March, 1918. Washington,
    DC: Government Printing Office, 1918.
Seeckt, Hans von. Gedanken eines Soldaten. Leipzig: K. F. Koehler, 1935.
Seidel, Alfred, ed. Die Beziehungen zwischen Deutschland und der Sowjetunion, 1939–
    1941: Dokumente des Auswärtigen Amtes [Relations between Germany and the
    Soviet Union, 1939–1941: Documents from the German Foreign Office]. Edited by
    Alfred Seidl. Tübingen: H. Laupp'sche Buchhandlung, 1949. Cited as BZDS.
Sontag, Raymond James, and James Stuart Beddie, eds. Nazi-Soviet Relations, 1939–
    1941: Documents from the Archives of the German Foreign Ministry. Washington,
    DC: US Department of State, 1948. Cited as NSR.

OTHER PRIMARY SOURCES

Bechhofer-Robert, Carl Eric. Through Starving Russia, Being a Record of a Journey to Moscow
    and the Volga Provinces, in August and September 1921. London: Methuen, 1921.
Boeckel, Richard M. "Military and Naval Expenditures." In Editorial Research Reports, 1930,
    Volume III. Washington, DC: CQ Press, 1930. Digitized at http://library.cqpress.
    com/cqresearcher/cqresrre1930072500.
Bór-Komorowski, Tadeusz. The Secret Army. London: Victor Gollancz Ltd., 1951.
Cockburn, Claud. In Time of Trouble. An Autobiography. London: Rubert Hart-Davis, 1957.
Corum, James S., and Richard R. Muller, eds. and trans. Heeresdienstvorschrift 487,
    Führung und Gefecht der verbundenen Waffen, Teil I (1921), Teil II (1923) [Army
    Regulations 487: Leadership and Battle with Combined Arms]. Baltimore: The
    Nautical and Aviation Publishing Company of America, 1998.
Dirksen, Herbert von. Moscow, Tokyo, London: Twenty Years of German Foreign Policy.
    Norman: University of Oklahoma Press, 1952.
Douhet, Giulio. "The War of 19—" and "The Command of the Air." In The Command of The
    Air, translated by Dino Ferrari, 292–405. Washington, DC: Air Force History and
    Museums Program, 1998.
Dulles, Allen W. "Germany and the Crisis in Disarmament." Foreign Affairs, 12:2 (Jan.,
    1934): 260–270.
Fedorov, Lev. "Voenno-khimicheskie poligon v Moskve: Interview with Lev Fedorov" [The
    Military Chemical Testing Grounds in Moscow]. By Marina Katys. Radio Liberty, 20
    December 2000. http://www.svoboda.org/content/transcript/24197763.html.
Fries, Amos A., and Clarence J. West. "The Future of Chemical Warfare." In Chemical
    Warfare, 435–439. New York: McGraw-Hill, 1921.
Frunze, Mikhail. "Unified Military Doctrine and the Red Army." Translated by David
    Stone. Originally published in Armiia i revolutsiia, 1 (July 1921). http://www-
    personal.k-state.edu/~stone/FrunzeDoctrine.

Goebbels, Joseph. *The Diaries of Joseph Goebbels*. Edited by Jana Richter. Munich: KG Saur, 2001.

Gorbatov, A. V. *Years Off My Life: The Memoir of General of the Soviet Army A. V. Gorbatov*. Translated by Gordon Clough and Anthony Cash. New York: W. W. Norton, 1965.

Groener, Wilhelm. *Lebenserinnerungen: Jugend, Generalstab, Weltkrieg* [Memoirs: Youth, General Staff, World War]. Göttingen: Vandenhoeck & Ruprecht, 1957.

Guderian, Heinz. *Die Panzerwaffe: Ihre Enwicklung, ihre Kampftaktik, und ihre operativen Möglichkeiten bis zum Beginn des grossdeutschen Freiheitskampfes* [The Panzer Force: Its Development, Battle Tactics, and Operational Opportunities until the Beginning of the Greater German Struggle for Freedom]. Stuttgart: Union Deutsche Verlagsgesellschaft, 1943.

Guderian, Heinz. *Panzer Leader*. Translated by Constantine Fitzgibbon. Cambridge, MA: Da Capo, 1996.

Heinkel, Ernst. *Stormy Life: Memoirs of a Pioneer of the Air Age*. Edited and translated by Jürgen Thorwald. Boston: Dutton Press, 1956.

Hilger, Gustav, and Alfred G. Meyer. *The Incompatible Allies: A Memoir-History of Soviet-German Relations, 1918–1941*. New York: Hafner, 1971.

Hindenburg, Paul von. *Out of My Life*. Translated by F. A. Holt. 1920, Reprint; London: Forgotten Books, 2013.

Hitler, Adolf. *Mein Kampf*. New York: Reynal and Hitchcock, 1941.

Hitler, Adolf. *Hitler's Second Book: The Unpublished Sequel to "Mein Kampf."* Edited by Gerhardt Weinberg. Translated by Krista Smith. New York: Enigma Books, 2003.

Hitler, Adolf. "Official Speech on the Enabling Act to the Reichstag." 23 March 1933. *World Future Fund Historical Documents Collection*, Accessed 1 May 2012. http://www.worldfuturefund.org/Reports2013/hitlerenablingact.htm.

Horne, Charles F. *The Great Events of the Great War: A Comprehensive and Readable Source Record of the World's Great War, Vol. III*. New York: J. J. Little and Ives, 1920.

Isserson, G. S. *G. S. Isserson and the War of the Future: Key Writings of a Soviet Military Theorist*. Edited and translated by Richard W. Harrison. Jefferson, NC: McFarland, 2016.

Ipatieff, V. N. "Original Manuscript of 'My Life as a Chemist.'" 1946, Ipatieff Collection, Boxes 1 and 2, Hoover Institution at Stanford University.

Köstring, Ernst. *General Ernst Köstring: Der militärische Mittler zwischen dem Deutschen Reich und der Sowjetunion 1921–1941* [General Ernst Köstring: The Military Intermediary between the German Reich and the Soviet Union, 1921–1941]. Edited by Herman Teske. Frankfurt: E. S. Mittler und Sohn, 1966.

Lenin, V. I. "First Session Speech." In *Second Congress of the Communist International. Minutes of the Proceedings*. Moscow: Publishing House of the Communist International, 1921.

Lenin, V. I. *Collected Works: Volume 28, July 1918–March 1919*. Translated and edited by Jim Riordan. Moscow: Progress Publishers, 1965.

Levichev, V. N. *Voina i voennoe delo: Posobie po voennomu delu dlya partiinogo, sovetskogo i profsouznogo aktiva* [War and Military Affairs: A Handbook on Military Affairs for Party, State, and Trade Union Activists]. Moscow: Government Military Publishing House, 1933.

Lipski, Jozef. *Diplomat in Berlin, 1933–1939: Papers and Memoirs of Jozef Lipski*. Edited by Wacław Jedrzejewicz. New York: Columbia University Press, 1968.

Maisky, Ivan. *The Complete Maisky Diaries, Volumes I, II, and III*. Edited by Gabriel Gorodetsky. Translated by Tatiana Sorokina and Oliver Ready. New Haven, CT: Yale University Press, 2007.

Martens, L. K, ed. *Tekhnicheskaya entsiklopedia* [Technical Encyclopedia], Vol. IV. Moscow: Joint Society for the Soviet Encyclopedia, 1928.

Melville, Cecil F. *The Russian Face of Germany: An Account of the Secret Military Relations between the German and Soviet-Russian Governments*. London: Wishart Publishing, 1932.

Meretskov, Kirill. *Na sluzhbe narodu* [In the Service of the People]. Moscow: Politizdat, 1968.

Müller, Klaus. *So lebten und arbeiteten wir 1929 bis 1933 in Kama* [So We Lived and Worked at Kama, 1929–1933]. Unpubl. memoir, 1972.

Nehring, Walter. *Die Geschichte Der Deutschen Panzerwaffe 1916 bis 1945*. Berlin: Propyläen Verlag, 1969.

Noske, Gustav. *Von Kiel bis Kapp: Zur Geschichte der deutschen Revolution* [From Kiel to Kapp: The History of the German Revolution]. Berlin: Verlag für Politik und Wirtschaft, 1920.

Pilsudski, Jozef. *Year 1920 and Its Climax Battle of Warsaw during the Polish-Soviet War, 1919–1920*. New York: Pilsudski Institute of America, 1972.

Porsche, Ferry. *We at Porsche: The Autobiography of Dr.Ing. H. C. Ferry Porsche*. New York: Doubleday, 1976.

Prentiss, A. M. *Chemicals in War. A Treatise on Chemical Warfare*. New York: McGraw Hill, 1937.

Provisional Field Regulations for the Red Army, 1936. Springfield, VA: National Technical Information Service, 1987.

Raeder, Erich. *Admiral Erich Raeder: My Life*. Translated by Henry W. Drexel. Annapolis, MD: United States Naval Institute, 1960.

Resis, Albert, ed. *Molotov Remembers: Conversations with Felix Chuev*. Chicago: Ivan R. Dee, 1993.

Schleicher, Kurt von. "The Conception of Defense in Present Day Germany." *World Affairs*, 95:3 (Dec. 1932): 160–161.

Sennikov, B. *Tambovskoe vosstanie 1918–1921 gg. i raskrestyanivanie Rossii 1929–1933 gg.* [The Tambov Rebellion of 1918–1921 and the Russian Peasantry, 1929–1933]. Moscow: Posev Publishing, 2004.

Sokoloff, Boris. *The White Nights: Pages from a Russian Doctor's Notebook*. Edited by Ian Ona Johnson. Tyler, TX: Bowen Books, 2018.

Speidel, Wilhelm, writing under the "pseudonym" Helm Speidel. "Reichswehr und Rote Armee," in *Vierteljahrshefte für Zeitgeschichte* [Quarterly Journal for Contemporary History], 1:1 (1953): 10–48.

Stalin, Joseph. "A Year of Great Change: On the Occasion of the Twelfth Anniversary of the October Revolution," in *Works*, Volume 12, April 1929–June 1930, 124–141. Moscow: Foreign Languages Publishing House, 1954.

Sultanbekov, Bulat. "Kama na Volge" [Kama on the Volga]. *Nauchno-dokumentalniy zhurnal "Gazirlar avazi"* [Scientific-Documentary Journal Gasirlar Avazi]. Issue 2 (2005).

Trotsky, Leon. *The Suppressed Testament of Lenin, with "On Lenin's Testament" by Leon Trotsky*. New York: Pioneer Publishers, 1946.

Trotsky, Leon. *The Military Writings and Speeches of Leon Trotsky, Volume I: 1918*. Translated and annotated by Brian Pearce. London: New Park Publications, 1979.

Trotsky, Leon. *The Military Writings and Speeches of Leon Trotsky, Volume V, The Years 1921–1923*. Translated and annotated by Brian Pearce. London: New Park Publications, 1979.

Trotsky, Leon. *The History of the Russian Revolution*. Translated by Max Eastman. London: Haymarket Books, 2008.

Tukhachevsky, Mikhail. "The March beyond the Vistula." In Jozef Pilsudski, *Year 1920 and Its Climax Battle of Warsaw during the Polish-Soviet War, 1919–1920*. New York: Pilsudski Institute of America, 1972.

Tukhachevsky, Mikhail. "The Battle of the Bugs," "Preface to J. F. C. Fuller's *The Reformation of War*," "New Questions of War," "Red Army's New (1936) Field Service Regulations." In Richard Simpkin, *Deep Battle: The Brainchild of Marshal Tukhachevskii*, 85–88, 125–135, 135–154, 159–176. London: Brassey's Defence Publishers, 1987.

Vansittart, Robert. *The Mist Procession: The Autobiography of Lord Vansittart.* London: Hutchinson, 1958.

Volckheim, Ernst. *Die deutschen Kampfwagen im Weltkriege* [German Tanks in the World War]. Berlin: Ernst Siegfried Mittler und Sohn, 1923.

Volckheim, Ernst. "Gas und Kampfwagen" [Poison Gas and Tanks]. *Der Kampfwagen*, Issue Nr. 4 (January 1925), 1.

Weimar Republic Document Collection. "Gesetz über die Bildung einer vorläufigen Reichswehr" [Act on the Formation of the Provisional Reichswehr]. 6 March 1919. Accessed 2010. http://www.documentarchiv.de/wr/vorl-reichswehr_ges.html.

NEWSPAPERS CITED

Chicago Daily News
The Globe
Izvestia
The Manchester Guardian
The New York Times
The New York Herald Tribune
The Pittsburgh Post-Gazette
Pravda
The Saturday Review
Der Spiegel
Vorwärts
Die Zeit

SECONDARY SOURCES

Adamthwaite, Anthony. *France and the Coming of the Second World War, 1936–1939.* London: Frank Cass, 1977.

Adamthwaite, Anthony. *Grandeur and Misery: France's Bid for Power in Europe, 1914–1940.* London: Bloomsbury, 1995.

Aitken, Hugh G. J. *The Continuous Wave: Technology and American Radio, 1900–1932.* Princeton, NJ: Princeton University Press, 1985.

Angelucci, Enzo. *The Rand McNally Encyclopedia of Military Aircraft, 1914–1980.* New York: The Military Press, 1983.

Applebaum, Anne. *Red Famine: Stalin's War on Ukraine.* New York: Penguin, 2017.

Aselius, Gunnar. *The Rise and Fall of the Soviet Navy in the Baltic, 1921–1941.* London: Frank Cass, 2005.

Avrich, Paul. *Kronstadt 1921.* New York: W. W. Norton, 1970.

Baikov, Alexander. "Voenno-promyshlennoye sotrudnichestvo SSSR i Germanii—kto koval sovetskiy mech" [Military-Industrial Cooperation between the USSR and Germany—Who Forged the Soviet Sword?]. In *Nepravda Viktora Suvorova* [The Untruth of Victor Suvorov], 218–302. Moscow: Yauza, 2008.

Barnett, Vincent. "As Good as Gold?: A Note on the Chervonets." *Europe-Asia Studies,* 46:4 (1994): 663–669.

Bayer, Philip A. *The Evolution of the Soviet General Staff, 1917–1941.* New York: Garland, 1987.

Bean, Tim, and Will Fowler. *Red Army Tanks of World War Two: A Guide to Soviet Armored Fighting Vehicles.* London: Amber Books, 2002.

Beaupré, Nicolas. "Occuper l'Allemagne après 1918" [The Occupation of Germany after 1918]. *Revue historique des armées,* 254 (2009): 9–19.

Beevor, Anthony. *The Battle for Spain: The Spanish Civil War.* London: Weidenfeld and Nicolson, 2006.

Beevor, Anthony. *The Second World War.* London: Little, Brown and Company, 2012.

Bennett, Edward W. *German Rearmament and the West, 1932–1933.* Princeton, NJ: Princeton University Press, 1979.

Beyerchen, Alan D. *Scientists under Hitler: Politics and the Physics Community in the Third Reich*. New Haven, CT: Yale University Press, 1977.

Beyerchen, Alan D. "From Radio to Radar: Interwar Military Adaptation to Technological Change in Germany, the United Kingdom and the United States." In *Military Innovation in the Interwar Period*, edited by Williamson Murray and Allan Millett, 265–299. Cambridge, UK: Cambridge University Press, 1996.

Bird, Keith W. *Erich Raeder, Admiral of the Third Reich*. Annapolis, MD: Naval Institute Press, 2006.

Birstein, Vadim J. *The Perversion of Knowledge: The True Story of Soviet Science*. Cambridge, MA: Perseus Book Group, 2001.

Boelcke, Willi I. *Die Kosten von Hitlers Krieg: Kriegfinanzierung und finanzielles Kriegserbe in Deutschland 1933–1948* [The Cost of Hitler's War: War Financing and the Financial Legacy in Germany, 1933–1948]. Paderborn: Schöningh, 1985.

Boemeke, Manfred F., and Gerald D. Feldman. *The Treaty of Versailles: A Reassessment after 75 Years*. Cambridge, UK: Cambridge University Press, 1998.

Bond, Brian, and Williamson Murray. "The British Armed Forces, 1918–1939." In *Military Effectiveness, Volume II: The Interwar Period*, edited by Allan R. Millett and Williamson Murray, 98–130. Boston: Unwin Hyman, 1988.

Boyd, John R. "The Origins of Order No. 1." *Soviet Studies*, 19:3 (Jan., 1968): 359–372.

Broadberry, Stephen, and Mark Harrison. *The Economics of World War I*. Cambridge, UK: Cambridge University Press, 2005.

Budrass, Lutz. *Flugzeugindustrie und Luftrüstung in Deutschland 1918–1945* [The Aircraft Industry and Air Armaments in Germany, 1918–1945]. Düsseldorf: Droste, 1996.

Burleigh, Michael, and Wolfgang Wippermann. *The Racial State: Germany, 1933–1945*. Cambridge, UK: Cambridge University Press, 1991.

Burns, Russell W. *Communications: An International History of the Formative Years*. London: Institution of Engineering and Technology, 2004.

Byers, Richard. *Flying Man: Hugo Junkers and the Dream of Aviation*. College Station: Texas A&M Press, 2016.

Carr, Edward Hallett. *German-Soviet Relations between the Two World Wars, 1919–1939*. Baltimore: Johns Hopkins Press, 1951.

Carroll, Berenice A. *Design for Total War: Arms and Economics in the Third Reich*. The Hague: Mouton, 1968.

Carsten, F. L. *The Reichswehr and Politics, 1918–1933*. Berkeley: University of California Press, 1966.

Carter, G. B. *Chemical and Biological Defence at Porton Down, 1916–2000*. Norwich: The Stationery Office, 2000.

Chamberlain, Peter, and Hilary L. Doyle. *Encyclopedia of German Tanks of World War Two: A Complete Illustrated Directory of German Battle Tanks, Armoured Cars, Self-Propelled Guns and Semi-Tracked Vehicles, 1933–1945*. New York: Arco, 1978.

Chamberlain, Peter, and Terry Gander. *Weapons of the Third Reich: An Encyclopedic Survey of All Small Arms, Artillery and Special Weapons of the German Land Forces 1939–1945*. New York: Doubleday, 1979.

Cherushev, Nikolai Semyonovich. *Rasstrelyannaya elita RKKA: Kombrigi i im ravnie, 1937–1941* [The Elite of the Red Army Who Were Shot, 1937–1941]. Moscow: Kukovo Pole, 2014.

CIA Historical Review Program. "The Lohmann Affair." 9 September 1993. Accessed 1 November 2014. https://www.cia.gov/static/57c8b16fd41a83887a104f85c27 b1e32/The-Lohmann-Affair.pdf.

Cienciala, Anna. *From Versailles to Locarno: Keys to Polish Foreign Policy, 1919–1925*. Lawrence: University Press of Kansas, 1984.

Cienciala, Anna. "The Nazi-Soviet Pact of August 23, 1939: When Did Stalin Decide to Align with Hitler, and Was Poland the Culprit?" In *Ideology, Politics, and Diplomacy in East Central Europe*, edited by M. B. B. Biskupski, 147–226. Rochester, NY: University of Rochester Press, 2003.

Cienciala, Anna. "The Foreign Policy of Jozef Pilsudski and Jozef Beck, 1926–
1939: Misconceptions and Interpretations." *The Polish Review* 56:1/2
(2011): 111–151.

Clarke, Jeffrey J. "The Nationalization of War Industries in France, 1936–1937: A Case
Study." *Journal of Modern History*, 49:3 (Sep., 1977): 411–430.

Citino, Robert M. *The Path to Blitzkrieg: Doctrine and Training in the German Army, 1920–
1939*. Boulder, CO: Lynne Rienner Publishing, 1999.

Citino, Robert M. *The Quest for Decisive Victory: From Stalemate to Blitzkrieg in Europe,
1899–1940*. Lawrence: University Press of Kansas, 2002.

Citino, Robert M. *The German Way of War: From the Thirty Years' War to the Third Reich*.
Lawrence: University Press of Kansas, 2005.

Condell, Bruce, and David T. Zabecki. *On the German Art of War: Truppenführung*. Boulder,
CO: Lynne Rienner Publishers, 2001.

Conquest, Robert. *The Great Terror: Stalin's Purge of the Thirties*.
New York: Macmillan, 1973.

Conquest, Robert. *The Great Terror: A Reassessment*. New York: Macmillan, 2008.

Coombs, Benjamin. *British Tank Production and the War Economy, 1934–1945*.
London: Bloomsbury, 2013.

Coopersmith, Jonathan. "Failure and Technology." *Japan Journal for Science, Technology
and Society*, 18 (2009): 93–118.

Coox, Alvin. *The Anatomy of a Small War: The Soviet-Japanese Struggle for Changkufeng/
Khasan, 1938*. Westport, CT: Greenwood Press, 1977.

Coox, Alvin. *Nomonhan: Japan against Russia, 1939*. Stanford, CA: Stanford University
Press, 1985.

Coox, Alvin. "The Lesser of Two Hells: NKVD General G. S. Lyushkov's Defection to Japan,
1938–1945, Part I." *Journal of Slavic Military Studies*, 11:3 (1998): 145–186.

Coox, Alvin. "The Lesser of Two Hells: NKVD General G. S. Lyushkov's Defection to Japan,
1938–1945, Part II." *Journal of Slavic Military Studies*, 11:4 (1998): 72–110.

Cordts, Georg. *Junge Adler: Vom Luftsport zum Flugdienst, 1920–1945* [Young Eagles: From
Air Sports to Flight Duty, 1920–1945]. Munich: Bechtle Verlag Esslingen, 1988.

Corum, James S. *The Roots of Blitzkrieg: Hans von Seeckt and German Military Reform*.
Lawrence: University Press of Kansas, 1992.

Corum, James S. "The Luftwaffe and the Coalition Air War in Spain, 1936–1939." *Journal
of Strategic Studies*, 18:1 (1995): 68–90.

Corum, James S. *The Luftwaffe: Creating the Operational Air War*. Lawrence: University
Press of Kansas, 1997.

Corum, James S. "Devil's Bargain: Germany and Russia before World War Two." *World War
Two Magazine*, 8 March 2018. http://www.historynet.com/devils-bargain-germany-
and-russia-before-wwii.htm.

Courtois, Stephane, Nicolas Werth, Jean-Louis Panne, Andrzej Paczkowski, Karel
Bartosek, and Jean-Louis Margolin. *The Black Book of Communism: Crimes, Terror,
Repression*. Translated by Jonathan Murphy and Mark Kramer. Cambridge,
MA: Harvard University Press, 1999.

Craig, Gordon A. *Germany, 1866–1945*. Oxford: Oxford University Press, 1979.

Croddy, Ed, and James Wirtz. *Weapons of Mass Destruction: Chemical and Biological
Weapons*. Santa Barbara, CA: ABC-CLIO, 2005.

Croll, Neil Harvey. *Mikhail Tukhachevsky in the Russian Civil War*. University of Glasgow.
Unpubl. PhD thesis, 2002.

Davies, Norman. *White Eagle, Red Star; the Polish-Soviet War, 1919–1920*.
London: Macdonald, 1972.

Davies, Norman. *God's Playground: A History of Poland, Volume II: 1795 to Present*. Oxford,
UK: Oxford University Press, 2005.

Davies, R. W. *Soviet Economic Development from Lenin to Khrushchev*. Cambridge,
UK: Cambridge University Press, 1988.

Davies, R. W. "Soviet Military Expenditure and the Armaments Industry, 1929–33: A Reconsideration." *Europe-Asia Studies*, 45:4 (1993): 577–608.

Davies, R. W., Mark Harrison, and S. G. Wheatcroft. *The Economic Transformation of the Soviet Union, 1913–1945*. Cambridge, UK: Cambridge University Press, 1994.

Davies, R. W., and Stephen G. Wheatcroft. *The Years of Hunger: Soviet Agriculture, 1931–1933*. New York: Palgrave Macmillan, 2009.

Debo, Richard K. *Survival and Consolidation: The Foreign Policy of Soviet Russia, 1918–1921*. Montreal: McGill–Queen's University Press, 1992.

Deist, Wilhelm. *The Wehrmacht and German Rearmament*. Toronto: University of Toronto Press, 1981.

Deist, Wilhelm. "The Rearmament of the Wehrmacht." In *Germany and the Second World War, Volume I: The Build-up of German Aggression*, edited by the Militärgeschichtliches Forschungsamt (Research Institute for Miltiary History), 373–540. Translated by P. S. Falla, Dean S. McMurry, and Ewald Osers. Oxford: Clarendon Press, 1990.

Demchak, Tony. *Reform, Foreign Technology, and Leadership in the Russian Imperial and Soviet Navies, 1881–1941*. Unpubl. diss., Kansas State University, 2016.

Deutsch, Harold. *Hitler and His Generals: The Hidden Crisis, January–June 1938*. Minneapolis: University of Minnesota Press, 1974.

Diehl, James M. *Paramilitary Politics in Weimar Germany*. Bloomington: Indiana University Press, 1977.

DiNardo, R. L. *Germany's Panzer Arm*. Westport, CT: Greenwood Press, 1997.

Doepgen, Peter. *Die Washingtoner Konferenz, das Deutsche Reich und die Reichsmarine: Deutsche Marinepolitik 1921 bis 1935* [The Washington Conference, the German Empire, and the Reichsmarine: German Naval Politics 1921–1935]. Bremen: Verlag H. M. Hauschild GmbH, 2001.

Doughty, Robert A. *The Seeds of Disaster: The Development of French Army Doctrine, 1919–39*. Hamden, CT: Archon Books, 1985.

Doughty, Robert A. "The French Armed Forces, 1918–1940." In *Military Innovation in the Interwar Period*, edited by Williamson Murray and Allan Millett, 39–69. Cambridge, UK: Cambridge University Press, 1996.

Dorpalen, Andreas. *Hindenburg and the Weimar Republic*. Princeton, NJ: Princeton University Press, 1964.

Duffy, Paul, and Andrei Kandalov. *Tupolev: The Man and His Aircraft*. Hong Kong: SAE Printing, 1996.

Durkata, Alan, Tom Darcey, and Viktor Kulikov. *The Imperial Russian Air Service: Famous Pilots and Aircraft of World War One*. Mountain View, CA: Flying Machines Press, 1996.

Dyck, Harvey L. "German-Soviet Relations and the Anglo-Soviet Break, 1927." *Slavic Review*, 25:1 (Mar., 1966): 67–83.

Edwards, Robert. *The Winter War: Russia's Invasion of Finland, 1939–1940*. New York: Pegasus, 2008.

Erickson, John. *The Soviet High Command: A Military-Political History, 1918–1941*. London: Westview Press, 1962/1984/2001.

Eschenburg, Theodor. "The Role of the Personality in the Crisis of the Weimar Republic: Hindenburg, Brüning, Groener, Schleicher." In *Republic to Reich: The Making of the Nazi Revolution*, edited by Hajo Holborn, 3–50. New York: Random House, 1972.

Esser, Willi. *Dokumentation über die Entwicklung und Erprobung der ersten Panzerkampfwagen der Reichswehr* [Documentation about the Development and Testing of the First Reichswehr Tanks]. München: Krauss Maffei AG, 1979.

Evans, Richard J. *The Third Reich in Power: 1933–1939*. New York: Penguin, 2005.

Faith, Thomas Iain. "Under a Green Sea: The US Chemical Warfare Services, 1917–1929." Unpubl. diss., George Washington University, 2008.

Fedorov, Lev Aleksandrovich. *Khimicheskoe oruzhie v Rossii: Istoria, ekologia, politikia* [Chemical Weapons in Russia: History, Ecology, Politics]. Moscow: Center for Ecological Policy of Russia, 1994.

Fedoseev, Semen. *Tanki pervoi mirovoi voini* [Tanks of the First World War]. Moscow: Eskmo Publishing, 2010.

Fest, Joachim C. *Hitler.* Orlando, FL: Harcourt, 1974.

Fiddick, Thomas. *Russia's Retreat from Poland: From Permanent Revolution to Peaceful Coexistence.* London: Macmillan, 1990.

Figes, Orlando. "The Red Army and Mass Mobilization during the Russian Civil War 1918–1920." *Past & Present,* 129 (Nov., 1990): 168–211.

Figes, Orlando. *A People's Tragedy: A History of the Russian Revolution.* New York: Penguin, 1997.

Fink, Carol. *The Genoa Conference: European Diplomacy, 1921–1922.* Chapel Hill: University of North Carolina Press, 1993.

Fischer, Conan. *The Ruhr Crisis, 1923–1924.* Oxford, UK: Oxford University Press, 2003.

Fischer, Conan. *Europe between Democracy and Dictatorship: 1900–1945.* Hoboken, NJ: John Wiley and Sons, 2011.

Fitzpatrick, Sheila. *Stalin's Peasants: Resistance and Survival in the Russian Village after Collectivization.* Oxford, UK: Oxford University Press, 1994.

Fitzpatrick, Sheila. *On Stalin's Team: The Years of Living Dangerously in Soviet Politics.* Princeton, NJ: Princeton University Press, 2015.

Forczyk, Robert. *Tank Warfare on the Eastern Front: Schwerpunkt.* Barnsley: Pen and Sword, 2013.

Forsgren, Jan. *Messerschmitt Bf 109: The Design and Operational History.* London: Fonthill Media, 2017.

Förster, Gerhard. *Totaler Krieg und Blitzkrieg: Die Theorie des totalen Krieges und des Blitzkrieges in der Militärdoktrin des faschistischen Deutschlands am Vorabend des zweiten Weltkrieges* [Total War and Blitzkrieg: The Theory of Total War and Blitzkrieg in the Military Doctrine of Fascist Germany on the Eve of the Second World War]. Berlin: Deutscher Militärverlag, 1967.

Förster, Jürgen. "Hitler's Decision in Favour of War against the Soviet Union." In *Germany and the Second World War, Volume IV: The Attack on the Soviet Union.* Edited by the Militärgeschichtliches Forschungsamt, 13–51. Translated by Dean S. McMurry, Ewald Osers, and Louise Willmot. Oxford, UK: Clarendon Press, 1998.

Fowkes, Ben, ed. *The German Left and the Weimar Republic: A Selection of Documents.* Leiden: Brill, 2014.

Franks, Norman, and Greg Van Wyngarden. *Fokker D VII Aces of World War I, Part 2.* Oxford, UK: Osprey Publishing, 2004.

Garrett, Benjamin C., and John Hart. "Fishman, Yakov Moiseevich (1887–1962)." In *Historical Dictionary of Nuclear, Biological and Chemical Warfare,* 76–77. Lanham, MD: Scarecrow Press, 2007.

Gatzke, Hans W. *Stresemann and the Rearmament of Germany.* Baltimore: Johns Hopkins Press, 1954.

Gaworek, Norbert H. "From Blockade to Trade: Allied Economic Warfare against Soviet Russia, June 1919 to January 1920." *Jahrbücher für Geschichte Osteuropas, Neue Folge,* 23:1 (1975): 39–69.

Gellerman, Günther. *Der Krieg, der nicht stattfand. Möglichkeiten, Überlegungen und Entscheidungen der deutschen Obersten Führung zur Verwendung chemischer Kampfstoffe im zweiten Weltkrieg* [The War That Never Happened: Options, Considerations, and Choices of the German Supreme Command Regarding the Use of Chemical Weapons in World War II]. Bonn: Bernard und Graefe, 1986.

Gerwarth, Robert. *The Bismarck Myth: Weimar Germany and the Legacy of the Iron Chancellor.* Oxford, UK: Clarendon Press, 2005.

Gerwarth, Robert. *The Vanquished: Why the First World War Failed to End.* New York: Farrar, Straus & Giroux, 2016.

Geyer, Michael. *Deutsche Rüstungspolitik, 1860–1980* [German Armaments Politics, 1860–1980]. Frankfurt am Main: Suhrkamp, 1984.

Gilbert, Martin. *The Roots of Appeasement.* London: Wiedenfeld and Nicolson, 1966.

Ginsburg, George. "The Soviet Union as a Neutral, 1939–1941." *Soviet Studies*, 10:1 (Jul., 1958): 12–35.

Glantz, David M. *Soviet Military Operational Art: In Pursuit of Deep Battle.* Portland, OR: Frank Cass Publishing, 1991.

Glantz, David M. "Chapter 1: Introduction." In *The Evolution of Soviet Operational Art, 1927–1991: The Documentary Basis, Volume 1, Operational Art, 1927–1964,* translated by Harold S. Orenstein, xiii–xx. London: Frank Cass Publishing, 1995.

Glantz, David M. *Stumbling Colossus: The Red Army on the Eve of World War.* Lawrence: University of Kansas Press, 1998.

Glantz, David M. *Companion to Colossus Reborn: Key Documents and Statistics.* Lawrence: University Press of Kansas, 2005.

Glantz, David M., and Jonathan M. House. *When Titans Clashed: How the Red Army Stopped Hitler.* Lawrence: University Press of Kansas, 2015.

Głowacki, Albin, "The Red Army Invasion and the Fourth Partition of Poland." In *White Spots—Black Spots: Difficult Matters in Polish-Russian Relations, 1918–2008,* edited by Adam Daniel Rotfeld and Anatoly V. Torkunov, 161–182. Pittsburgh: University Press of Pittsburgh, 2015.

Goldman, Aaron L. "Sir Robert Vansittart's Search for Italian Cooperation against Hitler, 1933–36." *Journal of Contemporary History*, 9:3 (Jul., 1974): 93–130.

Goldman, Stuart. *Nomonhan, 1939: The Red Army's Victory That Shaped World War Two.* Annapolis, MD: Naval Institute Press, 2012.

Gordon, Harold J. *The Reichswehr and the German Republic, 1919–1926.* Princeton, NJ: Princeton University Press, 1957.

Gorlov, Sergey Alexeyvich. *Sovershenno sekretno: Alianz Moskva-Berlin, 1920–1933* [Top Secret: Alliance Moscow-Berlin, 1920–1933]. Moscow: Olma Press, 2001.

Gorodetsky, Gabriel. *Grand Delusion: Stalin and the German Invasion of Russia.* New Haven, CT: Yale University Press, 1999.

Gorodetsky, Gabriel, ed. *Soviet Foreign Policy, 1917–1991: A Retrospective.* London: Frank Cass Publishers, 1994.

Grant, Jonathan A. *Big Business in Russia: The Putilov Company in Late Imperial Russia, 1868–1917.* Pittsburgh: University of Pittsburgh Press, 1999.

Grechko, Andrei Antonovich, ed. "Voenno-vozdushnie sil [Air Force]." In *Sovetskaya voennaya entsiklopedia* [The Soviet Military Encyclopedia], 245. Moscow: Voenizdat, 1980.

Guardia, Mike. *Junkers Ju 87 STUKA.* Oxford, UK: Osprey, 1924.

Gudmundsson, Bruce I. *Stormtroop Tactics: Innovation in the German Army, 1914–1918.* Westport, CT: Praeger Publishers, 1989.

Gunsburg, Jeffrey A. "The Battle of the Belgian Plain, 12–14 May 1940: The First Great Tank Battle." *Journal of Military History*, 56:2 (Apr., 1992): 207–244.

Gunston, Bill. *The Osprey Encyclopedia of Russian Aircraft 1875–1995.* London: Osprey, 1995.

Güth, Rolf. *Die Marine des deutschen Reiches, 1919–1939* [The Navy of the German Reich]. Frankfurt am Main: Bernard und Graefe, 1972.

Habeck, Mary. *Storm of Steel: The Development of Armor Doctrine in Germany and the Soviet Union, 1919–1939.* Ithaca, NY: Cornell University Press, 2003.

Haigh, R. H., D. S. Morris, and A. R. Peters. *German-Soviet Relations in the Weimar Era.* Totowa, NJ: Barnes and Noble Books, 1985.

Hall, Hines H., III. "The Foreign Policy-Making Process in Britain, 1934–1935, and the Origins of the Anglo-German Naval Agreement." *The Historical Journal* (Cambridge, UK), 19:2 (Jun., 1976): 477–499.

Hantke, Max, and Mark Spoerer. "The Imposed Gift of Versailles: The Fiscal Effects of Restricting the Size of Germany's Armed Forces, 1924–1929." *The Economic History Review*, 63:4 (November 2010): 849–864.

Harris, John Paul. *The War Office and Rearmament 1935–1939*. Unpubl. diss., King's College London, 1983.

Harris, Robert, and Jeremy Paxman. *A Higher Form of Killing: The Secret History of Chemical and Biological Warfare*. New York: Random House, 2002.

Harrison, Mark. "The Market for Inventions: Experimental Aircraft Engines." In *Guns and Rubles: The Defense Industry in the Soviet State*, edited by Mark Harrison, 210–229. New Haven, CT: Yale University Press, 2008.

Harrison, Mark. *Soviet Planning in Peace and War, 1938–1945*. Cambridge, UK: Cambridge University Press, 2002.

Harrison, Mark, and John Barber. *The Soviet Home Front, 1941–1945: A Social and Economic History of the USSR in World War II*. London: Longman, 1991.

Harrison, Richard W. *The Russian Way of War: Operational Art, 1904–1940*. Lawrence: University Press of Kansas, 2001.

Harrison, Richard W. *Architect of Soviet Victory in World War Two: The Life and Theories of G. S. Isserson*. Jefferson, NC: McFarland, 2010.

Hartley, Harold. "Speech at the Royal Society Club Dinner." 14 November 1968, *Notes and Records of the Royal Society of London*, 24:1 (June 1969).

Hart, Russell A. *Guderian: Panzer Pioneer or Myth Maker?* Washington, DC: Potomac, 2006.

Harvey, James Neal. *Sharks of the Air: Willy Messerschmidt and How He Built the World's First Operational Jet Fighter*. Havertown, PA: Casemate, 2011.

Haslam, Jonathan. *Soviet Foreign Policy, 1930–1933: The Impact of the Depression*. London and Hong Kong: Macmillan, 1983.

Haslam, Jonathan. *The Soviet Union and the Struggle for Collective Security in Europe, 1933–1939*. New York: St. Martin's Press, 1984.

Haslam, Jonathan. "Litvinov, Stalin, and the Road Not Taken." In *Soviet Foreign Policy, 1917–1991: A Retrospective*, edited by Gabriel Gorodetsky, 55–64. London: Frank Cass, 1994.

Hauner, Milan. "The Sudeten Crisis of 1938: Beneš and Munich." In *The Origins of the Second World War: An International Perspective*, edited by Frank McDonough, 360–373. London: Continuum, 2011.

Hayes, Peter. "A Question Mark with Epaulettes?: Kurt von Schleicher and Weimar Politics." *Journal of Modern History*, 52:1 (Mar., 1980): 35–65.

Hayes, Peter. *From Cooperation to Complicity: Degussa in the Third Reich*. Cambridge, UK: Cambridge University Press, 2009.

Heaton, Colin D., and Anne-Marie Lewis. *The German Aces Speak: World War II through the Eyes of Four of the Luftwaffe's Most Important Commanders*. Minneapolis, MN: Zenith Press, 2011.

Heiber, Helmut. *The Weimar Republic*. Translated by W. E. Yuill. Munich: Deutscher Taschenbuch Verlag GMBH, 1966.

Herrick, Robert W. *Soviet Naval Theory and Policy: Gorshkov's Inheritance*. Washington, DC: Government Printing Office, 1988.

Hett, Benjamin Carter. *Burning the Reichstag: An Investigation into the Third Reich's Enduring Mystery*. Oxford, UK: Oxford University Press, 2014.

Heywood, Anthony. *Modernizing Lenin's Russia: Economic Reconstruction, Foreign Trade and the Railways*. Cambridge, UK: Cambridge University Press, 1999.

Higham, Robin. *Two Roads to War: The French and British Air Arms from Versailles to Dunkirk*. Annapolis, MD: Naval Institute Press, 2012.

Himmer, Robert. "Soviet Policy towards Germany during the Russo-Polish War, 1920." *Slavic Review*, 35:4 (December 1976): 665–682.

Hoerber, Thomas. "Psychology and Reasoning in the Anglo-German Naval Agreement, 1935–1939." *The Historical Journal* (Cambridge, UK), 52:1 (2009): 153–174.

Hoffmann, David L. *Peasant Metropolis: Social Identities in Moscow, 1929–1941*. Ithaca, NY: Cornell University Press, 1994.

Holborn, Hajo, and Ralph Manheim, eds. *Republic to Reich: The Making of the Nazi Revolution. Ten Essays*. New York: Knopf-Doubleday, 1972.

Homze, Edward L. *Arming the Luftwaffe: The Reich Air Ministry and the German Aircraft Industry, 1919–1939*. Lincoln: University of Nebraska Press, 1976.

Hopkirk, Peter. *Like Hidden Fire: The Plot to Bring Down the British Empire*. Tokyo: Kodansha International, 1994.

Hyde, Charles Cheney. "The City of Flint." *American Journal of International Law*, 34:1 (Jan., 1940): 89–95.

Jackson, Robert. *The Red Falcons: The Soviet Air Force in Action, 1919–1969*. Brighton, UK: Clifton Books, 1970.

Jäger, Herbert. *German Artillery of World War One*. Ramsbury, Marlborough, Wiltshire: Crowood Press, 2001.

James, Harold. *The German Slump: Politics and Economics, 1924–1936*. Oxford, UK: Clarendon Press, 1986.

James, Harold. *Krupp: A History of the Legendary German Firm*. Princeton, NJ: Princeton University Press, 2012.

Jeffreys, Diarmuid. *Hell's Cartel: IG Farben and the Making of Hitler's War Machine*. New York: Metropolitan Books, 2008.

Jenkins, Brian. "The Six Fevrier 1934 and the 'Survival' of the French Republic." *French History*, 20:3 (4 August 2006): 333–335.

Jentz, Thomas L. *Panzertruppen: The Complete Guide to the Creation and Combat Employment of Germany's Tank Force, 1933–1942*. Atglen, PA: Schiffer Military History, 1996.

Johnson, Gaynor, ed. *Locarno Revisited: European Diplomacy, 1920–1929*. New York: Routledge, 2004.

Johnson, Ian Ona. "The Fire of Revolution: A Counterfactual Analysis of the Polish-Bolshevik War, 1919 to 1920." *Journal of Slavic Military Studies*, 28:1 (Mar. 2015): 156–185. https://www.tandfonline.com/.

Johnson, Ian Ona. "The Secret School of War: The Secret Soviet-German Armored Warfare Academy at Kama, 1919–1933." *Journal of Global War Studies*, 13:2 (Spring 2017): 1–39.

Johnson, Ian Ona. "Prophet of Poison Gas: Yakov Fishman and the Soviet Chemical Weapons Program, 1924–1937." *Vulcan: The International Journal of the Social History of Military Technology*, 6:1 (August 2018): 1–25.

Johnson, Ian Ona. "Technology's Cutting Edge: Futurism and Research in the Red Army, 1917–1937." *Technology and Culture*, 59:3 (August 2018): 689–718.

Johnson, Ian Ona, ed. *The White Nights: Pages from a Russian Doctor's Notebook*. Tyler, TX: Bowen Press, 2018.

Jones, Mark. *Founding Weimar: Violence and the German Revolution of 1918–1919*. Cambridge, UK: Cambridge University Press, 2016.

Kalb, Stefanie. *Wilhelm Neumann (1898–1965)—Leben und Werk unter besonderer Berücksichtigung seiner Rolle in der Kampfstoff-Forschung* [Wilhelm Neumann 1898–1965)—Life and Work with a Special Emphasis on His Role in Poison Gas Research]. Unpubl. diss., University of Würzburg, 2005.

Kane, Robert B. *Disobedience and Conspiracy in the German Army, 1918–1945*. Jefferson, NC: McFarland and Company, 2002.

Kantor, Iuliya. *Voina i mir Mikhaila Tukhachevsogo* [The War and Peace of Mikhail Tukhachevsky]. Moscow: Ogonyok, 2005.

Kantor, Iuliya. *Zaklyataya druzhba: Sekretnoe sotrudnichestvo SSSR i Germanii 20–30kh godov* [Vow of Friendship: Secret Cooperation between the USSR and Germany in the 1920s and 1930s]. Moscow: Rosspen, 2014.

Kay, Antony. *Junkers Aircraft & Engines 1913–1945*. London: Putnam Aeronautical Books, 2004.

Kershaw, Ian. *Hitler.* London: Longman Group UK, 1991.

Keylor, William. "Versailles and International Diplomacy." In *The Treaty of Versailles: A Reassessment after 75 Years,* edited by Manfred Boemeke, Gerald Feldman, and Elisabeth Glaser, 469–505. Cambridge, UK: Cambridge University Press, 1998.

Keylor, William. "France and the Illusion of American Support." In *French Defeat, 1940: Reassessments,* edited by Joel Blatt, 204–244. New York: Berghahn Books, 2006.

Keylor, William, ed. *The Legacy of the Great War: Peacemaking, 1919.* Boston: Houghton Mifflin, 1998.

Keynes, John Maynard. *The Economic Consequences of the Peace.* New York: Harcourt, Brace and Howe, 1920.

Khromov, S. S. *Innostrannie kontsessii v SSSR: Istoricheskii ocherk. Dokumenti, Chast I* [Foreign Concessions in the USSR: Historical Essay, Documents, Part I]. Moscow: Rossiiskaya Akademiya Nauk Institut Rossiiskoi Istorii, 2006.

Khrunichev State Research and Production Space Center. "History." August 2012. Accessed 17 October 2013. http://www.khrunichev.ru/main.php?id=36.

Klinova, M. V. *Gosudarstvo i chastnyy kapital v poiskakh pragmatichnogo vzaimodeystviya.* [The State and Private Capital Searching for Pragmatic Cooperation]. Moscow: IMEMO RAN, 2009.

Kojevnikov, Alexei. "The Great War, the Russian Civil War, and the Invention of Big Science." *Science in Context,* 15:2 (2002): 239–275.

König, Wolfgang. *Volkswagen, Volksempfänger, Volksgemeinschaft: "Volksprodukte" im Dritten Reich, vom Scheitern einer nationalsozialistischen Konsumgesellschaft* [The People's Car, the People's Radio Receiver, the People's Community: "People's" Products in the Third Reich, from the Failure of a National Socialist Consumer Economy]. Paderborn: Schöningh, 2004.

Koop, Gerhard, and Klaus-Peter Schmolke. *Pocket Battleships of the Deutschland Class: Warships of the Kriegsmarine.* Barnsley, UK: Seaforth Publishing, 2014.

Korbel, Jeffrey. *Poland between East and West: Soviet and German Diplomacy toward Poland, 1919–1933.* Princeton, NJ: Princeton University Press, 2015.

Kotkin, Stephen. *Stalin, Volume 1: Paradoxes of Power, 1878–1928.* New York: Penguin, 2014.

Kotkin, Stephen. *Stalin, Volume II: Waiting for Hitler, 1929–1941.* New York: Penguin, 2017.

Köves, A. "Chapters from the History of East-West Economic Relations." *Acta Oeconomica,* 17:2 (1976): 159–176.

Kowalsky, Daniel. *Stalin and the Spanish Civil War.* New York: Columbia University Press, 2004. Ebook: http://www.gutenberg-e.org/kod01/index.html.

Krause, Joachim, and Charles K. Mallory. *Chemical Weapons in Soviet Military Doctrine: Military and Historical Experience, 1915–1991.* Boulder, CO: Westview Press, 1992.

Kunz, Rudibert, and Rolf-Dieter Müller. *Giftgas gegen Abd El Krim: Deutschland, Spanien und der Gaskrieg in Spanisch-marokko, 1922–1927* [Poison Gas against Abd El Krim: Germany, Spain, and the Gas War in Spanish Morocco, 1922–1927]. Mannheim: Rombach, 1990.

Kurowski, Franz. *Panzer Aces: German Tank Commanders of World War II.* Mechanicsburg, PA: Stackpole Books, 1992.

Lafleur, Thomas M. *Mikhail Frunze and the Unified Military Doctrine.* Unpubl. MMAS thesis, US Army Command and General Staff College, Fort Leavenworth, KS, 2004.

Laurens, Franklin D. *France and the Italo-Ethiopian Crisis, 1935–1936.* The Hague: Mouton, 1967.

Layton, Roland V., Jr. "The 'Völkischer Beobachter,' 1920–1933: The Nazi Party Newspaper in the Weimar Era." *Central European History,* 3:4 (Dec., 1970): 353–382.

Lebedeva, Natalia S. "The Red Army Invasion and the Fourth Partition of Poland." In *White Spots—Black Spots,* edited by Adam Daniel Rotfeld and Anatoly V. Torkunov, 182–208. Pittsburgh: University Press of Pittsburgh, 2015.

Leitenberg, Milton, and Raymond Zilinskas. *The Soviet Biological Weapons Program, a History*. Cambridge, MA: Harvard University Press, 2014.

Lemay, Benoit, and Erich von Manstein. *Hitler's Master Strategist*. Havertown, PA: Casemate, 2010.

Lenoe, Matt. "Did Stalin Kill Kirov and Does It Matter?" *The Journal of Modern History*, 74:2 (June 2002): 352–380.

Lenoe, Matt. *The Kirov Murder and Soviet History*. New Haven, CT: Yale University Press, 2010.

Leonard, Raymond W. *Secret Soldiers of the Revolution: Soviet Military Intelligence, 1918–1933*. Westport, CT: Greenwood Publishing Group, 1999.

Leontiev, Yaroslav. "From Peace—to Bang, the Fate of Yakov Fishman." *Russian Life Journal*, 10 September 2008.

Lerner, Warren. *Karl Radek: The Last Internationalist*. Palo Alto, CA: Stanford University Press, 1970.

Lindert, Peter H., and Steven Nafziger. "Russian Inequality on the Eve of Revolution." *Journal of Economic History*, 74:3 (Sept. 2014): 767–798.

Lindner, Ralf, and Rainer-Olaf Schultze. "Germany." In *Elections in Europe: A Data Handbook*, edited by Dieter Nohlen and Philip Stöver, 723–806. Baden-Baden: Nomos Verlagsgesellschaft, 2010.

Liulevicius, Vejas Gabriel. *The German Myth of the East: 1800 to Present*. Oxford, UK: Oxford University Press, 2009.

Locksley, Christopher C. "Condor over Spain: The Civil War, Combat Experience and the Development of Luftwaffe Airpower Doctrine." *Civil Wars*, 2:1 (1999): 69–99.

Lukes, Igor. *Czechoslovakia between Stalin and Hitler: The Diplomacy of Edvard Beneš in the 1930s*. Oxford, UK: Oxford University Press, 1996.

Lukes, Igor. "The Czechoslovak Partial Mobilization in May 1938: A Mystery (Almost) Solved." *Journal of Contemporary History*, 31:4 (Oct., 1996): 699–720.

Luther, Craig W. H. *The First Day on the Eastern Front*. Guilford, CT: Stackpole Books, 2019.

Lutz, Martin. "L. B. Krasin und Siemens: Deutsch-sowjetische Wirtschaftsbeziehungen im institutionenökonomischen Paradigma" [L. B. Krasin and Siemens: German-Soviet Economic Relations in the Institutional Economic Paradigm]. *Vierteljahrschrift für Sozial- und Wirtschaftsgeschichte*, 95. Bd., H. 4 (2008): 391–409.

Macksey, Kenneth. *Tank Warfare: A History of Tanks in Battle*. Oxford, UK: Osprey, 2013.

Macksey, Kenneth. *The Tank Pioneers*. London: Jane's, 1981.

MacMillan, Margaret. *Paris 1919: Six Months That Changed the World*. New York: Random House, 2001.

Maddison, A., J. Bolt, and J. L. Van Zanden. "Global Economic Statistics Database," *Angus Maddison Project*. Accessed 2014. http://www.ggdc.net/maddison/maddison-project/home.htm.

Maingon, Claire, and David Campserveux. "A Museum at War: The Louvre 1914–1921." *L'Esprit créateur*, 54:2 (Summer 2014): 127–140.

Maiolo, Joe. *The Royal Navy and Nazi Germany, 1933–1939: A Study in Appeasement and the Origins of the Second World War*. London: Macmillan, 1998.

Maiolo, Joe. *Cry Havoc, The Arms Race and the Second World War, 1931–1941*. London: John Murray, 2011.

Marks, Sally. "Mistakes and Myths: The Allies, Germany, and the Versailles Treaty, 1918–1921." *The Journal of Modern History*, 85:3 (September 2013): 632–659.

Marks, Steven G. "War Finance (Russian Empire)." In *1914–1918: International Encyclopedia of the First World War*, edited by Ute Daniel, Peter Gatrell, Oliver Janz, Heather Jones, Jennifer Keene, Alan Kramer, and Bill Nasson. Berlin: Freie Universität Berlin Digital Press, 2014. http://dx.doi.org/10.15463/ie1418.10159.

Martinetz, Dieter. *Der Gaskrieg, 1914–1918: Entwicklung, Herstellung und Einsatz chemischer Kampfstoffe* [The Gas War, 1914–1918: The Development, Production, and Use of Chemical Weapons]. Bonn: Bernard und Graefe, 1996.

Mawdsley, Evan. *The Russian Civil War*. New York: Pegasus, 2005.

McElligott, Anthony. *Weimar Germany*. Oxford, UK: Oxford University Press, 2009.

McKay, John. *Pioneers for Profit: Foreign Entrepreneurship and Russian Industrialization, 1885–1913*. Chicago: University of Chicago Press, 1970.

McKercher, B. J. C. "Deterrence and the European Balance of Power: The Field Force and British Grand Strategy, 1934–1938." *The English Historical Review*, 123:500 (Feb., 2008): 98–131.

Mearsheimer, John. *Conventional Deterrence*. Ithaca, NY: Cornell University Press, 1983.

Medvedev, Roy. *Let History Judge: The Origins and Consequences of Stalinism*. New York: Columbia University Press, 1989.

Meier-Welcker, Hans. *Seeckt*. Frankfurt am Main: Bernard und Graefe, 1967.

Meilinger, Phillip S. "Giulio Douhet and the Origins of Airpower Theory." In *The Paths of Heaven: The Evolution of Airpower Theory*, edited by Phillip S. Meilinger, 1–40. Maxwell Air Force Base, AL: Air University Press, 1997.

Menzel, Thomas. "Lipezk. Die geheime Fliegerschule und Erprobungsstätte der Reichswehr in der Sowjetunion" [Lipetsk: The Secret Reichswehr Flight School and Testing Facility in the Soviet Union]. 2013, Bundesarchiv.de, https://www.bundesarchiv.de/DE/Content/Virtuelle-Ausstellungen/Lipezk-Die-Geheime-Fliegerschule-Und-Erprobungsstatte-Der-Reichswehr-In-Der-Sowjetunion/lipezk-die-geheime-fliegerschule-und-erprobungsstatte-der-reichswehr-in-der-sowjetunion.html.

Menning, Bruce W. "Introduction." In Georgii Samoilovich Isserson, *The Evolution of Operational Art*, i–xxiii. Translated by Bruce W. Menning. Leavenworth, KS: Combat Studies Institute Press, 2013.

Messerschmidt, Manfred. "German Military Effectiveness between 1919 and 1939." In *Military Effectiveness, Volume II: The Interwar Period*, edited by Allan R. Millett and Williamson Murray, 218–255. Boston: Unwin Hyman, 1988.

Messerschmidt, Manfred. "Foreign Policy and Preparation for War." In *Germany and the Second World War, Volume I: The Build-up of German Aggression*, edited by the Militärgeschichtliches Forschungsamt (Research Institute for Military History), 541–717. Translated by P. S. Falla, Dean S. McMurry, and Ewald Osers. Oxford, UK: Clarendon Press, 1990.

Milsom, John. *Russian Tanks, 1900–1970: The Complete Illustrated History of Soviet Armoured Theory and Design*. New York: Galahad, 1975.

Mitcham, Samuel W. *Eagles of the Third Reich: Men of the Luftwaffe in World War II*. Mechanicsburg, PA: Stackpole Books, 1997.

Mitcham, Samuel W. *The Men of Barbarossa: Commanders of the German Army*. Havertown, PA: Casemate, 2009.

Mitchell, B. R. *International Historical Statistics: Europe, 1750–2000*. New York: Palgrave Macmillan, 2003.

Mitchell, Donald W. *A History of Russian and Soviet Sea Power*. New York: Macmillan, 1974.

Mommsen, Hans. *The Rise and Fall of Weimar Democracy*. Translated by Elborg Forster and Larry Eugene Jones. Chapel Hill: University of North Carolina Press, 1996.

Montefiore, Simon Sebag. *Stalin: Court of the Red Tsar*. New York: Vintage, 2003.

Moorhouse, Roger. *The Devils' Alliance: Hitler's Pact with Stalin, 1939–1941*. New York: Basic Books, 2014.

Moorhouse, Roger. *Poland 1939: The Outbreak of World War II*. New York: Basic Books, 2020.

Mueller, Gordon H. "Rapallo Reexamined: A New Look at Germany's Secret Military Collaboration with Russia in 1922." *Military Affairs*, 40:3 (1976): 109–117.

Muller, Richard R. "Hitler, Airpower, and Statecraft." In *The Influence of Airpower upon History: Statesmanship, Diplomacy, and Foreign Policy since 1903*, edited by Robin Higham and Mark Parillo, 85–114. Lexington: University Press of Kentucky, 2013.

Müller, Rolf-Dieter. "From Economic Alliance to a War of Colonial Exploitation." In *Germany and the Second World War, Volume IV: The Attack on the Soviet Union*, edited by the Militärgeschichtliches Forschungsamt, 118–224. Translated by Dean S. McMurry, Ewald Osers, and Louise Willmot. Oxford, UK: Clarendon Press, 1998.

Müller, Rolf-Dieter. *Der Feind steht im Osten. Hitlers geheime Pläne für einen Krieg gegen die Sowjetunion im Jahr 1939* [The Enemy in the East. Hitler's Secret Plan for a War against the Soviet Union in 1939]. Berlin: Ch.Links, 2011.

Müller, Rolf-Dieter. *Enemy in the East: Hitler's Secret Plans to Invade the Soviet Union.* Translated by Alexander Starritt. London: I. B. Tauris, 2015.

Mulligan, William. *General Walther Reinhardt and the Weimar Republic, 1914–1930.* New York: Berghahn Books, 2005.

Murray, Williamson. *Strategy for Defeat: The Luftwaffe, 1933–1945.* Maxwell, AL: Air University Press, 1983.

Murray, Williamson. *The Change in the European Balance of Power, 1938–1939: The Path to Ruin.* Princeton, NJ: Princeton University Press, 1984.

Murray, Williamson. *A War to Be Won: Fighting the Second World War.* Cambridge, MA: Harvard University Press, 2009.

Murray, Williamson, and Alan Millett. *Military Innovation in the Interwar Period.* Cambridge, UK: Cambridge University Press, 1996.

Naimark, Norman. *Stalin's Genocides.* Princeton, NJ: Princeton University Press, 2010.

Niebrzydowski, Paul. "Das Deutsche Polenbild: Historicizing German Depictions of Poles, 1919–1934." Unpubl. thesis, Ohio State University, 2012.

Neiberg, Michael S., and David Jordan. *The Eastern Front 1914–1920: From Tannenberg to the Russo-Polish War.* London: Amber Books, 2008.

Nekrich, Aleksander. *Pariahs, Partners, Predators: German Soviet Relations, 1922–1941.* Edited and translated by Gregory Freeze. New York: Columbia University Press, 1997.

Nowarra, Heinz J. *Heinkel He 111: A Documentary History.* London, Jane's, 1980.

Officer, Lawrence H. "Bilateral Exchange Rates: 1913–1999" [Consistent Currency Units]. In *Historical Statistics of the United States, Earliest Times to the Present: Millennial Edition,* edited by Susan B. Carter, Scott Sigmund Gartner, Michael R. Haines, Alan L. Olmstead, Richard Sutch, and Gavin Wright, Series Ee662–678. New York: Cambridge University Press, 2006. https://hsus.cambridge.org/HSUSWeb/search/simpleSearch.do?id=SIMPLE&searcField=lawrence%20officer.

O'Connor, Timothy. *The Engineer of Revolution: L. B. Krasin and the Bolsheviks, 1870–1926.* New York: Westview Press, 1992.

Oswald, Werner. *Kraftfahrzeuge und Panzer der Reichswehr Wehrmacht und Bundeswehr* [Armored Vehicles and Tanks of the Reichswehr, Wehrmacht, and Bundeswehr]. Stuttgart: Motorbuch Verlag, 1971.

Ottanelli, Fraser M. *The Communist Party of the United States: From the Depression to World War Two.* New Brunswick, NJ: Rutgers University Press, 1991.

Overy, Richard. *Russia's War.* London: Penguin, 1997.

Overy, Richard, and Andrew Wheatcroft. *The Road to War.* London: Macmillan, 1989.

Philbin, Tobias R., III. *The Lure of Neptune: German-Soviet Naval Collaboration and Ambitions, 1919–1941.* Columbia: University of South Carolina Press, 1994.

Phillips, Hugh D. *Between the Revolution and the West: A Political Biography of Maxim M. Litvinov.* Boulder, CO: Westview Press, 1992.

Polmar, Norman, and Jurrien Noot. *Submarines of the Russian and Soviet Navies, 1718–1990.* Annapolis, MD: Naval Institute Press, 1991.

Post, Gaines, Jr. *The Civil-Military Fabric of Weimar Foreign Policy.* Princeton, NJ: Princeton University Press, 1973.

Preston, Paul. *The Spanish Civil War: Reaction, Revolution and Revenge.* London: Harper Perennial, 2006.

Prümm, Karl. *Die Literatur des soldatischen Nationalismus der 20er Jahre (1918–1933): Gruppenideologie und Epochenproblematik* [The Literature of Soldier Nationalism in the 1920s (1918–1933): Group Ideologies and Epochal Problems]. Kronberg, Taunus: Scriptor, 1974.

Pyta, Wolfram. "Kurt von Schleicher." In *Neue Deutsche Biographie* [New German Biography], edited by Otto Stolberg-Wernigerode, 50–52. Berlin: Duncker und Humblot, 2006.

Pyta, Wolfram. *Hindenburg: Herrschaft zwischen Hohenzollern und Hitler* [Hindenburg: The Reign between the Hohenzollerns and Hitler]. Munich: Seidler, 2007.

Rabenau, Friedrich von. *Hans von Seeckt: Aus seinem Leben (1918–1936)* [Hans von Seeckt: From His Life]. Leipzig: Hass und Koehler, 1940.

Rahn, Werner. *Reichsmarine und Landesverteidigung 1919–1928: Konzeption und Führung der Marine in der Weimarer Republik* [Reichsmarine and Defense 1919–1928: Conception and Leadership of the Navy in the Weimar Republic]. München: Bernard und Graefe, 1976.

Raths, Ralf. "German Tank Production and Armoured Warfare, 1916–18," *War and Society*, 30:1 (2011): 24–47.

Read, Anthony, and David Fisher. *The Deadly Embrace: Hitler, Stalin and the Nazi-Soviet Pact, 1939–1941.* New York: W. W. Norton, 1988.

Reese, Roger. *Stalin's Reluctant Soldiers: A Social History of the Red Army, 1925–1941.* Lawrence: University Press of Kansas, 1996.

Resis, Albert. "The Fall of Litvinov: Harbinger of the German-Soviet Non-Aggression Pact." *Europe-Asia Studies*, 52:1 (Jan., 2000): 33–56.

Revich, B., E. Aksel, T. Ushakova, I. Ivanova, N. Zhuchenko, N. Klyuev, B. Brodsky, and Y. Sotskov. "Dioxin Exposure and Public Health in Chapaevsk, Russia." *Chemosphere*, 43 (2001): 951–966.

Revyakin, Aleksandr V. "The Interwar Period: Poland and the Soviet Union in the Late 1920s and Early 1930s." In *White Spots—Black Spots: Difficult Matters in Polish-Russian Relations*, edited by Adam Daniel Rotfeld and Anatoly V. Torkunov, 79–104. Pittsburgh: University Press of Pittsburgh, 2015.

Richhardt, Dirk. *Auswahl und Ausbildung junger Offiziere 1930–1945: Zur sozialen Genese des deutschen Offizierkorps* [The Selection and Training of Young Officers, 1930–1945: The Social Genesis of the German Officer Corps]. Unpubl. diss., Philipps-Universität Marburg, 2002.

Ritschl, Albrecht. "Deficit Spending in the Nazi Recovery, 1933–1938: A Critical Reassessment." *Journal of the Japanese and International Economy*, 16 (2002): 559–582.

Roberts, Geoffrey. *The Unholy Alliance: Stalin's Pact with Hitler.* London: I. B. Tauris, 1989.

Roberts, Geoffrey. "A Soviet Bid for Coexistence with Nazi Germany, 1935–1937: The Kandelaki Affair." *International History Review*, 16:3 (Aug., 1994): 466–490.

Robertson, E. M. *Hitler's Pre-war Policy and Military Plans, 1933–1939.* London: Longmans, Green and Co., 1963.

Rohwer, Jürgen, and Mikhail S. Monakov. *Stalin's Ocean-Going Fleet: Soviet Naval Strategy and Shipbuilding Programmes, 1935–1953.* London: Frank Cass Publishers, 2001.

Rorlich, Azade-Ayse. "Fellow Travellers: Enver Pasha and the Bolshevik Government 1918–1920." *Asian Affairs*, 13:3 (1982): 288–296.

Rudman, Stella. *Lloyd George and the Appeasement of Germany, 1919–1945.* Newcastle, UK: Cambridge Scholars Publishing, 2011.

Rupieper, Hermann J. *The Cuno Government and Reparations 1922–1923: Politics and Economics.* The Hague: Martinus Nijhoff Publishers, 1979.

Sammartino, Annemarie H. *The Impossible Border: Germany and the East 1914–1922.* Ithaca, NY: Cornell University Press, 2010.

Samuelson, Lennart. "Mikhail Tukhachevsky and War-Economic Planning: Reconsiderations on the Prewar Soviet Military Buildup." *Journal of Slavic Military Studies*, 9:4 (1996): 804–847.

Samuelson, Lennart. *Soviet Defence Industry Planning: Tukhachevskii and Military-Industrial Mobilization, 1926–1937.* Stockholm: Stockholm Institute of East European Economies, 1996.

Schäfer, Kirsten. *Werner von Blomberg: Hitlers erster Feldmarschall, eine Biographie* [Werner von Blomberg, Hitler's First Field Marshal, a Biography]. Munich: Paderborn, 2006.

Schmerling, Lewis. *Vladimir Nikolaevich Ipatieff, 1867–1952, a Biographical Memoir.* Washington, DC: National Academy of Sciences, 1975.

Schönrade, Rüdiger. *General Joachim von Stülpnagel und die Politik: Eine biographische Skizze zum Verhältnis von militärischer und politischer Führung in der Weimarer Republik* [General Joachim von Stülpnagel and Politics: A Biographical Sketch on the Relationship between Military and Political Leadership in the Weimar Republic]. Berlin: Carola Hartmann Miles, 2007.

Schuker, Stephen A. *The End of French Predominance in Europe: The Financial Crisis of 1924 and the Adoption of the Dawes Plan.* Chapel Hill, NC: The University of North Carolina Press, 1976.

Schuker, Stephen A. "France and the Remilitarization of the Rhineland, 1936." *French Historical Studies,* 14 (1986): 299–338.

Schuker, Stephen A. *American "Reparations" to Germany, 1919–33: Implications for the Third-World Debt Crisis.* Princeton University: Princeton Studies in International Finance Publication Series, 1988.

Schweer, Henning. *Die Geschichte der chemischen Fabrik Stoltzenberg bis zum Ende des zweiten Weltkrieges* [The History of the Stolzenberg Chemical Factory until the End of World War II]. Stuttgart: Diepholz Verlag für Geschichte der Naturwissenschaften und der Technik, 2009.

Sebestyen, Victor. *Lenin: The Man, the Dictator, and the Master of Terror.* New York: Pantheon, 2017.

Seidt, Hans-Ulrich. *Berlin, Kabul, Moskau: Oskar Ritter von Niedermayer und Deutschlands Geopolitik* [Berlin, Kabul, Moscow: Oskar von Niedermayer and German Geopolitics]. Munich: Universitas Press, 2002.

Selyanichev, A. K. *V. I. Lenin i stanovlenie Sovetskogo Voenno-Morskogo Flota* [V. I. Lenin and the Foundation of the Soviet Military-Naval Fleet]. Moscow: Izdatelstvo Nauka, 1979.

Semiryaga, Mikhail. *Taini Stalinskoi diplomatii* [The Secrets of Stalin's Diplomacy]. Moscow: Vysshaya Shkola, 1992.

Service, Robert. *A History of Modern Russia, from Nicholas II to Putin.* London: Penguin, 2003.

Shirer, William. *The Rise and Fall of the Third Reich.* New York: Simon & Schuster, 1960.

Shore, Zach. "Hitler, Intelligence and the Decision to Remilitarize the Rhine." *Journal of Contemporary History,* 341 (Jan., 1999): 5–18.

Showalter, Dennis. *Instrument of War: The German Army, 1914–1918.* New York: Bloomsbury, 2016.

Shuster, Richard J. *German Disarmament after World War I: The Diplomacy of International Arms Inspection, 1920–1931.* London: Routledge, 2006.

Siegel, Jennifer. *For Peace and Money: French and British Finance in the Service of Tsars and Commissars.* Oxford, UK: Oxford University Press, 2014.

Simpkin, Richard. *Deep Battle: The Brainchild of Marshal Tukhachevskii.* London: Brassey's Defence Publishers, 1987.

Sinnott, Colin S. *The RAF and Aircraft Design: Air Staff Operational Requirements, 1923–1939.* London: Routledge, 2001.

Slusser, Robert M., and Jan F. Triska. *A Calendar of Soviet Treaties, 1917–1957.* Stanford, CA: Stanford University Press, 1957.

Smele, Jonathan D. *Historical Dictionary of the Russian Civil Wars, 1916–1926.* New York: Rowman and Littlefield, 2015.

Smith, J. R., and Antony L. Kay. *German Aircraft of the Second World War.* London: Putnam, 1972.

Snyder, Louis, ed. *Encyclopedia of the Third Reich.* New York: Marlowe and Company, 1976.

Snyder, Timothy. *Bloodlands: Europe between Hitler and Stalin.* New York: Basic Books, 2010.

Sobelev, D. A., and D. B. Khazanov. *Nemetskii sled v istorii otechestvennoi aviatsii* [The German Imprint on the History of Domestic Aviation]. Moscow: Rusavia, 2000.

Spielberger, Walter. *Panzer III and Its Variants.* Atglen, PA: Schiffer Publishing, 1993.

Spielberger, Walter. *Panzer IV and Its Variants.* Atglen, PA: Schiffer Publishing, 1993.

Spielberger, Walter. *Die Motorisierung der Deutschen Reichswehr 1920–1935* [The Motorization of the German Reichswehr 1920–1935]. Stuttgart: Motorbuch, 1995.

Steiner, Zara. "The Soviet Commissariat of Foreign Affairs and the Czechoslovakian Crisis in 1938: New Material from the Soviet Archives." *The Historical Journal,* 42:3 (Sep., 1999): 751–779.

Steiner, Zara. *The Lights That Failed: European International History, 1919–1933.* Oxford, UK: Oxford University Press, 2005.

Steiner, Zara. *The Triumph of the Dark: European International History, 1933–1939.* Oxford, UK: Oxford University Press, 2010.

Stephenson, Donald. *Frontschweine and Revolution: The Role of Front-Line Soldiers in the German Revolution of 1918.* Unpubl. diss., University of Kansas, 1986.

Stolzenberg, Dietrich. *Fritz Haber: Chemist, Nobel Laureate, German, Jew.* Philadelphia: Chemical Heritage Press, 2004.

Stone, David J. A. *Hitler's Army: The Men, Machines, and Organization: 1939–1945.* Minneapolis: MBI Publishing Company, 2009.

Stone, David J. A. *The Kaiser's Army: The German Army in World War One.* London, Conway-Bloomsbury, 2015.

Stone, David R. "Tukhachevsky in Leningrad: Military Politics and Exile. 1928–31." *Europe-Asia Studies,* 48:8 (Dec., 1996): 1365–1386.

Stone, David R.. *Hammer and Rifle: The Militarization of the Soviet Union.* Lawrence: University Press of Kansas, 2000.

Stone, David R. "The Prospect of War?: Lev Trotskii, the Soviet Army, and the German Revolution in 1923." *International History Review,* 25:4 (Dec., 2003): 799–817.

Stone, David R. *A Military History of Russia: From Ivan the Terrible to the War in Chechnya.* Westport, CT: Praeger Security International, 2006.

Stone, Norman. *The Eastern Front, 1914–1917.* London: Hodder and Stoughton, 1975.

Strang, G. Bruce. "Once More unto the Breach: Britain's Guarantee to Poland, March 1939." *Journal of Contemporary History,* 31:4 (Oct., 1996): 721–752.

Strenge, Irene. *Kurt von Schleicher: Politik im Reichswehrministerium am Ende der Weimarer Republik* [Kurt von Schleicher: Politics in the Reich Ministry of Defense at the End of the Weimar Republic]. Berlin: Duncker und Humblot, 2006.

Strohn, Matthias. "Hans von Seeckt and His Vision of a 'Modern Army.'" *War in History,* 12:3 (2005): 318–337.

Strohn, Matthias. *The German Army and the Defence of the Reich: Military Doctrine and the Conduct of the Defensive Battle 1918–1939.* Cambridge, UK: Cambridge University Press, 2011.

Suny, Ronald Grigor. *The Soviet Experiment: Russia, the USSR, and the Successor States.* Oxford, UK: Oxford University Press, 1998.

Sutton, Antony C. *Western Technology and Soviet Economic Development, 1917–1930.* Stanford, CA: Hoover Institution on War, Revolution and Peace Press, 1968.

Svirin, Mikhail. *Bronya krepka: Istoria sovetskogo tanka 1919–1937* [The Armor Is Strong: The History of the Soviet Tank 1919 to 1937]. Moscow: Iauza i Eksmo, 2006.

Tampke, Jürgen. *A Perfidious Distortion of History: The Versailles Peace Treaty and the Success of the Nazis.* Melbourne: Scribe, 2017.

Tarrant, V. E. *The U-Boat Offensive, 1914–1945.* London: Arms and Armour Press, 1989.

Taylor, A. J. P. *The Origins of the Second World War.* New York: Touchstone, 1961/1991.

Taylor, Bryan D. *Politics and the Russian Army: Civil-Military Relations, 1689–2000.* Cambridge, UK: Cambridge University, 2003.

Taylor, Telford. *Munich: The Price of Peace.* New York: Doubleday, 1979.

Thompson, Richard J. *Crystal Clear: The Struggle for Reliable Communications Technology in World War II.* Hoboken, NJ: Wiley, 2011.

Tooley, T. Hunt. *National Identity and Weimar Germany: Upper-Silesia and the Eastern Border 1918–1922*. Lincoln: University of Nebraska Press, 1997.

Tooze, Adam. "Weimar's Statistical Economics: Ernst Wagemann, the Reich's Statistical Office, and the Institute for Business-Cycle Research, 1925–1933." *Economic History Review*, 52:3 (Aug., 1999): 523–543.

Tooze, Adam. *The Wages of Destruction: The Making and Breaking of the Nazi Economy*. New York: Viking Penguin, 2007.

Turner, Henry Ashby. *Stresemann and the Politics of the Weimar Republic*. Princeton, NJ: Princeton University Press, 1965.

Turner, Henry Ashby. *Hitler's Thirty Days to Power: January 1933*. New York: Basic Books: 1996.

Turner, Henry Ashby. The Myth of Chancellor Von Schleicher's Querfront Strategy. *Central European History*, 41:4 (Dec., 2008): 673–681.

Ueberschär, Gerd R. *Hitlers militärische Elite: 68 Lebensläufe*. Zürich: Primus Verlag GmbH, 2011.

Uldricks, Teddy. "Soviet Security Policy in the 1930s." In *Soviet Foreign Policy, 1917–1991: A Retrospective*, edited by Gabriel Gorodetsky. London: Frank Cass Publishers, 1994: 65–74.

Ute, Daniel, Peter Gatrell, Oliver Janz, Heather Jones, Jennifer Keene, Alan Kramer, and Bill Nasson, eds. *The First World War*. Berlin: Freie Universität Berlin Digital Press, 2014. http://dx.doi.org/10.15463/ie1418.10159.

Vásárhelyi, Györgyi, and László Földi. "History of Russia's Chemical Weapons." *Journal of Academic and Applied Research in Military Science*, 6:1 (2007): 135–146.

Vasilieva, Larisa, Igor Zheltov, and Galina Chikova. *Pravda o tanke T-34: Fakti, dokumenti, vospominania i raznie tochki zrenia ob odnom iz chudes XX veka* [The Truth about the T-34: Facts, Documents, Reminiscences and Different Points of View about One of the Wonders of the 20th Century]. Moscow: Atlantida–XXI Veka Press, 2005.

Veterans Association of the Third Panzer Division (Collective Authorship). *Armored Bears: Volume I: The German 3rd Division in World War II*. Mechanicsburg, PA: Stackpole, 2012.

Vilensky, Joel. *Dew of Death: The Story of Lewisite, America's World War I Weapon of Mass Destruction*. Bloomington: Indiana University Press, 2005.

Viola, Lynne. *Peasant Rebels under Stalin: Collectivization and the Culture of Peasant Resistance*. Oxford, UK: Oxford University Press, 1999.

Viola, Lynne, V. P. Danilov, N. A. Ivnitskii, and Denis Kozlov, eds. *The War against the Peasantry*. Translated by Steven Shabad. New Haven, CT: Yale University Press, 2005.

Volkogonov, Dmitri. *Lenin: A New Biography*. New York: Free Press, 1994.

Volkogonov, Dmitri. *Trotsky: The Eternal Revolutionary*. Translated and edited by Harold Shukman. New York: Free Press, 1996.

Volkmann, Hans-Erich. "The National Socialist Economy in Preparation for War." In *Germany and the Second World War, Volume I: The Build-up of German Aggression*, edited by the Militärgeschichtliches Forschungsamt, 157–372. Translated by P. S. Falla, Dean S. McMurry, and Ewald Osers. Oxford, UK: Clarendon Press, 1990.

Vourkoutiotis, Vasilis. *Making Common Cause: German-Soviet Secret Relations, 1919–1922*. New York: Palgrave Macmillan, 2007.

Wagner, Wolfgang. *Hugo Junkers Pionier der Luftfahrt—seine Flugzeuge* [Hugo Junkers, Pioneer of Aviation: His Aircraft]. Bonn: Bernard und Graefe, 1996.

Waite, Robert G. L. *Vanguard of Nazism: The Free Corps Movement in Postwar Germany 1918–1923*. New York: W. W. Norton, 1952.

Warren, Christopher A. "GAS, GAS, GAS!: The Debate over Chemical Warfare between the World Wars." *Federal History*, 4 (Jan. 2012): 43–60.

Watson, Alexander. *Ring of Steel: Germany and Austria-Hungary in World War One*. New York: Basic Books, 2014.

Watt, Donald Cameron. *Too Serious a Business: European Armed Forces and the Approach to the Second World War*. Berkeley: University of California Press, 1975.

Watt, Donald Cameron. *How War Came: The Immediate Origins of the Second World War*. London: Pantheon Press, 1989.

Webster, Andrew. "From Versailles to Geneva: The Many Forms of Interwar Disarmament." *Journal of Strategic Studies*, 29:2 (2006): 225–246.

Wegner, Bernd, ed. *From Peace to War: Germany, Soviet Russia, and the World, 1939–1941*. Providence, RI: Berghahn Books, 1997.

Weinberg, Gerhard L. *The Foreign Policy of Hitler's Germany: Diplomatic Revolution in Europe, 1933–36*. Chicago: University of Chicago Press, 1970.

Weinberg, Gerhard L. *The Foreign Policy of Hitler's Germany: Starting World War II, 1937–1939*. Chicago: University of Chicago Press, 1980.

Weinberg, Gerhard L. *Hitler's Foreign Policy, 1933–1939: The Road to World War Two*. New York: Enigma Books, 2010. This is a synthesis of the two above works.

Wette, Wolfram. "Ideology, Propaganda, and Internal Politics as Preconditions of the War Policy of the Third Reich." In *Germany and the Second World War, Volume I: The Build-up of German Aggression*, edited by the Militärgeschichtliches Forschungsamt, 11–155. Translated by P. S. Falla, Dean S. McMurry, and Ewald Osers. Oxford, UK: Clarendon Press, 1990.

Whaley, Barton. *Covert German Rearmament, 1919–1939: Deception and Misperception*. Frederick, MD: University Publications of America, 1984.

Wheeler-Bennett, John. *Hindenburg: The Wooden Titan* (London: Macmillan, 1936/1967).

Wheeler-Bennett, John. *Brest-Litovsk: The Forgotten Peace*. London: Macmillan, 1938.

Wheeler-Bennett, John. *The Nemesis of Power*. London: Macmillan, 1967.

Wildman, Allan K. *The End of the Russian Imperial Army, Volume I: The Old Army and the Soldiers' Revolt*. Princeton, NJ: Princeton University Press, 2014.

Williams, Robert C. "Russian War Prisoners and Soviet-German Relations, 1918 to 1921." *Canadian Slavonic Papers*, 9:2 (Autumn 1967): 270–295.

Williamson, David G. *The British in Interwar Germany: The Reluctant Occupiers, 1918–1930*. London: Bloomsbury, 2017.

Wiskemann, Elizabeth. "The Night of the Long Knives." *History Today*, 14:6 (Jun. 1, 1964): 371–380.

Wright, Jonathan. "Stresemann and Locarno." *Contemporary European History*, 4:2 (Jul., 1995): 109–131.

Wright, Jonathan. *Gustav Stresemann: Weimar's Greatest Statesman*. Oxford, UK: Oxford University Press, 2002.

Young, Robert J. *In Command of France: French Foreign Policy and Military Planning, 1933–1940*. Cambridge, MA: Harvard University Press, 1978.

Zabecki, David T., ed. *Germany at War: 400 Years of Military History*. Santa Barbara, CA: ABC-CLIO, 2014.

Zaloga, Steven J. *Panzer IV vs. Char B1 bis: France 1940*. Oxford, UK: Osprey, 2011.

Zaloga, Steven J., and Grandsen, James. *Soviet Tanks and Combat Vehicles of World War Two*. London: Arms and Armour Press, 1988.

Zaloga, Steven, and Madej, Victor. *The Polish Campaign*. New York: Hippocrene, 1985.

Zaloga, Steven J., and Morshead, Henry. *T-26 Light Tank: Backbone of the Red Army*. Oxford: Osprey, 2015.

Zeidler, Manfred. *Reichswehr und Rote Armee, 1920–1933: Wege und Stationen einer ungewöhnlichen Zusammenarbeit* [The Reichswehr and the Red Army, 1920–1933: Paths and Facilities of an Unusual Collaboration]. Munich: Oldenbourg Verlag GmbH, 1994.

Zeidler, Manfred. "German-Soviet Economic Relations during the Hitler-Stalin Pact." In *From Peace to War: Germany, Soviet Russia, and the World, 1939–1941*, edited by Bernd Wegner, 95–113. Providence, RI: Berghahn Books, 1997.

Ziemke, Earl. "The Soviet Theory of Deep Operations." *Parameters: Journal of the US Army War College*, 13:2 (1983): 23–33.

Ziemke, Earl. *The Red Army, 1918–1941: From Vanguard of World Revolution to America's Ally*. New York: Routledge, 2001.

INDEX

For the benefit of digital users, indexed terms that span two pages (e.g., 52–53) may, on occasion, appear on only one of those pages.

Figures are indicated by *f* following the page number.

grain shortage, in Russia
    under Lenin, 41–42
    under Stalin, 122–23, 137–38
Grandsen, James, 312n.16
Great Britain
    attempt at trade negotiations by Soviets,
        306–7n.2
    Battle of Britain, 224
    efforts to contain German rearmament,
        165, 176–78
    naval agreement with Germany, 178,
        179–80
    Non-Intervention Agreement in Spanish
        Civil War, 182
    rearmament program of, 191
    security guarantee for Poland, 203–4
    Soviet purchase of tank designs, 286n.21
    warnings to Soviets of German invasion,
        231
Great Depression, 120–22, 289n.10
Great Terror, 184–88
Groener, Wilhelm, 248n.8
    end of First World War, 17–18
    Freikorps, integration of, 22
    as Minister of Defense, 104–5
    opposition to Hitler, 145–46
    reaction to Treaty of Versailles, 26–27
    Second Armaments Program, 289n.9
Grosstraktor prototype
    design of, 110–12
    modifications to, 126
    testing of, 116–17, 125, 130, 141
    three-man turret design, 134
Grotte, Eduard, 148
Gruhn, Erna, 194–95
Grundherr, Alexander von, 106
Gryaznov, Ivan, 148
Gubanov, N. S., 163
Guderian, Heinz, 97
    in Batttle of France, 222–23
    in invasion of Poland, 213, 214
    in Operation Barbarossa, 232–33
    visits to Kama, 130, 141
Guernica, Spain, 183–84, 297n.13

Haber, Fritz, 54–56, 69, 133
Hacha, Emil, 202–3
Hackmack, Hans, 89, 91
Hagelloch, Georg, 126, 150, 274n.7
Halder, Franz, 229
Hamburg uprising, 61–62
Hammerstein-Equord, Kurt von, 117–18,
    162
Harpe, Josef, 112
Hartmann, Otto, 160, 161, 164

Haslam, Jonathan, 301–2n.5
Hasse, Otto, 43, 47–48, 50
He-111 airplane, 58–59
Heavy Bomber-3 (TB-3), 147
Hefter, Ekkehard, 151–52, 183
Heinkel, 127, 128, 292n.37
Heinkel, Ernst, 86–87
Heinkel 51 (He-51) aircraft, 168–69,
    292n.37
Heinkel Flugzeugwerke, 58–59
Heinkel HD-17 airplane, 87
Henrich, Otto, 57
Henschel, 278n.20
Herwarth, Johnnie von, 304n.71
Heye, Wilhelm, 43–44, 90, 99–100
High Command of the Armed Forces
    (OKW), 195
Hilger, Gustav, 36, 205, 210
Hindenburg, Paul von, 171
    appointment of Hitler to chancellorship,
        154, 157
    assumption of presidency, 78–79
    death of, 173
    end of First World War, 17–18
    resignation of Groener, 145–46
    resignation of Papen, 153
    retirement of Seeckt, 89–90
Hitler, Adolf, 121, 303n.31
    annexation of Austria, 195–96
    appointment as chancellor, 154, 157
    Battle of Britain, 224
    Battle of France, 222–23
    Beer Hall Putsch, 62–63
    beginning of dictatorship, 157–58
    Boundary and Friendship Treaty,
        216–18
    diplomatic efforts to contain German
        rearmament, 176–78
    dissolution of relationship with Soviet
        Union, 161–64
    as Führer, 173
    German-Soviet Commercial Agreement,
        220–21
    goal to destroy Soviet Union, 251n.20
    Hossbach Conference, 189–90
    invasion of Czechoslovakia, 202–3
    invasion of Poland, 212–15
    invitation for Soviet Union to join
        Tripartite Pact, 224–28
    Molotov-Ribbentrop Pact, 210–11, 212f
    Munich Agreement, 198–200
    naval agreement with Great Britain, 178,
        179–80
    Night of the Long Knives, 172–73
    nonaggression pact with Poland, 166–67

VOKhIMU (Military Chemical Directorate), 68–71, 90
Volckheim, Ernst, 97
von Kühlmann, Richard, 12
Voroshilov, Kliment, 83–84, 107–8, 117–18, 119, 166–67
VVS. *See* Air Force of the Red Army

Waffenamt (Weapons Office), 32, 126–28, 141–42
Wa.Prüf 8, 87
War Communism, 41
war-guilt clause in Treaty of Versailles, 26–27
Watt, Donald Cameron, 301–2n.5
Weapons Office (Waffenamt), 32, 126–28, 141–42
Wehrmacht, 174–75
    annexation of Austria, 195–96
    Batttle of France, 222–23
    invasion of Poland, 212–13
    Operation Barbarossa, 229–34, 237–38
    plan to invade Czechoslovakia, 198–200
Weimar Republic. *See also* Treaty of Versailles
    Beer Hall Putsch, 62–63
    communist uprising in Hamburg, 62
    Reichswehr, relationship with, 31–32
    Treaty of Berlin, 85
    Treaty of Rapallo, 47–49

White Russian forces, 14–15, 36, 245n.42
Wilberg, Helmuth, 57–58, 74–75, 85–86, 126
Wilhelm II (Kaiser), 17–18
Wilson, Woodrow, 26
Wimmer, Wilhelm, 87, 169
Winter War, 218–19
Wirth, Fritz, 74, 105–6
Wirth, Joseph, 42–43, 48
Woelfert, Erich
    Grosstraktor prototype, 110–11
    LaS tank design, 141–42, 150, 169
    Panzer design and production, 169–70, 190
    testing prototypes in Kama, 125–26
Wurtzbacher, Ludwig, 50, 57

Yakir, Iona, 185
Yellow Cross, 133–34
Young Marks, 108–9
Yugoslavia, 230
Yurenev, Konstantin, 187

Zaloga, Steven J., 312n.16
Zeidler, Manfred, 243n.6
Zhigur, Jan Matiseevich, 140–41, 284n.29
Zhukovsky Air Force Engineering Academy, 79–80
Zindel, Ernst, 51–52, 168–69, 257n.38
Zinoviev, Grigory, 41–42
Zyklon B, 73–74, 269n.18